T&T Clark Studies in Systematic Theology

Edited by

John Webster
Ian A. McFarland
Ivor Davidson

Volume 18

TRINITY, FREEDOM, AND LOVE

An Engagement with the Theology of Eberhard Jüngel

Piotr J. Małysz

For Rich,

with love and
gratitude,

t&t clark

Published by T&T Clark International
A Bloomsbury Imprint
50 Bedford Square   80 Maiden Lane
London   New York
WC1B 3DP   NY 10038

www.continuumbooks.com

British Library Cataloguing-in-Publication Data
A catalogue record for this book is available from the British Library

ISBN: HB: 978-0-567-57235-6

Typeset by Deanta Global Publishing Services, Chennai, India
Printed in Great Britain

Contents

Acknowledgments

The idea for this study began to take shape during my early years as a doctoral student at Harvard Divinity School. I owe an immeasurable debt of gratitude to my *Doktorvater*, Professor Ronald Thiemann, who from the very beginning was more than supportive of this project and has continued to show a keen interest in my work. Where necessary, he prodded gently, critiqued constructively, encouraged patiently, and praised more than I deserved. Yet, in doing so, he always allowed me the space to pursue questions of interest to me. For his wise guidance and his friendship I cannot thank him enough.

I am also gratefully indebted to Professor Sarah Coakley, now of Cambridge University. From my very first days at Harvard, she took an active interest in my work and was always more than generous with her time. I am immensely thankful for her confidence in me, which she expressed early on by inviting me to contribute to several of her book projects. Over the years, Professor Coakley has remained for me a model, where combining rigorous theological engagement with pastoral sensitivity is at stake.

Much of who I am, as a theologian as well as a teacher, I owe, likewise, to the unfailing support of Professors David Lamberth and Francis Schüssler Fiorenza, both of whom served on my dissertation committee and provided essential feedback. In addition, Professors Helmut Koester and Stephanie Paulsell have both, in important ways, left a mark on my teaching and my thinking about Christian theology.

I would also like to take this opportunity to acknowledge colleagues and friends who have, over the years, offered much support, especially as conversation partners. My very first conversations about Jüngel were with Roland Ziegler and William Weinrich at Concordia Theological Seminary in Fort Wayne, Indiana. At Harvard, I could not have done without the friendship of Susan Abraham, Faye Bodley-Dangelo, Philip Francis, Paul Dafydd Jones, Tamsin Jones, Mark McInroy, Mark Scott, Charles Stang, Bryan Wagoner, and Mara Willard. A special debt of gratitude goes to Rich

Fair, who, though not a theologian, has offered most enthusiastic support. Many thanks are also due to the congregations of Our Savior Lutheran Church in Westminster, Massachusetts, and Messiah Lutheran Church in Fitchburg, Massachusetts, which I had the privilege to serve and which challenged me to theological engagement in a register different from that of the academy.

Further, I must also thank Harvard Divinity School for a dissertation fellowship and the Lilly Fellows Program at Valparaiso University in Valparaiso, Indiana, for taking me under its wing with a dissertation not quite finished. At Valparaiso, I benefitted from the friendship and insight of Professor Matthew Becker and from incisive conversations with Linn Tonstad.

Last but not least, I wish to thank the editors of the "Studies in Systematic Theology" series: John Webster, Ian A. McFarland and Ivor Davidson. Tomas Kraft and Anna Turton at T&T Clark/Continuum have been a delight to work with and, likewise, deserve a special word of appreciation. Finally, I am very grateful to Dr. Alexander Maßmann for his assistance with the *Zusammenfassung*.

This study is dedicated to my parents, Danuta and Edward, as a small token of gratitude for everything they have given me – most importantly, their unfailing love.

Good Friday
2012

Abbreviations

B&T	Martin Heidegger, *Being and Time*, trans. J. Macquarrie and E. Robinson (New York: Harper and Row, 1962). German pagination will be cited.
Becoming	Eberhard Jüngel, *God's Being is in Becoming: The Trinitarian Being of God in the Theology of Karl Barth. A Paraphrase,* trans. John Webster (Grand Rapids: Eerdmans, 2001).
BR	Eberhard Jüngel, *Beziehungsreich: Perspektiven des Glaubens* (Stuttgart: Radius-Verlag, 2002).
CD	Karl Barth, *Church Dogmatics,* ed. G. W. Bromiley and T. F. Torrance, 14 vols. (Edinburgh: T&T Clark, 1936–75).
Death	Eberhard Jüngel, *Death: The Riddle and the Mystery,* trans. I. and U. Nicol (Edinburgh: St. Andrew Press, 1974).
EmE	Eberhard Jüngel, *Erfahrungen mit der Erfahrung: Unterwegs bemerkt* (Stuttgart: Radius-Verlag, 2008).
Essays I	Eberhard Jüngel, *Theological Essays I,* trans. J. B. Webster (Edinburgh: T&T Clark, 1989).
Essays II	Eberhard Jüngel, *Theological Essays II,* ed. J. B. Webster (Edinburgh: T&T Clark, 1994).
FoC	Eberhard Jüngel, *The Freedom of a Christian: Luther's Significance for Contemporary Theology,* trans. R. A. Harrisville (Minneapolis: Augsburg, 1988).
GGW	Eberhard Jüngel, *Gott als Geheimnis der Welt* (1977; Tübingen: Mohr Siebeck, 2001).
Justification	Eberhard Jüngel, *Justification: The Heart of the Christian Faith: A Theological Study with an Ecumenical Purpose,* trans. J. F. Cayzer (Edinburgh: T&T Clark, 2001).
LW	*Luther's Works,* ed. J. Pelikan and H. T. Lehmann, 55 vols. (St. Louis: Concordia, and Philadelphia: Fortress Press, 1955–1986).

Mystery	Eberhard Jüngel, *God as the Mystery of the World: On the Foundation of the Theology of the Crucified One in the Dispute between Theism and Atheism*, trans. D. L. Guder (Edinburgh: T&T Clark, 1983).
TE I	Eberhard Jüngel, *Unterwegs zur Sache. Theologische Erörterungen I* (1972; Tübingen: Mohr Siebeck, 2000).
TE II	Eberhard Jüngel, *Entsprechungen: Gott – Wahrheit – Mensch. Theologische Erörterungen II* (1980; Tübingen: Mohr Siebeck, 2002).
TE III	Eberhard Jüngel, *Wertlose Wahrheit. Zur Identität und Relevanz des christlichen Glaubens. Theologische Erörterungen III* (1990; Tübingen: Mohr Siebeck, 2002).
TE IV	Eberhard Jüngel, *Indikative der Gnade – Imperative der Freiheit: Theologische Erörterungen IV* (Tübingen: Mohr Siebeck, 2000).
TE V	Eberhard Jüngel, *Ganz Werden: Theologische Erörterungen V* (Tübingen: Mohr Siebeck, 2003).
WA	*D. Martin Luthers Werke*, 69 vols. (Weimar: Böhlau, 1883–1993).

A Note on Citations

Page references to Kant's works will be followed by the German pagination in *Kants gesammelte Schriften* given in square brackets. References to Heidegger's *Being and Time* will be given only according to the German pagination.

A Note on Translation

Wherever a quotation is followed solely by a reference to a German edition, the translation is always mine. Wherever the edition referred to is English, the citation comes from that edition unless indicated otherwise.

Introduction

This study explores freedom: God's as well as human. But, insofar as its focus is on freedom, it is also an investigation of love. One of the goals of what follows will be to show an indissoluble connection between freedom and love, and their mutual indispensability, while at the same time arguing for a fundamental distinction between them. This exploration will have significant implications both for theological anthropology and especially for the doctrine of God. Thus another, broader goal that this study has in view is to provide conceptually for a close and, above all, coherent integration of the two.

The investigation undertaken here will take the form of a close reading of, and critical engagement with, the thought of the German Lutheran theologian, Eberhard Jüngel (b. 1934). Jüngel's doctrine of God will constitute an important test case, both where the relation of divine freedom to love is concerned, and in regard to the anthropological effects that Jüngel attributes to God's being. Despite the impressive achievement that Jüngel's doctrine of God, beyond all doubt, is – it will, in the end, be found wanting on both counts. This conclusion will then enable this study constructively to address itself to the question of how one can maintain God's freedom in the interest of *divine spontaneity and creativity*, while remaining committed to *intersubjective vulnerability* which the cross of Jesus entails as an event of divine love.

To accomplish these critical and constructive goals, it is necessary to begin by situating Jüngel's interest in freedom in its historical and intellectual context. This is one of the purposes of this Introduction. What this larger backdrop will, in turn, bring into sharp relief is the *anthropological* significance of *divine* freedom. I wish to draw particular attention to this significance. Finally, the Introduction will locate Jüngel's views on freedom, both human and divine, within the coordinates of his larger project of articulating God's speakability and thinkability in a milieu where God has ostensibly become unnecessary. In the remainder of this Introduction, I shall return to the significance of what this study proposes to undertake and outline the course of the argument to follow.

Freedoms: Human and Divine

More than human

Freedom was the Reformation's first, pithy statement of what it perceived to be the truth of the gospel. In 1520, Martin Luther published his famous pamphlet, *The Freedom of a Christian*, in which he offered a sustained elaboration of the concept and its relevance to Christian self-understanding and the conduct of the Christian life. The following year Philip Melanchthon, Luther's colleague and fellow faculty member at Wittenberg University, declared, in what was to become the nascent reform movement's first dogmatics, that "*libertas est Christianismus* [freedom is Christianity]."[1] It was only gradually and for reasons political, as well as theological, that the enthusiastic affirmation of freedom yielded the spotlight to the doctrine, or rather doctrines, of justification.[2] The latter, though no doubt hotly debated, did not have as wide a purchase on the minds of the nontheological public. This, to be sure, significantly reduced the possibility of an overenthused misunderstanding,[3] even though, as the tumultuous course of the sixteenth century showed, it did not eliminate it entirely. However, it also unduly concealed the potential for freedom inherent in the proclamation of Christ crucified.

Eberhard Jüngel has been among those consciously seeking to retrieve a *this-worldly* relevance of the early Reformation's rallying cry, without, however, sacrificing the precision and critical edge that the doctrine of

---

[1] Philip Melanchthon, *Loci communes theologici* (1521). In *Melanchthon and Bucer*, ed. Wilhelm Pauck (Philadelphia: Westminster, 1969), 123; *Corpus Reformatorum* 21:195. Cited by Jüngel, among other instances, in "Befreiende Freiheit – als Merkmal christlicher Existenz," *Anfänger: Herkunft und Zukunft christlicher Existenz* (Stuttgart: Radius-Verlag, 2003), 14; and "Die Freiheit eines Christenmenschen: Freiheit als Summe des Christentums," Michael Beintker et al. (eds), *Wege zum Einverständnis. Festschrift für Christoph Demke* (Leipzig: Evangelische Verlagsanstalt, 1997), 119.

[2] The primacy of freedom, as well as the plurality of understandings of justification that were put forth during the Reformation, has recently been emphasized by Volker Leppin, "Martin Luther, reconsidered for 2017," *Lutheran Quarterly* 22:4 (Winter 2008), 373–86; see also Berndt Hamm and Michael Welker, *Die Reformation: Potentiale der Freiheit* (Tübingen: Mohr Siebeck, 2008).

[3] Mark Edwards has provided an overview of representative misconstruals of Luther's call to freedom. In the early Reformation, Luther's conception was frequently seen either as a rejection of man-made laws, political as well as ecclesiastical, in favor of obedience to God's law, or, on the contrary, as an abandonment of all law-governed living. The former interpretations, for all their social radicalism, failed to grasp the far-reaching character of what Luther meant by freedom; the latter, by contrast, deliberately blurred the soteriological specificity of Luther's conception. Neither quite appreciated Luther's insistence that faith alone, rather than works of the law, is the determinant of the sinner's justification and salvation; neither was, therefore, able to spell out Christian freedom's precise worldly import. See Mark U. Edwards, Jr., "The Reception of Luther's Understanding of Freedom in the Early Modern Period: The Early Years," *Lutherjahrbuch* 62 (1995), 104–20.

justification gives to the concept of freedom. Though the proper understanding of justification became again a topic of debate in the twentieth century – with much of it focused on discerning the various strands of Reformation theology and ultimately aiming at ecumenical rapprochement – Jüngel has drawn attention more broadly to the significance of freedom. "If contemporary theology has any central theme at all, it is Christian freedom," he observes in his commentary on Luther's *Freiheitsschrift*.[4] On one level, this observation constitutes Jüngel's explicit programmatic assertion that freedom remains an inalienable dimension of the gospel – one with continued, if not increased, relevance. But as such it must be thought through theologically with all the rigor that such thinking demands. Hence, on another level, Jüngel's statement also expresses his critical theological assessment of the social, political, and above all intellectual landscape of modernity.

Before we turn to the specific import of Jüngel's statement, we must note several factors that have contributed, in Jüngel's case, to his placement of freedom in the center of the theological enterprise, factors beyond the obvious centrality of freedom to the gospel (Galatians 5:1)[5] and its reception as a potent theological notion in the Reformation. Theologies of liberation, so prominent on the theological scene in recent decades, definitely did not go unnoticed. Jüngel himself remarks that an experience of South African townships in the apartheid era changed his initial skepticism toward political theologies, such as the project initiated by Jürgen Moltmann, Jüngel's colleague at the University of Tübingen, and the Roman-Catholic theologian Johann Baptist Metz. Still, in Jüngel's case, his insistence that "the Christian is . . . commanded, to work against an unjust system, not only with thoughts and words but even with deeds" is accompanied by an equally strong concern, whose roots lie in the Reformation tensions, that Christianity must not be bound to a particular political course, let alone elevate revolution to a theological principle. "The political activity required of the church aims, above all else, to assist the cause of truth," Jüngel observes. He then goes on to warn that "in no instance should anyone be coerced theologically to take up violence."[6]

---

[4] *FoC*, 19.

[5] What will become the central, freedom-oriented themes of Jüngel's theological anthropology figure prominently already in his 1961 doctoral dissertation which explores the relationship between Paul's doctrine of divine justification of the ungodly and Jesus' parabolic proclamation of the Kingdom of God, as preserved in the synoptic tradition. See *Paulus und Jesus: eine Untersuchung zur Präzisierung der Frage nach dem Ursprung der Christologie* (Tübingen: Mohr Siebeck, 1962), esp. 62–6.

[6] "Toward the Heart of the Matter," *Christian Century* 108:7 (February 27, 1991), 229–30.

What Jüngel's theological commitment to freedom means, considering his praise of political involvement and simultaneous refusal of politicization, can be clarified by placing his commitment in the context not of liberation theologies but of political and philosophical concerns native to the European scene. Those very concerns actually underlie Jüngel's later critical receptivity to political theologies. The fact that Jüngel was born in Nazi Germany and spent his adolescence and adulthood, into his early 30s, in the former communist German Democratic Republic has played a formative role in leading him to explore the potential that *theology* offers for conceptualizing freedom.[7] A political declaration of freedom does not necessarily bring freedom with itself, as Hitler's rise to Reich's chancellorship, followed by the liberation of the German people by the Red Army twelve years later, both showed in very different ways. Yet, precisely because of the deceptiveness of politically fashioned freedom, Jüngel does not believe that freedom can be made separate from the socio-political realm, or that theology can remain politically uninvolved. In this he follows in the footsteps of his mentor, Karl Barth, or, to be even more specific, the *Barmen Declaration* (1934). There is no freedom without an impact on human beings as social and political creatures. Freedom does not pertain merely to the individual, and even less so to some circumscribed aspect of an individual's existence. A freedom that one might claim to enjoy within one's self is as illusory as the politically-decreed freedom that has led one, in the first place, to the creation of a private oasis of liberty within the self. In *this* particular sense, the peasants and nobles alike who responded with enthusiasm to Luther's proclamation of freedom were right: freedom concerns the *totus homo*, the human person in every aspect of his or her existence, both individual and social.

But, Jüngel insists, it concerns *more* than merely the total person or this or that group brought together by common interest. To see why and how that is the case, it is necessary, first, to consider freedom in its strictly anthropological dimension. One need not even look as far as the totalitarian regimes of the twentieth century to realize how easily freedom wrested from

---

[7] Jüngel's own reflections on his upbringing in a nontheological home, his subsequent turn to theology, and theological development can be found in a booklet-length interview he gave to the Italian theologian, Fulvio Ferrario: *Die Leidenschaft Gott zu denken: Ein Gespräch über Denk- und Lebenserfahrungen* (Zürich: Theologischer Verlag, 2009). A shorter, and older, autobiographical account can be found in "Toward the Heart of the Matter," 228–33. Derek Nelson has written a concise introduction, offering both biographical information and an overview of major theological themes; see his "The Indicative of Grace and the Imperative of Freedom: An Invitation to the Theology of Eberhard Jüngel," *Dialog: A Journal of Theology* 44:2 (Summer 2005), 164–80.

hostile and oppressive powers – whether political or ecclesiastical – degenerates into an even worse unfreedom. It is enough to call attention to the various socio-political experiments that the Reformation's call to freedom inspired: from the notorious, though rather marginal, Anabaptist Kingdom of Münster to Calvin's influential reorganization of Geneva's social and political life. Yet something even subtler is involved here. The Reformation, as some scholars have pointed out, left in its wake a regime of moral discipline and religious duties far stricter than what had come before – stricter because deprived of the cultic props and salvific motivation. In place of one system of values, the Reformation installed another and naturalized it by rooting it not only in the will of God but in the immutable divine law reflected in nature.[8] What the post-Reformation era shows is the remarkably easy ossification of freedom into new, often sinister legalisms.

With a sobering perspective on the twentieth century, one would be rather naïve simply to blame the Reformation, as one could still do in the nineteenth century, for providing the originary, but, unfortunately, incomplete (Hegel) and even self-defeating (Marx) impulse for freedom.[9] Rather, something altogether different is involved here. For at the culmination of modernity, despite its claim to completing the Reformation's unfinished project, there has, likewise, lain anything but freedom; and to hold the reformers culpable for this state of affairs would amount, at best, only to scapegoating propaganda. If there should have been a failure on the part of Luther and his successors, it had rather to do with soft-pedaling the temporal implications of Luther's bold, yet highly precise, notion of gospel freedom. This move, precipitated by misinterpretations and oft-enslaving abuses of Luther's call, served to make room for alternative articulations of freedom and, ironically, contributed to the enduring preeminence of freedom in modernity's self-consciousness. But the general notion of freedom that captured the minds of the moderns was one that, at bottom, differed quite drastically from what Luther had called for. Freedom turned, first and foremost, into a human undertaking in a world of ossified

---

[8] Cf. Euan Cameron, *The European Reformation* (Oxford: Clarendon Press, 1991), 389–416; and Diarmaid MacCulloch, *The Reformation* (New York: Viking Penguin, 2004), 531–683.

[9] Hegel saw in the philosophy of the French Enlightenment a completion of "the Reformation that Luther began" (G. W. F. Hegel, *Lectures on the History of Philosophy*, vol. 3: *Medieval and Modern Philosophy*, trans. E. S. Haldane [Lincoln, NE: Bison, 1995], 398). Marx's evaluation of Luther's Reformation was far less positive: "Luther, to be sure, overcame servitude based on devotion, but by replacing it with servitude based on conviction" (Karl Marx, *Critique of Hegel's Philosophy of Right*, trans. Joseph O'Malley [Cambridge: University Press, 1972], 138). Both are cited by Jüngel in "Die Freiheit eines Christenmenschen: Freiheit als Summe des Christentums," 120.

structures – a task. . . And it has never ceased to be one. It has to be won, and the very moment it is won, it must be gained again. It is a penultimate that never quite ushers in the ultimate. In other words, it is not that the Reformation failed to produce a compelling and robust notion of freedom and, for this reason, is to blame for subsequent unfreedoms that modernity has had to do away with. From the vantage point of the turn of the twenty-first century, it is rather the case that any anthropologically grounded freedom turns into its own opposite with uncanny ease. Human freedoms, whether early or late modern, are all precariously elusive and, once gained, turn out to be inherently unstable and ambiguous.

Given this ease with which even hard-won freedoms morph into cumbersome legalisms, Jüngel is interested less in revolutionary contestation than in the ways every individual must daily undertake the task and negotiate his or her freedom in the face of the world's impingement. Two broad sets of strategies are involved here. One either seeks freedom in variously conceived detachment, such as a retreat into one's inner rationality; or one must exert one's will over against the world and, instead of securing one's self against the world, one must make the world secure for oneself. Of particular importance for appreciating Jüngel's critique and re-envisioning of freedom's meaning is the fact that modernity makes a virtue of this precariousness of the human relation to the world. Society incorporates into its structures, and harnesses for its own ends, the human impulse toward self-possession, self-actualization, and self-determination. It thus renders it even more compulsive and relentless.

It is against this backdrop of the modern obsession with self-determination and, what is largely only implicit in Jüngel's critique, the elevation of this compulsion to socially expected norm in consumerist society that Jüngel retrieves the Reformation's call to freedom as *more* than an anthropological reality. Just as Luther accused Erasmus of turning people into "reckless workers" (*temerarii operarii*),[10] so also Jüngel holds modernity responsible not only for effectively reducing humans to the sum of their achievements but also for offering no respite from the incessant push toward achieving. Modernity's vaunted freedom conceals nothing but slavery, Jüngel holds. We shall examine this claim in more detail in the course of this study. What is important to note here is that, for Jüngel, the solution to freedom's contradictions does not lie in worldly actuality, in trying even harder but rather in God's act of unconditionally embracing and acknowledging humanity in the crucifixion of Jesus of Nazareth. It is that event, Jüngel

---

[10] Martin Luther, *The Bondage of the Will* (1525), *LW* 33:34–5; *WA* 18:613.

maintains, that has the capacity *elementally to interrupt* the continuity of human existence, and in doing so to distance one from oneself, and to open up entirely new possibilities for freedom amidst the compulsiveness of actuality.

Liberating God

From the more localized perspective of freedom, then, Jüngel's project concerns thinking human freedom together with God's justifying act, and thus thinking together God and humanity. Jüngel's *larger* concern, however, has to do with thinking and speaking God in a milieu where "God cannot be an intelligible theme for the person whose self is realized through activity."[11] What is this milieu? Jüngel blames the metaphysical elements in the theological tradition of the West – its assertion of God's "absoluteness and independence, his being over us as absolute causality, his infinity and his omnipotence, his immutability and his immortality"[12] – for the eventual impossibility of thinking God. Modernity's fetishization of self-possession is thus, for Jüngel, part of a *larger* trend of the exhaustion of the metaphysical concept of God, a trend to which Christian theology has contributed.

According to Jüngel it was Descartes who, without quite realizing the far-reaching theological implications, first made explicit the built-in self-destructiveness of the entire conception of God as the Absolute, that is, a being which is absolutely superior, to the exclusion of any imperfection or becoming, and absolutely simple. Absolute simplicity was meant further to shore up God's superiority: on the one hand, God is incapable of being affected by the world, and, on the other, because God's existence belongs to God's essence, God exists necessarily and, as such, affects all else. Now, as long as human thought found its ground in the thinking of the divine intellect, the scholastic, merely *rational* distinction between God's essence and God's existence – made not only to prove but simply to think God – remained quite innocuous. Things changed, however, when, in Descartes' relieved declaration, *Cogito ergo sum*, human thought discovered its ground in itself and then unceremoniously proceeded to enlist God in the process of securing the world for itself. The thinking ego thus "found its natural place between God's essence and God's existence."[13] What Descartes accidentally demonstrated was human mediation between the assertion of God's absolute essence and the conclusion that God exists. "God, when he is conceived of by

---

[11] *FoC*, 81.
[12] *Mystery*, 184; *GGW* 249.
[13] Mystery, 109; *GGW* 143.

me *as* God, must in terms of his *essence* be *above me* and with himself, *only with himself.* But in terms of his *existence*, as this essence, God must be *with me* and *only with me*, because only *through me* can he be present," Jüngel explains.[14] This contradiction in effect dismantles the absolute being of God: If His highest essence over me has its existence in and through me, then the highest essence may not be high enough. The declaration of God's unknowability, in Kant's philosophy, and ultimately God's unthinkability, in the thought of Johann Gottlieb Fichte, were, ironically, last-ditch attempts to secure God's divinity, his freedom from the confines of human conceptuality – but attempts whose practical upshot was no different from the atheistic pronouncement of God's death. In all, it may have been political fears that evacuated the doctrine of justification by grace through faith of its worldly liberating relevance and inadvertently made room for competing anthropological conceptions; but it was the trajectory of Western metaphysics that ultimately consigned the doctrine of a justifying God itself to the rubbish heap.

In order to be able to oppose modernity's deceptive freedom, by thinking freedom together with God's justifying act, one must reestablish the possibility of thinking God. Jüngel's recovery of this possibility, however, is not a resuscitation (were it even possible) of pre-Cartesian metaphysics. Jüngel turns, instead, to Luther and St. Paul. In their thought, he finds resources that allow him to appropriate the cross as the locale of God's self-revelation where God both subverts human conceptions of the divine and is known unambiguously as being *pro nobis*. For Luther, one finds assurance of one's salvation, and so a respite from the compulsion toward self-justifying works, at the cross, in Christ's saving work on humanity's behalf. Jüngel radicalizes Luther's insight by pointing out that the cross concerns not merely the revelation of God's attitude to humanity; it is not just the place where God discloses something of God's self. Rather, the cross is the locale where God happens (*ereignet sich*) for humanity. In this sense Jüngel may be considered to be a continuator – with the help of the early Christian *kerygma* and via the derailment of the metaphysical tradition – of the Reformation's project of thinking God from the cross.

The cross, according to Jüngel, makes it impossible to think God's essence and existence in separation from each other. It opposes to the metaphysical death of God a death that concerns God's very being and discloses that "the metaphysically postulated essence of God [is] a contradiction to the true deity of God."[15] In the event of the cross, God reveals God's being as

---

[14] *Mystery*, 125–6; *GGW* 166.
[15] *Mystery*, 203; *GGW* 276.

vigorously personal – as triune. By identifying with the crucified Jesus of Nazareth, God comes to stand as Father over against the Crucified One, declared, in this identification, to be the Son; yet both, despite their separation, are brought together by the Spirit. God's triunity, revealed in the cross, is "the event of the unity of life and death for the sake of life,"[16] or, to put it more conventionally, the event of God's being as *love*. In love there is no distinction between essence and existence.[17]

The cross makes it possible to think and speak God again, insofar as the triune God is not tied to dead-ended conceptions of divine absoluteness. Those, in any case, are little more than projections of perceived human deficiencies and desires and, as the story of modernity also illustrates, eventually become burdensome even for humanity. Jüngel expresses this *freedom of thinking God* – but, crucially, also the *freedom of God* who is thus thought – with the adage that God is "more than necessary" in relation to the world.[18] More than necessary does not mean unnecessary but rather that God is free to come to the world on God's own terms, that is, terms given neither by the world nor by the divine essence, as if God simply could not help himself, but, instead, given solely by God's free disposal over God's being. As more than necessary, God comes to the world closer than the world can come to itself. In revealing God's self, God can reveal the world to itself – both in the untruth of its pursuits and in the possibilities that God's coming opens up for it. In fact, the cross shows that God has already come to the world and in doing so unconditionally affirmed the world. And it shows that God simply is in coming and by being so desires elementally to interrupt the continuity of human being with ever-new possibilities. God desires to share *God's* freedom with humanity.

We shall investigate all this in more detail in the following pages. What concerns us here is that God, as God without absolutes, is neither a prisoner nor a jealous guardian of that which properly characterizes and belongs to God: freedom and love (the way the highest essence had to remain in all respects superior to everything else). All the divine attributes are communicable, Jüngel insists.[19] Yet their communication does not divinize humanity. On the contrary, participating in the freedom of God makes

---

[16] *Mystery*, 317; *GGW* 434.

[17] Jüngel does not reject divine simplicity per se but only the notion of absolute simplicity, which makes God into a being both necessary and incapable of interaction with the world. Cf. Paul J. DeHart, *Beyond the Necessary God: Trinitarian Faith and Philosophy in the Thought of Eberhard Jüngel* [AAR Reflection and Theory in the Study of Religion] (Atlanta, GA: Scholars Press, 1999), 66, 127, 160–1.

[18] *Mystery*, 24; *GGW* 30, *et passim.*

[19] E.g., "Der Geist der Hoffnung und des Trostes," *TE V*, 317 [Thesis 4.752].

humans more human. It establishes their humanity in a manner that is
beyond the reach of the spurious freedoms that humans try to wrest from
the world. This, in turn, enables humans, as already open to God, to open
themselves to the world, even though the world impinges on their fragile
being. As the event of God's freedom in action, the Trinity is "the sum of the
gospel,"[20] because in God's coming to the cross human freedom is also to
be found.

The Objectives of This Study in Light of Jüngel's Work

My principal goal in the pages that follow is to think, with Jüngel's help,
through the intimate connection of the doctrine of God and anthropology,
and to do so from the perspective of both the doctrine of God and
anthropology. This larger goal contains within itself two objectives. The first
is investigative and has to do with critically analyzing the divine-human
togetherness in Jüngel's theology through the lens of freedom. The second,
constructive objective will be critically to ask whether Jüngel's doctrine of
God is able to support the anthropological effects that Jüngel ascribes to
God's being; and, in light of this study's findings, to put forth a way of
intertwining even more closely and seamlessly trinitarian and anthropological
conceptualities.

The argument will unfold in four major moves. First, I shall examine
Jüngel's critique of the modern notion of freedom as rooted in self-securing
and self-possession. In this inquiry, I shall pay particular attention to the
subject's alleged autonomy. Second, I shall analyze Jüngel's account of
divine freedom. This analysis will show Jüngel's construal to be ultimately
dissonant in its two central emphases: the inalienable spontaneity and
creativity of God's being, on the one hand, and the intersubjective character
of God's self-determination as a trinitarian event of love, on the other. God's
subjectivity will be shown to border, as a result, on predominant self-
relatedness, which Jüngel rejects as unfreedom in anthropological terms.
In its third move, the argument will then turn to the being of the person as
elementally interrupted and so not only freed but brought into
correspondence with God. My focus here will be chiefly on the person's two
acts of existence. Finally, I shall develop the ontological implications of the
two existential acts of the free person. With their help I shall offer a way of

---

[20] Cf. "Das Verhältnis von »ökonomischer« und »immanenter« Trinität," *TE II*, 269.

resolving the ambiguity present in Jüngel's account of God's self-determination. This study's central, constructive claim will be that in God there also are two acts of existence, grounded in two distinct manners of trinitarian relationality. Next to what I call the logic of love, there is the logic of freedom. Without sacrificing God's originary creativity, it enables God to enter into a successful togetherness with the humanity God liberates and thus to determine God's self in an intersubjective manner as an event of love.

The Tübingen theologian and historian of dogma, Isaak Dorner (1809–84), remarked quite perceptively that the Reformation managed successfully to integrate human freedom into the process of salvation, in the sense that the unconditional and personal relation of God-in-Christ to humanity establishes also the freedom of the person. But, according to Dorner, the Reformation never succeeded in thinking beyond Christology to the doctrine of God's triunity and likewise rethinking the latter from a personalist and ethical, rather than substantive, perspective.[21] Jüngel's trinitarian thought is a commanding and intellectually rigorous attempt at such a necessary reformulation. In this regard, Jüngel, of course, follows the lead of Karl Barth, though, as we shall see, not uncritically and with a notable change of emphasis. The contribution that this study seeks to make is very modest by any account, yet it should, nonetheless, be seen as part of this larger trajectory that seeks to think through the Reformation's principal insights.

The work that contains Jüngel's sustained engagement with the doctrine of God is his *magnum opus, God as the Mystery of the World* (1977), bearing the subtitle, *On the Foundation of the Theology of the Crucified One in the Dispute between Theism and Atheism.* Besides Luther and Barth, it draws on a staggering host of critically appropriated influences and conversation partners, with Hegel, Heidegger, Rudolf Bultmann, Ernst Fuchs and Gerhard Ebeling being the chief among them. This study will not investigate these influences, except where the argument demands it.[22]

Unlike Jüngel's contribution to the doctrine of God, Jüngel's engagement with anthropological themes has to be gleaned largely from a host of essays, as well as his monographs, *Death: The Riddle and the Mystery* (1971) and *Justification: The Heart of the Christian Faith* (1998). This is not to suggest, as we have shown, that anthropology is a less important theme, whether for

---

[21] Isaak Dorner, *Divine Immutability: A Critical Reconsideration,* trans. Robert P. Williams and Claude Welch (1856–8; Philadelphia: Fortress Press, 1994), 99–100, and 132ff.
[22] For a brief overview, see DeHart, *Beyond the Necessary God,* 5–8.

Jüngel himself or within the repertoire of the theologian, in general. Jüngel insists that "[t]heology . . . is obligated to speak definitively about humanity"[23] – if for no other reason than that God has already done so in Jesus Christ. Jüngel concludes *God as the Mystery of the World* by laying what he considers to be a "foundation for a theology which narrates the being of God as the mystery of the world." This foundation, he opines, has to do with the manner in which "human acts and modes of being . . . correspond to the divine self-movements." He then proceeds briefly to discuss faith, love and hope as such anthropological correspondences.[24] What this study wishes to contribute in this regard is a precise account of the "divine self-movement" and the manner in which human being – as elementally interrupted by God's act in Christ – responds with its own correspondences.

A Note on Jüngel Scholarship

John Webster's *Eberhard Jüngel: An Introduction to His Theology*, first published in 1986, remains to this day the only comprehensive, book-length introduction to Jüngel's thought.[25] It is still a very valuable, though somewhat dated, survey of the major motifs of Jüngel's oeuvre. This said, it situates Jüngel in close – I believe too close – proximity to Barth. One of the side objectives of this study will be to problematize the Jüngel–Barth relationship, while drawing attention to Jüngel's conscious appropriation of, and copious indebtedness to, Luther, which Webster largely overlooks.

More specialized scholarship on Jüngel has focused chiefly on his doctrine of God, especially the formal, methodological assumptions underlying it. Particularly valuable here is Paul DeHart's monograph, *Beyond the Necessary God* (1999). DeHart focuses on Jüngel's engagement with the theological tradition, an engagement whose goal is to expose this tradition's unexamined theistic assumptions. DeHart carefully traces the way modern intellectual and cultural atheism – as a product of metaphysical theism's collapse – forms the context in which Jüngel constructs a trinitarian conceptuality of the divine being as speakable and thinkable and thus seeks to recover the possibility, indeed the indispensability, of faith. DeHart's study is not, however, a *direct* engagement with Jüngel's trinitarian theology; moreover, it, too, assumes that Jüngel's entire project is little

---

[23] *FoC*, 45.
[24] *Mystery*, 390ff; *GGW* 535ff.
[25] (Cambridge: Cambridge University Press, 1986).

more than an interpretation of Barth's trinitarianism. Other studies in this broad category include critical evaluations of God's subjectivity in terms of Jüngel's reception of Hegel.[26]

Interpreters have also explored Jüngel's understanding of religious language in general, and his concept of analogy more specifically.[27] Roland Zimany has furnished an overview of the contemporary theological and philosophical influences on Jüngel's thought.[28] Both Mark Mattes[29] and Arnold Neufeldt-Fast[30] have signaled the importance of Heidegger for Jüngel's thought. Both agree that Heidegger provides Jüngel with a hermeneutical key by means of which Jüngel diagnoses modernity's ills, comes to reject a causal view of God's being, and proposes instead a nonfoundational view of divine-human interconnection. Mark Mattes has also situated Jüngel's trinitarianism against the backdrop of contemporary trinitarian theologies of divine relationality, arguing, importantly, that Jüngel offers no convincing resolution to the incongruence of the subject paradigm and communal paradigm in his doctrine of God.

As far as anthropological themes are concerned, Neufeldt-Fast has offered an assessment of Jüngel's Christological thought in terms of the tension that the influences of Luther and Barth bring into it. In another study, Mark Mattes has evaluated Jüngel's understanding of justification as a critical appropriation of Luther and his successors' doctrine.[31] Several interpreters have noted that Jüngel's understanding of justification undercuts human agency[32] but have not correlated this fact with any particular ambiguity in Jüngel's construal of God as Trinity, as this study proposes to do.

None of these studies is devoted to a sustained exploration of the topic of freedom in Jüngel's theology. None, moreover, attempts to critique, let alone constructively to engage, Jüngel's doctrine of God from the

---

[26] Much of the German scholarship on Jüngel, as well as some of that produced in Anglo-Saxon circles, touches on this dimension of Jüngel's thought. This scholarship will be discussed in Chapter 2.

[27] Joseph Palakeel, *The Use of Analogy in Theological Discourse: An Investigation in Ecumenical Perspective* (Rome: Gregorian University, 1995).

[28] Roland D. Zimany, *Vehicle for God: The Metaphorical Theology of Eberhard Jüngel* (Macon, GA: Mercer University Press, 1994).

[29] Mark C. Mattes, *Toward Divine Relationality: Eberhard Jüngel's New Trinitarian, Postmetaphysical Approach* (unpublished Ph.D. thesis, University of Chicago, 1995).

[30] Arnold V. Neufeldt-Fast, *Eberhard Jüngel's Theological Anthropology in Light of His Christology* (unpublished Ph.D. dissertation, University of St. Michael's College, Toronto, 1996).

[31] Mark C. Mattes, *The Role of Justification in Contemporary Theology* (Grand Rapids, MI: Eerdmans, 2004).

[32] Zimany, Neufeldt-Fast; as well as John Webster, "Justification, Analogy and Action: Passivity and Activity in Jüngel's Anthropology," (ed.), *The Possibilities of Theology: Studies in the Theology of Eberhard Jüngel in his Sixtieth Year* (Edinburgh: T&T Clark, 1994).

perspective of the anthropological effects that Jüngel attributes to it. To say this is by no means to diminish their genealogical and critical contribution but rather to signal what sort of location the present study seeks to occupy.

Chapter Outline

This study's argument will be developed in the four chapters that follow. Chapter 1 will expound anthropological notions of freedom which Jüngel rejects. Those, as we shall see, all involve securing oneself against what one perceives as the vulnerability of one's own humanity and consist in a totalizing self-relation which dominates or crowds out one's relations to others. For Jüngel, both detachment from and control over the world not only involve one in a self-contradiction; they actually lead to the subjection of the ego to its own tyranny. This captivity manifests itself in the relentless imperative to self-realization which never affords one any rest and effectively reduces the person to his or her own works. The being of the person who exists in a totalizing self-relation thus becomes indeterminate, neither quite human nor yet divine.

In light of these conclusions, I shall then, in Chapter 2, investigate Jüngel's construal of God's freedom. I shall argue that Jüngel aims at, and offers rich resources for, the conceptualization of God's self-determination at the cross in a robustly intersubjective manner that involves both God and humanity in what he calls "a successful togetherness."[33] However, despite the care with which he articulates God's being as a cruciform event of love, Jüngel's proposal is undercut, and that for three reasons. First, Jüngel largely takes for granted the response of the beloved, that is, Jesus and, in Jesus, humanity, within the divine-human relationship. This is all the more surprising considering that Jüngel emphasizes divine creativity as accompanying God's identification with the crucified man. Second, in his construal of freedom's two moments: independence and determinateness, Jüngel does not discriminate between the inalienable spontaneity and creativity of God and the fact that love entails a reception of being also on the part of the lover. The latter ends up overridden for the sake of the former. Finally, Jüngel construes God cruciform determinateness as entirely anticipated within God's immanent subjectivity. Consequently, God appears to be a subject who merely determines God's self in relation to the other and incorporates

---

[33] "Ganzheitsbegriffe – in theologischer Perspektive," *TE V*, 51.

the other into God's self-relatedness. Not only is Jüngel's doctrine of God dissonant, but as a subject God seems to mirror the types of self-related subjectivity that Jüngel identifies anthropologically as unfree. Largely responsible for all this, I shall argue, is the fact that Jüngel considers freedom's two constitutive moments (and by extension both divine freedom and love) to be rooted in a single underlying subjective structure: what I call the logic of love.

In order to suggest ways of clarifying the relation between freedom and love in God's being, Chapter 3 will turn again to anthropology. My focus will be on the experience of the elemental interruption: its subjective manifestations and its ontological consequences. Of particular significance for this investigation will be the elementally interrupted person's existence in two acts of being. In the first, passive act, the person is granted determinateness by being effectively removed from the self and so also inhabiting the possibilities that flow from God's being. Immersed in those, the person is able to experience anew, with acute insight, his or her own being and the being of the world. In the second, active act, the person, as free from him- or herself, is able concretely to determine the person's self for the sake of another. The person, in sum, is both in being and in becoming.

Chapter 4 constitutes the constructive portion of the argument. On the basis of Jüngel's assertion that divine freedom is an attribute that is communicable and actually communicated to the person in the event of elemental interruption, I shall propose that God's being is inherently characterized by two subjective acts of existence: the logic of love and the logic of freedom. Those exhibit different types of trinitarian self-relatedness. I shall give a detailed account of the logic of freedom as reflective of God's subjectivity *a se* and intimately connected, precisely in its distinctiveness, to God's trinitarian, intersubjective self-determination and self-disclosure in the event of the cross. My contention will be that the two subjective structures introduce clarity into the doctrine of God, while at the same time doing justice to all of Jüngel's concerns. In particular, the logic of freedom enables the logic of love in the latter's full potential for intersubjectivity. So much so that the lover becomes threatened by the possibility of nonbeing, should the beloved not reciprocate the lover's love.

In addition to resolving ambiguities in the doctrine of the Trinity, this study will, as indicated, contribute to a deepened appreciation for human being in the world. It will show the fundamental relevance of human works of love on behalf of those afflicted by oppressive social structures and doomed to a dehumanizing pursuit of self-possession. Further, it will offer a precise analysis of the self in the two acts of existence and thus show that it is not merely the person's acts that correspond to God but the person, as a subject and God's partner, corresponds to God. Finally, worldly actions of the person will be shown to be indispensable, not only from the world's perspective but also from God's in that through them God's love is reciprocated and God's being is returned to God.

Chapter 1

Human Relationality and Unfreedom

In regard to human freedom, the task of this chapter is primarily a negative one: to analyze Jüngel's engagement with anthropological conceptions of freedom that he then unmasks as unfreedom. However, before we embark on this task, it may be useful to paint in broad strokes the landscape of which the following discussion is a part. Jüngel understands human freedom primarily as being true to the relational character of human being. What is crucial to note is that freedom remains beyond the reach of an individual, or even humanity as such. For Jüngel, one becomes free, and so true to oneself, only when liberated through what he calls "an elemental interruption of the continuity of being."[1] Thanks to this interruption, of which faith is an essential part, one can actualize one's freedom as love in the world and on the world's behalf. This richly relational existence is one in which the free person corresponds to God.

At the foundation of Jüngel's understanding of *un*freedom lies the Augustinian conception of sin as self-love. It is mediated to Jüngel via Luther's ontological interpretation, which sees the sinner as an imploding human being, one who is turned in on him- or herself (*incurvatus in se ipsum*).[2] However, Jüngel is not so much interested in merely asserting that such a hubristic posture exists or in presenting it in exclusively theological terms. He is, as we shall see, principally preoccupied with uncovering self-love's specifically modern manifestations and doing so in a manner that does not presuppose acceptance of the Christian notion of sin. To this end, he seeks to show that modernity's much-vaunted banners – self-possession and self-securing – do not deliver the freedom they promise but its opposite. Though they are highly

---

[1] "Value-Free Truth: The Christian Experience of Truth in the Struggle against the 'Tyranny of Values'," *Essays II*, 206.

[2] Cf. Martin Luther, *Lectures on Romans* (1515–16), *LW* 25:291, 313, 345; *WA* 56:304, 325, 356. Jüngel cites Luther's phrase, for example, in "On Becoming Truly Human. The Significance of the Reformation Distinction between Person and Works for the Self-Understanding of Modern Humanity," *Essays II*, 222; and *Justification*, 114, 145.

prized and sought after, they actually leave one no alternative other than their incessant pursuit. They are inescapable. The inescapability is what enslaves one, what turns one in on oneself. This unfreedom manifests itself as a persistent self-contradiction evident in a self-securing existence. However, the full extent of the damage – the fact that self-possession destroys the *person* – does not become quite apparent prior to the event of elemental interruption.

Jüngel, as noted earlier, does not offer a sustained consideration of theological anthropology. His views need to be gleaned from a variety of sources, some presenting lengthy and in-depth engagement with a theme, others a handful of casual remarks. The central ideas, such as Jüngel's disavowal of self-possession as a path to freedom, are relatively straightforward. But much is also left to interpretive inference and arrangement of the material.

Our discussion will begin with an account of how Jüngel understands the fundamental and primordial relationality of human beings. I will investigate why this relationality necessarily subverts itself and gives rise to the predominance of one's self-relation. Second, I will discuss, on the basis of human action and rationality, how the primordial relationality does offer glimpses of itself by showing human self-securing to be a contradiction of the self. Finally, under the rubric of unfreedom, I will address the toll that self-securing takes on the being of the human subject, and gesture toward a potential resolution of the self-contradiction.

Human Relationality and Its Subversions

Humans, according to Jüngel, are relational beings. Human relationality is not a matter of transcendence of, or addition to, some prior self-contained subjectivity. Relationality is not a function of an already established subject, an existential posture that the subject may, or may not, choose to assume. Rather, the opposite is the case: "*Personal being is being in relation.* Personal identity is relational identity, and consequently identity full of tension. . . . The relations in which a person exists do not exist independently of the life of the person; rather, they *are* the life of the person."[3] Jüngel distinguishes four kinds of fundamental relations that together constitute the human being as relational. These are: (1) relationship to self, (2) relationship to one's social environment, (3) relationship to one's natural environment, and (4) relationship to (one's) God.[4] Importantly, all of these, although never

---

[3] "The Dogmatic Significance of the Question of the Historical Jesus," *Essays II,* 112.
[4] "Hoffen, Handeln – und Leiden. Zum christlichen Verständnis des Menschen aus theologischer Sicht," *BR,* 19; "Zum Wesen des Friedens," *TE V,* 32.

separate, are distinct dimensions of human relationality. By asserting this distinctiveness, however, Jüngel does not mean to indicate what is necessarily the case in the way one exists. What is the case will more often than not belie this rich relationality. Yet neither is Jüngel's assertion unreflectively axiomatic. He is at pains to show *how* these relations emerge as constitutive dimensions of human being, woven into its very fabric. What Jüngel intends to establish is a "fundamental ontology," to borrow a term from Heidegger.[5] Subjectivity, one's self-aware relation to oneself, emerges because one already exists in relation. Rich relationality is primordial. It is, therefore, beyond, or rather prior to, actual choice.

That relationality is integral to one's being is evident, according to Jüngel, in the fact that even when humans believe themselves, and act as if they were, self-contained and isolated subjects, the relational nature of their being can at most be perverted and obscured. It cannot, however, be eradicated.[6] Consequently, an attempt to absorb all the other relations into one's self-relation, or to secure one's self-relation against them – even though it may *seem* like an assured pathway to freedom – is bound to involve one in a self-contradiction. The more one tries to possess oneself, the more the fundamental relationality of one's being will stand in the way. This possibility of self-contradiction is what, according to Jüngel, distinguishes human beings from all other creatures.[7] The self-contradiction creates fissures in one's self-securing that allow one a glimpse into the fundamental human relationality. But those faint manifestations are insufficient to furnish a precise and comprehensive diagnosis of the human condition, let alone point to a resolution. It is because of the indeterminacy that self-possession brings with itself, as well as the relentlessness with which humans double their efforts in response, that self-possession will lead to bondage instead of freedom.

---

[5] *B&T*, 132.

[6] "Zur Verankerung der Menschenrechte im christlichen Glauben," *Außer sich. Theologische Texte* (Stuttgart: Radius-Verlag, 2011), 132. Jüngel would no doubt agree with Heidegger that it is not required "that the ontological structure of existence should be theoretically transparent" (*B&T*, 12). Still, in each and every individual case, the human being situates his or her existence within and vis-à-vis this relational structure.

[7] "On Becoming Truly Human," *Essays II*, 218. It must be noted in this connection that, although Jüngel is highly critical of the Cartesian turn to the subject and Descartes' elevation of doubt to the status of a hermeneutical principle (see esp. *Mystery*, 111–26; *GGW* 146–67), Jüngel's emphasis on the fundamental relationality of human being does not grow out of critiques of Descartes which underscore the priority of the relation between consciousness and the world to any attempt at their conceptual isolation. As will be shown, for Jüngel relationality is a *theological* assertion grounded in the possibility of a human being existing in self-contradiction – a possibility whose entire destructive potential becomes visible, so to speak, only in light of God's revelation but glimpses of which are nonetheless anthropologically available.

Let us analyze this dynamic in more detail. I shall first discuss the linguistic conditions under which humans emerge as relational beings. We shall observe how these very conditions lead to the rise of the relation to self as the dominant relation. This will then enable us to examine the fissures that open up within the totalizing self-relation, in its attempt both to secure the world for itself and to secure itself against the world.

The human as a linguistic being

According to Jüngel, it is language that is constitutive of human relationality.[8] On the one hand, it is through language that one makes sense of one's own being in the world, or, to put it more precisely, of oneself as a world-being (*Welt-Wesen*) – and in so doing relates to oneself. On the other hand, the fact that the self-relation is achieved through none other than *language* is in itself an indicator that relations to others, which one's being-in-the-world necessarily entails, are given with one's self-relation yet as distinct from it. In both of these dimensions of self- and other-relation, the primary task of language is the granting and securing of recognition, including self-recognition.

In a set of theses, dealing with "The Limits of Being Human,"[9] Jüngel points out that the world, as experienced by humans, is disjoined into the past, present, and future. It is this very disjunction, in all its inevitability, that gives rise to the human as a language-being (*Sprach-Wesen*). Humans must protect the unity of their world, that is, they must safeguard the continuity of their being (*Seinszusammenhang*), by relating to it and appropriating it linguistically. Out of their ever-present life, humans acknowledge their own history, not only by making it their own through speech but also by relating it to present actions and states. Out of the same ever-present life, humans give themselves a future by allowing their thoughts to transcend the present moment.[10] In other words, they recognize themselves in, and discursively come to own, their past and their future. This makes time a form of human self-relation. But the past and the future

---

[8] Cf. "Humanity in Correspondence to God," *Essays I*, 145. In keeping with our anthropological point of departure, we are leaving aside for the moment the question of God's prior address as the enablement of language.

[9] "Grenzen des Menschseins," *TE II*, 355–61; cf. *Mystery*, 171ff; *GGW* 230–1.

[10] In Books XI–XIII of *The Confessions*, Augustine speaks of the human soul's ability to hold present the modes of time by remembering (*memoria*) perceiving (*contuitus*) and expecting (*expectatio*). Jüngel makes a brief reference to Augustine's discussion in "The Emergence of the New," *Essays II*, 53. As will become clear in subsequent chapters, Jüngel opposes to this understanding of time the never-waning newness of the elemental interruption present in the Christian understanding of time.

both presuppose relating to others. After all, a distinction between past, present, and future makes little sense in "splendid isolation." Insofar as relations to others are also given with temporality, space, too, is a form of human self-relation. "Man relates to himself *temporally* in that he already always relates *spatially* to *other* people and things," Jüngel comments.[11]

What Jüngel's account hints at is an essential fragility of human being. This fragility, understood here in a neutral sense, is what characterizes the very spatiotemporal structure of human being. But it concerns not only the plurality of relations involved but, above all, the self-relation as grounded in the spatiotemporal structure. It concerns the self-relation as the locale of one's identity. The entire spatiotemporal structure of human being is what enables the self-relation, that is, makes it possible for humans to manifest themselves as language-beings for the sake of the continuity of their being. But crucially, the structure does hardly more than enable. Without actively appropriating one's past and assuring one's future, there is only discontinuity and no identity. Put differently, the self-relation, while given with one's being, demands constant actualization. It is not automatic. Rather, it is constantly re-established through awareness and recognition of one's past, present, and future. To be sure, the self-relation is always also accompanied by relations to others, and, as we have noted, Jüngel argues it cannot exist without them. Yet it is only the self-relation for which one is *personally*, as it were, responsible, as one comes to own one's past and one's future. An actualized self-relation is the condition of one's being oneself.

As can be seen, the very spatiotemporal structure of human being is what makes it possible for the subtle balance between the self- and other-relations to be easily upset. The self-relation, as one's personal responsibility, can crowd out, dominate, and absorb into itself one's relations to others. In fact, it will inevitably seek to do so. Human world-being (*Welt-Wesen*), with its plurality of erratic relations, cannot but appear as a threat to one's being. One will come to see oneself as, in effect, threatened by oneself: by the past one must own, even though it is not entirely one's own, and by the future, even though it unpredictably involves others. One will come to see oneself as threatened by one's own humanity, by its susceptibility to impingement and interference. The self-relation will then cease to be a simple dimension, one of several, of one's world-being and the structural locus of identity. Instead, it will seek to establish itself as the be-all and end-all of one's existence – a totalizing relation for the sake of oneself. The essential human fragility will thus turn into an all-consuming and daunting *task* of making

---

[11] "Grenzen des Menschseins," *TE II*, 358.

sense of one's existence in the face of its ever-looming disintegration. One will become consumed by the dual project of securing oneself against the world and, at the same time, securing one's world, making it controllable, and predictable. All this ultimately with a view to removing one's mistrust of oneself.[12]

To put it more precisely, the self-relation will take upon itself the project of assuring human wholeness: what it perceives as an infallible closure of being that makes it impregnable and invulnerable to outside influences beyond one's control. Jüngel indicates this when he writes: "Without his relation to other humans, without his relation to his natural and social environment, and without his relationship to God, the human being is something other than whole."[13] Crucially, this ought not to be understood merely as a statement of fundamental ontology, or a programmatic assertion on Jüngel's part. Being "something other than whole" is an ontic reality, one that is readily available to the human being who sees him- or herself as threatened by the world. When the world is perceived as a threat, the ontological truth that human being cannot be whole without openness to its own worldly dimension is transformed – not entirely incorrectly – into a realization that humanity in and of itself suffers from an acute lack of wholeness. Left to itself, it is incomplete and, as it were, unfinished. Where things go wrong is with the diagnosis that the world is to blame for this state of affairs and the conclusion that, to prevent its own dissolution, humanity must remedy this lack of wholeness out of its own resources. It now appears to be self-evident that humanity must transform itself into a new humanity, able at all times to prevail against the world. The self-relation – precisely on account of its very humanity, correctly diagnosed as less than whole – will thus seek to establish and define itself beyond what it perceives as human vulnerability. Toward this contradictory goal – in which it is always *ahead* of its *human* self – it will direct all of its energy.[14]

---

[12] Cf. *Mystery*, 197; *GGW* 266.

[13] "Zum Wesen des Friedens," *TE V*, 32.

[14] Jüngel does not enter into dialog with contemporary critical theory and its accounts of selfhood. Yet it is obvious that his account could be significantly enriched if brought into conversation with the works of such figures as Michel Foucault or, more recently, Judith Butler. They all share some continental antecedents as well as intellectual opponents. Beyond this genealogical overlap, which of course as such carries no obligation to dialog, there is, I believe, a genuine possibility for conversation and mutual enrichment of perspectives. To give only one example, in her *Giving an Account of Oneself* (New York: Fordham University Press, 2005), Butler discusses the emergence of the ego in the context of what she calls "ethical violence," which is mostly the world's impingement on one, understood as guilt formation. Jüngel, for his part, is interested in the way the individual responds to this impingement by doing violence to the world and, not least, to him- or herself. Those two viewpoints could profitably be brought together.

A key consequence of this is withdrawal of the foundational relationality underlying human being: not merely in the sense of its nonnegotiability as a fundamental fact beyond one's choice but, above all, in the sense of *hiddenness* and *obscurity*. For a human being consumed by his or her self-relation, the rich relationality of humanity is neither self-evident nor empirically accessible. The very idea seems, in fact, to be a denial of humanity. It is so because a change has taken place in the person's being, a "radical negation . . . not simply logically but ontologically."[15] This change has the character of the sharpest possible disjunction between the ontic level (what is) and the now hidden ontological relationality. It manifests itself ontically in the privatization of language. Language becomes a casualty, in that its communicative character yields priority to rational thought (by definition, interior) in the service of self-actualization. This leads, further, to the prioritization of action as indispensible for the maintenance of the self-relation. Action no longer follows on the heels of speech as a vehicle of interrelation, but instead, subjected to the exigencies of the self-relation, it becomes a means of thought's externalization.

Before we discuss action and rationality further, what needs to be made clear is that we have here a vicious circle that has no anthropological resolution: humans use their relational potential, as speech- and world-beings, to obscure this very relational potential. Herein lies the chief self-contradiction of human being. It is by means of none other than language, despite and in the face of its capacity for interrelation, that humans reduce all of their relations to their own self-relation and so come to see themselves, ostensibly for their own sake, as subjects in isolation from others. Yet an all-dominating self-relation, despite appearances to the contrary, cannot simply do away with the fragility of human existence. Its exertions continue rather to be a testimony to this fragility. Human world-being, now seen as dangerous vulnerability, cannot be dissolved or absorbed by means of language and the self-relation, which this worldliness has given rise to in the first place. However, because humans are by themselves unable to take a step back from themselves, so to speak, and to see their world-being and other-relation as fundamentally belonging alongside of their self-relation, they feel compelled even further down the isolationist path in order to assure the integrity of their being. Needless to say, this obscures humanity's essential relationality even further.

---

[15] "The World as Possibility and Actuality. The Ontology of the Doctrine of Justification," *Essays I*, 106.

Keeping in mind that, for Jüngel, language is inextricably linked with human relationality, let us now turn to the symptoms of this relationality's contradiction. Those are the *primacy of action* and the self's *entrenchment in rationality*. Jüngel views both as perversions of human language-being. Our aim will be to show how, according to Jüngel, *action* and *language* – even when they fall victim to human relationlessness – do not cease to attest to human fragility and continue to offer glimpses of humans' primordial relationality.

Homo faber

Jüngel considers the primacy of action largely in its collective dimension. But it is assumed that what happens on the collective level has its parallel and prototype in the emergence of the self-securing subject. For an individual, the goal of action is to make an identity for him- or herself, an identity that is free from unwanted interference, genuinely his or her own. An individual seeks to transcend his or her fragile world-being, now considered old, and to construct a new, impregnable self – which can be done only by pushing back against the world. Importantly, as suspended between the old and the new, the self-securing person cannot refrain from action, as that would be tantamount to admitting defeat and allowing one's being to disintegrate. Action comes to define the person; it is the *sine qua non* of being.

Modernity has made action into its defining characteristic. In its collective dimension, the primacy of action, however, concerns not only aggregated individuals, each pursuing his or her own self-contained and secured subjectivity. The primacy of action, Jüngel holds, also concerns humanity as such. It manifests itself as (1) the absence of meaning, the *meaning of humanity*, and (2) the compulsion to construct this meaning at the world's expense. It is the rise of action in response to human meaninglessness that is of particular concern to Jüngel. This area of Jüngel's anthropological critique is perhaps the most dated, but that is a risk which inevitably attends any contextualization of theological concepts. Let us examine Jüngel's views first, before we determine whether one may still speak of the self's contradiction brought about by the self's orientation to action. We shall pay particular attention to the ways in which the fundamental human relationality continues to reassert itself by subverting the human quest for meaning.

In asserting humanity's meaninglessness, Jüngel zeros in on the Enlightenment project of human emancipation and this project's eventual failure to secure the meaning of human being. The roots of Jüngel's critique can, however, be found already in Luther's skepticism of reason's capacity to grasp itself or humanity as such. In his 1536 *Disputation Concerning Man,* Luther invokes a long-standing definition of the human: "Philosophy or human wisdom defines man as an animal having reason, sensation, and body [*animal rationale, sensitivum, corporeum*]." Luther notes that reason, "the principal part of man," appears to be that which essentially distinguishes humans from animals. However, reason has no *a priori* access to itself and thus cannot know whether it is corrupt or not. It knows itself *a posteriori* through its engagement with contingent realities – with the rationalities and irrationalities of human existence. Consequently, it is by itself unable maintain a strict distinction between human and animal. And so, when it comes to reason, as the material cause of humanity, "it will appear that we know almost nothing about man." Things, Luther alleges, get only more desperate when it comes to the efficient and final causes, which in each case point beyond the human as the source and locus of humanity's definition.[16]

But what do they point to? "The origin of human existence can be a question neither of mere chance nor of pure necessity." With these words, Jüngel gives expression to the pervasive sentiment that can be traced from the late modern "radical questionableness" of humanity all the way back to the Enlightenment.[17] He notes that it is far easier to assert where humanity is *not* from. We know of no higher necessity that mandates human existence. Yet it is impossible for us to insist with certainty that our humanity is simply a product of chance, especially when one considers human ability to transcend the element of chance in our individual lives.[18] If then both chance and necessity are out of the question, this implies that a definition of humanity is absent but not impossible; it is absent only in the sense of not being immanent and thus self-evident. This combination of absence and

---

[16] *LW* 34:137–8; *WA* 39¹:175. With very much the same point in mind, Jüngel cites the philosophical anthropologist Helmuth Plessner's article on anthropology from a philosophical perspective in *Die Religion in Geschichte und Gegenwart,* 3rd ed., vol. 1 (Tübingen: Mohr Siebeck, 1960), 411, where Plessner states there that humans are "beings whose origin and destination are equally obscure" ("Humanity in Correspondence to God," *Essays I,* 129). In *FoC,* 44, Jüngel offers another citation to the same effect, this time coming from Ernst Bloch's work, *Experimentum mundi: Frage, Kategorien des Herausbringens, Praxis* (Frankfurt am Main: Suhrkamp, 1975), 239.

[17] Jüngel's comment appears in an exegetical passage on Gotthold Lessing: "Humanity in Correspondence to God," *Essays I,* 128, 130; cf. "On Becoming Truly Human," *Essays II,* 222–3.

[18] Jüngel illustrates this by quoting Saladin's words to Nathan from Lessing's *Nathan the Wise:* "A man like you stands not where accident/Of birth has cast him. If he so remain/It is from judgment, reasons, choice of best" (Act III, Scene V; trans. E. Frothingham [New York: Henry Holt, 1892], 110).

possibility, acutely felt, makes the *meaning* of humanity – who or what it is – into a question that will not go away and a problem that humanity cannot avoid facing.[19]

It is in the ambiguous location between necessity and chance that the *homo faber* finds his origin. For the modern self-securing subject, the ambiguous location of humanity between chance and necessity constitutes a challenge to attempt a *positive* self-determination. Humanity is important enough to assert its own importance. What Luther meant, of course, was one's relationship to God as Creator. But, to the modern human ensconced within his or her self, the same absence of immanent meaning promises only one thing: the possibility of self-creation. And this can be done only by wresting one's identity from the world. For the *homo faber* the world is no longer something that is encountered and *welcomed* in the process of encountering oneself; nor is it a place, as it were, which actually enables one truly to encounter oneself. Instead, the world's expanse threatens to disrupt one's self-relation and to reduce humanity to insignificance. The world's openness imperils the precarious security and self-importance of the subject. It must, therefore, be done away with, subjugated by one's self-relation, and harnessed for its purposes. At the end of this process, one hopes, humanity will finally be all in all, having come to itself totally and in foolproof security.

Contrary to this modern conviction, Jüngel does not see humanity's indefinability as a temporary misfortune, eventually to be rectified by action. He argues rather that, from an immanent perspective, indefinability is both inevitable and insurmountable. When human action, which was to reflect the relational, linguistic make-up of the human, is employed for the purposes of self-determination, language (*Sprache*) becomes a means of violence through which the threat the world poses to one's self-relation is diffused – only to reemerge in a most unexpected way. How does this happen? For the *homo faber*, Jüngel observes, nothing has meaning in and of itself.[20] Bent on acquiring self-meaning, the human seeks to gain it by manufacturing it for everything around. "When things are transferred into concepts, they are acted upon."[21] Jüngel calls this a "gnostic flight from the

---

[19] *FoC*, 45.

[20] "Hoffen, Handeln – und Leiden," *BR*, 20.

[21] "Humanity in Correspondence to God," *Essays I*, 146. Jüngel does not wish to exclude altogether the stating function of language as it is reflected in our ability to act on the world and to make use of it. There is responsible dominion over the world. But for mastery over the world to become responsible, human action must first find its own limits, it must, to put it more precisely, be freed from its limitlessness. Only in this way will one be liberated for an *encounter* with the world in which one will be able to make something both of the world and of one's self. I will speak to this in Chapter 3.

world" which renders the world as a whole "a completely human work, in every respect a manufactured and artificial world."²² Yet precisely here one encounters a contradiction that offers a glimpse into the true nature of humanity. A totally humanized world turns out to be positively inhuman and uninhabitable. A fabricated world is a world without openness, over-familiar and utterly predictable; it turns out to be a stifling and dehumanizing world.²³ This world holds up a mirror to humanity, but it is doubtful whether, in the end, its makers can, or would even wish to, recognize themselves in it. Human action, aimed at colonizing the world, thus proves unable to solve human indefinability. It at best affords another negative determination, indicating that humanity, to put it simply, is not a product of its action. Human action cannot heal human fragility.

At bottom, the failure to overcome humanity's indefiniteness is a failure of language when the latter is enlisted in the forcible overcoming of the world's openness and used conceptually to subjugate the world. Employed discursively, rather than for the purpose of facilitating encounter, addressing, and doing justice, language shows itself to be limited. The fact that it can be (mis)used to impose meaning on the world does not entail that it is capable of bestowing the same kind of meaning on humanity. Jüngel underscores this by drawing attention, in his discussion of Luther's *Disputation Concerning Man*, to the necessarily partial, piecemeal nature of conceptual definitions which, as discursive, are unable to grasp the "*homo totus et perfectus*."²⁴

This inherent shortcoming of conceptual discourse finds its reflection in the modern sciences. Their very plurality, Jüngel notes, while advancing specialized knowledge of numerous dimensions of human existence, appears to indicate that "a definition of humanity as a whole seems to have become impossible." What has remained glaringly unanswered is "our question about ourselves," which the "multitude of positive findings" simply fall short of answering, unless the findings are pushed to "say more than they really signify."²⁵

The entire scientific enterprise, when viewed in light of Jüngel's critique of the *homo faber*, appears to be suspended between the poles of chance and

---

²² "Humanity in Correspondence to God," *Essays I*, 149. In *Justification*, 263, Jüngel comments: "We *manufacture* meaning by so reducing the excessive complexity of the world that we are able to fit in with the world." Cf. also *Mystery*, 178; *GGW* 240.

²³ This point, echoing the later Heidegger, has been made especially well by Leszek Kołakowski in *The Presence of Myth*, trans. Adam Czerniawski (1972; Chicago: The University of Chicago Press, 1989), 74–7.

²⁴ "Ganzheitsbegriffe – in theologischer Perspektive," *TE V*, 43–5.

²⁵ "Humanity in Correspondence to God," *Essays I*, 128–9; cf. "On Becoming Truly Human," *Essays II*, 223.

necessity. The "multitude of positive findings" may lead one to believe that a critical mass will eventually be reached and disclose humanity to itself in keeping with its aspirations. But, where human self-making is concerned, science seems immovably lodged in the ambiguous zone where it constantly undermines and reestablishes human uniqueness. In doing so, it continues to fuel the compulsion to overcome humanity's indefinability. Thus, admittedly, science has made this indefinability all the more egregious. The sciences, from biological through psychological to sociological ones, have in important respects undermined humans' claim to uniqueness within their own environment. But science, in principle, has not excluded the possibility of establishing human uniqueness. The sciences continue to demonstrate this uniqueness, without, however, being able to specify what it *all* means. Unlike (wild) animals, for example, humans are found to be open to the world, incomplete, as it were, in their instinctual constitution and throughout their lives exhibit an attitude of curiosity toward the world which in animals is present only at a young age and is later replaced instinct. Humans have also been shown to be capable of gratuitously inflicting pain on, maiming, and even killing members of their own species.[26] Finally, as already hinted at by Luther in his discussion of reason, the scientific enterprise continues in itself to be testimony to humanity's uniqueness,[27] even as it appears constantly to undermine it.[28] Thus, the sciences – like the reduction of language to concepts in general – do not simply exacerbate human indefinability, but

[26] In his essay, "Humanity in Correspondence to God," Jüngel offers a brief list of ambivalent animal-human distinctions. He makes a cursory reference only to Max Scheler, the philosopher Helmuth Plessner and the anthropologist Hans Weinert (129). In a Reformation Day sermon on "Freedom under God's Protection" (*Von Zeit zu Zeit* [München: Keiser, 1976], 92), Jüngel makes a general observation that in comparison to animals humans are without inherent restraints, since nature does not restrain them. This harks back to Kant's defense of the essential and distinctive role of reason in human nature: the task of reason it is not to assure human happiness and the satisfaction of needs, which could be done far more effectively by means of instinct, but to regulate moral behavior; see *Groundwork of The Metaphysics of Morals* (1785). In *Practical Philosophy*, trans. and ed. Mary J. Gregor (Cambridge: University Press, 1996), 50–2 [4:395–6].

[27] I realize that this is not an uncontroversial point, esp. when one considers, as does Leszek Kołakowski, the generation of scientific theories to be "a shorthand technique of recording the performed experiments" in which humans make use of the same capacity that is available to all beings equipped with a nervous system, namely, the ability to acquire conditioned reflexes; see *The Presence of Myth*, 111. For a different account that emphasizes the personal, idiosyncratic element in the formulation of scientific theories, see Michael Polanyi, *Personal Knowledge: Towards a Post-Critical Philosophy* (Chicago: University of Chicago Press, 1962).

[28] A better example of the ambivalence of scientific findings is furnished by the work of the Austrian zoologist and Nobel Prize laureate, Konrad Lorenz. In *The Foundations of Ethology: The Principal Ideas and Discoveries in Animal Behavior* (trans. K. Z. Lorenz & R. W. Kickert [New York & Wien: Springer, 1981]), Lorentz notes that "Except for the one great evolutionary step leading from nonlife to life, the coming into existence of conceptual thought certainly

also, in doing so, they simultaneously hold out a promise to overcome it. As such, for the *homo faber* science constitutes a summons, as it were, to doing, to continued self-determination in the hope that humanity's felt uniqueness will in the end yield the meaning of being human.

Let me conclude this discussion of action's primacy, as it emerges from Jüngel's own account, with a few general observations. The indefinability, or, as Jüngel puts it, "radical questionableness," of humanity, is not simply the outcome of humans' losing sight of the fundamental relationality of their being. Rather, it is a product of humanity's own pursuit of self-actualization in the face of that loss. It is an inevitable corollary of human self-understanding as a *homo faber*. The *homo faber* labors under the delusion that, because language can impose meaning, it will also give meaning to humanity, or, in the case of science, that, because its findings do not entirely undermine human uniqueness, those findings will eventually reach a critical mass that will yield humanity's overall meaning. One must simply press on. Three things must be emphasized in this context. First, for a human being bent on self-actualization, action is the *sine qua non* of being; it is primary *and* inescapable. Second, the contradiction between action's promise and what it actually delivers is an indication of the underling self-contradiction in which the *homo faber* exists. Third, the fact that linguistic colonization fails at the most crucial point, that of providing humanity's meaning, coupled with the fact that even for the *homo faber* self-meaning is not immanent, is itself a glimpse into the fundamental relationality of human being. Humanity's meaning is to be found through world-being, but it is questionable whether it can be wrested from the world for the sake of self-creation.

---

creates *the most essential distinction known to science*" (emphasis added). Conceptual thought possesses "*unprecedented* systematic characteristics" that constitute "a difference in *essence*, not only in degree." But, importantly, it does so like "*every* major step in evolution." Thus Lorenz immediately hastens to qualify his observation by adding that "it is no miracle . . . Like all other evolutionary events, [the rise of conceptual thought] consists of integrating pre-existing and independently functioning systems to form a new, superordinated one . . . " Having thus qualified what might seem like absolute human uniqueness, Lorenz is again compelled to qualify his qualification: this new system, to be sure, "possesses unprecedented and previously unpredictable systemic properties." Lorenz is careful to emphasize that it is "impossible [in advance] to infer the possibility of a superordinated system from studying the characteristics of its potential components" (339–40). As he applies these methodological observations, Lorenz is able, on the one hand, to claim that what is distinctive about humans is their capacity for common knowledge, for the accumulation of tradition from generation to generation. On the other hand, he also insists that "in the passing on of cultural information from one generation to the next, processes are at work that are entirely independent of rational considerations and . . . in many respects, are functionally analogous to the factors maintaining invariance in genetic inheritance" (343, 346).

As noted earlier, Jüngel's critique of the *homo faber* constitutes his response to humanity's questionableness. This questionableness, as humanity's inability to establish its own meaning, is a direct outcome of the Enlightenment assertion of humanity's autonomy. However, at the turn of the third millennium, it is doubtful whether humanity, or Western society to be more specific, experiences anxiety over the absence of its own meaning. This may very well be due to the fact that ours is a "culture of analgesics," as Leszek Kołakowski put it.[29] But it seems more plausible that the contradiction of self-securing is today simply more evident in individual lives, rather than in the presumption of humanity's sense of senselessness.

Zygmunt Bauman points out that in late, "liquid" modernity the *outcomes* of human actions have become not only inscrutable but also random. Human actions can no longer be trusted as capable of moving toward their intended goal, for example, that of humanity's security. Today's society is one in which power is increasingly global and exterritorial and so free from institutional constraints. Ours is, moreover, a "risk society" in which modernization, in minimizing the unpredictability of the natural world, has manufactured its own unpredictability and a new host of risk factors. The late-modern society, according to Bauman, is characterized by a fundamental uncertainty, the absence of ready-made recipes for a decent life, and the pervasive threat of the future. In this setting, autonomy no longer constitutes the promise of self-security, whether collective or individual, but a fate that dooms a person to confront systemic uncertainties and contradictions on an individual basis and so to attempt a biographical solution to them. What late modernity shares in common with its earlier avatars is thus the relentlessness of action – action is simply not a choice, even if it now seems to be deprived of a specifiable course and horizon. The self-contradiction in which liquid-modern autonomy involves a self-securing individual is defined by a disjunction between self-assertion, from which one cannot withdraw, and self-constitution, of which one is now decidedly incapable. One's actions are able at best only *temporarily* to stave off the risk of the future, because they themselves are part of the volatility of social settings in which they take place and which they perpetuate.[30]

---

[29] Kołakowski, *The Presence of Myth*, 83–109.

[30] See especially Zygmunt Bauman, "Freedom and security: The unfinished story of a tempestuous union," *The Individualized Society* (Cambridge, UK: Polity, 2001), 41–56. Cf. Ulrich Beck, *Risk Society: Towards a New Modernity*, trans. Mark Ritter (London: Sage Publications, 1992); and Ulrich Beck, *World at Risk*, trans. Ciaran Cronin (Cambridge, UK: Polity, 2009).

To conclude that today the contradiction of self-securing manifests itself primarily in *individual* lives is by no means to discount the fact that late-modern society, as such, has also become desensitized to its own sense of senselessness: it is a "culture of analgesics." Its being such must, likewise, be related to the pervasive uncertainty and risk. For late modernity's global volatility – in which one finds oneself caught up and which contributes to the unreliability even of communal actions – brings to light what was once only an oblique characteristic of the *homo faber*, namely, the absorption of the individual within the world. What characterizes the late-modern form of this absorption is that it has reached a level where the very human openness to the world becomes dissolved. The Italian philosopher, Giorgio Agamben, has provided conceptual resources for articulating this transition from humanity's indefinability as an insurmountable problem to an indefinability which is no longer perceived as a problem and, as such, poses a vital threat to humanity.

To begin with, Agamben emphasizes the characteristic of openness to the world as peculiar to humans – though he does not thereby exclude some putative animal nature. Based on his reading of Heidegger, Agamben notes that the human "is simply an animal that has learned to be bored; it has awakened" *from* being utterly captivated by its environment *to* the fact of this captivation. "This awakening of the living being to its own being-captivated," Agamben writes, "this anxious and resolute opening to a not-open, is the human."[31] Importantly, on Agamben's account, this definition does not yield some exclusive *essence* of humanity. What is grasped is nothing but animal captivation, rather than "a further, wider, and brighter space, achieved beyond the limits of the animal environment, and unrelated to it."[32] What Agamben thus articulates is humanity's indefinability, with awareness of this fact being the only mark of human uniqueness. This leads him to call for resolute contentment with indefinability so understood, with "the central emptiness, the hiatus that – within man – separates man and animal." He advocates "risk[ing] ourselves in this emptiness."[33] Now, whether a Sabbath rest from self-creation is actually possible, as Agamben would like his readers to believe, is an altogether different story.

The sole alternative to coming to terms with the senselessness at the core of human life, Agamben seems to indicate, is an obliteration of our

---

[31] Giorgio Agamben, *The Open: Man and Animal*, trans. K. Attell (Stanford: Stanford University Press, 2004), 70.
[32] Agamben, *The Open*, 68.
[33] Agamben, *The Open*, 92.

humanity, the annihilation of human openness to the world, and thus a *forced indefinability* that precludes any Sabbath rest whatever. That this remains the sole alternative stems from the failure of what Agamben calls "the anthropological machine": the complex deployment of humanity's cultural resources in the service of self-knowledge. The machine's purpose, more specifically, was to produce man through conceptual and technological mastery of the relation between man and animal; or, to put it simply, the salvation of man from animal. But the machine has failed. In the process of creating man, it has reduced humanity to precisely that which was to be excluded: the animal. This has happened because of the pervasive uncertainty of late modernity – an uncertainty brought about by the very operation of the anthropological machine in the confidence that humanity could eventually overcome its indefinability. For it has become doubtful that humanity can, in the end, recognize itself in its self-creation. Given this pervasive uncertainty, it is no longer possible to set before communities their historico-political destiny. In any case, poetry, religion or philosophy, by means of which this used to be done, have all become irreparably privatized. Instead, Agamben notes, "natural life itself and its well-being seem to appear as humanity's last historical task." The management of this bare, biological life takes place, according to Agamben, through the genome project, global economy and humanitarian ideology. "It is not easy to say," Agamben concludes, "whether humanity that has taken upon itself" – that, we might add, is left with nothing but – "the mandate of the total management of its animality is still human," at least in the sense of humanness aspired to by the *homo faber*.[34] The securing of biological life and the not unrelated provision of instant gratification are, to be sure, a humanization of the animal. Yet the fact that the *homo faber* has been reduced to this task, that no other, higher human task is available to him only confirms humanity's surprising closure to its own openness. The humanization of the animal is, in a striking reversal, the animalization of man – the absorption of man in the world, in the provision for the contingencies of man's biological existence. It is in the face of this destruction of human openness to the world that Agamben calls for halting the anthropological machine altogether and simply and knowingly coming to terms with humanity's indefinability. The salvation of humanity lies in acknowledging that neither the human nor the animal, as such, can be saved. The *homo faber* must leave

[34] Agamben, *The Open*, 76–7.

himself behind and allow himself to become obsolete. Only thus, according to Agamben, will he find rest.

This is only a brief sketch of how Jüngel's critique of the *homo faber* and the primacy of action could be developed. I believe that Bauman's and Agamben's assessment of the late-modern condition actually reinforces the notion of self-contradiction inherent in the existence of a would-be autonomous human being. While Agamben conjures up the promise of contentment in resignation, Bauman points to an even heightened and more desperate inescapability of action. More importantly, Bauman's analysis provides an account of this contradiction that not only focuses on its collective and social manifestations but also convincingly translates those into individual predicaments. Jüngel – as we are about to see also in his account of human rationality – has the tendency to view the self-contradiction in collective and universal terms, which makes the passage to freedom as the elemental interruption of an individual existence not as developed theoretically as it could be. A more detailed exploration of the possibilities offered by recent critiques of late modernity is, however, beyond the scope of this study. At this point, we must rather turn to the corollary of making the world secure for oneself, that is, to the construal of the self in rational terms and Jüngel's interpretation of it.

Retreat into rationality

The enlistment of speech in the project of colonizing the world betrays the elevation of rationality to the status of the command center of one's self-securing as well as its fundamental locale. Subjected to the exigencies of self-determining action, language comes to coincide with thought. It assumes, as Jüngel puts it, a commending (*empfehlen*) function, that is, "it makes recommendations to thinking," whereas the commanding (*befehlen*) role is reserved for thought. The communicative function of language is thus absorbed into, or at best made subservient to, the conceptualizing power of thought. The "fundamental linguistic structure of human beings," when harnessed for the purposes of self-determination, becomes a modality of rationality.[35]

The privileging of rationality over relationality as the defining characteristic of humanity necessarily accompanies self-securing. Self-securing (through action) logically presupposes control over the self, if not quite

---

[35] "Humanity in Correspondence to God," *Essays I*, 147–8.

self-possession (through reason). This is not to say that rational self-possession can simply be taken for granted. The two are rather simultaneous undertakings that constantly reinforce each other.[36] The self's disentanglement from the world more often than not enables one to impose one's will on the world, though it may also be the case that it is the failure of one's attempt to browbeat the world into submission that fuels a retreat into rationality and the self's detachment.

Yet even if restricted to mere rationality, self-possession is impossible in the end – and that in a way analogous to the failure of action. The imposition of meaning on the world does not give one meaning, at least it does not yield the sort of meaning in which one would, in the final analysis, recognize oneself, showing in a surprising reversal that one ought perhaps to receive oneself from the world. Likewise, a rational retreat, when relentlessly pursued, opens up in the rational self a dimension beyond reason's control. The project of rational securing posits a "beyond" which becomes the domain of faith, and about which nothing can be done. Jüngel appeals to Kant to make this point. Before we examine Jüngel's engagement with Kant, we must, however, situate the reason-centered understanding of the self more broadly.

The rational animal

Following Heidegger, Jüngel occasionally invokes the ancient Greek definition of the human as a ζῷον λόγον ἔχον.[37] Thanks to a largely etymological analysis of the noun λόγος, Heidegger came to believe that the phrase, in its original meaning, denoted a "living thing whose Being is essentially determined by the potentiality for discourse." It was only later,

---

[36] Thus, in *FoC*, 81, Jüngel argues that *complete* self-possession is also the overarching goal of action.

[37] E.g., "Humanity in Correspondence to God," *Essays I*, 146; "Value-Free Truth," *Essays II*, 207; *FoC*, 90. The question of Jüngel's indebtedness to Heidegger is a complicated one, and, since it is beyond the scope of this project, it cannot be given full attention. According to Jüngel, theology has indubitably benefitted from attentiveness to Heidegger's thought. This being said, Jüngel underscores, against uncritical appropriation, that "Theology is not ontology, although every theological statement has its ontological implications. Theology asks not about *being as such*, but about *the being of God, human being and the being of the world*. It asks, further, because it *has heard*, not because it is after something that remains yet to be interrogated" ("Gott entsprechendes Schweigen? Theologie in der Nachbarschaft des Denkens von Martin Heidegger," *Martin Heidegger: Fragen an sein Werk* [Stuttgart: Philipp Reclam, 1977], 41). For Jüngel's view of the theological relevance of Heidegger's thought, see, in addition, his article, co-authored with Michael Trowitzsch, "Provozierendes Denken: Bemerkungen zur theologischen Anstößigkeit der Denkwege Martin Heideggers," *Neue Hefte für Philosophie* 23 (1984), 59–74.

according to Heidegger, that the phrase became synonymous with an *animal rationale*, something living (understood as an object) which has reason (understood as "some superior endowment"). Heidegger did not consider the later definition to be false but clearly parasitical on the earlier one and with a tendency to conceal this indebtedness.[38] Jüngel believes that what paved the way for the emergence of the ζῷον λόγον ἔχον in its rational meaning was Plato's distinction between the soul's parts, of which the highest, divine one must achieve mastery over the entire human being, in order for one's life to be happy and self-sufficient. The distinction was given further currency by Plato's insistence that this mastery involved a subordination of sensuous desires to knowledge and reason.[39] Plato's views – originally expressed in the context of his indictment of an unjust, tyrannical life – were taken over by a line of epigones (of whom Plotinus was one) and gave rise, as Jüngel notes, to a school. The school emphasized the need for the rational inner man to exist apart from sensuous entanglement. It was the inner man that was then identified with the human being proper.[40]

Jüngel situates his ontology of the person in general opposition to what he sees as the Platonic notion that the human is a "being destined for knowledge," that is, one whose "true essence is deduced from what is

---

I shall here limit myself to several methodological comments. First of all, Jüngel's indebtedness has been variously judged as "unthematized" (Mark Mattes, *Toward Divine Relationality: Eberhard Jüngel's New Trinitarian, Postmetaphysical Approach* [unpublished Ph.D. thesis, University of Chicago, 1995], 310) or, on the contrary, principled and well thought through. The latter view is that of Arnold V. Neufeldt-Fast, who argues that Heidegger's thought has provided "*the Anstoß* – that is, both impulse and offence . . . driv[ing] Jüngel's assessment of modern anthropology . . . and creatively provok[ing] Jüngel's own nonmetaphysical theological constructions" (*Eberhard Jüngel's Theological Anthropology in Light of His Christology* [unpublished Ph.D. thesis, University of St. Michael's College, 1996], 72). I believe there are other influences at play which the spotlight on Heidegger obscures. Jüngel is also strongly and independently influenced by Luther's attempts to overcome Aristotelian substance metaphysics in favor of a relational ontology of the person, and the same influence can be demonstrated for Heidegger (e.g., Benjamin D. Crowe, *Heidegger's Religious Origins: Destruction and Authenticity* [Bloomington: Indiana University Press, 2006], esp. 35–66). Neufeldt-Fast's view is somewhat problematic in that he tends to reduce Luther's impact on Jüngel to the former's rather narrowly construed and artificially isolated doctrine of justification, and does not at all register Luther's influence on Heidegger's philosophy.

[38] *B&T*, 25, 48, 165. Cf. Luther's philosophical definition of man above. It must be noted that the *definition* of the human as a rational animal is commonly attributed to Aristotle; Jüngel himself takes this attribution for granted in his article "Der Mensch – im Schnittpunkt von Wissen, Glauben, Tun und Hoffen," *Zeitschrift für Theologie und Kirche* (2004), 329. It is questionable, however, whether Aristotle's theory of predication, where this definition is allegedly found, yields an actual definition of this sort (cf., e.g., the opening pages of Aristotle's *Categories*).

[39] *FoC*, 89–90; cf. *The Republic*, Book IX, 588–91 and 586–7 respectively.

[40] *FoC*, 90.

understood to be the essence of knowledge."[41] He specifically objects to the corollary understanding of the human as a being that is composed, on the one hand, of an immaterial soul, alone capable of being grasped by knowledge, and, on the other, of an animal body, which is not only largely negligible but actually constitutes an impediment on the soul's path toward its epistemic destiny. Thus, with his call for a theological "de-Platonising of Christianity," Jüngel,[42] like Heidegger, situates himself in opposition to the metaphysical tradition which views the human as, first and foremost, an *animal rationale*.

Of course, Jüngel is not opposed to rationality as such, just as he is not opposed to human action in the world. He comments positively on humanity's intellectual and technological achievement in very much the same spirit as Luther's affirmation of the "majesty of reason" in *The Disputation Concerning Man*.[43] These are not rhetorical ornaments. What Jüngel does oppose is rationality, insofar as it implies self-possession and constitutes the basis of human self-realization. Neither self-realization nor, for that matter, self-possession offers a solution to humanity's ills. Jüngel's entire philosophical-theological endeavor may be seen as directed toward constructing a reasoned argument to that effect.[44] A large portion of this task involves theological engagement with philosophy through a respectful, yet uncompromising, "conflict of the faculties."[45]

---

[41] *Death*, 43.

[42] *Death*, 53.

[43] E.g., "Befreiende Freiheit – als Merkmal christlicher Existenz," *Anfänger: Herkunft und Zukunft christlicher Existenz* (Stuttgart: Radius-Verlag, 2003), 21–2. Like Luther, Jüngel has been accused of undervaluing human agency (e.g., John Webster, "Justification, Analogy and Action. Passivity and Activity in Jüngel's Anthropology," John Webster (ed.), *The Possibilities of Theology: Studies in the Theology of Eberhard Jüngel in His Sixtieth Year* (Edinburgh: T&T Clark, 1994), 140–1; and, in a less nuanced manner, Neufeldt-Fast, *Eberhard Jüngel's Theological Anthropology*, 394ff). One of the goals of this study is to show that that is not the case.

[44] Jüngel writes: "Though Christian theology is certainly indebted to Western thought, faith recognizes that Western thought is following a path beset with difficulties, insofar as it reduces reason to rational activity and to its own model of rationality, in which perceiving reason falls victim to the independent and self-securing activity of the knowing subject" ("'My Theology' – A Short Summary," *Essays II*, 9).

[45] In his essay, "Der Mensch – im Schnittpunkt von Wissen, Glauben, Tun und Hoffen: Die theologische Fakultät im Streit mit der durch Immanuel Kant repräsentierten philosophischen Fakultät," Jüngel develops the parameters for such a theological-philosophical engagement. He does this by taking as his point of departure Barth's three models of theology's engagement with Kant. Like Barth, Jüngel opts for the third model, which has theology "stand on its own feet in relation to philosophy . . . recognizing the point of departure for its method in revelation, just as decidedly as philosophy sees its point of departure in reason." The goal is theology's "dialogue with philosophy." In regard to Kant, this entails specifically "at least questioning not only the application of the Kantian conception of the problem, but that conception itself, and therefore the autocracy and

According to Jüngel, Kant's is the crowning effort in the anthropological tradition whose trajectory starts with Plato. What characterizes the tradition, broadly speaking, is the disproportionate importance it attaches to rationality as the determinative trait of humanity. This tradition embraces not only thinkers, such as Boethius and those following his famous definition of the person, most notably, Thomas Aquinas.[46] It includes Descartes and his now infamous reduction of the "I" to a *res cogitans*.[47] More interestingly, especially when one considers the practical nature of Kant's emphasis on reason, the tradition also includes a host of Christian thinkers, such as Meister Eckhart, who might be described broadly as proponents of mystical theologies. In its mystical strand, whose preoccupation is with the cultivation of a proper existential posture, the tradition translates this singling out of rationality into a detachment of what it often terms the "inner man" from distracting and harmful sensuous entanglement in the world. In consequence of this detachment, the inner man, identified with reason (and usually also the divine spark in the soul), attains to superior and supramundane epistemic insight. In detachment, the person becomes truly him- or herself. The person – which is significant for this study – becomes truly free.

What the mystical tradition leaves largely concealed is that the self-emptying it calls for and seeks to cultivate, oftentimes described as an "annihilation of self," constitutes the ultimate act of self-possession – a triumph of reason over desire and, further still, a triumph of the human self over God, insofar as, in the words of Meister Eckhart, "God must of necessity give himself to a heart that has detachment."[48] In Kant's case, there no longer is any doubt that an act of the human self is involved through and through. As a result, Kant views the human as only an *animal rationabile* ("an animal endowed with the *capacity of reason*") who then, through an act

its competence to judge human reason in relation to the religious problem" (Karl Barth, *Protestant Theology in the Nineteenth Century*, trans. B. Cozens and J. Bowden [Grand Rapids, MI: Eerdmans, 2002], 292–3; cited partially by Jüngel in "Der Mensch," 316–17). Jüngel develops this method further, in that he allows theology to stand in the wings, as it were, thus, on the one hand, priming the stage for the universality of its claim. On the other hand, by delaying theology's entrance, he pushes philosophy toward a level of exhaustion, at which point it, too, begins to manifest its fissures.

46 Boethius: "*Persona est naturae rationalis individua substantia*" (*Liber contra Eutychem et Nestorium*, IV.8); Aquinas: "*omne individuum rationalis naturae dicitur persona*" (*Summa Theologica*, I, q. 29, a. 1).

47 Rene Descartes, *Discourse on Method*, Part IV, in *The Philosophical Writings of Descartes*, trans. J. Cottingham et al. (Cambridge: University Press, 1985), 127.

48 Meister Eckhart, "Counsels on Discernment," and "On Detachment," *The Essential Sermons, Commentaries, Treatises, and Defense*, ed. E. Colledge and B. McGinn (Mahwah, NJ: Paulist, 1981), 280 and 286 respectively.

of the will motivated by pure reason, achieves the status of an *animal rationale*.[49] Only in this way can an individual attain to "the worth [*Werth*] of the person."[50] In this way, it could be said, one becomes a human worth the name. What is significant, an act of self-possession, also for Kant, is at the same time an inevitable actualization of God. In Kant's words: "I *will* that there be a God."[51]

It is this dimension of belief that appears at the apex of self-possession that is of particular interest to us here as another fissure through which, according to Jüngel, the fundamental human relationality can be glimpsed.

Reason's faith

As we are about to engage Kant more closely, it is important not to lose sight of his (and this study's) overarching concern. Kant's critical exploration of the extent of human knowledge, properly motivated human action, and the role of religion in human life is at bottom animated by the more fundamental

---

[49] Immanuel Kant *Anthropology from a Pragmatic Point of View*, ed. R. B. Louden (1798; Cambridge: University Press, 2006), 226 [7:321]. Jüngel emphasizes this point in "Der Mensch," 329–30.

[50] Immanuel Kant, *Critique of Practical Reason* (1788). In *Practical Philosophy*, 258 [5:147].

[51] Kant, *Critique of Practical Reason*, 255 [5:143]. In *God as the Mystery of the World* (esp. 105–52; *GGW* 138–203), Jüngel is occupied chiefly with demonstrating that Western (substance) metaphysics – beginning with Aristotle's argument for God as a necessary being, moving through Aquinas, Descartes and Kant, and culminating with Feuerbach and Nietzsche – posits, with increasing self-awareness but also discomfort, the securing of God's essence and existence through the thinking human I. Human reason, as *cogitans*, guarantees the existence of God while determining the essence of God as exclusively perfection on the basis of that which humans lack. Kant represents a turning point in the trajectory, in that he relegates God beyond the realm of the cognizable in order to avoid self-contradictions of rational, knowledge-oriented thought. By thus taking the trajectory to its logical conclusion, Kant inadvertently paves the way for the subsequent atheistic denial of God's existence.

My reference here to the medieval affective traditions as antecedents to Kant has in view, first of all, the correspondence between their understanding of freedom as rational detachment and the Kantian conception of freedom as located in the practical exercise of pure reason. More importantly, for Kant (as is, of course, true of the mystics), the nexus of rational self-possession and self-actualizing action gives rise to a dimension of faith that escapes the all-conquering dominance of the human self-relation. For all of Jüngel's criticism of Kantian rationality and its disastrous consequences for the thought of God, this emergence of *belief*, despite all the ambiguity it entails, is seen by Jüngel as a *good* thing. Finally, Jüngel's critique of the Kantian notion of self-possessed freedom, together with the dimension of belief that inadvertently opens up within it, has its parallel in Luther's critical appropriation of the mystical tradition. Just as Jüngel critically appropriates Kant, so also did Luther critically appropriate the mystics. These two appropriations share significant emphases, with Jüngel following Luther's lead.

Jüngel's theology represents in many respects a conscious extension of Luther's project to overcome the anthropologically harmful influences of Aristotelian substance metaphysics by constructing in its place a relational ontology. Luther based this new ontology on the

question, "What is man?"[52] In this sense, Kant is part of the intellectual tradition that views rational self-possession as the *differentia specifica* of humanity. We shall first consider Kant's view of rational self-possession as freedom from empirical entanglement. Then, drawing on some of the critical points Jüngel raises, we shall investigate the dimension of faith that opens up in Kant's conception of essential human rationality.

According to Kant, an individual realizes his or her rational potential and so attains to humanity worth the name and to freedom only when the individual's acts of will are *not* grounded in the individual's world-being. They must not have their basis in a pursuit of happiness, not even ostensibly universal happiness. Happiness, Kant explains, is dependent on objects of experience. Thus, although the notion can rise to a level of generality, it cannot achieve universality.[53] Even less so can acts of the will be governed by inclination. The will must rather act in accordance with a purely formal law that cannot proceed from anywhere else other than pure reason – the moral law. This is an overarching law that requires all the principles that direct the will's activity to be of such a nature that they could be made into universal laws. The moral law alone, according to Kant, has the capacity to keep the specific rules of volitional engagement under control, assuring that they are not empirically conditioned. This does not mean, of course, that volitional acts will be devoid of a worldly object; it is rather that the acts cannot be motivated by such objects. Kant writes: "The sole principle of morality consists in independence from all matter of the law (namely, from a desired object) and at the same time in the determination of choice through the mere form of giving universal law that a maxim must be capable of."[54] Reason, and with it the will, becomes autonomous only through the moral law. Reason's freedom is both negative, in the sense of its independence

---

affective traditions, which he appreciated for their ambiguous attitude to the self-contained human self (the apex of self-realization brings into view the divine element in the soul and is often ecstatic). Luther, however, modified those traditions at one absolutely crucial point: the immanent divinized rationality was replaced with relationally understood faith (see my "Luther and the Lutherans," in the forthcoming *Oxford Handbook to the Reception History of Christian Theology*, ed. Sarah Coakley and Richard Cross). Jüngel's conscious, though not uncritical, treading in Luther's footsteps sheds light on his ambivalent attitude to Kant: he remains critical of Kant as a successor of the metaphysical tradition of rationality, while he is cautiously appreciative of Kant for exploding that very tradition in its practical dimension and for bringing belief back through the back door, so to speak, as an integral part of the human self. But Jüngel, like Luther, will seek to replace Kant's belief with relationally construed faith.

[52] A question Kant himself poses in his *Logic*, trans. R. S. Hartman and W. Schwarz (1800; New York: Dover, 1988), 29 [9:25]; cited in "Der Mensch," 318.

[53] Kant, *Critique of Practical Reason*, 168–9 [5:35–6].

[54] Kant, *Critique of Practical Reason*, 166 [5:33].

from empirical conditioning and positive in the sense of its *self*-legislating capacity. A rational individual alone is thus self-sufficient, notes Kant, insofar as the determination of his or her will is free, at least in its origin, from inclinations and needs. This self-sufficiency is analogous to that ascribed to the supreme being.[55]

It is against this backdrop that Jüngel asks critically: "How can reason, which does not ask after goals but commands unconditionally, say, as it were, to itself: et respice finem [keep in mind the goal]?"[56] What is it that keeps reason engaged in its endeavor? To answer this question, it is necessary, first, to consider how Kant explodes the traditional understanding of the human being as an *animal rationale*. It is true, on the one hand, that Kant espouses and takes to its logical conclusion the idea of self-possession, which analytically is part and parcel of the rationality-centered understanding of humanity. Kant cements the tradition, as it were. But, on the other hand, Kant's critical engagement with reason, precisely with a view to elevating rational self-possession, leads him to conclude that the human is not a being of knowledge! Human being, human rationality cannot be reduced to a concept of knowing. Even when we think of the human as a rational animal, Jüngel observes, this entails a careful division of thought into opinion, knowledge, and faith.[57] What motivates this division is not primarily reason's self-legislating capacity, which is, after all, withdrawn from the empirical. The division of thought is, above all, motivated by the fact that reason's ideas do not originate in empirical data processed by the understanding and, therefore, need not always find support in such data, as Kant argues in his *Critique of Pure Reason*. "Reason . . . is the faculty of inferring."[58] In the absence of empirical, experiential data, reason's inferences must be taken as only that: inferences, regulative ideas. They must not, however, be confused with knowledge.

Further, this precise circumscription of rational activity allows Kant to affirm God, but in such a way that God will not compromise but rather aid the project of human self-possession. Jüngel draws attention to the fact that, for Kant, morality must not be derived from religion, undergirded by its seeming dogmatic certainties, which religion tries to pass off as knowledge. To derive morality from religion would compromise the person's rational character, making his or her conduct machine- or puppet-like. Kant readily admits that religion, with its capacity to impose a moral code, could elicit

---

[55] Kant, *Critique of Practical Reason*, 235 [5:119].
[56] "Der Mensch," 332.
[57] "Der Mensch," 324–5.
[58] Immanuel Kant, *Critique of Pure Reason* (1781, 1787). Trans. and ed. Paul Guyer and Allen W. Wood (Cambridge: University Press, 1998), 403 [B386].

moral behavior. But, in Kant's words, "most actions conforming to the law would be done from fear, only a few from hope, and none at all from duty, and the moral worth of actions . . . would not exist at all."[59] Only when morality does not proceed from religion, but from self-legislating reason alone, will human beings finally come into their own and emerge from their "self-incurred minority," as Kant famously put it in his essay "What is Enlightenment?"[60] It is at this point that Kant allows God back into the picture as a purely rational inference. God is necessary because, as the author of all, God makes it possible to view the self-legislating human reason as consonant with the purposes of the world. To put it differently, by postulating God, Kant is able to naturalize rational self-possession as the promotion of the world's highest good and the execution of the divine will itself. However, as a postulate of reason without empirical grounding, God remains hidden. Kant, as Jüngel observes, considers this hiddenness to be grace. By remaining hidden, God allows, and Himself appears, to take seriously human self-possession and so also human freedom.[61] In all, though Jüngel is quite critical of "the ambiguous invisibility of a God who becomes definable primarily through human activity,"[62] he regards Kant's insistence that "Morality . . . *inevitably* leads to religion"[63] as a significant and intriguing assertion one must not simply gloss over.

This is the answer to our question: What keeps reason engaged in its endeavor? How does reason keep in mind the goal and yet remain pure? Reason, as Kant shows, *respicit finem* in the very exercise of its self-legislating, moral capacity. The imperative to rational self-possession, as that which makes one human and free, brings with itself the conviction that self-possession is precisely what harmonizes with the very structure of reality. Because the goal that reason keeps in mind is itself a rational inference, otherwise veiled in hiddenness, reason's self-legislation stands immune to ever being tainted by that which does not belong to reason, or by ever being tempted to fall back on a familiar prop. Kant can thus say: "the belief in a God and another world is so interwoven with my moral disposition that I am in as little danger of ever surrendering the former as I am worried that

---

[59] Kant, *Critique of Practical Reason*, 258 [5:147]; cited in "Der Mensch," 330.

[60] Immanuel Kant, *An Answer to the Question: What is Enlightenment?* (1784). In *Practical Philosophy*, 17 [8:35].

[61] "Der Mensch," 330–1.

[62] *FoC*, 31.

[63] Immanuel Kant, *Religion within the bounds of mere reason* (1793). In *Religion and Rational Theology*, trans. and ed. Allen W. Wood and George di Giovanni (Cambridge: University Press: 1996), 59 [6:6]. Cited in "Der Mensch," 332.

the latter can ever be torn away from me."[64] Belief in God is, for Kant, an inalienable aspect of reason's impulse toward self-possession.[65]

In the final analysis, Jüngel finds "unacceptable" Kant's definition of religion as "the sum of all our duties regarded as divine *commands*."[66] But, from Jüngel's perspective, it is significant that Kant's radical notion of rational self-possession acknowledges a dimension of faith within human rationality, a dimension which is beyond what can be known and thus beyond human (conceptual) control. Significantly, it is this dimension, as the presence of God in God's hiddenness, that makes possible human self-possession. Consequently, though Kant insists that what decides about our humanity is shutting out all external influence, with none but reason determining the will, more than reason's determination of the will is required for one to become moral, and thus human, and thus free. The Kantian faith, Jüngel notes, is a moralistically inflected faith, but it is faith all the same: "a virtuous atheist is in fact unthinkable for Kant." While this faith does not constitute human identity, it, nonetheless, preserves human identity (i.e., worth the name human,).[67]

Concluding remarks

Our discussion thus far has focused on explicating Jüngel's assertion that humans are fundamentally relational beings. Jüngel, as we have seen,

---

[64] Kant, *Critique of Pure Reason*, 689 [B857].

[65] Jüngel notes that, in the philosophy of Kant, the combative and expansive reason of the Enlightenment was led reluctantly to acknowledge what it had sought so desperately to overcome, namely, the once peaceful scholastic distinction between faith and reason. "In the ultimate consequence of the Enlightenment," Jüngel observes, "we are dealing with a reason which is restricted to being the *antithesis of the absolute*, and yet it cannot absolutely posit that antithesis." What Jüngel means is that reason voluntarily and yet quite unexpectedly excluded itself from discursively grasping "its noblest subject." Worse still, reason – withdrawn and yet colonizing – in the end turned out to know *only itself*; in the words of Kant, it "has insight only into what it itself produces according to its own design" (*Critique of Pure Reason*, 109 [Bxiii]). *Mystery*, 68–71; *GGW* 90–3. In Jüngel's anthropology, as we have already seen, this observation goes beyond epistemology and becomes part of an ontological critique. Humans, obsessed with self-possession and self-determination cannot gain self-meaning from the world; they only remake the world in their own image, after their own conceptualization. So remade the world does not yield any surplus which could provide the meaning of humanity but a surprising deficit; it becomes an inhuman world.

[66] Immanuel Kant, *The Conflict of the Faculties* (1798). In *Religion and Rational Theology*, 262 [7:36]. Discussed in "Der Mensch," 343.

[67] "Der Mensch," 327–8. One must not forget Kant's oft-invoked adage from the second preface to the *Critique of Pure Reason*: "I had to deny *knowledge* in order to make room for *faith*," 117 [Bxxx]. For Jüngel's less appreciative interpretation of Kant's rationalization of faith, with faith seen as still located within the perimeter of knowing, see an earlier essay, "Womit steht und fällt heute der christliche Glaube?" *Spricht Gott in der Geschichte?* (Freiburg: Herder, 1972), 157; as well as the relatively recent "Glaube und Vernunft," George Augustin and Klaus Krämer (eds), *Gott denken und bezeugen. Festschrift für Kardinal Walter Kasper zum 75. Geburtstag* (Freiburg: Herder, 2008), 25.

locates this fundamental relationality in the linguistic character of human being as being in the world. We have observed that it is this very worldly structure that enables one's relation to self. But it also makes possible the eventual transformation of one's self-relation into the totalizing relation. In the latter case, the self-relation will strive simultaneously to submit one's other world-relations to itself, and to secure itself against their impingement. This undertaking, perceived as a pursuit of freedom, transforms language from a medium primarily of recognition and address to a medium of meaning imposition. Action, rather than receptivity, becomes the individual's dominant mode of relating to the world, while rational thought becomes the locale of the self's entrenchment.

However, it is the fundamental relationality that also stubbornly prevents one from making the world secure for oneself, or from securing oneself against unwanted impingement. It thus involves the self-securing individual in a self-contradiction and so creates fissures through which human relationality can be glimpsed. We have analyzed two broad instances of this self-contradiction. The first, pertaining to action, shows that a secured world, whose otherness and unpredictability are annihilated, will only disclose human potential for dehumanization but will not yield a positive meaning of being human. What is thus disclosed is humanity's vital relation to the world as something that one cannot simply fabricate but must rather receive. In a similar fashion, rationality posits a beyond, a domain of faith, within reason itself. This domain shows itself as being beyond reason's control; at the same time reason is shown to depend on it for its own self-control. What the self-contradiction of reason discloses is that faith is a fundamental mode of receptivity in which, before all else, one must first receive oneself. Yet neither fissure offers a solution to the problems it poses, leaving fragile humans with no choice but to continue down the desperate path of self-securing and self-possession.

Self-Actualization as Unfreedom

Humans in pursuit of self-securing and self-possession are, according to Jüngel, neither here nor there. They are always transcending the old self, perceived as hopelessly fragile, and constructing a new, impregnable self. This undertaking, as we have seen, consists in simultaneously withdrawing from, and pushing back against, the world. What is crucial to note is that self-securing requires constant maintenance. And it demands one's entire self. The essence of self-securing lies in constant *actualization* of the self as a self-possessed self. The relentlessness of this process is precisely what helps to obscure its futility.

Jüngel declares the freedom promised by self-actualization to be nothing but captivity. We shall examine this claim from two angles. First, we shall consider the self as withdrawing from the world in order rationally to possess itself. The basis for this investigation will be Jüngel's critique of Kant's understanding of freedom. Second, we shall analyze the toll that the actualization of one's freedom takes on the human subject. Here, we shall pay particular attention to the subject's indeterminacy.

Kantian withdrawal into rationality

Jüngel agrees with Kant in one basic point, namely, that freedom denotes "the faculty of beginning a state *from itself* [*das Vermögen, einen Zustand* von selbst *anzufangen*]."[68] This is, however, as far as the agreement goes. Jüngel believes that, when understood in this manner, that is, as absolute spontaneity, freedom can be properly predicated of God alone, yet, crucially, it can also be communicated to humans.[69] Kant, for his part, insists that freedom can never be a matter of sense experience, and so of knowing oneself as a being in the world. Though Jüngel, as we have seen, does give a qualified approval to Kant's removal of God from the realm of knowledge to the realm of moral belief, he is far less appreciative of Kant's relegation of freedom to that same domain. He sharply criticizes Kant's conception. Kant, according to Jüngel, misses the target, in that his notion of freedom proves simultaneously too little and too much.

Let us begin with the under-determination of the Kantian conception. What Kant calls "freedom in the cosmological sense" is, by his own admission, a "pure transcendental idea." Freedom does not arise out of experience. The reason for this is that there is nothing in the entire field of experience that is not subject to the universal law of causality. One's ability to make sense of experience, according to Kant, actually depends on this law. Experience cannot grasp anything uncaused. However, as reason also strives to make sense of natural causality in its totality, it creates the idea of

---

[68] Kant, *Critique of Pure Reason*, 533 [B561]; cited in "Befreiende Freiheit," *Anfänger*, 17, cf. 7; and "*Credere in ecclesiam*: eine ökumenische Besinnung," *Zeitschrift für Theologie und Kirche* 99 (2002), 177. In the latter essay, though Jüngel readily acknowledges the totally philosophical orientation of Kant's conception, he also points out its "genuinely Christian background," in that, so understood, freedom necessarily entails a *creatio ex nihilo*.

[69] *Mystery*, 36–7; *GGW* 45–7; and "Die Freiheit eines Christenmenschen: Freiheit als Summe des Christentums," Michael Beintker et al. (eds), *Wege zum Einverständnis. Festschrift für Christoph Demke* (Leipzig: Evangelische Verlagsanstalt, 1997), 124–5.

spontaneity to raise itself above the realm of nature and to account for its causality. In *practical* terms, human freedom, as we have seen, consists in the will's submission to reason's moral law alone, the law that commands the will to act only in accordance with such principles which, in acting on them, one would also wish to become universal laws. For Kant, freedom lies in reason's ability to give this law to the will independently of experience (since experience always entails one's being-in-the-world). In the practical sense, explains Kant, freedom "is the independence of the power of choice from *necessitation* by impulses of sensibility." By contrast, an action that is brought about by sensibility reduces the human power of choice from freedom to animality.[70] Hence, Kant's assertion that only in possession of the moral strength is an individual "'free,' 'healthy,' 'rich,' 'a king,' and so forth and can suffer no loss by chance or fate, since he is in possession of himself and the virtuous man cannot lose his virtue."[71] What is important to observe here is that, for Kant, not only is freedom not derived from experience but, even more importantly, it is *located* and *realized* outside of experience, in the self-legislating capacity of reason.

Jüngel agrees with the critiques of the Kantian understanding of freedom put forth by Herbert Marcuse and Max Scheler.[72] In his 1919 essay, "Von zwei deutschen Krankheiten," Scheler criticizes Kant's distinction between the *homo phaenomenon* and the *homo noumenon*. Before we address Scheler's (and by extension Jüngel's) criticism, let us look briefly at how this distinction – to some degree, a restatement of the *animal rationale* conception of the human – functions in Kant's anthropology. With this distinction, Kant alleges that humans exist, on the one hand, as sensible beings, endowed with reason understood simply as a theoretical faculty, which exerts a causal influence on their actions. They are rational animals in the empirical sense of the phrase. But, according to Kant, humans also exist as intelligible beings "cogniz[able] only in morally practical relations, where the incomprehensible property of *freedom* is revealed by the influence of reason on the inner lawgiving will." This dimension of human existence is that of personality, where the human, disclosed as "a being endowed with *inner freedom*," can place him- or herself under obligation.[73] It is in this

---

[70] Kant, *Critique of Pure Reason*, 532–3 [B560–2].

[71] Immanuel Kant, *The Metaphysics of Morals* (1797–8). In *Practical Philosophy*, trans. and ed. Mary J. Gregor (Cambridge: University Press, 1996), 534 [6:405]; cited partially in "On Becoming Truly Human," *Essays II*, 234.

[72] "On Becoming Truly Human," *Essays II*, 217–18, and the longer discussion in *FoC*, 50–6. In those pieces, Jüngel's primary goal is to show, *contra* Marcuse and Scheler, that Luther was not a harbinger of the Kantian conception.

[73] Kant, *The Metaphysics of Morals*, 544 [6:418].

dimension that one can elevate oneself from an *animal rationabile* to an *animal rationale* in the proper sense. (It must be noted that Kant introduces this distinction to account for the apparent paradox of placing oneself under obligation to oneself. The placement of oneself under obligation happens purely within the intelligible dimension of one's being. It is there that, in separation from the sensible self, one has the freedom to dispose over oneself, as it were, and to determine oneself. It is there that one can be one's own.) Once one has exercised this inner freedom, one can then project it toward the sensible animal self, in order to provide for it and to rein it in. As can be seen, the self-related person is, for Kant, non-sensible and nonempirical; it is knowable only in this practical moral self-determination. And if that does not take place, the human, even when otherwise rational, is little better than an animal.

Scheler points out that the Kantian distinction between the *homo phaenomenon* and *homo noumenon* does not entail that, even in the properly rational person, there has to be any correspondence between the sensible and the personal. Kant's "good intention" (i.e., the noumenal act of self-disposition, of giving a moral law to oneself), notes Scheler, can by definition be linked to any material content, whatever this content's origin. As Kant himself put it, virtue "is not a property of [empirical, material] choice but of the [immaterial] *will*, which is a faculty of desire that, in adopting a rule, also gives it as a universal law."[74] Thus, on the one hand, an individual can absolve him- or herself of wrongdoing by pointing out that he or she did nothing other than dutifully obey orders. On the other hand, Kant's distinction does not prevent material exploitation of fellow humans. After all, human worth has its seat "in the unknown and unrecognizable sphere of the thing-in-itself," from where it cannot be taken away.[75] In sum, whatever one does, as long as it is done out of duty, and whatever is done to one, which can only be done in the empirical realm, cannot compromise the freedom of the perpetrator or sufferer. Freedom is a purely inward, detached reality.

Marcuse's critique focuses less on the question of justifying wrongdoing and mistreatment, and more on how, through the Kantian doctrine of freedom, "actual [social] unfreedom is subsumed into the concept of freedom" – which "makes it possible entirely to depreciate 'outer' misery

---

[74] Kant, *The Metaphysics of Morals*, 535 [6:407].
[75] Max Scheler, "Von zwei Deutschen Krankheiten," *Gesammelte Werke*, vol. 6: *Schriften zur Soziologie und Weltanschauungslehre* (Bern & München: Francke, 1963), 213–14; cited partially by Jüngel in *FoC*, 102.

and to justify it 'transcendentally.'" Kantian freedom, notes Marcuse, precedes all of the person's acts and does not require acting either on the part of the person, or on the person's behalf. Only one act (of sorts) is required: one must make oneself free by submitting one's will to reason's formal law, "but this liberation leaves all types of actual servitude untouched."[76] Marcuse is especially interested in how this understanding of freedom entails submission, out of freedom, to political authority by voluntarily limiting one's freedom as part of duty to oneself as a social being. At best this produces, empirically and phenomenally, a purely intellectual exercise of social freedom: freedom becomes freedom of thought. A notorious illustration is provided by Kant's statement in "What is Enlightenment?": "Argue as much as you will and about whatever you will, but obey."[77]

In light of these criticisms, Jüngel finds the Kantian understanding of freedom as self-possession and self-determination to be woefully under-determined. Kantian freedom can be used to absolve oneself either of wrong action, or inaction (provided the intention is right), or even of instrumentalization of fellow humans. Any type of content can be governed by a formal, moral law that finds its satisfaction purely in the realm of rational interiority. What is more, freedom, understood only as antecedent to all action, must remain without any practical impact on the structure of society. "The concrete world with its good and evils, and the concrete human being in this world, become *ethical abstractions*," Jüngel argues.[78]

In addition to the under-determination of Kant's conception of freedom, Jüngel clearly also considers it over-determined. Whereas the under-determination has to do with the location of freedom and the impact, or rather lack thereof, that it has on one's world being, the over-determination concerns the impact of Kant's notion on the self. Kant asserts: "two things are required for inner freedom: being one's own *master* in a given case (*animus sui compos*), and *ruling* oneself (*imperium in semetipsum*), that is, subduing one's affects and *governing* one's passions." Therefore, "unless reason holds the reins of government in its own hands, [man's] feeling and inclinations play the master over him."[79] Because in this conception freedom

---

[76] Herbert Marcuse, "A Study on Authority: Luther, Calvin, Kant," Eduardo Mendieta (ed.), *The Frankfurt School on Religion: Key Writings by the Major Thinkers* (New York & London: Routledge, 2005), 141.

[77] Kant, *An Answer to the Question: What is Enlightenment?* 18 [8:37]; cited in "Der Mensch," 321.

[78] "Value-Free Truth," *Essays II*, 198.

[79] Kant, *The Metaphysics of Morals*, 535–6 [6:407–8].

precedes all of the person's acts, it renders the individual, in a sense, doomed to freedom. The individual, as an empirical entity, will have to live with the consequences of the fact that he or she is an empirical entity, always going against him- or herself, always torn, and never quite able to catch up with his or her intelligible self, always struggling for mastery, and never being given a respite from the struggle. Jüngel hints at the oppressiveness of the Kantian conception of freedom in his discussion of the Last Judgment, at which Christ will finally put an end, for the humanity bent on self-possession, to the inevitable discrepancy between the "*quaestio facti*," that which, in actuality, is, and the "*quaestio iuris*," that which, in fact, ought to be.[80] What Jüngel's statement implies is that Kantian freedom is an overburdened conception that inevitably and relentlessly has humans fall short of the categorical imperative, of the "ought" which the moral law commands, and yet leaves them with no choice but only to double their effort.

The Doer's indeterminacy

What our discussion of Jüngel's critique of the Kantian understanding of human freedom has shown is that the location of freedom in rational self-possession is indeed a Pyrrhic victory. It leaves out aspects of human being that cannot by any account be considered negligible. Humans are not Platonic souls trapped in the material world. Humanity's world-being cannot be simply bracketed or wished away. In this regard, as we have seen, there is more to Kant's notion that Jüngel finds problematic than its implied justification of various types unfreedom in the world. What Kant's view shows is that – in a very practical, day-to-day manner – one's empirical existence will not let itself be made negligible. Even when embodied existence is by definition excluded from the essence of freedom, what human freedom amounts to in practice is a relentless browbeating of the passions into submission and never being able to relax one's grip on oneself. One can possess oneself only against oneself!

This latter dimension (what I referred to above as freedom's over-determinateness) is one that Jüngel is particularly interested in. In Kant's case, it has to do with the constant actualization of one's self-possession through the reining in of the passions. But the above critique of Kant should

---

[80] "Das jüngste Gericht als Akt der Gnade," *Anfänger*, 61–2; "Der Geist der Hoffnung und des Trostes," *TE* V, 319.

be taken as no more than a signal case of the problems evident in the conceptualization of freedom as self-possession. Jüngel is interested in much more than simply critiquing Kant.[81] As we have already seen, the actualization of one's self-possession may take the form not only of (attempted) detachment from the world's impingement but also of controlling one's relations to others and even fabricating the world – all in the hope of coming to oneself with new, foolproof security.

Regardless of the specific manner in which one reacts against the world's impingement, what is of importance here is the fact that the actualization of one's self-possession is an ongoing activity. It needs to be undertaken over and over again. It thus reduces the person to the person's activity, insofar as it is only through that activity that a semblance of self-possession is created. It is in this sense that Jüngel warns that "unassailable self-possession damages human persons."[82] Jüngel associates unfreedom not primarily with narrowly construed freedoms but precisely with the disappearance of the distinction between person and works. As captive, the person becomes indeterminate. Let us take a closer look at Jüngel's explication of unfreedom from this perspective.

The tyrannies of self-actualization

Jüngel's critique of action, as we have seen, proceeds from the fundamental insight that humans do have the capacity to determine the world, a capacity they should by all means exercise – but they are not "determining subjects in relation to themselves."[83] Even "will to power" is not wrong in and of itself, much as it is through this will that humans enslave themselves to themselves.[84] Only when the self's capacity for action becomes harnessed for the purpose of self-determination does action damage the self. This damage manifests itself, first of all, as being tyrannized.

---

[81] Scattered as Jüngel's references to Kant are, there is no doubt that Jüngel singles out Kant's conception of freedom as paradigmatically too narrow in focus and too excessive in its mechanics. It comes as somewhat of a surprise that he simply takes for granted other conceptions of freedom put forth since the Enlightenment and, seemingly, assumes that they will exemplify one or both of Kant's failures. It may very well be the case that all humanly posited freedoms place the would-be free person under a law (*Gesetz des Handelns*) that demands constant action – both safeguarding and actualization – on the person's part, and, as such, they all fall short of the gospel freedom from compulsion to deed (*Zwang zur Tat*); cf. "Die Freiheit eines Christenmenschen: Freiheit als Summe des Christentums," 131. But this still requires broader engagement and unpacking.

[82] "On Becoming Truly Human," *Essays II*, 235.

[83] "On Becoming Truly Human," *Essays II*, 225.

[84] "Befreiende Freiheit," *Anfänger*, 21.

The first type of tyranny, to which we have already alluded, may be called a tyranny of the future. It has to do directly with the fact that self-determination, as a state, is always on the horizon of self-determining action, always within reach – but never quite reachable. Action holds out a promise, but never quite delivers on it, relentlessly spurring self-seeking humans on to further self-directed works. Self-determination through action never offers any respite – it never leads to a mission accomplished.[85]

However, what tyrannizes the self-actualizing individual is not only works that seemingly still remain to be done, for the ever-receding goal to be reached. Works already accomplished also have a tyrannical effect. As Jüngel notes, for humans unassailably to possess themselves, "they would have to be equally the sum of their acts – and *no single act* could speak *against them.*"[86] This applies to both reprehensible and praiseworthy acts. Because humans not only have a past, but also exist in a necessary identity-relation to this past, there are always past accomplishments to live up to and failures to live with. It is not only past transgressions that we have to live with, but it is also the good that we may have done and now, for whatever reason, fail to do. Success obligates as strongly as failure indicts. Jüngel calls this "the tyranny of the past."[87] This tyranny is also, in a sense, a tyranny of the future (of a different kind from the one just noted), in that a past that has become an integral part of one's works-identity will tend to impact, and even crucially determine, one's future actions.[88] In this way, the human individual remains in bondage to actuality, and his or her self-realization does not produce

---

[85] Simply put, self-determination as an accomplished state of affairs is "an impossible actuality" (a phrase that is Jüngel's more precise restatement of Karl Barth's definition of sin as an "impossible possibility"). This should be related to Jüngel's insight that "now and not yet," as a hermeneutical principle for eschatological statements, reflects more the structure of human self-determining action rather than the presence/absence of the kingdom of God; "The World as Possibility and Actuality," *Essays I*, 99–100, 111. Interestingly, Zygmunt Bauman renders this modernist goal even more problematic when he points out that in "liquid modernity" the pressure exerted on the individual is no longer about the construction of an identity which, once constructed, could bring all self-determining efforts to their end. Rather, in its distinctly postmodern form, the pressure has as much to do with the construction as with a timely discarding of identities. There is thus no longer any horizon but only the inner compulsion toward, and outer pressure on, never-ending performance. See Bauman's "Identity in the globalizing world," *The Individualized Society*, 140–52.

[86] "On Becoming Truly Human," *Essays II*, 235.

[87] "Umgang mit der Vergangenheit in theologischer Perspektive," *BR*, 43–4. In this essay, Jüngel offers a brief cultural-historical sketch of how distance to one's past and so also the possibility of relating to it developed and was represented in Ancient Greek literature and philosophy. See also "Die Wahrheit des Christentums," *BR*, 122–3; and "Die Freiheit eines Christenmenschen: Freiheit als Summe des Christentums," 123–4.

[88] "Befreiende Freiheit," *Anfänger*, 26–9; "Hoffen, Handeln – und Leiden," *BR*, 27.

anything new beyond the replication of existent actuality in ever "new" actions. A totalizing self-relation is trivial in its actualization.

The tyranny of the past in its most acute form is the tyranny of guilt. One may try to diffuse it by appealing to mitigating factors, or by otherwise explaining one's past wrongdoing, or mistakes away. (It does not matter whether they were objectively such, or are only subjectively perceived as such.) The actions themselves, however, cannot be revoked. And so the conscience can at best only be anesthetized. In the midst of coming to oneself one is thus repelled by oneself. I believe guilt's tyranny is what Jüngel has in mind when he observes that "the sinful person can no longer agree with himself."[89]

Guilt and self-justification together point to yet another type of tyranny. Self-determination, even when it concerns fabricating a world, more often than not involves some standard by which one's works are judged. One thus comes under the "the tyranny of values." The phrase, as Jüngel notes, was coined by Nicolai Hartmann (1882–1950), as part of a program to oppose Kant's ethical formalism, as well as the materialism and empiricism implicit in Kant's epistemology.[90] Hartmann distinguishes between stratified real being and ideal being, with the latter understood not as a lofty sphere of which the former is but a shadow, but, in more Hegelian terms, as the ground of the real. It is to this sphere that values belong, and their knowledge is, therefore, a priori, like mathematical or logical knowledge. "Hartmann's ethics are in essence an effort to . . . vindicate the premodern conception that values cannot be invented but can merely be found, and are therefore objective and absolute."[91] This does not mean, however, that real being always corresponds to ideal being. Values must be laid hold of affectively by the conscience and real-ized. However, the realm of values can never be grasped in its entirety. Instead, individual values tend to demand absolute commitment and dull the sense of other values in the person or community they grip. They have a tyrannical tendency. What co-exists in the sphere of ideal being generates potentially conflict-laden situations in the sphere of the real.

Jüngel could not be more skeptical that the restoration of value discourse constitutes a remedy to the self's disembodiedness in Kant's ethical theory and the *de facto* unfreedom lurking in it. Jüngel bases his critique of

---

[89] *Justification*, 108.
[90] Jüngel's discussion can be found in "Value-Free Truth," *Essays II*, 198–204.
[91] Andreas A. M. Kinneging, "Introduction," Nicolai Hartmann, *Ethics*, trans. S. Coit, vol. 1 (of 3): *Moral Phenomena* (New Brunswick: Transaction, 2002), xvii.

Hartmann on the observations of the political theorist Carl Schmitt (1888–1985), who developed Hartmann's notion of "the tyranny of values."[92] In all, Jüngel agrees with Schmitt that recourse to values was a self-deceptive program on the part of some who sought to overcome the nihilistic crisis of the late nineteenth century. Value is at bottom an economic term, and it cannot be applied indiscriminately. For this reason, states Jüngel, "Value thinking is thoroughly aggressive," and to claim that values exist objectively is only to strengthen this potential for aggression. "No one can valuate without devaluing, revaluating, and evaluating."[93] The tyranny of values emerges when one's conscience presumes to judge, as it inevitably will, what another is to do or to allow. Out of this arises political conflict, which leads to the disappearance of (political) community: "the terror of value" is the "end of political culture."[94] Thus, Jüngel concludes, "[t]he determination of values only empowers the threat against which humanity seeks to protect itself precisely by determining values." This is all aside from the fact that, when it comes to persons, they "*have no value [Wert] but rather dignity [Würde].* And dignity is precisely not amenable to valuation."[95]

Value discourse, in other words, may offer a quick fix to the under-determinateness of the Kantian conception of freedom, but, contrary to expectations, an emphasis on values (and morality) neither alleviates guilt nor creates a community. It is true that values inhibit some (chiefly negative) actions. However, value discourse only exacerbates further the identification of person and work by making explicit what was largely implicit for Kant: the criterion of worth, the worth of a person. Hence, values leave the "I" solitary and burdened even more by the self's works.

All of these tyrannies – of the future, of the past, and of values – in the end come down to one fundamental tyranny, that of the "I." Mastery over oneself means "being mercilessly delivered up to [oneself]."[96] What Jüngel has in mind specifically is the havoc self-love wreaks not only with one's fundamental relationality but also with one's being in the world – humans are often the most effective destroyers of their own dignity.

---

[92] Carl Schmitt, "Die Tyrannei der Werte," Eberhard Jüngel and Sepp Schelz (eds), *Die Tyrannei der Werte* (1960; Hamburg: Lutherisches Verlagshaus, 1979), 11–43. ET: *The Tyranny of Values*, trans. S. Draghici (Washington, D.C.: Plutarch Press, 1996).

[93] "Value-Free Truth," *Essays II*, 203.

[94] "Wertlose Würde – Gewissenhafte Gewissenlosigkeit. Eine Erinnerung an den fortwirkenden christlichen Ursprung lebensorientierender Begriffe," *EmE*, 102–3.

[95] "Value-Free Truth," *Essays II*, 201; *TE III*, 98 (emphasis original).

[96] *Justification*, 144; cf. "Befreiende Freiheit," *Anfänger*, 26, where Jüngel states: "Von allen Tyrannen ist unser eigenes Ich der mächtigste und listenreichste."

But there is also another, subtler dimension of this tyranny implicit in Jüngel's anthropology. It has to do with the fact that one's self-determination always takes place within a larger social and political context, in a milieu where self-determination is the way to be. Because humans seek to define themselves by means of their works, they must inevitably compete with others, who, armed with works of their own, perhaps even better works or better executed ones, threaten the *uniqueness* of one's painstakingly built identity. Self-determination becomes in this context subject to an "ought," an unrealistic demand that one's works furnish the sort of uniqueness to which works, by nature reproducible, simply cannot attain. Jüngel indicates this broader framework of self-realization when he states that "To realize oneself means to procure recognition of oneself."[97] The tyranny of the "I" is thus a tyranny of the I, which has absorbed all of its worldly relationality into itself and now stands in judgment on one not in some private, subjective, and negotiable verdict of conscience but as a proxy for the mercilessly competitive public arena. The "I" demands and indicts, but its demand and indictment are those of a public verdict.

This paradox of self-realization – the fact that it cannot be accomplished unless the uniqueness of one's identity, and thus one's irreplaceability, is also publically confirmed – leads to two other modalities of the I's tyranny: the compulsion toward self-judgment in anticipation of what is perceived as the impending public judgment, and toward self-justification in its face. One justifies oneself by claiming that, despite appearances, one's actions do conform to the current valuational law, or by claiming exemption from the law, or by forcefully opposing new valuations to the existent law. In doing so, we must also judge others, whether fairly or unfairly. The world of self-possessed humans, notes Jüngel, is a world of judgment, of self and of others, from which there is no human release.[98]

Lack of boundaries

The unfreedom of self-securing concerns not only one's *self-experience*, however oppressive it may turn out to be. The predominance of one's self-relation also gives a particular shape to the self, which sets it on a course of

---

[97] "On Becoming Truly Human," *Essays II*, 235.
[98] "Das jüngste Gericht," *Anfänger*, 60, 68. Cf. Jüngel's statement in *Justification*, 140: "We use our knowledge of good and evil to divert attention from our own evil nature by identifying others as evil. . . . It is no longer a case of *being able* to decide between god and evil. Now we are *forced* to do so."

progressing *relationlessness*. Self-actualization through works entails a loss of
boundaries, resulting in violence both to one's self and to God, yet in such
a way that it is fellow humans that bear the brunt of one's unfreedom.

Let us consider the human dimension first. Jüngel claims: "When we
cease *to set ourselves limits* and to affirm the limits imposed upon us by our
societary ontological structure we deny our humanness *de facto*."[99] According
to Jüngel, there are three types of boundaries that pertain to our humanity.
The first two are the Word of God, a boundary which we shall take up in
Chapter 3, and time and space, that is, the world in its totality as a boundary.
These two are ontologically inviolable, in that they establish our *humanity*.
The third type of boundary includes humanly established boundaries within
the world.[100] These boundaries are meant to be transcended in acts of
genuine, nontotalizing lordship over the world; each act of such
transcendence leads to the creation of new limits which, in turn, call for
further acts of transcendence.[101] Problems arise when one's self-relation
becomes a totalizing force behind human action, a pursuit of lordship
without limits. This brings about a simultaneous collapse and destructive
distendedness of our *human* being.

Our being collapses, because the "I," as tyrannized by itself, cannot avoid
self-alienation, as we have seen. This is only exacerbated when responsibility
for this self-alienation is shifted onto others. They are seen as those who
have deprived one of self-security and from whom this security must be
wrested back. "Sinners," writes Jüngel, "are characterized by a belief that
they must and can seize their own right."[102] And they take it away from
others. They secure themselves at others' cost. A self-actualizing individual
will seek to control his or her worldly relations, to bring them within the
confines of his or her self-relation. By attempting to do this, one destroys
those other relations, insofar as they entailed a togetherness which is now
perverted into suspicion and often hostility. In the end, the fragility and the
apparent enmity even of one's self-relation find their expression and
confirmation in death, which, as Jüngel points out, is the "definitive end of
all relations."[103] In death, the relationlessness of the sinner's being is
exposed, as the sinner's final relationship, that to self, is undercut.

Beyond day-to-day human interaction, Jüngel does have some interest
in how this implosion of relationality affects the structure of entire human

---

[99] "Humanity in Correspondence to God," *Essays I*, 142.
[100] "Grenzen des Menschseins" *TE II*, 360.
[101] "Lob der Grenze," *TE II*, 376; "Humanity in Correspondence to God," *Essays I*, 148.
[102] "Living out of Righteousness: God's Action – Human Agency," *Essays II*, 252.
[103] "Living out of Righteousness," *Essays II*, 252; *Death*, 115ff.

communities. The most radical and notorious communal manifestations are, of course, totalitarian regimes with their methods of control and surveillance.[104] But less ominous social structures, founded on a mutual restraint of individual egoisms, do not constitute an exception. Where the "wolf-nature of man" is given up for the sake of a higher entity responsible for order, this higher entity, the state, can very easily become "the super-beast."[105] Even in more "agreeable" instances, societally reconciled egoisms are ultimately driven by self-interest, too – a patronizing self-interest that wishes to be seen as care.[106] Where one's individual being implodes, there communities fare no better.

In addition to this all-pervading collapse, self-actualizing human being is also disproportionately distended, overblown to the point of limitlessness, even to the point of divinity (or what it misperceives as divinity). "The unfree human being is a god-less human being who does not wish to be able to renounce his god-lessness and precisely by this understands himself as his own god. But no one can be god by himself and play god for himself alone," Jüngel notes. Admittedly, one may wish to play god with ostensibly the best of intentions, and for the sake of another who, seemingly, does not know any better. But that hardly changes the status of the other vis-à-vis one's self-relation. Hence, Jüngel's sobering equation: "homo homini deus = homo homini lupus."[107] This god-lessness, in the end, does violence to God – not only because the human sets him- or herself up in place of God, often thus incapacitating others. It does violence to God also because it suggests that to be like God is to exercise totalizing control. Through reckless self-actualization, humans not only leave no room for God, as they ride roughshod over *all* boundaries, but they also seek sanction for this by lying about who and what God is (or should be). Jüngel comments: "human beings miss the *nature* of the God they assume to exist because they themselves want to be as God. They desire those very predicates of deity which apart from God's loving self-emptying as easily create a devil as a god."[108]

All in all, an individual bent on self-possession, Jüngel notes, has become *verhältnislos* in both senses of the German term: self-indulgent and knowing

---

[104] "Böse – was ist das?" *EmE*, 73.

[105] For Jüngel's critique of Hobbes' *Leviathan*, see "Zum Wesen des Friedens," *TE V*, 18–22.

[106] Like any law, such social structures inhibit certain actions but do not resolve the problem of person vs. works; they do not make people any less self- and control-seeking.

[107] "Freiheitsrechte und Gerechtigkeit," *TE I*, 248; cf. "Zum Wesen des Friedens," *TE V*, 18–22.

[108] *FoC*, 24. Cf. *Justification*, 138: "Unbelief mistrusts God's goodness by insinuating that God does not really give to human beings everything which is good for them. This is why their distrust of God is at the same time a lust for what is apparently being withheld. And this is not God's divinity; it is what sinners imagine it to be."

no restraint (*maßlos*), as well as relationless (*beziehungslos*).[109] One's pursuit of self-securing not only makes one unfree but makes others hostage to one's unfreedom.

Concluding remarks

For Jüngel, as the foregoing investigation has shown, self-determination does not deliver the freedom it promises but only reinforces one's unfreedom. This captivity has a number of facets. The location and realization of freedom within one's rational self is simply a case of under-determined freedom, because what is bracketed cannot simply be ignored. Freedom must extend beyond rational self-possession into one's world-being, or have its necessary correspondence therein – unless, in one's praise of freedom, one is prepared to turn a blind eye to all manners of worldly unfreedom. But even if one is not prepared to do so, the compulsion constantly to actualize one's freedom is likewise unfreedom, according to Jüngel. It makes little difference whether this actualization concerns the will's submission to reason's control, or one's action in the world. At bottom, self-actualization is unfreedom, in that it makes the individual captive to his or her works. It reduces the person to works. Again, it does not matter whether the work is understood as making an *animal rationale* out of an animal that is merely *rationabile*, or whether one's ability to have the world submit to one's will is concerned. Self-actualization means self-destructive existence under the tyranny of one's own ego.

What our discussion has also drawn crucial attention to is that, as unfree, humans remain indeterminate. This lack of determinateness stems from the suppression of human world-being, which, as we have noted, gives rise to one's self-relation in the first place. As bent on self-securing, humans lose all proportion. The totalizing self-relation is simultaneously imploding and distended. Humans remain suspended between creating themselves as self-secure and overcoming their fragility, between progressing relationlessness and making others hostage to their self-relation.

This indeterminacy has not only an individual dimension but also a collective one. In its collective manifestation, it means, according to Jüngel, that humanity as whole lacks a definition. It has become mysterious to itself. "[W]e moderns," Jüngel writes, "understand ourselves exclusively on the model of our relation to the world: namely as subjects who determine

---

[109] "Befreiende Freiheit," *Anfänger*, 19; cf. "Das jüngste Gericht," *Anfänger*, 69.

ourselves by our acts" – and that regardless of whether this self-understanding is idealist, materialist, existential, or positivist?[110] Yet, despite the fact that humanity is increasingly (and sometimes frighteningly so) able to impose meaning on the world as its object, that is, to manufacture the world, which it can then navigate securely and control, it remains unclear what being human – in the world and together with fellow humans – really means.

By Way of a Conclusion: (Theological) Anthropology

Jüngel's goal, as he engages the modern conception of freedom as self-possession and self-actualization, is to uncover the contradictions in which the pursuit of self-possession involves both individuals and humanity in general. By drawing attention to these contradictions, Jüngel wishes both to pose the question of the truth of human being and to underscore the absence of an immanent solution to the contradictions he has identified.

In what follows, I shall briefly situate Jüngel's procedure against the backdrop of his claim that God is more than necessary and then, in that light, evaluate the status of this chapter's findings. This discussion is intended as a foray into our analysis of Jüngel's doctrine of God in the following chapter.

God as a selfless concept

Jüngel's view of God as more than necessary finds its reflection in properly oriented theological discourse. Specifically, it means that the idea of God can be used to critique worldly contingencies without the need to be made explicit. Theological discourse can have an ostensibly anthropological point of departure, thanks to which its claims may become universally recognizable; yet this point of departure in reality reflects the character of God and is governed by the doctrine of God. How does this work?

Jüngel argues that theological language, when properly oriented by God's Word, possesses universal anthropological intelligibility.[111] This fact is arguably far from self-evident, especially if one takes seriously Jüngel's insistence that God must be defined with the highest possible specificity, that is, through the cross of Christ. Jüngel counters this fear by pointing out

---

[110] "On Becoming Truly Human," *Essays II,* 227, 224.
[111] "Humanity in Correspondence to God," *Essays I,* 126.

that, because it is none other than the concept of *God* that is involved, and so one capable of "theoretical selflessness," statements in theological anthropology are, in fact, possible without an explicit reference to God.[112] This "secularized modus loquendi," Jüngel claims, can speak to the reason even of those who are without God and, in the end, enables them to affirm the validity and justifiability of such statements.[113]

But, significantly, this sort of entry-level universality does not come without a price. When employed in this manner, theological-anthropological language will retain its analytical capacity – but, what is crucial, its findings will remain "inherently ambiguous [*in sich ambivalent*]."[114] What Jüngel means is not so much that anthropological discourse will somehow suffer from a lack of clarity, but rather that this discourse will do little more than point to a lack of clarity in the being of those it addresses. The discourse will bring to light contradictions and inconsistencies woven into the lives of those to whom it speaks. But it will do so without "making things good [*eindeutig wohltun*]." By raising questions and awakening anxiety – without, however, providing an answer or remedy – such anthropologically centered theological statements will perform a function that Protestant theology has traditionally associated with the proclamation of the law.

The disambiguation of theological-anthropological statements can only be achieved through the gospel: God's Word of address in which God makes God's self known. Only when the identity of God is made explicit in its utmost concreteness will the un-clarity and self-contradiction that is a universal predicament of human being find a resolution.[115] This said, it should be noted carefully that the gospel here is not a type of discourse that

---

[112] "Humanity in Correspondence to God," *Essays I*, 126.

[113] Cf. "Zur Verankerung der Menschenrechte im christlichen Glauben," 138.

[114] "Humanity in Correspondence to God," *Essays I*, 126.

[115] I remain skeptical of Mark Mattes's sharp distinction between preaching and what he perceives as Jüngel's "ordering between the divine and the human . . . established by theory." Preaching, Mattes believes, is the sole way to accomplish this ordering (Mark C. Mattes, *The Role of Justification in Contemporary Theology* [Grand Rapids: Eerdmans, 2004], 45; for this view Mattes is actually indebted to Steven D. Paulson's study *Analogy and Proclamation: The Struggle over God's Hiddenness in the Theology of Martin Luther and Eberhard Juengel* [unpublished Th.D. dissertation, Lutheran School of Theology, Chicago, 1992]). However, to say that Jüngel is a theoretician and that what he theorizes about does not lend itself to, or is not derived (in part at least) from, proclamation is unfair. Jüngel, it seems to me, makes a conscious effort to indicate the proclamatory value and dimension of his theological thought. But, like Barth, Jüngel is less interested in the proper distinction of law and gospel than in their proper relation, specifically the relation of the law to the gospel; see "Gospel and Law: The Relationship of Dogmatics to Ethics," *Karl Barth: A Theological Legacy*, trans. Garrett E. Paul (Philadelphia: Westminster, 1986), 105–26. I will return to the alleged disjunction between proclamation and theory in Chapter 4.

follows upon the law's pronouncements as a solution to the lack which the law identified and defined. God is not a quick fix to problems that emerge *from within* human identities, whereby the identities themselves determine the character of the solution. Rather, the gospel is that which clarifies what has been true all along and what the law was able to grasp only in an incomplete and distorted manner. The gospel, in other words, clarifies its own truth, the truth.[116]

Intimations of the problem

Our analysis in this chapter has drawn attention to the way in which one's self-relation emerges from one's world being. We have also indicated why the self-relation inevitably becomes the dominant relation, crowding out or seeking to control all one's world-relations. Briefly put: because one is personally responsible for assuring the continuity of one's being, which one does by relating to one's past and one's future. Self-possession is thus not a modern phenomenon, as both the Augustinian notion of self-love and Luther's *homo incurvatus in se ipsum* demonstrate. What makes modernity distinct is that it defines itself by the concepts of self-possession and self-actualization – which in part has to do with the unthinkability and unspeakability of God likewise characteristic of modernity.

Our analysis has shown, further, that self-possession is, in fact, impossible. It requires constant actualization. Yet, even if one throws oneself into it with abandon, not only does this not alleviate the world's impingement, but, in addition, renders one hopelessly mired and tyrannized by one's own self, by the past, which one has to own, and the future, which only tries to live up to or live down the past. In its impossibility, self-possession renders one's being indeterminate and trivial. Besides this, self-possession is impossible, further, in that it leads one to a self-contradiction. This self-contradiction – evident in the case of both human action and rationality – discloses vaguely that perhaps human being lies in receptivity. Yet this disclosure only sends one back, and with a vengeance, down the path of self-securing. To allow oneself to receive one's self from the world is to allow one's self to be destroyed by a world hell-bent on self-securing. To allow oneself to believe is to throw oneself down an abyss of unknowability

---

[116] Cf. "Value-Free Truth," *Essays II*, 206. '*Lichtung*' is a Heideggerian term with its roots in antiquity; see, e.g., *B&T* 170. Jüngel can also speak more conventionally about the elucidation [*Aufklärung*] of our lives lived through the light [*Licht*] of the gospel; see "Das jüngste Gericht," *Anfänger*, 56.

with no guarantee that in its depths one will encounter a god who might grant one the self-security one seeks.

Reduced to its purely anthropological dimension, Jüngel's critique of modernity offers only vague intimations of the problematic situation of humanity. But it does not make the nature of the human predicament specific. Thus, even when one accepts the validity of Jüngel's argument, one's desire will still be for self-possession as the only possible way of human being in the world. Anything else is pure fantasy. One's desire will be for a solution to the problem as one sees it, and the problem concerns how one can *make oneself free*. Given the vague intimation of the problem, even less so, then, can such anthropological critique offer a solution to the contradiction of the fundamental human relationality.

According to Jüngel, one can become free, both from one's delusion in regard to oneself and from one's impossible way of being, only through being addressed about oneself by the Word of the gospel. Through this Word, God elementally interrupts the continuity of one's being. In doing so, *God liberates* one as a language being and unfolds the fullness of one's relationality.

Our critical task in this study – which explains its own seemingly anthropological point of departure – is to ask whether, in Jüngel's formulation of the doctrine of God, God can have the anthropological impact that Jüngel ascribes to God. Or does God dangerously border on what this chapter has described as a totalizing self-relation? With these questions, we now turn to Jüngel's doctrine of God.

Chapter 2

The Contradictions of Divine Freedom

When left to their own devices, humans, Jüngel argues, plunge deeper and deeper into unfreedom. Unfreedom consists in the fundamental human relationality being inflected by, and absorbed into, one's relation to self. It is a surprising, yet in the end not so unexpected, product of a quest to overcome one's human fragility and in this overcoming to possess and secure oneself as more than human. Jüngel sees genuine human freedom in God's interruption of this distended relation to self. This, as he calls it, "elemental interruption" restores proper proportion and role to one's self-relation. It makes one's ontic being true to human ontological relationality, which, though suppressed, has manifested itself in the impossibility of final self-securing and the failure of complete self-possession.

Though Jüngel's case for human unfreedom draws on both anthropological and theological resources, Jüngel's point is ultimately a theological one. Only a relation to God, as one who is more than necessary, can restore proper balance between one's self- and other-relations. God alone makes humans free. For Jüngel, freedom is, properly speaking, a divine predicate. Like all divine predicates, however, it is communicable. Humans come to share in God's freedom and so become truly free. They do not become divinized, but rather, by sharing in God's freedom, they become properly human. "The human being may be in a human way what God is in a divine way, namely, a free lord over all things and subject to none, and a willing servant in all things and subject to everyone."[1]

I shall postpone further consideration of human freedom till the next chapter. This chapter will take up, instead, God's freedom. My reason for this ordering has to do not only with the fact that God's freedom is the *ratio*

---

[1] "Theses on the Relation of the Existence, Essence and Attributes of God," *Toronto Journal of Theology*, vol. 17:1 (Summer 2001), 67. The statement is, of course, an echo of Luther's 1520 treatise, *The Freedom of a Christian*. Cf. also "Die Freiheit eines Christenmenschen: Freiheit als Summe des Christentums," Michael Beintker et al. (eds), *Wege zum Einverständnis. Festschrift für Christoph Demke* (Leipzig: Evangelische Verlagsanstalt), esp. 124–5.

cognoscendi and presupposition of human freedom. More important for me is subjecting Jüngel's understanding of God's freedom to close scrutiny. The argument I wish to advance in this chapter is that Jüngel is unable to provide a coherent account of what he identifies as two moments of divine freedom: independence and determinateness. As a result, God emerges from Jüngel's account, despite his intentions to the contrary, as a fundamentally self-related subject. It is with this particular problem in mind that we shall, in the chapter to follow, return to human freedom as divinely communicated. On the basis of the anthropological impact of divine freedom, thanks to which humans, in their very humanity, correspond to God, I shall then propose a way of eliminating the incoherence in Jüngel's account of divine freedom, as well as its excessively self-relational overtones.

The argument of the present chapter will unfold as follows. I shall begin by locating Jüngel's discussion of divine freedom in the broader context of his critique of the metaphysical tradition, drawing attention in particular to the freedom of God in God's revelation vis-à-vis the only-apparent freedom of the God of metaphysical theism. I shall then outline Jüngel's understanding of divine freedom, following which I shall analyze, in quite some detail, its constitutive moments: determinateness and independence. This chapter will conclude, first, with a discussion of what I take to be Jüngel's attempt, an unsuccessful one, to resolve the tension in his account of God's freedom. Second, I shall present an overview of external evidence, drawn from Jüngel's interpreters, for the tension analyzed in this chapter, pointing out the one-sidedness of their interpretations and their tendency to collapse one of freedom's moments into the other. This will prepare the ground, in subsequent chapters, for taking Jüngel's account of freedom beyond his *formal* elaboration as a way of preserving divine freedom's complexity and giving the concept internal coherence. What I believe is ultimately responsible for the disjointedness and ambiguity is Jüngel's purely formal analysis of God's freedom. He never considers whether freedom might itself have a concrete, trinitarian structure in a manner similar to love.

God's Freedom

Jüngel's opposition to the metaphysical tradition

The Introduction has already touched on Jüngel's doctrine of God in the context of the overall design of his project. Jüngel's intention, it will be recalled, is to trace the trajectory of western metaphysics – a trajectory at whose end one finds, in the works of Kant and Fichte, a declaration of the unknowability and eventually also unthinkability of God. This declaration, according to Jüngel, is hardly a surprise. Theism conceives of God as the *absolute* and *necessary* essence. However, this conception has its starting point not in God but in the self-reflection of the human subject, who sees itself as imperfect; it is rooted in the speculation of the human subject who determines God's divinity and then seeks to secure God's existence but in truth strives, above all else, to secure itself through the God it postulates. From an absolute God, existing at the mercy of human reason, it is but a small step to atheism, as Jüngel shows. And even if one does not wish to take this step, one cannot but recognize that God's sublime divinity can only be spared its dependence on human rationality when the human subject simply gives up all thought of God. Atheism, for its part, is all too eager to pronounce the death of the God of theism, as was done by Nietzsche, and to announce liberation from metaphysical thought-forms that, allegedly, have only stifled human flourishing. In atheism, the human subject discovers that self-securing does not require the theistic God after all. One is actually encouraged to reclaim from this God humanity's best qualities which have become alienated as a result of their misguided projection onto the divine.

Against this backdrop, Jüngel enquires into the conditions under which God can be thought and spoken of again. He concludes that the atheistic pronouncement of the death of God is premature, to say the least. It is premature because theism, of which atheism is but a logical outgrowth, has never seriously entertained the biblical witness to God's identification with the crucified man Jesus. Theism has never seriously considered God's death – not as atheism's pronouncement but as an event of God's self-definition that contradicts all human speculation about God. Faced with the mirror alternatives of theism and atheism, Jüngel turns to the cross as the locale of God's self-disclosure par excellence.

In this section, I wish to revisit Jüngel's opposition to the metaphysical tradition. But I will do so not so much from the perspective of God's thinkability and speakability as from the perspective of honoring divine freedom. Freedom, Jüngel maintains, properly belongs to none but God; yet, in His freedom, God chooses truly to share freedom with His creatures. Jesus' cross, according to Jüngel, not only enables speech and thought about God; it is the site where God determines God's own being. God determines God's being as, among others, liberator and does so freely, on God's own terms, and thus against the better judgment of the theistically-minded defender of God's divine absoluteness. Jüngel opposes traditional metaphysics because it practically deprives God of His freedom. It excludes the sharing of freedom by God, and, by doing so, it leaves Him at the mercy of human use and abuse.

The metaphysical notion restricts freedom to God alone.[2] It does so because any communication of freedom on God's part would undermine God's divinity, which consists in being absolutely distinct from all that is not God. The metaphysical tradition conceptualizes God in terms of an infinite substance, pure energy, a prime mover, or a perfect and necessary being. Even when it concludes that God's essence is ultimately unspeakable (or precisely because it makes this claim), it still insists that God is singular, allowing of no division, no self-communication, let alone inner opposition or contradiction.[3]

A super-being of this sort must necessarily be in competition with His creatures whose very existence, not to mention self-assertion, poses a direct threat to His godhood. This threat is diffused through a number of conceptual moves. It is claimed, for example, that if God is, then humans are not.[4] If God acts, then human action is negligible, being only a modality of divine action (unless it is sinful or evil, but even so, to the chagrin of His defenders, God, in order to remain God, cannot be entirely absolved of involvement).[5] If God wills, then humans are an externalization of the divine will, obedient to the point of dissolving their will in God's, or else they are willful, which is a sin and for which they will eventually pay.[6] If God is free, then humans have no freedom (with the apparent exception of some mundane choices where the bondage of the human is happily negligible).[7]

---

[2] Consider, for example, Luther's assertion contra Erasmus: "free choice is plainly a divine term, and can be properly applied to none but the Divine Majesty alone" (*The Bondage of the Will* [1525], *LW* 33:68; *WA* 18:636; cited in *Mystery*, 36; *GGW* 45).

[3] Jüngel traces this tradition back to Parmenides and Aristotle; see "Nemo contra deum nisi deus ipse: Zum Verhältnis von theologia crucis und Trinitätslehre," *TE V*, 244–5.

[4] For example, Pseudo-Dionysius the Areopagite, *The Divine Names* 5.4 (817D); 5.10 (825B).

[5] For example, Luther, *The Bondage of the Will*, *LW* 33:176; *WA* 18:709 and, paradigmatically, Jean Calvin, *Institutes of the Christian Religion*, I.xvi.2, I.xvi.8, III.xxiii.7. The problem of evil is a conundrum *par excellence* for the metaphysical doctrine of God. See in this context Jüngel's essay, "Gottes ursprüngliches Anfangen als schöpferische Selbstbegrenzung. Ein Beitrag zum Gespräch mit Hans Jonas über den »Gottesbegriff nach Auschwitz«," *TE III*, 151–62. Jüngel speaks here of God's ongoing creativity; yet it is precisely as Creator that God also limits himself for the creature, makes room for the creature, gives the creature time, suffers with the suffering, all of which gives suffering eternal value and creates new possibilities where all possibility seems to be extinguished. More to this below.

[6] For example, *The Theologia Germanica of Martin Luther*, ed. Bengt Hoffman (Mahwah, N.J.: Paulist, 1980), 138–9.

[7] For example, Luther, *The Bondage of the Will*, *LW* 33:68–70; *WA* 18: 636–8. Even Barth's doctrine of election lends itself to such interpretations. For a discussion and critique, see Hans Theodor Goebel, *Vom freien Wählen Gottes und des Menschen* (Frankfurt am Main: Peter Lang, 1990), 281–92.

This situation is hardly improved when one attempts to make a virtue out of human self-negation and maintains that it is only out of love that God desires to draw all to God's self and that in the face of such love one simply can do no other but surrender one's self. If anything, this claim relativizes the notion of love by turning it into a modality of divine omnipotence. It preempts any possible protest by insisting, quite axiomatically, that one simply cannot quarrel with love. But it does not diffuse the totalizing and exclusive dimension that characterizes God's relation to his creation. Jüngel offers this comment on the unenviable fate of the ill-fated competitor: "One could then become unstable – yes, so frightened, by such a divine lord whose essence solely consists in a concept of abstract omnipotence that one then is only silent about Him in powerless rage or in powerless contempt."[8] To speak of human partnership with this God would not only be presumptuous but also oxymoronic.

This singular and imperious divinity seems, at first sight, to be completely removed from all things human as their absolute antithesis. The God of the metaphysical tradition remains solitary in His godhood. For the sake of His perfection, He cannot be affected by transient human affairs; nor does He have any real need of humans, not even by His own decision. Without injury to His perfection, He can truly love only Himself: "*Neminem amat deus nisi deum ipsum.*"[9] Yet, precisely as supremely divine, this God is also supremely manipulable by humans to browbeat others into submission. Human distendedness need not always be openly godless and usurping godhood for itself. It may, in fact, appear to be very pious and even self-deprecating, and, under that mask, be expansive and colonizing. In interhuman relations the word "God" may be used to justify all manners of unfreedom that humans inflict on others. Humans may seek their own self-security at others' expense, as well as control over their world – both in the name of God and with the word "God" on their lips. Jüngel observes, in the context of his discussion of human liberation, that tyrannical and being-destructive interruption with the *word* "God" is possible. The latter, however, is not a *divine* interruption, and the being of God it discloses is, in reality, a mask hiding nothing but humanity's own distendedness.[10] Humans can easily interrupt others' lives with the word "God" but, instead of wholeness, leave

---

[8] "What does it mean to say, 'God is love'?" T. Hart and D. Thimell (eds), *Christ in our Place: The Humanity of God in Christ for the Reconciliation of the World. Essays Presented to Prof. James Torrance* (Exeter, UK: Paternoster, 1989), 301.

[9] Jüngel credits Spinoza with finally saying it firmly and clearly: "Deus . . . neminem . . . amat" (*The Ethics*, Part V, prop. 17; cited in "Nemo contra deum nisi deus ipse," *TE V*, 245; see also *Mystery*, 329; *GGW* 451).

[10] "What does it mean to say, 'God is love'?" 300–1.

only brokenness in their wake. Here I again call attention to Jüngel's equation: "homo homini deus = homo homini lupus."[11]

God lends Himself to this (ab)use even, and perhaps especially, in the name of love, which, because it has no real mooring in God's being, becomes a handy veil for power claims and an excuse for violence. The philosophical reason why this distant and totalizing divinity, antithetical to everything human, can be manipulated with such ease lies in the fact that it is nothing but a product of human reason. Theologically speaking, it is a product of "lust for what is apparently being withheld. And this is not God's divinity; it is what sinners imagine it to be."[12] The God of the metaphysical tradition embodies the unassailable godhood for which self-securing humans quest. His godhood, represented by the classical "ways" of negation (*via negationis*), eminence (*via eminentiae*), and causality (*via causalitatis*), constitutes a repudiation of that which is fragile and an intensification of that which is scarce and hence valued in human existence. And it remains a thinly veiled image of humans' own relationlessness and lack of all proportion even when, in a seemingly final act of deference, human thought stops short of the divine, calls into question the three ways, and, through a second act of negation, proclaims God to be infinitely superior to every predicate and incapable of definition (*deus definiri nequit*).[13]

God's free self-determination

It is out of concern for divine freedom that Jüngel affirms, in opposition to the metaphysical tradition, that God is *more than necessary* in relation to the world. Now, this must not be taken to mean that God is *un*necessary. Rather, God's being more than necessary overcomes the false alternatives of (theistic) presence or (atheistic) absence, both equally forced.[14] It allows for divine *self*-determination and, in this way only, for *self*-disclosure on God's part. In freedom, "God is present as the one who is absent in the world"[15] and so really present – as God and on God's own terms.

Jüngel defines God's freedom as consisting of two, *in themselves abstract*, moments: "(a) self-determination [*Selbstbestimmung*] as the opposite of alien determination [*Fremdbestimmung*], but also (b) self-determination as the opposite of indeterminateness (arbitrariness) [*Unbestimmtheit*

---

[11] "Freiheitsrechte und Gerechtigkeit," *TE I*, 248.
[12] Justification, 138.
[13] Cf. *Mystery*, 231ff, esp. 257–8; *GGW* 314ff, esp. 350–2.
[14] *Mystery*, 55; *GGW* 71.
[15] *Mystery*, 62; *GGW* 81.

(*Beliebigkeit*)]."[16] In brief, freedom consists in independence and determinateness, inseparably conjoined.

As more than necessary, God is *independent*. God is not determined by worldly contingencies, and, as such, He has nothing to do with human reason's flights of fancy. God is neither the ultimate solution to the world's perceived imperfections nor the final conclusion of rational calculation. In other words, God is not an object necessitated by or proceeding from humanity's need. Jüngel makes this point pithily: "God comes from God."[17] This assertion, often repeated by Jüngel, constitutes the core of his trinitarian doctrine. It expresses the freedom of God to reveal God's self on God's terms instead of being a worldly given. And, as far as God's being is concerned, it affirms that God, and not others, decides who or what God should be. God's coming from God means that "God stands under no conditions of any kind."[18] Jüngel adds that divine freedom, so understood, implies independence not only of outer but also inner necessity. God is not determined by worldly contingencies; more than that, He is under no compulsion, in His own being, to reveal Himself in any way, let alone to identify with the man Jesus and to make this man integral to God's being.[19]

But freedom also entails *determinateness* – an actual decision with regard to one's own being. For "without the goal of determinateness [freedom] would be an impermissible abstraction" warns Jüngel.[20] God is free, truly free, in that He actually allows Himself to be experienced, "on the basis of his self-revelation," as the one who comes to humanity, the one who loves, and the one who bestows gifts.[21] God's determinateness consists even more

---

[16] *Mystery*, 36; *GGW* 46.

[17] *Mystery*, 34, 381ff; *GGW* 43, 522ff.

[18] *Mystery*, 35; *GGW* 44.

[19] This is contra Hegel. Jüngel remains much appreciative of Hegel's "grand theological accomplishment . . . a philosophically conceived theology of the Crucified One *as* the doctrine of the Triune God." It is precisely this achievement that, in Jüngel's judgment, enables God's speakability in the wake of Kant. The theological criticism that Jüngel levels at Hegel is that "Hegel's God needs man" in order to come to himself. This not only compromises divine freedom and love but also exploits and destroys humanity by divinizing it. Hence Jüngel's insistence on God's being moved by no inner necessity toward identification with the crucified Jesus. See *Mystery*, 63–97, esp. 94–5; *GGW* 83–128, esp. 124–5. Jüngel, to be sure, avoids making humanity necessary to God's self-realization, but whether he can give as unambiguous an account of divine love as he wishes to is, as this chapter will show, quite another story.

[20] *Mystery*, 36; *GGW* 46.

[21] *Mystery*, 34; *GGW* 43. This is not to say that traditional metaphysics aprioristically excluded any special revelation. What, according to Jüngel, saves theism from complete derailment, is an inconsistency that must be recognized as such: what theistic speculation arrives at and identifies *as* God *remoto deo*, it frequently conflates *with* a notion of God obtained from another source, namely, divine revelation. Distortion, however, is inevitable and it is usually revelation that bears its brunt by being thrust into the alien mold cast by theistic speculation. See Jüngel's critique of Aquinas' "five ways" and his relative preference for Anselm's proof in "Theses on the Relation of the Existence, Essence and Attributes of God," *Toronto Journal of Theology* 17:1 (Summer 2001), 58–60.

specifically in "the christological identity of God with the crucified Jesus."[22]
It is important to underscore here that the import of the cross, for Jüngel,
is ultimately not merely negative and polemical but also positive. The cross
is not only the site of the retrieval of God's speakability; as the event of
God's identification with the man Jesus, the cross gives expression to the
basic presupposition of Jüngel's doctrine of God, namely, divine freedom.
In His freedom, God is that which God and God alone decides to be: "God
not without man,"[23] God in relation to an other.

Tension-fraught freedom

What can already be gathered from this preliminary foray into Jüngel's
construal of divine freedom is that, on the one hand, God is a single subject,
with sole prerogative over God's self. Freedom is a correlate of God's
subjectivity, in that in freedom God remains who God is. This will be
especially important for an understanding of God's creativity and God's
prevalence over death. On the other hand, God enters into a relationship
with otherness. This relationship, as we shall see, is not only one of self-
limitation but also, as love, one that involves reciprocity. From the viewpoint
of divine determinateness, God's subjectivity is a relational subjectivity,
realized supremely in God's love for humanity, which leads God to
identification with the dead Jesus, in such a manner that "God himself
is dead."[24]

Together these two moments – independence and determinateness – are
said to constitute God's freedom. In Jüngel's words, "Only as one who is
determined on the basis of his self-determination is God a concrete reality
[*konkret*]."[25] However, already a mere theoretical consideration of the two
moments leads one to ask whether – and if so, then how – they can be
maintained simultaneously as equally weighted focal points. Freedom
invariably exhibits the characteristics of one at the expense of the other.
And it does so in such a way that the gravitational pull of the one moment
distorts, or even contradicts the other. This lack of equilibrium is thus
clearly not a mere matter of emphasis. It must rather be attributed, in part

---

[22] *Mystery*, 40; *GGW* 51.
[23] *Mystery*, 37; *GGW* 47.
[24] Jüngel traces the origin of this pronouncement via Hegel, the seventeenth-century chorale,
    "O Traurigkeit, O Herzeleid," back to Tertullian; see *Mystery*, 64–5; *GGW* 84–5. The *Lutheran
    Service Book* (St. Louis: Concordia, 2006) restores the more controversial version of the cho-
    rale's second stanza: "O sorrow dread! Our God is dead, Upon the cross extended" (#448).
[25] *Mystery*, 36; *GGW* 46.

at least, to a serious discordance between the two foci, as well as the absence of a clear set of principles to specify how and under what circumstances one of the moments should be highlighted or privileged, so that the other one is not undermined.

What is this discordance? To begin with, it needs to be noted that independence is a presupposition for self-executed determinateness. It is the point of departure for determinateness. As such, it represents a range of possibilities, infinite perhaps, prior to their closure. As independence, freedom is a potentiality that appears to be undone through its actualization. By contrast – and somewhat counter-intuitively – freedom, understood as self-posited determinateness, is not *possibility* but the *act* itself of closure of all possibilities but one. These are very different dimensions: the one implies detached self-preservation, the other committed self-limitation.

Abstractly, it may seem possible to maintain the two foci: freedom as the *logical presupposition* of, or the *conclusion* to be drawn from, self-determination. The tension between them is diffused (though not eliminated) when only one of the foci is concretized while the other remains merely logical or rational. But God's freedom, Jüngel insists, is a reality, an *ongoing reality*, a reality permeating God's entire being-in-act; no dimension of it is just a logical construct. The question then remains how freedom is both a state presupposed by the act of self-determination and the reality established in particular determinateness that is intersubjective to boot? How is independence at once overcome through specific actualization only to be re-established with new vigor? What is the concrete reality of divine freedom – concrete precisely in that it accommodates the two tension-fraught dimensions: self-preservation and self-limitation?

Before these questions can be addressed constructively, we must examine how Jüngel maintains the two focal points of divine freedom and, in so doing, demonstrate that the tension just identified is indeed present in Jüngel's doctrine of God. That is, we must show that in his discussion Jüngel does in fact oscillate between the one and the other understanding of freedom, without accounting for how they cohere with each other. We must also show that, as a result, there occurs a distortion of the other moment.

Freedom's Determinateness

We begin our analysis with Jüngel's articulation of God's determinateness. When Jüngel's writings are considered against the backdrop of their theological milieu, one can discern a push, on Jüngel's part, toward asserting not only the determinateness of God's being but a particularly robust sort of determinateness. Jüngel locates God's self-determining decision in time. This then enables Him to propose a vigorously relational, cruciform account of God's subjectivity and to mine the rich mutuality that God's being a temporal event of love entails. The following discussion will take up three aspects of God's relational determinateness, as those are articulated by Jüngel: decision, cruciform subjectivity, and love.

Determinateness as God's decision

Jüngel emphasizes, first and foremost, that God's determinateness is grounded solely in God's decision. This leads him to reject two splits present in traditional metaphysical formulations of the locus *de Deo*. The first split is that between God's essence and God's existence. Jüngel, as we have seen, blames this conceptual split for the trajectory of Western theism, in that the split enabled the human subject to lodge itself between God's essence and existence, declare what God's essence was to be, and then stand in judgment over God's existence. Jüngel's rejection of the split, however, is not driven by polemic alone. The dismissal is intended to underscore that, where God's determinateness is concerned, there is no essence that is given apart from the concrete manner in which God exists. God's particular existence, His more-than-necessary existence out of Himself, is His very essence. In other words, God determines God's self through God's very existence. God alone, in His existence, disposes over God's being.

To underscore that God's self-determination is indeed *God's self* determination, Jüngel rejects a further split: between God's being in God's self and God's being in relation. There is no disquieting *deus absconditus* behind and beyond the *deus revelatus*.[26] Nor is there divine aseity that, though somehow knowable, remains indifferent to God's relational self-determining. We shall discuss this in more detail when we consider Jüngel's account of divine independence. It will suffice to say here that, for Jüngel, self-determined determinateness belongs to God in God's self.

The above two points are of particular significance for Jüngel's understanding of divine freedom. To recapitulate: God alone determines

---

[26] To Jüngel's appropriation of Luther's categories that avoids the ethical and ontological split within the being of God, a split the threatens to undermine the genuineness of God's self-disclosure, see "The Revelation of the Hiddenness of God. A Contribution to the Protestant Understanding of the Hiddenness of Divine Action," *Essays II*, 120–44; and "Quae supra nos, nihil ad nos: Eine Kurzformel der Lehre vom verborgenen Gott – im Anschluss an Luther interpretiert," *TE II*, 202–51. This is not to say that Jüngel leaves no room for divine hiddenness altogether – a point to which I shall return in Chapter 4.

God's self and for this reason it truly is God's own determinateness. This fundamental insight owes much to Barth's influence on Jüngel. But Jüngel wishes to emphasize even more: determinateness is not only grounded in God's decision, but it is grounded in a specific type of decision. This is where Jüngel and Barth diverge, and Jüngel offers his own, temporal construal of God's self-determining decision.

For Barth, the divine election is God's primal decision – of fundamental significance for both humanity and God himself. As Barth famously expressed it, "God was not alone, nor did He work alone, at that beginning of all His works and ways. He was not without man."[27] This means that the humanity of Jesus Christ, in Barth's Christology, is emphatically not "a contingent fact of history."[28] Very likely it may mean, in addition, that election constitutes not only the ground of Christ's human being but also the ground of God's own triune being: God is eternally triune because He *is* his primal electing decision. Jüngel's own interpretation of Barth tends in this direction. He writes, for example, "we have to understand God's primal decision as an *event* in the being of God which differentiates [*unterscheidendes Ereignis*] the modes of God's being."[29]

The focus changes when Jüngel states his own position: "The death of Jesus Christ . . . forced a differentiation [*zu unterscheiden zwang*] between God and God. . . [T]he divine modes of being, Father, and Son, . . . in this death separated into such a great differentiation than which nothing greater can be imagined."[30] Though God's identification with the dead Jesus was, it must be added, effected wholly by God, with the resulting differentiation being uncoerced[31] – it must likewise be pointed out that, in Jüngel's formulation, there no longer is any sense of God's decision as a primal, inner-trinitarian event aimed at that which *only is to be* beyond God (*opus ad extra internum*). Jüngel accentuates, instead, the event of divine love and God's historical engagement culminating in God's self-differentiating

---

[27] *CD* IV/2, 32.

[28] *CD* IV/2, 31.

[29] *Becoming*, 86. For this reason, Jüngel is eagerly enlisted by Bruce McCormack in support of McCormack's own reading of Barth in a debate which has, particularly within the last decade, exercised a number of Barth scholars in the United Sates. The issue being debated concerns the logical relation of Trinity and election. See Bruce McCormack, "God *Is* His Decision: The Jüngel-Gollwitzer 'Debate' Revisited," Bruce L. McCormack & Kimlyn J. Bender (eds), *Theology as Conversation: The Significance of Dialogue in Historical and Contemporary Theology. A Festschrift for Daniel L. Migliore* (Grand Rapids: Eerdmans, 2009), 48–66; and "Election and the Trinity: Theses in response to George Hunsinger," *Scottish Journal of Theology* 63:2 (2010), esp. 207–8.

[30] *Mystery*, 374; *GGW* 513.

[31] *Mystery*, 363; *GGW* 498.

identification with the dead man Jesus: "in the event of Jesus' death, and thus at the point where God-forsakenness reached its apex, God became *one* with this man. God *identified* himself with Jesus, with this mortal man, so that, in *unity* with the dead man, he might be there for all mortal humans."[32] Not only is there an arguably stronger emphasis on actuality over against (its corresponding) possibility, but what is emphasized is a specific, unambiguously historical actuality, into which God enters. This actuality is not a mere repetition or realization in time of what has been resolved and determined eternally. Rather, it expresses itself both in the contingency of Jesus' death[33] and in the resultant – yet entirely gratuitous – self-identification of God with the dead Jesus. In other words, when Jüngel's theology is seen in the context of Barth's, by which it is undoubtedly influenced, there is a marked shift from that which is largely intradivine – that is, the proleptic presence of the man Jesus in God's eternal self-determining decision – to that which is temporal: God's triune "happen[ing] as love in the death of Jesus."[34]

What these two christological elaborations of the doctrine of God share in common is a fundamental commitment to God's own self-determination. God's decision alone is the ground of God's being. As such, this decision is the ground of human being only because God makes room for humanity – for Jesus – in his self-determination: "the triune God affirms us and himself with one and the same yes."[35] What thus constitutes the fundament of God's "ways and works" – for Barth as well as for Jüngel – is God's uncompromisable subjectivity. In his discussion of Barth's theological development, Jüngel credits Barth with the insight and insistence that "the doctrine of the Trinity should be formulated in terms of 'the problem of the inalienable subjectivity of God in his revelation.'"[36] For his part, Jüngel, too, affirms that "God is the unconditional subject of himself [*unbedingtes Subjekt seiner selbst*] and as such is accessible only because and to the extent that he makes himself accessible."[37]

---

[32] "Was ist 'das unterscheidend Christliche'?" *TE I*, 298 (emphases added).

[33] Jüngel discusses the various historical dimensions of Jesus' death in "Das Sein Jesu Christi als Ereignis der Versöhnung Gottes mit einer gottlosen Welt: Die Hingabe des Gekreuzigten" *TE II*, 279.

[34] *Mystery*, 221; *GGW* 301.

[35] "Unterbrechung des Weltlebens: Eberhard Jüngel über »Gottes Sein ist im Werden« (1965)," Henning Ritter (ed.), *Werksbesichtigung Geisteswissenschaften: Fünfundzwanzig Bücher von ihren Autoren gelesen* (Frankfurt am Main: Insel Verlag, 1990), 138. Cf. *Becoming*, 103.

[36] As Barth put it in a 1924 letter to Eduard Thurneysen; cited in Jüngel's *Karl Barth: A Theological Legacy*, trans. Garrett E. Paul (Philadelphia: Westminster, 1986), 38.

[37] *Mystery*, 158; *GGW* 212.

God's cruciform subjectivity

Though the point on which Jüngel differs from Barth seems to echo the standard and rather superficial Lutheran criticisms of Barth, according to which Barth locates the entire salvation drama outside of history, Jüngel knows better than that.[38] His temporalization of God's self-determination is not meant, therefore, to be a corrective of Barth in this regard, that is, a relocation of the salvation story from the eternity of God's election into history.

Rather, Jüngel's move has to do, as I will show, with the specific character of God's triune subjectivity. Despite the fundamental commitment, on both Barth's and Jüngel's part, to God's being the subject of his own determination, it is on the issue of divine subjectivity that Barth's and Jüngel's construals of God's triunity ultimately part ways. Jüngel's views, as we shall see in due course, are not always as clear as one might wish, and one of the tasks of this project is to propose a way in which such clarity can be achieved. However, what remains quite clear is that, whereas Barth's understanding of God's subjectivity is clearly incarnation-oriented, Jüngel's understanding of God as subject is distinctly cruciform. This has considerable implications, for two different modes of subjective being are, in fact, involved here. Jüngel, I wish to argue, aims at a more unambiguously and robustly relational understanding of God's being.

To appreciate the difference between Barth and Jüngel in their respective conceptions of the divine subject, let us, first, compare the accounts the two theologians offer of God's subjectivity in revelation. On this basis I will then provide a precise description of what the relationality of the divine subject means for Jüngel.

For Barth, Jesus of Nazareth is present to God "even before the dawn of his own time." In fact, "[a]t no level or time can we have to do with God without having also to do with this man."[39] Significantly, however, even though Barth comes astonishingly close, as McCormack points out, to identifying the second mode of God's triune being (i.e., the Son) with Jesus, he does in the end shrink back from doing so.[40] The Logos and Jesus, though inseparable,

---

[38] A good summary of, as well as a response to, the Lutheran critique can be found in Gerald McKenny, *The Analogy of Grace: Karl Barth's Moral Theology* (Oxford: University Press, 2010), 173–5.

[39] *CD* IV/2, 33.

[40] Bruce McCormack, "Participation in God, Yes, Deification, No," Ingolf U. Dalferth, et al. (eds), *Denkwürdiges Geheimnis: Beiträge zur Gotteslehre. Festschrift für Eberhard Jüngel zum 70. Geburtstag* (Tübingen: Mohr Siebeck, 2004), 369.

remain distinct.[41] The eternal Logos, as a mode of God's triune being, constitutes, by virtue of God's primal decision, a stopgap for the historical man Jesus of Nazareth.[42] Both the presence of Jesus to God in God's eternity and the carefully maintained distinction between the divine Logos and the humanity of Jesus mean that God's revelation in Jesus of Nazareth amounts to a temporal realization of the eternally constituted determinateness of God as subject. The being of God as subject is eternally oriented to Jesus who, in addition to being human, is also the incarnate God the Son.

By contrast, Jüngel views God's revelation as *more* than an execution of a subjectivity which enters history in its eternally established self-determination and orientation. God's revelation is, for Jüngel, not only God's self-interpretation in time. It is also a self-definition: "*God defines himself* when he identifies himself with the dead Jesus."[43] As self-definition, God's revelation has two dimensions: first, God, as is to be expected, can be located only in a particular historical, that is, spatiotemporal, locality, in a particular event; and, second, this event is not without impact on the being of God, which, aside from God's revelatory will, is the reason why God is available only in the locale of that event. In the backdrop here is Luther's emphatic insistence that God not only is known but actually "wish[es] . . . to be recognized in suffering." In fact, according to Luther, "God can be found only in suffering and the cross."[44] Human salvation crucially depends on "God's death and a dead God."[45] Jüngel takes these Lutheran insights to their logical conclusion. In the cross, God defines himself so completely and exhaustively[46]

---

[41] "in the eternal election of God [Jesus Christ] is *with* [*mit*] God's Son the first, that is, the primary object and content of the primal and basic will of God" (*CD* IV/2, 33, emphasis added).

[42] *CD* II/2, 96.

[43] *Mystery*, 363–4, see also 221; *GGW* 498, see also 300.

[44] Martin Luther, *The Heidelberg Disputation* (1518), *LW* 31:52–3; *WA* 1:362 [Theses 20 and 21].

[45] Martin Luther, *On the Councils and the Church* (1539), *LW* 41:103; *WA* 50:590. The guiding concern behind Luther's turn to the cross, a turn exemplified programmatically in both the *Heidelberg Disputation* (1518) and *The Bondage of the Will* (1525), is to critique the works-obsessed piety of the late middle ages. Luther believed that it not only encouraged foolhardy confidence in one's natural powers in relation to salvation but also, in doing so, obscured the redemptive dimension of Christ's death. When confidence eventually gives way to despair over the quality and quantity of one's works, the person is left with nowhere to turn to. For Luther, the cross is the only source of certainty of one's salvation; such certainty, Luther holds, can never be afforded by works and is, therefore, achieved not through doing but only in faith. Jüngel's appropriation of Luther's theology of the cross shifts the focus from human guilt before God and the question of the certainty of one's salvation to what are largely epistemological concerns with regard to God's being. Yet, as I will show in the following chapter, Jüngel does draw substantially on the Reformation's critique of works and on its lifting up of faith as constitutive of the person in his anthropology. In his doctrine of God, this influence is more oblique.

[46] "Das Sein Jesu Christi," *TE II*, 277.

that God's being can be understood in no other way than on the basis of the integration of Jesus' death into it. This endows the event of the cross not only with epistemological reliability (pertaining to God's revelatory will) but also ontological reliability (pertaining to God's very being), so much so that "one can experience who or what God actually is only on the basis of this event."[47] Jüngel offers the following systematic-theological elaboration:

> Christ's death can be understood no more as a salvation event, one among others, or, for that matter, as an event *sui generis* to be interpreted through a presupposed concept of God. . . Rather, God's being is to be understood from the event of this death. . . Because when, in Jesus' death, God has defined himself *as* God, then death has *ontological relevance* for the being of God and also for the life of Jesus Christ. For God defines himself not with propositions, but with his own being.[48]

As Jüngel puts it elsewhere, the freedom in which God identifies God's self with the dead Jesus constitutes "a *substantive* moment of [God's] self-definition."[49]

Jüngel appeals to the Easter proclamation of the resurrection of the crucified Jesus to support his view of "the Crucified One as the self-definition of God."[50] The Easter *kerygma*, especially as formulated by St. Paul (Romans 1:4) and his Lutheran interpreters,[51] constitutes, according to Jüngel, the *material* necessity of locating God's own being in the crucifixion of Jesus. The *formal* necessity of doing so lies in the consequences of modern metaphysics and has to do with the recovery of the thinkability and speakability of God. These two necessities, Jüngel claims, exist in fruitful tension.[52] Presumably, the formal necessity gives sharpness to the proclamatory impulse and extends the scope of its application.

But what specifically, in terms of God's subjectivity, does it mean that the crucified Jesus is the self-definition of God? How is Jesus's death integrated into God's being? According to Jüngel, God's free self-determination becomes "concrete freedom,"[53] in that what takes place in the event of the

---

[47] *Mystery*, 221; *GGW* 300.
[48] "Vom Tod des lebendigen Gottes: Ein Plakat," *TE I*, 119
[49] *Mystery*, 221; *GGW* 300.
[50] *Mystery*, 364; *GGW* 498.
[51] E.g., *Mystery*, 37, 205–7; *GGW* 47, 279–82.
[52] *Mystery*, 193, cf. 185; *GGW* 261, cf. 250.
[53] *Mystery*, 221; *GGW* 300.

cross is God's self-differentiation as Father, Son, and Spirit. Jüngel explains God's self-differentiation thus:

> By [God's] identification [with the crucified, dead and buried man Jesus] is . . . understood an event, in which God, who relates himself to himself, so relates himself to the man Jesus, who is distinct from him, that, in complete unity with this man, God – in the distinction between Father and Son – opposes himself; yet in this opposition, which has become unsurpassable through the antithesis of divine life and human death, God – as Spirit – remains related to himself.[54]

It is also at the cross, one might add, that the man Jesus is defined as the Son of God.[55]

Thus far we have shown that Jüngel posits a temporal location for God's self-determination. The chief implication of this is that, in contradistinction to Barth, it is in history, as God reveals God's self, that God establishes his determinateness as a triune subject. This is a crucial point that raises further considerations about Jüngel's cross-centered articulation of God's triunity. These considerations have to do – beyond the *that* or the *how* of God's subjectivity yet on the basis of these two – with the *what*. The question, in other words, is: What exactly does Jüngel gain through this particular trinitarian construal? What is the divine subjectivity that emerges from God's self-determination as subject in this particular, temporal manner?

To answer this question, I shall mention here two influences on whom Jüngel draws and from whom he chooses to differ: Barth, to whose critical (though not uncritical) impact on Jüngel we have already given some attention, as well as the Roman-Catholic theologian Karl Rahner. But before we consider the two theologians, let me situate my comments against the broader backdrop of Jüngel's criticism of traditional trinitarian dogma. Jüngel writes:

> That God became *man* was for the classical trinitarian doctrine not the constitutively determining event of the trinitarian being of God, although it [= classical trinitarian doctrine] then derived from that event as a further consequence of the basic thought [that God became man]. One could think God as God without having thought of the Crucified One as God. The death of Jesus concerned the concept of deity, the divine nature, as

[54] "Das Sein Jesu Christi," *TE II*, 276; cf. *Mystery*, 363; *GGW* 498.
[55] *Mystery*, 364; *GGW* 498.

little as the life of this man was significant for the concept of divine being. According to this view, God comes to himself even apart from Jesus. *God's freedom, therefore, was conceived of without his concrete self-determination.*[56]

What is interesting about this passage is the subtle shift from the incarnation to the death of Jesus. Jüngel is, of course, right that the death of Jesus, in classical trinitarian dogma, was not "the constitutively determining event of the *trinitarian being of God.*" But he is only partially right when it comes to the incarnation. (I shall here use the term "incarnation" and its adjectival form more narrowly, as oriented to the beginning of Jesus' human life.) Luther's thought, for example, offers resources that call for understanding the *being of God* from the incarnation, or, to be more precise, from the communication of properties between the divine and human natures in the person of Jesus Christ (as opposed to the more narrow death of Jesus). I believe it is significant that, for all his appeals to Luther, Jüngel does not wish to develop Luther's incarnational model into a full-blown trinitarianism. Why?

Let us keep in mind Jüngel's preference for the cross versus the incarnation, as we now turn to the more contemporary influences who actually share Jüngel's criticism concerning the theological irrelevance and consequent marginalization of classical trinitarianism. Jüngel enthusiastically endorses Rahner's axiom that the Trinity in revelation is none other than the triune God as He is in God's self, and that the triune God in Himself is none other than the God revealed.[57] "The Trinity is a mystery of salvation," Rahner insists famously, "otherwise it would never have been revealed."[58] If so, "the doctrine of the 'missions' is from its very nature the starting point for the doctrine of the Trinity."[59] So far, so good: Jüngel echoes these comments closely in his own emphasis on God's self-revelation as the source of God's knowability. But, for Rahner, more specifically, it is the *unio hypostatica*, not the cross that makes sense of and warrants trinitarian dogma. Jesus as the Father's Word in the flesh discloses the eternal procession of the Word from the Father. This raises Jüngel's concern in that Rahner achieves the identity of the immanent Trinity and economic Trinity by viewing the Logos as essentially characterized by the property of incarnability. To put it differently, if Jesus is the Father's Word in the flesh, then, for

[56] *Mystery,* 37; *GGW* 46–7 (emphasis added).
[57] *Mystery,* 369–70; *GGW* 506–7.
[58] Karl Rahner, *The Trinity,* trans. Joseph Donceel (New York: Crossroad, 1997), 21.
[59] Rahner, *The Trinity,* 48.

Rahner, the Logos alone must be both enfleshable and to be enfleshed. The identity of the Logos rests in his predisposition to become incarnate. Jüngel worries that the incarnation, as so grounded in God's eternity, carries with itself overtones of necessity and inevitability. It does not have the same force of a historical and contingent demand as does Jesus' death. Jüngel asks "whether Rahner has considered the hypostatic character of the Son also in the sense of a soteriological predisposition, namely, that to the Son of God belongs, as his ontological quality, not only the incarnation but also becoming flesh (in the Pauline sense)." If the latter indeed belongs there, as Jüngel maintains, "there can be no compulsion towards the ontic execution of this ontological property."[60] God's freedom must not be compromised. For only in freedom – understood as God's own decision with regard to God's self – can God's identification with humanity be a *gracious* identification. Jüngel's polemic with Rahner is ultimately carried out in the interest of the gratuity of divine grace.

Jüngel's worry in regard to Barth has a somewhat different orientation because of Barth's central emphasis on God's primal decision of election, in which God determines Himself for humanity and humanity for Himself. The divine election is, for Barth, explicitly "an election of grace."[61] But, given Jüngel's departure from Barth, there clearly is some uneasiness on his part also with Barth's incarnation-centered understanding of God's triune being. As we have seen, Jüngel considers the grace of God's self-determination for humanity to be of fundamental importance. But for him, this grace has a very specific dimension. It is directed not to humanity which has yet to be, or to humanity in its humanness; it is directed to humanity afflicted by sin, to humans whose lives desperately need God's elemental interruption of the continuity of worldly being. For Jüngel, God's grace shows itself as grace, in that it embraces, first and foremost, the disgraced and God-forsaken one, the crucified Jesus of Nazareth.[62]

In order to evaluate Jüngel's critical reception of both Barth and Rahner, it is important to recognize the fundamental commitment of all the three theologians to making trinitarian doctrine directly relevant to God's self-revelation in Jesus Christ. God's revelation in Jesus cannot be understood in

---

[60] "Das Verhältnis von »ökonomischer« und »immanenter« Trinität," *TE II*, 272. Cf. Reiner Dvorak, *Gott ist Liebe: Eine Studie zur Grundlegung der Trinitätslehre bei Eberhard Jüngel* (Würzburg: Echter Verlag, 1999), 315.

[61] E.g., *CD* IV/2, 31, 37.

[62] *Mystery*, 360–1; *GGW* 393–5. The irony, of course, is that "Jesus suffers the death which the law foresees for the godless, *because* he identified this godlessness as such" (*Mystery*, 367; *GGW* 503).

any other way than as the revelation of the *triune* God. On this basis, all three would agree that God must not be viewed as "the *absolutely* self-related essence [*das* schlechthin *selbstbezogene Wesen*]."[63] Now, what Jüngel's reception of Barth and Rahner evidences in this context is a desire to open up God's triune being, as it were, by providing a stronger account of God's relation to otherness. The incarnation, because it can be variously anticipated in the eternity of God's being, remains fraught with lingering overtones of God's self-contained subjectivity which merely or straightforwardly actualizes itself in time. When God's self-determination only anticipates history – even if in this anticipation it should already presuppose a relationship to an other – this self-determination remains imbued excessively with notions of lordship, self-possession, and self-control. In addition, it renders the genuinely historical dimension of the other – the other's God-forsakenness and death – of lesser importance. Hans Küng's warning is pertinent here: "Christology is not only the theology of the incarnation which would anticipate the event of redemption and make the suffering and death of Jesus a mere appendix."[64]

Bruce McCormack claims that the concept of identification, though not entirely clear in Jüngel's thought, is intended by Jüngel to do the work of the traditional language of incarnation, hypostatic union, etc.[65] In support of this claim, McCormack invokes Jüngel's discussion of the resurrection *kerygma*: in Jesus's death, says Jüngel, "God himself happened" by identifying himself with the dead man, with his God-forsakenness, *and with his life*.[66] McCormack is, of course, right that Jüngel employs the concept of identification in place of the more traditional christological notions to express God's unity with Jesus. But, I believe, more than Christ's theanthropic unity is at stake in Jüngel's preference, especially when one observes that the language of identification is more conducive to Jüngel's cross-centered interpretation of God's unity with humanity, whereas the traditional categories call for an incarnational construal of this unity. Jüngel, as we have seen, does not wish to interpret Jesus' identity through the incarnation. In this, as I have shown, lies his difference from Barth and Rahner. He follows, instead, Wolfhart Pannenberg, according to whom only in the resurrection does God confirm Jesus' pre-Easter claim to divine authority.

---

[63] *Mystery*, 369; *GGW* 506 (emphasis added).

[64] Hans Küng, *The Incarnation of God: An Introduction to Hegel's Theological Thought as Prolegomena to a Future Christology* (Edinburgh: T&T Clark, 1987), 448.

[65] McCormack, "Participation in God, Yes, Deification, No," Dalferth, et al. (eds), *Denkwürdiges Geheimnis*, 368.

[66] "... sich in diesem Tod Gott selbst ereignete" (*Mystery*, 363, translation altered; *GGW* 497).

Importantly, this event of confirmation, for Pannenberg, possesses retroactive ontic force.[67] The resurrection *establishes* Jesus' status has having been God's Son *all along*. Despite a different placement of emphasis, Jüngel's claim is essentially the same. God identifies with Jesus' death, and with his life only retroactively, insofar as He identifies with Jesus death. Jesus' life belongs to, and can only be made sense of in the context of, his death. His death, its particular manner, is not subsumed under his life as its inevitable outcome; it is rather his death, *as it has been taken up by God*, that now makes sense of his life.

Why this reluctance to construe Jesus' identity on the basis of the incarnation? I am persuaded that what ultimately is at stake here is the triune being of God. Jüngel wants there to be no doubt as to the robustly *relational and intersubjective* character of God's triune being, and he strives to give such an account of God's trinity in the belief that the incarnational model of God's triunity is ambiguous in its relationality and not as clearly intersubjective.[68] On Jüngel's cruciform model, therefore, "the incarnation

---

[67] Wolfhart Pannenberg, *Jesus – God and Man*, trans. L. L. Wilkins and D. A. Priebe (Philadelphia: Westminster, 1968), 135–6. Cf. *Mystery*, 363; *GGW* 497–8.

[68] In an early essay, "Jesu Wort und Jesus als Wort Gottes" (1966), Jüngel still employs Barth's concepts of anhypostasia and enhypostasia to define Jesus' humanity. For Barth the two terms convey that Christ's human nature is, inseparably and simultaneously, without its own personal center of subsistence and subsists in the person of the eternal Logos. Significantly, already in this early essay, Jüngel distances himself from Barth's usage and opts for a "historical [*geschichtlich*]" ordering of the two notions, with Easter marking the point of transition. He writes: "We ought not to balk at thinking about the historicity of Jesus Christ's being as a history, in which the ontologically identical relations of an- and enhypostasis become, within the horizon of time, historically separate as ontic relations, without thus falling apart ontologically" (*TE I*, 138).

However historically conscious and qualified Jüngel's adoption of Barth's categories might be, it still requires him to posit a primal relation of obedience between the eternal Logos and God the Father. This relation of obedience constitutes a prevenient turning of the Logos to Jesus and, as such, makes possible Jesus' relation to God the Father. Hence Jüngel expresses his agreement with Pannenberg only insofar as "Jesus' *relation to God the Father* constitutes his personal oneness with *God the Son*." But he "cannot . . . say with Pannenberg: Jesus 'did not live in dependence upon the Son'," even though Jüngel acknowledges that "Pannenberg denies 'this obvious understanding of the enhypostasis of Jesus' because it 'does not do justice to the historical accomplishment of his existence'" (cf. Pannenberg, *Jesus – God and Man*, 339). Jüngel explains that "that the relation to the Father, which constitutes the oneness of Jesus' person with the Son, is *already grace*. And so this relation is only possible, because the eternal Son, for his part, relates obediently to the Father and in this obedient relation to God the Father . . . preveniently turns towards the man Jesus. In doing so, he is the One who makes possible Jesus' personal oneness with himself and Jesus' human being" (*TE I*, 140–1).

In the decade following "Jesu Wort," Jüngel seems to have reconsidered whether the historicization of the anhypostasis-enhypostasis schema suffices unambiguously to do justice to Jesus' status as subject and agent. This led him to speak, with Pannenberg, not about the Logos' enabling "Jesus' personal oneness with himself and Jesus' human being," but about God's cruciform identification with the dead Jesus which retroactively makes the life of this dead man God's own. Correspondingly, Jüngel draws attention to the "*fellowship* [*Gemeinschaft*] with God which made Jesus, in an incomparable way, an individual, a special,

of God cannot be deduced from his being as triune God."[69] Only God's death can, as in the event of His triunity God resolves to identify with the crucified man taking into Himself all of the latter's God-forsakenness.[70]

A strongly intersubjective, relational character of God's subjectivity is what Jüngel's emphasis on the cross ultimately aims at. To undergird this divine relationality, Jüngel underscores, first of all, the freedom of God to engage otherness. Not inner necessity but only sheer grace motivates God to make Himself available to the other. At the same time, the cross, with all its force of historical contingency, assures the robust otherness of the other. Both of these dimensions – the gratuity of God's relationship and the radical otherness of the other – are brought out unambiguously by the inimical character of the other. Identification with the dead Jesus – though it by no means leads to a distortion of God's being – does, nevertheless, entail for God a struggle. Confrontation with nothingness forces God to stand against God in this self-identification.[71] As God stands against God's self, God stands unambiguously for the other, and, more importantly, does so *for the other's sake.*

---

unmistakable person in his individual existence and thus, in a certain way, the loneliest of men" (*Mystery*, 354; *GGW* 485). The anhypostasia/enhypostasia schema has given way to an assertion, already present in the earlier essay (*TE I*, 136), that "Jesus' life and death was an ek-sistence from the coming reign of God and an insistence on God's fatherly will" ("Das Sein Jesu Christi," *TE II*, 283). What is noteworthy is that the language of Jesus' unparalleled obedience to God's will – emphasizing his subjective act considered from the perspective of his death – comes to supersede the rather incarnationally oriented language of Jesus' anhy-postatic/enhypostatic subsistence. This not only clearly underscores Jesus' status as subject and agent in his own right, but also – and more importantly – opens up the being of God for intersubjective engagement.

[69] *Mystery*, 221; *GGW* 300.

[70] It may be worth drawing another contrast with Barth. In a recent study (*The Humanity of Christ: Christology in Karl Barth's Church Dogmatics* [London: T&T Clark, 2008]), Paul Dafydd Jones has defended quite vigorously the "ontological and agential integrity" (170) of Christ's humanity in Barth's theology, "suggest[ing even] that God organizes the temporalized eternity of God's second way of being around Christ's contingent existence" (192). Yet, despite this robust construal of Christ's humanity, Jones' model cannot avoid what from Jüngel's perspective are the weaknesses of the incarnational view: it may be relational but it is doubtful whether it allows for genuine intersubjectivity. Thus, on Jones' reading of Barth, "Christ's human essence . . . actualizes itself alongside the actualization of the divine Son, *realizing the identity assigned to it* in an act of self-constitution" (142, emphasis added); it "take[s] up and enact[s] the identity that God proposes" (143); "Christ humanly 'finalizes' the identity that God assigns him, positing himself as the human assumed by God – even as this action renders his human essence 'secondary' to that of the divine Son" (143); Christ "enacts perfectly the history that God intends" (157). For Jüngel, by contrast, God's identification with Jesus only at Jesus' crucifixion allows for a consideration not only of Jesus' *subjectivity*, unencumbered by some constitutive mission, but, consequently, also of the *intersubjectivity* of God's trinitarian self-determination through identification with the Crucified One.

[71] *Mystery*, 221, 363; *GGW* 300, 498. Jüngel makes use here of "Goethe's mysterious statement" – "*Nemo contra deum nisi deus ipse*" – which functions as the epigrammatic clasp holding together trinitarian explication and the theology of the cross. To the genealogy and the theological utility of the saying, see Jüngel's "*Nemo contra deum nisi deus ipse*: Zum Verhältnis von theologia crucis und Trinitätslehre," *TE V*, 231–52.

God is love

An uncoerced and selfless embrace of the other, for the other's sake, is what, according to Jüngel, characterizes love. The cross thus allows one to give an account of divine subjectivity not only as relational and intersubjective in a further unspecified sense but specifically as a subjectivity in which love plays a constitutive role.

Before we explore what it means for God to be a loving subject, it is important to clarify the relation between God's love and human love. "To think God as love is the task of theology," Jüngel insists, its task par excellence.[72] As we embark on this task, we will invariably work with a "preunderstanding" of love. There is nothing wrong with this: we actually must, says Jüngel, "first ask[] about the essential meaning of the *word* 'love.'" Care must be taken, however, not to deduce the being of the triune God merely "from the logic of the essence of love," apart from God's historical self-determination. To affirm that God is love can be done only on the basis of the New Testament proclamation of the cross. This procedure is observed, for example, in 1 John (4:8); we have tried to observe it here, as well. It respects God's self-determination, God's own subjective act.[73] It is then God's identification with the dead man Jesus that discloses that God's "being as subject in a trinitarian way" coincides with what humans know as the essence of love. Moreover, it gives further specificity to our essential understanding, particularly when we consider that, while humans love, God *is* love. Taking all this into account, Jüngel warns that theology, in its task of thinking God as love, must, on the one hand, make sure that the essence of love is preserved: as love is predicated of God, it "may not contradict what people experience as love." On the other hand, even in this coincidence and especially because of it, it is necessary to distinguish between the event

---

[72] *Mystery*, 315; *GGW* 430. This entire paragraph is based on *Mystery*, 315–17.

[73] Jüngel is generally rather scathingly critical of Ludwig Feuerbach, but it is criticism not without appreciative points. The fundamental lesson that, according to Jüngel, must be learned from Feuerbach, is "not to differentiate God and love ontologically in the sense that God's being is not *defined* by love" (*Mystery*, 316; *GGW* 432). But Jüngel immediately cautions, *contra* Feuerbach, that it is illegitimate to conclude, on the basis of God's being his self-determination as love, that God and love are interchangeable: while one must assert that God is love, one is not thereby authorized to declare that love is God. Love must not be transferred to the subject position and God made the predicate. God is not Feuerbach's logical subject of a logical predicate, which enables transference between the subject and the predicate. He is not, to put it differently, shorthand for human phenomena. God is a nontransferable ontological subject. Because God is more than necessary, God's inalienable subjectivity can be acknowledged only in faith. Unlike reason, with all its objectifications, faith acknowledges God's fundamental ontological subjectivity. See "Nihil divinitatis, ubi non fides," *Zeitschrift für Theologie und Kirche* 86 (1989), 219.

of God's love and human love, with a view to doing justice to God's ontological subjectivity.

In what follows, I shall, first, discuss Jüngel's articulation of the essence of love, from both a formal and a material angle. Particular attention will be paid to Jüngel's stipulation of reciprocity. I shall then focus on that which, in the event of God's love, exceeds the speculative definition supplied by Jüngel, namely, divine love's spontaneity and creativity. Here I shall emphasize the impact of divine love on the creature. This will, finally, lead me to pose the question of reciprocity again and the impact of God's relation to the creature on God Himself.

Love and death

In his discussion of love, Jüngel focuses not only on the impact of the lover's selflessness and other-regard on the *beloved*; his preoccupation is with the *subject of love*, God. Where the lover is concerned, Jüngel is careful to note, love has as its two dimensions both agape and eros – it is not wholly devoid of a relation to oneself. But it is a self-relation of a particular sort. Love involves both estrangement from, and newness to, oneself.[74] As one relates to the beloved, one surrenders oneself to the beloved, and receives one's being from the beloved – and only in this way does one relate to oneself. "I am united with myself in a new way in that . . . the beloved Thou, coming closer to me than I am able to be to myself, brings me close to myself in a new way," asserts Jüngel.[75] Significantly enough, when Jüngel speaks of the beloved coming closer to me than I am able to come to myself, this is not a mere trope. He suggests rather that love inevitably involves a self-differentiation – not only in the case of God but also humans. "Self-differentiation as the implication of identification with another is . . . the expression of the fact that that other profoundly defines my own being from outside of myself. That other one steps between me and me, so to speak."[76] Hence, love consists in allowing room for the other – for the beloved – within one's own being. I will discuss the anthropological implications of this statement in the next chapter. Here we must note that all of the above statements can be summed up in Jüngel's *structural, formal* definition of love "as a still greater selflessness in the midst of a great (and

---

[74] "Eros is to be understood as the process of attraction to another person without which a person knows that he is not complete. . . . [L]ove . . . will not exclude eros from itself. . . . [A]gape is a power which integrates eros" (*Mystery*, 337–8; *GGW* 461–4).
[75] *Mystery*, 324; *GGW* 444.
[76] *Mystery*, 363; *GGW* 498.

justifiably so) self-relatedness, and accordingly as a self-relation that, in freedom over itself, goes out of itself, shares itself and gifts itself."[77]

In *material* terms, love, declares Jüngel, is "the event of the unity of life and death for the sake of life."[78] It is important to observe what Jüngel means by death here. In anthropological terms, death has to do with the radical change that love brings with itself, a complete change of one's way of being-in-the-world. In love one relates to the beloved, in order unreservedly to give oneself, more than that, to surrender oneself to the beloved Thou. One thus dies to one's old self.[79] And one receives oneself, as we have observed, as a new, self-differentiated being. But, crucially, the dimension of death seems to linger. There is an apparent vulnerability that comes with *love as such*: "The existence from the other is an existence which is burdened with *the potential of [the lover's] own nonbeing*."[80]

The lover's vulnerability evident in these definitions is worth noting. It expresses itself in a scarcity of being, in that the lover surrenders his or her being to the beloved; and it manifests itself in a simultaneous plentitude of being which is the lover's but only as received from, and together with, the beloved. The lover thus not only has died to him- or herself, insofar as both essentially and existentially he or she is a new (kind of) being, but the lover never ceases to be in this state of death-to-self and self-reception. Only because the lover relates to the beloved does he or she also relate to him- or herself. The lover, of course, does all this gladly.

God's creative love

God's self-determination through identification with the crucified Jesus does appear to correspond to the above definitions. There is a sense in which the beloved, when embraced, impacts the being of God in God's triune self-differentiation. But there is also a curious shift, as far as I can tell completely unacknowledged by Jüngel, that is evident at two points: where Jüngel locates *death* and where he locates the *reception* of being. God's self-determination does not involve death, as it functions in the essential definition of love, that is, as a threat of nonbeing in the face of the beloved. It involves instead the very real death of the beloved, the human death of Jesus of Nazareth. This death, in addition to its actual, biological dimension, is the cursed death of one who, for his righteousness, is unjustly judged to

---

[77] "Das Verhältnis von »ökonomischer« und »immanenter« Trinität," *TE II*, 270. Cf. *Mystery*, 317; *GGW* 434.

[78] *Mystery*, 317; *GGW* 434.

[79] *Mystery*, 323; *GGW* 442.

[80] *Mystery*, 324; *GGW* 443.

be a criminal and who experiences the violent irony of this judgment as God-forsakenness. It is with this death of *another* that God identifies in His self-determination. He identifies with it to such a degree that, in the self-differentiation between the Father and Son, Jesus' death becomes God's own death, a death that God makes God's own. In consequence of this self-differentiation, God makes room for death itself in His triune being.[81] But, oddly enough, it is not God who receives His being in vulnerable openness to the other. Rather, it is the vulnerable other on whom being is bestowed. As for God, God's identification with Jesus remains an exclusive self-determination. At no point does God's existence seem like an "existence from the other . . . burdened with the potential of [God's] own nonbeing," whereby "the other profoundly defines [God's] own being from outside of [God's] self."

To appreciate why this shift happens, as Jüngel at this crucial juncture conflates the various modalities of death, and moves rather too easily from one to the other, we must keep in mind that there are two things which Jüngel wishes to do justice to: the spontaneity and the creativity that he associates with God's love. The shift is intended to demonstrate that God loves out of Himself and does so in an inherently creative manner. God does not need a lovable object to spark His love.[82] For this reason, God is able to involve Himself with the utter lovelessness of a particular man, with the very inimical force – nothingness – that has rendered this man loveless beyond all hope. And in that desperate situation, against all odds, love prevails over death and enables life to triumph.

What happens when God's love ventures into nothingness? Jüngel holds that when God prevails over nothingness – when God makes room for nothingness and its representative, death, within God's being[83] – He does not leave nothingness to itself. Rather, "he contradicts and resists the annihilating power of nothingness" and, in doing so, defines it. In itself, nothingness is unlocatable, indeterminate, and without being. Because of this, it is aggressive and expansive – "it wants everything."[84] But, as it annexes being to itself, it annihilates it: it extinguishes not only the actuality of being but also all possibility. From nothingness, nothing can be salvaged or derived. God's act of defining nothingness as integral to God's self involves both nothingness and God in what becomes a struggle between being and nonbeing. In this

---

[81] *Mystery*, 364; *GGW* 498.

[82] *Mystery*, 327; *GGW* 448. Jüngel follows here in the footsteps of Luther, who, in the final thesis of his *Heidelberg Disputation*, stated famously: 'The love of God does not find, but creates, that which is pleasing to it' (*LW* 31:57; *WA* 1:365).

[83] *Mystery*, 221; *GGW* 300.

[84] *Mystery*, 219; *GGW* 297.

struggle, nothingness is transformed, in unity with God, into perishability. And what, according to Jüngel, is distinctive about perishability is possibility: "The perishable tends, as what is perishing, back toward the possibility out of which it came."[85] God's reining in of nothingness thus gives rise to possibility. And possibility, Jüngel insists, must not be understood in Aristotelian terms as a deficiency, but as the absolutely creative power which opens up new avenues, even where nothingness seems to have carried the day and, which is equally important, even in dead-ended actuality. Possibility has to do with capacity and promise. In the cross, possibility takes the form of belief in the resurrection of Jesus from the dead.[86]

Divine self-relatedness or selflessness?

Keeping in mind this creative impact that God's love has on the beloved, let me now return to the issue of love's intersubjectivity in regard to God's own being. I have underscored Jüngel's localization of God's cruciform self-determination in temporality not only in negative terms, as a counter-(a)theistic move, but also in positive terms as an attempt to give expression to the intersubjective character of God's self-revelation. This intersubjectivity is particularly evident in the early Christian *kerygma*, and it is preserved in its later reception in the two-natures Christology. What lends further support to this construal is Jüngel's interpretation of God's revelation as love, more

---

[85] *Mystery*, 216; *GGW* 293.
[86] *Mystery*, 216–18; *GGW* 293–6. Jüngel's approach to nothingness, in contradistinction to Barth's, further highlights the cruciform, relational nature of God's subjectivity. God defines and determines, "contradicts and resists the annihilating power of nothingness" *in and for the sake of* his relationship with the crucified Jesus. God does not involve himself in nothingness, Jüngel holds, "in order to destroy nothingness but rather so that nothingness will be drawn into God's history" (*Mystery*, 219; *GGW* 297). As that which has engulfed Jesus and thus become the beloved's defining characteristic, nothingness is taken on by God and transformed into a fount of possibility. Thus, because of God's relational intervention into the struggle between being and nonbeing (specifically, into the death of Jesus by crucifixion), God is in no other way than in unity with perishability, whereas the dead Jesus is now the risen Son of God. In his struggle with nothingness, God establishes his subjectivity as unquestionably relational. By contrast, Barth views God's assault on nothingness as grounded in the incarnation. This means that God's struggle against nothingness is not constitutive of God's self-determination as such; it is rather carried out by the incarnate Word on behalf of humanity in "ratification of the faithfulness which [God] pledged to the creature when He made it." Barth writes: "when the Word of God became flesh, God took up the cause of sinful man enslaved to nothingness [*das Nichtige*] and subject to sin, putting His creative will into operation. . . Himself becoming a creature, and attacking and overcoming that which offended Him, He has dealt with it also as an offence to His creature, and completely destroyed it" (*CD* III/3, 309). Two corollaries are worth noting here. First, for Barth, the whole life of Jesus, not just the crucifixion, constitutes God's exposure to nothingness: "In the incarnation God exposed himself to nothingness even as this enemy and assailant . . . [and] the last and true form in which Jesus exposed himself to this total enemy is that of His crucifixion" (311). Yet, despite this exposure, nothingness has no impact on God. The divine subjectivity is already

than that, as love that is not fundamentally different from the human experience of love.

Love, to state the obvious, involves a lover and a beloved. This said, what strikes one in Jüngel's account of love as such is the remarkable passivity of the beloved. Admittedly, the beloved "comes closer to me" and "profoundly defines my own being." Yet what is not obvious is whether this involves any actual action on the beloved's part, or whether it is merely a self-perception in the lover's act of turning one's whole being to the beloved. True, "the I who truly loves promises itself nothing." It is also true that "Love itself promises new being."[87] But the emphasis should be on the word "promises." The threat of the lover's own nonbeing is a real threat, as Jüngel points out. But it can only be real because the beloved is a *subject*, rather than mere object, of the lover's love. What distinguishes love from both abstract eros and abstract agape is the togetherness that love gives rise to. For such togetherness to take place, however, the beloved must respond to the lover's love. The beloved must recognize him- or herself in the lover's self-determination for the beloved's sake and, in turn, affirm it for the lover's sake. The beloved's reciprocation can neither be taken for granted, nor can it be dispensed with, as some of Jüngel's statements might suggest. To be sure, love is not motivated by this response, but even unconditional love aims at this response. In short, there is no love – understood as a genuine intersubjective relation – without reciprocity.[88]

determined, and what defines it is its lordship and claim on humanity. It comes as no surprise, therefore, that Barth makes no mention of either God's unity with perishability or the transformation of nothingness into possibility – both of which, for Jüngel, are constituents of God's relational subjectivity in its temporal self-definition. Second, with there being no room or role for nothingness, however transformed, it can only be destroyed. As "that which God does not will", as the "negation of his grace," and simply put "evil" (352–3), nothingness is in Christ "consigned to the past . . . destroyed . . . routed and extirpated" (363). Barth's treatment of nothingness reinforces his incarnational view of God's subjectivity that lacks the bold intersubjective dimension of Jüngel's view.

[87] *Mystery*, 321; *GGW* 439–40.

[88] It is not only togetherness, as the goal of love, that calls for reciprocity but also Jüngel's integration of eros within agape, a move whose reciprocal potential Jüngel does not quite realize. Jüngel, as noted earlier, integrates eros within agape for the sake of the lover's transformation – a renewed self-relation on the lover's part that only follows on the heels of the lover's relation to the beloved. But this integration of eros cannot be seen as merely bringing one's self-relation within the purview of agape. It also, I wish to argue, eliminates abstract agape that simply erases the particularity of the beloved. By itself, while agape does not instrumentalize the other in the same way as eros does, it, nonetheless, remains unable to regard the other as an end. Neera K. Badhwar has shown that Andreas Nygren's influential conception of agape as unconditional love, insofar as it denies the worth or lovability of the individual, denies that the individual is loved for his or her sake ("Friends as Ends in Themselves," Alan Soble [ed.], *Eros, Agape, and Philia: Readings in the Philosophy of Love* [St. Paul, MN: Paragon House, 1989], 172–3). The integration of eros within agape thus allows not only for a radical transformation of the lover's self-relation, but, more specifically, it allows for a transformation of the lover in which, crucially, the beloved plays a reciprocal role in his or her subjective particularity.

Two objections could be raised here. First, one could point out astutely that in the event of the cross the beloved cannot reciprocate. The beloved is dead. But one could retort that Jüngel's emphasis on creativity should allow all the more for the beloved's response. Jesus is – in all his graceless God-forsakenness – graciously caught up into the livingness of God. God prevails over death. Yet, despite this victory of life and selflessness, reciprocation does not seem to be among the possibilities that arise from it. Second, one could also object that, in the death of Jesus, God actually identified with the history of Jesus, with Jesus' entire life, which he had lived by receiving himself from God.[89] Though one could indeed read this as intersubjective mutuality, on God's part it appears to come inexplicably late, when the possibility of reciprocal togetherness is extinguished and not quite revived. In response to both of these objections, it is necessary to insist that to the early Christian *kerygma* (as Jüngel knows, of course) belongs not only the cross but also the proclamation that the Crucified One had been raised from the dead by God (the Father) (1 Corinthians 15:1–8). Jüngel's account of God's being as a cruciform event of love, as we have seen, emphasizes the beloved's, rather than the lover's, death and reception of being, and does so explicitly for the sake of divine creativity. So it comes as somewhat of a surprise that this creativity is presented only in terms of nothingness becoming perishability and the rather vague assertion that "in the event of the resurrection of Jesus from the dead" God ascribed "an eternal future to this period of time [i.e., Jesus' life]."[90]

The point I am making here is that Jüngel's account of God's self-determination as an event of love does not seem to go much further than God's self-differentiation which includes the crucified man, to whom God

---

[89] *Mystery*, 301; *GGW* 411. Jesus' entire existence, as evidenced in his proclamation of God's kingdom, exhibits "the being of the Son of God . . . [who] receive[s] himself totally and completely from God the Father . . . [and] want[s] to be nothing for himself," who, in other words, understands himself as conditioned by the in-breaking of the kingdom of God ("The Dogmatic Significance of the Question of the Historical Jesus," *Essays II*, 113–14; cf. 103). The cross then represents the final recognition of Jesus' existence as God's Son and conclusive definition of this status through God's self-differentiating embrace of the dead man. It bears repeating that Jüngel understands Jesus' theanthropic personhood in this precise manner, that is, relationally. In so doing, he continues the Lutheran transformation of Chalcedon's rigid understanding of Christ's two natures. They are to be distinguished. But distinction may lead to a surprising nearness. Luther understood this nearness in terms of the *communicatio idiomatum*; Jüngel construes it as a mutually determining relation. Jesus is divine precisely in his humanity. By not usurping (false) godhood for himself, Jesus distinguishes himself from God. In this self-distinction, he remains truly human. As truly human, however, "Jesus . . . ek-sists totally and completely from the Father and therefore in-sists on God's parental will." As such, as God's Son, he is, at his crucifixion, to be identified with God Himself. *Ibid.*, 116–17.

[90] *Mystery*, 301; *GGW* 411.

relates, as one crucified, in God's definition of God's own being. The crucified Jesus, as already mentioned, moves the eternal being of God to a trinitarian self-definition. But can one speak here also of God's openness to *receive* one's being from the beloved, of a real threat by the possibility of nonbeing?

Before we answer this question, we must keep in mind the following. First of all, Jüngel characterizes the cross as divine self-limitation. In God's identification with the dead Jesus there takes place a self-limitation (*Selbstbegrenzung*) on God's part – a self-limitation that is willed by God. God's freedom, Jüngel claims, can, in fact, limit itself. What is this self-limitation? At the cross, divine power withholds itself, as it were, for the sake of God's identification and unity with the depotentiated; but, because this self-identification is a *relational* event – involving a *differentiation* between God and God – it opens up new and powerful possibilities, as God the Father, through God the Spirit, relates to him who now is the Father's Son in the Son's utterly desperate predicament. Powerlessness thus turns out to be true power – the power of God's love, the power of creative possibility.[91] The stage, it would seem, is set for the beloved's role. This point is reinforced when one considers, further, that, in so identifying with the dead Jesus, God

---

[91] John Webster claims that Jüngel "somewhat confusingly" uses the language of identity and unity alongside of that of God's identification with Jesus. Identification, unlike the former two, is an event, Webster points out. The concept, therefore, "serves additionally to highlight the freedom of God in the event of Jesus' death. God is not in any *simple* way *the same as* the crucified; his manifestation of himself does not mean complete disclosure or availability" (John Webster, "Jesus in Modernity: Reflections on Jüngel's Christology," *Word and Church: Essays in Christian Dogmatics* [Edinburgh: T&T Clark, 2001], 176; cf. Webster's *Eberhard Jüngel: An Introduction to his Theology* [Cambridge: Cambridge University Press, 1986], 145). While Webster is correct that "God is not in any *simple* way *the same as* the crucified," what he identifies as the point of contrast (identity vs. identification) misses the point Jüngel seeks to make and leads to confusion about Jüngel's language. Jüngel is actually quite precise in his employment of all these terms. Simple identity and unity of God with Jesus would mean a self-emptying on God's part. The language of *identification* and the concomitant *self-differentiation* on God's part ensures that God's *identity* and *unity* with Jesus are not at the same time a kenosis. They indicate rather that the beloved plays a constitutive role in the lover's self in such a way that the lover does not exist other than with the beloved. In trinitarian terms: as the Son, God is completely and truly one with Jesus; as the Father, God stands against God's-self-in-God's-identity-with-Jesus and yet, in the Spirit, God continues to relate to God's self as Father and Son, and so remains one God in God's intersubjectivity. "In light of God's identification with one of his creatures, even with the man Jesus, trinitarian thought, if nothing else, allows one to escape having to think of God's *relationless* identity with his creation and enables one to think God *in relation* to his creation, *in praedicamento relationis*," says Jüngel ("Gottes ursprüngliches Anfangen," *TE III*, 159). Failure to comprehend the precision with which Jüngel uses language here lies also at the bottom of Michael Murrmann-Kahl's rather unfair claim: "Jüngel's speech of 'God's identification with' remains the logic of a monadic, but not trinitarian Subject and arrests his inner movement towards identity" (*"Mysterium trinitatis?" Fallstudien zur Trinitätslehre in der evangelischen Dogmatik des 20. Jahrhunderts* [Berlin: Walter de Gruyter, 1997], 127).

does not contradict God's being. Rather, God corresponds (*entspricht*) to Himself.[92] Jüngel draws attention to God's self-correspondence so as to rule out any notion of self-abandonment (*Selbstaufgabe*) on God's part.[93] The cross is emphatically not an act of divine *kenosis*, an act in which God divests Himself of His deity. To interpret the cross this way would be to miss its point and to draw a mistaken conclusion. As an act of divine love, the cross is an act of God's self-correspondence that discloses the *uncompromisedly relational* character of God's subjectivity, so uncompromisedly relational that it reaches into, and takes into itself, lovelessness and the expansive ugliness of death.[94] By embracing it, God does not abandon His being, contradict Himself, or become something other than God. Self-limitation, Jüngel declares, belongs to the "mystery of love."[95]

---

[92] *Mystery*, 346; *GGW* 474.

[93] "Säkularisierung – Theologische Anmerkungen zum Begriff einer weltlichen Welt," *TE II*, 289; *Becoming*, 122.

[94] It is against this backdrop that we must understand Jüngel's claim that God is against God in his identification with the Crucified One. Jüngel's assertion is an indication of God's robustly interpersonal subjectivity, a subjectivity that opens itself up to another even in this other's deformity. This can be seen even more clearly once we have contrasted Jüngel's view with Barth's rejection of the possibility of God's being against God in Barth's incarnational construal of God's subjectivity (*CD* IV/1, 184–6). To be sure, the incarnate Word "enters into *our* being in contradiction . . . [and] takes upon Himself its consequences"; yet, Barth insists, "It is not for us to speak of a contradiction and rift in the being of God" (186, emphasis added). Barth emphatically rejects the view that it pleased God, in his redemptive work, "to deny the immutability of His being, His divine nature, to be in discontinuity with Himself, to be against Himself, to set Himself in self-contradiction" (184). For Barth, God acts always "within God's nature" (186). The possibility of the incarnation cannot thus lie in God's determination to be "God against God" (184). What is interesting about these statements is that they presuppose an identity – the Word, whether incarnate or to be incarnated – within God's eternal triunity. This identity is closed, as it were, in its determinacy. Consequently, what Barth focuses on is not divine *subjectivity* in its relational unfolding but a potential change of God's essence or nature, which he denies. Barth affirms a nonnegotiable self-consistency on God's part: by becoming human God does not deny his divinity. Jüngel likewise considers it essential to affirm that God's actions are never out of character: to identify with the dead Jesus is not inconsistent with God's being. But this does not mean that, in the actual commitment to the beloved, God cannot be against God. With this, Jüngel shifts his consideration of the axiom from substantive to *subjective* being. In his identification with the crucified Jesus, we indeed have to do with God's being against God, with death, in its many dimensions, impacting the being of God as subject. God is now identical with the Crucified One, but this identity is at the same time manifested as God's being the Son standing over against God's being the Father. Both subjective identities, however, are united in their mutual opposition by the Spirit, the bond of love. Even with God against God, "God does not contradict himself" – the doctrine of the Trinity gives expression to this fact (*Mystery*, 346; *GGW* 474). Thus, in God's identification with the crucified Jesus, we have to do with an event of divine love which leads to a trinitarian self-differentiation of God's being, whereby the "*maxime contraria*" (Luther's phrase, *LW* 5:219; *WA* 43:580) become accommodated by an even stronger relationality. See especially "*Nemo contra deum nisi deus ipse*," *TE V*, 251–2.

[95] "Gottes ursprüngliches Anfangen als schöpferische Selbstbegrenzung," *TE III*, 156. Jüngel formulates this view in response to the kenotic notion of God put forth by Hans Jonas in a 1984 lecture at Tübingen University (ET: "The Concept of God after Auschwitz. A Jewish

Given that God's self-limitation is also God's self-correspondence, the crux of the matter lies in *how one interprets the originary relationality* that characterizes God's being and comes to expression in the event of the cross. God identifies with the dead man and so comes to stand, as Son, against God, as Father; though this opposition between life and death within God's being is, by all appearances, insurmountable, God overcomes it for the sake of life, in that God, as Spirit, continues to relate to Himself by being the bond of love between the Father and His dead Son. What is of particular interest to us here is the sudden appearance of the Spirit. Does the Spirit's reconciling presence as the bond of love reflect a divine self-relatedness that is there *prior* to the event of the cross? It would appear so. Because God is *fundamentally relational,* God can identify God's self with the dead Jesus without self-abandonment. Further, God can identify with Jesus spontaneously, out of God's very self. God does not require a love-worthy object to take God out of God's self. Hence, there is no death-to-self that God undergoes and which is sparked by such an object. Just as one must not speak of God's renunciation of divinity, one must likewise, with reference to the material dimension of love, not speak of God as somehow redeemed from a prior absolutizing self-relation by an act of love. Finally, because God is fundamentally relational, God can love in a creative way. God can love the loveless; He can love that where the human possibility for relations has been extinguished. In sum, love has its beginning and inexhaustible source in God alone.

Yet, having said all this, we must now crucially ask: But does the Spirit also belong to God's cruciform self-determination? In other words, is the Spirit now also the Spirit of the Crucified One who must respond to the Spirit's procession from the Father through which the Father embraces the Son? Should God's relation to the beloved, *once established,* not allow for reciprocity in such a way that God also receives God's being from the other and God's "existence from the other . . . is burdened with the potential of

Voice," *The Journal of Religion* 67:1 [January 1987], 1–13). For Jonas, God, by virtue of the creative act, abdicates his omnipotence and, as a result, ends up being not only limited but also essentially altered. Jonas affirms, in this context, a self-renunciation and a becoming that God undergoes. Both of these ideas are superficially quite close to what Jüngel himself advocates in his cruciform makeover of the doctrine of God. It is, therefore, important for Jüngel to emphasize, in contradistinction to Jonas, that the self-surrender and being-in-becoming of which he speaks are a surrender and becoming which are essential to love, rather than a renunciation of divine omnipotence. As love in action, God does not renounce his identity but rather remains consistent with himself. Then, as Jüngel explains in *God as the Mystery of the World,* "God's omnipotence is understood as the power of his love. Only love is almighty" (22; *GGW* 26).

[God's] own nonbeing?" Jüngel, it seems, does wish to do justice, in addition to God's creative initiative, also to the essence of love, which, he claims, God's historical self-determination exhibits. He actually appears to speak of God's death with the full force that that notion has in the essential definition of love. He posits a self-surrender (*Selbstpreisgabe*), even a self-sacrifice (*Selbsthingabe*) on God's part.[96] God, he writes, "allowed the continuity of his own life to be interrupted through the death of Jesus Christ. For the cross of Jesus Christ is that event through which the living and eternally alive God accepted death for himself."[97] Though Jüngel is generally reluctant to use the notion of risk, especially when it is applied to God's being,[98] Jüngel does, nonetheless, affirm it. He writes: "God . . . lets himself be interrupted in an elemental way by humanity threatened by the possibility of nonbeing. . . *risks himself* for them [*sich . . . für diesen Menschen einsetzt*]."[99] Elemental interruption, as we shall also see in the following chapter, is, for all its creative possibilities "a negation that deeply endangers that which is interrupted. It exposes a being to the possibility of non-being."[100]

This latter dimension of God's love, though posited in the essential definition, remains rather undeveloped in Jüngel's doctrine of God. It becomes submerged by his preoccupation with divine love's spontaneity and creativity. Because Jüngel does not seem to notice the shift that occurs as he reads God's historical self-determination through the lens of love's essential definition, he conflates that which is unique about God's love with that which actually points to its being love in the first place – to the detriment of the latter. No attempt is made at distinguishing the two dimensions and theorizing their interrelation. This is unfortunate. In consequence, Jüngel's exposition depicts God's love as by all means relational, but it is doubtful whether this relation is one of "a still greater selflessness in the midst of a great (and justifiably so) self-relatedness," or rather of a still greater self-relatedness in the midst of a great selflessness.

---

[96] "Value-Free Truth: The Christian Experience of Truth in the Struggle against the 'Tyranny of Values'," *Essays II*, 209. In *God as the Mystery of the World*, Jüngel speaks also of God's "*Dahingabe*" (369; *GGW* 505).

[97] "The Truth of Life: Observations on Truth as the Interruption of the Continuity of Life," Richard W. A. McKinney (ed.), *Creation, Christ, and Culture: Studies in Honour of T. F. Torrance* (Edinburgh: T&T Clark, 1976), 235–6.

[98] Hans Jonas speaks of "an endangered God, a God who runs a risk" ("The Concept of God after Auschwitz," *The Journal of Religion* 67:1 [January 1987], 8). For Jüngel's trinitarian, anti-kenotic critique, see "Gottes ursprüngliches Anfangen," *TE III*, 157.

[99] "Value-Free Truth," *Essays II*, 209 (emphasis added).

[100] "Value-Free Truth," *Essays II*, 207.

Concluding remarks

As the foregoing has shown, Jüngel construes God's subjective determinateness in a robustly relational manner. He does so, first, by locating God's self-determining decision in time. This move is not intended as a stock Lutheran criticism of Barth, changing the setting of salvation drama from God's eternal being back into temporality; instead, it is meant to draw attention to the otherness of the one with whom God comes to identify God's self, to his historical particularity. This otherness is underscored further by the fact that it is with the crucified man Jesus that God identifies Himself in God's self-determination. Jüngel's preference for the cross, rather than the incarnation, as the locale of God's trinitarian self-determination precludes the otherness of the other as somehow anticipated within God's being. This is reinforced by the inimical character of the other. Hence, Jüngel's articulation of the New Testament *kerygma* of the Crucified One as the Son of God aims not only at a relational but an unambiguously intersubjective view of God's self – God's cruciform subjectivity, as I have termed it here. In absolute freedom over his being, God determines Himself to be intersubjective in his existence.

Jüngel identifies Gods intersubjective determinateness as love. But it is here that his entire effort is, rather unexpectedly, called into question. Although Jüngel does speak of God's self-surrender in God's act of trinitarian identification with the crucified Jesus, it does not seem that, in his specific determinateness, God in any meaningful sense receives his being from another. Jüngel unreflectively collapses the reciprocity of divine love into this love's unique characteristics: spontaneity and creativity. As a result, God's relation to the other borders on a modality of God's self-relation. God's intersubjective determinateness appears in the end as nothing but subjective determination, performed by a subject who makes a show of the risk he faces when, in fact, he does not seem to face any.

Having said all this, let me now return to the two moments – independence and determinateness – by which Jüngel characterizes divine freedom. Jüngel's program is rooted in a passionate defense of God's freedom. Jüngel declares, for example, "God is the unconditional subject of himself and as such is accessible only because and to the extent that he makes himself accessible."[101] But the goal of this program, in its orientation to the early Christian *kerygma*, is not to distance God from humanity but to announce that God has come to humanity closer than it is able to come to itself. *In the*

---

[101] *Mystery*, 158; *GGW* 212.

act of revealing Himself, God no longer is "the unconditional subject of himself," because He reveals Himself as one resolving not to be that kind of subject. But for all his talk about love and its reciprocal impact, Jüngel shies away from this conclusion. He shies away from it in the interest of affirming the spontaneous and creative dimension of God's love. This shows how tension-fraught his understanding of God's freedom as independence and determinateness is. It is tempting to make independence a mere logical precondition of God's determinateness, whereby God Himself surrenders Himself to his creature, comes to rely on His creature, and receives His being from the creature in all the vulnerability that such a relationship entails. But Jüngel cannot take this step because divine independence means precisely loving initiative and creative power. These are nonnegotiable as an abiding reality of the divine life. The only alternative is to articulate a relationship of determinateness and independence that transcends their abstract conceptualization as freedom's constitutive moments. This task I shall undertake in Chapter 4.

The task at hand is to examine Jüngel's construal of divine independence. It will be shown that just as independence, in the end, distorts divine determinateness, so also determinateness leads to a distortion of divine independence in Jüngel's account.

Divine Independence

Jüngel is concerned that divine independence not be reduced to a mere logical postulate, or given the status of a divine past that is overcome through God's taking upon God's self human destiny gone awry. Jüngel wants to preserve independence as an *actual* dimension of God's being. For to divinity belongs not only the self-surrender of love but also, in the midst of this self-surrender, God's unimpaired and ongoing capacity to create. Jüngel, as noted in the previous chapter, shares Kant's view that freedom denotes "the faculty of beginning a state *from itself* [*das Vermögen, einen Zustand* von selbst *anzufangen*]" and, as such, can be properly predicated of God alone.[102] It is this absolute spontaneity that Jüngel wishes to safeguard for the sake of God's creativity.

---

[102] Immanuel Kant, *Critique of Pure Reason*, 533 [B561]; cited in "Befreiende Freiheit," *Anfänger: Herkunft und Zukunft christlicher Existenz* (Stuttgart: Radius-Verlag, 2003), 17, cf. 7. See also *Mystery*, 36–7; *GGW* 45–7.

Safeguarding divine independence would not, of course, seem like such a pressing issue, were it not for Jüngel's own insistence on the intersubjective relationality of God's love. Even as one determined by a human other, determined to the point of being in God's self determined for and by the other and stamped with the other's nothingness – God must remain God. As love, God must, to be sure, be the one who embraces utter desperation and plunges into death itself; but God must also be the one who, against all odds, overcomes nothingness and brings into being new possibilities.

Jüngel, as I have noted, remains largely unaware that his account of God's love and God's intersubjective self-determination is *not* as robust as it might at first appear. This lack of awareness leads him to take God's cruciform subjectivity for granted and prevents him from articulating the precise relation between love's intersubjectivity and divine creativity. Both of these aspects then come to play a role in Jüngel's construal of divine independence. How does this happen? To begin with, because he simply takes for granted God's intersubjective determinateness, Jüngel is presented with a problem that emerges from his localization of God's trinitarian self-determination in time. The question, now posed with particular acuteness, concerns the subject of this temporal determination. Who is the God who determines God's self through trinitarian identification with the crucified Jesus of Nazareth? It is this ontological concern that becomes paramount in Jüngel's construal of God's independence. Jüngel's response to this concern is, in turn, shaped by his failure to articulate the distinction between love's intersubjectivity and God's inalienable spontaneity. In Jüngel's account of divine determinateness, we will recall, God's intersubjectivity became ultimately submerged in God's independence, that is, in the spontaneous and creative dimension of God's being. This called into question the genuineness of divine love. By contrast, in Jüngel's account of divine independence, it is the moment of independence that, as we are about to see, receives its content from God's determinateness. To be more precise, determinateness is transposed into independence. The result, oddly enough, is the same: the robustness of Jüngel's model of divine subjectivity loses plausibility.

In what follows I shall trace this in more detail. I shall look closely at Jüngel's postulates of divine self-consistency, the sufficiency of God's love, and God's trinitarian immanence. The thesis I wish to advance is, in short, that Jüngel's construal renders divine independence needlessly over-determined to the detriment of divine love.

God's temporal self-determination and its challenge to divine subjectivity

Jüngel's temporalization of God's trinitarian self-determination leads to a head-on confrontation with a problem that in Barth's doctrine of God has the status of a largely speculative exercise.[103] For Barth, it will be recalled, God's eternal self-determining decision of election takes place in eternity. God's triune being is thus none other than the unfolding of God's eternal decision. One may be led to inquire, in this context, if the Trinity logically, and perhaps even ontologically, precedes God's being his simultaneous self- and other-electing. But whether one affirms such precedence at all, and in whatever manner, changes very little about the *actuality* of God's being a God who eternally elects both the man Jesus and his own, so electing, being. For this reason, in his paraphrase of Barth's doctrine of God, Jüngel does not even take up the issue of the relation of God's triune being and God's electing decision. If a position were to be teased out of Jüngel's exposition, it would be that there is at best only a logical precedence of the Trinity over God's decision: God's being from eternity to eternity is none other than that of His electing decision. This is God's becoming: His eternal volitional self-enactment.

Instead of the question of a prior subjectivity preceding the electing actuality of God's being, Jüngel's attention in the *Paraphrase* is focused rather on the implications of the actuality of God's simultaneous self- and other-election. Jüngel is preoccupied (as McCormack correctly recognizes) with "the relation of God's being 'in and for himself' to God's being in the mode of a Subject who suffers and dies."[104] What motivates this preoccupation is Jüngel's desire to affirm God's aseity – God's independence – in face of God's revelatory commitment. But he wishes to do so without separating God's being "in and for himself" from this commitment or making this commitment irrelevant to who God is.[105] How then is God "in and for

---

[103] This is not to say that it has not been debated quite vigorously.

[104] McCormack, "God *Is* His Decision," 60.

[105] The safeguarding of God's aseity is aimed against Bultmannian existentialism, whose orientation to Christian experience one-sidedly reduces legitimate God-talk to accounts of God-for-us. By contrast, Jüngel's insistence on not separating the objective reality of God, once it has been affirmed, from the revelatory experience of God-for-us critiques most of the Western formulations of the dogmatic locus *de Deo*. What occasioned the actual writing of Jüngel's *Paraphrase* was a debate between Herbert Brown, a New Testament scholar in the tradition of Bultmann, and Helmut Gollwitzer, a Barthian systematic theologian. Jüngel feared that Gollwitzer, in his reaction to Brown, came out too strongly in favor of God's fundamental being in-and-for-himself, thus threatening to make revelation irrelevant to who God is. Jüngel's *Paraphrase* is intended to demonstrate that Barth himself offers resources with which one can establish a truly mediating position.

himself," even as He is for humanity? In answer to this question, Jüngel draws attention to Barth's distinction between God's primary and secondary objectivity. God's secondary objectivity – that is, His revelatory giving Himself to be known as the man Jesus – is rooted in God's intratrinitarian, incarnation-oriented objectivity. God's self-disclosure in history is, in other words, anticipated by the fact that the man Jesus is caught up into how God eternally wills and knows God's own self. This primary objectivity – that is, God's own self-knowledge that includes the man Jesus – assures God's independence from history and his Lordship over history. At the same time, it does not result in a metaphysical split between God as He is in God's self and the God revealed in Christ; it does not relegate revelation to the status of an ontologically irrelevant appendage where God's being, as such, is concerned. God's secondary objectivity is an *irreducible* dimension – but still only a *dimension* – of His one eternal decision.

Now, in *God as the Mystery of the World*, Jüngel temporalizes God's self-determination. He does so, as we have observed, to give a more robust account of God's intersubjectivity. This temporalization critically radicalizes the two sets of questions just mentioned that emerge out of Barth's account of God's triunity. For one thing, the implicit question of the relation of God's decision to God's triune being comes to the fore with all explicitness and urgency. It is no longer a speculative matter of gingerly peeking behind God's eternity, as it were, to find a prior – logical or ontological – subject and thereby to satisfy one's curiosity. In Jüngel's account, it becomes a question that asks about the subjectivity of the God who in time identifies God's self with the crucified man, with the result that God is now against God. Is it only this very identification that effects a triune differentiation within God's being? And if so, how can one speak of the continuity of God's being?

Second, as for the question which Jüngel judged to be *the* critical issue in Barth's doctrine of God, namely, the question of linking together God's commitment to humanity and God's being in and for himself, one now has every reason to ask whether Jüngel has all but given up on the elegant structure of his Barthian interpretation and jettisoned any notion, however qualified, of God's being *a se*. On Jüngel's account, God's temporal self-determination seems conclusively to do away with God's independence. As an event of self-disclosive commitment, an event of love, God's self-determination appears to have no primary objectivity to ground it; the very idea that it should have such a ground seems self-contradictory. After all, this is what makes it truly an event of love. It "happens," erupts in a concrete temporal situation, a situation which, moreover, is hopeless; and it involves a concrete other, the crucified man Jesus, whose specificity is further underscored by his lovelessness. God's being "in and for himself" and God's identification with Jesus of Nazareth thus appear to denote two different *phases* in the being of God, with the former dissolved in the unfolding of God's triune being as love. Jüngel does not, of course, wish to reintroduce a metaphysical split within God's being but apparently avoids such a split only thanks to the temporalization of God's self-determining decision (In time God becomes!) instead of, like Barth, seeing the temporal as inalienably rooted in and presupposed by the eternal.

This, of course, cannot be the case. God's being in-and-for-himself must remain a matter of actuality rather than mere logic or a bygone past (however such divine past might be understood). In this way, what in Jüngel's account of love was a problem of distinguishing and relating the reciprocity of love with divine love's spontaneity has now been transformed into a problem of divine subjectivity. Can one speak of God as a subject in such a way that his subjectivity constitutes the ground of his intersubjective being, and yet this intersubjective determinateness is not reduced to a mere modality of divine subjectivity but persists alongside of it, undiminished and constantly reinforced in its reception of being by God's independence? How would these two dimensions of God's subjectivity be linked and at the same time remain essentially distinct?

As I will demonstrate in Chapter 4, divine subjectivity is indeed the issue and the key to solving it. Here, however, we must evaluate Jüngel's own solution to the problem. Because Jüngel has conflated the uniqueness of God's love with its essential dimension, characteristic also of human love, he seeks to safeguard divine independence in an overdetermined manner. This progressing overdetermination begins with the question of divine self-consistency.

The self-consistency of the divine subject

It may, at first blush, seem that Jüngel is not really interested in the self-consistency of God as a subject. For example, he regards as harmful "the axiom of immutability," which in principle bars any change in God's being. Yet, in reality, he regards the axiom as harmful precisely because the axiom undermines the self-consistency of the divine subject and thus fails to do justice to the Christian doctrine of God. Specifically, it renders God's being indifferent to God's act at the cross. This drives a wedge between God's being in God's self and God's being in relation to humanity.

The axiom of divine immutability thus, at the very least, turns God, in God's very being, into a *deus absconditus, exlex* who, as Feuerbach famously put it, is "a subject who even without love is something by himself, an unloving monster."[106] When viewed through the lens of Jüngel's antimetaphysical polemic, the axiom makes God's being uncertain and, as such, constitutes a concession to atheism. It must thus be destroyed, together with other metaphysical attributes of God, through the cross of Christ because "Only the God who is identical with the Crucified One makes us certain of his love and thus of himself."[107] Jüngel thus extends the Reformation's emphasis on the certainty of God's favorable attitude to humanity, a certainty obtainable at the cross, into the very heart of the doctrine of God.[108] It is necessary, he insists, to submit "God's absoluteness and independence, his being over us as absolute causality, his infinity and his omnipotence, his immutability and his immortality . . . to *perishability* and to the negating reality of *death*."[109]

---

[106] The quote from Feuerbach, together with Jüngel's comments, can be found in "*Nemo contra deum nisi deus ipse,*" *TE V*, 251; cf. *Mystery*, 336; *GGW* 460. In its larger context, Feuerbach's criticism reads as follows: "So long as love is not exalted into a substance, into an essence, so long there lurks in the background of love a subject who even without love is something by himself, an unloving monster, a diabolical being, whose personality, separable and actually separated from love, delights in the blood of heretics and unbelievers, – the phantom of religious fanaticism" (*The Essence of Christianity*, 2nd ed., trans. Marian Evans [London: Trübner, 1881], 52–3).

[107] *Mystery*, 373; *GGW* 511.

[108] Jüngel's rejection of the immutability axiom may seem, like his entire project, to be spurred by post-Enlightenment epistemological concerns. But this is only part of the picture. At the center of Jüngel's critical engagement with the metaphysical tradition lies a *soteriologically driven* epistemological concern that has its roots in the Reformation's question of where one can find assurance that God is gracious, an assurance that liberates one from an obsession with doing and so also from a debilitating preoccupation with one's own self. Jüngel inquires about the basis of thinking and speaking God which can furnish faith's certainty that God is love, such that one is elementally interrupted in one's being. Now, metaphysically construed immutability seems to exclude any personal attributes, let alone the sort of mutuality that characterizes love. It is incompatible with love. Worse still, it actually indicates nothing specific about God's ethical character. For Jüngel, as for the Reformers, it is the cross, as opposed to intellectual speculation, that is *the* locale where God discloses himself and, moreover, where God discloses himself as "God the Justifier and Savior" ("*deus iustificans vel salvator,*" in Luther's famous words from his exposition of Psalm 51, *LW* 12:311; *WA* 40[II], 328). But if the cross is this kind of event in which God is infallibly to be found and recognized as love, then the cross must have an impact not only on the believer but also on God, who cannot remain indifferent to the cross. Jüngel's christologically-oriented doctrine of God is thus to be seen as a continuation – in formal, if not quite material, terms – of the project of aligning the doctrine of God with Luther's fundamental christological emphasis, a project never accomplished during the Reformation. This project, formulated specifically as an engagement with divine immutability, was first undertaken by Isaak Dorner in his *Divine Immutability: A Critical Reconsideration*, trans. Robert P. Williams and Claude Welch (1856–8; Philadelphia: Fortress Press, 1994); see esp. 99–100.

[109] *Mystery*, 184; *GGW* 249.

For all its pointedness, this programmatic statement does not, therefore, call for a blanket dismissal of divine immutability. The destruction of immutability through perishability does not usher an indiscriminate surrender of, or fluctuation within, God's being. Rather it assures that God Himself can be present in the event of the cross, and that God's act in this event neither changes God beyond *all* recognition nor is somehow uncharacteristic. As we said earlier, God corresponds to Himself in the event of the cross. Jüngel comments: "in the special event of God's identification with the Crucified One, God expresses himself as *the one who he has always been,* in himself"; and further on Jüngel adds: "In unity with the man Jesus, God differentiates himself from himself, *without ceasing to be the one God* in this self-differentiation."[110] In McCormack's words, "the being of God undergoes real change. To be sure, in his insistence that the origin is not left behind, Jüngel is making it clear that the being of God is the same being both before and after the death/resurrection of Jesus Christ but it is the same being *differently.*"[111] McCormack is, of course, essentially correct, just as he is right in pointing out that Jüngel's doctrine of God owes its shape not only to the direct influence of Hegel but also, in quite substantial terms, that of Luther. But McCormack falls short of explaining what sort of divine being undergoes a change in the event of the cross and yet remains the same. It is also unclear what kind of change it is: Is it a transformation? An addition? To be fair to McCormack, Jüngel does not shed enough light on this matter, either.

The change must obviously concern God's subjective being. Since Jüngel rejects the metaphysical split between God's essence and God's existence, the change cannot be a change of substance.[112] It must relate to God's being love. Even more so when one considers that it was for the sake of being certain that God *is* love that the axiom of immutability had to be destroyed in the first place.

Love

"God has shown himself to be human in the execution of his divinity," writes Jüngel.[113] This statement points to the extent of God's love,

---

[110] *Mystery,* 220, 221; *GGW* 299, 300 (emphasis added).

[111] McCormack, "Participation in God, Yes, Deification, No," Dalferth, et al. (eds), *Denkwürdiges Geheimnis,* 372.

[112] At best, such a change would have to entail a kenotic self-emptying, which Jüngel opposes, or a temporal eclipse of the prior substance, which is precisely what Jüngel wishes to avoid; at worst, positing a substantive change would mean a plunge into incoherence.

[113] *Mystery,* 288; *GGW* 393.

which will not shrink even from human death. God establishes a loving relationship where all seems to be lost, where inhumanity seems to have prevailed, where nothingness seems to have carried the day. God, moreover, exposes God's self to this relationship and, by identifying with the Crucified One, allows this relationship to reconfigure, as it were, God's self. In the event of the cross, God defines God's self as the loving relationship forged between the Father and the Son, whose mutual dissimilarity is overcome by the Spirit, binding together the Father and his human – yet because of this bond also divine – Son. Such is the extent of God's love.

But Jüngel's statement also draws attention to the fact that God's act of love – God's becoming human – is at the same time an execution of God's divinity. The *event* of love is anticipated within God's divinity, which is thus characterized, at the very least, by a predisposition for love. A predisposition and an event are not, of course, one and the same phenomenon. In the distinction between loving Father and beloved Son, considered a-historically, "God is still not *love itself,*" comments Jüngel. "The identifying statement 'God is love' can be made only on the basis of the fact that . . . the loving one separates himself from his Son . . . [and] subjects himself to lovelessness in the beloved."[114] Jüngel's assertion points to love as an abiding characteristic of divine subjectivity, without at the same time detracting from the decisive role of the cross in God's being love.

But elsewhere Jüngel's language is more radical. Responsible for this, as I have mentioned several times, is Jüngel's failure to make the necessary distinction in his exposition of God's love and of God's self-correspondence in the event of the cross. Jüngel actually goes on to assert not only a mere predisposition but also sufficiency of divine love, whose actuality now also appears to be independent of the event of the cross: "God *happens as love* in the death of Jesus but did not first *become love* there."[115] On the face of it, Jüngel's claim seems to put in question the authenticity and strength of God's commitment to the man Jesus, as well as the genuineness of the divine self's specific determination which takes place in God's identification with the dead man. Still, the ambiguity of Jüngel's language notwithstanding, it may be possible to understand his claim that God is love in and of himself without at the same time undermining the significance of the cross, or rendering the cross into a mere function of a

---

[114] *Mystery,* 327; *GGW* 448.
[115] *Mystery,* 221; *GGW* 301 (emphasis added).

prior and fixed subject.[116] If I am indeed correct in identifying the pivotal element of Jüngel's doctrine of God (namely, that at the cross God determines his subjectivity in a cruciform manner that entails mutuality), then Jüngel's affirmation of God's being love ought to be interpreted against the backdrop of the difficulties that Jüngel's view of God's self-determination raises. Among these difficulties is the question of the nature of the subject who so determines itself – a question which, as we have noted, Jüngel cannot avoid. And so, to say that God is love in and of himself is not to detract from the cruciform self-determination of God, but to draw attention to the self-consistency of God in this act. God's identification with the crucified Jesus is not out of character. Further, to affirm the self-sufficiency of divine love is not to turn the cross into a manifestation of what has been the case all along, or an instrument through which an already determined subject merely becomes visible, so to speak. The self-sufficiency of divine love underscores instead the initiatory and creative character of God's love, its self-generating and overflowing nature that exists and persists in the midst of God's self-defining commitment to another: "that God is love is the reason that anything exists at all" because "God is the one who loves out of himself, who does not have to be loved by man in order to love."[117] Because God is love "in and of himself," He can also be the event of love in which He involves Himself with "nothingness and its representative, death."[118] In short, with his claim that God is *love in a fundamental and creative manner*, Jüngel provides divine independence with specific content, yet without detracting from the radicalness of God's commitment to the Crucified One.

Thus far we have observed how God's subjectivity unfolds itself in the event of love *par excellence*, the cross. What still remains to be seen is what sort of subject God, as love, is prior to God's self-determining identification with the crucified Jesus, and in what way this subjectivity persists in, even as it becomes imprinted with and critically related to, God's commitment to the creature.

---

[116] Jüngel has been charged by some of his German interpreters with ultimately turning the cross – despite his own protestations to the contrary – into a mere epiphenomenon of a formalistically understood divine love, complete in itself prior to the event of the cross. This, Jüngel's opponents hold, in turn renders the cross into a function, rather than constitutive element, of divine subjectivity. See especially Murrmann-Kahl, *"Mysterium trinitatis?"* 108–35; Michael Korthaus, *Kreuzestheologie: Geschichte und Gehalt eines Programmbegriffs in der evangelischen Theologie* (Tübingen: Mohr Siebeck, 2007), 308–9; Matthias Haudel, *Die Selbsterschliessung des dreieinigen Gottes: Grundlage eines ökumenischen Offenbarungs-, Gottes- und Kirchenverständnisses* (Göttingen: Vandenhoeck & Ruprecht, 2006), 277.

[117] *Mystery,* 223, 327; *GGW* 303, 448.

[118] *Mystery,* 222; *GGW* 302.

Jüngel's conception of God becomes increasingly problematic, as he attempts to answer this question. He wishes to affirm – against the backdrop of God's cruciform self-determination – the self-consistency of the divine subject and, ultimately, divine independence. But he appears to do so in a way that actually threatens to undermine the robust view of God's mutuality-driven relationship to his creature. He rather indiscriminately transposes God's determinateness into divine freedom's moment of independence. This renders his account of God's being love ambiguous, though a generous reading is still possible. This ambiguity disappears in Jüngel's conceptualization of God's immanent triunity, to which such interpretive generosity can no longer be extended.

The immanent and economic trinity

Jüngel not only claims (somewhat ambiguously, as we have seen) that God is love in and of Himself, prior to and in distinction from the event of divine love that takes place at the cross. He actually goes as far as affirming God's immanent triunity, prior to and in distinction from God's trinitarian self-definition and self-determination through identification with the crucified Jesus. On the whole, such an affirmation, on Jüngel's part, is not entirely unexpected. If the *event* of love entails triunity on God's part, then the divine subject who is love in and of Himself must already also be triune. To assert this – that is, to distinguish between the economic and immanent Trinity – does indeed cut the knot of God's subjectivity: it gives concrete shape to the subject's independence. But whether independence, predicated on God's immanent triunity, can make room for the reciprocity of love and give centrality to God's cruciform self-definition as Father, Son, and Spirit is a different question. Let us examine the answer that Jüngel gives.

To begin with, it must be granted that Jüngel's postulate of God's immanent triunity has to do with divine independence *within* the actuality of revelation. This can be seen from Jüngel's explicit dismissal of two wrongheaded conceptualizations of the immanent and economic Trinity. First of all, Jüngel emphatically rejects the notion that the economic Trinity is merely synonymous with the Trinity-in-revelation, or the revealed Trinity, while immanence stands for the unrevealed. On the one hand, the Trinity in its immanence belongs as much to revelation, because it is none other than God Himself who reveals God's self in the event of Jesus' crucifixion and resurrection. On the other hand, to God's economy, to His dealings with the world belongs also God's hiddenness – understood as both the God-forsakenness of the cross, as God's death in identification with the crucified Jesus and, more generally, as "the reality of lacking knowledge of God."[119] Jüngel's goal in making these clarifications is to emphasize that God truly reveals Himself, but He reveals Himself on His own initiative and His own terms. Second, it is erroneous, as Jüngel has already argued in his *Paraphrase* of Barth, to view the immanent Trinity as referring to "God himself with no regard for his relationship to man," while the economic Trinity is said to comprehend "God's being in its relationship to man and his world."[120] God's acts with regard to humanity are not detached from God's acts with regard to God's self. In summary, God's independence is intimately related to God's revelation. It actually safeguards the actuality of revelation as *revelation*. It is, therefore, important that independence remain *in some manner* an actuality within divine revelation.

This is all well and good. However, the distinction between the immanent and economic Trinity, once introduced, raises more questions than simply

---

[119] *Mystery*, 346; *GGW* 474. Ralph Stolina notes that the distinction between 'immanent Trinity' and 'economic Trinity' makes a rather late appearance in the conceptual repertoire of theologians. It was unknown as late as the age of Protestant orthodoxy and appeared for the first time in the work of Johann August Urlsperger (1728–1806), with the actual phrases making an explicit appearance in the 1837–41 discussion between August Detlev Christian Twesten, Friedrich Lücke and Carl Immanuel Nitzsch. See Stolina's essay "»Ökonomische« und »immanente Trinität«? Zur Problematik einer trinitätstheologischen Denkfigur," *Zeitschrift für Theologie und Kirche* 105 (2008), 170–94; Wolfhart Pannenberg also credits Urlsperger with introducing the distinction: *Systematic Theology*, vol. 1, trans. Geoffrey Bromiley (Grand Rapids: Eerdmans, 1991), 291. In light of this provenance, Stolina rejects Jüngel's claim (*Mystery*, 346) that the distinction between the immanent and economic Trinity corresponds to the patristic distinction between *theologia* and *oikonomia*. The latter distinction, Stolina claims, juxtaposes God's triune being and perichoretic nature with God's concrete actions and works in creation and salvation. Those actions and works, however, do not become properties of the divine subject which are then, in a circular manner, correlated with historical-revelation (195–6). Jüngel acknowledges Stolina's point but regards it as a piece of "conceptual scholasticism" – former conceptualities must be subjected to critical reception, he insists. See Jüngel's response to Stolina: "»Was ist er inwerds?«" *Zeitschrift für Theologie und Kirche* 105 (2008), esp. 451.

[120] *Mystery*, 346; *GGW* 474–5. In light of Stolina's genealogy of the distinction between the immanent and economic Trinity, Jüngel is thus to be seen, in keeping with the goals of his project, in a line of post-Enlightenment German theologians for whom the affirmation of the immanent and economic Trinity functions as an abstract device to guarantee the reality and reliability of God's revelation, against threats such as pantheism. If anything, the distinction between, and subsequent correlation of, God's trinitarian immanence and economy makes clear God's control over his revelation. What is noteworthy is that God is now endowed primarily with the features of an absolute personality: he is an "immanent process of self-consciousness which repeats and replays itself in revelation" (Twesten; cited by Stolina, "»Ökonomische« und »immanente Trinität«? *Zeitschrift für Theologie und Kirche* 105 [2008], 183), an absolute subject engaged in self-knowledge and self-love (Nitsch; Stolina, 185), or a personal spirit whose trinitarian revelation does not, in the end, do justice to his absolute oneness (Lücke; Stolina, 189). Echoes of such an understanding of God are very strong in Jüngel, though the indebtedness, with the exception of Hegel, goes largely unacknowledged. It is not coincidental that Jüngel has also been frequently charged by his German critics with positing what ultimately ends up being a superficially trinitarian, monadic understanding of God's subjectivity.

an affirmation of divine independence. Most fundamentally: How is one to think of God's being triune and His being love in and of Himself, without at the same time undermining God's triune self-determination at the cross and the mutuality that God's identification with the crucified beloved entails? Can one conceptualize God's subjectivity in such a way that, *in* His being love and *in* His triunity, God remains both independent and self-sacrificially open to another? At bottom, what I am inquiring into is the nature of the distinction, and so also of the identity of the economic and immanent Trinity.

Jüngel holds that the distinction between the immanent and economic Trinity is merely a *distinctio rationis* whose purpose is to assure that God's revelation is a divine act through and through. This enables him to give robust expression to God's independence. Specifically, Jüngel insists that "the economic doctrine of the Trinity deals with God's history with man, and the immanent doctrine of the Trinity is *its summarizing concept.*"[121] Note that he does not mean that the immanent Trinity, as a "summarizing concept," is less important. On the contrary: while it is true that one derives one's knowledge of God in God's self (the immanent Trinity) solely from the divine economy, it is divine immanence that, in the order of being, determines the economy. Jüngel makes this point more clearly elsewhere: God's "identification with the man Jesus is . . . the *revelation* of the *eternal* being of God."[122] Hence, for Jüngel, the immanent and economic Trinity are ontologically one. The conceptual distinction between them is introduced only for the sake of making clear God's independence and thoroughgoing control over his self-disclosure.

Jüngel's comes very close to Barth's schema of God's primary and secondary objectivity, in which God's *history* with humanity is simply encapsulated in God's own *historicity.*[123] Jüngel's affirmation of the eternality of God's being – its eternal anticipatory completeness – does represent, I believe, a Barthian strand in his doctrine of God, a strand that, for all his indebtedness to it, Jüngel has wished to submit to a cross-centered critique and reconstruction. In Jüngel's account of divine love and God's triune intersubjectivity which unfolds itself in the event of the cross, Jüngel's application of the corrective is largely successful, even though not entirely so. But when he takes a step back from the radicalness of his notion of love, in order to assert divine independence, he does this in a rather Barthian

---

[121] *Mystery*, 346; *GGW* 475.
[122] *Mystery*, 221; *GGW* 299 (emphasis original).
[123] To Jüngel's use of these terms, see *Mystery*, 346–7; *GGW* 475.

fashion: by falling back on the notion of God's eternal subjectivity playing itself out in temporality. Jüngel speaks explicitly of "the repetition of eternity in time (*repetitio aeternitatis in tempore*)."[124] And in an essay contemporary with *God as the Mystery of the World,* Jüngel defines God's triunity thus: "As God the Son, God is identical with Jesus, as God the Father, God is the ground of this identification, as Holy Spirit, God is the *eternal and temporal event* of this identity."[125] Noteworthy is not only the sequence, eternal and then temporal, but also the fact that the very *event* (a term Jüngel ordinarily reserves for the temporal) of identity is described as taking place eternally.

What is one to make of all these statements? Jüngel's appeal to the immanent Trinity (which he makes for the sake of safeguarding divine independence), coupled with his subsequent declaration of a mere *distinctio rationis* between the immanent and economic Trinity, tilts Jüngel's doctrine of God disproportionately and undesirably toward God's independence. Admittedly, Jüngel does manage to resolve the knotty issue of God's subjectivity. An appeal to God's trinitarian immanence enables him to specify the nature of the subject who at the cross, consistently with himself, defines and determines himself as triune. Jüngel thus gives concrete content to God's self-consistence. But he does so at the price of undermining his own proposal for God's cruciform intersubjectivity. With eternity repeating itself in time, there appears to be little room for the reciprocity of love that God's self-defining identification with the crucified Jesus calls for. Instead, the divine subject appears to be thoroughly self-possessed and self-determining, rather than self-sacrificing and intersubjective. The notion of *time* repeating itself in eternity (*repetitio temporis in aeternitate*) does not even enter into consideration. God's self-determination at the cross is thus little short of tautological, at least as far as divine subjectivity is concerned.

Jüngel's own warning against tautology, paradoxically, only reinforces this perception. He writes:

> To assert the unity of the "immanent" and "economic" Trinity is theologically legitimate only then when this unity is not misjudged tautologically

---

[124] *Mystery,* 383; *GGW* 525. To be sure, Jüngel does assert that this is the sole basis for insight into God's eternal nature: one can speak of an eternal triune self-differentiation of God (*repetitio aeternitatis in aeternitate*) only on the basis of God's self-differentiating disclosure in history (*repetito aeternitatis in tempore*). But this precedence of history is true only of the noetic, epistemological ratio. It does not indicate the ontic ratio, the primary location of God's being. That Jüngel's statement here speaks only to the noetic order is corroborated further by Jüngel's choice of the noun *repetitio* – eternity only *repeats* itself in time. In other words, God can be *known* solely on the basis of his self-revelation. But, in the ontic order, it is eternity that has precedence. And eternity – even in, or rather because of, its identity with temporality – stands for the fixity and self-possession on the part of the divine self.

[125] "Das Sein Jesu Christi," *TE II,* 276.

in the sense that makes unthinkable the *freedom* and gratuitous *grace* of God's self-communication, as well as this self-communication's *capacity for happening*. Therefore, one should maintain theologically the *distinctio rationis* between the "economic" and "immanent" Trinity, just in order to be able to *articulate as a mystery* the *real* identity of "immanent" and "economic" Trinity.[126]

What Jüngel is saying is that God's trinitarian revelation, which is noetically primary, does not authorize one to make ontic statements to the effect that in his being God was under an inner compulsion to reveal God's self to humanity. The anti-Rahnerian thrust of this statement is probably the reason why Jüngel never pauses, in his attempt to safeguard divine independence, to consider whether tautology is perhaps not located also elsewhere and in such a manner as to call into question his own elucidation of God's being love. The caution that we might wish to express in connection with Jüngel's doctrine of God's trinitarian immanence and economy would thus run as follows: the unity of God's eternity and temporality is not to be misjudged tautologically in the sense that excludes God's reciprocal commitment to another and the impact of God's history on God's eternal being. In short, God by all means corresponds to himself, yet not in a way that leaves him prisoner to mere self-repetition.

Concluding remarks

The conclusion to be drawn from all this is *not* that Jüngel's distinction between the immanent and economic Trinity is altogether mistaken. Not necessarily. Jüngel is right in seeking to give concrete, subjective shape to divine independence. In affirming God's being love and God's triunity prior to God's self-determining identification with the crucified Jesus, Jüngel assures the relational self-consistency of the divine subject, which was raised as a question by his robust view of divine temporality. What is problematic is rather that Jüngel's specific appeal to the immanent Trinity, made in the interest of giving concrete form to the independence of the divine subject, is coupled with his insistence on the merely conceptual character of the distinction. This renders his formulation of divine independence needlessly overdetermined, as determinateness, rooted in an unreflective concept of love, is transposed into independence. The overdetermination manifests itself in Jüngel's legitimate concern about safeguarding God's creative initiative being swallowed up by what

---

[126] "Das Verhältnis von »ökonomischer« und »immanenter« Trinität," *TE II*, 275.

emerges as an absolute divine personality. This, in turn, nullifies the intersubjectivity and mutuality of divine love, which Jüngel has advocated so vigorously.

Resolving the Tension? Jüngel's Proposal

Jüngel, it seems, is not entirely unaware that his construal of divine independence stands in tension with his postulate of God's cruciform, self-surrendering determination as Father, Son, and Spirit. *God as the Mystery of the World* contains passages that, I believe, ought to be interpreted as Jüngel's own proposal to resolve this burning tension. For, in addition to, on the one hand, explicit statements of divine reciprocity and cruciform intersubjectivity and, on the other, clear affirmations of God's independence, Jüngel speaks also of the realization or consummation (*Vollziehung*) of God's being in his existence with the man Jesus. While this latter, milder language is certainly oriented to the continuity and conservation of God's being, it also, in its context, draws attention to the fact that God's being "happens" in what is for God a new situation. In what follows, I shall take a look at Jüngel's proposal. My conclusion will be that, for all its promise, it cannot undo the mutual contradictoriness of the focal points of God's freedom in Jüngel's theology.

In order not to compromise God's historical self-definition, but also not to leave God's being indefinite (*deus absconditus*), Jüngel posits a kind of protodeterminateness in God prior to the event of the cross. Being unconditioned does not mean that in his being God is arbitrary. Independence (*Unabhängigkeit*) does not mean "complete lack of motivation [*völliger Unmotiviertheit*]," such that the majesty of God is "the majesty of a[n unpredictable] tyrant."[127] In addition to "motivation," Jüngel also, rather enigmatically, calls this protodeterminateness "divine motive [*ein göttliches Motiv*]."[128] This motivation does not – Jüngel is quite adamant – have the character of inner necessity. Rather, its character, in Jüngel's own words, is that of "innermost involvement [*innerste Beteiligung*]."[129] It moves God to self-determination by identification with the Crucified One. "In this *existence* of God with the man Jesus, the divine *being* realizes itself [*vollzieht sich*]."[130]

---

[127] *Mystery*, 35–6; *GGW* 45.
[128] *Mystery*, 363; *GGW* 498.
[129] *Mystery*, 221; *GGW* 300. The provenance of the general idea can be traced back to Barth, who speaks of God's "lean[ing] towards . . . unity with our life" (*CD* II/1, 274).
[130] *Mystery*, 191 (translation altered); *GGW* 259.

What exactly Jüngel might have in mind here is not easy to ascertain. The language appears to be Hegelian save Jüngel's insistence on the absence of inner necessity. The inner motivation is, of course, established from the reality of revelation – revelation is noetically primary. But what we must inquire after is the ontic antecedence of this inner motivation to God's identification with the crucified Jesus. What does it accomplish? For one thing, it gives content (of sorts) to God's being. In doing so, it assures that, in the event of revelation, God reveals Himself on His own terms and by His own initiative. In His self-determination "God *is motivated by God*," as Jüngel puts it.[131] Further, it assures that in the event of revelation one has to do with God Himself: revelation neither compromises, nor is irrelevant to, the being of God. The postulate of an inner motivation thus enables Jüngel to shore up divine independence along the lines we have seen above. Outside of, and prior to, His intersubjective involvement in history, there is in God neither indeterminateness nor yet a necessity but an inner motivation to make room for and become involved in that which is not God. This is intended to guarantee that, in all his entanglement with history and death, God is and remains who He is: God. Nevertheless, revelation is not, at least not in any straightforward sense, a reiteration of God's "innermost involvement." It is rather an outworking and realization, overlaid with grace and freedom, of the "divine motive." Room thus appears to be made for a historical self-determination and self-definition of the divine subject, as motivation gives way to specific determinateness.[132]

If Jüngel's postulate of an inner "divine motive" is indeed to be seen as an attempt at negotiating the contradictoriness of his construal of divine intersubjectivity and divine independence, then it seems that Jüngel does manage to lessen the tension between the two foci of divine subjectivity. Inner motivation constitutes a more modest construal of divine independence than Jüngel's otherwise rather rigid understanding. Its goal, by and large, is to point to the initiative and self-involvement of God in revelation. So understood, divine independence allows for a more robust account of God's love, without the two accounts being in conflict.

But one is still led to ask whether Jüngel does not perhaps miss the mark here, and whether the tension his proposal appears to banish does not come back with a vengeance. To be sure, Jüngel's polemic succeeds in deflecting the Enlightenment pronouncement of the uncertainty and unthinkability of God's being. But does it also succeed in assuring God's

---

[131] *Mystery*, 36; *GGW* 45.
[132] *Mystery*, 36; *GGW* 45–6.

ongoing capacity to create and be the origin of ever-new possibilities? I argue it does not. First, the "divine motive" appears, in Jüngel's proposal, to be utterly dissolved in God's cruciform self-differentiation. It becomes *aufgehoben*. God's intersubjective determinateness thus puts an end to divine independence. Second, what makes this *aufhebung* inevitable is not only a sequential construal of the "divine motive" but also the fact that, as an expression of divine independence, it is simply under-determined. Construed as prerevelatory initiative and revelatory self-investment, it lacks the continuing creative dimension that Jüngel otherwise wishes to ascribe to God's subjectivity. It is too thin – incomparably thinner than an assertion of God's ability to love out of God's self and to create. There is no reason for its persistence. But it is not only God's independence, and with it the creative dimension of God's being, that suffers. So does Jüngel's construal of God's being love. The "divine motive" is posited primarily in bare terms of initiative and control over self-realization. It may be understood either as closely related to the event of love, that is, in a Hegelian manner as a tendency toward relationality through which the divine being becomes complete; or as essentially unrelated to love, such that the event of love is only a stepping stone, as it were, on the path of the subject's self-realization. In other words, love seems either necessary or practically accidental, but in either case devalued.

By postulating the "divine motive," Jüngel seeks to emphasize the grace but also the naturalness of God's identification with the crucified Jesus. But it is well-nigh impossible to tell what exactly this motivation is. The connection between the "divine motive" and God's trinitarian self-determination in time is too tenuous. How does the inner motivation relate to God's being love? How does it relate to God's being triune? What exactly is it in terms of God's very being? As can be seen, Jüngel's mediating proposal (or what I take to be one) actually reinstates the tension and ambiguity evident in his more robust elaboration of God's determinateness and independence, and reinstates it with yet further questions that remain unanswered.

Evidence from Jüngel's Interpreters

Jüngel's interpreters do not generally seem to notice that there is a *real* tension between the focal points of divine freedom – between God's intersubjective determinateness and God's independence – in Jüngel's doctrine of God. A notable exception is Nicolaus Klimek, who cursorily points out the inconsistency between the ontological self-possession and the relationality of God. Jüngel, he opines, is unable to reconcile those convincingly.[133] Other interpreters tend to view Jüngel as simply erring on either the side of one or the other, and tend to criticize Jüngel's construal of God's subjectivity for its one-sidedness, rather than, as I have done here, for its failure to give a *coherent* account of the two dimensions of divine subjectivity. It is only by surveying a number of interpretations of Jüngel's doctrine of God that one can both see the tension reemerge and appreciate the difficulty that it poses.

Some interpreters in the English-speaking world emphasize the primacy of the relational being of God in Jüngel's thought and conclude that it inevitably undermines God's aseity. To this camp belong, in very different ways, Bruce McCormack and Paul Molnar. The former, as we have seen, juxtaposes Jüngel with Barth, concluding that, for Barth, God's being – as God's eternal decision that involves history – is in becoming but does not become. Barth wishes to safeguard divine immutability. By contrast, for Jüngel, notes McCormack, God indeed becomes. McCormack seems to interpret this becoming along the lines of Jüngel's own mediating proposal: in His becoming God does not leave His origin behind yet "is the same being *differently*."[134] McCormack is largely appreciative of Jüngel. Paul Molnar is less so. He alleges that Jüngel has compromised his commitment to the freedom of revelation by introducing "a kind of mutual conditioning"[135] into God's being. For Molnar, Jüngel's doctrine of God, especially Jüngel's claim that God's love "may not contradict what people experience as love,"[136] shatters the integrity of the divine self, reducing its existence to the intersubjective dimension in the economy.[137]

---

[133] Nicolaus Klimek, *Der Gott, der Liebe ist: zur trinitarischen Auslegung des Begriffs "Liebe" bei Eberhard Jüngel* (Essen: Verlag Die Blaue Eule, 1986), 110.

[134] McCormack, "Participation in God, Yes, Deification, No," 372.

[135] Paul D. Molnar, *Divine Freedom and the Doctrine of the Immanent Trinity* (London: T&T Clark, 2002), 268, 270.

[136] *Mystery*, 315; *GGW* 430–1.

[137] I find Molnar's interpretation problematic, in that he locates the problem with Jüngel's theology in Jüngel's collapsing of the immanent Trinity into the economic Trinity. Molnar does not quite appreciate the vigorous defense of divine independence that Jüngel undertakes through his appeal to God's trinitarian immanence, and he entirely overlooks Jüngel's insistence, contra Rahner, on the gratuitous character of divine revelation, and thus Jüngel's only conditional acceptance of Rahner's axiom. Molnar's goal, it must be said, is to defend divine freedom, a project that in his opinion can succeed only by means of a robust doctrine of the immanent Trinity. This is well and good. My goal is ultimately to give a coherent account of both divine independence and the intersubjective reality of God's love. This, as I hope to have shown already, cannot be done through a simple appeal to the immanent Trinity.

An opposing view, namely, that Jüngel has compromised his commitment to the robust intersubjectivity of divine love, is put forth largely by Jüngel's German interpreters. Michael Korthaus, Michael Murrmann-Kahl, Wolfhart Pannenberg, as well as Michael Welker, all allege that Jüngel's insistence on God's aseity ultimately undermines and renders merely apparent any genuinely relational involvement on God's part. Jüngel is charged with positing God's triunity on the basis of an abstract notion of love and thus antecedently to the cross.[138] This, in turn, is said to turn God into a self-possessed and self-controlled entity[139] which is none other than an all-relations-absorbing, self-referential hypostasis of the Father.[140] These interpreters generally blame Jüngel's alleged failure truly to integrate the cross into the doctrine of God on Jüngel's inability to free his doctrine of God from what they see as Barth's eternally self-determined subject.[141]

One interpreter has even concluded that Jüngel fails both on the side of love's reciprocity and on the side of independence. According to Michael

---

[138] Rather absurd in this regard is Murrmann-Kahl's claim of having uncovered a "concealed immanent Trinity" in Jüngel's doctrine of God; see *"Mysterium trinitatis?"* 117, cf. also 118, 126, 130; and Korthaus, *Kreuzestheologie*, 314. For a view that denies this, see Dvorak, *Gott ist Liebe*, 333.

[139] Wolfhart Pannenberg concludes that Jüngel's doctrine of the Trinity entails a view of "God as a transcendent person for whom love is a quality or activity" (*Systematic Theology*, trans. Geoffrey W. Bromiley, vol. 1 [Grand Rapids: Eerdmans, 1991], 298). To this Jüngel replies that God, to be sure, is a subject (an ontological one, contra Feuerbach's claim that God's subjectivity is merely logical, denoting human love), but God's subjectivity is none other than his concrete self-determination as love ("Nihil divinitatis, ubi non fides," *Zeitschrift für Theologie und Kirche* 86 [1989], 219). God's subjectivity is located precisely in his making humanity integral to his divinity. It is not certain whether Jüngel has managed to escape Pannenberg's charge, given Jüngel's strong account of divine independence. Michael Welker (*God the Spirit*, trans. John F. Hoffmeyer [Minneapolis: Fortress, 1994], 298) applauds Jüngel's call to give up the Aristotelian idea of God as pure actuality, "as the pure activity of having always already actualized oneself." But, notes Welker, Jüngel's affirmation of the primacy of possibility over actuality still leaves unquestioned the notion of actuality itself, and so also of God's actualization. For Jüngel does not contest that actuality is appropriately defined as self-actualization, "as *intellectual self*-possession." Even with the primacy of possibility Jüngel's God thus remains, at least where divine independence is concerned, a self-contained subject.

[140] Michael Murrmann-Kahl charges: "Despite the crucifixion of the Son in the personal unity with Jesus, the hypostasis of the Father remains identical with itself, a precondition for the event of the crucifixion . . . Therefore, at the foundation of Jüngel's conception lies an understanding of God as an almighty acting and governing subject, superior to the world – a subject which continues and upholds itself regardless of self-renunciation in temporality and perishability. God's being ends up painted in the hues of almightiness and aseity of the Father's hypostasis, which is identical with God's being. The trinitarian explication of the event of the cross falls back into the area of the abstract doctrine of God and consequently belies the program of a staurocentrically-mediated doctrine of the Trinity" (*"Mysterium trinitatis?"* 124).

[141] Murrmann-Kahl, *"Mysterium Trinitatis?"* 124.

Schulz, Jüngel's construal of the identity of the immanent and economic Trinity, both essentially and structurally, remains no different from the movement of Hegel's Spirit. The immanent Trinity finds its necessary perfection in its economic unfolding. This does away not only with genuine love but also with the freedom of the divine subject who is dependent on otherness for his ultimate self-actualization.[142]

Finally, there are interpreters who brush aside the ambiguity inherent in Jüngel's doctrine of God by attributing this ambiguity to Jüngel's not always precise and careful use of certain terms. Key here are terms such as identity and identification, with identification judged to be the more correct notion.[143] These interpreters tend to read Jüngel's doctrine of God in close proximity to Barth's. They put a high premium on the conservation of God's being along the same lines as those suggested by the schema of primary and secondary objectivity.[144] History, to be sure, is incorporated in God's self-willing, but its role is carefully circumscribed by the divine will. What goes unappreciated is that what Jüngel is perhaps searching after is an understanding of God as subject, different from Barth's, that allows for both the intersubjectivity and reciprocity of love *and* continued

---

[142] Michael Schulz, *Sein und Trinität: systematische Erörterungen zur Religionsphilosophie G.W.F. Hegels im ontologiegeschichtlichen Rückblick auf J. Duns Scotus und I. Kant und die Hegel-Rezeption in der Seinsauslegung und Trinitätstheologie bei W. Pannenberg, E. Jüngel, K. Rahner und H. U. v. Balthasar* (St. Ottilien: EOS Verlag, 1997), 562–80. Schulz's criticism, while not unfounded, seems to me overstated, in that he makes no distinction between the noetic and ontic ratio. From a noetic point of view, God's being in and for himself finds its necessary perfection in the economy; God has made himself knowable. That this is the case noetically need not automatically imply that it is also the case ontically.

[143] Ivor J. Davidson ("*Curx probat omnia*: Eberhard Jüngel and the Theology of the Crucified One," *Scottish Journal of Theology* 50:2 [1997], 174–5) claims that Jüngel fails to distinguish between the two terms. As a result, God's identity with Jesus reduces Jesus' humanity to an appearance (docetism) and renders Jesus only divine (monophysitism). According to Davidson, the only way to salvage Jüngel's construal, and Jesus' humanity within it, would be to reduce identification to mere moral support. John Webster, as already noted above (fn. 91), considers Jüngel's use of the terms 'identity' and 'unity' confusing and believes 'identification' is the only proper term to use. Unlike the former two terms, 'identification' "highlight[s] the freedom of God in the event of Jesus' death," and, together with Jüngel's concept of God's coming to the world, "retains a sense of God's nonidentity with the world even in the midst of his intimacy with it in the person of Jesus" ("Jesus in Modernity," 176).

[144] John Webster writes, for example, "God retains his freedom in self-renunciation, because his submission to the cross is voluntary, the exercise of his will. In giving himself up to the cross, God actualizes, and does not deny, his freedom" (*Eberhard Jüngel: An Introduction to His Theology*, 66). What is interesting about this passage is the conceptual shift that the word 'freedom' undergoes. The second sentence is, of course, true – especially so when we take into account Jüngel's understanding of freedom as both independence and self-determination. The first sentence, however, juxtaposes self-renunciation with freedom, thus restricting the meaning of freedom to independence. It inscribes self-renunciation within self-control and suggests that self-renunciation lies exclusively within the perimeter of God's will.

independence of the subject. What goes unappreciated is that Jüngel need not be "careless" in his use of terms such as identity and identification but may be pursuing a program that has resulted in a tension, a contradiction even, that needs to be taken with all seriousness.[145]

As can be seen, Jüngel's interpreters are generally too hasty in dismissing the tension evident in his construal of God's freedom. The tendency is to declare one of freedom's dimensions predominant and collapse the other into it. Accusing Jüngel of terminological imprecision is only a variation on this theme.

Conclusion

The overarching argument of this chapter has been that Jüngel's formal articulation of God's freedom as independence and determinateness is insufficient. The intersubjectivity of divine love that emerges from Jüngel's account of God's trinitarian self-determination in the cross is made ambiguous by his one-sided elaboration of the essence of love and then appears to be unexpectedly (and rather unnecessarily) undercut through his construal of divine love's spontaneity and creativity. Without theorizing the interrelation between divine love's intersubjectivity and divine creativity, Jüngel inadvertently allows the latter to overshadow the former. Unaware of this, Jüngel actually proceeds to safeguard divine independence. Owing to the same untheorized interrelation, Jüngel's account of divine independence becomes overdetermined through an unreflective transposition of divine determinateness. Without the necessary distinction between the

---

[145] Jüngel's theology is often – in my judgment too often – presented as simply developing what is implicit in Barth (with a sprinkling of Lutheran emphases). This point has been made, for example, by John Thompson in his article "Jüngel on Barth" (in John Webster [ed.], *The Possibilities of Theology: Studies in the Theology of Eberhard Jüngel in his Sixtieth Year* [Edinburgh: T&T Clark, 1994], 143–89). In his assessment of Jüngel's christological contribution (171–3), Thompson opines that Jüngel's emphasis on God's identification with the dead Jesus "scarcely . . . lift[s] what Jüngel says about Jesus beyond a jesuology to a Christology." This leads Thompson to conclude that there "does not seem to be a better way" than Barth's own. This is problematic, for to say this is to assume that Jüngel simply shares Barth's christological concerns. Judged by those, Jüngel's project will inevitably fall short. It does not seem to occur to Thompson that Jüngel may have concerns of his own, and that the incarnational model that Barth puts forth, while more explicitly Chalcedonian, may represent the type of subjectivity that Jüngel wishes to overcome. To claim that Jüngel's construal of Jesus' place in God's self-determination amounts to a jesuology is to underestimate the vigorously relational model of divine and human subjectivity that Jüngel seeks to put forth; in this model the place of Jesus is construed differently from Barth's understanding of divine subjectivity.

essential dimension of God's love and this love's specifically divine *propria*, all that belongs to God's love is transposed into the subject's being-in-itself.

It is difficult to escape the impression that – when considered in light of the anthropological types of freedom which Jüngel rejects as actually concealing unfreedom – Jüngel's construal of divine freedom stands in rather too close proximity to those. His elaboration of divine determinateness, insofar as there seems to be no use for the beloved's reciprocation – borders on the view that freedom lies in the self-relation's control over that which comes, or is allowed, into it. By contrast, Jüngel's account of God's independence as an unfolding of divine immanence in the economy is, in its own peculiar way, reminiscent of freedom understood as detachment. In consequence, Jüngel's entire undertaking is imbued with overtones of an essentially self-related divine subject entirely in control of his temporal self-determination.

All of this yields a highly ambiguous doctrine of God, as is evidenced by the range of available interpretations. On the one hand, there is Jüngel's vigorously intersubjective conception of God's being and all his protestations; but, on the other hand, there is a drastically overburdened view of God's independence, no longer focused on the spontaneity and creativity of divine love, but threatening Jüngel's entire cruciform construal. Our task ahead will be to bring the uniqueness of divine love into view again and articulate the relation that obtains between God's spontaneity and creativity, on the one hand, and the intersubjective vulnerability of love, even divine love, on the other. This, I believe, can only be done by going beyond a mere formal conception of divine freedom and by asking – once more – about the subject who in correspondence to himself determines himself in a trinitarian fashion by identifying with a crucified man.

Chapter 3

Freedom as Interruption of the Continuity of Being

In this chapter, we return to anthropology. It will be remembered, however, that the discussion ultimately has in view the doctrine of God, which I shall take up again in the following chapter. Our present task is to examine human freedom, in particular human subjectivity, as grounded in the event of elemental interruption, which penetrates into the core of one's being. Since in freedom humans correspond to God, our findings will eventually enable us to propose a reconstruction of divine subjectivity that avoids the contradictions identified in the previous chapter.

Jüngel's articulation of what it means for humans to be free stands in explicit opposition to spurious freedom, characterized by a totalizing predominance of one's relation to self. Jüngel rejects the idea that freedom can be rooted in self-possession and self-actualization. As was argued in Chapter 1, a self-relation that seeks to absorb all other relations into itself for the sake of its own preservation leads at best to freedom *de iure* but not freedom *de facto*, thus belying the spontaneity it promises. The reason for this, as will be recalled, is that humans cannot simply retreat from the world into their inner rationality. Instead, as not only rational but also corporeal beings, they must push back against the world; they must wrest their security and their significance from the world and at the world's expense. But for all their effort, the world's impingement will not be eclipsed, thus exposing the intractable vulnerability of human being. Crucially, in one's striving to overcome one's humanness, one reduces oneself to one's self-making. One's works then begin to tyrannize one. Their actuality exerts an impact on present possibilities. There are not only failures, which must be lived down or concealed, but also successes, which obligate. At bottom, the person bent on self-possession is a person threatened by the world and tyrannized by his or her own "I," a person at odds with him or herself, relationless and shapeless, neither here nor there.

Before I turn to Jüngel's own constructive proposal for human freedom, I wish to stress again that Jüngel remains in basic agreement with the conceptions of freedom he rejects. For him, too, spontaneity is essential. But for freedom to become freedom *de facto*, he insists, the self-relation must be stopped in its sterile self-securing and undergo an elemental interruption (*elementare Unterbrechung*).

I shall begin by taking a brief look at how this interruption is anticipated in humans' ontological constitution, as well as in human proneness to interruptibility. Everything else that follows will concern the elemental interruption as a specifically Christian event of being liberated by God's word of address. This part of my investigation will focus primarily on the interrupted self: its self-perception, structure, and situatedness.

The Human Being as Fragile

Ontological interruptibility

According to Jüngel, "human beings are ontologically connected with and ontically directed toward" an "elemental interruption of the continuity of life."[1] The interruption's ontological inescapability may, at first blush, seem strange, especially when one considers that it falls to humans to assure the continuity of their own being. Some of the perplexity, I believe, stems from Jüngel's approach to interruption exclusively in terms of an event. Before we follow him in that approach, we ought, however, to attend to two more basic questions: What does it mean that human beings are "ontologically connected" to interruption? And how does this connection to interruption relate to the need for assuring the continuity of one's being?

To answer the first question, let us return to the fundamental spatio-temporal structure of human existence. In Jüngel's personal ontology, the self-relation, as a temporal phenomenon, is actually enabled and remains persistently accompanied by spatial relations to other people and objects. These relations differentiate one's present into past, present, and future, out of which the self-relation then arises as an integrative mechanism providing human existence with continuity. To put it simply, one relates to oneself because others already relate to one. Interruptedness is then what thematizes the spatiotemporal structure of existence by uncovering the plurality of relations inextricably woven into its fabric.

---

[1] "Value-Free Truth: The Christian Experience of Truth in the Struggle against the 'Tyranny of Values'," *Essays II*, 205.

This is confirmed on the ontic level by the impossibility of securing oneself in one's self-relation. From an ontic perspective, relations to others intractably impinge on one's self-relation, appearing as an ontic threat to one's being, rather than as its precondition. And yet, in face of this threat, one cannot turn the self-relation into the exclusive relation, or make relations to others into its modalities. Inevitably, one must realize that one can neither completely flee from the world nor recast the world in one's image. Precisely this failure reveals interruptedness to be an ontological characteristic of human being, manifested on the ontic level by the persistent interruptibility of one's self-relation, by what I referred to earlier as human fragility. Humans do not own themselves, but relate to themselves by relating to others and by having others relate to them. Appearances notwithstanding, the continuity of one's being is always continuity in the midst of, and thanks to, human ontological interruptedness. To seek it in solitary self-securing is not only to fail but ultimately to lose oneself.

In sum, interruptedness constitutes the logical precondition of the continuity of human being, and it is in interruption that this continuity must be sought. But will any interruption do? Clearly, a human being who has no alternative but to secure his or her self-relation, or else to allow his or her being to disintegrate has good reason to see the world's impingement as a threat.

Interruptions

The purpose of what Jüngel understands by "elemental interruption of the continuity of being" is the bursting apart of one's totalizing self-relation and of one's flight from interruptibility. The purpose of the interruption is to ask – in light of the glaring and persistent interruptibility of one's self-relation – what it is that *truly* constitutes the continuity of one's being and to align this continuity with the human being's fundamental interruptibility. In other words, the purpose of the interruption is to enable one to grasp one's existence in all of its untruth and to restore one's being to its relationality.

There are, Jüngel notes, events which come close to doing just that and so offer a glimpse of the fundamental interruptibility of human being. Among those events are experiences of ecstasy or pain, not infrequently accompanied by verbal exclamations. Those interjections function quite differently from the conceptual language of thought: "exclamation or silence is an interjection in which the I . . . breaks out of itself and thereby gives voice to the fact that something has stepped in between me and

myself."[2] The exclamation will often consist in a swearword, expressing
one's irritation with the unruly nature of one's self-relation or the world.
Whether uttered in ecstasy or in frustration, the exclamation is address-
like in character. It may even be an (unwitting) invocation of God. Having
said this, we must note that Jüngel makes a careful distinction between
broadly understood *religious* experiences and the *Christian* experience of
interruption.[3] It is not one's (mis)use of the word God, let alone a short-
lived ecstasy, that can undo the self-contradiction of human being. Even
less so can this self-contradiction be undone by pain. Although pain has
the capacity to interrupt the continuity of one's being, sometimes
permanently, it is unable to bring about wholeness in the wake of this
interruption.

Subjective experiences of interruption, including those that lead to an
accidental invocation of God, in themselves serve only as a reminder of the
interruptibility of human being. The expletives which they elicit are merely
an expression of frustration with one's humanity, which will not allow itself
to be fully secured from the world; or they are an expression of short-lived
forgetfulness on the part of the self-relation which, in a moment of rapture,
unwittingly allows somebody or something else to step into its midst and
thus to uncover its vulnerability.

These subjective experiences can become an experience of elemental
interruption if and only if, in the midst of the crisis caused by the
interruption, it is God's Word that is heard, that is, a Word by which God,
in and through Christ, addresses the human. This christological dimension
cannot be overestimated. It is perfectly possible, as touched on in the
previous chapter, to interrupt the continuity of a person's being with a
concept of "God" which has little or nothing to do with God. The monadic
and perfect god of the metaphysical tradition – whose love for humans
alternates between an appearance and possessiveness and whose omnipotence can only terrify – cannot bring about human freedom, let alone
flourishing, unless he is pushed out of the world and out of human thought.
Faced with this god, humans can only cower in their brokenness. Yet, by
securing their selves against and without god, by coming, as it were, into
their own, they repeat in their own actions and conduct toward others all
that the dethroned deity stood for. On Jüngel's account, the god of the

[2] "Value-Free Truth," *Essays II*, 205. Jüngel cautions against an indiscriminate condemnation
   of and flight from pain at all costs precisely on account of its being-interrupting capacity;
   see "Hoffen, Handeln – und Leiden. Zum christlichen Verständnis des Menschen aus
   theologischer Sicht," *BR*, 31–2.
[3] "Value-Free Truth," *Essays II*, 208.

metaphysical tradition is, after all, only a mask for human self-actualization and desire to dominate. Simply stripping off the mask does not change the one wearing it or the one who has seen through it. In sum, the god of the metaphysical tradition serves only the twin purpose of interrupting and leaving broken at the hands of someone else bent on self-securing. To experience this god is not yet to experience the elemental interruption of the continuity of being.

Be that as it may, the word "God," when subjectively invoked at a time of desperation or spoken in a moment of delight, does, according to Jüngel, effect an interruption that could be called elemental. He comments: "'God' is a word of invocation, an interjection, because it has its *Sitz im Leben* in highly existential exclamatory statements before it appears in theological declaratory statements . . . we can *elementarily interrupt* our life with this word of exclamation and salutation so that we are no longer solely and uninterruptedly by ourselves. Rather, being truly and elementarily interrupted in our egocentricity, we are, from now on, close to God." This statement, as well as the context in which it appears, is somewhat ambiguous and does not seem to denote an elemental interruption in the technical sense of the concept, namely, as a lasting and being-altering interruption of the continuity of being.[4] What Jüngel appears to have in mind, however, is that, even when the word "God" serves as an invocation in a context in which it is little understood or is misused, it does effect a closeness to God. One could interpret this as follows: It is true that no Word of God in Christ may have been heard by the person who makes the invocation. But this does not change the fact that the invocation, as such, constitutes a plea for solidarity that comes from the very depths of one's humanity and is addressed to the God who one wishes had also, in God's very self, shared in the nothingness, brokenness, and sheer unpredictability of an interrupted life. It is a cry of God-forsakenness in which there takes place a lingual closeness to God. Yet this lingual relation is, in fact, real closeness, for the address which effects it is possible only because God has, in fact, already addressed himself to the person. When the person, with his or her desperate plea for solidarity, reaches into the depths of her relationality, he or she

---

[4] Jüngel offers his remark following a lengthy quote by Martin Buber in which the latter discusses the widespread misuse of the word 'God' coupled with the fact that even its abusers at times feel compelled to address the one whom they have abused. It is not entirely clear who exactly Jüngel means by the pronoun 'we' which is the subject of his statement. "What does it mean to say, 'God is love'?" T. Hart and D. Thimell (eds), *Christ in our Place: The Humanity of God in Christ for the Reconciliation of the World. Essays Presented to Prof. James Torrance* (Exeter, UK: Paternoster, 1989), 298 (emphasis original); see also *Mystery*, 11–12; *GGW* 12–13.

comes into the sphere of God's prior address. This is not to say, however, that such an interruption revels God. God, Jüngel warns, is not a predicate of interruption.[5]

To sum up, an interruption may not yet be an *elemental* interruption strictly speaking, but, in that it breaks up one's totalizing self-relation, it brings to light, however ephemerally, one's humanity. This humanity is characterized by a simultaneous fragility and persistence, because it will not allow itself to be turned into a super humanity, and any such self-securing attempts can only lead to an exasperated expletive or an invocation of God, with which one interrupts the continuity of one's own being and tacitly affirms one's relationality. One's humanity, which thus comes into view, appears to be curiously suspended between chance and necessity: one does not possess oneself, and yet, despite the failure of one's self-securing, one exists. It is this suspension that raises the possibility of a prior address to which one's invocation of God is merely a response. An interruption, despite all the expletives it may lead one to utter, may also be a realization that one ought first to hear. By virtue of this realization, it may become an elemental interruption in the strict sense.

The Elemental Interruption

Freedom as being liberated

Jüngel holds, as we have just seen, that it is possible for one temporarily to interrupt one's life by invoking God – usually in response to a crisis or a situation where the world breaks into the self-relation and, in doing so, produces either terror or aesthetic gratification. Through such invocation one often catches a glimpse of one's humanity as radically different, richer, and more mysterious than that which emerges from obsessive self-securing and colonizing self-actualization. What requires some clarification is that it is only derivatively that one interrupts the continuity of one's being: human interruptions presuppose interruptedness and anticipate the elemental interruption.

Even though the invocation proceeds from one, ontologically the whole experience presupposes a prior relation; it presupposes the fact that, at a level *inaccessible* to the agent bent on self-possession, the human being already exists as primordially recognized, as a partaker of divine-human

---

[5] This is contra Lévinas. "The Dogmatic Significance of the Question of the Historical Jesus," *Essays II*, 91–3.

togetherness. The invocation of God, uttered in a moment of exasperation, gives expression to this in the form of an ontic longing for such divine-human solidarity; it is a longing for a God in whose nature it is to come into human brokenness and who, therefore, would already have done so. It is important to note this aspect in order to draw attention to what our discussion has frequently signaled only obliquely, namely, that humans cannot free themselves: they cannot free themselves *through* self-possession, and, what is particularly important in the present context, they cannot free themselves *from* their compulsion toward self-possession. When *they* interrupt their lives with an invocation of God, the invocation presupposes that it is God's nature to be liberator *par excellence*. But on the ontic level, such an interruption is only an expression of forlorn hope made amidst depictions of God that belie it. On the level accessible to the person, every such interruption is thus only a longing for liberation. In brief, freedom for human beings means being liberated: letting go of one's freedom, or whatever one imagines it to be, and accepting it from another, with all the risk it entails. But for this freedom to be more than a matter of longing, the liberator must first reveal himself.

This inevitably raises the question of how freedom on someone else's terms can be true freedom. Jüngel does not need to look for an experience of liberation turning out to be the worst kind of bondage any further than the experience of his own nation in the wake of its "liberation" from Nazi dictatorship by the Soviet Red Army in 1945.[6] We must attend to this concern before we may continue our exploration of human freedom as divine liberation. Of crucial significance here is the distinction, already adumbrated, between God and the world in relation to human subjectivity. Because of the triune God's more than necessary character at the ontic level, that is, in relation to worldly contingencies, God does not impinge on human subjectivity in the same way the world does as both this subjectivity's precondition and a seemingly deadly threat to it. Thus, in the power of his self-disclosure, God has the freedom to address humanity in its tug-of-war with the world, to put an end to the reciprocal violence, and to establish mutuality between one's self- and other-relations. This ontic togetherness, maintained through the divine-human relationship, is, as we shall see, structurally constitutive of freedom. It makes one true to one's ontological

---

[6] "Befreiende Freiheit – als Merkmal christlicher Existenz," Anfänger: *Herkunft und Zukunft christlicher Existenz* (Stuttgart: Radius-Verlag, 2003), 11; see also *Die Leidenschaft Gott zu denken: Ein Gespräch über Denk- und Lebenserfahrungen* (Zürich: Theologischer Verlag, 2009), 14.

being, which the event of divine revelation discloses both in its newness, that is, in the ontic *reality* of freedom, and in its always having been the case, in that, "also as a sinner" one has always been ontologically "determined for freedom to begin something with oneself and one's world."[7] In brief, freedom, when it is rooted in the triune God's revelation, is not an imposition of that which is alien but a disclosure of that which is intimately one's own. It shows that the self-contradiction in which one lives is not an affliction to which one is intrinsically doomed.

As we move on to investigate in more detail the disclosive character of the event and experience of elemental interruption, it is important to keep in mind the distinction between the *ontic*, which is interrupted, and the *ontological*. At its disclosure, as we shall see, the ontological is not merely elevated to the ontic surface, but it, too, undergoes a transformation, in that it receives specificity and becomes anchored in the *event* of God's elemental interruption. As a result, the distinction between the ontological and the ontic is reconfigured into two distinct acts of being.

The elemental interruption as self-disclosure of God and disclosure of humanity

An interruption that leads to wholeness and flourishing, Jüngel insists, takes place when, in an act of faith, one acknowledges the triune God's relationship to one. What is this relationship? It corresponds to the longing implicit in human self-interruptions, but it corresponds to it with the force, precision, and excess of a historical occurrence.

The elemental interruption finds its *raison d'être* in the events of Good Friday and Easter morning. Those events, recognized as God's self-disclosure, constitute the basis of the elemental interruption as a subjectively disclosive experience. The interruption is an experience in which those events present themselves as being of immeasurable significance to the one who undergoes the experience. What specifically is disclosed? In the first place, that God has, in fact, in God's very self experienced the nothingness and brokenness of an interrupted human life, that in His very self God does not exist apart from this once-broken life, and that through this life, lovingly taken up into God's self, He acknowledges all of humanity. Hence, the interruption reveals the freedom of God to embrace the nothingness of human death within God's self.

---

[7] "Hoffen, Handeln – und Leiden," *BR*, 24.

In addition, what is disclosed is also the being of humanity. God's act of self-identification with the suffering of Christ constitutes an affirmation of the moribund human. It shows that a human being need not be doomed to futile self-securing but rather "lives from God's recognition."[8] It shows, further, that Christ's humanity, affirmed by being taken up into God's very life, is humanity which precisely *as humanity* is made in God's image. The human being is shown to exist in a fundamental relation to God, thanks to which it can rest in its humanity, which, in turn, is shown to be infinitely more than what any self-transcendence can promise.

Both living from God's recognition and thus being renewed in God's image result in human freedom, or rather the sharing, on humanity's part, in the freedom of God. God's freedom – as freedom that realizes itself in bestowal – liberates humanity from the compulsion toward self-affirmation. "Easter," Jüngel asserts, "makes it certain that God himself not only is the embodiment of all freedom but also uses his infinite freedom in order to free us humans from our self-inflicted unfreedom. In the person of Jesus Christ – that is where freedom is. Christ, risen from the dead – he is free and he makes free; he is the freeing freedom in person."[9] Christ is the person in whom and as whom God discloses Himself and, in doing so, discloses humanity to itself as beings that can be renewed in God's image.

In subjective terms, one experiences this disclosure as God's justifying Word which He – *in* Christ's death and resurrection, and as the Word *about* Christ's death and resurrection – addresses to the sinner.[10] In the Lutheran tradition, this particular Word is known as the gospel. It proclaims to the sinner, in the midst of his or her compulsive self-securing, that not merely Christ, as if his humanity were something different and remote from one's

---

[8] "On Becoming Truly Human. The Significance of the Reformation Distinction between Person and Works for the Self-Understanding of Modern Humanity," *Essays II*, 237. Commenting on Barth's anthropology, Jüngel writes: "The apparent deficiency in Jesus' humanity [that is, its living from God] turns out to be the achievement of a true humanity in the coexistence of the God-man" (*Karl Barth: A Theological Legacy*, trans. Garrett E. Paul [Philadelphia: Westminster, 1986], 134; cf. *Mystery*, 358; *GGW* 491). As noted earlier, what distinguishes Jüngel from Barth, and what makes Jesus unique in Jüngel's own theology, is the fact that, as he lives from God, Jesus does not realize a prior identity assigned to him (see Chapter 2, fn. 70); his life is rather retroactively claimed by God and made God's own at Jesus' death. God's identification with Jesus renders God's self-determination intersubjective.

[9] "Befreiende Freiheit," *Anfänger*, 13–14.

[10] Jüngel emphasizes the significance of the narrative character of the Word: "[historical] narrative [*Erzählen*] is a powerful kind of talk which should result in past history liberating its most authentic possibilities anew" (*Mystery*, 305f; *GGW* 417f). More specifically, the Jesus story has, for Jüngel, a "sacramental function" through which the hearer wins freedom (*Mystery*, 309; *GGW* 422).

own, but the sinner, too, already is "an irrevocably affirmed and recognized person."[11] One experiences Christ's humanity as one's own humanity: his God-forsakenness as one's own God-forsakenness, his affirmation by the Father in the Spirit as one's own affirmation by God. And one experiences the fragility of one's human being as so transcended through God's act of recognition that one can now allow oneself simply to be human in all the relational fragility that being human entails. It is this experience that interrupts, according to Jüngel, the continuity of one's being, renews one in God's image and makes one free, and, finally, calls one to a life of freedom after God's image.

Let us now turn to the human being who has, in his or her very being, experienced the elemental interruption. My discussion, as indicated earlier, will elaborate on the self-experience, structure, and situatedness of the interrupted self.

The Free Person

What does it mean for a person to be free? This question can be answered in a threefold manner. Seen from one perspective, the question directs us to the *experience* and *self-perception* of the free person, whose ontic existence has been aligned with humanity's fundamental relationality. It asks about the person's identity. And it asks this while explicitly guarding against the danger of human self-contradiction and the spurious freedoms that issue from it. From another perspective, the question asks about the ontology of human freedom as established by the relationship between the triune God, who is more than necessary vis-à-vis worldly contingences, and the human being who is relationally constituted through participation in God's freedom. Put forth this way, the question calls for an analysis of the divine-human relationship as constitutive of the structural framework and underpinnings of freedom. Finally, the question may also concern the ontic self-expression of the free person as an agent. It can be phrased as follows: What is the *ontic* reality of freedom for which one has been determined all along and which is more than a wild goose chase? I shall analyze these three dimensions in turn.

---

[11] "Hoffen, Handeln – und Leiden," *BR*, 24. Cf. "Wertlose Würde – Gewissenhafter Gewissenlosigkeit," *EmE*, 98; and "Living out of Righteousness: God's Action – Human Agency," *Essays II*, 256.

The experience of interruption

Crisis

Jüngel is quite emphatic that the impact of the elemental interruption extends beyond the realm of action and conduct and concerns its very ground. God's unconditional recognition of humanity does not respond to humanity's loss of self- and world-meaning by aiding the human project of meaning-imposition. Instead, the entire project – what Jüngel refers to as the "the meaning of meaning" – is called into question by God's justifying act. "Justification is something other than satisfaction of needs. It is something more like transforming needs," Jüngel writes.[12] With this, he wants to affirm that the elemental interruption concerns life at its very core.[13] It spurs not moral betterment, such that the goal of self-securing comes more within human reach; rather, it is a radical ontological negation of the being that humans bent on self-possession strive to actualize. It is a repudiation of the very idea of self-actualization. Only in this way can agency itself, in all its self-seeking and attempted self-actualizing, be restructured and liberated. In brief, the elemental interruption involves a radical contradiction of what human beings perceive as their own freedom and wholeness.

This is not to say that what the sinner desires is entirely misdirected. Hence, I believe, Jüngel's emphasis on the seemingly weaker *transformation* of needs, as opposed to eradication or replacement. Humans involved in an ontological self-contradiction by all accounts do desire wholeness and freedom. But the point is that wholeness is not to be found in superhumanity, that is, through overcoming one's own human fragility, while freedom is not to be found in self-security, that is, through simultaneously doing violence to the world and securing oneself against it. What the elemental interruption accomplishes is human wholeness and freedom – but it neither makes one superhuman nor enables the self to turn into a solitary fortress. Wholeness and freedom, as they issue forth from the elemental interruption, contradict human notions of wholeness and freedom. They are, on the one hand, wholeness and freedom on God's terms. On the other hand, by resolving humans' ontological self-contradiction, they are wholeness and freedom that intimately, and now also really, belong to humanity.

The revelation of this intimate belonging comes only later, however. As a transformation that entails negation of being, the elemental interruption

---

[12] *Justification*, 263.
[13] "Living out of Righteousness," *Essays II*, 243.

ushers itself in, first of all, as an experience of an all-enveloping crisis. It is
an event which calls into question one's entire life.[14] One may ask why this
is the case, since the news, after all, is good news. This is true. The gospel
message of God's self-identification with nothingness for humanity's sake is
ultimately a comforting one. But before it brings comfort, it first discloses,
with no room for doubt or self-deception, that the *nothingness* which God
takes up into God's being is none other than one's life's quest for self-
security.[15] God's self-identification with "the scandalously murdered man
Jesus,"[16] who as righteous dies accused of unrighteousness, puts into sharp
relief the project of human self-securing and reveals its destructiveness. The
project is shown to be neither a partial success that can still, with some aid,
be brought to completion nor a temporary failure that one can eventually
overcome. In the cross, this project is disclosed as a contradictory and
destructive abandonment of one's human being, in all its relational richness,
for a pernicious pipe dream. It is disclosed as nothingness that is expansive,
self-indulgent, and incapable of relationships, a nothingness that not only
has taken over one's entire life but also has no regard for the life and
humanity of another.

Thus, the elemental interruption shows sin to be far more egregious than
mere misconduct, which, when brought to one's attention, one can strive to
correct. Recognition of the gravity of sin, of one's own deformity, must
bring with itself vulnerability. It throws the would-be superhuman back onto
his or her own mere humanity and, in doing so, exposes one to injury or
misuse. It entails a loss of control.[17] "Elemental interruption is a negation
that deeply endangers that which is interrupted. It exposes a being to the
possibility of nonbeing." It discloses more than the futility of one's self-
securing; it shows its deadly nature. In consequence, the interruption
appears to leave one suspended between the seemingly impossible life of
human vulnerability and the even more damaging pursuit of super-
humanity. "But just this possibility of nonbeing," says Jüngel, "is creative in
the most powerful way."[18] The elemental interruption would be an entirely
negative experience, a life-shattering event "only if the continuity of life
remained permanently interrupted," if the sinner were left with nothing
but his or her own vulnerability. But, as Jüngel underscores, it is an

---

[14] "Value-Free Truth," *Essays II*, 204.
[15] Jüngel's christologically-oriented doctrine of sin follows in the footsteps of Barth; see *Karl
Barth*, 116.
[16] *Mystery*, 329; *GGW* 451.
[17] "What does it mean to say, 'God is love'?" 300.
[18] "Value-Free Truth," *Essays II*, 207.

interruption not for the sake of a crisis but for the sake of a qualitative "*enhancement* of the continuity of life." It makes life newer and richer.[19]

Faith

How specifically is life's continuity enhanced? The short answer is: on account of faith. The proclamation of the Christ narrative not only reveals the nothingness of the sinner's solitude and vulnerability but, above all, it proleptically discloses the sinner's identity as one affirmed and unconditionally recognized. One embraces God's act, as well as human identity which it discloses, in an act of faith. In faith one lets go of one's futile self-securing; yet, by doing so, one does not become insecure. To understand why faith does not lead to insecurity, we must, first, return to Jüngel's engagement with Kant, discussed in Chapter 1.

Kant's insight that Jüngel highlights is that faith is an inevitable, albeit unwelcome, product of a rationality that aims at self-possession. A consistent pursuit of rational self-securing will eventually subvert itself by positing a dimension of faith over which reason has no control. This leads Kant to conclude that faith constitutes an essential part of human identity – an inescapable corollary of reason's theoretical separation from sense experience and practical withdrawal from empirical conditioning. Be that as it may, the Kantian faith rests in divine hiddenness, which Kant, with thankfulness, regards as mercy. This hiddenness guarantees that the moral law is obeyed for its own sake, rather than because of an expected reward or out of fear of punishment. As far as Jüngel is concerned, humans are thus thrown back on their own self-securing, which, however impossible, is reinforced as an inevitable pursuit.[20] In other words, while Kant's faith points to the impossibility of rational self-securing, it cannot put an end to the all-embracing pursuit of such self-security. It only makes the compulsion toward self-possession more reckless and more desperate. Kant's celebrated categorical imperative is nothing but making a virtue out of necessity.

Jüngel concurs that faith is a dimension that ineluctably opens up in the midst of a totalizing self-relation and destabilizes it. But for faith to become not just a vague intimation of a problem but the solution to the self-contradiction of a self-securing existence, faith must be more than Kant's moral belief. It must be grounded in God's revelation. It must thus be understood as Luther understood it, in terms of a divine-human relation,

---

[19] "Value-Free Truth," *Essays II*, 205, 207.

[20] Jüngel asks: "Is not ultimately the categorical imperative the grand attempt to establish the morally understood security of the human race as its highest good?" (*Mystery*, 196; *GGW* 265).

foundational for one's entire being.[21] So understood, faith is a fissure
through which humanity's ontological relationality breaks forth and gains
specificity. The faith that attends the elemental interruption, Jüngel holds,
is an acknowledgment of, and response to, recognition by God. It is a letting
go of oneself and a reception of oneself from God. It is trust. Trust, notes
Jüngel, is the opposite of control.[22] Yet, what is significant, though trust
removes security for the sake of a relationship, it does not make one
insecure. Trust in God entails certainty and, as such, is "the basic process
between man and God." It, so to speak, unturns the ego from its compulsion
toward itself. Trust does not make one insecure but free.[23] "Put
anthropologically, faith is the emergence of freedom."[24]

One's faith relation to God brings with itself a new perspective on oneself.
The sterility of one's self-relation comes into view but does so as transcended.
One sees oneself as unconditionally recognized, recognized precisely in
one's nothingness. One looks at oneself from a distance, through the eyes
of the one whose judgment is unconditional recognition. The disruptions
and discontinuities of one's relation to the world are comprehended in a
continuity that remains unaffected by them.

Experience with experience

As one looks at oneself through the eyes of faith, there takes place "an
experience with experience." Jüngel explains: "faith distinguishes itself
from an array of worldly experiences not (in a negative sense) because it is
beyond experience, but it distinguishes itself from an array of worldly
experiences (in a positive sense) because it is *an experience with experience*
[*Erfahrung mit der Erfahrung*], a peculiar experience with the very act of
experiencing." More than that, "faith makes ever anew an experience with
experience so that the plural, experiences with experience, is by implication
plausible."[25] Elsewhere Jüngel states this more briefly: "I experience again all
that is and all previous experiences of self and world."[26]

---

[21] "true faith is not . . . an absolute . . . quality in the soul, but it is something which does not
allow itself to be torn away from Christ" (*Against Latomus* [1521], *LW* 32:239; *WA* 8:114).

[22] "every interpersonal relationship, every contact from person to person, would be destroyed
by the performance of that securing process which provides for control" (*Mystery*, 196; *GGW*
266).

[23] *Mystery*, 197; *GGW* 267. These ideas are an echo of Luther, e.g., "Experience also teaches
that even though a man may work himself to death, his heart has no peace until he begins
to yield himself to God's grace, and takes the risk of trust in it" (*Defense and Explanation of All
the Articles* [1521], *LW* 32:54; *WA* 7:386).

[24] *Mystery*, 164; *GGW* 220.

[25] *EmE*, 9–10; cf. *Mystery*, 168; *GGW* 225.

[26] "Value-Free Truth," *Essays II*, 208.

This new perception that springs into being at the event of elemental interruption makes "new things . . . self-evident."[27] It manifests itself as awareness of one's nonbeing and the possibility of nonbeing in general – this is the dimension of crisis. But this gives way to an awareness of the fullness of being that exceeds anything that self-possession can aim at. One realizes that one's true being is not that which is now perceived in its untruth but rather that from whose perspective one now perceives, that is, humanity unconditionally affirmed by God. "Faith," comments Jüngel, "is a self-discovery that begins at the same time as we discover God. It is the discovery of a self-renewal that affects the whole person" who now "experiences God as the inexhaustible mystery of [the self] and of all things."[28] As someone who has experienced anew all of his experiences, the person can now distinguish between being and nonbeing, a distinction that begins with the person him- or herself.

The person as separate from works

What is experienced as nonbeing are one's efforts aimed at self-securing and, more generally, the capacity of human actions to effect such self-securing. What is experienced as being is the unconditional affirmation by God – affirmation in the midst and in spite of the restless and expansive nothingness which one's totalizing self-relation engenders. This experience of distance to self, such that the perceiving self and the self which is perceived are not mere mirror images, effects a separation between person and works, or, to be more precise, the ontic emergence of the person vis-à-vis the person's works. One experiences oneself as infinitely more than the sum total of one's actions. In the words of Luther, which Jüngel quotes, "*Fides facit personam . . . opus non facit personam, sed persona facit opus.*"[29] The person is now seen as having priority over any work of his or hers, purely by virtue of faith in God's justifying work and word. In this sense, "*faith is irreplaceable.*"[30] As in Kant's case, faith preserves human identity; more than that, it establishes it. But it does so not by directing humans back to their own doing, but by freeing them from the compulsion toward it.

The immediate consequence of this is liberation from the tyranny of works (and its modalities in the form of the tyrannies of the past, future,

---

[27] "Value-Free Truth," *Essays II*, 214.

[28] *Justification*, 241; "My Theology," *Essays II*, 7.

[29] *Zirkulardisputation de veste nuptiali* (1537); WA 39^I:283; cited partially in "On Becoming Truly Human," *Essays II*, 231; and "Hoffen, Handeln – und Leiden," *BR*, 24. Cf. also Luther's *Lectures on Galatians* (1535), *LW* 26:256; WA 40^I:402.

[30] *FoC*, 30 (emphasis original).

and values). Self-securing, together with the underlying relationlessness, is forgiven, and conclusively relegated to the past. This does not mean, however, that one's past is erased. Rather, the fact that one has a past, which one must relate to and appropriate, ceases to be a source of oppression and personhood-destroying struggle. One can now deal with the past out of one's God's given identity, instead of having the past inexorably impinge on one's identity-in-the-making.[31] Jüngel expresses this idea by means of mystical concepts, as those were appropriated and substantially reworked by Luther: there has now emerged a genuine distinction between the inner and the outer in a person. The inner and the outer are no longer mirror images of each other, replicating each other in an endless reverberation, with actuality necessarily producing only more of itself. Faith has brought a surplus into the self-relation. One consequence of this is that the outer man – understood as a *totus homo* and not just the sensible dimension of human existence – is always in the process of becoming old. As the inner person, who is infinitely more than the sum of works, never ceases to be renewed in faith, the outer man is no longer able perilously to linger in the present. The outer man, together with all his works, can safely become old.

In terms of self-experience, all this means that one is freed from guilt. With this assertion, Jüngel consciously opposes both Heidegger and Hartmann. He disagrees with Heidegger that guilt belongs to the primordial structure of human being.[32] For Heidegger, wanting to have a conscience is part of authentic existence. Conscience continually calls one face to face with oneself and, in doing so, attests to one's very own potential for true being.[33] It seems the motivation behind Jüngel's rejection is not dissimilar from his dismissal of Kantian freedom: a conscience that conjures up a fullness of being as something one must never stop pressing toward, makes freedom incomprehensible at best and incoherent at worst. Freedom, for Jüngel, is no longer an oppressive and being-destroying imperative, a command to possess oneself. Instead the cross proclaims the "sovereign indicative of freedom."[34] Freedom brings with itself a dimension of rest, in

---

[31] Hence Jüngel's rejection, as deficient, of John Locke's understanding of the person as "a thinking intelligent Being, that has reason and reflection, and can consider itself as itself, the same thinking thing, in different times and places." *Essay Concerning Human Understanding* (1689), Bk. II, Ch. XXVII, §9. For Jüngel, a self-relation rooted in memory is by itself insufficient to decide the question of one's status as person or one's personal dignity. Cf. "Hoffen, Handeln – und Leiden," *BR*, 23, 39.

[32] This disagreement is registered very briefly in "Wertlose Würde," *EmE*, 101.

[33] *B&T*, 285–9.

[34] "Befreiende Freiheit," *Anfänger*, 13.

which the person comes into view, whereas the person's works recede into the background.

Jüngel's dismissal of Hartmann has to do not so much with guilt as a structural characteristic of human being as with an actual feeling of guilt which persists as long as values do. According to Hartmann, guilt assures that one remains a moral being, and, therefore, its removal would be an evil greater than its fostering for the sake of continued actualization of values.[35] Jüngel responds by affirming categorically that "The gospel so touches the conscience that it is not tranquillized, but rather cancelled and relieved of its post."[36]

Jüngel's juxtaposition between the tranquilization and the cancellation of conscience requires further explanation. Here Jüngel agrees with Kant that the conscience is a faculty of judgment, which adjudicates on the basis of what is given to it by another authority. But he questions whether this authority should be reason judging itself. The task, he maintains, should rather be accorded to God's Word of the gospel.[37] To understand what motivates Jüngel, one must consider the authority of the law and how its seeming irrevocability translates into the law's capacity for anesthetizing the conscience. Legal penalties, to be sure, inhibit transgression. If one obeys the law, one's conscience is tranquilized. A human being who considers him- or herself to be law-abiding is obviously a self-satisfied person. Yet even in the case of such a person the demand of the law inescapably towers over the conscience and splits the person. It does not, in the end, matter whether the law is understood as an extraneous, civil code or as an immanent human characteristic (purely formal, as in Kant, or bearing a particular content). For even an individual who "appeals to his or her conscience in order to gain freedom from the law's universal reach follows another law, namely, the law of his or her conscience."[38] A person, however law-abiding, who lives under the ever-impending judgment of the law – even if this law is only a law of one's conscience and its sole demand is to make oneself free – is a person at odds with him- or herself, a person who

---

[35] "Value-Free Truth," *Essays II*, 2010–11. Hartmann writes: "The state of being guilty on account of a bad deed cannot be taken away from anyone, since it is inseparable from the guilty man – one would need to deny his guiltiness and impugn his accountability" (*Ethics*, trans. S. Coit, vol. 3: *Moral Freedom* [New Brunswick: Transaction, 2002], 271).

[36] *Justification*, 230.

[37] "Der Mensch – im Schnittpunkt von Wissen, Glauben, Tun und Hoffen," *Zeitschrift für Theologie und Kirche* (2004), 343. Cf. Kant, *Religion within the bounds of mere reason* (1793). In *Religion and Rational Theology*, trans. and ed. Allen W. Wood and George di Giovanni (Cambridge: University Press: 1996), 203 [6:186].

[38] "Ordnung gibt der Freiheit einen Raum," *Evangelische Freiheit – kirchliche Ordnung: Beiträge zum Selbstverständnis der Kirche* (Stuttgart: Quell, 1987), 110.

is never relieved of the task of making sure that no single work speaks against him- or herself. Tranquilizing the conscience simply will not do. The conscience can only be cancelled.

Jüngel's distinction between the (rational) law and the gospel, with only the latter being able to bring peace to the conscience, is a self-aware continuation of the Reformation's heritage. Salvation cannot come through the law of works, the Wittenberg reformers insisted in the spirit of St. Paul. Peace, as opposed to short-lived self-satisfaction, cannot be effected through a demand, regardless of who issues it, Jüngel holds. He extends this insight to more modern notions, pertaining to human being in the world, such as dignity, uniqueness, personhood, and wholeness. None of these must be conditioned on one's conformity to a law. None of these is subject to achievement. They are possible only through unconditional recognition. Because it goes ahead of the person's works, unconditional recognition distinguishes the person from his or her works and thus cancels the person's conscience.[39]

God's affirmation of humanity, when believed, brings about the freedom of conscience. "Christian freedom in its primary form is *freedom of conscience*," Jüngel declares. This freedom must not be understood in the same manner that the phrase "freedom of conscience" is employed in contemporary political discourse in the West. Seen against the backdrop of Jüngel's anthropology, the political understanding seems to exhibit some of the weaknesses that have led Jüngel (via Marcuse) to dismiss Kant's understanding of freedom. What Jüngel wishes to recover is Luther's understanding of the freedom of conscience as "the royal freedom of the person to be separated from his or her guilt and thus liberated for the transformation of the world."[40] Luther, Jüngel notes, offers the first known

---

[39] Jüngel's thinking on law and gospel has been shaped as much by Luther as by Barth. The gospel and the law are diametrically opposed to each other (which is the traditional Lutheran position), but only, Jüngel avers, where the law remains unrestricted by the gospel. In other words, if individuals are bent on determining themselves definitively through their acts, there is no room for the gospel, and, consequently, the demand of the law becomes "an excessive demand," which the gospel opposes with full force. Jüngel views the gospel – as does Luther in his catechetical explanation of the Creed's first article and as more self-awarely does Barth – as the basic dimension of the entirety of human history, evident already in the divine act of creation. Though Jüngel gives only a qualified approval to Barth's designation of "the law as sum and form of the gospel" (*CD* II/2, 509; *Karl Barth*, 119), he agrees that one can speak of the "imperatives of freedom" only in the context of the "indicative of grace." Jüngel explains: "The gospel does not contradict the law's demand, but it certainly contradicts the excessive demand of the law by proclaiming the justification of sinners and thereby the distinction between person and work" ("On Becoming Truly Human," *Essays II*, 236).

[40] "Wertlose Würde," *EmE*, 101.

instance of the phrase "*libertas conscientiae.*"[41] It goes without saying that it by no means follows from this cancellation of conscience that one can now be immoral (to allay Hartmann's fear).

The person as distinguished from God

The distinction between person and works is related to another fundamental distinction. In irrevocably affirming the person, God also distinguishes between God and the person in his or her humanity. One no longer needs, as a justified person, to secure oneself against one's human fragility by seeking to transcend it. As recognized by God, one is freed from the urge to remake oneself in the image of what one understands God to be. "To be justified means to be unconditionally distinguished from God for one's own good," Jüngel observes.[42] One's relation to God does not divinize one but, precisely on account of God's closeness, one becomes specific as a *human* person, a creature. "The *righteous person* is . . . nothing other than the *truly human person* [*der menschliche Mensch*]."[43]

The humanness of the free person cannot be overestimated. In my engagement both with Jüngel's critique of Kantian freedom and with Jüngel's construal of divine freedom, I noted that freedom consists not only in independence and the capacity to determine oneself but also in determinateness. Freedom involves not only spontaneity but also defining what exactly one is as a spontaneous being in the world.

The freedom of a human subject bent on self-actualization seems to be incapable of determinateness. Human self-determination (in the word's active sense) does not achieve determinateness but rather makes humans lose whatever determinateness they have. They become relationless, at the

---

[41] Luther writes: "Christian or evangelical freedom, then, is a freedom of conscience which liberates the conscience from works. Not that no works are done, but no faith is put in them. For conscience is not the power to do works, but to judge them. The proper work of conscience (as Paul says in Romans 2[:15]), is to accuse or excuse, to make guilty or guiltless, uncertain or certain. Its purpose is not to do, but to pass judgment on what has been done and what should be done, and this judgment makes us stand accused or saved in God's sight. Christ has freed this conscience from works through the gospel and teaches this conscience not to trust in works, but to rely only on his mercy. And so, the conscience of a man of faith depends solely and entirely on the works of Christ" (*The Judgment of Martin Luther on Monastic Vows* [1521], *LW* 44:298; *WA* 8:606–7; cited partially in "Die Freiheit eines Christenmenschen: Freiheit als Summe des Christentums," Michael Beintker et al. [eds], *Wege zum Einverständnis. Festschrift für Christoph Demke* [Leipzig: Evangelische Verlagsanstalt, 1997], 128).

[42] *FoC,* 26.

[43] "On Becoming Truly Human," *Essays II*, 216. Cf. "Grenzen des Menschseins," *TE II*, 358; and *Justification*, 199–200 n. 121.

same time tyrannized and controlling, as well as boundaryless, moribund in the simultaneous collapse and distendedness of their being. This lack of determinateness results from the fact that – for a human in a totalizing self-relation – self-actualization, self-meaning and so also the self's freedom are not grounded in that which is given and which is perceived as fragile. They have to be seized from the world and over against the world, whose unpredictability and impingement pose a threat to the security of the self-relation; they have to be wrested from the world by manufacturing the world. Self-determination entangles humans in an inescapable self-contradiction, as, through their own humanity, their own capacity for world-being, they seek to get ahead of their own humanity and leave behind its world-being, now seen as deadly vulnerability. Thus, at best, self-determination amounts to compulsion toward action. But it cannot bring about determinateness. In this process, humans destroy their relational identity.

The elemental interruption, by contrast, renders humans specific and makes human determinateness possible. As it exposes the self-contradiction of human being, the unfreedom and futility of human self-determination, it also reestablishes one's fundamental humanity in its relation to God. God is now revealed as the *boundary* of the human, as the one who gives humanity its proper place and proportion. But this boundary is one of freedom, whereby humanity is shown to be infinitely more than mere fragility and limitedness. The human person is essentially a creature, related both to his or her Creator and to everything else, now understood as God's creation. Yet, because God relates to the contingent as one who is more than necessary, the human being, precisely qua creature, is infinitely bounded: "Der Mensch *ist unendlich* begrenzt."[44]

---

[44] "Grenzen des Menschseins," *TE II*, 360. Jüngel follows here in the footsteps of Barth, who states: "Man as such . . . has no beyond. Nor does he need one, for God is his beyond" (*CD* III/2, 632; cited in *Karl Barth*, 46). This may be a good place to indicate that the concept of interruption, too, appears already in Barth, though not as a technical term and in a manner that is generally unthematized. The following quotation from the *Church Dogmatics* illustrates both Jüngel's indebtedness to Barth, as well as how significantly he develops themes which have only an inchoate presence in Barth: "we can and must realise that this participation [in God's revelation] is achieved in our own experience and activity, in that act of self-determination which we call our human existence. This participation has nothing whatever to do with a magical invasion of the interrelated totality of our physico-psychical human life by supernatural factors and forces. It does signify a limitation and interruption [*Unterbrechung*], a most concrete limitation and interruption, of our existence. Our existence is confronted by something outside and over against it, by which it is . . . totally determined. But it is determined as the act of our self-determination in the totality of its possibilities. Yet not in such a way that we know in advance and can usually tell what form the fulfilment of this self-determination will take" (*CD* I/2, 266, translation altered). Elsewhere Barth also speaks of God's invading, reaching and piercing; see *CD* III/2, 141–2.

The human person is a being determined in a most creative way – by and for possibility that embraces actuality in hitherto unforeseen ways. This becomes apparent when we again contrast the sinner's existence with that of the free person. The sinner's quest for self-possessed subjectivity, for the closure, so to speak, of the self, renders the sinner's being open, shapeless, and indeterminate. At the same time, the sinner's world becomes increasingly closed and predictable, a product of one's attempted mastery over it. This fundamental closure of the world in its unruliness – that is, the sinner's inability to receive from the world despite the sinner's worldly involvement – makes the sinner's being trivial. It only reproduces itself in its indeterminateness. By contrast, the person, who in faith has received his or her determination from another, from God, remains open to the world. As the distendedness of one's self-securing being recedes, space is opened up for otherness. In this openness, the world is allowed to exist for its own sake and for the sake of one's action on its behalf. It comes into one's self-relation, interrupts the self-relation, calling for ever-new possibilities for reception and for action, possibilities that cannot be assimilated but only enjoyed, and hence ever fresh and new possibilities.[45] Therefore, paradoxically, even though one's being is specific, it is hardly trivial in its determinateness. I believe this is what Jüngel has in mind when he states that "one is . . . taken away from oneself, is destined to *be* and to *become*."[46]

In sum, it is the God-effected distinction of the human from God that allows the person to relate to God and to fellow humans and, more than that, to be constantly enriched in those relations. God's relation to the person restores an equilibrium between one's relations to others and one's relation to self.

With these last remarks, we have already transcended the realm of self-perception and ventured into the territory of Jüngel's relational ontology. It is to this that we now turn.

Human being is in becoming

The elemental interruption does not exhaust itself simply in subjective perception. This would make it hardly different from Kant's inner freedom as interpreted and critiqued by Marcuse and Scheler. Jüngel is quite

---

[45] "Humanity in Correspondence to God. Remarks on the Image of God as a Basic Concept in Theological Anthropology," *Essays I*, 150.
[46] *FoC*, 82 (emphasis added).

emphatic that the elemental interruption is, so to speak, ontically available. It manifests itself as a particular relational structure of the person's being-in-the-world.

A creature of distance

A person's freedom from dependence on works for his or her identity is, in fact, grounded in a real separation that takes place in the person's being. In interrupting the sinner's totalizing self-relation, God has, in fact, come closer to the human than the human is to him- or herself.[47] As a result of God's coming, the person has been distanced from him- or herself. This, in turn, has enabled the emergence of a discrete, specific identity. Personhood, dignity, and uniqueness – which hitherto remained beyond the reach of the self-relation's trivial exertions – are now granted to the person in a nontrivial fashion. They are granted out of divine excess: not as a possession but as a relation, precisely so that they would not become mirror images of the person's ontic existence.

Because my identity is found in God, as in faith I claim as mine God's identification with the dead Jesus, God's closeness to me is also my existence outside of myself. A justified person ek-sists (*ek-sistiert*) – exists from another and, as we are about to see, also for another.[48] "Faith," writes Jüngel, "is a participation in God himself."[49]

---

[47] "*In the gospel* . . . God . . . draws *near* to me, indeed *nearer to me than I am able to be to myself*" ("Living out of Righteousness," *Essays II*, 245).

[48] Jüngel comments: "Eine Person sein heißt vielmehr von Anderen her und auf Andere hin existieren und in solcher Ek-sistenz ab aliis und ad alios *bejaht* und *anerkannt* sein" ("Hoffen, Handeln – und Leiden," *BR*, 23). In a manner analogous to Jesus, one comes to exist in the world in a way that has already surpassed the totality of one's worldly existence. One has "eschatological spiritual presence" (*Mystery*, 174; *GGW* 235). This means that God has made an *eschatological* claim on, and has vindicated, one's entire life. The consequence of God's claim, of one's standing in this fashion before God, is that one's life in the here and now is already lived out of eschatological excess, out of a future that transcends any future one could ever give to oneself.

The language of ek-sistence is, of course, of Heideggerian provenance. But it is important to stress that, for Jüngel, this language is unmistakably christological (cf. Chapter 2, fn. 68) and harks back to Luther's understanding of human personhood as constituted through a faith-relation to God. As a matter of fact, Jüngel's location of the truth of human relationality in the person of Christ (who is to be understood in the larger context of the event of God's triune being) represents a way in which Jüngel disambiguates the ontological character of human being in Heidegger's thought. Heidegger's shying away from either making or presupposing theological claims in *Being and Time*, arguably, produces an insurmountable ambivalence in his view of Dasein. The ambivalence has to do, first of all, with whether Dasein's fallenness is its ontic or, more seriously, ontological dimension. On the one hand, if authenticity, taking responsibility for one's existence and opening oneself up for relational encounter with beings, is indeed attainable for humans, fallenness must belong merely to the realm of the ontic. On the other hand, if inauthentic existence in the they, that is, merely

Thus I am "constituted from outside the self"[50] and, as such, become a "creature of distance [*Wesen der Ferne*]" (a Heideggerian phrase that Jüngel invokes[51]). The dialectic of distance and nearness has several modalities in Jüngel's thought. As a person, I now exist in a distance from myself, which means that I can no longer destroy myself with my actions, whatever they might be, by becoming their sum total. Yet, in this, I am also identical with myself, insofar as I inhabit my ontological humanity.[52] I no longer exist in a distance from myself and from God, where distance meant my inability to

within socially defined and culturally transmitted roles, precedes individual human identity and as such is primordial, as Heidegger claims, then it is questionable whether authenticity is in fact achievable. In short, the ambiguity has to do with Heidegger's insistence that fallenness is more than a mere accident and yet less than a necessity. It comes down to which is the primary characteristic of Dasein: authenticity, as Heidegger wishes to assert, or inauthenticity, as he seems to be arguing. Second, the ambivalence manifests itself in Dasein's being as being-in-the-world. On the one hand, thanks to its world-being, Dasein can and indeed must assume responsibility for its existence in the world and acknowledge its own relationality and realize the possibilities it brings with itself. On the other hand, it is this very worldly existence that entangles Dasein in inauthentic being. In short, in Heidegger's account, world-being is for Dasein both a possibility of true being-in-the-world and a hindrance to it. For a more detailed analysis of this ambivalence, see Stephen Mulhall, *Philosophical Myths of the Fall* (Princeton: Princeton University Press, 2005), 49–56.

Jüngel resolves this ambiguity by locating the truth of human relationality in God's relation to humanity, and, even more specifically, in the event of the cross. Relationality is thus more than necessary in relation to inauthentic human existence. What this means is that, by themselves, humans must remain a mystery to themselves. At best they sense, as we have shown, that there is something self-contradictory about human world-being. But inauthentic existence does not by itself lead to relationality, it produces all the wrong solutions to its own worldly entanglement: turning against the world or away from it. In this sense, for Jüngel, fallenness is primordial and humanly insurmountable. Yet it is primordial only as an "impossible actuality." More primordial is the presupposition of human relationality in God's relational being, which alone can give rise to authenticity and care for the world. Cf. in this context Luther's reference to God's truth (*veritas*) as that "which makes us truthful [*qua nos veraces facit*]" in the *Psalmenvorlesung* (1513/15), WA 4:15.

[49] *Mystery*, 176; *GGW* 237–8.

[50] *FoC*, 61.

[51] Heidegger writes: "man, as existing transcendence abounding in and surpassing toward possibilities, is a *creature of distance*. Only through the primordial distance he establishes toward all being in his transcendence does a true nearness to things flourish in him. And only the knack for hearing into the distance awakens Dasein as self to the answer of its Dasein with others. For only in its Dasein with others can Dasein surrender its individuality in order to win itself as an authentic self" (Martin Heidegger, *The Essence of Reasons*, trans. T. Malick [Evanston, IL: Northwestern University Press, 1969], 131). Jüngel comments: "Martin Heidegger's determination of human being can by all means be also received theologically, provided one understands 'distance' as the origin of God's *coming close* to us: so close that God comes closer to me than I am ever able to be close to myself (*interior intimo meo*) and that, because of this closeness, I win freedom to distance myself from myself without thus losing myself" ("Glaube und Vernunft," George Augustin and Klaus Krämer (eds), *Gott denken und bezeugen. Festschrift für Kardinal Walter Kasper zum 75. Geburtstag* [Freiburg: Herder, 2008], 28–9; cf. "On Becoming Truly Human," *Essays II*, 234, with a mistaken page reference to Heidegger's work).

[52] "In being accepted by God the human person *becomes* that which he or she is determined *to be*: a whole human person, one who is identical with him- or herself" ("The Mystery of Substitution," *Essays II*, 161).

catch up with the secured, god-like self I conjured up and quested for. That I no longer exist in this latter distance (actually effected by an excessive closeness to myself) is because God has come closer to me than I am able to be to my self. God's coming cancelled the illusory being-destructive distance (animated by the self-identification of person with achievement) and effected another (between person and work), for my sake.[53] What all these modalities of nearness and distance are meant to emphasize, from various angles, is that divine justification, in the end, amounts to liberation from the self, from the tyranny of the "I," from "the drive of the ego toward itself."[54] What matters above all is that the self has been radically opened up and unfolded, as it were, in its relational capacity.

Love

Being "elementally interrupted" involves not only closeness to God and a simultaneous distance from self, which have largely occupied us thus far. The elemental interruption has as much to do with the closeness of the world, in the sense that the world is now able to come close to the person. (By "world" I mean the totality of one's relations other than those to God and to self.) The world, especially fellow humans are now no longer perceived as a threat to the person's being, a threat against which the person needs to secure him- or herself or because of which the person needs to remake the world in a way he or she finds palatable. The world can now come close to the person in its own otherness, which lies beyond the person's control. The world is, as I have mentioned above, allowed to exist for its own sake and for the sake of the person's action on its behalf. Because God has elementally interrupted the continuity of the person's being, the justified human can now allow the world to interrupt him or her and enter the space which God has opened up in the person's self-relation.

What I have just described is really none other than the essence of love. In love, we may recall, "the beloved Thou, com[es] closer to me than I am able to be to myself."[55] This is, of course, paradigmatically true of God. God alone loves out of God's self and, as God's love penetrates into nothingness

---

[53] "As the one who distances us from ourselves, God is certainly the one who is farthest away from the man who seeks to exist in and of himself, who seeks to will in and of himself, and who thus insists on himself. The converse is simultaneously true: this fundamental 'us being outside ourselves' (*nos extra nos esse*) is as such identical with the nearness of God" (*Mystery*, 183; *GGW* 246).

[54] *Mystery*, 197; *GGW* 267.

[55] *Mystery*, 324, cf. 321; *GGW* 444, cf. 440.

and lovelessness, frees those tyrannized by their own selves. God steps between me and me in the most originary way, in that He is the prime mover, so to speak, of love, and His loving act of liberation is unsurpassed. I come to rest in the infinity of God's unconditionally affirming love and participate in the ever-new possibilities that flow from it. This is all true. But, we must also ask, what else could the freedom, bestowed through God's act of elementally interrupting the continuity of my own being, the freedom that differentiates between me and me, be other than freedom for love? *My love.* Jüngel writes: "To believe in God means to believe in the victory of love *in view of* triumphs of lovelessness and hate and in trust in this divine victory of love (which we don't have to procure) to now oppose in a human way the lovelessness in this world with deeds of love."[56]

Therefore, it is not only God who "profoundly [*zuinnerst*] defines my own being from outside of myself."[57] To be sure, the person always rests in God's definition, being unconditionally acknowledged. But precisely because the person has his or her God-given, human specificity, because the person already *is* – the person can now also *become* by allowing others profoundly to define him or her from outside the self. Free human being is thus a being in becoming. "Whoever really is *for others* and seeks to *be* himself in that, always subjects himself immediately to nothingness," notes Jüngel.[58]

It must be noted that the potential of the lover's own nonbeing in this context transcends the "anticipative exchange of being [*Seinswechsel*]" in which "the self-loss in the event of love is already surpassed by the new being which the loving I receives from the beloved Thou in the act of surrender."[59] The risk is real that, as one ventures into the loveless world, one's love will be rejected, that one's deeds of love will meet only with incomprehension or hostility. In face of such impingement, the loving I may be tempted to retreat from his or her self-surrender and again to secure him- or herself within the self-relation. The dimension of death inherent in love is, in this situation, far from metaphorical.

Yet it is precisely "*in view of* triumphs of lovelessness and hate," as Jüngel puts it, that the risk of love is worth taking. Not because of any benefit that might accrue to the lover, but because "a *life* that is *loveless* is already *in death.*"[60] Elsewhere Jüngel adds that "By himself man likely is the least

---

[56] "What does it mean to say, 'God is love'?" 310.
[57] *Mystery,* 363; *GGW* 498.
[58] *Mystery,* 219; *GGW* 298.
[59] *Mystery,* 322; *GGW* 441.
[60] "Nemo contra deum nisi deus ipse: Zum Verhältnis von theologia crucis und Trinitätslehre," *TE V,* 250.

secure" and goes on compare self-securing to a fortress that unavoidably turns out to be one's prison.[61] The free person knows all this and cannot simply go back. And, despite appearances, going forward has much to recommend it. "[L]ove does not even fear its own weakness"[62] – for it knows its weakness to be a strength that has already, against all odds, transformed one's self and cannot but transform the world.[63]

Community

Love has already brought about a "successful togetherness [*Zusammensein*] of man with God."[64] What, in turn, emerges from it is a worldly togetherness: what Jüngel calls the "connectedness of life [*Lebenszusammenhang*]."[65] It emerges as already a reality but also an ever-present task. What characterizes this togetherness is peace. Not the precarious peace of reconciled self-interests but *shalom*, characterized by "creative security . . . ability to trust and . . . responsibility through which the indicative of peace [i.e., its givenness] is preserved."[66] Such peace by definition implies a community, a tapestry of relations epitomized in lingual recognition, in the greeting of peace. In the "Peace be with you!" – Jüngel observes – the statement "homo homini lupus" is falsified and replaced with the statement "homo homini homo." All this is possible because, fundamentally speaking, "Deus homini homo."[67]

The creative security of *shalom* refers to that activity which celebrates the human person's rich relationality and strives to enhance it and make the most of it. Such creative security is the very essence of freedom; it is the capacity to "begin something with oneself and one's world"[68] – again, to become. The free person lives out of the unconditionally justifying divine affirmation. This means that the free person lives out of the infinite horizon of divine possibility, out of the future, unconstrained by the present, yet embracing the present

---

[61] "Zum Wesen des Friedens," *TE V*, 34–5.

[62] *Mystery*, 325; *GGW* 445.

[63] Martin H. Thiele (*Gott – Allmacht – Zeit: Ein theologisches Gespräch mit Johann Baptist Metz und Eberhard Jüngel* [Münster: Aschendorff, 2009], 255–65) perceptively correlates the worldly impact of God's justifying act with the de-apocalypticization of eschatology, a development which Jüngel discerns already in the preaching of Jesus and which, since Paul, has lain at the foundation of the Christian notion of time. For Jüngel, this de-apocalypticization becomes a theological program, whose central concept is God's elemental interruption of the continuity of one's life. Thus established, God's rule gives rise to an *existential* time for love *within* worldly time and, in doing so, establishes itself also as the latter's limit.

[64] "Ganzheitsbegriffe – in theologischer Perspektive," *TE V*, 51.

[65] "Zum Wesen des Friedens," *TE V*, 26.

[66] "Zum Wesen des Friedens," *TE V*, 33.

[67] "Zum Wesen des Friedens," *TE V*, 31.

[68] "The Emergence of the New," *Essays II*, 57.

as a nothingness that is yet to become something. Resting in God's affirmation free person is able to bring the unexpected and the unforeseen into being. "Christian existence is existence out of nothingness, because it is all along the line existence out of the creative power of God who justifies."[69] Living out of God's creative power, and thus no longer doomed to trivial self-creation, one can now "begin something with oneself and one's world." The free person is an inherently creative person.

This creativity takes the form of affirming another's dignity, or, to put it in more theological terms, of sharing one's righteousness, the righteousness which one, together with all humanity, has received through God's recognition. One is called to grant the same recognition to others, however extreme their otherness, in "the peaceful wholeness of good order, where every single person seeks the rights of the other."[70] Jüngel insists on "the communicability of not only divine but also of human righteousness, which does not allow those who exist outside our community to remain there, but draws them in, and in this way, for example, allows the foreigner to participate in one's own social justice."[71]

Significantly, it is through this affirmation of others for their sake that one, as an unconditionally affirmed person, also affirms oneself. One's self-relation is thus reconfigured and aligned with the fundamental human relationality. It is constituted by one's attentive relations to others. Jüngel writes: "In his created being-other vis-à-vis the Creator man is irrevocably affirmed and authorized to affirm himself. Self-affirmation, however, means to have the freedom to begin something with oneself and one's world." It is by allowing others to interrupt one that one enriches, and begins something with, oneself. It is by engaging otherness in love that one begins something with one's world. One finds one's being's continuity in one's very interruptibility. "In this freedom of being able to begin," Jüngel adds, "the human is the image of the divine creator."[72]

The free person as agent

Passivity and activity

Our discussion of freedom's communal expression has already touched on the importance of human action as a significant dimension of human

---

[69] "The World as Possibility and Actuality," *Essays I*, 108–9.
[70] *Justification*, 273; cf. "Living out of Righteousness," *Essays II*, 260; and "Ordnung gibt der Freiheit einen Raum," 118–19.
[71] "Living out of Righteousness," *Essays II*, 262.
[72] "Hoffen, Handeln – und Leiden," *BR*, 23.

freedom in Jüngel's thought. Freedom, as we have shown, consists, first and foremost, in being interrupted, that is, in passivity through which both recognition and new being are granted to the person. But freedom does not exhaust itself in this passivity. "The gift [*Gabe*] of peace becomes a task [*Aufgabe*]."[73] Jüngel is careful to emphasize that we are *not* lifted "out of the connection of person and works but simply out of the lordship of the works over the person."[74]

These two aspects of freedom, active and passive, correspond to the interrupted and nontrivially differentiated self. Jüngel offers the following elaboration in his exposition of Luther's 1520 treatise, *The Freedom of a Christian*:

> that distance which is rich in connection and is opened up by the distinction between the inner and outer man – i.e., between being and what ought to be, between receiving one's person and acting, between one's most intensive, not lifeless, but most vital passivity and wildest activity – is strategic for an understanding of Christian freedom and with it for a theological understanding of human being as such.[75]

Though Jüngel, following Luther, uses here the mystical categories of inner and outer, both of these stand for the *total* human being, who exists simultaneously in two different modes, as it were. It would be a mistake to associate the inner with the rational and the outer merely with one's sensory and historical existence, or to treat one as desirable and the other as unnecessary and burdensome, or, finally to think of one as free and the other as enslaved. To be sure, the outer – understood more generally as one's self-relation, as that which is active – exists prior to the act of faith, exists in a totalizing and exclusive manner, and so is unfree. Yet properly speaking the outer is enabled only by the emergence of the inner. As such, both of these dimensions belong to freedom.[76]

---

[73] "Zum Wesen des Friedens," *TE V*, 33. This important motif appears as early as Jüngel's doctoral dissertation where Jüngel not only distinguishes between the being (*Sein*) and existence (*Existenz*) of the Christian, but also correlates those with the indicative and imperative modes respectively. *Paulus und Jesus: eine Untersuchung zur Präzisierung der Frage nach dem Ursprung der Christologie* (Tübingen: Mohr Siebeck, 1962), 63.

[74] "Humanity in Correspondence to God," *Essays I*, 150.

[75] *FoC*, 83.

[76] To Luther's adaptation of these mystical categories – with a view to expressing the ecstatic nature of the believer's existence and a relational, rather than substance-centered, understanding of personhood, see Karl-Heinz zur Mühlen, *Nos extra nos: Luthers Theologie zwischen Mystik und Scholastik* (Tübingen: Mohr Siebeck, 1972), 155–60. Jüngel's focus, in contrast to Luther, is not so much on the outer dimension simply being caught up in the inner, as on the transfiguration of the outer through the emergence of the inner.

This intimate connection between passivity and activity in the self ought to make clear once again that freedom has everything to do with worldly existence. It cannot be otherwise, given that Jüngel's entire anthropology is constructed in opposition to apparent freedoms which, when it comes to human being in the world, turn out to be unfreedom. Hence Jüngel's insistence that, though freedom becomes concrete in faith, this concreteness unfolds itself as part of human being-in-the-world. Freedom rooted in the elemental interruption is not a mere name that can mask all sorts of bondage. For Jüngel, the freedom of faith and worldly freedom are essentially identical. There is no duality.[77] God may be more than necessary in relation to worldly contingencies, but this means the exact opposite of divine irrelevance or idleness.[78] It means that freedom, which lives out of faith in God, is not determined or hamstrung by worldly actuality. Precisely because of this, it is very much relevant, as it makes one free to respond and lovingly to embrace and transform what is actual.

To understand this potency of freedom more precisely, we may recall here the observations, made in the Introduction, about the fate of freedom during and after the Reformation. This will help us appreciate the active dimension of freedom, its capacity for worldly engagement – as none other than an outworking of God's justifying act. Owing, in part, to enthused misunderstandings, socio-political circumstances and, finally, the reformers' timidity and their successors' self-satisfaction, the Reformation's call to freedom, I have argued, gave way to alternative, anthropological conceptions. A purely anthropological understanding may, at first blush, seem appealing in all its urgency. But it makes freedom into a ceaseless undertaking whose goal is to win freedom and, once it has been gained, to combat its relentless ossification into its opposite. Because it lacks an indicative mode, such freedom not only shows itself to be constrained by worldly actuality but, above all, ends up being preoccupied with itself. Its energies are largely self-referential. By contrast, God's gift of freedom, as always fresh and always the case, becomes a task of *love* which can embrace and engage actuality. When freedom is a gift of God, its activity is creatively directed beyond itself. This worldly relevance of divinely imparted freedom manifests itself through deliberateness and responsibility, which come to characterize the free human's actions in the world.

---

[77] "Freiheitsrechte und Gerechtigkeit," *TE I*, 246–7.
[78] "Umgang mit der Vergangenheit in theologischer Perspektive," *BR*, 48.

Deliberateness

As a being whose personhood, dignity, and uniqueness are already infinitely more than the sum of his or her actions, the free person is liberated from compulsion toward action. The free person can thus act as a genuine agent – no longer relentlessly compelled to act by actuality but called by possibility to "begin something." Being able to begin means that the free person has been given time to think. He or she can reflect on the range of creative possibilities that open up. And having taken the time to deliberate, the free person can thus truly make a difference by his or her actions. Jüngel expresses this sentiment in a somewhat narrower context when he criticizes the impatience with theological thinking and the singular privileging of activism that characterize some parts of contemporary Christianity.[79]

Jüngel's call to deliberateness and his plea on behalf of theological reflection are not intended to downplay the role of activism, or action in a more general sense. On the contrary, he makes his plea *because* action matters. He does admit that "Possibility, which unconditionally concerns actuality as a future which results from outside and from nothing – from no tendency in the actual – is open to suspicion of being irrelevant to or even altogether impossible for actuality."[80] But it is precisely here, in the deliberative passage from possibility to actuality, that genuine space for human action opens up. "We now have to make distinction within actuality, we must *act*, we must *decide* according to the necessity of the time constituted by possibility, sometimes, even, decide for a politics . . . of revolution."[81]

The distinction that the possible enables one to make within actuality is a differentiation between the possible and the impossible. The possible enters actuality as "a space for freedom . . . critically differentiating between actualities." The possible can, therefore, openly call the impossible – such as an inhuman, self-preserving form of government – the impossible, without thereby evoking despair over that which actuality has to offer as an alternative.[82]

---

[79] "the evidence of ethical immediacy to action may not be permitted to tyrannize over the stringency and consequence of the dogmatic mediation of truth" (*Mystery*, xi; *GGW* xv).

[80] "The World as Possibility and Actuality," *Essays I*, 117.

[81] "The World as Possibility and Actuality," *Essays I*, 121.

[82] "The World as Possibility and Actuality," *Essays I*, 120. The distinction between possibility and actuality is important for Jüngel, especially when it comes to possibility's impact on actuality in the actions of the free person. But what Jüngel regards as "incomparably more fundamental" is the distinction between the possible and the impossible because the latter "concerns the distinction between God and the world. And in the distinction between God and the world we are not concerned primarily with actuality, but with truth" (110–11). It is in light of the distinction between the possible and the impossible that the worldly distinction between the actual and the possible as not-yet-actual is disclosed in all its triviality and unfreedom, while the notion of the possible as preceding and transcending actuality is revealed as a dimension of creative, God-given freedom.

Even as it is actualized, the possible never exhausts itself as the possible. It thus continues to exercise its critical function. On the one hand, it constantly calls one to trust in the possible. On the other hand, it empowers the person who wishes deliberately to engage actuality, and especially that actuality which, in light of the possible, is disclosed in all its untruth and impossibility. It is important to note that, in this respect, the actualization of the possible is quite different from the actualization of values in Hartmann's ethical system. The possible, once actualized, does not become one actuality among many which then asserts itself by tyrannizing and crowding out actuality's other dimensions. Rather, the possible never exhausts itself but always enters actuality as a surplus, as new possibilities that, when reflected on, subject actuality to constant critique, to becoming old, or simply reveal its impossibility. "The authority of the possible is [instead] the authority of given freedom."[83] This freedom is one in which deliberation leads to precise and meaningful engagement.

Responsibility

The deliberative and critical posture is, we must remember, inscribed into the interruptedness of the self, which the world, too, now interrupts, showing itself – even in its brokenness and self-seeking – as interesting and worthwhile for its own sake. Underlying all deliberation and criticism is thus ultimately responsibility for actuality. Without it, we would be dealing merely with another case of a self-relation lording it over actuality and, worse still, enlisting God for that purpose.

How does responsibility manifest itself? Primarily in attentiveness to another, not unrelated distinction that God's act at the cross has effected within actuality: the distinction between person and works, mentioned earlier. Precisely because there is a distinction between person and works, persons can be addressed about their works. Works can be critiqued and, if need be, even condemned, without reducing the person to the sum of his or her works. Jüngel writes: "The dignity of the person is secured by God and therefore inviolable; his or her works are, by contrast, subject to discussion, criticism, praise or condemnation. The human is answerable for his or her works. God, however, answers for the human's personhood".[84] This means specifically that "The right to judge the being of *the person* is withheld from all earthly persons and authorities."[85] The consequences are

---

[83] "The World as Possibility and Actuality," *Essays I*, 119.
[84] "Wertlose Würde," *EmE*, 99.
[85] "On Becoming Truly Human," *Essays II*, 229 (emphasis added).

far-reaching not only for daily human interaction but also for the political dimension of human societies: "in justifying the sinner, God's righteousness attaches *inviolable value to the human person* whose worldly protection must be expressed in a number of *human rights* which ought to be introduced into every constitution."[86] This impacts how the elderly and children are to be treated: "In dealing with the person who is not yet capable of, or no longer capable of, achieving anything, we have a *criterion* for the humanity of our society," Jüngel insists.[87] It also impacts the treatment of criminals, with the abolition of the death penalty being of particular urgency.[88] For the sake of this broader social impact, Jüngel is very much concerned about the preservation of social times and spaces where God's Word of being-interrupting address can be heard, such as holy days and worship services. Without such reinforcement, he opines, "in the end a society that destroys institutions in which such elemental interruptions have their Sitz im Leben will become overburdened with lack of hope."[89]

Conclusion

Our analysis of the ontology of human freedom has shown that God's act of elemental interruption, as apprehended through faith, brings about a fundamental restructuring of a person's being-in-the-world. Freedom for Jüngel is, above all, freedom from the tyranny of the ego. God's interruption of the ego's totalizing self-relation effects a nontrivial differentiation within the self: the person, as unconditionally recognized, becomes distinct from the person's works and conclusively distinguished in his or her humanity from God. The person thus gains specificity, which was unavailable through self-actualization. This renders the person free to commit her actions, the self's other dimension, to the neighbor for the neighbor's sake. As fundamentally related to God, the self thus becomes a fully relational self. As interrupted by God, one can now allow oneself to be interrupted by the world. With a specificity bestowed through God's affirmation, one is now able to receive being from another and to act on another's behalf. One is,

---

[86] *Christ, Justice and Peace: Toward a Theology of the State* (Edinburgh: T&T Clark, 1992), 68. Jüngel discusses theology's potential for contributing to and strengthening human rights discourse in his essay, "Zur Verankerung der Menschenrechte im christlichen Glauben," *Außer sich. Theologische Texte* (Stuttgart: Radius-Verlag, 2011), 124–38.

[87] "On Becoming Truly Human," *Essays II*, 239.

[88] *Death*, 134; "Living out of Righteousness," *Essays II*, 257–8; "Hoffen, Handeln – und Leiden," *BR*, 36–7.

[89] "Wertlose Würde," *EmE*, 100; cf. "Living out of Righteousness," *Essays II*, 255.

and one becomes. Luther's statement of this very idea, found in his *Freiheitsschrift*, remains unsurpassed both in theological insight and rhetorical beauty: "a Christian lives not in himself, but in Christ and in his neighbor. Otherwise he is not a Christian. He lives in Christ through faith, in his neighbor through love. By faith he is caught up beyond himself into God. By love he descends beneath himself into his neighbor. Yet he *always remains* in God and in his love."[90]

Our discussion has also shown that freedom is a reality in close proximity to love. It finds its perfect and natural expression in love, while love's capacity for transformation expresses itself in the freedom it bestows on another. Ultimately, it is not merely the case that a person is freed and transformed through God's act of elemental interruption, but rather that a peaceful community comes into being. In Jüngel's words, "The personalism of love . . . transforms, along with loved persons, their being-in-the-world and in this sense also the being of the world."[91] Love is that thanks to which freedom not only is granted but also becomes woven into the structure of the world.

With this fundamental human relationality in mind, Jüngel rewrites Kant's famed questions by means of which the Prussian philosopher seeks to capture the essence of the human. Kant's central question is "What is man?" In order to answer it, he examines the intersection of knowledge, action, and faith. What he finds there is a self-possessed rational subject. Jüngel does not view the nexus itself as wrong but questions the possibility of such a subject at this, or any other, nexus. He argues that to do justice to human freedom, Kant's original questions must explicitly take into account the fundamentally relational character of humanity, which the intersection of knowledge, action, and faith actually calls for. Thus, "What can I know?" becomes "Who, when I cry, hears me?" "What ought I to do?" becomes "Who is reliable?" "What can I hope?" becomes "Who is my hope?" Most importantly, the question "What is man?" becomes "In whom can I believe?"[92] – in affirmation of faith's being humanity's most fundamental constituent. "Faith . . . is an act of freedom," insists Jüngel, qualifiedly registering his own agreement with Kant.[93] But it is such an act not because

[90] *The Freedom of a Christian*, LW 31:371; WA 7:69; cited partially in "Befreiende Freiheit," *Anfänger*, 35.
[91] "What does it mean to say, 'God is love'?" 311.
[92] "Hoffen, Handeln – und Leiden," *BR*, 18. Kant's first three questions can be found in his *Critique of Pure Reason* (1781, 1787). Trans. and ed. Paul Guyer and Allen W. Wood (Cambridge: University Press, 1998), 677 [B833]. The final question comes from Kant's *Logic*, trans. R. S. Hartman and W. Schwarz (New York: Dover, 1988), 29 [25].
[93] "Der Mensch," 344.

faith cannot be commanded, as Kant maintains, but because in faith one becomes free.

With this emphasis on faith as a relation, we come back to the question of God, God's freedom, and human correspondence to it. These will be taken up in the next, final chapter of this study.

Chapter 4

The Trinitarian Logic of Freedom

Jüngel, as we have seen, articulates his doctrine of God and his anthropology in very close proximity to each other, far closer than what the traditional metaphysical approach can allow. The death of Jesus is essential for the understanding of God's trinitarian being as the event of love. The elemental interruption, which reorients one's being toward God's act at the cross, is the *sine qua non* of human freedom.

All this notwithstanding, it has been my contention throughout the present study that Jüngel's doctrine of God and his anthropology do not fit together as neatly as Jüngel expects. The problems lie in Jüngel's doctrine of God and are both internal and external to it. Internally, Jüngel's elaboration of divine freedom's two constitutive moments – independence and determinateness – is afflicted by a contradiction. They distort each other, or rather blend into each other, producing in the case of each the same result: a divine subject that appears to be self-related and self-actualizing. It all happens despite Jüngel's resolve to uphold God's robustly intersubjective determinateness, which he postulates theoretically in his account of love's essence and for which he makes conceptual room in the notion of God's trinitarian self-differentiation as withdrawal. Besides this internal distortion, the self-possessed divine subject seems to be the embodiment not of freedom but what Jüngel might rather consider unfreedom in anthropological terms, that is, freedom conceived either in voluntarist terms or as detachment. The upshot of all this is that, at best, the freedom of the divine subject remains ambiguous, as love's reciprocity is called into question; at worst, God's self-determination at the cross is shown to be nothing but a predetermined scenario of which God remains the author, director, and principal actor.

The task of the present chapter is to remove this ambiguity. I shall draw heavily on the resources that Jüngel provides, but ultimately it is a constructive undertaking. I shall take quite seriously Jüngel's insight that in freedom God determines Himself as a trinitarian event of love by identifying with the crucified man Jesus. God's determinateness is intersubjective and is characterized by openness to another, the reception of being from this other, and thus also by a real threat of nonbeing. At the same time, however, God remains the one who loves out of himself in a spontaneous and creative fashion. Even where actuality is all but moribund and all possibility seems to be extinguished, God gives rise to new possibilities. To do justice to both of these dimensions of divine subjectivity I shall develop a trinitarian logic of freedom – an explication of divine freedom that goes beyond a mere formal specification in terms of independence and determinateness.

Essential in the retrieval of freedom's logic will be Jüngel's articulation of the anthropological effects of the elemental interruption, here understood in the precise sense of communication of freedom, which brings humans into correspondence with God. My focus will be especially on the ontology of human freedom and human agency as those follow on the heels of the interruption. Through this appeal to anthropology, I hope not only to advance trinitarian thought but also to articulate a more robust notion of human freedom in correspondence to God. All in all, the constructive project which I am about to undertake involves rethinking the interface of trinitarian doctrine and anthropology – not with a view to once again distancing the two *loci* but rather to achieving their even better integration (without, of course, collapsing one into the other).

The argument of this chapter will proceed as follows. I shall, first, evaluate and enlarge on those elements and conclusions of my discussion thus far that point toward the necessity of understanding freedom beyond its mere formal specification and suggest ways in which such a construal could be obtained. The second section will then develop an ontological understanding of divine freedom as a logic of the divine subject's self-relation. I shall test its plausibility in light of Jüngel's theological commitment to God's self-determination as an event of love, as well as to God's abiding creativity.

Freedom: Beyond the Formal Definition

As I argued in Chapter 2, Jüngel unwittingly undermines his own proposal for a robustly intersubjective character of God's self-determination at the cross. Let me begin by reviewing the reasons why this happens, followed by a brief assessment of the consequences for Jüngel's doctrine of God. This will enable me to outline a *conceptual* distinction between God's love and freedom. I shall emphasize, at the same time, that Jüngel's trinitarian construal will avoid incoherence only if the distinction has actual ontological grounding. I shall conclude this section by drawing attention to how the free person, in corresponding to God, exhibits in his or her own being the distinction between love and freedom. The being of the free person will be of great significance for the proposed reconstruction of the doctrine of God.

Taking stock: Divine creativity and love's self-surrender

Jüngel's doctrine of the Trinity is informed by a desire to give expression to the richly relational nature of God's subjectivity. To be sure, there are also other concerns. Jüngel's critique of the metaphysical tradition intends to combat the latter's distancing of God from all things human and eventual banishment of God from thought – both accompanied by God's supreme manipulability. In positive terms, Jüngel's critique is meant to underscore the freedom of God over God's self – the freedom of God to reveal God's self on God's own terms and thus truly to reveal God's self. By locating the event of God's triune being at the cross, in God's identification with the unjustly and cruelly murdered Jesus, Jüngel preserves and radicalizes the Reformation's emphasis on the objective certainty of God's being for his people (*pro nobis*). But there is more to Jüngel's cruciform emphasis than the issue of God's knowability and the certainty of that knowledge, important as those are. Unlike the incarnation, which can be anticipated in the eternal structure of God's being, God's identification specifically with one crucified as a criminal leaves no doubt as to the intersubjective character of God's self-determination. As an "unconditional subject of himself,"[1] God determines Himself in an intersubjective manner. God determines Himself as a triune event of love by embracing the dead man.

The event of divine love, Jüngel insists, is not essentially different from human love. Love consists in "the beloved Thou, coming closer to me than I am able to be to myself" and thus "profoundly defin[ing] my being from outside of myself."[2] In love, there takes place a "self-surrender" and a "self-sacrifice" on the lover's part, such that one's "existence from the other is an existence which is burdened with the potential of [one's] own nonbeing."[3] Jüngel elaborates:

> The lover does not *exist* on the basis of what he has been until now or has made of himself. Instead, in receiving himself from another, the lover *exists*. Thus he *exists* only because of the existence which is *given* to him,

---

[1] *Mystery*, 158; *GGW* 212.
[2] *Mystery*, 324, 363; *GGW* 444, 498.
[3] "Value-Free Truth: The Christian Experience of Truth in the Struggle against the 'Tyranny of Values'," *Essays II*, 209; and *Mystery*, 324; *GGW* 443.

and apart from that he is nothing. The loving and beloved I is then totally related to the beloved Thou, and thus to his own nonbeing. . . . Love conceals within itself a dimension of death in that it grants new being.[4]

What characterizes love is radical openness to another in the depths of one's very self, a desire to receive one's self form the beloved, and so also a togetherness at which all love aims. Yet, even when the togetherness is successful, the potential of nonbeing is real, insofar as the togetherness is not simply reducible without remainder to two individual selves. What alleviates this burden, Jüngel notes, is the fact that "the self-loss in the event of love is already surpassed by the new being which the loving I receives from the beloved Thou in the act of surrender."[5] However, the lover cannot count on being met by the beloved with a surplus of being. This makes the burden of potential nonbeing real regardless of whether love is requited or not. Love does not calculate before it loves. Jüngel, as we have seen, admits that believers will find themselves "oppos[ing] . . . the lovelessness in this world with deeds of love."[6] The cross, at first blush, also makes it rather difficult to speak of an "anticipative exchange of being"[7] between the lover and the beloved. There, Jüngel writes, God . . . lets himself be interrupted in an elemental way by humanity threatened by the possibility of nonbeing . . . [and] risks himself for them."[8] In sum, what, according to Jüngel, is central to love, be it requited or not, is the lover's posture of openness to the beloved and desire, a real need in fact, to receive one's being from the beloved as the basis for an entirely new self-relation. It is not loving that ultimately contents the lover but the mutual togetherness of lover and beloved.

Jüngel affirms all this about love in general and God's love in particular. But he also, as we have seen, wishes to affirm characteristics that are unique to God's being: God's ability to love out of Himself and the creativity that attends God's love. It is this dimension that comes to the fore in God's self-differentiating identification with the crucified Jesus. Where death had all but won and all possibility had been extinguished, God intervened with new possibilities untethered to the deadly actuality. God brings life.

---

[4] *Mystery*, 323; *GGW* 442.

[5] *Mystery*, 322; *GGW* 441.

[6] "What does it mean to say, 'God is love'?" T. Hart and D. Thimell (eds), *Christ in our Place: The Humanity of God in Christ for the Reconciliation of the World. Essays Presented to Prof. James Torrance* (Exeter, UK: Paternoster, 1989), 310.

[7] *Mystery*, 322; *GGW* 441.

[8] "Value-Free Truth," *Essays II*, 209.

Jüngel, as I argued in Chapter 2, conflates these two dimensions. His entire cruciform construal of God's subjectivity – with its emphases on God's self-determination in time and on the radical otherness of Jesus – aims at the intersubjective openness of divine love. But Jügnel wishes also, in his consideration of the cross, to emphasize the spontaneity and creativity of divine love. Because he provides no articulation of the interrelation of these two aspects, the essential definition of love is all too easily swallowed up by the divine *propria*. Specifically, Jüngel displaces – from the lover to the beloved – love's death-to-self and the attendant reception of being. God's being, to be sure, is impacted by God's identification with the crucified Jesus: God now stands, as Son, over against God, as Father, and yet as Spirit binds together the Father and Son, in order, in this cruciform determinateness, to correspond to God's self. There is even, as I have also observed, a self-limitation on God's part, in that God withholds His power so as to become one, as Son, with the crucified man. All this is true and must be taken quite seriously. But one wonders whether this really is a self-surrender in which God "risks himself" for humanity, perhaps even without any anticipatory guarantee, and receives His being from humanity. It is difficult to see how God, in any real sense, exposes Himself to the possibility of nonbeing. What is quite certain – and this is what Jüngel ends up emphasizing – is that the expansiveness of death is checked, and the nothingness of a literally dead-ended human life is turned into new possibility. But what is this rather vaguely articulated possibility? Throughout God remains in full control of his determinateness. In the final reckoning, given Jüngel's effort to articulate God's being as intersubjective – as love, one is led to conclude that at the last, but absolutely crucial, step Jüngel unwittingly undermines his own position. He undermines it, when the emphasis on divine creativity actually offers ways of strengthening it, provided this creativity is thought through. As I suggested in Chapter 2, Jüngel's elucidation of God's cruciform self-determination is not so much a case of "a still greater selflessness in the midst of a great (and justifiably so) self-relatedness,"[9] as a case of a still greater self-relatedness in the midst of a great selflessness.[10]

---

[9] "Das Verhältnis von »ökonomischer« und »immanenter« Trinität," *TE II*, 270.

[10] Nicolas Klimek makes this point somewhat differently by hinting at the disregard for reciprocation that characterizes Jüngel's God: "What is involved in the self-externalization is at most an ecstatic agape, but never an eros, who is fascinated with the other" (*Der Gott, der Liebe ist: zur trinitarischen Auslegung des Begriffs "Liebe" bei Eberhard Jüngel* [Essen: Verlag Die Blaue Eule, 1986], 108).

The consequences of Jüngel's failure to theorize the two dimensions of God's being – its spontaneity and its capacity for intersubjective determinateness – are quite far reaching. Most immediately, as we have seen, it is the intersubjective determinateness entailed in God's being love that is adversely affected. It is absorbed by those attributes that express God's independence and self-relation. And yet the latent presence of intersubjective determinateness, subsumed under God's self-actualization, does eventually resurface. It makes itself known when Jüngel sets out to articulate God's independence. This time it is independence that suffers. Recall that Jüngel's location of God's self-determination in time forces him to account for God's independence in a twofold manner: as a subject who, out of Himself, becomes the event of cruciform love and as one who amidst his intersubjective determinateness retains His capacity for spontaneity and creativity. The issue, in other words, has to do with articulating the priority and simultaneity of divine independence vis-à-vis God's trinitarian self-determination at the cross. It is here that determinateness reappears with a vengeance and renders Jüngel's construal over-determined.

As he defines the nature of the subject who, in identifying with the dead Jesus, corresponds to himself, Jüngel does not even pause to consider, in a more focused fashion, God's spontaneity and creativity as the essence of divine independence. Instead, he indiscriminately transposes the entire event of love and God's triune self-differentiation into the subject's eternity and immanence. This done, it then becomes Jüngel's fear that this transposition may undermine God's freedom and grace by placing God under an inner compulsion. He, therefore, insists on the necessity of maintaining a merely *rational* distinction between God's trinitarian immanence and economy.

However, Jüngel overlooks a far more serious problem. The transposition so impacts God's self-correspondence that the *real* identity of God's trinitiarian immanence and economy is now understood as God's immanence having ontic priority over God's temporal determinateness. Let me be clear: I am not suggesting that somehow the immanent now constitutes a separate and self-contained aspect of God's being of which the economy is but a mere shadow. The temporal, to be sure, does constitute the one subject's real determinateness. But it is a determinateness within the parameters of God's immanence, commandeered by its own eternal anticipatedness in the structure of the subject's being. This renders Jüngel's claim much stronger than God's self-correspondence. It not only is about God's identification with the Crucified One not being out of character for God, but it is about ontological conservation. God is turned into a self-possessed and self-actualized subject whose temporal becoming proceeds strictly in accordance with the prior coordinates of his subjectivity. God's cruciform self-determination, when inscribed into God's eternity, is only trivial. The upshot of this is that no room is left for the intersubjectivity of love, or a genuine, even risk-fraught openness to and reception of being from another.

It is deeply ironic, as I noted earlier, that Jüngel's push to secure God's freedom from metaphysical confines, for the sake of none other than God's robustly relational, intersubjective self-determination in time, should in the end lapse into the Barthian schema of primary and secondary objectivity. This schema is far better suited to an incarnational understanding of God's subjectivity, whereby the subject's openness to another is determined in advance and directed by the subject himself. Here God is, first and foremost, the Lord. It bears repeating, against the stock Lutheran criticism of Barth, that the issue is not that history is emptied of salvific significance and that salvation drama has already played itself out in the eternity of God's being. Rather, the issue here is whether the cross, in its historical actuality, truly is the event of God's self-determination, such that, in face of the dead other, God is now intersubjective in his determinateness. Is the cross truly the event of God's *love*, whereby God enters into a reciprocal relationship with humanity? This is how, I believe, one should understand Michael Korthaus's warning: "Nothing less than Jüngel's entire doctrine of the Trinity depends on a genuine integration of the life and suffering of Jesus into the doctrine of God."[11] That is, one should understand it as a call not for the integration of the temporal in God's determinateness (that is not the problem) but as a call for the intersubjective character of God's determinateness. The credibility of divine love depends on this integration.

Freedom and love: Distancing divine creativity and love's self-surrender

Jüngel ultimately fails to arrive at a robustly cruciform construal of divine subjectivity despite his location of God's self-determination not only in time but also in God's identification with the crucified other. Jüngel's failure is predicated on the fact that, in his account of God's cruciform self-determination, he overlooks early on the distinction between that which pertains to the essence of love and that which constitutes the unique dimension of God's being love. He thus remains inattentive to the shift that

---

[11] Michael Korthaus, *Kreuzestheologie: Geschichte und Gehalt eines Programmbegriffs in der evangelischen Theologie* (Tübingen: Mohr Siebeck, 2007), 309.

occurs in his interpretation of the cross – a shift of focus from the reciprocity of love and its impact on the being of the lover (what might properly be termed the death of God) to the bestowal of being on the beloved (the dead Jesus). My contention here is that the failure of Jüngel's cruciform construal of divine subjectivity can be avoided by attending to the distinction between God's determinateness as an event of love, on the one hand, and the inalienable spontaneity and creativity of God's being, on the other. Those dimensions of God's being must not be conflated. Providing a coherent account of God's subjectivity will thus have to do, first of all, with establishing conceptual clarity. Ultimately, however, conceptual distinctions will seem only arbitrary unless they can be shown to have an ontological foundation, as well.

Let me tackle concepts first. It seems that, from a *formal* point of view, love and freedom, when it comes to God's being, remain indistinguishable, not to say tautological. So far I have spoken of Jüngel's overlooking the distinction between the essential aspect of God's love and this love's specifically divine dimension. I have also argued that, when confronted with the problem of the self-determining subject, Jüngel transposes God's entire determinateness, that is, all that pertains to God's being the event of love, into God's independence. And I have suggested in response that an account of divine independence must be more focused and concern itself only with the spontaneity and creativity of God's love. What is important to note here is that God's *love*, like *freedom*, has been shown to involve two moments: independence and determinateness. Recall that God's freedom, as was noted in Chapter 2, has to do not only with independence from any outer or inner compulsion but also concrete determinateness to be an event of love by relating to another. Jüngel tacitly acknowledges that love likewise consists in determinateness: "God is (to be sure) the one who involves himself in nothingness and as such is love"; but it also involves independence: "God is (however) love in and of himself and not only through the nothingness with which he involves himself."[12]

That love and freedom are formally indistinguishable is corroborated by the fact that whether Jüngel speaks of freedom or love seems to be determined largely by the context. He discusses God's freedom and its two abstract moments when he engages the metaphysical tradition. His goal is to establish and secure God's subjectivity in revelation. He also, to be sure, acknowledges freedom's importance as a necessary correlate of love. For the most part, however, his focus remains on God's love as

---

[12] *Mystery*, 221; *GGW* 301.

sufficient to do justice to God's being (with the distinction between love's intersubjectivity and divine love's *propria* playing little role in his account). Jüngel's concentration on love stems, I believe, from his identification of the cross as the locale that makes God certain – both thinkable and speakable. It stems also from the ontological grounding of love in God's being that characterizes the Western theological tradition: God is love, in that the Father is related to the Son in the Spirit, who, as the bond of love, proceeds from both. Finally, it is grounded in his affirmation of the distinction between immanent and economic Trinity as a distinction in thought alone.

I have, for the most part, tacitly acknowledged this formal coincidence of freedom and love. The question is, however: Should freedom and love be distinguished? Jüngel insists that one must "think God's love as freedom, but also . . . think his freedom in no other way than love."[13] In this he follows in the footsteps of Karl Barth, who asserted famously that God is "the one who loves in freedom"[14] – although Barth does differentiate between God's freedom and love by categorizing the divine perfections as more properly belonging to one or to the other. The point here is not to deny the supreme closeness of freedom and love. That they ought to be thought together is an indispensable insight. But I wish to identify this togetherness precisely as closeness, and then clarify the relation without collapsing either of the relata into the other in a tautological manner.

For all the formal coincidence of love and freedom in Jüngel's theology, I have shown that there are aspects of God's subjectivity that – on the *conceptual* level – more properly belong to divine freedom or divine love. Take God's ability to be in relation and to receive being from another. As we have seen, this dimension could be regarded as the determinateness of divine freedom, insofar as freedom is the opposite of self-possession and self-actualization, and insofar as love, in order to be love, must be set in freedom. But there is little doubt that this dimension of God's being is more properly described as simply love. By contrast, spontaneity and creativity could be regarded as an expression of love, insofar as true freedom is freedom from the self and for another, and insofar as it is out of love that God comes into nothingness so as to engender new possibilities within it. But there is little doubt that a more proper designation for this aspect of God's being is freedom, because it implies independence from actuality, including the transcendence of one's own self. In sum, the determinateness

---

[13] *Mystery*, 221; *GGW* 301.
[14] *CD* II/1, 257 *et passim.*

of God's being is more properly correlated with love, whereas independence is to be correlated with freedom.

This means that, as long as we acknowledge that there are two focal points in God's subjectivity: independence and determinateness, we must also recognize freedom and love as two distinct dimensions of God's being. My argument thus far has been in favor of nontrivially differentiating between independence and determinateness. I have argued that the ambiguity and incoherence of Jüngel's doctrine of God, as well as its contradiction of Jüngel's conception of human freedom, all stem from the fact that Jüngel does not *in practice* distinguish between independence and determinateness. He assigns the same ontological content to both. As a result, he does not move beyond the formal coincidence of freedom and love, and his preference for one term over the other depends wholly on the context.

I, by contrast, with to suggest that freedom and love, for all their closeness and necessary relatedness, are to be differentiated. They represent two distinct, yet mutually informing and indispensable *dimensions of God's being*, rather than two different contextual lenses through which God's being can be seen. The distinction, in other words, is not a matter of more or less proper categorization of attributes, or, as one might say uncharitably, logomachy. If it is only that, it will not forestall *actual* conflation of distinct aspects of God's being, and it will in the end produce an incoherent picture of God's freedom, as well as rendering divine love ambiguous. This said, we must, therefore, inquire into the ontological manifestation of this distinction. Is there such a thing? Are freedom and love ontologically distinct? And if so, what is the order of being corresponding to each?

To show that a distinction between freedom and love is, in fact, ontologically viable, I shall first take up the being of the elementally interrupted person. Jüngel's construal of it demonstrates quite clearly the ontological difference between love and freedom. As elementally interrupted, it will be recalled, the person corresponds to God. On the basis of this correspondence, I shall eventually propose how God's subjectivity is to be construed in its dual aspect of spontaneity and creativity, on the one hand, and the reception of being in love, on the other.

Freedom and love: The human person in correspondence to God

Two acts of existence

The elemental interruption, as I showed in Chapter 3, does not exhaust itself in an experience, a subjective self-perception. It is, to be sure, accompanied by a dimension of crisis; this, in turn, is followed by faith – a relational sort of certainty, rooted not in self-securing but in trust. However, the elemental interruption also has consequences that pertain to the very being of the person. Those fall into two categories, representing, as it were, two acts of existence: the person *is* and, at the same time, *becomes*. It is these two ontological aspects of an interrupted existence that we must examine here.

It will be recalled that self-securing cannot, according to Jüngel, produce a discrete identity; it rather distorts one's being into shapelessness. The reason for this is that self-securing, as a quest for super-humanity, even divinity (or what is understood as such), is a quest that is perpetually thwarted by the impingement of the world upon one's fragile being. One cannot overcome this impingement either by securing oneself against the world or by making the world absolutely safe and secure for oneself. Freedom lies neither in subjecting the world to one's will nor in subjective detachment from the world. In ontological terms, one cannot turn the self-relation into the exclusive relation, or turn relations to others into its modalities. Even the Kantian route, though it restricts the scope of self-possession to rationality, simultaneously establishes rationality's boundaries and requires faith as a condition *sine qua non* for self-possession. Yet precisely because of the hiddenness of faith's object, it throws one back, and with a vengeance, onto incessant self-realization. The individual is never free from pressing toward an ever-receding horizon. The restlessness and relentlessness of the imperative to self-realization render one's self-relation trivial; it becomes suspended in inconclusiveness. And this triviality is only reinforced, as one comes under the "dictatorship of the imperative, which people receive in part from others, and in part give to themselves."[15] One begins to be tyrannized by one's past, one's works, be they good or bad, and by values by means of which one's doing is judged. Past works inflect one's present doing, and actuality spirals into echoing sameness.

By contrast, as elementally interrupted, the person is given an identity that transcends human action and comes to rest in God's. One is "irrevocably affirmed and recognized."[16] This recognition transposes one "out of [one's] *activities* into a very lively, very intensive, indeed highly *creative passivity*"; one comes to inhabit "the oasis of the indicative."[17] The givenness of one's identity manifests itself in the emergence of the person as separate from works. And it manifests itself in the person's being separate from God,

---

[15] "On Becoming Truly Human. The Significance of the Reformation Distinction between Person and Works for the Self-Understanding of Modern Humanity," *Essays II*, 238.
[16] "Hoffen, Handeln – und Leiden," *BR*, 24.
[17] "On Becoming Truly Human," *Essays II*, 238.

insofar as one no longer feels compelled to overcome one's humanity but in it comes to enjoy God's unconditional affirmation. God's recognition exceeds the sum total of even the best works.

Jüngel makes it clear that being elementally interrupted involves an actual distance to self. The totalizing self-relation is burst apart. More than that, it is burst apart in a particular fashion. In elementally interrupting the continuity of one's being, God comes closer to one that one is able to come to oneself. "[O]ne is . . . taken away from oneself."[18] Through faith one comes to participate in God Himself. This means that the poles of one's self-relation become distinguished. They are no longer trivial – mere mirror images of each other. Rather, there is now the inner and the outer human who relate to each other indirectly. "Self-differentiation as the implication of identification with another is . . . the expression of the fact that that other profoundly defines my own being from outside of myself. That other one steps between me and me, so to speak."[19] One relates to oneself only insofar as God first relates to one. One, first and foremost, receives being, and thus one is "constituted from outside the self."[20]

What is crucial to note here is that, as free, the human is a tri-polar being, with God's relation to one constituting the first, most important aspect of the self. It is in this tri-polarity – as a human in relation to God – that the person *is*. "In love, *having*, because it is inherently also a *being had*, becomes a *being*."[21] This is the person's identity. But it is an identity of a peculiar sort. Yes, it consists in liberation from the tyrannous vacuity of the ego. It consists in the celebration of one's humanity. But it also consists in sharing in God's freedom. Participation in God, as I have noted, is participation in that which is more than necessary. By participating in God, one comes to share in God's creativity, in the possibilities untethered to the frequently dead-ended actuality. Therefore, the free person, precisely as human, is "infinitely bounded."[22] One is a creature of openness – not only as elementally interrupted in the continuity of one's being but also as a person who can now "begin something with oneself and one's world."[23] Because one *is*, one can now also *become*.

---

[18] *FoC,* 82.
[19] *Mystery,* 363; *GGW* 498. Jüngel considers the distinction between the outer and inner self to have a primary function and to be of ultimate significance; the distinction is indispensable, even if the terms themselves are not appropriated; see *FoC,* 67.
[20] *FoC,* 61.
[21] *Mystery,* 391; *GGW* 537.
[22] "Grenzen des Menschseins," *TE II,* 360.
[23] "The Emergence of the New," *Essays II,* 57.

The free person's becoming is not the opposite of action but is the "wildest activity."[24] As such, however, it is to be differentiated from the becoming associated with self-realization. Now that the world and especially fellow humans are no longer regarded as a threat to the integrity of one's being, one can allow the world to come close to one in its own otherness. One can allow oneself to be interrupted. As a matter of fact, one actually anticipates this interruption by going beyond one's self "to now oppose in a human way the lovelessness in this world with deeds of love."[25] As Luther puts it, one "descends ... into [one's] neighbor."[26] In other words, the becoming associated with the elemental interruption has to do not with preemptively striking against the world but with self-surrender and affirming the world in its otherness. It has to do with being there for others, for their sake subjecting oneself to nothingness, and finding oneself in that.[27] Becoming is love.

The implications of this becoming, I believe, are even more specific. It involves assumption of responsibility for the world in concrete social and vocational relationships. Note that one unconditionally affirms others, for their own sake, only in specific situations. This affirmation is none other than the opening up of new possibilities – above all, the possibility of liberation. As *unconditional* affirmation, love is always liberating. Hence, the granting of freedom inevitably performs a differentiating function: It brings to light what is possible and what is impossible. And so, as one penetrates into the concreteness of a given actuality and comes closer to it than it can come to itself, one is called to social and vocational responsibility. In this task, one may find oneself where one least expects to be – ever called to become, ever called to express one's love through the liberation of fellow humans and care for the world.

Still, the possibilities that God brings into human existence are fully actualized not merely in the unfolding of human relationality but, above all, in the flourishing of actual relationships. God, as Creator, is the inexhaustible fount of possibility. But its actualization is never individualistic; rather, it takes place within horizontal relationships. One naturally hopes that the other will reciprocate one's becoming-for-the-other's-sake. For one, too, wishes to be unconditionally recognized. One hopes that, in freedom, the neighbor will affirm one in the concreteness of the identities one has assumed for the other's sake. In short, in one's self-surrender on another's behalf, one wishes likewise to be granted being. God's creativity is one of

---

[24] *FoC*, 83.
[25] "What does it mean to say, 'God is love'?" 310.
[26] *The Freedom of a Christian*, *LW* 31:371; *WA* 7:69.
[27] *Mystery*, 219–20; *GGW* 298.

love, and it finds its perfection in human love. The essence of love, in each and every relation, is reciprocity.[28]

One's works of love, as we have observed, have the capacity to liberate others. Hence, God's elemental interruption gives rise to a relational structure that transcends the individual: being liberated expresses itself in love, which liberates another for love, which liberates, etc. Personal wholeness, bestowed through God's relationship to the person, brings about a togetherness, a community which is held together through the self-giving and mutual affirmation of its members.

As can be seen, the elemental interruption, as well as the relationality it gives rise to, is characterized by two distinct, yet inseparable and mutually informing acts of existence. One is passive; the other is active. The former consists in being liberated, when one, in faith, recognizes oneself as embraced by God's event of love at the cross. This act establishes the person's identity as independent from the tyranny of the person's own self. As such, it is not only a participation in, but also a communication of, divine freedom. Distanced from one's self, one comes to share in the infinite possibilities of God's being.[29] The elementally interrupted person is characterized by spontaneity and creativity. The other act, then, consists in the exercise of this creative spontaneity through works of self-giving. In one's God-given identity – in one's freedom – one can allow oneself to be concretely determined for the sake of another and by another. What is important to note here is that the two acts are not discontinuous. Rather, the free person, as a loving agent, *corresponds* to his or her *identity-in-God.*

Taken together, the two acts can be considered from the perspective of either freedom or love. The act of being elementally interrupted, however, is more properly categorized as freedom, which, as freedom from the self, naturally brings about the self-surrender for another's sake; whereas the act of self-surrender is more properly categorized as love, which would not be love if the self-surrender did not flow out of freedom. Formally, then, the being of the elementally interrupted person as a *totus homo* can be described as either freedom or love, both consisting in a moment of independence

---

[28] That recognition will be given to one and one's self-giving reciprocated is by no means a foregone conclusion. It is for this reason that Luther identified the cross as a mark of the Christian life. Luther writes: "the holy Christian people are externally recognized by the holy possession of the sacred cross. They must endure every misfortune and persecution, all kinds of trials and evil from the devil, the world, and the flesh... They must be pious, quiet, obedient, and prepared to serve the government and everybody with life and goods, doing no one any harm. ... *No one has compassion on them*" (*On the Councils and the Church* [1539], *LW* 41:164–5; *WA* 50:641–2, emphasis added).

[29] Luther, though with a more narrowly soteriological focus, speaks of the communication of divine omnipotence to the believer. See *The Freedom of a Christian, LW* 31:355; *WA* 7:57.

and intersubjective determinateness. Yet neither freedom nor love can be collapsed into the other without being compromised.

Self-correspondence: The ontology of the person

What is of particular interest to us here is the ontology of the person in both of these acts. In both the person is a relational being, but differently in each.

First, as elementally interrupted, the person, as we have noted, is a tri-polar subject: The person relates to his or her self only insofar as God is present in the person's self-relation and first relates to the person. The person is independent and free, as his or her self-relation is no longer trivial and threatened by the world's impingement but imbued with the most creative possibility.

Second, as one who, on account of one's freedom, affirms another rather than oneself – the person is not only a *self-differentiated* but an *intersubjective* being. The person surrenders his or her self for another's sake. That is, in an act of love the person assumes a socio-vocational role and becomes a doer of works for this other's sake. To put it more precisely, one can speak here of the person's self-withdrawal, accomplished insofar as the inner self has its being in God, and the person's simultaneous identification of his or her self – that is, the self's active, outer dimension – with the other. Jüngel acknowledges this withdrawal of the self when he writes: "The event of love is the most intensive event of self-withdrawal [*Selbstentzogenheit*] and of new and creative self-relatedness [*Selbstbezogenheit*]."[30] What needs to be underscored more strongly is that the new self-relatedness that emerges can only be intersubjective. The person trusts that the love that motivates his or her self-surrender will so free that other that he or she will, in turn, likewise affirm the person in his or her self-giving. Each act of love is performed, as it were, from the horizon of being anticipated by the other's reciprocity – not in the sense of *do ut des* but in the conviction that "love . . . is as strong

---

[30] *Mystery*, 391; *GGW* 537. The idea expressed here, it may be useful to add, has its precedent in Luther. In his treatise, *The Freedom of a Christian*, Luther both articulates the logic of one's vocational identification with the neighbor and grounds this logic in the capacity of Christ, according to his *human* nature, to become our servant, precisely on account of His human nature residing in the very form of God (cf. Philippians 2). Luther writes: "I will therefore give myself as a Christ to my neighbor, just has Christ offered himself to me; I will do nothing in this life except where I see is necessary, profitable, and salutary to my neighbor, since through faith I have an abundance of all good things in Christ. ... [T]he good things we have from God should flow from one to the other and be common to all, so that *everyone should 'put on' his neighbor and so conduct himself toward him as if he himself were in the other's place*" (*LW* 31:367, 371; *WA* 7:66, 69; emphasis added).

as death and thus stronger."[31] Love makes one into a being of hope in the certainty that love does bring freedom.

Earlier I drew attention to the *self*-correspondence of the person in these two distinct, yet inseparable existential acts of freedom and love. To recognize this correspondence is to affirm the conceptual continuity of freedom and love, while assuring that there is a logical pause between them. What our ontological consideration of the elementally interrupted person has shown is that this logical pause is, in fact, ontological in character. There first takes place a withdrawal of the self to God, whereby the subject is established as tri-polar. This then enables the ecstatic self-identification with the beloved, whereby the outer self surrenders itself for the sake of the beloved so that a new relational reality might come into being through the beloved's participation. One can now appreciate not only *that* but also *how* one's independence as a subject does not stand in opposition to one's intersubjectivity.

Jüngel only in passing mentions the *self*-correspondence of the elementally interrupted person.[32] I emphasize it here, because it will help us clarify the subjective, ontological nature of God's self-correspondence in the event of the cross. This clarification will become possible, however, only because of the even more fundamental fact that the elementally interrupted person, first and foremost, corresponds to God.

Correspondence to God

The correspondence is established by God's Word of address to which the person responds with faith. God speaks (*Gott spricht*) – the human co-responds (*der Mensch entspricht*). Jüngel explains this as follows:

> The essence of faith is the speech event of faith in which God speaks [*spricht*] and the human co-responds [*entspricht*] to God's speech. God speaks as the one who called the crucified Jesus into life and now calls the human into life. The human co-responds to the speech of God by confessing the dead Jesus as the living Lord and, faced with the crucified Jesus, follows him into life. This is faith's abundance.

---

[31] *Mystery*, 392; *GGW* 538. Cf. Song of Solomon 6:8.
[32] His focus is on the bare fact (the *that* rather than the *how*) of a nontrivial relation of the inner and outer self, which makes correspondence, as such, possible in the first place; see *FoC*, 64–5.

What is initially a fact of address, becomes, through the elemental interruption, a fact of being. In faith's abundance, a response becomes a correspondence.[33]

I have thus far drawn attention to humans' correspondence to God under the rubric of participation in, and communication of, God's freedom. But participation and communication are none other than the correspondence of the human subject, in one of the person's existential acts, to the subjectivity of God. They can be correlated as follows. Participation is the human counterpart of God's elementally interrupting identification with humanity as the event of love. Communication is the event in which the human beloved becomes a lover descending into the neighbor. Jüngel himself notes, albeit with less clarity, the elementally interrupted person corresponds to God both as lover and beloved.[34]

It ought to be clear by now that humans do not simply correspond to God by virtue of the bare fact of their relationality, by simply desisting from self-actualization. Jüngel points out that human relationality unfolds itself analogically to God's relationality. But the correspondence, as I claim here more specifically, extends also to the ontological structure of human relationality. This is the dimension that Jüngel largely overlooks, and which is of particular interest for the project at hand. Thus, I argue that being in the image of God (*imago dei*) has the twofold sense of agreement in mode of being and being's structure, so to speak.

Let me, first, comment on relationality as such. Humans correspond to God, Jüngel argues, in the very mode of their relational existence. Just as God corresponds to God's self by identifying with the dead Jesus, so also humans, embraced in God's cruciform act of affirmation, correspond to God by affirming fellow humans. In other words, God's relation to humanity gives rise to relations between humans, which as its counterparts are also embedded within it and propelled by it.[35] The elementally interrupted person thus becomes a partner of God.[36] He or she is not only a considerate agent who initiates and brings into being – who makes a difference. More specifically, the free person's actions become "parables of the kingdom of

---

[33] "Theologische Wissenschaft und Glaube," *TE I*, 26; see also Jüngel's essay, "Humanity in Correspondence to God. Remarks on the Image of God as a Basic Concept in Theological Anthropology," *Essays I*.

[34] *Mystery*, 392; *GGW* 538.

[35] Jüngel discerns a more complex, election-centered chain of correspondences in Barth's *Church Dogmatics*; see his "Die Möglichkeit theologischer Anthropologie auf dem Grunde der Analogie," *Barth-Studien* (Zürich: Benziger Verlag, 1982), 225.

[36] "Zum Wesen des Friedens," *TE V*, 37.

God on earth."[37] Jüngel writes: "Everything which serves love makes man more human, brings man further along the way of becoming a humanity which corresponds to God."[38]

Correspondence is here none other than an analogy of relation (*analgia relationis*), which Jüngel has learned from Barth. It preserves the distinction between God and humans and, in doing so, creates a sphere in which human activity is indeed indispensable. It assures that human liberation of fellow humans for communal togetherness is truly a human work, which, only as such, must be said to have its impetus in and give expression to God's work in elementally interrupting the continuity of human being. More to this below.

The other type of correspondence – which is also analogical, but which Jüngel does not consider – is the *ontological* correspondence of the *totus homo* to God. Human love and freedom, like God's, consist, as I have shown, of two formal moments of independence and determinateness. In the case of the elementally interrupted person, these moments are rooted in what clearly are two ontologically distinct, yet intimately interrelated acts of existence: one subjective, the other intersubjective. All this is quite different from Jüngel's attempt, in the doctrine of God, to transpose the structure of love into God's freedom. What is, however, present in Jüngel's doctrine of God (though only as an abstract notion), and what we have also uncovered in his anthropological construal, is the self-correspondence of the subject in love and freedom. Ontologically speaking, human correspondence to God, as we have observed, hides within itself a self-correspondence of the person that parallels God's self-correspondence. As interrupted by God and thus a tri-polar being sharing in God's possibilities, the person actualizes his or her identity by surrendering his or her self in love for another, by effectively allowing another to actualize it. The self-differentiated person is able, through a withdrawal of his or her self, to give his or her self away. The anthropological reality of this self-correspondence shows that, even if love and freedom were founded on two distinct ontological acts of existence, those acts need not be discontinuous.

These two facts – first, of the differentiated ontological underpinnings of human freedom and love and, second, of the self-correspondence of the person in these two differentiated structures of being – lend support to our conviction that Jüngel's doctrine of God requires an ontological elaboration of divine freedom as distinct from God's being the event of trine love. Only such an explicit ontological formulation can prevent freedom and love from undermining each other as the theologian tries to do justice to both. To do justice to God's being both freedom and love, we must thus go beyond

---

[37] "My Theology," *Essays II*, 16.
[38] *Mystery*, 392; *GGW* 538.

a mere formal specification of freedom and love as independence and determinateness, underwritten by one and the same structure of being. This said, we must now finally inquire into what the trinitarian logic of freedom should look like.

The Logic of Freedom

As the vehicle of God's spontaneity and creativity, the logic of freedom, I submit, has a trinitarian structure. It is trinitarian, however, in a manner distinct from God's trinitarian self-determination at the cross. In what follows I shall outline this structure. My original contention was that, despite Jüngel's intersubjective construal of divine love, love's reciprocity is unexpectedly (though inevitably, given the single underlying ontological structure) swallowed up by divine independence in Jüngel's doctrine of God. In this light, the purpose of the logic of freedom is twofold. It gives expression to God's inalienable spontaneity and creativity, which Jüngel rightly does not wish to surrender. At the same time, however, the logic of freedom makes possible the mutual bestowal of being within the divine-human relationship. It, so to speak, enables the trinitarian logic of love. In short, God's freedom and God's love will be shown in what follows to be centered in two distinct structures of subjectivity that, for all their distinctiveness, remain mutually indispensable, with love corresponding to freedom and freedom reinforcing love.

Freedom's triunity

The elemental interruption and God's tri-polar subjectivity

The human person who has been elementally interrupted in the continuity of his or her being becomes, as we have noted, self-differentiated in a tri-polar fashion. The third pole, which interrupts the person's self-relation, is constituted by none other than God, who as Son is identical with the crucified Jesus. The self-relation undergoes this self-differentiation when the elementally interrupted person believes that in Jesus' humanity his or her own humanity is likewise embraced by God and unconditionally affirmed. Importantly, the human person is this tri-polar – and thus free – being only as related to God, who overcomes the person's totalizing self-relation. I have emphasized God's decisive role before by speaking of the free person as, first and foremost, liberated.

In the case of God, by contrast, freedom simply belongs to God's being. God can begin something with God's self – be spontaneous and creative – out of God's self. This means that God's being is inherently tri-polar, rather than self-absorbed and trivial in a di-polar fashion. God's self-relation is a naturally open self-relation and as such is the source of inexhaustible possibility. Jüngel hints at a subjective structure of this sort when he insists that "in that God is, he is already beyond himself. And in precisely that, he is God."[39] In a manner of speaking (and only so!) God exists then in what seems like an eternally interrupted self-relation. It is to this divine tri-polarity that the interrupted human self-relation must correspond. No less than such subjective correspondence can make the communication of divine freedom to the person a reality.

What we have just done is indicate, on the basis of human correspondence to God, the kind of self-relation that, above all, characterizes divine freedom. Now we must turn to the divine subject to provide this tri-polarity with specific content. As we do so, we must keep in mind that the subject – in his cruciform intersubjective determinateness – actually *corresponds* to himself. Freedom's tri-polarity, which we are seeking to specify, actually reinforces the intersubjectivity of God's love. We should, therefore, turn to the subject's determinateness for the specification of freedom's tri-polarity as divine.

God's self-correspondence

The easiest way to provide the tri-polar structure of freedom with content would be to copy God's determinateness as love and, on the basis of God's self-correspondence, to transpose it into the divine subject's determinateness. This, as I showed in Chapter 2, is exactly what Jüngel does. The result is an over-determination of divine independence, which, in turn, undermines the reality of God's intersubjective being. The reciprocity of love is reduced to a function of the subject's self-actualization. Freedom swallows up love. And Jüngel's doctrine of God becomes fraught with ambiguity and contradictoriness. The irony, as we have observed, is that the very temporal self-determination of God, which was to underscore the robust character of God's love, is what in the end threatens to subvert this very love by demanding an account of the subject's independence.

How then are we to construe the tri-polarity of the subject's independence in such a way that it precedes, accompanies and, not least, translates itself into God's determinateness as love, without undermining the latter? To answer this question, let us begin with what I shall call here the logic of love – the specific trinitarian relationality through which God determines God's self as love.

---

[39] *Mystery*, 222; *GGW* 302.

On the face of it, Jüngel's construal of love's trinitarian logic represents the understanding of God's triune being that has predominated in Western theology and dates at least as far back as Augustine. This understanding is enshrined in the *filoque*, the distinctly Western assertion of the procession of the Spirit from the Father and the Son as "the common charity by which the Father and the Son love each other."[40] However, Jüngel's assertion that God *determines* God's self as triune and does so *in time* introduces a *novum*. According to Jüngel, God becomes determinate as the event of love at the cross, by identifying God's self with the crucified Jesus. In this identification, God defines God's self as the Father and Son, who despite their maximal opposition are bound together by the Spirit of love. As observed, Jüngel's move is motivated by his desire in part to oppose the trajectory of Western metaphysics and in part to give expression to what Jüngel understands as the early Christian *kerygma*. But fundamentally it is motivated by his desire to do justice to God's being love – to allow for intersubjectivity that transcends the self-relatedness of the divine subject and for the elevation of the human, in love, to partnership with God. It is because of this latter concern that the Augustinian construct undergoes a modification. As I noted in Chapter 2, the relationship between the Father and the Son is, according to Jüngel, one in which God limits God's self, limits his freedom, for the sake of love. Self-differentiated in the face of the crucified Jesus, God withdraws as Father, so that as Son He might be united with the dead man; yet, in this maximal opposition, God as Spirit makes possible the self-correspondence of God in his identity with Jesus. What was a withholding of divine power becomes an eruption of divine life.

What we see here closely parallels the self-correspondence of the elementally interrupted person in the two existential acts. The person's *inner self* is withdrawn into God. This makes possible the nontrivial determination of the *outer self* by another, who can now step in and concretely differentiate me from my own self. One identifies (*identifizieren*) oneself with the other in one's outer self, allowing the other profoundly to define one's own being from outside the self. The identification takes place for the other's sake and, as I have stressed with particular care, in the hope that this other will affirm and reciprocate one's self-giving and thus return one's being in a loving togetherness. But the unity of the lover with the beloved does not hinge on the prior assurance of such reciprocation: love does not first calculate the odds in order to be loving. For this reason, Jüngel simply

---

[40] Augustine, *The Trinity*, trans. Edmund Hill, O.P. (Hyde Park, NY: New City Press, 1991), 418 [Bk. XV, Ch. 5]. Cf. *Mystery*, 388; *GGW* 532.

[41] *Mystery*, 363; *GGW* 498.

(and somewhat unreflectively) assumes the lover's unity with the beloved. He contends that "one does not have to be in disunity with oneself in order to be quite unified [*ganz einig*] with another person."[41] Though Jüngel's focus in this comment is on the absence of subjective disunity, we must keep in mind that all the while the determination of the outer self by another is nothing but the actualization of the possibilities that inhere in the elementally interrupted self-relation, where the self has been differentiated into the inner and outer and where one's freedom from oneself has its locale.

What does this mean for the logic of freedom we are trying to establish? If the human self is so interrupted that, in the differentiation that ensues, the inner assures that there is no self-abandonment, no renunciation of one's fundamental human identity – then, when we read God's self-determination through this lens, it must mean that the inner corresponds to the Father. In more conventional trinitarian language, the Father is the source of God's triune life, the eternal "*fons et principium divinitatis et omnium rerum.*"[42] The outer then – as determined by, and in unity with, another – corresponds to the Son. The mode of Sonship is God's determination for Jesus's sake. (In what sense we have to do here also with reciprocal affirmation is still for us to establish.) What is of immediate interest to us is how these modes of God's being, revealed in God's cruciform determinateness as *love*, are represented in the tri-polarity of God's *freedom*. To invoke the human analogy again, what is the trinitarian structure of freedom to which there corresponds the elementally interrupted human self-relation?

The only answer to this question seems to be that the trinitarian logic of freedom has the form of the Father's fundamental relation to the Spirit which is, as it were, eternally interrupted by the Son. Put differently, the triune logic of freedom posits and shows that there is a fundamental relationship between the Father, as origin, and the Spirit, as "goal" of God's being.[43] This relationship is, or rather would be, self-referential in nature, but it exists eternally only as interrupted and re-directed by the presence of that mode of divine subjectivity which, for Jesus' sake, is revealed as the Son. The logic of freedom thus indicates that there is in God a capacity for love and, further, for genuine creaturely interruption, because from eternity to eternity,

---

[42] Cf. "Nemo contra deum nisi deus ipse: Zum Verhältnis von theologia crucis und Trinitätslehre," *TE V*, 252.

[43] Note that Jüngel ordinarily speaks of the Son as the goal of the Father (e.g., *Mystery*, 382ff; *GGW* 524ff), since for Jüngel the only ontological structure in the Trinity is the logic of love.

from origin to goal, God's being does not have the form of a di-polar self-relation aimed at self-maintenance but is rather a triune self-transcendence. God is free even with regard to his own freedom, free from the compulsive preservation of his freedom. This makes God a living subject, one that can go into otherness and bring its livingness with it. In brief, God's being in freedom is such that God inclines to define the other not by God's own goal, God's future (a fundamentally self-related subject), but rather to define God's own future by the other (a subject open to self-differentiation and inter-subjectivity).[44] Or, to put it in terms of established trinitarian conceptualities, *in the logic of divine freedom the Spirit proceeds from the Father but does so only through the Logos, the creative word that God speaks out of God's self.*[45]

Before I enlarge on this logic and its relationship to the logic of love, it must be briefly noted here that Jüngel, for his part, speaks of God's coming from God, to God and as God.[46] This complex assertion constitutes his own, more robustly relational restatement of the Augustinian logic of love. God comes from God – as Father, to God – as Son, and as God – that is, as Spirit, who as the chain of love (*vinculum caritatis*) binds the Father and the Son together. God comes in such a way that temporality plays a constitutive a role in his coming. However, Jüngel's elaboration of this construal suffers from the same ambiguity as his doctrine of God in general. What Jüngel ostensibly wishes to convey is the logic of love, but any reciprocity or threat of nonbeing seems to be excluded even as a mere possibility. There is to be sure relationality, even a relation to an other, but is all submerged in the even greater self-relatedness (self-coming) of the divine subject. Now, it may be possible to read Jüngel's' trinitarian construct as an expression of the logic of freedom. He writes: "God is eternally his own goal . . . wherever he goes, he always comes to God." Jüngel explains further that God "is as goal distinct from himself as origin,"[47] even though he "does not leave himself as origin behind."[48] These statements may be interpreted as affirmations of God's being the inexhaustible fount of possibility who, as one who is always in coming, prevails even over nothingness yet does so for another's, rather than his own, sake. That something akin to the logic of freedom is indeed implied in Jüngel's construal is supported by the fact that

---

[44] I borrow this notion, though with considerable freedom, from Immanuel Lévinas' *Time and the Other* (1947). Cf. Seán Hand (ed.), *The Levinas Reader* (Oxford: Basil Blackwell, 1989), 47.

[45] The echo of the traditional Eastern construal of the Spirit's procession, as opposed to the Western model, is quite deliberate.

[46] *Mystery*, 380–9; *GGW* 521–34.

[47] *Mystery*, 383; *GGW* 525.

[48] *Mystery*, 380; *GGW* 521.

God's coming to God's self at the cross forms the basis, as *analogans*, for the elementally interrupted person's renewed relationship to the world, as *analogatum*. In other words, God's coming to Jesus in an act of love liberates one for a loving relationship to the world.[49] However, if the logic of freedom is indeed implied here, then we shall still have an incomplete depiction of God's subjectivity, because the focus rests on God's spontaneity and creativity. God's being is in coming – in this liberating act God *is*; but there seems to be no corresponding act of *becoming*. Love, in the robust sense of reciprocal togetherness, remains conspicuously absent.

My claim here is that, *where God's revelation is concerned,* God's being exhibits two subjective structures. Just as the elementally interrupted human being exists in two distinct acts, so does God in God's revelation. These ontological structures, corresponding to both creative spontaneity and love, must, therefore, be accounted for in order to do justice to God's subjectivity. What follows is an account of the subjective interrelation of freedom and love. I shall develop it by, first, speaking to three issues which are also potential objections. The first concerns the question of determinateness, the second God's self-realization through temporal self-determination, and the third the logic of freedom's self-sufficient character. This discussion will then be a springboard for further elucidation of freedom's distinctive role within God's subjectivity.

Determinateness

With God's freedom specified as the originary relational openness, whereby the Spirit proceeds from the Father but does so only through the Logos, it may seem that we are detracting from God's determinateness as love. After all, I have maintained all along that it is in the event of love that, by identifying God's self with the crucified Jesus, God defines God's self as Father, Son, and Spirit. In addition, I have repeatedly pointed out that Jüngel's doctrine of God becomes contradictory, in part, when he transposes God's triunity from love into independence; he is thereby able to account for the temporally self-determining subject but at the cost of effectively undermining divine love in its temporal dimension. In order to clarify this issue, we need to ask about the triunity of freedom in relation to that of love, as well as whether it can in any way be regarded as (and so confused with) God's cruciform determinateness.

---

[49] For Jüngel's extended discussion of what he terms "the analogy of advent," see *Mystery*, 281–98; *GGW* 383–408.

To begin with, it should be noted that what gives rise to confusion in Jüngel's doctrine of God is not so much the transposition of God's triunity as the transposition, more specifically, of the triune logic of love into God's freedom. There is, as I pointed out in Chapter 2, a legitimate way of conceptualizing God's freedom as triune, prior to, and alongside of, God's trinitarian self-determination at the cross. But there are two caveats: first, this conceptualization cannot be merely a matter of predication concealing the same ontological structure, or else freedom and love will both become ambiguous; and second, this conceptualization must let love be love and center rather on the divine *propria*, spontaneity and creativity. When one takes those into account, it turns out that no transposition is actually necessary. Only a subject whose self-relatedness is tri-polar is a free subject who can then determine him- or herself through a reciprocal relation with another. Only a tri-polar subject has the capacity to interrupt others' totalizing self-relation. No human being is such a subject out of him- or herself. Only God is. Thus, only God can in freedom determine God's self as love and through this love free creatures who are hopelessly mired in themselves. The bottom line, then, is that there is in God an original triunity of sorts, a triunity that belongs to the divine subject prior to his cruciform self-determination. It factors, as we have seen, into the subject's self-determination, in that the poles of this triune self reconfigure in a logic of love yet do so in accordance with their original openness. It is this triunity – the original, exclusive and vital freedom of God – that needs to be conceptualized in itself.

Jüngel actually suggests that there may be an originary structure to God's being, distinct from God's self-determination as an event of love, when he puts forth his mediating proposal for an inner motivation that leads God, without any inner necessity, to a cruciform self-determination. But motivation is simply too vague a concept. It may help dispel the shadow of a Hegelian inner necessity but not quite that of the subject's development. Unlike the over-determination through transposition of the logic of love, it leaves God's freedom under-specified. Who is the subject of this gracious motivation? Does this motivation give way to relationality? More promising is Jüngel's use of the term "modes of being" (*Seinsweisen*), which he takes over from Barth. It is Barth's preferred way of referring to the trinitarian *hypostases*, in order to rule out their misunderstanding as persons in the modern sense of an autonomous personality. In Jüngel's case, the term *may* be taken to imply the subject's self-relatedness, what I have called here the logic of freedom, prior to God's intersubjective self-determination at the cross. Jüngel writes, for example: "The death of Jesus Christ . . . forced a

differentiation between God and God. . . [T]he *divine modes of being*, Father
and Son, which in this death *separated* into such a great differentiation than
which nothing greater can be imagined, now so differentiated related to
each other anew: *in the Holy Spirit.*"[50] However, this construal also seems not
specific enough. It is not merely a matter of what kind of dimensions make
up God's subjectivity as free, but of their particular configuration, their
particular logic, their apparent interruptedness, which will allow us to
glimpse how the subject – in freedom over himself – determines himself in
an intersubjective way.

What contributes to the impression that divine freedom, conceptualized
as a distinct triune structure, may detract from God's determinateness as a
triune event of love is the fact that we can only speak of God's freedom in
the revelatory concreteness of God's being. The only noetically admissible
starting point is God's self-determination in its totality as independence and
determinateness. It is, first and foremost, God's love that leads us to pose
the question of God's freedom. Only as one confesses God's identity with
the crucified Jesus is one led to ask about the identity of the God who is
capable of such selflessness. As one experiences oneself as freed through
God's love and having now the capacity to be selfless and so free others for
love – one is led to ask about the unsurpassable freedom of God which has
made it possible for God in love to embrace the utterly loveless corpse of
one crucified as a criminal and through him to embrace all of humanity in
its compulsive self-seeking. In short, only on the basis of God's
determinateness as love is one led to ask about the freedom which has made
the actuality of such love possible. Second, God's determinateness as love
also enables us to name the modes of being that constitute the triune
structure of divine freedom. This is done not by copying the logic of love
but by tracing the intersubjective character of God's determinateness to the
creative spontaneity which alone can make love into what it is, a self-giving
bestowal of being.

Yet even with this much specificity, divine freedom is not, strictly speaking,
determinateness and thus cannot in itself be a source of knowledge of God
or certainty of God's being. All one can really do is specify divine freedom's
tri-polar structure, and, with reference to God's intersubjective
determinateness, name the free subject's modes of being. Besides this,
freedom remains characterized primarily by hiddenness. For in freedom

---

[50] *Mystery*, 374; *GGW* 513 (the first two emphases added). Reiner Dvorak claims that Jüngel
actually uses the terms 'person' and 'mode of being' interchangeably; see *Gott ist Liebe: Eine
Studie zur Grundlegung der Trinitätslehre bei Eberhard Jüngel* (Würzburg: Echter Verlag, 1999),
321.

God is the fount of possibility that is unconstrained by actuality. God is spontaneous, "the unconditional subject of himself."[51] Only because this hiddenness belongs to revelation is it shown to be a hiddenness that is in the service of love – not merely spontaneity but also creativity.[52] But it remains hiddenness, the liveliest of possibility. The logic of freedom is decidedly not determinateness.[53]

Subjective development?

The other point of clarification, in addition to the question of where to locate divine determinateness, has to do with the proper way to understand God's self-realization through temporal self-determination. The notion of God coming into view from within divine hiddenness may suggest that God's cruciform self-determination constitutes an unfolding of the being of God akin to that of the movement of the Hegelian *Geist* toward self-consciousness. It may imply the subject's incompleteness or deficiency, and thus an inner compulsion toward self-determination. This mistaken impression is inadvertently strengthened by Jüngel's own mediating proposal, despite his protestations that no inner compulsion is involved. "In this *existence* of God with the man Jesus, the divine *being*

---

[51] *Mystery*, 158; *GGW* 212.

[52] Jüngel warns that "If God's hiddenness as such (and with it the hidden God himself) is not identified concretely, the hiddenness of God escalates. A godhood that cannot be identified concretely," even if that identification is only of divine hiddenness, "is of the devil" ("Zum Begriff der Offenbarung," Gerhard Besier and Eduard Lohse (eds), *Glaube – Bekenntnis – Kirchenrecht* (Hannover: Lutherisches Verlaghaus, 1989), 218. Elsewhere he cautions: "there may well be something like the 'hidden work of God' (*opus dei absconditum*). But if God is the one who speaks of himself, then there is no *deus absconditus* ('hidden God') in the sense of the principle of the unrecognizability of God" (*Mystery*, 177; *GGW* 238).

[53] For Jüngel's account of God's creative hiddenness in the world, put forth in conversation with Luther, see *FoC*, 34–7. I am largely in agreement with Daryl Ellis's spirited defense of divine hiddenness as an essential element of Jüngel's doctrine of God ("God's Hiddenness as Trinitarian Grace and Miracle: A Response to Christopher R. J. Holmes's Critique of Eberhard Jüngel's Conception of Divine Hiddenness," *Neue Zeitschrift für Systematische Theologie und Religionsphilosophie* 52:1 [2010], 82–101). Ellis makes his argument against Christopher R. J. Holmes, who has argued that any residue of divine hiddenness detracts from the clarity of God's self-disclosure in Jesus ("Disclosure without Reservation: Re-evaluating Divine Hiddenness," *Neue Zeitschrift für Systematische Theologie und Religionsphilosophie* 48:3 [2006], 367–79). My only quibble with Ellis's interpretation is that he views Jüngel's insistence on divine hiddenness largely through the lens of Jüngel's polemic with post-Cartesian theism: God's primary hiddenness is the unspeakable excess of God's being that cannot be mediated to creatures. I argue here that hiddenness belongs to divine revelation and its chief function is not so much polemical as *kerygmatic*. Hiddenness stands for the logic of freedom, for the spontaneous creativity of God, which, as separate from the logic of love, both makes possible God's revelation as an event of *love* and assures that the ensuing intersubjectivity is none other than God's actualization of his freedom. In brief, hiddenness is a corollary of Jüngel's view of divine self-limitation for the sake of love, rather than for the sake of speakability.

realizes itself [*vollzieht sich*]," Jüngel writes.[54] He portrays God's trinitarian self-determination as an unfolding of a proto-determinateness, a "divine motive."[55] At issue here, then, are the necessity of God's temporal self-determination and its apparent sequentiality, whereby the subject transitions from one developmental stage to another.

The advantage of positing a fundamental and inalienable structure of freedom is that it actually rules out the divine subject's incompleteness prior to identification with the crucified Jesus. It does so in two ways. First, excluded in God's case is the notion of transformation from a subjectivity centered on self-possession to intersubjectivity, after the fashion of human liberation. What the logic of freedom indicates is that the relationship between the Father and the Spirit does not, and cannot, as such constitute the possibility of an interrupted, triune, being of God, but rather its impossibility. A purely self-referential relationship like that cannot interrupt itself, since the interruption must come from outside the relationship. It thus cannot exist. Even when such dualist self-determination is said to exist, as is the case with sinful humanity, it is precisely in its impossibility that it exists, in so far as there exists a triune God who upholds it in its ontological relationality and guarantees the possibility of its interruption (only thanks to God does the sinner exist, though even then only as a possible impossibility). In sum, the logic of freedom shows that God's subjectivity is fundamentally complete aside from God's cruciform self-determination. The latter is a self-realization of the divine subject in an event of love but is not a perfecting of divine subjectivity's imperfections.

Second, the subject's incompleteness is likewise ruled out by the fact that God's being is simply *not motivated by self-interest*. The logic of freedom shows that God is not like a human being questing for self-possession, suspended between a humanity that has been discarded and the godhood that has not yet been gained. God does not need actuality to be neutralized by incorporating it into His self-relation; nor does He need to render His self-relation immune to actuality's invasiveness. God's freedom lies in originary openness, which makes God the inexhaustible fount of possibility. It is in this manner that God's self-sufficiency must be understood. God is a subject who, out of God's self, can be there for another, and whose spontaneity is creativity for another's sake. It is rather creaturely actuality that has no freedom, no *being* without God and needs God as its redeemer. Out of love, by sheer grace, God can grant it freedom and a share in His being by so

---

[54] *Mystery*, 191 (translation altered); *GGW* 259.
[55] *Mystery*, 363; *GGW* 498.

determining Himself for its sake that it can now be there for His sake and so be liberated and thus also *be*: not through its jealously guarded freedoms but through God's freedom. God's involvement in creaturely actuality is, therefore, not an addition to God of something God is not but the self-sameness of God who in all His relations makes new actuality possible and relegates old actuality to the past. Briefly put, the logic of divine freedom allows for the deepest involvement with otherness, but it reveals God's involvement to be always grace.

Freedom's self-sufficiency

The ascription of determinateness solely to God's identification with the crucified Jesus, coupled with the structurally irreducible character of freedom, places the two existential acts of the self in a rather complex relation. To recapitulate: that determinateness does not belong to God's freedom, whose chief characteristics are openness and hiddenness, might suggest that determinateness is then a necessary completion of an otherwise incomplete subjectivity. However, as we have seen, the structure of divine freedom prevents one from considering freedom as an incomplete dimension of God's subjectivity, a dimension that must then of necessity be submerged in God's determinateness as the cruciform event of love. Freedom's logic does not show that, as free, God's subjectivity requires completion; instead the logic makes possible God's *gracious self-realization* for another's sake. Let me clarify this particular role further.

It may be useful to draw again the anthropological parallel based on the correspondence of the liberated person to God. Recall that human love – that is, acts of becoming through (reciprocal) identification with fellow humans – does not detract from the person's liberating rootedness in God's love. On the contrary, the deeper one's involvement in the other's otherness, the more is human freedom a reality. Freedom becomes magnified precisely because of the works of self-giving which flow from it. The same is true the other way round: the interruptedness of the human self-relation and one's participation in God's freedom do not diminish one's commitment to the other or make it any less serious (à la Marcuse's critique of Luther). Rather, actuality's ever-narrowing range of options finds its refreshment in freedom's new possibilities. Freedom does not undermine commitment but renews it and gives it unexpected depth. In the same manner, God's loving identification with the crucified Jesus neither does away with nor detracts from the tri-polar structure of God's independence. And vice versa: the trinitarian structure of the subject's freedom does not diminish the robustness of the event of love, which God is, but reinforces it as an event of *love*. Love is what it is – grace and solidarity – only in freedom.

This general compatibility of love and freedom, with freedom reinforcing love and love manifesting freedom, must by all means be emphasized. But we must also consider freedom and love in their specificity. For it is here that we shall still find some lingering questions about freedom and love as two co-present subjective acts. Jüngel, as I showed earlier, conflates the two dimensions and consequently undercuts love. In response, it will not do simply to separate the two structurally and then assert their theoretical compatibility. We must rather consider the actual concerns that lead Jüngel to make the moves he makes and respond to those. Thus, when it comes to the intersubjective character of God's identification with the crucified Jesus, an identification through which God's being becomes an event of love – Jüngel, nonetheless, wishes to uphold God's spontaneity and creativity. Jüngel's account of the temporally self-determining subject, however, manifests a different concern. It is driven by a desire not to leave the subject in himself as simply blank. Jüngel aims to protect the subject's self-consistence and so also the graciousness of the subject's cruciform self-determination. In our construal of the trinitarian logic of freedom, we must take these concerns into account and do justice to the two dimensions of God's freedom which they represent, namely, (a) freedom's distinctiveness as a subjective structure alongside of love and (b) its precedence in relation to God's determinateness. Only then will we be able to turn to love to find out whether a subjective structure of freedom thus posited allows for and makes the most of the intersubjective, robust character of divine love.

Let me address the latter concern first, since it is a corollary of what I referred to above as the subjective self-sufficiency of divine freedom. (I will speak to the former in the following sub-section.) The point that was made was that God's is not a half-formed subjectivity that must necessarily find its completion in the logic of love. Freedom does not morph into love. Rather, out of freedom God graciously determines God's self to be a temporal event of love. In God's determination, freedom does not give way to love but rather persists as a subjective structure alongside of love, so that in his revelation God exists in two simultaneous subjective acts.

Although this eliminates a crassly Hegelian understanding of God's subjectivity, characterized by a progressing phasal perfection of the subject, it does not quite do away with the lingering impression that necessity is nonetheless involved. What creates this impression, first of all, is the fact that, though freedom's tri-polar structure is in no way incomplete or imperfect, it nonetheless precedes God's temporal determinateness. It is its *sine qua non* condition. What then turns the possibility into a distinct impression that necessity is involved after all is the character of the elementally interrupted human person in correspondence to God. As free, a human being not only comes to *be* but necessarily also *becomes*. Works of love, whereby one allows another to determine one's self, necessarily follow upon the event of interruption. Of course, necessity here has nothing to do with coercion but with the fact that as elementally interrupted one is so freed from the tyranny of one's ego that one can, and one does, now relate to the world in a new way.

It would seem that the anthropological analogy calls into question the gracious character of God's cruciform self-determination. On its strength, God's freedom seems to require God's commitment to another: God's freedom requires an event of love, and so God, as subject, needs the world. I wish to argue, however, that this objection to the sufficiency of divine freedom is only apparent, and that for two reasons. First of all, as I pointed out in Chapter 1, human existence, regardless of its modality, is inextricably bound with the existence of the world. Human being is always given together with that of the world, whereas God's being, by contrast, does not presuppose the existence of the world. Even prior to the elemental interruption, humans already exist in a necessary relation to the world, insofar as one's self-securing is aimed at the world's impingement on one's self-relation and also insofar as it remains an ever-elusive goal. The elemental interruption only changes how one now relates to the world, rooting this relation in freedom, that is, in the power of God-given possibilities and in the absence of fear for one's self-relation. Instead of securing oneself against the world's self-securing, one can now go with love's works into places devoid of love. In other words, humanity's relation to the world is never merely a possibility that becomes real with the elemental interruption. Rather, it is simply given with being human. Thus, the inextricability of becoming for the world's sake does not, strictly speaking, flow from the freedom bestowed by the elemental interruption but from the person's very humanity, as it is re-established through God-given freedom.

Second, we must also take into account humanity's relation to God, which is of even greater significance for settling the question of the nonnecessity of God's determinateness as an event of love in contradistinction to the necessary character of human becoming. Humans, as I have emphasized on a number of occasions, can only be liberated. The elemental interruption thus automatically puts a person in a relationship with God.

This relationship is one of love, in that God has determined God's self for humanity's sake. He has moreover done so in such a manner that the only appropriate response to the elementally interrupting capacity of God's self-determination is a recognition of God's love. In the freedom which God's love has bestowed, one is called to reciprocate the love offered. God, by contrast, is a free subject in God's self. God's freedom is not established through a relationship. Thus, while it enables God to enter into a creative relationship with humanity, there is no compulsion, either internal or external, for God to do so. God's identification with the crucified Jesus is an act of grace.

The logic of freedom as subjective creativity

In addition to freedom's *antecedent* self-sufficiency, its *persistence* as a distinct subjective structure is important if one wishes to uphold God's (and by extension also human) spontaneity and creativity. This matters especially when one considers that love, in its essence, has to do with self-surrender. It manifests itself in death to self and in the desire to receive oneself from, through, and with the beloved. Putting it rather pointedly, the lover is reduced to nothing so that he or she might be recreated as a new kind of self alongside of the beloved. The lover desires to become. Love thus brings with itself, as Jüngel repeatedly underscores, the threat of nonbeing. We must take this dimension of the subject's existence in all seriousness. But if we do, how then is freedom to be conceptualized alongside of such robustly understood love?

To begin with, we must make sure that freedom, as a distinct structure of subjectivity, does not constitute an escape hatch for the subject to avoid love's risk when it becomes too perilous. Freedom is not a structure that guarantees the subject's self-maintenance. It is not there to assure that, regardless of the risk, the subject will at the last moment still come out relatively unscathed. In its most perverse form, we will recall, this would be the mechanism that, according to Marcuse, is evident in Luther's view of Christian freedom. The subject submits to the coerciveness of social structures, perhaps justifying it as an act of love; at the same time the subject disengages from this act of submission, maintaining that he or she remains free in the inner self. Jüngel, as we have seen, denies that this is Luther's view, or the proper view of freedom in general (though he does associate it with Kant). Freedom does not turn love into a low-commitment relationship, or one that splits the self. God's freedom is not escapist, even though it deals with possibility.

Freedom does not safeguard *the subject's self-maintenance*, not even in the interest of the subject's creativity. Rather, freedom safeguards *the subject's creativity*. This, I believe, is how one must interpret the assertion that love is what it is only in freedom. That is, freedom does not accompany love to make it uncoerced but at the same time to place it under one's control, so that one might disengage from, and secure oneself against, a love that turns out too threatening or too hopeless. Instead, freedom radicalizes love. The structure of freedom, with its self-transcendence, is the locus of creativity. Through its presence alongside of love's concrete determinations, the structure gives love a particular orientation – toward the loveless, and thus gives love the widest possible scope. In freedom one loves not only that which is already lovable but above all that which is unlovable and undeserving of love. Freedom makes love into an *agape*. Paradigmatically such, according to Luther, is God's love.[56] It is such because God loves in freedom. To put it more specifically, freedom enables the lover to turn to the unlovable in a situation where there is self-evidently no guarantee, not even the slightest indication, that one's being for another's sake will be recognized and returned to one. Moreover, freedom gives meaning to love in situations where no compassion is offered in return and where one might consequently be tempted to withdraw into one's self. Freedom constantly refreshes love where calculation of personal cost, which suddenly invades one's vulnerability, seems to be the only soberly real thing amidst the stubborn unreality of love. In those situations, freedom, instead of being an escape hatch, upholds the lover with the force of its creativity in the conviction that no one is beyond the reach of love and in the certainty that love is stronger. Buoyed by freedom, God's identification with the dead man Jesus is not merely an act of solidarity with one unjustly condemned but a creative act from which surely life must spring again.

Before I say more about God, let me underscore freedom's creativity from an anthropological angle. This is best expressed, I believe, by the biblical affirmation that a person's "life is hidden [κέκρυπται] with Christ in God" (Colossians 3:3). In the context of our discussion of freedom, one could interpret this verse in the following manner. One's identity lies in God's love, in the concreteness of God's cruciform self-determination for the sake of moribund humanity – that is, one's identity lies in Christ. This christological location of human identity is not to be overestimated. One is

---

[56] "The love of God does not find, but creates, that which is pleasing to it" (Martin Luther, *Heidelberg Disputation* [1518], *LW* 31:57; *WA* 1:365 [Thesis 28]). It is this particular aspect that is captured by Jüngel's ultimately rather imprecise definition of God's being as "*a se in nihilum ek-sistere*" (*Mystery*, 223; *GGW* 303).

defined by God's love, in that *God has defined God's self* for the sake of one. As an elementally interrupted person, whose self is thus withdrawn into God, not only is one free, but what this freedom means more specifically is that one has now become a creature of hiddenness. One is no longer trivially indeterminate. Rather, one has gained quite remarkable specificity – one's life is hidden in God. One shares in the creative hiddenness through which one may now likewise become determinate through love for another. One may perhaps invoke here St. Paul's words from his First Letter to the Corinthians (9:19–23; a passage Luther echoes in his *Freiheitsschrift*): "though I am free with respect to all, I have made myself a slave to all. . . To the Jews I became as a Jew. . . To those under the law I became as one under the law. . . To those outside the law, I became as one outside the law. . . To the weak I became week. . ." This is how freedom is creative, as a hiddenness that enables one to become determinate for – and, as is to be hoped, also together with – another.

A human being becomes a creature of hiddenness only because of God's love. God, however, in the freedom that belongs to His being, has this creative hiddenness in Himself. On its account, God can not only determine God's self as an event of love but, above all, can be this event for the sake of a loveless, dead man and in him for the sake of sinful humanity. As free God is not motivated by anticipated reciprocation; God does not, so to speak, play it safe. His love can, therefore, penetrate into nothingness itself. In the power of divine freedom God's love is love imbued with the most creative and originary possibilities – possibilities that, first and foremost, touch God's very self. To those possibilities belongs God's self-determination for the sake of another, or to put it more specifically, becoming the other in God's own self. This is what God's identity with the crucified Jesus means. It means, moreover, that the other can now also be for the sake of God. I shall return to the issue of love's reciprocity presently. Here it will suffice to underscore briefly that God's freedom is hiddenness precisely because it enables the concreteness and determinateness of the self in no other way than as a loving self for the sake of the loveless.

The question of human reciprocation brings us at long last into the territory of the divine logic of love. As will be recalled, I have put forth an argument in favor of a distinct logic of freedom within God's subjectivity, in order precisely to do justice to God's self-determination as an event of love. In Jüngel's account of God's triune being, love – in its essential character of an act that involves a threat of nonbeing and calls for reciprocity – is ultimately sacrificed to the need to shore up God's spontaneity and creativity. Love falls victim to what I have referred to as the divine *propria*. The outcome is that, despite Jüngel's protestations to the contrary, God emerges as a subject who is fundamentally self-related and whose love is carefully circumscribed within the subject's self-control. This, I believe, is not an inevitable consequence. In what follows I shall give an account of divine love that does justice – in light of God's act of freedom – to its reciprocal character. At the same time, I propose, it does not surrender the creativity that properly belongs to God's being.

The reciprocity of divine love

As I have already briefly indicated, the obvious challenge to the possibility of reciprocating divine love is the fact the beloved with whom God identifies God's self is dead. The equally obvious riposte, however, is the creativity that accompanies God's identification with Jesus. This creativity has as its corollary the fact that, by virtue of this very identification, Jesus' humanity becomes a surrogate for all humanity. This happens in two ways. First of all, God's identification with Jesus vindicates Jesus' humanity as true humanity. Jesus' relation to God that defined his entire life exhibited the anticipative exchange that belongs to love. "In that Jesus existed completely from the kingdom of God, deriving his own being entirely from God's fatherly act of majesty, his life and then his death were emphatic insistence on God's coming."[57] Jesus' certainty of God made him "absolutely free" and allowed him to perform works of love with reckless abandon. The last of these, his death as a righteous man condemned for unrighteousness by self-righteous men, brought with itself a God-forsakenness which underscored, however, that the anticipatory character of love is never based on self-securing calculation. Still, even in his God-forsakenness, Jesus turned to God. At the moment when the risk undertaken by love must have appeared insuperable and the path of self-securing, belatedly, as the only one worth taking, Jesus turned to God with a reproachful plea for solidarity. Jesus' plea was for divine recognition, yet as such, as coming from the depths of his love, this was a plea based not on *do ut des*, calling on God to do his part of the bargain, but on the confession that without God all human love must falter. The moment of God-forsakenness, as Jesus final act of self-conscious love, was thus disclosed as a moment pregnant with the closeness of God. In that very moment, God vindicated Jesus' humanity by becoming identical (*identisch*)[58] with the

[57] *Mystery*, 359; *GGW* 493.
[58] Cf. *Mystery*, 280; *GGW* 382.

dead man in an act of all-embracing divine love. God has given Jesus' humanity a universal dimension by affirming that to be human means to love in the freedom of God.

Second, in addition to the vindication of Jesus' humanity as true humanity (*menschliche Menschlichkeit*), God's act of identification with Jesus enables one, through its capacity for elemental interruption, to recognize one's own humanity in this act. To begin with, in Jesus' God-forsakenness one recognizes the failure of one's own humanity. One sees this both by recognizing oneself in the self-righteousness of those condemning Jesus and by contrasting oneself with how Jesus reacts to his God-forsakenness. A self-relation that does not need God, as it seeks to construct its own security, pushes others into self-securing. God is pushed out of the world. But Jesus, even in a moment of his death, will not let this happen; Jesus calls on God even when all hope seems to be lost. Thus, in Jesus' death, one comes to see one's own sin with its dire consequences: one's bondage to self-remaking, one's active propagation of God-forsakenness, and one's lack of love. But in God's affirmation of Jesus' humanity one also sees what one's humanity can be as a humanity that lives from God. The death of Jesus discloses the persistent love that flows from it and offers forgiveness to those who know not what they do. And it discloses the living love that embraces it. In the death of Jesus, love, not death, is shown to have the last word. In his identity with God, Jesus is God's Word of love. As elementally interrupted, one now sees oneself as addressed by this Word and embraced by its unconditional forgiveness. Briefly put, in one's own frantic livingness, in one's self-securing, one now comes to perceive death, a death that affects not only one but also those one relates to; in the death of Jesus, by contrast, one comes to see life: a love that is stronger than death. I shall address how one is led to this perception later.

As can be seen, the death of the beloved may not really be an obstacle to considering the issue of reciprocating divine love. Jesus' death makes possible humanity's inclusion within his own humanity, both because God acknowledges Christ's humanity as true humanity and because this recognition, in turn, enables the self-identification of the elementally interrupted person with Christ's humanity. Jesus' death thus actually constitutes the possibility of a far wider reciprocation – indeed, a reciprocation that aims at all of humanity. Besides clarifying this point, the above introduction has also suggested two ways for human reciprocation of divine love to take place. One has to do with counteracting God-forsakenness, the other with the recognition of the dead Jesus as the Son of God. Let me explore those in turn.

Partnership with God

Jüngel's critique of the metaphysical tradition, as we have observed, is intended to highlight that the tradition itself, with its "false presupposition" of the absolute necessity of God vis-à-vis the world,[59] has laid the foundation for God's eventually being pushed out of the world. Where the actuality of God is merely the guarantee of the actuality of humanity, there may come a time – and such time has indeed come – when humans "understand[] [themselves] on the basis of [themselves], whether accidentally or necessarily."[60] There is no more need for the hypothesis of God to aid human self-securing: "if God has been established as the *securing factor* for man, has not then the decision been already made that from now on the securing must become the *god of man*?"[61] The awareness that such indeed had been the function of God's absoluteness came too late in the course of Western metaphysics. When it did, humans no longer had much reason to appeal to God, while the metaphysical enterprise had for the most part plunged into silence in a desperate attempt to safeguard God's divinity from the straightjacket of human conceptualizations. The result was in both cases exactly the same: the God who was absolutely necessary became quite unnecessary.

Jüngel, as we have seen, does not regard this metaphysical death of God as a tragedy but rather as a welcome opportunity to think afresh God's relation to the world from the perspective of that death of God which took place on Good Friday. It is by returning to and thinking through the early Christina *kerygma* that Jüngel comes to assert the more than necessary character of God in relation to the world. He intends this claim to counter humans' self-serving objectification of God in the metaphysical tradition and to uphold the subjective freedom of God in the act of divine revelation. Being more than necessary, conceptually speaking, liberates God's divinity from dependence on the being of some other being, or the being of being as such. But it would be illicit to infer that God is, therefore, unnecessary, as if God's being were accidental and thus irrelevant to the being of the world. Rather, more than necessary means that in freedom, coming out of God's self, God "disposes over being and nonbeing."[62] This latter statement indicates that Jüngel's assertion is not only aimed critically and polemically at metaphysical constructs but also has a positive role to play in the doctrine of God. Let us consider its implications.

---

[59] *Mystery*, 59; *GGW* 78.
[60] *Mystery*, 16; *GGW* 19.
[61] *Mystery*, 196; *GGW* 265.
[62] *Mystery*, 33; *GGW* 41.

That God's relation to the world is one of freedom means, first of all, that the rigid and, in fact, competitive relation between God and world, posited by the metaphysical tradition no longer obtains. According to the latter, God is the *ens realissimum*, to whom supremely belong being, agency, and above all freedom. For humans to claim those in any real sense dissolves the boundary between humanity and God and constitutes an assault on God's omnipotence, omniscience and omnipresence. These realities can, of course, be ascribed to humans but as such are only feeble shadows of the attributes which not only are properly God's but can really be affirmed only of God. Ironically, as I noted earlier, this absolutely necessary deity, for all his jealously guarded attributes, submits with absolute ease to ruthless and self-seeking manipulation. That human self-deprecation in the face of God's power should hide within itself exploitative self-empowerment is actually a corollary of the nonnecessity of God concealed within his absolute necessity. By contrast, when God is thought as more than necessary, the relation between God and humanity is not given in the order of being to which even God must submit. It is thus a relation of greater distance, a relation over a chasm that is humanly untraversable. But at the same time, it is a relation of unparalleled nearness, in that, in the absence of a predetermined relation between God and world, God himself can negotiate it and come to the world closer than the world can come to itself.

This, according to Jüngel, is how one must understand God as Creator. To be sure, the world necessarily presupposes a creator if it is to be thought of as created. But, as such, this assertion goes only so far as making humanity "the product of creative arbitrariness."[63] It has, of course, been made as a corollary of God's absoluteness, which "was in an earlier age the guarantor of the coherence of the world and human societies."[64] But now, that the absolute God has been at best rendered unspeakable and at worst revealed as a figment of human desire for security, the assertion has become irrelevant. In any case, as Jüngel points out, "the absoluteness of God . . . now appears to modern man to be a power which paralyzes responsibility for the world and society."[65] Therefore, it belongs to our affirmation of God as Creator that "God would have us know that we must live as [humans] who manage our lives without him."[66] Yet this living without God must not be understood as living *without God*! For in freedom God can come closer to

---

[63] *Mystery*, 38; *GGW* 48.
[64] *Mystery*, 40; *GGW* 52.
[65] *Mystery*, 40; *GGW* 52.
[66] Dietrich Bonhoeffer, "[Letter] To Eberhard Bethge, [Tegel Prison] 16 July [1944]," *Letters and Papers from Prison*, ed. Eberhard Bethge (New York: Touchstone, 1997), 360; cited in *Mystery*, 59; *GGW* 77.

us than we can come to ourselves. Indeed, God has done so, and the cross is the locale of God's coming.

The affirmation of God as Creator can be made meaningfully only on account of God's coming to the world from within divine hiddenness, that is, on the basis of God's cruciform self-determination. "[T]he theological concept of the Creator cannot simply be derived from the creation," Jüngel insists.[67] But God's creativity, although crucially rooted in the cross, extends beyond it. It is an integral dimension of divine subjectivity; it attends God's love. "Every creative act of divine power is as such an act of divine love in action, which not only establishes reality as realized possibility but also creates still more possibilities with every reality."[68] As a loving subject, God is Creator who continues to create, who brings new possibilities where nothingness seems to have gained the upper hand, or where actuality only replicates itself in its ugliness. As a loving subject, God continues elementally to interrupt the continuity of being which has fallen prey to the undertow of nothingness. Yet, crucially, all these creative acts return to the cross. The cross is the noetic source of one's self-recognition as a creature, in that it is the Word of the cross that, in the first place, raises the question of one's createdness, as it elementally interrupts human self-creation. In sum, it is to the cross that one must look for the meaning of God's relation, as Creator, to his creation.

What then does one affirm when, on the basis of the cross, one affirms God as Creator and oneself as a creature? First of all, one affirms the being of God and the being of humanity. God's coming to the cross is simultaneously a judgment over being and a revelation of being. God's coming is a judgment on human self-creation, the human quest for divinity, understood as securing oneself within one's self-relation. And it is a revelation of human being-in-relation to God. What faith perceives in the cross is God's self-limitation for the sake of self-identification, as Son, with the Crucified One. And, insofar as Christ's humanity is also true humanity, faith sees that inscribed into God's self-limitation is *God's ongoing concern for his creation.* Thus God's identification with the dead Jesus makes God's relation to his creatures one in which there likewise takes place a withholding, as it were, of God's overwhelming might for the sake of identification with those who are in Christ. On the one hand, this withholding, which is God's very relation to the creature, establishes the creature as only that, a creature. On the other hand, to be a creature of God means that the person is "hidden

[67] *Mystery,* 218; *GGW* 296.
[68] *Mystery,* 339; *GGW* 464–5.

with Christ in God" and is thus a being of possibility. As can be seen, the cross thematizes God's polemically established distance and capacity for closeness as love. It reveals God's being as an event of love and human being as freed through God's love.[69]

Second, in addition to this disclosure, the cross shows that it is *an act of God's love* that, also as free persons, we must manage our lives *without God*. To understand what is being said here, we must look more closely at the event of God's cruciform self-determination. Together with God's identification, as Son, with the crucified Jesus, there takes place a self-withholding of God, as Father, for the sake of this identification. This, as observed earlier, enables God to become the other in God's own self, yet in such a way that neither does God abandon God's self and transform into the other, nor is the beloved absorbed into God's self-relation. The beloved belongs to God's self, yet in such a way that the integrity of the beloved is preserved. God so determines God's self that God does not wish to have his self without the beloved. In short, the beloved is given a constitutive role within God's triune life. In Christ's death, all of humanity is addressed about this role and called to belong to God's self-determination. God's relation to humanity is thus to be seen as a self-determination for humanity's sake in such a way that humanity can now be there for God's sake.

This does not render humanity anything other than human. From the perspective of one loved by God, one experiences God's self-differentiation simultaneously as a call into being through God's identification with the creature and as God's self-withholding. As elementally interrupted, one participates in God through faith. One stands continually before God. At the same time, one finds oneself in a world which is without God. "The God who lets us live in the world without the working hypothesis of God is the God before whom we stand continually," as Dietrich Bonhoeffer pointed out.[70] Yet when humans respond with love to God's loving self-determination for humanity's sake, when they acknowledge themselves as constituted by God's love which does not wish to be without them – they themselves become the presence of God in the world. "Loving, God shares his power with the creature he loves."[71] More than that: in love God entrusts himself

---

[69] God could, of course, have come to the world without withholding himself and identifying with a creature. But this would not have been a coming of love which brings the world to a turning point. Such a visible coming of God in majesty could only have been the end of the world. See *Mystery*, 379; *GGW* 519.

[70] Bonhoeffer, "To Eberhard Bethge," *Letters and Papers from Prison*, 360; cited in *Mystery*, 59; *GGW* 77.

[71] "Gottes ursprüngliches Anfangen," *TE III*, 159.

to humanity, God trusts humanity with God's own self.[72] The beloved who responds with love to the lover's love becomes the presence of the lover who does not wish to be himself without the beloved and who is his self only with the beloved. The love of the beloved becomes the lover's presence wherever the beloved is found. How do humans respond? By living their lives as lives embraced by God, by living out of God's creative possibilities. They respond by living out of their God-given freedom in such a way that they, like God, can become, for others' sake. Human works of love – as the actualization of possibilities inherent in one's being-in-God – are the presence of God in the world. In the visible works of human love, "God . . . as love works invisibly."[73] In this way God's being, God's self, is returned to God. In summary, that in this world humans must manage without God is an expression of God's love, for, as God's beloved, humans are the ones who actualize the lover's presence in the world. In doing so, humans reciprocate God's love and return God's being to God.

It is essential to emphasize at this point that it is not that, without human reciprocation, God would simply cease to exist. Rather, without human reciprocation the world would truly be without God. The reciprocity of love threatens the being of God, who is coming to the world, with nonexistence in the world and for the world's sake. This is best understood in terms of the two existential acts of the divine subject. The self-differentiation of God in the event of the cross is none other than the rise of a different logic of subjective being alongside of that of freedom – the logic of love. The subject's self-withholding attests to the persistence of the subjective structure of divine freedom. But it shows this structure to be not one of self-conservation but one that enables the going of God where the return of being cannot be guaranteed in advance. The logic of freedom enables God's going into what is engulfed in nothingness and becoming for the sake of another – without being motivated by the beloved's reciprocation. But, as self-withdrawal, it does make this reciprocation possible and, as we have just seen, even necessary. Without human reciprocation – without humans living the lives of freedom which God's love bestows – God would have no being in the world. God would be only a dead God. To be sure, the divine subject would continue in the subjective act which is the subject's freedom. But as such, God would remain hidden in God's being, not given by anything, not even Himself, indeterminate. The world without God

---

[72] On faith as both trust and trustworthiness, in a more general, less pointed way, see *Mystery*, 197; *GGW* 266–7.

[73] *Mystery*, 392; *GGW* 538.

would then cease to be the world which, as such, can become the object of God's love but would become a God-less and a God-forsaken world.

There is, of course, something counterfactual in the above scenario, counterfactual but not impossible. It is not impossible, because Jesus himself experienced the judgment of the godless and God-forsaken world. In what should be seen as an act of atonement, he freely took upon himself the violent assault of the world's God-forsakenness and responded to it in the least likely of ways – with love. Yet the above scenario is counterfactual precisely on account of the cross, that is, because God responded to the world's judgment on Jesus by comprehending it in a judgment and a determination of God's own. God uniquely embraced the dead man and gave an eternal significance to Jesus' atoning death, and with it to his entire life of love – all this so that humanity might not be mired all the more in its deadly and expansive God-lessness. In the crucified beloved, God claimed the world's self-chosen God-lessness and, in doing so, made it into an absence which, as such, is God's *presence through love.* By claiming Jesus' death and life as God's own, God has now put God's own love on the line.

Through the cross, God's love, for all its feebleness, has actually shown itself to be a force of liberation in a God-forsaken world. And it has shown itself to be this force in a world that already is a God-forsaken world. God persistently comes to the world out of the inexhaustible possibilities for love that spring from divine freedom. God comes, even though the world which is the aim of God's love is a world seeking its own divinity, a world whose gods are mere stepping-stones to its own self-divinization. This is a world in which a righteous man gets condemned for unrighteousness by self-righteous men, a world hell-bent on self-securing, and rife with triumphs of lovelessness. This world desires being but cannot tell the difference between being and nonbeing. Those whom God's love embraces in this world are not, therefore, encountered in the neutral condition of simply inhabiting a world to which God is coming. They must be elementally interrupted in the compulsion of their self-securing. They must be freed.

But this freedom is not an easy freedom. To be sure, "The human lives ontologically from the *indicative* of peace which God creates." This indicative is neither humanly constituted nor guaranteed. But for this reason "The moral *imperative* to make peace oneself . . . is in fact an unprecedentedly urgent, categorical imperative."[74] In describing the situation of those who in this world are freed by God's love, Jüngel appeals (via Dietrich Bonhoeffer)

---

[74] "Zum Wesen des Friedens," *TE V,* 30–1.

to the imagery of the Passion: "The God who is with us is the God who forsakes us."[75] I believe this statement needs to be interpreted in stronger terms than the highlighting of the world's autonomy suggested by Jüngel. It must be understood, closer to Bonhoeffer's context, through the lens of Jesus' Passion. If human works of love, too, involve a becoming for another's sake in such a way that the other, as one loved, plays a constitutive role in the existence of the self – then, like God, one becomes threatened with nonexistence at the hands of fellow humans. Love's vulnerability exposes one to lack of compassion and even outright hostility and abuse. One might be tempted to respond to this with similar self-securing. Jüngel recognizes this predicament when he writes: "Love does not yet *rule* on earth." But the ultimate test of love comes when love can dare to have the final word where prudence has all but given up. If it can, then "It can moderate the ruling powers and thereby make the ambivalences and ambiguities of life in the kingdoms of the world more bearable."[76] One is called, as a person free from the tyranny of the ego, to courage to oppose the world's lovelessness with deeds of love. One is called to turn the world's god-forsakenness, despite the world's prudent opinions, into the presence of God to the world. And if God's love has managed to free one, only God can tell how far its freeing power can reach.

What I have said here is not new. There are resources in the theological tradition of the Church that point to such robustly conceptualized human role in response to God's love. Here I wish to highlight only two: the apostle Paul and Martin Luther. Paul's harsh words, directed at the disunity of the Corinthian assembly in his First Letter to the Church at Corinth, do not merely indicate that those who believe in Christ come to form a community. Rather, Paul sets before the Corinthian assembly a vision of a community where specifically not only is each member attuned to the others' needs but the whole community, in its inalienable togetherness, becomes the presence of Christ's risen body (1 Corinthians 12). It is as a community that love's final Word, expressed in Christ's cry of dereliction, becomes the presence of the body of Christ embraced by God.

Somewhat different is Luther's emphasis in his less known, though not uncontroversial adage, "*fides creatrix divinitatis.*" According to Luther, when God justifies one by grace, one becomes incomparably more than one could ever make of oneself. One becomes a person, rather than the sum total of one's works. One becomes a doer who precedes actual doing[77] and who thus

---

[75] Bonhoeffer, "To Eberhard Bethge," *Letters and Papers from Prison*, 360; cited in *Mystery*, 59; *GGW* 77.

[76] "My Theology," *Essays II*, 16.

[77] Martin Luther, *Lectures on Galatians* (1535), *LW* 26:256; *WA* 40¹:402.

can direct one's works to the neighbor instead of one's self-making. As justified by God, one can now justify the neighbor – one can offer the neighbor one's righteousness.[78] In this way, that is, by first and foremost believing that God is "the Author and Donor of every good," Luther maintains, one also justifies God. One justifies God as the giver of freedom, which not only frees one from restless working but also enables one effectively to counter the unfreedom that surrounds one. Thus, Luther holds, "faith . . . consummates the Deity . . . it is the *creator of the Deity*, not in the substance of God but in us. For without faith God loses His glory, wisdom, righteousness, truthfulness, mercy, etc., in us; in short, God has none of His majesty or divinity where faith is absent."[79] For Luther, faith (and that includes the person's entire fundamentally reoriented life) is the presence of God among humans and the worldly actuality of God's kingdom. Through faith humans return God's being to God, they justify him as the giver of an enduring identity in which, to put it now in Jüngel's categories, are their freedom, their becoming, and the togetherness of the community.[80]

The spirit and faith

Luther, as we have just seen, points to faith as responsible for the transformation of one's entire being, thanks to which one can now counteract the world's God-forsakenness and, through works of love, actualize God's presence in the world. But Luther's emphasis on faith suggests also another mode in which humans reciprocate divine love – faith itself. Reciprocation

---

[78] "das groest [werck der liebe] ist das, wenn ich mein gerechtigkeit hyn gib und dienen lassz des nechsten sünde" (*Predigt am 3. Sonntag nach Trinitatis* [1522]; *WA* 10^III:217).

[79] *Lectures on Galatians*, *LW* 26:227, 233; *WA* 40^I:360, 369 (emphasis added). Cf. also the explanation of The Second Petition of the Lord's Prayer ("Thy kingdom come") in Luther's *Catechisms*.

[80] Jüngel does refer to Luther's adage, directly or indirectly, a handful of times, but he does not mine its potential for conceptualizing human reciprocation of divine love. In his essay, "Gott – als Wort unserer Sprache" (*TE I*, 101), Jüngel invokes the adage both to emphasize that God and faith belong inseparably together and to deny, therefore, the possibility of God's verification outside of faith. Jüngel admits in passing that "What it means that God and faith belong together is quite unfathomable." In his essay, "Die Freiheit der Theologie" (*TE II*, 25), Jüngel cites Luther's adage, while warning that one must, nonetheless, maintain a distinction between God and faith because it is God who creates faith. Our distinction between the logic of love and the logic of freedom has observed this distinction, while also allowing for the possibility of humans' returning God's self to God. Finally, in *The Freedom of a Christian*, Jüngel cautions that faith is not a doing, on the person's part, to which God responds with gifts. Faith, Jüngel writes, means "to allow oneself to be given something, to receive" (*FoC*, 67, 70). We have heeded this warning here by insisting that human actualization of God's presence in the world flows from the passivity of being liberated by God's Word.

here has to do specifically with the agency of faith and its connection to the Holy Spirit.

Interpreters generally point out a binitarian tendency in Jüngel's doctrine of God, in that it centers largely on the agency of God and Jesus. To be sure the Spirit is present in Jüngel's account of the events of Good Friday. But, unlike the Father, who lovingly identifies himself with the crucified Jesus, and unlike Jesus, who loves even when God-forsakenness appears to be overwhelming – the Spirit has no role to *play*. John Webster comments that Jüngel's "account of the Spirit is not so much an account of a personal agent as a description of a state of affairs, of the fact, that is, that 'God's being *remains* in coming.' Language about the Spirit as 'the relation between the relations of the Father and the Son' simply serves to denote the *quality* of relationship between the Father and the Son."[81]

This apparent passivity of the Spirit need not be seen as a weakness in the context of our re-articulation of the doctrine of God. Nor need it be seen as a weakness that the Spirit is introduced by Jüngel as a *deus ex machina* to provide a resolution to the drama of Golgotha. For Michael Murrmann-Kahl the fact that the Spirit appears suddenly in the function of the reconciling bond between the maximally alienated divine modes of Father and Son indicates that the Spirit belongs to the subject's self-relatedness into which Jesus is simply absorbed. The Spirit, in other words, guarantees the self-maintenance of the divine subject in the face of that which threatens it.[82] This, however, is not an inevitable conclusion. Just as the death of Christ made possible the reciprocation of God's love on the part of the entire community as the body of Christ, so also the Spirit, as the bond of love, may constitute an opening for human agency. The Spirit's coming from within God's freedom may then be viewed not as evidence of an absolute subject who reproduces his own self-relatedness in the economy but rather as the possibility of a spiritual response on humanity's part.

How would such a response be construed? I believe it has to do with faith's perception, with what faith proclaims on the basis of what it perceives, and with the locatedness of faith. To begin with, we should note that the identity of God and Jesus belongs to faith. It is faith that, so to speak, puts

---

[81] John Webster, *Eberhard Jüngel: An Introduction to his Theology* (Cambridge: Cambridge University Press, 1986), 77 (second emphasis added). The Jüngel citations come from *Mystery*, 387 and 375 respectively; *GGW* 531, 513. Michael Murrmann-Kahl concludes that "the perichoretic moment of the three hypostases is de facto identified with the hypostasis of the Spirit" (*"Mysterium trinitatis?" Fallstudien zur Trinitätslehre in der evangelischen Dogmatik des 20. Jahrhunderts* [Berlin: Walter de Gruyter, 1997], 132).

[82] Murrmann-Kahl, *"Mysterium trinitatis?"* 121, 125. See also 91 above.

two and two together and recognizes the brutally murdered Jesus as God's Son. To worldly eyes, Jesus is at best only a savior who in the end could not save even himself (Mark 15:29–30). But faith perceives in Jesus' cry of God-forsakenness the presence of God's love. The Father's love embraces Jesus' unwavering love and makes him the Father's own Word of love. Despite his repugnant death, faith insists, the Son is embraced by the Father through the Father's Spirit. Further, faith not only perceives – or thinks – the Word but also proclaims it for all its apparent foolishness and offensiveness, though to the world that is divinizing itself the Word of faith cannot seem anything other than scandalous. Jüngel suggests that this is indeed what faith does when he writes:

> Trust and faith are nothing other than those human acts with which man *affirms God for God's sake* (and not for the sake of some other necessity) in such a way that he *allows him to be there where he is*, which is with man. . . . *Faith preserves the identity of God's being and existence* in that it perceives God's being as a being with the man Jesus and thus as a being for all people.[83]

Jüngel means this passage in the weaker sense of doing justice to God, that is, recognizing God in Jesus death. But the passage could – and I believe, should – also be understood in Luther's stronger sense of doing justice, namely, that of justifying God and so actualizing God's self in the world.

For this sort of understanding it will not do, however, to speak merely of faith's perception and proclamation. Here we must take into account the locatedness of faith. What is significant is that the identity of God and Jesus belongs to the *Easter faith in the risen Christ.* What faith also perceives, therefore, is that Jesus' life has been saved – not in the sense that Jesus has been saved out of this life but rather that his life has been gathered into a believing community – the body of Christ – and so made eternal and made manifest.[84] It is as coming from this locale that faith turns out to be that act which, as it were, co-responds to the movement of the Spirit. In this broader context, it now becomes explainable why the Spirit in faith's proclamation of the cross may appear passive or a *deus ex machina.* If the Spirit were anything more than that, the Spirit would become a vehicle of absorption of the dead Jesus into God's subjectivity. As the Spirit is, however, the Spirit constitutes an opening for the agency of the believing community as the

---

[83] *Mystery*, 191; *GGW* 259 (emphases added).
[84] Cf. *Death*, 120–1.

body of Christ. The community actualizes its Spirit-role by now embracing the Father who, in God's eternal coming, embraced the Son on the cross of Golgotha. To the coming of God in Spirit there corresponds the present confession of the body of believers in such a way that both converge in the past event, which, in this convergence, gains an eternal significance in the here and now. The Spirit proceeds from the Father and the Son. Hence, it makes sense to speak of the Spirit only where God and the body of believers are involved together, just as it is proper to speak of faith only where both are involved as well. Spirit and faith become one and the same reality, insofar as, as two constituents of one intersubjective act, they actualize the presence of the triune God to the world.

But here one might, and actually should, ask: Whence faith? John Webster has perceptively pointed out that in Jüngel's theology "there is also need for some account of how we are able to recognise that it is *God* who is hidden in the cross, of how the cross comes to be seen as God's revelation rather than simply a human tragedy in which no features of divinity can be traced."[85] Here, I believe, the logic of divine freedom comes in good stead. What we have just outlined is the logic of love: the manner in which the believing community plays a constitutive role in the subjectivity of God, who does not wish, as subject, to be without the beloved. The community is the body of Christ, which – through its confession of God's identity with the crucified Jesus – makes God present. But for all this, the community does not create its own faith. Faith is not grounded in itself. To create faith belongs rather to God's Spirit, who, through the proclaimed Word, creates

---

[85] Webster, *Eberhard Jüngel*, 68. Webster's observation turns, in Steven Paulson's study of Luther and Jüngel, into a complex charge that Jüngel's analogy- and correspondence-based conception of the divine-human relationship is, fundamentally, an intellectual conception which does not lend itself to proclamation. Its essence is the narration of a past event which can at best only intellectually convince one of the thinkability of God and so also of the continuity of one's being with God's. But Jüngel's notion of analogy, Paulson claims, even as it makes God speakable, precludes God's speaking in the present through the word of the law and that of the gospel, through judgment and through grace. Paulson comments that Jüngel's "is a theology of the cross without proclamation. ... What is missing ... is the recognition that God's advent is always present in the *moment of preaching* to individuals, i.e., in an act or deed that is ... the actual God-happening, or doing of God to the hearers, with or without – but not because of – the thought that follows. The present act of proclamation is God's becoming ... God comes to love us, and proclamation done properly is where this love happens, not *in mentis*, but in actuality" (Steven D. Paulson, *Analogy and Proclamation: The Struggle over God's Hiddenness in the Theology of Martin Luther and Eberhard Juengel* [unpublished Th.D. dissertation, Lutheran School of Theology, Chicago, 1992], 470). What, according to Paulson, is responsible for the proclamatory deficiency of Jüngel's doctrine of God is its basis in analogy. Analogy inscribes the doctrine of God into an *exitus-reditus* schema and, through its principles of plentitude, continuity, hierarchy and theophany, "ontologically secures God's being for human thought" (249). For Paulson, then, Jüngel's entire doctrine of God is irredeemable for proclamation. This latter conclusion I wish to challenge here.

faith "*ubi et quando visum est Deo,*" as the Augsburg Confession aptly puts it.[86] What is implied here is that, in the actualization of God's self by the Church, God Himself is present also in the hidden act of His freedom. In this act God is not coming *to* the cross, but *through* the cross to humanity. Without the Spirit proceeding from the Father, yet through the Son, the Word of the community would not elementally interrupt a single existence. It would only sound scandalously foolish. In the logic of freedom, the Spirit is not the bond of love but the vehicle of eternity (*vehiculum aeternitatis*),[87] an eternity defined by the beloved, the Church, which is Christ's body. Without the Spirit's creative coming, the confession of the community would become less and less audible and more and more obsolete, and the community itself would dwindle into nonexistence. But with the Spirit's coming, the Church, as Jüngel puts it, represents God as the one who liberates from self-incurred slavery and immaturity by granting a share in His freedom. In this way, also, it represents God as the one who makes self-deceiving people true by granting a share in His truth. In this way, finally, it represents God as the one who reconciles the world by granting a share in the peace of His life as Father, Son, and Holy Spirit in which the deepest opposites are united.[88]

It is from the perspective of the logic of freedom that the Spirit is an agent in the Spirit's own right. God alone is the creator of faith, through which the community can proclaim the cross for the well-being of the world (cf. John 6:51).[89]

---

[86] "where and when it pleases God" (Article V; *Die Bekenntnisschriften der evangelisch-lutherischen Kirche* [Göttingen: Vandenhoeck & Ruprecht, 1930, 1991], 58).

[87] Cf. *Mystery*, 388; *GGW* 532.

[88] "My Theology," *Essays II*, 17.

[89] Steven Paulson is quite right to have identified a proclamatory weakness in Jüngel's formulation of the doctrine of God. This weakness has to do with the absence of an account of God's coming as belonging also to the proclamation of the cross and, further, with Jüngel's reluctance to distinguish between God's relation to the person as self-securing and as believing. However, I do not think this is a weakness that *necessarily* inheres in Jüngel's analogical conception of the human-divine relation. Paulson reads Jüngel in close proximity to Barth and does not quite appreciate the proclamatory significance of those points where Jüngel also distances himself from Barth, especially the temporal and intersubjective character of God's self-determination. It is the cruciform character of God's revelation that enables one to recover a notion of divine hiddenness (which Jüngel himself is loath to surrender) as integral to revelation. If divine hiddenness is to be correlated not only with the *sub contrario* of the cross but also, as I have suggested here, with the divine logic of freedom – then, on the one hand, the hiddenness of God's freedom makes conceptual room for God's continued coming to humanity, and, on the other, it *might* also make it possible to conceptualize an experience of God's wrath.

First, God's hidden act of being is revealed, in light of God's identification with the Crucified One, as a most creative hiddenness. For in the narration of the cross, as I have proposed, the Spirit proceeds from the Father through the Son and, in this procession, reaches into and interrupts human lives (the logic of freedom). In so creating faith, the Spirit then comes to proceed also from the Body of Christ, which here and now, embraced out of nothingness,

Concluding remarks

The foregoing discussion of the trinitarian logic of love has been intended to demonstrate that it is possible to hold to a robustly intersubjective view of divine love, without at the same time surrendering the spontaneity and creativity that properly belong to God's being. I have discussed two modes in which humans reciprocate God's love: love and faith. In both, humans not only recognize God's gracious self-determination for humanity's sake but also co-respond to it with their entire being and, in doing so, return God's being to God. Human agency is that which renders God present to the world, insofar as God does not wish to have God's self without the

---

embraces the Father (the logic of love). Why some believe and not others must remain the *crux theologorum*. Importantly, however, God's act of coming in freedom, even as hidden, does not stand at odds with God's act of love. This preserves Jüngel's emphasis on faith's certainty that God's being is as God has determined God's self, that is, none other than love. In contradistinction to Luther (and by extension Paulson), already the light of grace, rather than glory, shows the unity of God's being in hiddenness and in love. God's love is shown to presuppose the hiddenness of divine freedom and to correspond to it. Faith, in other words, does not believe, as it does for Luther, that God is love in spite of God who "saves so few and damns so many." For Luther, faith is indispensable, because one cannot understand how the same God is "righteous when by his own will he makes us necessarily damnable" (*The Bondage of the Will*, *LW* 33:62, cf. 292; *WA* 18:633, cf. 785). But, for Jüngel, faith is a mode of being in which the elementally interrupted person recognizes God in the crucified Jesus and lets go of him- or herself. This interplay of love and hiddenness, to be sure, is undeveloped by Jüngel. That being the case, it is still quite certain that Jüngel's analogical construal of the divine-human relationship does not in principle make it impossible to account for God's coming in the proclamation of the cross.

Second, it is likewise an overstatement to say that Jüngel's doctrine of God lends itself, at best, only to an intellectual argument, aimed at the self-proclaimed atheist, to the effect that faith in God is not only possible but intellectually reputable. Paulson notes that, by contrast, "In proclamation God's being changes from wrath to love, from naked hiddenness to hiddenness clothed in the word" (*Analogy and Proclamation*, 19). This need not be antithetical to Jüngel's account. According to Jüngel, the Word of God does not meet humans in a condition of intellectual unbelief but as hopelessly contradictory and afflicted beings. In this contradiction lies an impossible demand – to receive oneself, from the world and in faith – impossible precisely in face of God's absence. And yet, insofar as one's self-contradiction is a fissure into the underlying relationality, this self-contradiction, the fact that humans cannot create themselves from nothing, inescapably raises the question of humanity as given to itself. It is this nagging questions and the attendant experience of God's absence that *could* be seen as an experience of divine wrath, of God-forsakenness. As self-contradictory, one stands before the hiddenness of a God who has withdrawn from one. One thus stands before a God who judges one's self-securing and with his absence passes a death sentence: as you want it, so you shall have it. Yet God has withdrawn from humanity because God has already assured a place for humanity through God's self-determination. God's judgment can thus be overridden only by an equally unlikely faith in the impossible: the gospel of the God who is one with the dead Jesus. This faith only God's coming can create, as one is embraced by God's love to be God's beloved, without whom God can only be absent in the world under divine judgment. The logic of freedom – though it does not furnish (and for good reasons) as strong a sense of divine hiddenness and wrath as Paulson might wish – does, I believe, make it possible to proclaim the cross and, through this proclamation, to place a self-securing human being in a fundamentally different relation to God: as God's beloved.

beloved. Neither mode, however, renders the individual or the community divine. Both are thoroughly relational and intersubjective.

There is also an important difference between the two modes of human reciprocation. In works of *love*, human agency, established through participation in the very freedom of God, carries on (so to speak) the work of divine love. Human works of love, precisely as human, become the presence of God who is love and who wishes to be the event of love only together with beloved humanity. The Church's *faith* is similar only up to a point. It also has to do with actually making present God's Word of love, instead of merely retelling the community's founding story. Yet crucially, and this is where the difference appears, concealed in this act of spiritual re-presenting – in which the Church is the body of Christ, a community marked by the cross – is also God in God's freedom. It is this coming of God in freedom that makes faith-full participation in God's freedom for love's sake possible in the first place. In other words, the difference between love and faith, as human modes of reciprocating God's love, is that, in love human agency represents God's agency, insofar as God in God's being has determined to identify his agency with human agency and thus to entrust God's self to the beloved; in faith, however, divine and human agencies are most carefully distinguished, though without either being dissolved or made redundant. Faith ultimately depends not only on the act of the believing community but also on God's creative act of elemental interruption. Therefore, "faith does not force itself into a position *between* God and God," the way the self-securing Cartesian ego places itself between God's essence and God's existence and, in doing so, enlists God in its project. "It is [rather] the essence of faith to let God be who he is" – the one who in coming interrupts, and frees humans from, self-securing.[90] This status that faith has assures that Jüngel's Feuerbachian criticism is met: God is love, but love, the love of the believing community, is *not* God. It belongs to faith to recognize this.[91]

All in all, in contradistinction to the metaphysical tradition, analogy, for Jüngel, means being God's counterpart, rather than a feeble reflection of this or that attribute of the divine being.

[90] *Mystery*, 176; *GGW* 237.
[91] Cf. *Mystery*, 339; *GGW* 464–5.

Conclusion: Divine-Human Togetherness

My goal in this study of divine and human freedom has been to think through Jüngel's interweaving of the doctrine of God and anthropology – not with a view to distancing the two but rather for the purpose of bringing them more seamlessly together. In broad outline, the task involved, on the one hand, examining Jüngel's doctrine of God both in light of its internal coherence and clarity and in light of the anthropological effects that Jüngel ascribes to it. It was by recourse to the latter that I proposed to identify and remove the ambiguities pervading Jüngel's account of God's subjectivity. On the other hand, this engagement with the doctrine of God allowed us at the same time to put forth a precise and rich account of the anthropological correspondences that God enjoys as the world's mystery.

Central to Jüngel's construal of God's freedom is his insistence that freedom consists in both independence and determinateness. But these two moments, already on the conceptual level, exist in tension, insofar as God's being in either cannot be anything less than fully actualized. What the foregoing analysis has shown is that Jüngel does not, in practice, discriminate between freedom's two moments and is able to consider God's spontaneity and God's identification with Jesus under either rubric. This observation, while indicating a lack of clarity, has allowed us to cast Jüngel's rather marginal discussion of God's freedom (i.e., outside of his engagement with the metaphysical tradition) onto a much larger canvas. We have been able to restate it terms of broader concerns that underlie Jüngel's doctrine of God in its non-polemical aspect. To those concerns belongs the safeguarding of God's spontaneity and creativity, as well as the intersubjective character of God's self-determination as an event of love. This intersubjectivity, it must be said, is not always robustly articulated, insofar as the beloved's response often seems to be taken for granted, which makes the beloved appear rather impassive at times. Yet Jüngel's entire construal of love as successful togetherness, evident especially in his anthropologically oriented essays, calls quite unambiguously for such intersubjective mutuality. So does his location of God's trinitarian self-determination at the cross.

With Jüngel's concerns carefully distinguished, we have been able to examine freedom and creativity in their togetherness, as well as, more importantly, the possibility of the lover's own nonbeing in the event of love. My argument for two distinct subjective structures underlying and distinguishing these (as I called them) existential acts has involved, in part, a re-deployment of the immanent and economic Trinity as intimately connected yet distinct aspects of divine subjectivity. In support, I have also invoked the presence of such acts in the elementally interrupted human being who – in those two acts of being and becoming, freedom and love – corresponds to God. All this has allowed me to posit an inalienable tri-polarity by which God's subjectivity is primordially characterized. Through it, God is able – in a decision of unmerited grace – to generate a different set of self-relations that allows God, in God's very being, to identify with another, to free this other into partnership with God's self, and to depend on the beloved's free response for God's own being in the world.

The logic of freedom may be considered a development of Jüngel's mediating proposal which seeks to do justice both to the freedom of God's self-revelation (though without saying much more about this freedom) and to God's self-determination by identifying with the crucified Jesus. But the logic of freedom is not fraught with the necessitarian and developmental overtones that attend Jüngel's construal of an inner motivation in God. Besides this, there are other considerable advantages to positing a distinct logic of freedom within God's subjective being, that is, the Spirit's procession from the Father which, as the Father's self-future, is "interrupted" by the Son, in such a way that the Father's future is nontautologously defined by the Son and so truly is Spirit. What are those advantages?

First of all, the logic unambiguously rules out a variety of deficient subjectivities that may lurk in the shadows of Jüngel's articulation of the doctrine of God. To begin with, it does not leave the subject who determines himself as an event of love empty. Without leaving the subject indeterminate but not detracting from the subject's determinateness, the logic of freedom makes the subject specific in the most pregnant of ways. Further, the logic explicitly rules out that in God's self-determination God could be a self-related subject tenaciously in control of his self-determination, or a subject who out of his detachment merely actualizes himself in the world. It disambiguates statements such as "God indeed comes form God, but God does not want to come to Himself without having come to humankind."[1]

---

[1] "What does it mean to say, 'God is love'?" T. Hart and D. Thimell (eds), *Christ in our Place: The Humanity of God in Christ for the Reconciliation of the World. Essays Presented to Prof. James Torrance* (Exeter, UK: Paternoster, 1989), 307

What it all boils down to is whether the beloved is merely accommodated within God's fundamental relationality, or whether out of this subjective relationality there now arises a genuinely intersubjective relation. The logic of freedom points unambiguously to the latter.

Second, freedom's tri-polar structure at the same time does not turn God into a subject who needs the world. It rather shows God as self-sufficient *a se*. Specifically, it makes it possible to give an account of God as subject of God's self-determination. It shows precisely how God's self-determination as an event of love belongs intimately to God's being, so much so that God corresponds to, rather than abandons, God's self in the event. And it shows further that in God there is no self-love but a motivation for love that does not detract from the possibility of God's being an event of love in life-giving togetherness with another. It is in this manner – as a subject that overflows with being in his very subjectivity and so is able to love even the loveless – that God is love.

Third, the logic of freedom accounts for God's self-limitation for the sake of the beloved as that which enables this self-limitation. It indicates precisely *how* the self-limitation takes place within the divine being, so that God remains "in utmost *concord* with himself."[2] The self-limitation, in turn, involves God in a struggle between being and nonbeing. The logic of freedom renders the character of this struggle specific as a struggle for God's presence as the absent one – as lover – in the world. The logic of freedom thus makes possible a death on God's part, which is the possibility of the impossible – of God's nonexistence in the world and the world's dying in its godlessness and God-forsakenness.

Fourth, the logic of freedom demonstrates that divine immanence has a *concrete* function *alongside of* God's determinateness, instead of being a mere (ad hoc?) distinction in thought for the sake of divine grace. It is God's subjective act of freedom that is "the most specific hiddenness of God *in* this world."[3] It enables one to account for the elemental interruption, faith, and one's incorporation into the community, insofar as the logic of freedom, alongside of the logic of love, shows God to be in coming. God comes through the cross, through God's own determinateness, as the future defined by the other and always, on his account, creatively defining itself by the other. The immanent Trinity belongs firmly to God's revelation.

Fifth, the logic of freedom discloses how humanity, not merely in its actions, but in its very being – in the subjective acts of freedom and love – is

---

[2] *Justification*, 83.
[3] *FoC*, 34.

in correspondence to God. At the end of his magnum opus Jüngel only signals that there are "human acts and modes of being" in which one "enters into the fact that God is coming to the world and that therefore [one] is not destined to possess [oneself]."[4] Jüngel categorizes those correspondences as falling under faith, hope, and love. In our account, we have correlated those correspondences rather more precisely with the two subjective acts in which the elementally interrupted person exists. Those human acts, we have claimed further, are in correspondence to God's being subject both in God's act of freedom and in God's specific determinateness as an act of love.

I have not correlated hope with either of the human acts. But I have emphasized it throughout as belonging to both, or rather lying in-between them. I do think one can actually be more specific than that. Hope is the now and not yet of the worldly presence of the God who loves us in freedom and into freedom. It is the logical pause that connects the two acts of an elementally interrupted existence. It is the point at which freedom becomes love, without ever ceasing to be freedom; it is the moment where the self-relation of freedom gives rise to rich intersubjective relationality. Love does not calculate, *love hopes out of faith*. This makes it stronger than death. Both for God and for us.

Some Trinitarian and Christological Considerations

In closing, it is necessary to spell out some of the broader trinitarian and christological implications of the above investigation. I shall do so, first of all, by reiterating the conclusions of this study in light of Jüngel's comments on how properly to articulate divine self-relatedness. Second, I shall indicate how the two modes of divine self-relation developed in this study – the logic of freedom and the logic of love – do justice to the historical accomplishment of Jesus' life in the context of full-blown trinitarianism.

God's self-relatedness

In the concluding section of his Barth *Paraphrase*, Jüngel notes that "The doctrine of the Trinity is an attempt to think through the self-relatedness of God's being."[5] The doctrinal intent is to conceptualize God's being as

---

[4] *Mystery*, 390; *GGW* 535.
[5] This and the following quotations come from *Becoming*, 114–15.

relational, so that neither is God made to be dependent on some other, nor is that relation reduced to a mere accidental property of a self-related substance. To achieve this goal, Jüngel points out, one must think of God's being as "*doubly* relational." "God can enter into a relation (*ad extra*) . . . because God's being (*ad intra*) is a being *related to itself*." This self-relatedness is none other than "the *power* of God's being *to become* the God of another."

Since *God's Being is in Becoming* is Jüngel's paraphrase of Barth's doctrine of the Trinity, what Jüngel has in mind is God's eternal self-willing which includes the man Jesus. As primary objectivity this self-willing then anchors God's self-giving for the sake of being known in Jesus of Nazareth. I have argued in the present study that Jüngel's own project is rather different from his articulation of Barth's trinitarianism. Jüngel's cruciform conception of God's self-determination is driven by a complex notion of love as intersubjective determination. In its backdrop are the modern avatars of self-love – self-securing and self-possession – which Jüngel exposes as unfreedom. To do justice to love's intersubjectivity, Jüngel, as we have seen, locates God's self-determination in the event of the cross. This move enables him to allow for the historical accomplishment of Jesus' existence (a point to which we shall return presently). This, in turn, opens up conceptual room for reciprocity in humanity's relation to God. The argument of this study has been that – in order to maintain one's commitment to this view of divine love without incoherence or being at odds with theological anthropology – Jüngel's conception of divine self-determination does actually require one to posit a self-relatedness of the divine being: not a primary objectivity but the logic of freedom. This crucial difference between Jüngel and Barth notwithstanding, our construal is not, as such, exempt from the criteria for sound trinitarianism that Jüngel puts forth in his discussion of Barth.

It is important to note that by insisting on the self-relatedness of God's being, Jüngel wishes to exclude the dependence of God's being on another, as well as making the divine economy a mere accident of God's being. These stipulations are really only some of the historical concerns that propelled the development of trinitarian doctrine in the first place. The constructive proposal presented here, I believe, avoids both these pitfalls. Let me return to some of its central points. When it comes to the dependence criterion, it might appear that the logic of love belies it. But what Jüngel means by the exclusion of God's dependence on another, whether Jesus, or more broadly, humans, is not that God must not be viewed as identifying God's self with the dead man and so determining God's self for an intersubjective relation. What is at stake rather is that "God's becoming must [not] first take place through 'something other than God' . . . God's self-relatedness must rather be understood as a *becoming proper* to his *own* being." In other words, self-determination belongs to God's independence as its original and irreducible capacity. As was pointed out in Chapter 4, God is a self-sufficient subject. Only thus can God's being-for-us be an act of grace and love.

The second stipulation calls for an integral connection between the self-relatedness of God and the divine economy. What it means for this study is that it is impermissible to regard the logic of freedom as the general principle or underlying essence of the divine being; likewise, neither may one view the logic of love as a contingent, merely illustrative actualization of this underlying essence. Anything less than actual, and anything less than fundamental and close correspondence will not do. We have repeatedly drawn attention to this inseparability-in-distinction of freedom and love, as well as the ontological actuality of their structures, in the course of our investigation. Here I wish only to register agreement with Jüngel's rejection of attempts to determine God's abstract essence, unaffected by God's acts, by distinguishing between God's "existentiality" and God's "concrete actualization."[6] God's being cannot be considered in abstraction from God's self-determination, just as God's self-determination cannot be considered something different from the divine being. "God's being," comments Jüngel, "is as such *concrete* – that is the point of the Christian doctrine of the Trinity."[7] This study, as I have just noted, has argued for precisely such a fundamental actuality and mutual interlocking of both the trinitarain logic of love and the logic of freedom. Regarding Jüngel's concern about attempts to establish a pure existentiality, or a phenomenology of the divine being, it should be pointed out once more that the logic of freedom is not a construct developed *remoto Deo* by simply positing an idea of God best suited to some perceived human need. Instead, its articulation is informed by – and thinks after (*denkt nach*) – God's self-disclosure in the event of the cross and its anthropological effects. Thus, even when one speaks of God prior to God's

---

[6] This distinction, based on the philosophy of Charles Hartshorne, was once recommended by Schubert Odgen in his article "Bultmann's Demythologizing and Hartshorne's Dipolar Theism," W. Reese and E. Freeman (eds), *Process and Divinity: The Hartshorne's Festschrift* (LaSalle, IL: Open Court, 1964), 103–24. For Jüngel's discussion, see *Becoming*, 115. Cf. also Paul DeHart's analysis in *Beyond the Necessary God: Trinitarian Faith and Philosophy in the Thought of Eberhard Jüngel* (Atlanta, GA: Scholars Press, 1999), 165–9. Unfortunately, for all the merits of his penetrating analysis of Jüngel's theistic critique, in these pages DeHart rather hastily lumps *together* Jüngel's engagement with Barth *and* Jüngel's own trinitarian reconstruction.

[7] Emphasis added.

cruciform self-definition, one speaks only of an originary tri-polar openness whose coming to light cannot be severed from God's self-determination, not to mention that it is disclosed only as hiddenness, as the fount of creative possibility within God's intersubjective being. There is no underlying essence that can be determined or otherwise captured to the exclusion of God's own being-in-act. What there is an actuality intimately tided to God's self-determination as love.

For this reason Jüngel also denies that Heidegger's distinction between the ontological and the ontic can be applied to the being of God. Now, it may appear that this study's reconceptualization of God's being through the anthropological distinction between the passive and active acts of being is guilty of this very error. To be sure, the argument, advanced in Chapter 2, for the impossibility of self-securing drew on a fundamental ontology akin to Heidegger's. The impossibility of ontic self-securing was attributed to the relational character of humanity, to the persistence of an underlying ontological structure to which the various contingent failures and contradictions of self-securing point. However, the structure as such remains abstract and ungraspable.[8] It can only become manifest and gain specificity in God's act of elemental interruption. In the actuality of God's relation to one and one's resulting correspondence to God, the distinction between the ontological and the ontic is transcended and transformed into two concrete and closely corresponding anthropological acts of existence: freedom and love. The act of freedom, in other words, is not determined by stripping away the ontic layer but, once again, by thinking after God's creative self-disclosure. Consequently, what this study has applied to the being of God is not the Heideggerian schema but the concrete anthropological effects of God's relational self-determination, which leave this schema behind.[9]

Jesus and the triune being of God

To be sure, the interlocking of the logic of freedom and the logic of love, within the uncompromisable actuality of God's self-disclosure, indicates that Jesus *uniquely* belongs to God's self-definition. God's identification with the dead man does not stand alongside of humanity's participation in the triune life of God, or of believers' loving actualization of God's presence-as-the-absent-one, as the lover, in the world. Rather, it is God's cruciform

---

[8] Not to mention that its philosophical articulation seems to be fraught with insoluble ambiguity; see Chapter 3, fn. 48.
[9] See 124 above.

self-determination that enables human reciprocation in the first place. God's trinitarian self-definition for the sake of human freedom is that which makes possible this freedom's exercise in loving togetherness between the God who makes himself known and humans who through God's act are known better than they know themselves. The cross is the center of this togetherness.

We have explored the pivotal role of the cross in both the logic of love and the logic of freedom in quite some detail. We have also investigated the possibility of reciprocation that the cross opens up. Here we must reiterate the more specific presupposition of this reciprocation: The unique status of Jesus in God's self-definition is achieved without prejudice to the historical accomplishment of Jesus' life. It is only by identifying with Jesus' death that God also *retroactively* claims the life of this man as God's own. As noted earlier, Jüngel appropriates the notion of retroactive ontological consequences of Jesus' vindication by God from Wolfhart Pannenberg.[10] For Pannenberg, "Jesus' resurrection is not only constitutive for our perception of his divinity, but it is *ontologically constitutive* for that divinity. . . . [Only] from the perspective of the resurrection . . . is [Jesus] retrospectively one with God in his whole pre-Easter life."[11] Pannenberg's goal, informed by critical scholarship of the New Testament, is to illuminate how the history of Jesus – as a true human being firmly embedded in his own historical setting – came to play a constitutive role in the postresurrection community's confession of him as God's Son. Pannenberg does not believe that an account of this role should be preempted by abstract dogmatic considerations that have to do with unifying the divine with the human. Jesus, Pannenberg argues, must be considered and confessed to be God in no other way than as the human he was.

What characterized Jesus' life, according to Pannenberg, was not only the natural human openness to the world but above all a total openness to God. Jesus' message and actions had only one goal: to announce God's coming kingdom. In proclaiming it, "Jesus knew himself to be functionally one with God's will," so much so that he made others' fate in the imminent kingdom depend on their relation to himself as its proclaimer. In this way, he knew himself "to be one with God himself." Importantly, however, it was "with the Father – not a divine hypostasis differentiated from him – with whom Jesus

---

[10] To Jüngel's move away from the Barthian schema of Jesus' anhypostatic/enhypostatic existence in favor of Pannenberg's retroactive ontology, see Chapter 2, fn. 68.

[11] Wolfhart Pannenberg, *Jesus – God and Man*, trans. L. L. Wilkins and D. A. Priebe (Philadelphia: Westminster, 1968), 224 (emphasis added).

knew himself to be one."[12] This means that "his unity with God was hidden not only to other men but above all, which emerges from a critical examination of the tradition, for Jesus himself also."[13] God's future, begun in Jesus message, would only be consummated with the coming of the Son of Man, an eschatological figure whom Jesus announced but with whom he did not identify.[14] This consummation would then "decide the rightness or wrongness of [Jesus'] own activity."[15] Jesus' crucifixion as such must have seemed like Jesus' utter failure – instead of the kingdom's powerful arrival, its messenger was subjected to a gruesome execution. His fate, however, as the early Christian community perceived, was not a failure when all was said and done. Pannenberg comments: "The trust in the God who has been perceived in the clarity of the message of the immanent Kingdom, of the imminent Lordship of God, had to find its vindication precisely in the darkness of the failure of just this message." However, that Jesus' death in unflagging devotion to God was not a failure, after all, was determined by God alone. "Only by the resurrection is Jesus' personal community with God confirmed from God's side also."[16] So much so that Jesus is now recognized not only as identical with the coming Son of Man, in whom the kingdom is consummated, but above all as the divine Son who belongs to God's very being.

Jüngel agrees with Pannenberg in the placement of divine vindication at the end of Jesus' life. But his agreement is driven less by historical-critical concerns. This is not to say that those are unimportant, or that Jüngel must, therefore, fall back on abstract conceptualizations of Jesus' divinity and humanity. Rather, Jüngel tacitly accepts the critical research that drives Pannenberg's dogmatic construal, but Jüngel chooses to account for the conclusions of this research in terms of the intersubjectivity of love. Love, which allows another to play a role in one's self-determination and relies on the other's recognition, demands that justice be done to the accomplishment of Jesus' life as, above all, a human life. A concern for love's distance and nearness is what leads Jüngel to locate God's identification with, and vindication of, Jesus in the event of the cross.

If one were to venture a guess why it is the cross and not the resurrection that constitutes God's trinitarian self-determination, it could be said, in

---

[12] Pannenberg, *Jesus – God and Man*, 334. Cf. *Paulus und Jesus: eine Untersuchung zur Präzisierung der Frage nach dem Ursprung der Christologie* (Tübingen: Mohr Siebeck, 1962), 281–2.

[13] Pannenberg, *Jesus – God and Man*, 321.

[14] Cf. *Paulus und Jesus*, 262.

[15] Pannenberg, *Jesus – God and Man*, 332.

[16] Pannenberg, *Jesus – God and Man*, 335.

light of this study's constructive proposal, that Jüngel thus makes room for believers' participation. While the cross is the place of God's intersubjective self-definition as God-for-us, the resurrection comprehends the reciprocation of Christ's body, the church, which justifies God's being-for-us as *for us* indeed. The resurrection is the locale of the beloved's return of being to the lover, insofar as the body of Christ makes God present as the one who for the sake of this humanly actualized presence is absent. In short, Jesus' resurrection is also the rise of the believing, and so also loving, community as Christ's body – a rise enabled and called for by God's unique, cruciform self-determination.

Importantly, with its emphatic insistence on love, Jüngel's articulation of God's being emerges, from the constructive proposal of this study, as transcending the dichotomy between a christology from above and a christology from below. On the one hand, the doctrine of God presented here does justice to the historical development of trinitarian doctrine as postresurrection reflection on the life and death of Jesus – a fact to which Pannenberg's christology wishes to accord fundamental dogmatic significance. Jesus plays a constitutive role in God's triune being. On the other hand, this study thinks through the mutual loving recognition manifest in God's identification with Jesus' death and life-of-dedication-to-God, and on the basis of this reciprocity calls for the necessary articulation of trinitarian immanence, the logic of freedom, as its presupposition. Both Pannenberg and Jüngel have been charged with reducing the Logos to "a kind of eternally personified idea of self-surrender which becomes actual in Jesus' self-surrender to the Father without effectively determining this process. The unity of the Logos with Jesus would then be 'decided' only retrospectively."[17] Thomas Koppehl, who makes this charge, is right that neither for Pannenberg nor for Jüngel does the Logos determine Jesus' life. He may also be correct that, for Pannenberg, the Logos is for this reason only an idea of self-surrender. But this conclusion need not – and actually must not – follow for Jüngel. The logic of freedom shows the Logos to be far more than an idea. The Logos is the fundamental interruptedness of God's originary tri-polarity and creative actuality. The Logos – as the structural embodiment of the divine self's capacity intersubjectively to address God's self to that which is beyond God's self – plays a vital role in God's self-differentiation and identification with the Crucified One.

---

[17] Thomas Koppehl, "Die Christologie I. A. Dorners im Vergleich zu der E. Jüngels," *Die Wissenschaftliche Standpunkt der Theologie Isaak August Dorners* (Berlin: De Gruyter, 1997), 315.

What Jüngel's theology of divine freedom and love enables us to avoid is the sort of christology from below that ends up prematurely caught up in a christology from above, to the detriment of both. In the Introduction to this volume, it was stated that this study sees itself as, in a modest measure, responding to Isaak Dorner's call for articulating a personalist and ethical doctrine of God, a task ultimately neglected by the Reformation. Dorner himself attempts to put forth a christology that does justice to the human self-consciousness of Jesus; he does so by understanding the incarnation as a process. Yet there never appears an aspect of Jesus' developing self-consciousness that is not immediately united with the Logos. All that is human about Jesus is progressively assumed by the Logos and is, in fact, divine-human. In the unity of his person (Dorner is keen to avoid a double personality in Jesus), Jesus comes to know and will himself always as God-human.[18] This raises the issue of the genuineness of Jesus' humanity as a humanly accomplished existence. Likewise, when it comes to Jesus' relation to God, God appears simply to incorporate Jesus' developing humanity in the structures of God's own absolute personality, to the detriment of divine relationality. No room is left for loving self-determination with a view to allowing the other an active part in it. What Dorner accomplishes is an arguably confused welding together of a christology from below with one from above. He is not able, however, to transcend this binary paradigm, a possibility that is opened up through an interpretation of the cross as an event of divine love. By contrast, the proposal put forth here rests on the premise that it is through Jesus, in the concreteness of his human life and death, that God determines God's being as triune; but the love evident in the divine self-determination actually points to an original tri-polarity of the divine being as the presupposition of revelatory intersubjectivity. Hence, our critical appropriation of Jüngel's notion of God's cruciform self-definition has enabled us to place Jüngel's doctrine of God between an understanding of God's triunity rooted in a christology from below (such as that advanced by Pannenberg), and a trinitarianism that reflects a christology from above, where Jesus' humanity is immediately appropriated by the Logos. While preserving the insights of both approaches, our proposal succeeds in transcending their one-sidedness through a complex conceptualization of love.

This study's strong insistence on the integrity of Jesus' human life, coupled with the fact that it is claimed by God as God's own only at its end,

---

[18] Isaak August Dorner, *A System of Christian Doctrine*, trans. A. Cave and J. S. Banks, vol. 3 (Edinburgh: T&T Clark, 1885), 308–18.

leads perhaps to two questions: Who is the God whose kingdom Jesus proclaims? And is Jesus' being interrupted by God? The God whom Jesus proclaims and who is yet to determine God's self in Jesus' gruesome death is the one whose being alone is originary openness, who is a fount of possibility – the one who alone can interrupt the self-securing human existence. For human self-possession, on account of its contradictions, cannot possibly be the be-all-and-end-all of human being! Jesus' God is the God of Israel who is about to make himself clear – one might even say: disambiguate himself – in communion with Jesus as the one who is open to all of humanity, as the one who, in the coming of his kingdom, empowers humans to be God-lovers in a godless, but not God-forsaken, world. Jesus is one who, against overwhelming odds, believes in God's hidden power to interrupt human time with the time of God's kingdom. Yet, even as he takes upon himself the violent assault of the world's God-forsakenness and responds to it in the least likely of ways, with love, Jesus himself must await God's vindicating self-clarification. In this way, Jesus is uniquely "made sin for us [ὑπὲρ ἡμῶν ἁμαρτίαν ἐποίησεν]" (2 Corinthians 5:21),[19] who must experience the very real God-lessness of the world; yet mysteriously he believes in the hidden possibilities of God with an utterly unique "faith of Jesus Christ" (πίστις 'Ιησοῦ Χριστοῦ, Romans 3:22).[20] Jesus is not elementally interrupted; he is retroactively vindicated as God's Son. Thanks to Jesus' faith, the world's godlessness is *for us* only the presence of God who empowers us to be God's people; and our life of faith is our constant standing before God who has made His self clear *for us* by identifying God's self with Jesus, "the loneliest of men,"[21] in this man's death.

One might object perhaps that God's trinitarian self-determination understood as intersubjective identification with the crucified Jesus undercuts Christianity's fundamental commitment to the unity of God. Jüngel diffuses this criticism by pointing to the unity of love which God is: "Under the category of *love*, the being of the triune God is so understood that, with the three Persons of Father, Son, and Holy Spirit, defined as relations, one grasps at the same time one divine being."[22] To state the obvious, one might also add that, from the perspective of Christology, the doctrine of the Trinity is always in some (though rather vague) sense

---

[19] Cf. *Mystery*, 367; *GGW* 504.
[20] This is contra Jüngel's early treatment of this phrase, in *Paulus und Jesus*, 274, as an objective, rather than subjective, genitive.
[21] *Mystery*, 354; *GGW* 485.
[22] "Das Sein Jesu Christi als Ereignis der Versöhnung Gottes mit einer gottlosen Welt: Die Hingabe des Gekreuzigten," *TE II*, 277.

intersubjective, insofar as Christ is also fully human. What our investigation has made clear, however, is that in freedom relationality becomes the fabric of reality, so much so that reality can no longer be broken into self-contained selves, or persons, without an infinite loss. God is one in that God is freedom in and of God's self. But even as such God transcends the category of being, not only because God is not a creature but fundamentally because God is being that overflows itself. Insofar as we have shown that freedom never pertains to a self-contained subject, the rest is simply togetherness, or, to use Jüngel's phrase, "the order – of peace."[23]

---

[23] "Ordnung gibt der Freiheit einen Raum," *Evangelische Freiheit – kirchliche Ordnung: Beiträge zum Selbstverständnis der Kirche* (Stuttgart: Quell, 1987), 118.

Bibliography

Eberhard Jüngel's Works

A bibliography of Jüngel's writings, appended to his 2004 *Festschrift*, extends upto 45 pages and includes 581 items (many of which are reprints revisions and translations). The list below contains Jüngel's monographs, essay and sermon collections and the most important essays and articles published in journals and edited volumes. Those essays that were eventually collected in the five volumes of Jüngel's *Theologische Erörterungen* are, with a few exceptions, listed only as part of those volumes, with the original publication date alone included in parentheses. English translations are cross-referenced, with 'G =' denoting a reference to the German edition.

German

1962   *Paulus und Jesus: eine Untersuchung zur Präzisierung der Frage nach dem Ursprung der Christologie* (Tübingen: Mohr Siebeck; 7th edn. 2004).

1964   *Zum Ursprung der Analogie bei Parmenides und Heraklit* (Berlin: de Gruyter). [=1980 .3]

1965   *Gottes Sein ist im Werden: Verantwortliche Rede vom Sein Gottes bei Karl Barth. Eine Paraphrase* (Tübingen: Mohr Siebeck; 4th edn. 1986).

1968   *Predigten. Mit einem Anhang: Was hat die Predigt mit dem Text zu tun?* (München: Kaiser). [=2003/d]

1971/a   "Das Sakrament – Was ist das? Versuch einer Antwort," Eberhard Jüngel und Karl Rahner, *Was ist ein Sakrament? Vorstöße zur Verständigung* (Freiburg: Herder), 7–61.

1971/b   *Tod* (Stuttgart, Kreuz Verlag; 4th edn. Gütersloh: Mohn, 1990).

1972/a   *Unterwegs zur Sache. Theologische Erörterungen I* (Tübingen: Mohr Siebeck; 3rd edn. 2000).

       1 "Drei Vorbemerkungen," 7–10;

       2 "»Theologische Wissenschaft und Glaube« im Blick auf die Armut Jesu" (1964), 11–33;

       3 "Das Verhältnis der theologischen Disziplinen untereinander" (1968), 34–59;

4 "Gottes umstrittene Gerechtigkeit. Eine reformatorische Besinnung zum paulinischen Begriff δικαιοσύνε θεοῦ" (1968), 60–79;

5 "Gott – als Wort unserer Sprache" (1969), 80–104;

6 "Vom Tod des lebendigen Gottes: Ein Plakat" (1968), 105–25;

7 "Jesu Wort und Jesus als Wort Gottes. Ein hermeneutischer Beitrag zum christologischen Problem" (1966), 126–44;

8 "Das Gesetz zwischen Adam und Christus. Eine theologische Studie zu Röm 5,12–21" (1963), 145–72;

9 "Ein Paulinischer Chiasmus. Zum Verständnis der Vorstellung vom Gericht nach den Werken in Röm 2, 2–11" (1963), 173–8;

10 "Die Autorität des bittenden *Christus*. Eine These zur materialen Begründung der Eigenart des Wortes Gottes. Erwägungen zum Problem der Infallibilität in der Theologie" (1970), 179–88;

11 "Irren ist menschlich. Zur Kontroverse um Hans Küngs Buch »Unfehlbar? Eine Anfrage«" (1971), 189–205;

12 "Die Welt als Möglichkeit und Wirklichkeit. Zum ontologischen Ansatz der Rechtfertigungslehre" (1969), 206–33;

13 "Erwägungen zur Grundlegung evangelischer. Ethik im Anschluß an die Theologie des Paulus. Eine biblische Meditation" (1966), 234–45;

14 "Freiheitsrechte und Gerechtigkeit" (1968), 246–56;

15 "Der Schritt des Glaubens im Rhythmus der Welt" (1969), 257–73;

16 "Thesen zur Grundlegung der Christologie" (1969/70), 274–95;

17 "Was ist »das unterscheidend Christliche«?" (1971), 296–9.

1972/b "Womit steht und fällt heute der christliche Glaube?" F. H. Tenbruck, G. Klein, E. Jüngel und A. Sand *Spricht Gott in der Geschichte?* (Freiburg: Herder), 154–77.

1974 *Geistesgegenwart. Predigten* (München: Kaiser). [=2003/e]

1976/a *Anfechtung und Gewissheit des Glaubens: oder, Wie die Kirche wieder zu ihrer Sache kommt. Zwei Vorträge* (München: Kaiser).

1 "Anfechtung und Gewißheit des Glaubens. Wie bleibt die Kirche bei ihrer Sache?" 9–46 [=2003/c5];

2 "Die Bedeutung der Predigt angesichts unserer volkskirchlichen Existenz," 47–71.

1976/b *Gott – für den ganzen Menschen* (Einsiedeln/Zürich/Köln: Benziger).

1 "Gott – im Totentanz (Jes 53,3)," 9–17;

2 "Gott – für den ganzen Menschen (Jes 55,1–5)," 19–33;

3 "Der Gott entsprechende Mensch (Eph 4,24f.)," 35–45;

4 "Keine Angst vor der Angst (1 Joh 4,17b)," 47–58;

5 "Eine Trauerpredigt (Ps 121,4.7f.)," 59–63.

1976/c   Wolfgang Teichert (ed.), *Müssen Christen Sozialisten sein? Zwischen Glaube und Politik* (Hamburg: Lutherisches Verlagshaus).

– "Zukunft und Hoffnung. Zur politischen Funktion christlicher Theologie," 11–30;

– "Warum gleich mit dem Faß geworden? Über die Kunst, mit roter Tinte umzugehen. Offener Brief an Helmut Gollwitzer," 41–9;

– "Wer denkt konkret?" 111–17.

1976/d   *Von Zeit zu Zeit: Betrachtungen zu d. Festzeiten im Kirchenjahr* (München: Kaiser).

1 "Von Zeit zu Zeit," 5–7;

2 "Weihnachten – Freude am menschlichen Gott," 8–14;

3 "Karfreitag – Das dunkle Wort vom »Tode Gottes«," 15–63;

4 "Ostern – Das Geheimnis des Gekreuzigten," 64–72;

5 "Himmelfahrt – Gottes Offener Himmel über uns (Röm 10,6–8)," 73–82;

6 "Pfingsten – Aufruhr zur Treue," 83–7;

7 "Reformationsfest – Freiheit unter Gottesschutz (Röm 10,4)," 88–95.

1977/a   *Gott als Geheimnis der Welt. Zur Begründung der Theologie des Gekreuzigten im Streit zwischen Theismus und Atheismus* (Tübingen: Mohr Siebeck; 8th edn. 2010).

1977/b   "Gott entsprechendes Schweigen? Theologie in der Nachbarschaft des Denkens von Martin Heidegger," *Martin Heidegger: Fragen an sein Werk* (Stuttgart: Philipp Reclam), 37–45.

1977/c   *Der Wahrheit zum Recht verhelfen* (Stuttgart: Kreuz Verlag).

1 "Zu dieser Schrift," 7–12;

2 "Mit unserer Macht ist nichts getan," 13–25;

3 "Liebe zur Wahrheit," 26–39;

4 "Barmherzigkeit des Rechts – Recht der Barmherzigkeit," 40–51;

5 "Zur Wahrheit dem Recht verhelfen," 52–60;

6 "».. . daß nimmermehr loskomm der Große Krebs«, Pfingstsonntage 1977," 61–9;

7 "Der Mensch dem Menschen kein Wolf," 70–7;

8 "Was nicht wahr ist, macht auch nicht frei – was nicht frei macht, ist auch nicht wahr. Zum 500. Jubiläum der Eberhard-Karls Universität Tübingen am 9. Oktober 1977," 78–89.

9 "Betroffen," 90–3.

1978/a "Die Wirksamkeit des Entzogenen. Zum Vorgang geschichtlichen Verstehens als Einführung in die Christologie," Barbara Aland (ed.), *Gnosis. Festschrift für Hans Jonas* (Göttingen: Vandenhoeck & Ruprecht), 15–32.

1978/b *Zur Freiheit eines Christenmenschen. Eine Erinnerung an Luthers Schrift* (München: Kaiser). [=2000 .5]

1979 *Reden für die Stadt: zum Verhältnis von Christengemeinde und Bürgergemeinde* (München: Kaiser).

    1 "Salz der Erde. Zum Verhältnis von Christen Gemeinde und Bürgergemeinde," 13–47 [=2003/c8];

    2 "Segen für die Stadt," 48–59.

1980 *Entsprechungen: Gott – Wahrheit – Mensch. Theologische Erörterungen II* (Tübingen: Mohr Siebeck; 3rd edn. 2002).

    1 "Die Freiheit der Theologie" (1967), 11–36;

    2 "Theologie in der Spannung zwischen Wissenschaft und Bekenntnis" (1973), 37–51;

    3 "Zum Ursprung der Analogie bei Parmenides und Heraklit" (1964), 52–102 [=1964];

    4 "Metaphorische Wahrheit. Erwägungen zur theologischen Relevanz der Metapher als Beitrag zur Hermeneutik einer narrativen Theologie" (1974), 105–57;

    5 "Das Dilemma der natürlichen Theologie und die Wahrheit ihres Problems Überlegungen für ein Gespräch mit Wolfhart Pannenberg" (1975), 158–77;

    6 "Extra Christum nulla salus – als Grundsatz natürlicher Theologie? Evangelische Erwägungen zur »Anonymität« des Christenmenschen" (1975), 178–92;

    7 "Gott – um seiner selbst willen interessant. Plädoyer für eine natürlichere Theologie" (1975), 193–7;

    8 "Gelegentliche Thesen zum Problem der natürlichen Theologie" (1977), 198–201;

    9 "Quae supra nos, nihil ad nos. Eine Kurzformel der Lehre vom verborgenen Gott – im Anschluß an Luther interpretiert" (1972), 202–51;

    10 "Gottesgewißheit" (1979), 252–64;

    11 "Das Verhältnis von »ökonomischer« und »immanenter« Trinität. Erwägungen über eine biblische Begründung der Trinitätslehre – im Anschluß an und in Auseinandersetzung mit Karl Rahners Lehre vom dreifaltigen Gott als transzendentem Urgrund der Heilsgeschichte" (1975), 265–75;

12 "Das Sein Jesu Christi als Ereignis der Versöhnung Gottes mit einer gottlosen Welt: Die Hingabe des Gekreuzigten" (1978), 276–84;

13 "Säkularisierung - Theologische Anmerkungen zum Begriff einer weltlichen Welt" (1972), 285–9;

14 "Der Gott entsprechende Mensch. Bemerkungen zur Gottebenbildlichkeit des Menschen als Grundfigur theologischer Anthropologie" (1975), 290–317;

15 "Der alte Mensch – als Kriterium der Lebensqualität. Bemerkungen zur Menschenwürde der leistungsunfähigen Person" (1976), 318–21;

16 "Recht auf Leben – Recht auf Sterben: Theologische Bemerkungen" (1975), 322–6;

17 "Der Tod als Geheimnis des Lebens" (1976), 327–54;

18 "Grenzen des Menschseins" (1971), 355–61;

19 "Mut zur Angst. Dreizehn Aphorismen zum Jahreswechsel" (1978), 362–70;

20 "Lob der Grenze" (1973), 371–7.

1981 (with Ingolf U. Dalferth) "Person und Gottebenbildlichkeit," Franz Böckle et al. (eds), *Christlicher Glaube in moderner Gesellschaft* (Freiburg: Herder).

1982 *Barth-Studien* (Zürich: Benziger).

1 "Vorwort," 9–14;

2 "Karl Barth" (1969), 15–21;

3 "Einführung in Leben und Werk Karl Barths" (1981), 22–60;

4 "Die theologischen Anfänge. Beobachtungen," 61–126;

5 "Von der Dialektik zur Analogie. Die Schule Kierkegaards und der Einspruch Petersons," 127–79;

6 "Evangelium und Gesetz. Zugleich vom Verhältnis von Dogmatik und Ethik," 180–209;

7 "Die Möglichkeit theologischer Anthropologie auf dem Grunde der Analogie. Eine Untersuchung zum Analogieverständnis Karl Barths" (1962), 210–32;

8 "Der königliche Mensch. Eine christologische Reflexion auf die Würde des Menschen in der Theologie Karl Barths" (1966), 233–45;

9 "Karl Barths Lehre von der Taufe: Ein Hinweis auf ihre Probleme" (1968), 246–90;

10 "Thesen zu Karl Barths Lehre von der Taufe" (1971), 291–4;

11 "Zur Kritik des sakramentalen Verständnisses der Taufe," 295–314;

12 "Anrufung Gottes als Grundethos christlichen Handelns. Einführende Bemerkungen zu den nachgelassenen Fragmenten der Ethik der Versöhnungslehre Karl Barths" (1980), 315–31;

13 ". . . keine Menschlosigkeit Gottes . . . Zur Theologie Karl Barths zwischen Theismus und Atheismus" (1971), 332–47.

1983/a   *Schmecken und Sehen. Predigten III* (München: Kaiser). [=2003/f]

1983/b   "Zur Lehre vom heiligen Geist. Thesen," Ulrich Luz and Hans Weder (eds), *Die Mitte des Neuen Testaments: Einheit und Vielfalt neutestamentlicher Theologie: Festschrift für Eduard Schweizer zum siebzigsten Geburtstag* (Göttingen: Vandenhoeck & Ruprecht), 97–118.

1984   (with Michael Trowitzsch) "Provozierendes Denken: Bemerkungen zur theologischen Anstößigkeit der Denkwege Martin Heideggers," *Neue Hefte für Philosophie* 23, 59–74.

1986   "»Jedermann sei untertan der Obrigkeit . . . «: Eine Bibelarbeit über Römer 13,1–7," E. Jüngel, R. Herzog und H. Simon, *Evangelische Christen in unserer Demokratie: Beiträge aus der Synode der Evangelischen Kirche* (Gütersloh: Verlagshaus Mohn), 8–37.

1987   "Ordnung gibt der Freiheit einen Raum," *Evangelische Freiheit - kirchliche Ordnung: Beiträge zum Selbstverständnis der Kirche* (Stuttgart: Quell), 105–19.

1989/a   "Nihil divinitatis, ubi non fides. Ist christliche Dogmatik in rein theoretischer Perspektive möglich? Bemerkungen zu einem theologischen Entwurf von Rang" *Zeitschrift für Theologie und Kirche* 86, 204–35.

1989/b   *Unterbrechungen. Predigten IV* (München: Kaiser). [=2003/g]

1989/c   "Zum Begriff der Offenbarung," Gerhard Besier and Eduard Lohse (eds), *Glaube – Bekenntnis – Kirchenrecht* (Hannover: Lutherisches Verlaghaus), 215–21.

1990/a   "Unterbrechung des Weltlebens: Eberhard Jüngel über »Gottes Sein ist im Werden« (1965)," Henning Ritter (ed.), *Werksbesichtigung Geisteswissenschaften: Fünfundzwanzig Bücher von ihren Autoren gelesen* (Frankfurt am Main: Insel Verlag), 131–8.

1990/b   *Wertlose Wahrheit. Zur Identität und Relevanz des christlichen Glaubens. Theologische Erörterungen III* (Tübingen: Mohr Siebeck; 2nd edn. 2003).

1 "»Meine Theologie« – kurz gefaßt" (1985), 1–15;

2 "Glauben und Verstehen: zum Theologiebegriff Rudolf Bultmanns" (1985), 16–77;

3 "». . . Du redest wie ein Buch . . . «: Zum Verständnis der »Philosophischen Brocken« des J. Climacus, herausgegeben von *Sören Kierkegaard* (1813–55)" (1988), 78–89;

4 "Wertlose Wahrheit: Christliche Wahrheitserfahrung im Streit gegen die »Tyrannei der Werte«" (1979), 90–109;

5 "Anthropomorphismus als Grundproblem neuzeitlicher Hermeneutik" (1982), 110–31;

6 "Das Entstehen von Neuem" (1988), 132–50;

7 "Gottes ursprüngliches Anfangen als schöpferische Selbstbegrenzung. Ein Beitrag zum Gespräch mit Hans Jonas über den »Gottesbegriff nach Auschwitz«" (1986), 151–62;

8 "Die Offenbarung der Verborgenheit Gottes. Ein Beitrag zum evangelischen Verständnis der Verborgenheit des göttlichen Wirkens" (1984), 163–82;

9 "Gottes Geduld – Geduld der Liebe" (1983), 183–93;

10 "Der menschliche Mensch. Die Bedeutung der reformatorischen Unterscheidung der Person von ihren Werken für das Selbstverständnis des neuzeitlichen Menschen" (1985), 194–213;

11 "Zur dogmatischen Bedeutung der Frage nach dem historischen Jesus" (1988), 214–42;

12 "Das Geheimnis der Stellvertretung. Ein dogmatisches Gespräch mit Heinrich Vogel" (1983), 243–60;

13 "Das Opfer Jesu Christi als sacramentum et exemplum. Was bedeutet das Opfer Christi für den Beitrag der Kirchen zur Lebensbewältigung und Lebensgestaltung?" (1982), 261–82;

14 "Der evangelisch verstandene Gottesdienst," 283–310;

15 "Die Kirche als Sakrament?" (1983), 311–34;

16 "Einheit der Kirche – konkret" (1983), 335–45;

17 "Leben aus Gerechtigkeit. Gottes Handeln – menschliches Tun" (1988/89), 346–64;

18 "Hat der christliche Glaube eine besondere Affinität zur Demokratie?" (1985), 365–77;

19 "»Auch das Schöne muß sterben« Schönheit im Lichte der Wahrheit. Theologische Bemerkungen zum ästhetischen Verhältnis" (1984), 378–98;

20 "Was heißt beten?" (1982), 397–405.

1997/a "Die Freiheit eines Christenmenschen: Freiheit als Summe des Christentums," Michael Beintker, Eberhard Jüngel and Wolf Krötke (eds), *Wege zum Einverständnis. Festschrift für Christoph Demke* (Leipzig: Evangelische Verlagsanstalt), 118–37.

1997/b "Um Gottes willen - Klarheit! Kritische Bemerkungen zur Verharmlosung der kriteriologischen Funktion des Rechtfertigungsartikels – aus Anlaß einer ökumenischen, »Gemeinsamen Erklärung zur Rechtfertigungslehre«," *Zeitschrift für Theologie und Kirche* 94, 394–406.

1998/a "Amica Exegesis einer römischen Note," *Zeitschrift für Theologie und Kirche*, Beiheft 10, 252–79.

1998/b *Das Evangelium von der Rechtfertigung des Gottlosen als Zentrum des christlichen Glaubens. Eine theologische Studie in ökumenischer Absicht* (Tübingen: Mohr Siebeck; 5th edn. 2006).

1998/c "Zum Gewissen," *Communio viatorum* 40:1, 33–43.

1999/a "Hoffnung: Bemerkungen zum christlichen Verständnis des Begriffs," *Edith-Stein-Jahrbuch* 5, 55–62.

1999/b "Die Theologie als Narr im Haus der Wissenschaften," Johann Reikerstorfer (ed.), *Zum gesellschaftlichen Schicksal der Theologie. Ein Wiener Symposium zu Ehren von Johann Baptist Metz* (Münster: Lit), 60–72.

2000 *Indikative der Gnade – Imperative der Freiheit: Theologische Erörterungen IV* (Tübingen: Mohr Siebeck).

    1 "Zum Wesen des Christentums" (1994), 1–23;

    2 "Untergang oder Renaissance der Religion? Überlegungen zu einer schiefen Alternative" (1995), 24–39;

    3 "Die Wahrheit des Mythos und die Notwendigkeit der Entmythologisierung" (1991), 40–57;

    4 "Meine Zeit steht in Deinen Händen (Psalm 31,16). Zur Würde des befristeten Menschenlebens" (1997), 58–83;

    5 "Zur Freiheit eines Christenmenschen. Eine Erinnerung an Luthers Schrift," (1978), 84–160 [=1978/b];

    6 "Mit Frieden Staat zu machen: politische Existenz nach Barmen V" (1984), 161–204;

    7 "Die Wahrnehmung des Anderen in der Perspektive des christlichen Glaubens" (1997), 205–30;

    8 "Gewinn im Himmel und auf Erden. Theologische Bemerkungen zum Streben nach Gewinn" (1997), 231–51;

    9 "Häresis – ein Wort[,] das wieder zu Ehren gebracht werden sollte: Schleiermacher als Ökumeniker" (1999), 252–78;

    10 "Das Evangelium und die evangelischen Kirchen Europas" (1992), 279–95;

    11 "Kirche und Staat in der pluralistischen Gesellschaft," 296–311;

    12 "Strukturwandel der Öffentlichkeit. Herausforderung und Chance für die universitäre Theologie," 312–29;

    13 "Der Gottesdienst als Fest der Freiheit. Der theologische Ort des Gottesdienstes nach Friedrich Schleiermacher" (1984), 330–50;

    14 "Was ist die theologische Aufgabe evangelischer Kirchenleitung?" (1994), 351–72;

    15 "Thesen zum Amt der Kirche nach evangelischem Verständnis" (2000), 373–80.

2001/a   *... ein bißchen meschugge ... Predigten und biblische Besinnungen 5* (Stuttgart: Radius-Verlag).

2001/b   "Der Geist der Liebe als Gemeinschaftsgeist. Zur pneumatologischen Begründung der christlichen Kirche," Albert Raffelt (ed.), *Weg und Weite. Festschrift für Karl Lehmann* (Freiburg: Herder), 549–62.

2001/c   (with Richard Schröder) "Macht - Wissen – Vergewisserung," Christian Drägert (ed.), *Medienethik: Freiheit und Verantwortung. Festschrift zum 65. Geburtstag von Manfred Kock* (Stuttgart: Kreuz Verlag, 2001), 347–61.

2002/a   *Beziehungsreich: Perspektiven des Glaubens* (Stuttgart: Radius-Verlag).

    1   "Hoffen, Handeln – und Leiden: Zum christlichen Verständnis des Menschen aus theologischer Sicht," 13–40;

    2   "Umgang mit der Vergangenheit in theologischer Perspektive," 41–56;

    3   "Die Zukunft der Zehn Gebote," 57–70;

    4   "Bioethische Aporien," 71–90;

    5   "Glauben und Hoffen in einer sinnlosen Zeit: Theologische Meditation in einer sich selbst überholenden Neuzeit," 91–116;

    6   "Die Wahrheit des Christentums," 117–30;

    7   "Das Wunder des Glaubens," 131–54.

2002/b   "*Credere in ecclesiam*: eine ökumenische Besinnung," *Zeitschrift für Theologie und Kirche* 99, 177–95.

2003/a   *Anfänger: Herkunft und Zukunft christlicher Existenz*

    1   "Befreiende Freiheit – als Merkmal christlicher Existenz," 9–35;

    2   "Das jüngste Gericht als Akt der Gnade," 37–73.

2003/b   "Besinnung auf 50 Jahre theologische Existenz," *Theologische Literaturzeitung* 128:5, 471–84.

2003/c   *Ganz Werden: Theologische Erörterungen V* (Tübingen: Mohr Siebeck).

    1   "Zum Wesen des Friedens: Frieden als Kategorie theologischer Anthropologie" (1983), 1–39;

    2   "Ganzheitsbegriffe—in theologischer Perspektive" (1997), 40–53;

    3   "... unum aliquid assecutus, omnia assecutus .... Zum Verständnis des Verstehens—nach M. Luther, De servo arbitrio (WA 18, 605)" (1997), 54–75;

    4   "Bekennen und Bekenntnis" (1968), 76–88;

    5   "Anfechtung und Gewißheit des Glaubens. Wie bleibt die Kirche heute bei ihrer Sache?" (1976), 89–114 [=1976/a1];

    6   "Mission und Evangelisation" (1999), 115–36;

    7   "Zwei Schwerter—Zwei Reiche. Die Trennung der Mächte in der Reformation" (2000), 137–57;

8 "Das Salz der Erde. Zum Verhältnis von Christen Gemeinde und Bürgergemeinde" (1979) [=1979 .1];

9 "Zum Verhältnis von Kirche und Staat nach Karl Barth" (1986), 174–230;

10 "Nemo contra deum nisi deus ipse. Zum Verhältnis von theologia crucis und Trinitätslehre," 231–52;

11 "Thesen zum Verhältnis von Existenz, Wesen und Eigenschaften Gottes" (1999), 253–73;

12 "Sakrament und Repräsentation. Wesen und Funktion der sakramentalen Handlungen" (2001), 274–87;

13 "Auf dem Weg zur Eucharistiegemeinschaft" (1999), 288–305;

14 Der Geist der Hoffnung und des Trostes. Thesen zur Begründung des eschatologischen Lehrstücks vom Reich der Freiheit" (2000), 306–22;

15 "»Die Weltgeschichte ist das Weltgericht« aus theologischer Perspektive" (2001), 323–44;

16 "Die Ewigkeit des ewigen Lebens. Thesen" (2000), 345–53.

2003/d   . . . *weil ein gesprochenes Wort war. . . Predigten 1* (Stuttgart: Radius-Verlag). [=1968 without "Anhang"]

2003/e   *Geistesgegenwart. Predigten 2* (Stuttgart: Radius-Verlag). [=1974]

2003/f   *Schmecken und Sehen. Predigten 3* (Stuttgart: Radius-Verlag). [=1983/a]

2003/g   *Unterbrechungen. Predigten 4* (Stuttgart: Radius-Verlag). [=1989/b]

2004/a   "Der Mensch – im Schnittpunkt von Wissen, Glauben, Tun und Hoffen: Die theologische Fakultät im Streit mit der durch Immanuel Kant repräsentierten philosophischen Fakultät," *Zeitschrift für Theologie und Kirche* 101, 315–45.

2004/b   *Zum Staunen geboren. Predigten 6* (Stuttgart: Radius-Verlag).

2005/a   "Provozierende Theologie: zur theologischen Existenz Karl Barths (1921–35)," Michael Beintker et al. (eds), *Karl Barth in Deutschland (1921–35): Aufbruch – Klärung – Widerstand* [Beiträge zum Internationalen Symposion vom 1. bis 4. Mai 2003 in der Johannes a Lasco Bibliothek Emden] (Zürich: Theologischer Verlag), 41–55.

2005/b   "Religion, Zivilreligion und christlicher Glaube: das Christentum in einer pluralistischen Gesellschaft," Burkhard Kämper (ed.), *Religionen in Deutschland und das Staatskirchenrecht* (Münster: Aschendorff), 53–100.

2005/c   "Die schöpferische Kraft des Wortes," Gerhard Gläde (ed.), *Hören – Glauben – Denken. Festschrift für Peter Knauer S.J. zur Vollendung seines 70. Lebensjahres* (Münster: Lit), 7–24. [=2011 .3]

2005/d   *Unterwegs im Kirchenjahr. Predigten* (Stuttgart: Radius-Verlag).

2006/a   *"Caritas fide formata*: die erste Enzyklika Benedikt XVI. - gelesen mit den Augen eines evangelischen Christenmenschen," *Internationale katholische Zeitschrift "Communio"* 35:6 (November/December 2006), 595–614.

2006/b   "Gott selbst im Ereignis seiner Offenbarung: Thesen zur trinitarischen Fassung der christlichen Rede von Gott," Michael Welker and Miroslav Volf (eds), *Der lebendige Gott als Trinität: Jürgen Moltmann zum 80. Geburtstag* (Gütersloh: Gütersloher Verlagshaus), 23–33.

2008/a   *Erfahrungen mit der Erfahrung. Unterwegs bemerkt* (Stuttgart: Radius-Verlag).

        1   "Die wunderbaren Kraftakte des Jesus von Nazareth," 13–20;

        2   "Neu – Alt – Neu. Theologische Aphorismen," 21–7;

        3   "O Haupt voll Blut und Wunden. Zum 400. Geburtstag von Paul Gerhard," 28–41;

        4   "Erwachen," 42–8;

        5   "Licht in der Finsternis," 49–53;

        6   "Böse – was ist das? Versuch einer theologischer Begriffsbestimmung," 54–86;

        7   "Gibt es den gerechten Krieg?" 87–94;

        8   "Wertlose Würde – Gewissenhafte Gewissenlosigkeit. Eine Erinnerung an den fortwirkenden christlichen Ursprung lebensorientierender Begriffe," 95–103;

        9   "Passagen," 104–8;

        10 "Das Staunen bleibt," 109–14.

2008/b   "Glaube und Vernunft," George Augustin and Klaus Krämer (eds), *Gott denken und bezeugen. Festschrift für Kardinal Walter Kasper zum 75. Geburtstag* (Freiburg: Herder), 15–32.

2008/c   "»Was ist er inwerds?«" *Zeitschrift für Theologie und Kirche* 105, 443–55.

2008/d   "Zur Verankerung der Menschenrechte im christlichen Glauben," Günter Nooke et al. (eds), *Gelten Menschenrechte universal? Begründungen und Infragestellungen* (Freiburg: Konrad-Adenauer-Stiftung), 166–79. [=2011.8]

2009/a   *Allerneuende Klarheit. Predigten 7* (Stuttgart: Radius-Verlag).

2009/b   *Die Leidenschaft Gott zu denken: Ein Gespräch über Denk- und Lebenserfahrungen* (Zürich: Theologischer Verlag).

2011   *Außer sich. Theologische Texte* (Stuttgart: Radius-Verlag).

        1   "Mensch, wo bist Du? Glauben und Freiheit als Ortsbestimmungen des Christenmenschen," 13–40;

        2   "Außer sich. Zu 2. Korinther 5, 17–21," 41–50;

        3   "Die schöpferische Kraft des Wortes" (2005), 51–82 [=2005/c];

4 "Stille Nacht" (2009) 83–7;

5 "Ja. Vorbehaltlos, eindeutig, uneingeschränkt" (2010), 88–91;

6 "Sprachlose Freude? Eine Erinnerung an Schleiermachers Weihnachtsfeier" (2009), 92–8;

7 "Wirkung durch Entzug. Eine theologische Anmerkung zum Begriff der Wirkungsgeschichte" (2008), 99–123;

8 "Zur Verankerung der Menschenrechte im christlichen Glauben" (2008), 124–38 [=2008/d];

9 "Arbeit in biblischem Verständnis" (2006), 139–47;

10 "Hoffnung für das Alter" (2010), 148–67;

11 "Was hat des Menschen Glück mit seiner Seligkeit zu tun," 168–98;

12 "Nichts erzählen" (2010), 199–201;

13 "Letzte Worte?" (2008), 202–4.

English

1969   "Four Preliminary Considerations on the Concept of Authority," *The Ecumenical Review* 21:2 (April 1969), 150–66. [G=1972/a10]

1971   "God – as a Word of Our Language," Frederick Herzog (ed.), *Theology of the Liberating Word* (Nashville: Abingdon), 24–45. [G=1972/a5]

1974   *Death: The Riddle and the Mystery*, trans. Iain and Ute Nicol (Edinburgh: St. Andrew Press; Philadelphia: The Westminster Press, 1975). [G=1971/b]

1976/a   "The Relationship between 'Economic' and 'Immanent' Trinity," *Theology Digest* 24, 179–84. [G=1980 .11, summarized]

1976/b   "The Truth of Life: Observations on Truth as the Interruption of the Continuity of Life," Richard W. A. McKinney (ed.), *Creation, Christ, and Culture: Studies in Honour of T. F. Torrance* (Edinburgh: T&T Clark), 231–6.

1983   *God as the Mystery of the World: On the Foundation of the Theology of the Crucified One in the Dispute between Theism and Atheism*, trans. Darrell L. Guder (Edinburgh: T&T Clark). [G=1977/a]

1986   *Karl Barth: A Theological Legacy*, trans. Garrett E. Paul (Philadelphia: Westminster). [G=1982]

    1 "Introduction," 11–15 [G=1982 .1, edited];

    2 "Karl Barth: A Tribute at Death," 16–21 [G=1982 .2];

    3 "Barth's Life and Work," 22–52 [G=1982 .3];

    4 "Barth's Theological Beginnings," 53–104 [G=1982 .4];

5 "Gospel and Law: The Relationship of Dogmatics to Ethics," 105–26 [G = 1982 .6];

6 "The Royal Man. A Christological Reflection on Human Dignity in Barth's Theology," 127–38 [G = 1982 .8].

1988/a   "The Christian Understanding of Suffering" in *Journal of Theology for Southern Africa* 65, 3–13.

1988/b   *The Freedom of a Christian: Luther's Significance for Contemporary Theology*, trans. Roy A. Harrisville (Minneapolis: Augsburg). [G = 1978/b; 2000 .5]

1989/a   "Response to Josef Blank" in H. Kung and D. Tracy (eds), *Paradigm Change in Theology: A Symposium for the Future* (Edinburgh: T&T Clark), 297–304.

1989/b   *Theological Essays I*, trans. J. B. Webster (Edinburgh: T&T Clark).

1 "Metaphorical Truth. Reflections on Theological Metaphor as a Contribution to a Hermeneutics of Narrative Theology," 16–71 [G = 1980 .4];

2 "Anthropomorphism: A Fundamental Problem in Modern Hermeneutics," 72–94 [G = 1990/b5];

3 "The World as Possibility and Actuality. The Ontology of the Doctrine of Justification," 95–123 [G = 1972/a12];

4 "Humanity in Correspondence to God. Remarks on the Image of God as a Basic Concept in Theological Anthropology," 124–53 [G = 1980 .14];

5 "Invocation of God as the Ethical Ground of Christian Action. Introductory Remarks on the Posthumous Fragments of Karl Barth's Ethics of the Doctrine of Reconciliation," 154–72 [G = 1982 .12];

6 "*Extra Christum nulla salus* – A Principle of Natural Theology? Protestant Reflections on the 'Anonymity' of the Christian," 173–88 [G = 1980 .6];

7 "The Church as Sacrament?" 189–213 [G = 1990/b15];

8 "The Effectiveness of Christ Withdrawn. On the Process of Historical Understanding as an Introduction to Christology," 214–31 [G = 1978/a].

1989/c   "What does it mean to say, 'God is love'?" T. Hart and D. Thimell (eds), *Christ in our Place: The Humanity of God in Christ for the Reconciliation of the World. Essays Presented to Prof. James Torrance* (Exeter, UK: Paternoster), 294–312.

1990   "The Last Judgment as an Act of Grace," *Louvain Studies* 14, 389–405. [G = 2003/a2]

1991/a   "Life after Death? A Response to Theology's Silence about Eternal Life," *Word and World* 11, 5–8.

1991/b   "Toward the Heart of the Matter," *Christian Century* 108:7 (February 27, 1991), 228–33.

1992   *Christ, Justice and Peace: Toward a Theology of the State in Dialogue with the Barmen Declaration*, trans. D. B. Hamill and Alan J. Torrance (Edinburgh: T&T Clark). [G = 2000 .6]

1993   "The Gospel and the Protestant Churches of Europe: Christian Responsibility for Europe from a Protestant Perspective," *Religion, State and Society* 21:2, 137–49.

1994   *Theological Essays II*, ed. John Webster (Edinburgh: T&T Clark).

            1   "'My theology' – A Short Summary," 1–19 [G = 1990/b1];

            2   " ' . . . You talk like a book . . . ' Toward an Understanding of *Philosophical Fragments* by J. Climacus, edited by Sören Kierkegaard (1813–55)," 20–34 [G = 1990/b3];

            3   "The emergence of the new," 35–58 [G = 1990/b6];

            4   "'Even the beautiful must die' – Beauty in the Light of Truth. Theological Observations on the Aesthetic Relation," 59–81 [G = 1990/b19];

            5   "The Dogmatic Significance of the Question of the Historical Jesus," 82–119 [G = 1990/b11];

            6   "The Revelation of the Hiddenness of God. A Contribution to the Protestant Understanding of the Hiddenness of Divine Action," 120–44 [G = 1990/b8];

            7   "The Mystery of Substitution. A Dogmatic Conversation with Heinrich Vogel," 145–62 [G = 1990/b12];

            8   "The Sacrifice of Jesus Christ as Sacrament and Example," 163–90 [G = 1990/b13];

            9   "Value-Free Truth: The Christian Experience of Truth in the Struggle against the 'Tyranny of Values'," 191–215 [G = 1990/b4];

            10 "On Becoming Truly Human. The Significance of the Reformation Distinction between Person and Works for the Self-Understanding of Modern Humanity," 216–40 [G = 1990/b10];

            11 "Living out of Righteousness: God's Action – Human Agency," 241–63 [G = 1990/b17].

1998   "Trinitarian Prayers for Christian Worship," *Word and World* 18 (Summer 1998), 244–53.

1999   "On the Doctrine of Justification," *International Journal of Systematic Theology* 1:1 (March 1999), 24–52.

2000   "To Tell the World about God: The Task for the Mission of the Church on the Threshold of the Third Millennium," *International Review of Mission* (April 30, 2000), 203–15.

2001/a   *God's Being Is in Becoming: The Trinitarian Being of God in the Theology of Karl Barth – A Paraphrase*, trans. J. B. Webster (Edinburgh: T&T Clark); previously translated as *The Doctrine of the Trinity*, trans. H. Harris (Edinburgh: Scottish Academic Press, 1976). [G = 1965]

2001/b   *Justification: The Heart of the Christian Faith*, trans. Jeffrey F. Cayzer (Edinburgh: T&T Clark). [G = 1998/b]

2001/c   "Theses on the Relation of the Existence, Essence and Attributes of God," *Toronto Journal of Theology*, vol. 17:1 (Summer 2001), 55–74. [G = 2003/c11]

2002/a   "The Cross After Postmodernity," Uwe Siemon-Netto (ed.), *One Incarnate Truth: Christianity's Answer to Spiritual Chaos* (St. Louis: Concordia Publishing House).

2002/b   "Sermon on Matthew 25:1–12," *Toronto Journal of Theology* 18:1 (Spring 2002), 13–19.

2005   "Church Unity is Already Happening: The Path Toward Eucharistic Community," *Dialog: A Journal of Lutheran Theology* 44:1 (Spring 2005), 30–7. [G = 2003/c13]

2006   "Theses on the Eternality of Eternal Life," *Toronto Journal of Theology* 22:2 (Fall 2006), 163–9. [G = 2003/c16]

Select Secondary Literature on Jüngel

Barth, Ulrich, "Zur Barth-Deutung Eberhard Jüngels," *Theologische Zeitschrift* 40 (1984), 3:296–320 and 4:394–415.

Case, Jonathan P., "The Death of Jesus and the Truth of the Triune God in Wolfhart Pannenberg and Eberhard Jüngel," *Journal for Christian Theological Research* 9 (2004), 1–13.

Dalferth, Ingolf U., et al. (eds), *Denkwürdiges Geheimnis: Beiträge zur Gotteslehre. Festschrift für Eberhard Jüngel zum 70. Geburtstag* (Tübingen: Mohr Siebeck, 2004).

1 Hans-Christoph Askani, "Gott ohne Neid?" 1–21;
2 Michael Beintker, "' . . . es ist moralisch nothwendig, das Dasein Gottes anzunehmen': einige Erwägungen zu Kants moralischem Gottesbeweis," 23–39;
3 Rüdiger Bubner, "Descartes' Gottesbeweis," 41–50;
4 Ingolf U. Dalferth, "Gott für uns: die Bedeutung des christologischen Dogmas für die christliche Theologie," 51–75;
5 Reinhard Feldmeier, "Theos zōopoiōn: die paulinische Rede von der Unvergänglichkeit in ihrem religionsgeschichtlichen Kontext," 77–91;
6 Johannes Fischer, "Gott im Spannungsfeld zwischen Glaube und Wissen," 93–112;
7 David F. Ford, "The God of Blessing Who Loves in Wisdom," 113–26;
8 Hans-Peter Großhans, "Selbsterkenntnis als Gotteserkenntnis? Zum Verhältnis von schlechthinnigem Abhängigkeitsgefühl und schlechthinniger Ursächlichkeit bei Friedrich Schleiermacher," 127–44;

 9 Martin Hengel, "Abba, Maranatha, Hosanna und die Anfänge der Christologie," 145–83;

10 Hans-Jürgen Hermisson, "Von Zorn und Leiden Gottes," 185–207;

11 Bernd Jochen Hilberath, "Sender - Empfänger - Botschaft: der Heilige Geist als Kommunikator zwischen Gott und Welt," 209–23;

12 Otfried Hofius, "Gott war in Christus": sprachliche und theologische Erwägungen zu der Versöhnungsaussage 2Kor 5,19a," 225–36;

13 Wilhelm Hüffmeier, "Deus providebit? Eine Zwischenbilanz zur Kritik der Lehre von Gottes Vorsehung," 237–58;

14 J. Christine Janowski, "Cur deus homo crucifixus: zu René Girards kritischer Apologie des Christentums," 259–89;

15 Walter Kasper, "Ökumenisch von Gott sprechen?" 291–302;

16 Wolf Krötke, "Nicht 'auf Ebenteuer' beten: zur Frage der inter- und multireligiösen Anrufung Gottes," 303–19;

17 Hans Küng, "Christlicher Glaube und Weltreligionen," 321–9;

18 Karl Lehmann, "Karl Rahner und die Ökumene," 331–46;

19 Bruce McCormack, "Participation in God, yes, deification, no: two modern Protestant responses to an ancient question," 347–74;

20 Jürgen Moltmann, "Von Angesicht zu Angesicht: eine Meditation über die Gottesschau zu Ehren des Tübinger 'Mystikers mit offenen Augen'," 375–86;

21 Michael Moxter, "Gott als Künstler: Anmerkungen zu einer Metapher Schleiermachers," 387–404;

22 Helmut Obst, "Trinität? Zur Gotteslehre christlicher Sondergemeinschaften (Mormonen, Christian Science, Zeugen Jehovas)," 405–16;

23 Wolfhart Pannenberg, "Der eine Gott als der wahrhaft Unendliche und die Trinitätslehre," 417–26;

24 Trutz Rendtorff, "Vom Misston zur Polyphonie? Theologiehistorische Beobachtungen im Vorfeld der Gotteslehre," 427–42;

25 Jan Rohls, "Der Gott Spinozas," 443–64;

26 Dietrich Rössler, "Moral statt Metaphysik: Anmerkungen zur Bedeutung der theologischen Gotteslehre für die Perikopenpredigt," 465–77;

27 Richard Schröder, "'Du hast die Welt nach Maß, Zahl und Gewicht geordnet': über einen Konsens im astronomischen Weltbildstreit des 16. und 17. Jahrhunderts," 479–506;

28 Rudolf Smend, "Vom Ende der Gottesbilder: Predigt über Exodus 20,1–6 am 29. Oktober 1972 in der Universitätskirche St. Nikolai in Göttingen," 507–13;

29 Volker Spangenberg, "Der Gott, der mich sieht: zum Predigtwerk von Albrecht Goes," 515–37;

30 John B. Webster, "The immensity and ubiquity of God," 539–56;

31 Hans Weder, "Komparative und ein parataktisches kai: eine neutestamentlich orientierte Skizze zur transzendierten Notwendigkeit," 557–81;

32 Folkart Wittekind, "Gott - die alles bestimmende Wirklichkeit? Zum Verständnis von Bultmanns Deutung der Gottesvorstellung Jesu," 583–604;

33 "Bibliographie Eberhard Jüngels," 605–49.

Davidson, Ivor J., "*Curx probat omnia*: Eberhard Jüngel and the Theology of the Cru-cified One," *Scottish Journal of Theology* 50:2 (1997), 157–90.

DeHart, Paul, "Eberhard Jüngel on the Structure of Theology," *Theological Studies* 57 (1996), 46–64.

— *Beyond the Necessary God: Trinitarian Faith and Philosophy in the Thought of Eberhard Jüngel* [AAR Reflection and Theory in the Study of Religion] (Atlanta, GA: Schol-ars Press, 1999).

— "The Ambiguous Infinite: Jungel, Marion, and the God of Descartes," *The Journal of Religion* 82:1 (2002), 75–96.

Dvorak, Rainer, *Gott ist Liebe: Eine Studie zur Grundlegung der Trinitätslehre bei Eberhard Jüngel* (Würzburg: Echter, 1999).

Ellis, Daryl, "God's Hiddenness as Trinitarian Grace and Miracle: A Response to Christopher R. J. Holmes's Critique of Eberhard Jüngel's Conception of Divine Hiddenness," *Neue Zeitschrift für Systematische Theologie und Religionsphilosophie* 52:1 (2010), 82–101.

Fekete, David J., "Ancient echoes in modern halls: the recent erotic spirituality of Vatican II, David Matzko McCarthy, Karl Barth, and Eberhard Jüngel," *A Rhap-sody of Love and Spirituality* (New York: Algora, 2003), 237–66.

Fiddes, Paul S., *The Creative Suffering of God* (Oxford: Clarendon Press, 1988).

Ford, David, *Self and Salvation: Being Transformed* (Cambridge: Cambridge University Press, 1999).

Fuchs, Frank, *Konkretionen des Narrativen: am Beispiel von Eberhard Jüngels Theologie und Predigten unter Einbeziehung der Hermeneutik Paul Ricoeurs sowie der Textlinguistik Klaus Brinkers* (Münster: Lit, 2004).

Goebel, Hans Theodor, *Vom freien Wählen Gottes und des Menschen* (Frankfurt am Main: Peter Lang, 1990).

Haudel, Matthias, *Die Selbsterschliessung des dreieinigen Gottes: Grundlage eines ökumenis-chen Offenbarungs-, Gottes- und Kirchenverständnisses* (Göttingen: Vandenhoeck & Ruprecht, 2006).

Holmes, Christopher, "Disclosure without Reservation: Re-evaluating Divine Hiddenness," *Neue Zeitschrift für Systematische Theologie und Religionsphilosophie* 48:3 (2006), 367–79.

— "The Glory of God in the Theology of Eberhard Jüngel," *International Journal of Systematic Theology* 8:4 (2006), 342–55.

— *Revisiting the Doctrine of the Divine Attributes: In Dialogue With Karl Barth, Eberhard Jüngel, and Wolf Krötke* (Bern: Peter Lang Publishing, 2006).

Huber, Wolfgang, "'Theologie und Kirchenleitung' – Vortrag zu Ehren von Eber-hard Jüngel, Tübingen" (2005), available on website of the Evangelische Kirche in Deutschland, http://www.ekd.de/vortraege/050204_huber_ehrung_juengel. html (accessed January 17, 2012).

Kelsey, David H., "Two Theologies of Death: Anthropological Gleanings," *Modern Theology* 13:3 (1997), 347–70.

Klimek, Nicolaus, *Der Gott, der Liebe ist: zur trinitarischen Auslegung des Begriffs "Liebe" bei Eberhard Jüngel* (Essen: Verlag Die Blaue Eule, 1986).

Koppehl, Thomas, "Die Christologie I. A. Dorners im Vergleich zu der E. Jüngels," *Die Wissenschaftliche Standpunkt der Theologie Isaak August Dorners* (Berlin: De Gruyter, 1997), 290–326.

Korthaus, Michael, *Kreuzestheologie: Geschichte und Gehalt eines Programmbegriffs in der evangelischen Theologie* (Tübingen: Mohr Siebeck, 2007).

Küng, Hans, *The Incarnation of God: An Introduction to Hegel's Theological Thought as Prolegomena to a Future Christology* (1970; Edinburgh: T&T Clark, 1987).

Macken, John, *The Autonomy Theme in Karl Barth's Church Dogmatics and in Current Barth Criticism: Inaugural-Dissertation. . .* (Tübingen: Zeeb-Druck, 1984).

Mattes, Mark C., *Toward Divine Relationality: Eberhard Jüngel's New Trinitarian, Post-metaphysical Approach* (unpublished Ph.D. dissertation, University of Chicago, Chicago, IL, 1995).

— *The Role of Justification in Contemporary Theology* (Grand Rapids, MI: Eerdmans, 2004).

McCormack, Bruce, "God *Is* His Decision: The Jüngel-Gollwitzer 'Debate' Revisited," Bruce L. McCormack & Kimlyn J. Bender (eds), *Theology as Conversation: The Significance of Dialogue in Historical and Contemporary Theology. A Festschrift for Daniel L. Migliore* (Grand Rapids, MI: Eerdmans, 2009), 48–66.

— "Election and the Trinity: Theses in response to George Hunsinger," *Scottish Journal of Theology* 63:2 (2010), 203–24.

Molnar, Paul D., *Divine Freedom and the Doctrine of the Immanent Trinity* (London: T&T Clark, 2002).

Murrmann-Kahl, Michael, *"Mysterium trinitatis"? Fallstudien zur Trinitätslehre in der evangelischen Dogmatik des 20. Jahrhunderts* (Berlin: de Gruyter, 1997).

Nelson, Derek, "The Indicative of Grace and the Imperative of Freedom: An Invitation to the Theology of Eberhard Jüngel," *Dialog: A Journal of Lutheran Theology* 44:2 (Summer 2005), 164–80.

Neufeldt-Fast, Arnold V., *Eberhard Jüngel's Theological Anthropology in Light of His Christology* (unpublished Ph.D. dissertation, University of St. Michael's College, Toronto, 1996).

O'Donovan, Leo J., S. J., "The Mystery of God as a History of Love: Eberhard Jüngel's Doctrine of God," *Theological Studies* 42 (1981), 251–71.

Palakeel, Joseph, *The Use of Analogy in Theological Discourse: An Investigation in Ecumenical Perspective* (Rome: Gregorian University, 1995).

Pambrun, James R., "Eberhard Jüngel's *Gott als Geheimnis der Welt*. An Interpretation," *Église et Théologie* 15 (1984), 321–46.

Paulson, Steven D., *Analogy and Proclamation: The Struggle over God's Hiddenness in the Theology of Martin Luther and Eberhard Juengel* (unpublished Th.D. dissertation, Lutheran School of Theology, Chicago, IL, 1992).

Paulus, Engelbert, *Liebe, das Geheimnis der Welt: formale und materiale Aspekte der Theologie Eberhard Jüngels* (Würzburg: Echter, 1990).

Rohls, Jan, "Ist Gott notwendig? – Zu einer These von E. Jüngels," *Neue Zeitschrift für Systematische Theologie und Religionsphilosophie* 22 (1980), 282–96.

Royon, Claude, *Dieu, l'homme et la croix: Stanislas Breton et Eberhard Jüngel* (Paris: Éditions du Cerf, 1998).

Schott, Faye E., "Comparing Eberhard Jüngel and Wolfhart Pannenberg on Theological Method and Religious Pluralism," *Dialog: A Journal of Theology* 31:2 (Spring 1992), 129–35.

Schulz, Michael, *Sein und Trinität: systematische Erörterungen zur Religionsphilosophie G. W. F. Hegels im ontologiegeschichtlichen Rückblick auf J. Duns Scotus und I. Kant und die Hegel-Rezeption in der Seinsauslegung und Trinitätstheologie bei W. Pannenberg, E. Jüngel, K. Rahner und H. U. v. Balthasar* (St. Ottilien: EOS Verlag, 1997).

Spjuth, Roland, *Creation, contingency and divine presence in the theologies of Thomas F. Torrance and Eberhard Juengel* (unpublished Ph.D. dissertation, Lunds Universitet, Sweden, 1995).

— "Redemption without Actuality: A Critical Interrelation between Eberhard Jüngel's and John Milbank's Ontological Endeavours," *Modern Theology* 14:4 (1998), 505–22.

Stolina, Ralf, "Eberhard Jüngels Kritik negativer Theologie," *Niemand hat Gott je gesehen: Traktat über negative Theologie* (Berlin: de Gruyter, 2000).

— "Gott – Geheimnis – Kreuz," *Zeitschrift für Theologie und Kirche* 101:2 (Juni 2004), 175–97.

— "»Ökonomische« und »immanente Trinität«? Zur Problematik einer trinitätstheologischen Denkfigur," *Zeitschrift für Theologie und Kirche* 105 (2008), 170–94.

Thiele, Martin H., *Gott – Allmacht – Zeit: Ein theologisches Gespräch mit Johann Baptist Metz und Eberhard Jüngel* (Münster: Aschendorff, 2009).

Watts, Graham John, *Revelation and the Spirit: a comparative study of the relationship between the doctrine of revelation and pneumatology in the theology of Eberhard Jüngel and Wolfhart Pannenberg* (Milton Keynes, UK; Waynesboro, GA: Paternoster, 2005).

Webster, John, "Eberhard Jüngel: The Humanity of God and the Humanity of Man," *Evangel* 2:2 (Spring 1984), 4–6.

— "Eberhard Jüngel on the Language of Faith," *Modern Theology* 1:3 (1985), 253–76.

— "Bibliography: The Theology of Eberhard Jungel," *Modern Churchman* 28:3 (1986), 41–4.

— *Eberhard Jüngel: An Introduction to His Theology* (Cambridge: University Press, 1986).

Webster, John, (ed.), *The Possibilities of Theology: Studies in the Theology of Eberhard Jüngel in his Sixtieth Year* (Edinburgh: T&T Clark, 1994).

  1 John Webster, "Introduction," 1–6;
  2 Colin Gunton, "The being and attributes of God: Eberhard Jüngel's dispute with the classical philosophical tradition," 7–22;
  3 David F. Ford, "Hosting a dialogue: Jüngel and Lévinas on God, self and language," 23–59;
  4 G. O. Mazur, "On Jüngel's four-fold appropriation of Friedrich Nietzsche," 60–9;
  5 Werner Jeanrond, "The problem of the starting-point of theological thinking," 70–89;
  6 Geoffrey Wainwright, "Church and sacrament(s)," 90–105;
  7 John Webster, "Justification, analogy and action: passivity and activity in Jüngel's anthropology," 106–42;
  8 John Thompson, "Jüngel on Barth," 143–89;
  9 George Newlands, "The love of God and the future of theology: a personal engagement with Jüngel's work," 190–205;
  10 Arnold Neufeldt-Fast, "Eberhard Jüngel: a bibliography," 206–41.

— "Jesus Speech, God's Word: An introduction to Eberhard Jüngel (I)," *Christian Century* 112:35 (December 6, 1995), 1174–8.

— "Who God Is, Who We Are: An introduction to Eberhard Jüngel (II)," *Christian Century* 112:36 (December 13, 1995), 1217–20.

— "Jesus in the Theology of Eberhard Jüngel," *Calvin Theological Journal* 32:1 (1997), 43–71.

— "Jesus in Modernity: Reflections on Jüngel's Christology," *Word and Church: Essays in Christian Dogmatics* (Edinburgh: T&T Clark, 2001), 151–90. [=1997]

Zimany, Roland D., *Vehicle for God: The Metaphorical Theology of Eberhard Jüngel* (Macon, GA: Mercer University Press, 1994).

Other References

Agamben, Giorgio, *The Open: Man and Animal*, trans. K. Attell (Stanford, CA: Stanford University Press, 2004).

Aquinas, Thomas, *Summa Theologica*, trans. Fathers of the English Dominican Province (various editions available).

Augustine, *The Confessions*, trans. Henry Chadwick (Oxford: University Press, 1991).

— *The Trinity*, trans. Edmund Hill, O. P. (Hyde Park, NY: New City Press, 1991).

Badhwar, Neera K., "Friends as Ends in Themselves," ed. Alan Soble, *Eros, Agape, and Philia: Readings in the Philosophy of Love* (St. Paul, MN: Paragon House, 1989), 165–86.

Barth, Karl, *Church Dogmatics*, ed. G. W. Bromiley & T. F. Torrance, 14 vols. (Edinburgh: T&T Clark, 1936–75).

— *Protestant Theology in the Nineteenth Century*, trans. B. Cozens and J. Bowden (Grand Rapids, MI: Eerdmans, 2002).

Bauman, Zygmunt, "Freedom and security: The unfinished story of a tempestuous union," *The Individualized Society* (Cambridge, UK: Polity, 2001), 41–56.

— "Identity in the globalizing world," *The Individualized Society*, (Cambridge, UK: Polity, 2001), 140–52.

Beck, Ulrich, *Risk Society: Towards a New Modernity*, trans. Mark Ritter (London: Sage Publications, 1992).

— *World at Risk*, trans. Ciaran Cronin (Cambridge, UK: Polity, 2009). *Die Bekenntnisschriften der evangelisch-lutherischen Kirche* (Göttingen: Vandenhoeck & Ruprecht, 1930, 1991).

Bloch, Ernst, *Experimentum mundi: Frage, Kategorien des Herausbringens, Praxis* (Frankfurt am Main: Suhrkamp, 1975).

Boethius, *A Treatise contra Eutyches and Nestorius*. In *Theological Tractates*, trans. H. F. Stewart et al. (Cambridge, MA: Harvard University Press, 1973), 73–27.

Bonhoeffer, Dietrich, *Letters and Papers from Prison*, ed. Eberhard Bethge (New York: Touchstone, 1997).

Butler, Judith, *Giving an Account of Oneself* (New York: Fordham University Press, 2005).

Calvin, Jean, *Institutes of the Christian Religion*, ed. John T. McNeill, 2 vols. (Philadelphia: Westminster, 1960).

Cameron, Euan, *The European Reformation* (Oxford: Clarendon Press, 1991).

Crowe, Benjamin D., *Heidegger's Religious Origins: Destruction and Authenticity* (Bloomington, IN: Indiana University Press, 2006).

Descartes, Rene, *Discourse on Method*, Part IV, in *The Philosophical Writings of Descartes*, trans. J. Cottingham et al. (Cambridge: University Press, 1985).

Dorner, Isaak A., *Divine Immutability: A Critical Reconsideration*, trans. Robert P. Williams and Claude Welch (1856–8; Philadelphia: Fortress Press, 1994).

— *A System of Christian Doctrine*, trans. A. Cave and J. S. Banks, vol. 3 (Edinburgh: T&T Clark, 1885).

Edwards, Mark U., Jr., The Reception of Luther's Understanding of Freedom in the Early Modern Period: The Early Years," *Lutherjahrbuch* 62 (1995), 104–20.

Feuerbach, Ludwig, *The Essence of Christianity*, trans. George Eliot (1841; Amherst, MA: Prometheus Books, 1999).

Hamm, Berndt and Michael Welker, *Die Reformation: Potentiale der Freiheit* (Tübingen: Mohr Siebeck, 2008).

Hartmann, Nicolai, *Ethics*, trans. S. Coit, 3 vols. [v. 1. Moral phenomena; v. 2. Moral values; v. 3. Moral freedom, with introductions by Andreas A. M. Kinneging] (1926; New Brunswick, NJ: Transaction Publishers, 2002–4).

Hegel, G. W. F., *Lectures on the History of Philosophy*, vol. 3: *Medieval and Modern Philosophy*, trans. E. S. Haldane (Lincoln, NE: Bison, 1995).

Heidegger, Martin, *Being and Time*, trans. J. Macquarrie and E. Robinson (New York: Harper and Row, 1962).

— *The Essence of Reasons*, trans. T. Malick (Evanston, IL: Northwestern University Press, 1969).

Hendry, George S., "The Freedom of God in the Theology of Karl Barth," *Scottish Journal of Theology* 31:1 (1978), 229–44.

Jonas, Hans, "The Concept of God after Auschwitz. A Jewish Voice," *The Journal of Religion* 67:1 (1987), 1–13.

Jones, Paul Dafydd, *The Humanity of Christ: Christology in Karl Barth's Church Dogmatics* (London: T&T Clark, 2008).

Kant, Immanuel, *Critique of Pure Reason*, trans. and ed. Paul Guyer and Allen W. Wood (1781, 1787; Cambridge: University Press, 1998).

— *Prolegomena to Any Future Metaphysics: That Will Be Able to Come Forward as a Science*, trans. and ed. Gary Hatfield, revised edn. (1783; Cambridge: University Press, 2004).

— *An Answer to the Question: What is Enlightenment?* (1784). In *Practical Philosophy*, trans. and ed. Mary J. Gregor (Cambridge: University Press, 1996), 15–22.

— *Groundwork of The Metaphysics of Morals* (1785). In *Practical Philosophy*, 37–108.

— *Critique of Practical Reason* (1788). In *Practical Philosophy*, 133–271.

— *Religion within the bounds of mere reason* (1793). In *Religion and Rational Theology*, trans. and ed. Allen W. Wood and George di Giovanni (Cambridge: University Press: 1996), 39–215.

— *The Metaphysics of Morals* (1797–8). In *Practical Philosophy*, 363–603.

— *Anthropology from a Pragmatic Point of View*, ed. R. B. Louden (1798; Cambridge: University Press, 2006).

— *The Conflict of the Faculties* (1798). In *Religion and Rational Theology*, 237–93.

— *Logic*, trans. R. S. Hartman and W. Schwarz (1800; New York: Dover, 1988).

Kołakowski, Leszek, *The Presence of Myth*, trans. Adam Czerniawski (1972; Chicago, IL: The University of Chicago Press, 1989).

Leppin, Volker, "Martin Luther, reconsidered for 2017," *Lutheran Quarterly* 22:4 (Winter 2008), 373–86.

Lessing, Gotthold, *Nathan the Wise* trans. E. Frothingham (1779; New York: Henry Holt, 1892).

Lévinas, Emmanuel, *Time and the Other* (1947). In *The Levinas Reader*, ed. Seán Hand (Oxford: Basil Blackwell, 1989), 37–58.

Locke, John, *Essay Concerning Human Understanding*, ed. Peter H. Nidditch (Oxford: Oxford University Press, 1975).

Lorenz, Konrad, *The Foundations of Ethology: The Principal Ideas and Discoveries in Animal Behavior*, trans. K. Z. Lorenz & R. W. Kickert (New York & Wien: Springer, 1981).

Luther, Martin, *Dr. Martin Luthers Werke*, 69 vols. (Weimar: Böhlau, 1883–1993).

— *Luther's Works*, ed. Jaroslav Pelikan and Helmut T. Lehmann, 55 vols. (St. Louis: Concordia and Philadelphia: Fortress Press, 1955–86).

MacCulloch, Diarmaid, *The Reformation* (New York: Viking Penguin, 2004).

Małysz, Piotr J., "Luther and the Lutherans," eds Sarah Coakley and Richard Cross, *Oxford Handbook to the Reception History of Christian Theology* (Oxford: University Press, forthcoming in 2013).

Marcuse, Herbert, "A Study of Authority: Luther, Calvin, Kant," ed. Eduardo Mendieta, *The Frankfurt School on Religion* (New York and London: Routledge, 2005), 115–45.

Marx, Karl, *Critique of Hegel's Philosophy of Right*, trans. Joseph O'Malley (Cambridge: University Press, 1972).

McKenny, Gerald, *The Analogy of Grace: Karl Barth's Moral Theology* (Oxford: University Press, 2010).

Meister Eckhart, *The Essential Sermons, Commentaries, Treatises, and Defense*, ed. E. Colledge and B. McGinn (Mahwah, NJ: Paulist, 1981).

Melanchthon, Philip, *Loci communes theologici* (1521). In *Melanchthon and Bucer*, ed. Wilhelm Pauck (Philadelphia: Westminster, 1969).

Mulhall, Stephen, *Philosophical Myths of the Fall* (Princeton, NJ: Princeton University Press, 2005).

Ogden, Schubert, "Bultmann's Demythologizing and Hartshorne's Dipolar Theism," eds W. Reese and E. Freeman, *Process and Divinity: The Hartshorne's Festschrift* (LaSalle, IL: Open Court, 1964), 103–24.

Pannenberg, Wolfhart, *Jesus – God and Man*, trans. L. L. Wilkins and D. A. Priebe (Philadelphia: Westminster, 1968).

— *Systematic Theology*, 3 vols., trans. Geoffrey Bromiley (Grand Rapids, MI: Eerdmans, 1991–8).

Plato, *The Republic*, trans. Allan Bloom (New York: Basic Books, 1968).

Polanyi, Michael, *Personal Knowledge: Towards a Post-Critical Philosophy* (Chicago, IL: University of Chicago Press, 1962).

Pseudo-Dionysius the Areopagite, *The Divine Names*. In Pseudo-Dionysius, *The Complete Works*, ed. Paul Rorem (Mahwah, NJ: Paulist 1987), 47–131.

Rahner, Karl, *The Trinity*, trans. Joseph Donceel (New York: Crossroad, 1997).

Scheler, Max, "Von zwei Deutschen Krankheiten," *Gesammelte Werke*, vol. 6: *Schriften zur Soziologie und Weltanschauungslehre* (Bern & München: Francke, 1963), 204–19.

Schmitt, Carl, "Die Tyrannei der Werte," eds Eberhard Jüngel and Sepp Schelz, *Die Tyrannei der Werte* (1960; Hamburg: Lutherisches Verlagshaus, 1979), 11–43.

The Theologia Germanica of Martin Luther, ed. Bengt Hoffman (Mahwah, NJ: Paulist, 1980).

Welker, Michael, *God the Spirit*, trans. John F. Hoffmeyer (Minneapolis, MN: Fortress, 1994).

zur Mühlen, Karl-Heinz, *Nos extra nos: Luthers Theologie zwischen Mystik und Scholastik* (Tübingen: Mohr Siebeck, 1972).

Zusammenfassung

Der Hauptzweck dieser Arbeit besteht in einer Auseinandersetzung mit Eberhard Jüngels Interpretation der Freiheit und, darauf aufbauend, der Darstellung der engen Verbindung der Gotteslehre mit der Anthropologie. Diese übergeordnete Intention impliziert wiederum zwei Ziele. Das erste dient einer kritischen Rekonstruktion des gott-menschlichen Zusammenseins in Jüngels Theologie mit besonderem Augenmerk auf die Freiheitskonzeption. Das zweite, konstruktive Ziel besteht in der Beantwortung der kritischen Frage, ob Jüngels Gotteslehre mit den Auswirkungen in der Anthropologie harmoniert, die Jüngel dem Sein Gottes beimisst, und in der Formulierung eines Konzeptes, in dem Anthropologie und Trinitätslehre noch enger und einheitlicher miteinander verwoben sind.

Die Arbeit geht in vier Argumentationssträngen vor. Zunächst untersuche ich Jüngels Kritik an der modernen Vorstellung der Freiheit, die auf die Sicherung des Subjekts durch sich selbst und seinen Selbstbesitz abzielt. Zweitens analysiere ich Jüngels Darstellung der Freiheit Gottes. Diese Darstellung legt eine Spannung zwischen den beiden von Jüngel besonders hervorgehobenen Aussagen frei, einerseits der unveräußerlichen Spontaneität und der grundlegend schöpferischen Eigenart des Seins Gottes, andererseits dem intersubjektiven Charakter der Selbstbestimmung Gottes als dem trinitarischen Ereignis der Liebe. Gottes Subjektivität grenzt daher, so wird gezeigt, an eine vorherrschende Selbstbezüglichkeit, die Jüngel auf der anthropologischen Ebene wiederum als Unfreiheit ablehnt. Im dritten Argumentationsgang widme ich mich dem Sein der Person, das Jüngel unter dem Vorzeichen der elementaren Unterbrechung darstellt, wonach die Person nicht nur befreit wird, sondern in Entsprechung zu Gott gebracht wird. Hier geht es mir vor allem um die beiden Akte der Existenz der Person. Schließlich entwickele ich die ontologischen Implikationen der beiden existentiellen Akte der freien Person. Auf sie gestützt schlage ich eine Möglichkeit vor, die Ambivalenz aufzulösen, die Jüngels Darstellung von Gottes Akt der Selbstbestimmung Gottes kennzeichnet. Die zentrale, konstruktive These der Arbeit besteht darin, dass es auch in Gott zwei

Existenzakte gibt, die in zwei unterschiedlichen Varianten der trinitarischen Relationalität begründet sind. Neben der von mir so genannten Logik der Liebe ist auch die Logik der Freiheit zu bedenken. Ohne Gottes ursprüngliche Kreativität zu opfern, erlaubt sie es Gott, in ein erfülltes Miteinander mit der von Gott befreiten Menschheit einzutreten und sein Selbst auf intersubjektive Weise als Ereignis der Liebe zu bestimmen.

Index

DATE DUE

8/30	
9/11	

DEMCO, INC. 38-2931

RANDOM HOUSE

LARGE
PRINT

Also by Stephen Frey
available from Random House Large Print

The Chairman

THE PROTÉGÉ

THE
PROTÉGÉ

A NOVEL

STEPHEN
FREY

This is a work of fiction. Names, characters, places, and incidents are either the products of the author's imagination or are used fictitiously. Any resemblance to actual persons, living or dead, events, or locales is entirely coincidental.

For Diana . . . I love you so much.

ACKNOWLEDGMENTS

A special thank you to Dr. Teo Forcht Dagi, a very busy man who was always available to talk and to offer tremendous help with technical guidance; Mark Tavani, my editor, for his tireless efforts; Cynthia Manson, my agent, for her tireless efforts; and Matt Malone, my great friend, for his suggestions on this book.

Thank you also to my daughters Ashley and Christina, whom I love very much, and to those who have always been there to answer questions and give encouragement: Stephen Watson, Kevin "Big Sky" Erdman, Gina Centrello, Jack Wallace, Bob Wieczorek, Scott Andrews, John Piazza, Kristin Malone, Gordon Eadon, Chris Andrews, Andy Brusman, Jeff Faville, Marvin Bush, Jim and Anmarie Galowski, Courtney, Walter Frey, Tony Brazely, John Grigg, Bart Begley, Barbara Fertig, Pat and Terry Lynch, Chris Tesoriero, Baron Stewart, Gerry Barton, and Mike Pocalyko.

And to Diana. I love you, sweetheart. You're my angel.

PROLOGUE

DAVID WRIGHT'S eyes narrowed as he watched the woman struggle. She was standing on her tiptoes, hands high above her head, wrists chained to iron rings bolted into the ceiling. Her long dark hair cascaded past her naked shoulders as she held her head back, straining against the chains, trying to ease the pain.

Wright picked up the whip. Attached to its smooth wooden handle were ten narrow leather strands, each twelve inches long, each knotted at the tip. His breath turned quick and his heart raced as he drew the strands through his fingers, then passed them over her smooth skin. She moaned and shook her head when she felt the leather, trying to pull away, so afraid of what was coming. But her wrists were as high above her head as she could reach— she was almost hanging—so she could barely move. She was completely in his control.

Wright had first come to the sex store in the West Village several months ago, interested in toys to share with his wife, Peggy. After several visits, he'd gotten to know the owner, a slight, chain-smoking man with a thin mustache who'd casually asked from behind the counter one day if Wright would be interested in something "live." After a few moments, Wright had nodded and the man had led him through a hidden door in the back—into a bondage chamber.

Wright had watched the first session, then quickly decided to participate. Now he did it one-on-one, spending an hour alone with a woman he chose from a folder of photographs. The fee for the hour was five thousand dollars, but money like that was no object for him. This was his fourth session in the last six weeks. He took a gulp of water—it was hot in the room—as he gazed at the woman's slim arms and legs. He could see her muscles beginning to cramp, and he liked it.

He made the first lash hard, even though he'd been told to start slow. Not for her sake, but to excite him more. The owner had told Wright that if he took his time in the beginning, the thrill would build more consistently and thus be more intense when he began to deliver real pain. But he didn't care. He did what he wanted when he wanted.

The second lash was as hard as he could make it. She screamed into one arm, and a tremor shook her entire body. But there was no need to worry about anyone outside hearing her screams—the room was soundproof.

Wright took a deep breath. He'd used this woman the last three times. He liked her delicate features, her beautiful body, the way her skin rose quickly with the lashes. And he had no misgivings about the pain. She earned half the five grand—a lot of money for an hour's work, especially for a woman who by day was an administrative assistant at a law firm. She knew what she was getting into, she knew what he was going to do to her. There was no reason for remorse.

With the crack of the third lash, her head snapped back and she screamed at the top of her lungs, begging for mercy—which only made him want to hurt her more. He delivered the fourth, fifth, sixth, and seventh lashes in rapid succession, causing her skin to swell in long, narrow lines. After the seventh lash he rested, breathing hard, sweating profusely. He wiped the back of his hand across his forehead and took several more gulps of water, enjoying her sobs and moans.

When he was finished drinking, he put down the whip and forced the woman roughly up onto a block of wood, reaching for a noose hanging from a ceiling beam. Forcing it over her head and around her neck as she tried to keep it away by ducking. It was his first time doing this—the owner's suggestion. The owner had warned him to be very careful; things could easily go wrong. But he'd also told Wright what an incredible thrill it would be and how the woman had never had this done to her—so she'd be genuinely terrified.

Wright unhooked the woman's wrists from the iron rings, then brought her hands down behind her back and cuffed them. As he drew the noose firmly around her neck, she started to whimper. "Shut up!" he hissed, moving toward the wall where the other 'end of the rope was knotted to a cleat. He was going to tighten the rope, then pull the block of wood slowly out from under her and let her dangle for a few moments. Letting her think he was going to leave her there until she suffocated. Then push the block back beneath her feet when she started gasping hard. The owner was right: This was going to be incredible.

It was then that she panicked, struggling against the noose and screaming wildly.

He rushed toward her as she came perilously close to the edge of the wooden block, to steady her. But his foot slammed into the block as he reached for her, tripping him and knocking it from beneath her. He careened to the cement floor, then rolled quickly onto his back. Just in time to see her fall.

The drop was short, only eighteen inches. But it was enough.

Wright sprang up and rushed to the cleat on the wall, his fingers working madly to undo the knot. When he finally tore the loops free, he lowered her down, watching in horror as her limp body crumpled to the floor, the noose still draped around her broken neck. He knelt over her, staring into her empty eyes, his hands shaking horribly and blood pounding in his brain so hard that his vision blurred with each beat. "Christ," he whispered, sweat soaking his clothes. She wasn't breathing, and he couldn't find a pulse. He didn't know CPR, so he took her head in his hands and shook it gently. A pathetic attempt to revive her. But there was no response, not even a flicker of her eyelids. Just a dull, mannequin gaze. "Shit!" he whined, panic seizing him for real now.

He crawled quickly to the door and cracked it, peering into the main part of the store. It was dark, as if the owner were gone. Which was strange. The other times, the guy had waited until Wright was finished—three in the morning a week ago. It was only a few minutes before midnight now.

He opened the door wider, allowing light from the chamber to illuminate the store. Still no sign of the owner. So strange, but he didn't have time to think on it now. He needed to take advantage of the opportunity.

He crawled back to where the woman lay, removed the noose from her neck, the cuffs from her wrists, then found a rag and wiped down everything in the room, erasing his fingerprints. Then he dressed the woman and carried her through the store, laying her down in front of the door before climbing three steps to the sidewalk, peering up and down the darkened West Village side street to make certain it was deserted. When he was satisfied all was clear, he hurried back to her body, scooped it up, and ran down the sidewalk as fast as he could, gasping with each stride.

When he'd gone fifty yards, he moved in between two parked cars and put her body down between them. He stepped back slowly, gazing down at her lifeless form, remorse overtaking him, hoping he'd wake up from this nightmare. A sudden sob racked his body, and he shook his head, then turned and raced back to the shop. It was about survival at this point. He had to stay focused on getting out of here.

Back inside the shop, Wright gathered up the noose, the cuffs, and the rag he'd used to wipe down the place, then bolted. He dropped everything in a trash can several blocks away and headed for Seventh Avenue to catch a taxi. But when he reached the brightly lit area, he realized he didn't want a driver identifying him later. So he half walked, half ran across Manhattan to Lexington Avenue and caught the subway, not looking anyone in the eye all the way home.

Wright finally got back to his apartment on the Upper East Side a little before two in the morning. He didn't want to wake up his wife, so he lay down on the couch and stared at the ceiling. Wondering when the police would come for him.

PART
ONE

1

CHRISTIAN GILLETTE strode purposefully down the long main corridor of Everest Capital, the Manhattan-based investment firm he ran.

"Christian."

Gillette ignored the voice calling him from behind.

"Christian!"

Louder this time, but Gillette still didn't stop. He glanced over at his assistant, Debbie, pen and pad in hand. She was struggling to keep up.

"Mr. Chairman!" Faraday huffed, finally catching up with Gillette, and grabbing him by the back of the arm. Faraday was second in command at Everest. A talented money raiser from Great Britain who had an Outlook full of high-level connections in the Wall Street world. His accent was heavy, though he'd been in the States for fifteen years. "Wait a minute."

"Morning, Nigel," Gillette said politely.

"A fucking magnificent pleasure to see you, too," Faraday muttered, breathing hard. He inhaled ice cream constantly—to fight stress, he claimed—but he'd been thirty pounds overweight since graduating from Eton. Long before he'd ever dealt with the pressures of a private equity investment firm. "I sent you three e-mails this morning," he grumbled. "You haven't replied to any of them."

"No time."

"One of them was **extremely** important."

"I'll get to it when I can."

Faraday scowled. "I'm the number two person here, Christian. I need access to you."

Gillette jabbed a thumb over his shoulder. "I've got three conference rooms waiting for me. A guy representing the Wallace Family in One, one of our accounting firms in Two, and—"

"The **Chicago** Wallaces?"

"Yeah."

"Jesus, they're worth like twenty double-large."

Following Gillette's lead, people at Everest sometimes referred to a million as "large" and a billion as "double-large."

"More than that."

"But they keep to themselves," Faraday continued. "They don't talk to other investors. I've been trying to get to them for years, to have them invest with us. But nothing, not even a return phone call. They're very secretive."

"I know."

Faraday hesitated, waiting for an explanation that didn't come. "Well, what do they want?"

"To hire you."

"Really?" Faraday leaned back, putting a chubby, pale hand on his chest.

"No, not really," Gillette answered, grinning.

Faraday sighed. "Well, what **do** they want?"

"I'll tell you this afternoon at three, when we're **scheduled** to meet."

"But I have to talk to you **now**."

"All right," Gillette said, giving in. "Talk."

"Hey, it's fucking good news. I thought you'd want to hear right away."

Good news was always a welcome interruption. "What you got?"

"Two more commitments to the new fund," Faraday explained. "I got an e-mail late last night from the California Teachers Pension. They're in for six hundred large. And North America Guaranty agreed to invest one double-large five minutes ago." Faraday broke into a proud smile. "We're done, Christian. Everest Eight now has fifteen billion dollars of commitments. I'm happy to report to you that we've raised the largest private equity fund in history."

Incredible, Gillette thought. And fifteen billion of equity could be leveraged with at least sixty billion of debt from the banks and insurance companies that were constantly begging to partner with them.

Which meant he had seventy-five billion dollars of fresh money to buy more companies with. To add to the thirty Everest already owned.

"What do you think?" Faraday asked. "Great, right?"

"It took a while."

Faraday's expression sagged. "It took ten months. That's pretty **fucking** good."

Eleven years Gillette had known Faraday, and he was still amazed at the Brit's language. He didn't care if the guy dropped the F-bomb when it was just the two of them, but there were others around now.

"The original target was a year," Faraday reminded Gillette. "We beat that by two months!"

Gillette spotted one of the receptionists coming up behind Faraday, a middle-aged woman who was waving, trying to get his attention. "Yes, Karen."

"Mr. Gillette, the commissioner of the National Football League is holding for you."

Gillette watched Faraday's face go pale. They'd been waiting a long time for this call. Two years of work lay in the balance. "Transfer Mr. Landry to my cell," he instructed calmly, pulling the tiny phone from his pocket.

"Right away," Karen called, hurrying off.

Gillette moved to where Faraday stood and shook his hand. "You did a great job on the fund, Nigel. You really did."

Faraday looked down, caught off guard by the compliment. "Thanks, that means a lot."

Gillette's cell phone rang, and Faraday glanced at it apprehensively. "God, I hope we get this."

Gillette pressed the "talk" button and put the phone to his ear, still staring at Faraday. "This is Christian Gillette."

"Christian, it's Kurt Landry."

"Hi, Kurt. What's up?"

"Well . . . Christian . . . the owners met last night." Landry hesitated. "And they voted to award the new Las Vegas expansion franchise to you, to Everest Capital. **You got it.**"

A thrill rushed through Gillette. They'd offered the NFL four hundred and fifty million dollars. A tremendous sum of money for a franchise with no history in a city that was nothing more than a dot in the desert. Lacking a large, permanent population that might justify such a stratospheric price elsewhere. But with the strategy he and his team had devised, Gillette was confident the franchise could be worth five times that in a few years. Maybe more. Maybe **much** more.

"Well?" Faraday whispered.

Gillette silently mouthed, **We got it.** "I have some ideas for the team's name, Kurt," he said, watching Faraday pump his fists, then raise both arms above his head and do an embarrassing dance in front of Debbie. Shaking his head and laughing at the Brit's exuberance. "How about the Craps?"

"Christian, I don't think that's—"

"Or the Twenty-ones," Gillette kept going, enjoying Landry's anxious response. "I can see the Super Bowl trailer now: The Twenty-ones and the Forty-niners for the world championship. Whose number is up?"

"Had that ready for me, right? In case I had good news."

"I **assumed** you had good news."

"Don't start designing logos yet," Landry advised, chuckling. "How about lunch on Monday? We'll talk details then."

Gillette already had a lunch Monday, but this was much more important. "Sure. I'll have Debbie call your EA to arrange it."

"Thanks."

Gillette slid the phone back in his pocket. "We're done, Nigel, it's ours."

Faraday was beaming. "Pretty good morning, huh?"

Gillette checked his watch: ten-thirty. Still plenty of time in the day for things to go wrong. "We'll see."

"Don't get so excited," Faraday said. "Wouldn't want you to have a heart attack here in front of everyone."

But Gillette was already striding down the corridor toward Conference Room One. "Cancel Monday's lunch," he said to Debbie as she trotted beside him, scribbling on her pad. "Then call Kurt Landry's executive assistant and—"

"I heard, Chris. I'll take care of everything."

Debbie was one of his best hiring decisions. She

was always anticipating, always executing, and always pleasant—even when he wasn't. She was one of the few people he truly depended on. And one of the few people who called him Chris.

As Gillette reached the conference room door, his cell phone went off again. He pulled it out and checked the number: Harry Stein, CEO of Discount America, a fast-growing chain of megastores that had taken on Wal-Mart—and was winning. Everest Capital owned ninety percent of Discount America, and Gillette was chairman of the board. As chairman of Everest, Gillette also chaired many of the companies Everest owned.

"Go in and see if they need anything," Gillette instructed, motioning toward the conference room. "Drinks, whatever. Tell them I'll be right in."

Debbie shook her head as his cell phone continued to buzz. "It's amazing."

"What?"

"How you handle so many things at once and keep everything straight."

He froze, unprepared for the praise.

"Okay, okay," she said, rolling her eyes, taking his reaction as impatience. "I'm going."

Gillette grimaced as she moved inside the conference room and closed the door. He'd always been terrible at accepting compliments. Just like his father. "What do you need, Harry?"

"Damn, Mr. Chairman, not even a 'good morning'?"

"What do you need?"

"How do you know I **need** anything?"

"You always do. What is it now?"

"It's what I told you about last week, but it's gotten worse. We're up to our eyeballs in alligators down in Maryland."

Stein constantly alluded to animals in conversation—which drove Gillette up a wall. "Remind me."

"We're trying to put up this great new store in a town called Chatham on the Eastern Shore. That's on the other side of the Chesapeake Bay from Balt—"

"I know where the Eastern Shore is."

"Right. Well, this'll be our first store in the region, and if we get in there, we'll give Wal-Mart fits. It'll really put us on the map."

"So, what's the problem?" Gillette asked.

"The mayor's rallying everybody against us."

"Why?"

"Chatham's this old fishing town from before the Revolutionary War that's built on some river called the Chester. Lots of boring history the locals want you to love, you know? Anyway, it's centrally located, very strategic. We'll draw from lots of other little towns. But this woman's all hot and bothered about us being the eight-hundred-pound gorilla. Got a bee in her bonnet because she thinks when the store goes up we'll run all her quaint little waterfront shops out of business and turn her Garden of Eden into strip mall heaven. Typical misguided small-town paranoia, but the woman's a damn pit bull. She's actually making progress, getting everybody stirred up, and—"

"That's normal, Harry, we've seen it before. Let it run its course," Gillette said gently.

"But she's calling mayors and town councils in other places we're trying to get into. She's already talked to people in New Jersey, Pennsylvania, Virginia, and North Carolina. Hell, she started some Web site, and she's spreading rumors on it about a class-action sex-bias suit she's going to hit us with. There's nothing to the suit, but that kind of crap can spin out of control."

"Why are you calling me?"

"You need to meet with her," Stein explained.

"Why me? **You're** the CEO."

"I did meet with her," Stein muttered. "I didn't do very well."

"Why would I do any better?"

"You're the ultimate decision maker, and she's a bottom-line nut. She was pissed off when I told her I had to go to you for permission to get some of the things she said might change her mind. She didn't have much use for me after that."

"What's she looking for?"

"For starters, she wants us to build her a new elementary school and a retirement home."

People always had their damn hands out looking for freebies. Sometimes the world seemed like one big scamfest. "That's ridiculous," Gillette griped.

"But it's going to be an awesome store, Christian. A hundred thousand square feet of shelf-space heaven, our best location yet. A revolution in retailing. Everything a shopper could want under one roof in a region we've got to penetrate **right now.**" Stein took a deep breath. "And we've got to stop this woman from talking to other towns. I need your help."

Gillette knew what "help" meant. It meant a day of palm pressing and ass kissing big-ego, small-town officials who'd try to pry everything they could out of him over a lunch of rubber chicken and some local high-carb dish that won last year's church bakeoff. Nothing for the highlight reel and a black hole in terms of time, but Discount America was at a critical point. About to break out, about to make major noise in the retail industry. Which should enable Everest to take the chain public in the next twelve to eighteen months—or sell to Wal-Mart—at a **huge** profit.

"Call Debbie and set it up. Middle of next week sometime."

"Thanks, Mr. Chairman. You'll make the difference. You could charm a rattlesnake out of its fangs, and I—"

Gillette ended the call. He didn't have time for Stein's snow. The phone went off again as he was putting it back in his pocket. He cursed as he checked the display: Faith Cassidy. He was supposed to have called her earlier.

Faith was a pop star on a roll. Her first two albums had sold millions, and she was about to release her third. She was on the West Coast doing prerelease promotions. Her label was owned by an entertainment company controlled by Everest Capital and chaired by Gillette. She was also his girlfriend. Sort of.

"What's up?"

"Hi, Chris."

"Hi."

"God, you sound busy."

"Yeah. How's it going?"

"Great, it's going great. Thanks for calling the music execs out here. I'm getting the royal treatment."

"You should. You're hot."

"Well . . . I don't know about that," Faith said, being modest. "I miss you."

"Me too. When are you back?"

"I don't know yet. Depends on a couple of things. But I can't wait to see you."

"Yeah . . . it'll be nice."

"Just a bursting bud of romance this morning, aren't you?"

"Busy, baby. That's all."

She sighed. "I understand."

"Call me later, all right?"

"I love you, Chris."

He hesitated, waiting until a young associate heading up the hallway had passed by. "You too. See ya."

The man on the other side of the table stood up and held out his hand as Gillette walked into the conference room. "Gordon Meade, executive director of the Wallace Family office."

"Christian Gillette."

"It's a pleasure to meet you, Christian."

Meade looked to be in his late fifties, neatly groomed from his silver hair to his shiny shoes. For a man who managed over twenty billion, Meade had a relaxed air about him, and when he spoke he did so with a faint smile, as if he were recalling a secret about a Wallace Family member. Something that gave him job security, no matter what.

Families were always full of secrets, Gillette knew. Especially wealthy ones.

"The pleasure's mine," Gillette said, motioning for Meade to sit back down. "I know you don't talk to other firms very often, so I'm honored that you're here."

"Thank you." Meade gestured at the young woman sitting beside him. "Christian, this is Allison Wallace."

Allison was attractive, no two ways about it. Blond and slim, with pretty facial features: light blue eyes, a thin nose, full lips, and high cheekbones. Dressed conservatively in a dark blue skirt suit and a white blouse, top button buttoned. Late twenties, Gillette figured. "Hello."

She gave him a slight nod.

"Allison's on the board of the Wallace Family

Trust," Meade explained. "Along with her uncle and her grandfather. The trust is the vehicle the Wallaces make most of their investments with. I report to Allison." His smile grew forced.

As if it were irritating to report to a woman half his age, Gillette thought. "Thank you both for coming. Like I said, I'm honored, but also curious," he admitted, sitting at the head of the table. "You weren't clear about what you wanted when you called, Gordon. Frankly, I don't usually take a meeting without a specific agenda. But this is the Wallace Family."

"Representing the Wallaces does have its advantages," Meade acknowledged. "How much do you know about the family?"

"I know they're hypersensitive about publicity. So hyper they don't even have a Web site. Most family offices do."

"I've tried to get them to set one up," Meade responded. "Better to control the flow of information than have people guess. But they won't do it. Are you at all familiar with the family history?" he asked.

"I know that Willard Wallace founded the Chicago and Western Railway back in the 1850s." Gillette loved railroads, so the Wallace Family history had piqued his interest when Debbie dropped the prep memo on his desk yesterday. "The family sold it to what's now the Burlington Northern in the early 1900s, but they kept a lot of the land Willard originally purchased for the railroad. They made a killing off it, too, selling it parcel by parcel for major bucks over the years. Then they struck gold again with the cell phone explosion." Gillette could tell that Meade was impressed.

"Nice job, Christian. That stuff isn't easy to find."

Everest Capital owned an investigation and personal protection firm—McGuire & Company—that could dig up almost anything on anybody. McGuire's CEO, Craig West, reported directly to Gillette. "I believe the family's worth over twenty billion."

"Can't comment on that," Meade said quickly, his expression turning serious.

"Which means I'm close." Gillette glanced at Allison. She still hadn't said a word—or taken her eyes off him.

"One thing you also figured out is the Wallace Family's political affiliation." Meade gestured at photos on the bookcases of Gillette shaking hands with both President Bushes, Rudy Giuliani, George Pataki, and several other Republican stars. "The Wallaces are big GOP supporters." Meade smiled. "Is there a conference room with pictures of you shaking Democratic hands as well?"

"Both Clintons, Kerry, Cuomo, and a few others," Gillette replied. "We have one for the independents, too." He checked his watch: five after eleven. He was supposed to have met with the accountants in Conference Room Two at ten-thirty and the guy in Three five minutes ago. "So why did you want to get together?"

"You've become quite a story in the financial world," Meade began. "A hot commodity."

"We're a **team** around here, Gordon, no stars. My **team's** a hot commodity, not me."

"That's a nice piece of humble pie, Christian. Sincerely sliced, I'm sure. But you're the chairman of Everest Capital. You take hell for everyone's mistakes, so you get credit for their wins. That's the way it works." Meade eased back in his chair and crossed his legs at the knees. "How old are you?"

"Thirty-seven."

"So young." The older man sighed.

"I've done my time."

"Oh, I know. I saw that **People** magazine article a few weeks ago. The top fifty bachelors list issue. They called you one of the hardest-working men in America."

"I didn't speak to anyone at **People** about that list," Gillette said curtly. "They put it together on their own. They didn't even give me a courtesy call to tell me the article was coming out. I don't pay attention to that stuff, anyway."

Meade chuckled. "I guess it doesn't do much good to be one of the top fifty bachelors if you don't have time to do the things bachelors do."

"There's never enough time, Gordon."

Meade shook his head paternally. "I used to think that way, but I've learned to relax as my sun heads toward the horizon. Enjoy it while you can, Christian. Dust to dust, you know?"

"Uh-huh."

Meade flicked a piece of lint from his pants. "I want to ask you a few questions about Everest before I get into specifics of why Allison and I are here."

The people in the other conference rooms could wait. This man controlled twenty billion dollars, and Gillette smelled opportunity. "Go ahead."

"You took over as Everest's chairman, what? About a year ago?"

"Ten months."

"How long have you been here?"

"Eleven years." Gillette glanced over at Allison. She was still staring at him intently. "Before that I was with Goldman Sachs in their mergers and acquisitions department."

"Bill Donovan was chairman of Everest before you, right?"

"Yup. Bill founded Everest back in 1984 and was chairman until last November, when I took over. The first fund he raised was twenty-five million. We've raised seven more funds since then."

"Seven more?" Meade asked.

"Yes, eight in total since 1984."

"I thought Fund Seven was the last one you raised. That's what it says on your Web site."

"We just finished raising our eighth fund this morning. Literally right before I walked in here. The Web site should be updated by COB today."

"How big is this one?"

Out of the corner of his eye, Gillette noticed

Allison lean forward slightly in her chair. "Fifteen billion."

Meade whistled. "Jesus, that's got to be the largest private equity fund ever raised."

"It is," Gillette agreed. "We're lucky."

"You aren't lucky," Allison spoke up, finally breaking her silence. "You're good. Investors don't care about luck, they care about performance, and your performance has been outstanding. Your funds have done at least forty percent a year. I hear the return for Everest Six was over **fifty** percent a year. In the past nine months, you've sold your grocery store chain and your waste management company to industry buyers and taken two other companies public. Your information management business in Los Angeles and that chip maker in La Jolla. All at very fat gains. The profit on those deals alone was over three billion."

"Closer to four," Gillette corrected. Maybe there was more to Allison Wallace than just a bloodline. "It's been a good run."

"It's been an **incredible** run, and you still haven't sold your grand slam, Laurel Energy. That should be a four-to-five-billion-dollar profit by itself."

Laurel Energy was a Canadian energy exploration and production company Everest had bought several years ago. Last fall, Laurel engineers had discovered a major oil and gas field on several option properties the company had acquired cheaply. Everest had put just three hundred million into Laurel, and Allison was right: According to the engineers, it was worth around five billion now. "How do you know about Laurel?" he asked.

"We have some oil and gas investments up there, too," she explained. "People can't keep their mouths shut. Everybody's always got to tell somebody their secret."

"Yeah, everybody wants to feel like they're in the know."

"Which you wouldn't understand, Christian," Meade observed, "because you're **always** in the know." His expression turned grave. "Let's talk about what happened here last November."

Gillette's gaze moved deliberately from Allison to Meade.

"About how you became chairman of Everest. About Miles Whitman."

Miles Whitman. Gillette hadn't heard that name in a long time.

A year ago, Whitman had been the chief investment officer and a board member of North America Guaranty—the country's largest insurance company and Everest's biggest investor. But Whitman had lost billions on some terrible investments he'd secretly made with NAG funds and was facing a long prison sentence if the internal accountants and the other board members figured out what he'd done. So he'd hatched a desperate plot to cover up his losses—which involved gaining control of Everest.

The plot hinged on Whitman having his own chairman of Everest, a puppet who'd do exactly what he was told. It had also hinged on getting Bill Donovan—**and then Gillette**—out of the way with help from the men who'd once run McGuire & Company—Tom and Vince McGuire. They'd gotten Donovan, but ultimately the plot had been uncovered and the conspirators had fled. The authorities had taken Vince in, but Whitman and Tom McGuire were still out there somewhere.

Donovan had been murdered on a remote area of his Connecticut estate. One hell of a way to get promoted, Gillette thought, shaking his head. "What happened last November was all over the news for weeks, Gordon," he said quietly.

"Yes, but—"

"You can read all about it on the Internet." Gillette could see that Meade wasn't happy.

"Any hangover from all that as far as North America Guaranty goes?" Meade asked. "Did they invest in the fund you just finished raising? In Everest Eight?"

"A billion dollars," Gillette replied. "We just got that commitment this morning."

"Good. It's important to have a relationship with the biggest pot of money around."

"Believe me," Gillette said firmly, "I understand."

"How much of Fund Seven is left?" Meade asked.

"Two billion."

"So you have seventeen billion of equity right now. Two billion from Seven and fifteen in the new fund."

"Seventeen. Right."

"How many companies do you own?"

"Thirty. We also own shares of other companies we've taken public but don't control anymore."

"What's that in total revenues for the control companies?"

"About seventy billion."

"How many of the thirty companies are you chairman of?"

Meade wasn't going to like this answer. "Eighteen."

"Holy crap!" the older man exclaimed. "Do you really have time to chair that many companies, chair Everest, **and** put seventeen billion dollars of new equity to work?"

"No," Gillette admitted. "We're going to hire at least two more managing partners in the next few weeks. We'll probably open a West Coast office before the end of the year, too, and staff that up fast with experienced people we pick off from other private equity firms. It'll cost more to do it that way, but it'll save time."

"L.A. or San Francisco?"

Gillette checked the clock on the wall. "Look, are you going to tell me why you're here?"

"We want to coinvest with you," Allison broke in before Meade could say anything.

Gillette considered her answer for a few moments. "What exactly does that mean?"

"We want you to call us when you're about to buy a company and give us the option to invest in the equity alongside you."

Gillette considered what she'd said for a moment. "What do I get for doing all the work? For finding the company and structuring the deal. For recruiting a management team to run the company after we take it over. What's in it for me?"

"More equity," Allison answered. "We'll commit five billion dollars to you so you'll have twenty-two billion instead of seventeen. You'll be able to buy more and bigger companies."

"It didn't sound like you were giving me a commitment a minute ago."

"Why not?"

"You used the word **option.** You said you wanted the **option** to invest with us."

"If we don't like the company you want to buy, we won't invest."

"That's not how it works at Everest. If you commit to us, you **have** to wire your share of the money when we call it to buy the company. If you don't, you forfeit what you've already invested. This is the big leagues. It doesn't work for me unless I know you're unconditionally committed. When I negotiate, I need to know I have firepower."

"What's the annual fee on Everest Eight?" Allison asked.

"One percent."

"A hundred and fifty million a year?"

"Most funds charge at least one and a **half** percent," Gillette pointed out. "As much as two, in some cases. You both know that. It's just that we're so big, we felt it was fairer to our investors to charge less."

"We'll pay a half a percent on our five billion," Allison offered.

"I don't cut special deals for anyone. I don't have to." Gillette looked at Meade, who was gazing down into his lap, then at Allison. She was staring straight back. So she was the decision maker after all. He hadn't been sure until just now.

"All right," Allison said deliberately. "We'll invest five billion in Everest Capital Partners Eight under the same terms as everyone else."

"I'll have to go back to my investors," Gillette cautioned, "to the limited partners who've already committed to Eight. I have to make sure they're okay with the fund going from fifteen to twenty billion."

"At five billion, would we be your biggest investor?" Allison wanted to know.

"By far."

"Then I do want something."

Gillette figured this was coming. You didn't get five billion that easily. "What?"

"I want to be a managing partner here at Everest."

Including Faraday, four managing partners reported to Gillette. Beneath that were eight managing directors, then a number of vice presidents and associates reporting to the managing directors. One thing he hadn't anticipated from this meeting was adding anyone else to that pyramid.

"And I don't care about getting paid."

Ultimately, everybody wanted to get paid. Allison had some kind of angle here.

"I don't want a salary or a bonus," she continued. "I don't even want any of the ups."

Ups were pieces of profitable deals. When Everest made money—when it sold a portfolio company for more than it had paid—Gillette got to keep twenty percent of the gain. In the case of Laurel Energy, they'd paid $300 million. If they sold it for $5 billion, he'd keep twenty percent of the $4.7 billion gain—$940 million. As chairman, it was up to him to spread that around Everest as he saw fit. Under terms of the partnership's operating agreement, he could actually keep it all for himself if he chose to. He wouldn't, but he could.

"You want to see how we do it," Gillette said, thinking about Laurel. If the investment bankers could really get him five billion, it would be the best deal in Everest history. "You want to learn our secrets."

"Of course I do," Allison replied. "But in return you get five billion more of equity, fifty million more a year in fees, the ability to leverage that five billion with lots more debt, and a managing partner at no cost."

Gillette hesitated, going through the downside. As the biggest investor in the fund, Allison would assume she could barge into his office anytime. She'd probably feel she should have a bigger say than anyone else as far as strategy and investment decisions went, too. Still, as she'd pointed out, it was five billion in equity and fifty million a year in fees.

He took a deep breath. Major decisions all the time. "Done."

Moments later, Allison and Meade were gone and it was just Gillette and Debbie in the conference room.

"Well, that was interesting," Debbie said with a smug smile as they stood by the door.

"What was?"

"I've seen women try a lot of things to hook a man, but I've never seen one put up five billion dollars. That's a big piece of bait."

In the back of his mind he'd thought the same thing, but he didn't want to admit it to her. "It's not unusual for investors to want to have their people at a private equity firm when they make a huge commitment like that." Actually, it was, but she wouldn't know that. "And that's probably the biggest commitment any single investor ever made to a private equity firm."

Debbie groaned. "Give me a break. Did you see

the way she was looking at you? She didn't take her eyes off you the whole time."

"Please."

"Come on, you two would make an incredible couple. Tall, dark, and handsome—slim and blond. Chairman of Everest Capital—heiress to one of the greatest fortunes in this country. The dream couple, A-list for every party. That's what she was thinking, Chris. I could see it all over her face."

"You're just jealous."

Which they both knew wasn't true. Debbie was a lesbian. Gillette had been sure of that before he'd hired her—thanks to McGuire & Company. It was a perfect business relationship. No chance of her developing a silly crush on him, no chance of him getting any stupid ideas of his own.

"Do me a favor," he said. "Call Craig West over at McGuire and tell him to find out everything he can about Allison ASAP."

"Sure."

"And tell the guy in Three I'll be there in five minutes," he said over his shoulder as he moved toward the doorway. Then he stopped. "Oh."

Debbie looked up. "Yes?"

"What you said outside before we came in here."

She thought for a moment, trying to remember. "You mean about you being able to handle so much?"

Christian nodded. "Thanks," he said, his voice low. "That was nice."

"Christian!"

"Damn," Gillette muttered, almost running into David Wright as he turned to go.

Wright was an up-and-coming Everest managing director—thirty-one years old, tall and square-faced, with close-set eyes, short blond hair, and light skin. Aggressive to the point of arrogance, he was by far the most talented MD at the firm. And the only person at Everest who could give Gillette any competition at pool.

"I've got to talk to you, Christian. Now. **Right** now."

"What is it?" Gillette demanded. Seemed like everyone always needed to talk to him right away.

"We've got a chance to buy Hush-Hush Intimates," Wright explained. "You know, the Victoria's Secret competitor."

Gillette knew about Hush-Hush. The company was less than ten years old but had already racked up megasuccess by pushing the sex envelope even further than Victoria's Secret. Hush-Hush's catalog, published once a season, had become hotter than the **Sports Illustrated** swimsuit issue and the **Victoria's Secret** catalog combined.

"The company's privately held," Wright continued, "and the family just decided to sell."

"How do you know?"

"I just got off the phone with the guy who's head of corporate development there. His name's Frank

Hobbs. We were pretty good friends in business school. He says he can get us the inside track to buy the company, but we've got to move fast."

"How big is it?" Gillette asked.

Wright shrugged. "I don't know. Who cares? It's growing like a tech firm, and we can get our hands on it."

Gillette eyed Wright carefully. They'd worked closely together for several years, and Wright had a haggard look about him Gillette had never seen. "You okay?"

Wright's gaze dropped to the floor. "Yeah, fine."

Gillette hesitated a beat, waiting for the younger man to look up. But he didn't. "Uh-huh, well, get more information on it," he instructed, brushing past.

"Hi, Marvin," Gillette said loudly, moving into Conference Room Two. Marvin Miller was a partner at White & Cross, a large public accounting firm.

"Hello, Christian," Miller said enthusiastically, rising from his seat and pumping Gillette's hand. "This is—"

Miller started to introduce a young associate who'd come with him, but Gillette waved it off. There wasn't time. "Relax," he said, recognizing Miller's anxiety. A lot of money was at stake here. "Sit down."

A nervous smile played across Miller's face. "Relax? Why would I need to do that?"

"You know why I wanted to see you."

"What do you mean?" Miller asked innocently as they both sat down.

"Come on, Marvin, you said there was a problem with the Laurel Energy financial statements. A problem that could get in the way of a sale. I'm about to get five billion for Laurel. Nothing's going to screw that up."

"I said it **might** get in the way."

"You guys have been doing Laurel's financial statements for the last three years. How could there **possibly** be a problem?"

"We depend on your management team to give us good numbers, Christian. One of my guys has a question about a couple of the admin figures we got last month. They don't seem right."

Gillette started to say something, then stopped. This was going to be a quick conversation, no screwing around. "How many of our companies do you audit, Marvin?"

"Um, nineteen."

"What do you make off us a year?"

"I . . . I . . . I don't know exactly, I'd have to—"

"Give me an estimate."

Miller swallowed hard before answering. "Around a hundred million, maybe more."

"A hundred million. That's a lot of fees, Marvin. A lot of fees to lose." Gillette watched Miller swallow even harder. "And we just finished raising another fund this morning. It's twenty billion, so we're going to be buying a lot more companies. Big companies with lots of accounting needs. You can have first crack at auditing those companies." He hesitated. "Or not."

"Christian, I—"

"Very soon I'm going to start the process to sell Laurel," Gillette cut in. "I'm going to retain Morgan Stanley, and the financials better be in perfect order," he warned, rising from his seat. "Got it?"

Miller nodded, resigned to doing whatever was necessary to stay in Gillette's good graces. "Yes, Christian, there won't be any problems," he said quietly. "Take this off your issue list."

"I will."

Gillette glanced at his watch as he headed toward Conference Room Three. It was eleven-thirty. He hoped the guy had waited.

He hadn't.

"Damn it!" As Gillette turned to go back to his office, Debbie was standing in front of him.

"You didn't miss Mr. Smith," Debbie explained. "He never showed."

"What?"

"Yeah, he called reception while you were in with the Wallace people. He's waiting for you in his hotel room at the Intercontinental." The Intercontinental Hotel was a couple of blocks from the Everest offices. "Room 1241." She smirked. "As if you're really going to drop everything and go running over there."

Gillette rolled his eyes. "Yeah, as if."

. . .

"**MR. SMITH?**" Gillette asked, moving through the hotel room doorway.

After Gillette had passed, the other man leaned into the hallway and glanced in both directions, then shut and locked the door. "Thank you for coming here, Mr. Gillette." The man moved into the suite and sat on a small sofa in front of a dark wood coffee table. He pointed at the matching sofa on the other side of the table. "I know you're busy, but it has to be this way."

Gillette sat down, not taking his eyes off the other man.

"By the way, my name isn't Smith, it's Ganze. Daniel Ganze."

"Okay."

"Would you like something to drink, Mr. Gillette? Coffee, Coke?"

"No."

Ganze was short, no more than five six, with closely cropped black hair that was thinning on top. He had dark, straight eyebrows and a small mouth with thin lips that barely moved when he spoke. His voice was low and precise, each syllable perfectly articulated. He didn't face you when he talked—his chin was pointed off at an angle, left or right. He didn't look you straight in the eye, either. Almost, but not quite.

"Why all the secrecy, Mr. Ganze?" It was the

second time today Gillette had agreed to a meeting without a specific agenda, and it was killing him. "Senator Clark asked me to meet with you," he said when Ganze didn't answer right away. Michael Clark was the senior United States senator from California. Gillette had met Clark this past summer at a White House dinner, and they'd gotten together several times since to discuss ways in which Everest could do more business in California—and California could benefit. "I'm always happy to help the senator, but he didn't tell me what this was about. In fact, he didn't even tell me what you do, Mr. Ganze."

"I'm an attorney by training, but I don't practice anymore. Now I represent certain interests in Washington, D.C."

"Interests?"

"Yes, interests." Ganze leaned forward, over the table. "I appreciate Senator Clark setting this meeting up, and I appreciate your time. I know how busy you are."

It was the second time Ganze had said that. "How exactly do you know how busy I am?"

"I just do." Ganze folded his hands tightly. "As I said before, I'm sorry for all the secrecy, but it has to be this way. That's all I can tell you about me and the interests I represent right now. If we proceed, you'll learn more."

Gillette was about to say something when Ganze spoke up again.

"Your father was a senator, Mr. Gillette."

Gillette's eyes raced to Ganze's, and his pulse exploded. He fought to contain himself, but it was impossible. "Yes, he was." He tried to say the words calmly, but he could tell Ganze had noticed the electric reaction and the rasp in his voice as his throat went dry. He hated being transparent, but he couldn't help it. This was his father.

"His name was Clayton Gillette," Ganze continued. "He founded and built a very successful Los Angeles–based investment bank, then sold it to one of the big Wall Street brokerage firms for a hundred million. Stayed on for a while after he sold out, then ran for Congress. One term there, then he won a Senate seat. He was killed in a private plane crash in the middle of that Senate term. The plane went down just after takeoff from Orange County Airport. It was a clear day. The official record says pilot error, but that explanation seems thin to me. To other people as well," Ganze added, his voice low.

Gillette had wondered about the crash for years but figured grief was making him paranoid. "What **other** people?"

"We have more information you'll want to hear," Ganze said, dodging Gillette's question.

"Like what?"

"Like the identity and location of a woman you've been trying to find for years."

Gillette froze, understanding immediately. His blood mother. "Ganze, I—"

"Mr. Gillette," Ganze cut in, "I know this is hard,

but I can't tell you anything else at this time. I'm sorry. If you want to hear more, you'll have to come to Washington to meet with my superior and me. If that's agreeable, I'll be in touch." He hesitated, then motioned at the door. "Good-bye."

2

CLAYTON WAS lighting his pipe when Christian got to the den—a hallowed room in the Bel Air mansion. He hesitated at the doorway, waiting for his father to see him.

"Come on in, Chris," Clayton called from behind the desk, clenching the pipe tightly between his teeth as he held a silver lighter over the bowl and sucked the flame down. "Close the door so we aren't interrupted, will you?"

"Yes, sir."

Christian loved this room. Dark wood paneling, big furniture, photographs of his father on hunting and fishing expeditions in exotic places with other famous people, dim lighting, the aroma of that pipe, a classic pool table off in one corner. A man's room. He sat in the leather chair in front of the desk.

Clayton tossed the lighter on the desk and took his first deep breath of the pungent smoke. The lighter landed beside the text of a speech he'd be making to the full Senate when they reconvened after the holidays. "Nice to get away from all the hubbub, huh?"

They'd just finished eating: thirty guests at the mansion for a formal Christmas Eve dinner. "Yeah," Christian agreed. Even nicer to spend time alone with his father. That rarely happened now that he was away on the East Coast at college.

"Your mother did a heck of a job with dinner. The food was great, wasn't it?"

Christian wanted to stop himself, but he couldn't. "My **step**mother, you mean." He'd had another run-in with Lana that afternoon, over something he couldn't even remember now, but it had burned out of control quickly. Like a small flame in a bone-dry forest, fanned by so much history.

Clayton looked up. "Chris, there's no reason—"

"And **you** did a heck of a job with dinner, Dad. **You** paid for the caterer. Lana didn't lift a finger." Christian watched for any signs of anger, but his father's handsome face stayed calm.

"Let's play some pool," Clayton suggested, nodding toward the table.

Christian had been hoping his father would say that. They had a long-running score he wanted to settle. "Sure."

As they got up, there was a knock on the door. "Yes?" Clayton called, clearly irritated at the interruption. "Come in."

The door burst open and Nikki rushed in. Nikki was Christian's younger half sister. She was a pretty brunette with a bubbly personality. They'd always been close.

She went to Clayton first and threw her arms around his neck. "Sorry to interrupt, Daddy," she said breathlessly, "but I wanted to say good-bye. I'm going to Kim's house, then a bunch of us are going out."

"On Christmas Eve?" Clayton asked, winking at Christian over her shoulder, feigning anger.

"Thanks for the bracelet, Daddy," she said, moving quickly to Christian and hugging him. "It's exactly what I wanted."

"There'll be more tomorrow."

"I can't wait to spend more time with you while you're home, Chris," she said, kissing his cheek.

Christian leaned back and smiled. "Ah, you'll be out with your friends all the time."

"No way." She shook her head hard, then headed for the door. "Bye, you two. Have fun."

When she was gone and the door was closed, they moved to the table.

"Eight ball?" Clayton suggested, putting his smoldering pipe in a large ashtray, then picking out his favorite cue stick from the wall rack. "Best of three, you break?"

"Okay, but I don't want any charity. You break."

Clayton nodded. "Fine, I'll take all the charity I can get," he said, leaning down and lining up the cue ball with the top of the triangle at the far end of the table. Then he hesitated, smiling serenely and straightening up. Looking at the ceiling as if he were deep in thought. "You've never taken a match from me, have you?"

They both knew Christian hadn't. **And** they both knew that such a victory was Christian's white whale. Reminding him of the streak was his father's way of playing with his mind, but he wasn't going to let himself be manipulated tonight. "This'll be interesting, Dad. I played a lot last semester."

"Is that all you guys at Princeton do?" Clayton wanted to know, breaking up the balls with a loud crack. "Play pool?"

"I'm keeping my grades up," Christian said quickly, sizing up the way the balls had come to rest. None in for his father on the break. A good way to start. "I'm fine."

Clayton chuckled. "I know you are. Four A's and a B plus in advanced calculus last semester. You're still on track to graduate with honors this May."

Christian had been about to take his first shot, but he stopped. "How do you know?" The semester had just ended last week. Final grades hadn't been released yet.

"I called my friend John Gray. He's one of the—"

"One of the assistant deans," Christian broke in, setting up for the shot again. "Yeah, I know." He made it easily. "Checking up, huh?"

"It's what I do, son. **Which reminds me.** While

you're home I want you to have lunch with my friend Ted Stovall. He's a Stanford trustee. He'll be very helpful getting you into business school."

Stanford University had one of the nation's elite business schools. "I'll take care of that on my own, Dad," Christian said. "I appreciate it, but I don't need your help. Damn it!" He'd missed a shot he shouldn't have because he'd been distracted by the conversation.

"You mean you don't **want** my help," Clayton corrected, inhaling, then clenching the pipe between his teeth as he prepared to shoot. "Just have lunch with Ted," he pushed gently. "Okay?"

"Yes, sir."

"And when you graduate from Stanford, we're going to get you that job at Goldman Sachs. Mergers and acquisitions. That's the one you want, right?"

It was exactly the job Christian wanted after business school. The **only** job he wanted. "Yes, sir," he said, spying a large wooden box sitting on a table in front of the window. "Thanks." He knew this den like the back of his hand, and the box hadn't been there when he'd left for Princeton last September. "Is that a humidor?" he asked, pointing.

Clayton glanced in the direction Christian was pointing. "Yes."

"When did you start smoking cigars? I thought you hated them."

"I do. It's a gift from a friend in Cuba. I'm not

supposed to keep those things, but, well, it was just so pretty."

Christian watched his father sink seven balls in a row, tapping the butt end of his cue on the floor faster and faster, harder and harder, until the eight disappeared, too. "Damn," he muttered.

Clayton rose up as the black ball dropped and smiled from behind the pipe. "One down, one to go. This is going to be easy."

But Christian won the second game, and the third was hard fought. Finally, there were just three balls left on the tan felt—the cue, the eight, and a stripe—Clayton's. Christian smiled. His father was blocked. The striped ball lay directly on the opposite side of the eight from the cue, and his father couldn't use the eight in a combination.

Clayton grimaced. "Tough leave, huh? Nowhere for me to go."

Christian nodded, trying to mask the smile. His father had to do something, and the odds were good that once the cue ball came to rest, he'd have an easy next shot to win. The streak was almost over. He could feel it.

But Clayton did the impossible. He made the cue ball jump the eight and into the stripe, knocking the stripe cleanly into a far pocket. The cue ball caromed off two sides of the table and came to rest near the eight. Clayton dropped it into a side pocket easily for the win.

Christian just shook his head as Clayton replaced his cue stick in the rack on the wall and came around the table. He'd been so close.

"I know how you hate to lose," Clayton said, placing his hands on Christian's shoulders. "You're so much like me," he murmured, smiling. "So much."

"Christian."

Gillette heard the voice but didn't react. He was still far away, still in his father's study, wishing he could have an evening like that just once more. After pool, they'd talked until two in the morning. But there'd never be another evening like that. Six months later, Clayton was gone.

"Christian!"

Gillette finally looked up. Faraday was standing in his office doorway. "What is it, Nigel?"

"It's time for the meeting," Faraday replied, tapping his wristwatch. He cocked his head to one side. "You okay?"

"LET'S GO," Faraday snapped at the stragglers. "You're four minutes late."

The two managing directors hustled to their seats at the far end of the conference room table.

This was the Everest managers meeting: Gillette, four managing partners, eight managing directors, and Debbie; attendance required. The only exception—Gillette. If he needed to be elsewhere, Faraday was in charge.

Gillette ran the meeting from the head of the table, while the other managers sat down the sides in descending order of seniority. Debbie sat at the far end of the table, taking minutes. Donovan had never allowed anyone but the partners into this meeting, but Gillette had a different management style. He believed in open communication—most of the time, anyway.

"Everyone's here, Christian," Faraday reported. He sat immediately to Gillette's right.

Gillette had been reviewing a memo and glanced up into two rows of hungry eyes. They reminded him of a wolf pack. "A couple of updates," he began. "Nigel finished raising Everest Eight this morning. We now have fifteen billion dollars of signed commitments."

Everyone rapped the table with their knuckles—the customary show of approval. The news about Everest Eight had spread like wildfire this morning, so the announcement was just a formality.

"Nigel deserves more than that, people," Gillette urged as the sounds of congratulation faded. "I said **fifteen billion.**"

The room broke into raucous applause and loud whistles. Gillette usually wanted controlled responses to everything at this meeting, even big news, but when he gave permission to celebrate, people responded. And this was tear-the-roof-off stuff.

Historically, Everest had achieved at least a three-to-one return, with the firm keeping twenty percent of the profits. So if the people around the table could turn fifteen billion into forty-five over the next few years, Gillette would have six billion—twenty percent of the thirty-billion-dollar profit—to spread around. It would be the biggest payout ever for a private equity firm. Some of the money would go to the Everest rank and file, but most of it would go to the people in this room.

Gillette nodded approvingly at their reaction, watching the hungry looks turn ravenous. He could see people calculating their potential share of the ups—as they should. Money was their driver, their reward for the intense stress and sacrifice—eighty to ninety hours a week away from family and friends. If they didn't get to enjoy the reward, they wouldn't last.

"That's better," Gillette said, motioning for quiet as he turned to Faraday, who was beaming. "Nigel, it's a tremendous achievement. The largest private equity fund ever raised. Thank you."

"Thank **you,** Mr. Chairman."

People began to clap and whistle again, but Gillette shut them down with a flash of his piercing gray eyes. "It gets better," he continued when the room was silent. "This morning, I met with representatives of the Wallace Family. They're out of Chicago, for any of you who **don't** know," he said, effectively telling anyone who didn't that they better research the Wallaces right after the meeting. "They're one of the wealthiest families in the country." He paused. "They've committed an additional five billion to Everest Eight, so it's now a **twenty**-billion-dollar fund."

There were gasps.

"And they've made their investment on the same terms and conditions as the other limited partners."

"They don't want **anything** special?" Maggie Carpenter asked warily. Maggie was one of the managing partners. Six months ago, Gillette had hired her away from Kohlberg Kravis & Roberts, another high-profile private equity firm in Manhattan. Thirty-five, Maggie was thin with dark red hair, a pale, freckled complexion, and stark facial features. Besides Gillette, she was usually the first one to ask tough questions in this meeting. "That's an awfully big commitment for them not to get some sizzle."

"They want one of their people on the ground here at Everest," Gillette replied, catching the uneasy looks appearing on the faces around the table. "Allison Wallace will join us as a managing partner. That's the only extra they want."

"The **only** extra?" asked Blair Johnson. Johnson was another of the four managing partners. He was African American and had grown up in an upper-middle-class Atlanta suburb. The son of a physician, he'd gone to the right schools: Harvard undergraduate and Columbia Business School. He'd been with Everest for seven years, and Gillette had promoted him to managing partner nine months ago. "That seems like a lot."

"Worried about the money?" Gillette asked.

Johnson cased the room quickly, making certain he wasn't the only one concerned about Allison Wallace. "Not the salary and bonus, really," he answered hesitantly. "After all, it's a twenty-billion-dollar fund. At one percent, we'll make two hundred million a year in fees alone."

"So it's the ups you're worried about."

"Yeah, the ups."

"Well, here's the deal, Blair," Gillette said sharply. "Allison doesn't want **any** money. No salary, no bonus, no ups. All she wants is a front row seat at the game so she can see how her money's being used."

"What Allison Wallace wants," Tom O'Brien said in a professorial tone, "is to see how we do it." O'Brien was the fourth managing partner. He was forty-one but looked older. His hair was snow white, and he had a ruddy complexion. From Boston, he had a prickly New England accent. "She wants to go to school. She wants the keys to the castle."

"Of course she does," Gillette agreed. "But so what? Nigel and I planned on adding two more managing partners anyway. We'll need six of you to put twenty double-large to work in three years. At **least** six. This way we get one free, and we get an extra five billion to invest, plus the annual fee. It's like she's paying us fifty million a year to work here," he reasoned, liking the way it sounded. "It's a good deal, and it's not like she's going to be able to duplicate what we have when she goes back to her family office in Chicago." Gillette could see that people were apprehensive. "Another update," he said, switching subjects, not wanting to dwell on something that made people feel insecure. He'd made the decision about Allison Wallace, and it was final. "We got the Las Vegas NFL franchise."

"Hot damn!" yelled O'Brien, banging the table. He was a sports nut and had helped Gillette and Faraday during the bid process.

"Next week I'm meeting with Kurt Landry, the NFL commissioner, to work out a few things," Gillette continued, "but basically it's a done deal."

"And we're sure we've got the zoning to build the stadium?" Maggie wanted to know.

"Absolutely."

"Wait a minute," David Wright broke in. Typically, he was the only managing director that spoke without being asked a question by a managing partner first. "We're building the stadium?"

"I want to build it so we keep the extra revenue," Gillette explained. "Concessions, advertising rights, naming it. This way we have total control of everything."

"How much did we offer for the franchise?" Maggie asked. "I can't remember."

"Four hundred and fifty million."

"What's the strategy with this?" she continued. "I don't know much about sports teams, but four hundred fifty million seems like a lot, **and** you've got the cost of building the stadium. Which is what?"

"Three hundred million."

"So we're in for seven hundred and fifty million. Can we really get a decent return on that, Christian?"

Maggie was suspicious that this was just a "boys gone wild" investment, Gillette could tell. An excuse to jet to Las Vegas every few weeks and hang out with movie stars, corporate bigwigs, sports figures, politicians, and friends in a plush skybox. "The stadium will be finished in a year and a half, and it'll seat eighty thousand," Gillette answered, giving a quick overview of the numbers. "We'll charge an average of a hundred dollars a ticket. That's eight million dollars for each of the eight home games, sixty-four million a season. And that doesn't include a couple of preseason games we can probably get fifty bucks a ticket for. Plus, we get concessions, our share of the NFL TV contracts, and ad dollars. One of the big computer store chains already offered us ten million a year to put their name on the stadium. Nigel and Tom," he said, "figure we can generate at least three hundred million a year in revenues. Based on where other major league sports teams sell, that would make the franchise worth somewhere between two and three billion. That would be a hell of a return."

"But can you really fill up eighty thousand seats at a hundred bucks a pop in that city?" Maggie pushed. "Vegas isn't that big, it's probably only got around a million permanent residents. I don't think eight percent of the population is going to a football game eight times a year for that kind of money."

"The population is closer to a million five," Gillette corrected, "but I hear what you're saying. Which is why we're already negotiating with a couple of the major airlines to add flights from Los Angeles to Vegas on game weekends. Remember, as crazy as it sounds, L.A. doesn't have a football team, and we've got assurances from the NFL that it won't get one in the next few years, until we're established. I think L.A. will adopt the Vegas franchise. It's a nothing flight for those people—you're up, you're down. We're also working with the casinos on promotions, and we're pretty far along with several of them. In fact—and what I'm about to tell you has to stay in this room," he said, giving everyone a warning glare. "We're looking at opening a casino ourselves. We've gotten to know the city officials very well over the last two years, and they've told us they can persuade the state gaming commission to give us a license."

"What about the Mafia?" Maggie asked bluntly.

Gillette had figured someone would ask about that. "We're checking, but I doubt the NFL would greenlight the franchise if the Mafia was still a problem out there." He had better information than that but didn't want to alarm anyone. "I'll keep everyone up-to-date on what we find," he promised, looking around the room. It was time to end the cross-examination. Maggie was good, but she didn't get it this time. "This could turn out to be one of our best investments ever. Not Laurel Energy, but close."

People rapped on the table hard, nodding their approval, understanding that Gillette had ended the discussion on this topic.

"Another thing," he continued, holding up his hand for quiet. "I'm going to retain Morgan Stanley to sell Laurel Energy."

"Why Morgan Stanley?" Maggie asked.

"Why not?"

"I thought Goldman Sachs had the best mergers and acquisitions group for the energy industry."

"Morgan Stanley will do a great job for us," Gillette replied confidently.

"Is this payback?" Maggie looked over at Wright, then back at Gillette.

"For what?" Gillette demanded.

"You know what."

Gillette's eyes narrowed. "No." He stared at her for a few moments more, then resumed the meeting. "I want to get back to a point Blair made earlier. The fact that we'll be making two hundred million a year in fees on Everest Eight. I've decided to commit ten million of the first-year fee to St. Christopher's Hospital up on the West Side." He paused. "I want all of you to make personal contributions to your local charities, too. In your towns, your neighborhoods, whatever. That'll be something I'll talk about with each of you during your annual reviews in January.

Frankly, the more you donate the better. All of us are lucky when it comes to money. I know everyone works hard and makes a lot of sacrifices, particularly those of you who have spouses and children. You don't see them much," he said, his voice dropping. "But it isn't like we dig ditches, either. While I'm chairman, this firm is going to be socially responsible, understood?"

His words were met with nods.

"Good." Gillette checked his agenda, scratching out the NFL, Laurel Energy, and charitable contribution items. The next topic was the L.A. office. "Just so everyone's clear, Nigel and I are looking into opening a Los Angeles office, but we haven't made any final decisions yet. I don't want rumors going around. When we do make a decision, we'll let everyone know right away." He grinned. "Anybody want to volunteer to go?"

Wright raised his hand immediately. "Can I get promoted to managing partner if I do?"

Gillette shot Faraday a quick look and shook his head, still grinning.

Faraday rolled his eyes.

"Always looking for a deal, aren't you, David." Gillette turned back to face Wright. "Stop by later and we'll talk about it. We can talk more about that other thing, too."

"Stop by later" meant they'd talk about it during a game of pool in the room adjoining Gillette's office.

"I'd rather talk about Hush-Hush **now**," Wright said, taking advantage of the fact that Gillette was speaking to him. "I don't want to wait. It's too hot."

To bring up a prospective investment in this meeting, a managing partner or managing director was supposed to run it by Faraday first, then send around a short memo on the company so the group had the basic facts—what the company did, how big it was, how profitable it was. Wright hadn't talked to Faraday or sent around a memo.

"Hush-Hush?" O'Brien piped up. "The intimate-apparel company?"

"Yeah, that's it," Wright said.

"What's the deal?"

"We've got the inside track to buy it. I have a friend in senior management who can help us ink it." Wright nodded at Gillette. "I spoke to Christian about it earlier. He likes it."

"**What I said was,** you should get more information," Gillette reminded the younger man, irritated that Wright had jumped the gun and was trying to make people in the room think he was already on board.

"I'll vote against that investment on principle alone," Maggie spoke up. "I don't care how great a deal it is. Their catalog is basically a porn magazine. It's insulting to women."

"If it's so insulting," Wright shot back, "there must be a lot of women who like being insulted.

Hush-Hush is growing at over eighty percent a year, and—"

"I don't care how fast it's growing," Maggie interrupted. "It's not something we should get into."

"Hey, just because you don't care about looking sexy doesn't mean the rest of the female world doesn't—"

"David." Gillette's sharp rebuke cut Wright off instantly.

Maggie glared at Wright for several moments, then turned to look at Gillette when Wright didn't look away. "Besides, it's the fashion business," she said, her voice cracking with anger. "There can be big revenue swings." She took a deep breath. "Christian, for Everest to make an investment, you and all four managing partners have to vote yes. I'm telling you right now, I'd vote no. So we can all save ourselves a lot of time by cutting off this discussion right now."

Gillette folded his arms over his chest. Maggie was right. Buying any fashion business was risky, especially one like Hush-Hush. But he didn't appreciate the way she'd tried to take control of the meeting. "Let me remind you," he said, "the chairman of this firm can overrule any single negative vote. Got that?"

She nodded quickly, understanding what he was saying—so much more than that he might overrule her if she chose to vote against the investment. "Yes."

Gillette looked back at Wright, irritated. "David, you know you're supposed to talk to Nigel before you bring up something like that."

"But I thought—"

"David."

Wright's gaze fell to his lap. "Sorry."

"**YOU GIVE** David Wright a lot of fucking rope," Faraday muttered as he sat down in front of Gillette's desk.

It was six-fifteen. The managers meeting had broken up ten minutes before, and Gillette was checking out a story on the Internet. He put his shoes up on the desk and locked his fingers behind his head. "David's a star, easily our top managing director. We both know that. He deserves some extra rope."

"Not as much as you give him."

"He's a thoroughbred."

"He's cocky as hell."

"He's young, he'll mellow with age. You and I can help him with that."

"Some of the other managing directors are grumbling."

"About what?" Gillette demanded, dropping his shoes to the floor. "Making a million dollars a year?"

"There's more to it than just the fucking money," Faraday retorted. "People around here are like puppies, okay? They don't like it when you pay a lot of attention to one person."

"Tell the whiners to find some investments for us," Gillette suggested. "Right now, David's the only managing director who does. We've already bought two companies he found, and now he's got us in the hunt for Hush-Hush. Which despite Maggie's objections might be a good deal. It's three hundred million in revenues, growing like mad, too. And I think you told me once you know people at some big apparel company in Paris. Your family is friends with the CEO's family, right?"

Faraday nodded, understanding immediately where Gillette was headed. "That's a good idea, I'll get in touch with him."

"He'd probably salivate at the chance to own Hush-Hush," Gillette pointed out. "You know, increase his presence in the U.S. with a hot brand."

"Sure."

"It'll be an easy flip. We grab this thing quick, before other people find out it's on the block, then sell it in a few months for a couple-hundred-million-dollar gain. If it works, it'll be thanks to David."

"Yeah, but—"

"And remember, David's the one who got us in to see the California Teachers Pension," Gillette reminded Faraday. "The people who made that six-hundred-million-dollar commitment this morning. At one percent, that's six million a year of income for this firm. That ain't chump change."

"His fucking **father** got us in to see them."

Wright's father was a senior investment banker at

Morgan Stanley. He'd introduced Faraday to the executives of the West Coast pension fund several months ago.

"But David made it happen. Now we have a great relationship with one of the biggest institutional investors in the country. Hell, they could have committed a couple of billion to us if they wanted. And they will next time around, to Everest Nine."

Faraday shook his head. "Christ, the ink isn't even dry on the Everest Eight subscription agreements and you're already thinking about Nine." He smoothed his tie. "Can I ask you something?"

Gillette heard an unusual tone in Faraday's voice. "What?"

"Was Maggie on point today?"

"About?"

"She didn't spin it out all the way, and frankly, I don't blame her. God, you looked like you were going to bite her head off when she started talking."

"You mean the Laurel Energy thing?" Gillette asked. "Giving the sell-side mandate to Morgan Stanley?"

"Yeah. Was that payback for David's father introducing us to the California Teachers Pension? Was she right?"

"Morgan Stanley will do a great job for us. I'm confident they'll get us five billion for Laurel." Gillette raised one eyebrow. "But if I can show appreciation for a favor at the same time and give them an incentive to do us more favors, well, that's just good business."

"Laurel Energy is so important to—"

"Enough." Gillette checked a stock price on his computer. "I'm thinking about promoting David to managing partner."

Faraday groaned. "But he's only thirty-one."

"He's on seven of our boards, five with me. I'm chairman of those companies, but he basically runs the quarterly meetings. He does a great job, too. Nobody on those boards seems to care that he's thirty-one."

Faraday exhaled heavily. "I guess it's better to promote from inside; at least you know what you're getting." He looked up. "But I don't think it would be a good idea to promote him, then send him to L.A. to open the office. We need to see how he does as a managing partner first."

"Agreed."

Faraday chuckled. "Can you imagine letting him go to L.A., what with all that beautiful, barely dressed tail running around, right after we promote him to managing partner? Jesus, we'd never be able to find him. Neither would his wife."

"I **said,** I agree."

"I just don't want you changing your mind over a game of pool with him. David can be very convincing."

"Won't happen." Gillette thought back to this

morning when he was coming out of the conference room and he'd run into Wright. "Has David seemed a little off lately?"

"What do you mean?"

"Preoccupied. Subdued. Not himself."

Faraday hesitated, thinking. "No, I haven't noticed anything."

"I hope he's all right. I always worry that our top people are being wooed away."

Faraday's expression soured.

"What is it?" Gillette asked. He could tell that Faraday had started to say something but stopped.

"Nothing."

"Come on, Nigel."

Faraday fiddled with his tie for a moment, then dropped it on his shirt. "David Wright," he mumbled. "Are you grooming him to take over Everest when you leave?"

Gillette looked at Faraday hard for a few moments. "Every organization needs a succession plan."

"Why not me?" Faraday asked quietly. "You know I'm committed, and after all, I am second in command."

Gillette hesitated, thinking about whether or not to get into it. He needed Faraday to stay committed, and you had to be careful about how people would react if you were candid with them. Faraday might check out mentally if he thought he'd hit a ceiling. At the same time, you couldn't string someone along. Not someone as loyal as Nigel. Gillette took a deep breath. There were always so many major issues swirling around. So many split-second decisions he had to make.

"You're a hell of a money raiser, Nigel, and you've really come through for me over the last ten months as far as the admin side of the firm goes. But you don't have any deal experience," Gillette said gently. "You don't know how to find companies for us to buy, how to structure deals, or how to run the companies after we buy them."

"I can learn."

"That's a lot to learn."

"Listen, I'm—"

"Let's talk about Apex," Gillette interrupted.

Faraday hung his head, as though Apex were the last thing he wanted to talk about. "Not again."

"Yes," Gillette said strongly, "again."

"But we already have **twenty-two billion** to put to work now that you've got the Wallace Family in the corral. Do you really want more?"

"I always want more."

"And," Faraday kept going, "with Apex, we'd be inheriting more fucking problems. Why would you want to do that?"

Apex Capital was another large Manhattan-based private equity firm that owned twenty-two companies and had another five billion of dry powder—equity commitments from investors to buy more companies. Until last year, Apex had been run by a self-made moneyman named Paul Strazzi. But

Strazzi had become the second casualty of Miles Whitman's war of desperation. Strazzi's fatal error: making a play for Everest, too.

Since Strazzi's murder, Apex had been run by a man named Russell Hughes, who couldn't fight his way out of a wet paper bag. Hughes looked the part—tall and dark, with sharp facial features, like Gillette—so he made a good first impression. But he couldn't make a decision to save his life. He put off everything, and the lack of leadership was severely affecting Apex. The firm had made only one investment under Hughes, and several of the portfolio companies had run into trouble over the last six months because he'd hesitated to replace incompetent executives. Apex was vulnerable, and Gillette knew it.

"We can pick Apex off cheap," Gillette said. "All we have to do is pay the general partners par, what they originally put in. Then we've got five billion more of dry powder and twenty-two more companies, several of which we could combine with our portfolio companies. By doing that, we'll pick up big savings axing back office jobs and getting more purchasing power with suppliers. I think I can clean up their dogs fast, too. I've looked at them, and I don't think they're beyond repair. If we fire a few of the execs and replace them with people we know, we can save them. But the most important thing is to get that five billion of unused equity. At that point, we'd have twenty-seven billion dollars of equity. Then we'll lever that twenty-seven with debt from the banks and insurance companies that are all over us to partner with them. I'd say we could get at least four times, wouldn't you?"

Faraday considered Gillette's guess. "That's probably right."

"Four times would be almost a hundred and ten billion dollars. Combined with the twenty-seven of equity, we'd control over a hundred and thirty-five billion of capital."

"How do you know we'd be able to get Apex so cheap?" Faraday asked.

"I spoke to Apex's controlling general partner. They hate Russell Hughes. They'd sell to us in a heartbeat if we offer par because they figure if he stays at the top, the family's money isn't going to be worth **anything.**"

"Why don't they just replace Russell?"

"That would confirm to everyone in the financial world that Apex is in chaos. It would be impossible for them to raise any more funds, and who wants to be bought by a private equity firm in chaos?"

"I see what you're saying."

"So they're stuck with Russell," Gillette continued, "unless I show up. And I think I can get them to approve this thing fast."

"I bet you could," Faraday agreed. "How much would it cost?"

"A billion. It would have been a lot more a year ago, but Hughes has driven the thing into the ground."

"Would you collapse Apex into Everest after we bought it?"

"No. Not at first, anyway. I wouldn't give those people the opportunity to benefit from all the money you've raised. That wouldn't be fair."

"Good."

"Down the road, I might. Once you and I figure out who the keepers are over there."

"How are you going to do this? Who are you going to approach first?"

"Next week I'm meeting with Russell's largest limited partners, the institutional investors. I'm going to explain what I want, get their buy-in, and ask them to contact Russell and urge him not to fight us. Then I'm going back to the general partner, the Strazzi estate, to make a formal offer. After that I'll get a couple of the Apex managing partners in a room and make them an offer, too. Obviously Hughes won't want to sell his stake, but if I have everyone else in my corner, he won't have any choice."

"You've got it all figured out, don't you. Hughes is a dead man and he doesn't even know it."

"That's the way it has to be."

"You get what you fucking want, don't you, Christian."

"Usually. And one thing I want is you to watch your mouth."

Faraday raised both eyebrows. "Huh?"

"You don't even know you're doing it, do you."

"Well, I . . ." Faraday's voice trailed off.

"Like I told you before, I don't care if 'fuck' is every other word when you and I are one-on-one like this, but I don't want you saying it in front of others in the office, especially the women."

"When did I—"

"This morning, okay?"

Faraday groaned. "Well, excuse me for getting excited."

"I don't care if you get excited. I don't even care if you do that silly dance you did in the hall this morning, which by the way has to be one of the most embarrassing things I've ever had the misfortune of witnessing. Just don't drop the F-bomb in public anymore."

"All right, all right." Faraday started to get up, then dropped his pudgy form back into the seat. "Is Allison Wallace qualified to be a managing partner at Everest Capital? Did you check her out?" he pushed. "I mean, it's great to add another five double-large to the new fund, but I don't want deadwood walking around here. Especially deadwood as pretty as her. She'll be a big distraction."

Gillette sighed. It seemed he was always pushing things uphill. "When did you see her?"

"When she was walking out this morning, after you met with her. How could I miss her? The whole office stopped to look."

"Give me a break."

"Legs up to her neck and a short little skirt to show them off," Faraday said smugly, holding one hand below his chin.

"Her skirt wasn't short. She was dressed very conservatively."

"Yeah, maybe you're right." Faraday chuckled. "But the important question is, does she have game or is she where she is just because of all the money? Even more important, are you letting her in here to get into her piggy bank or her panties?"

"Maybe both."

"At least you're honest."

"Oh, come on, Nigel. You know me better than that." Gillette's tone turned serious. "I'd never do something like that."

"I know."

"Hey, she's on the board of the family trust with her uncle and her grandfather. There's plenty of others in that generation of the Wallace Family they could have put on the board. She's qualified."

"Did you call Craig West?"

"As soon as Allison was out the door this morning," Gillette confirmed. "Craig called me back before we went into this afternoon's meeting. Allison went to Yale undergrad and Chicago's business school. You don't get much better than that."

"But what fucking university isn't going to accept her? Think about what she probably donates to those schools every year."

"She was top of her class both places."

"Really?" Faraday hesitated. "Did she go right to the family trust after business school?"

"No, Goldman Sachs after Chicago. Same department I was in before I came to Everest. There's still a couple of guys over there I know. They said she was good. Said she didn't try to shirk anything because of who she was."

Faraday held up his hands. "Okay, okay. You convinced me. But she will be a temptation."

"I'm still with Faith. You know that."

"Ah, yes, the lovely Miss Cassidy. Do I hear wedding bells?"

Gillette glanced out the window into the fading late afternoon light of midtown Manhattan.

Faraday let it ride for a few moments, then gave up, rising from his chair with a groan and heading toward the door. "I'm going downstairs to get some mint chocolate chip," he announced. "Nothing like a little instant fucking gratification."

"You better start watching your weight," Gillette called after him, grabbing his computer mouse.

"What are you, my father? First I have to watch my mouth, now I've got to watch my weight. **Oh, Jesus.**" Faraday snapped his fingers and turned around as he reached the door. "I meant to tell you, Christian."

Gillette was focused on the computer. "What?"

"I had the strangest experience this morning."

Gillette grinned. "Don't tell me, you actually ate something healthy for breakfast."

"I thought I saw Tom McGuire on Park Avenue."

The computer screen blurred. Tom McGuire. The former CEO of McGuire & Company who had teamed with Miles Whitman to kill Bill Donovan—and tried to kill Gillette. McGuire was still out there somewhere—filled with hatred of Gillette for uncovering the plot and costing him hundreds of millions in the process. "That's not funny, Nigel."

"I know it's not, but that's what I saw. At least I think I did. I was walking up Park Avenue from the subway, and I was almost to our building. I happened to look up, and he was coming the other way. I'm pretty sure it was McGuire, anyway. I mean, he'd put on some weight and his hair was longer, but I wouldn't forget that face. It was weird, too. I was going to start yelling for the cops, but when I turned around he was gone. It was like he'd evaporated into thin air." Faraday shrugged. "Hey, maybe I'm wrong, maybe it wasn't him."

Gillette glanced back at the screen. He had a bad feeling Faraday wasn't wrong.

3

NORMAN BOYD studied Gillette's head shot. Black hair parted on the left side as he faced you, combed neatly back over the ears. Sharp facial features—a thin nose, strong jaw, prominent chin, defined cheekbones, and intense gray eyes that caught you right away, even from a photograph. It was the fourth time today Boyd had looked at Gillette's picture, trying to glean anything he could from the image. So much depended on his ability to manipulate this man. Based upon what he knew so far, that wasn't going to be easy. Not like many others he'd dealt with.

"How did it go?" Boyd asked, setting the photograph on the desk of the sparsely furnished office.

"Fine," Ganze answered. "He left Everest right away to come to my hotel room when he found out I hadn't shown up."

"He's interested."

"Very."

"You mentioned his father's plane crash, right?" Boyd asked.

"Yes. He wants to know more."

"Good."

"Much more," Ganze continued. "You should have seen his reaction when I mention Clayton. Gillette's thought about that crash every day for the last sixteen years. It's haunted him."

"**Haunted** him, Daniel?"

"A father's death haunts every son."

Boyd hesitated, thinking about his own father's death last year. Hadn't haunted him. "Tell me about Gillette."

Ganze reviewed his notes. "Went to Princeton under—"

"Yeah, yeah. Princeton undergrad, Stanford business school, Goldman Sachs M and A, then Everest. I read the short file. Tell me about the **man.**"

"He's got a half-brother and a half-sister."

Boyd's eyebrows rose. **"Half?"**

"Thirty-eight years ago, Clayton Gillette had an affair with a nineteen-year-old Hollywood wannabe. The affair was short but important. That woman is Christian's blood mother."

"Does Gillette have a relationship with her?"

"He doesn't even know who she is." Ganze grimaced and shook his head. "It's got to be tough, you know?"

Boyd sneered. "It isn't **that** tough. Most of the

planet would trade places with him in a heartbeat."
Ganze came across as a cold fish when you first met
him, Boyd knew, but beneath that plywood exterior
was a compassionate heart. Which bothered Boyd.
You couldn't be sentimental in this business. If
Ganze wasn't such a tremendous sleuth, Boyd would
never have kept him around all these years. "Does he
know that Clayton's wife is his stepmother? Does
he know he was born out of wedlock?"

"He found out when he was a teenager."

"I assume we know who Gillette's blood
mother is."

"We do."

"Excellent."

"Christian's stepmother agreed to raise him,"
Ganze continued, "but she always hated him."

"What's her name?"

"Lana, after the actress. Lana's father was a Hollywood producer back in the fifties and sixties," Ganze
explained. "He had a couple of boys, too. Named
them Wayne and Kirk."

"How do you know Lana hated Gillette?"

"She carved Christian out of the fortune as soon
as Clayton was dead. The will, monthly allowance,
credit cards, bank accounts. Everything. She didn't
even send him cash to get home."

"Wow."

"Christian had just graduated from Princeton
and was motorcycling back across the country to
California. He'd stopped in a small town in western

Pennsylvania to visit his grandfather. The second day he was there was the day of the crash. Lana called an hour after the plane went down to tell Christian he was cut off completely. The motorcycle was in the shop, and he had to sell it to the owner because he didn't have cash on him for the repairs. He had to ride freight trains back to the West Coast, had to take out big loans to pay for business school, had to get Goldman Sachs to advance him two months' salary so he could put down a security deposit on an apartment in a crappy section of Brooklyn. The irony is that he comes from a ton of money, but he's completely self-made. Everything he has he's earned himself."

"Tough?"

"As tungsten. And careful and calculating. But he's got a big heart."

Boyd scoffed. "Sure he does."

"No, no. I'm serious. He gives a lot to charity, personally and through the firm. He had Everest donate ten million dollars to a hospital in New York so it could build a new wing for kids with cancer."

"It's called publicity," Boyd observed. "You said he was calculating."

"People he's close to are very loyal to him," Ganze argued.

"He probably pays them a lot more than they could make anywhere else."

"Yeah, he does," Ganze agreed grudgingly.

Boyd bit his lower lip, thinking. "Lana Gillette

sounds like a cold one. Do you think she was involved?"

Ganze's expression turned curious. "Involved, sir?"

"In Clayton's plane crash."

"Nothing I've turned up indicates that."

Music to Boyd's ears. "How did Lana and Clayton meet?"

"Lana's father sent her east for college, to the University of Virginia. His family was originally from Virginia. Richmond, I believe. Clayton was at UVA on a football scholarship. He was a star quarterback in high school, but his college career wasn't anything to write home about. He and Lana married a month after graduation and moved to Los Angeles, actually lived with her parents for a year. Clayton went to work for a local brokerage house that was owned by a friend of Lana's father. He got the hang of selling stocks and bonds fast and opened his own shop a few years later."

"Let me guess," Boyd spoke up. "He took all the guy's clients with him."

"Yup. He was smooth, could sell anything. That was his talent. After a few years, he got the firm into investment banking, too. Sold it for a hundred million dollars before he went into politics."

"So Lana's set financially."

"I haven't nailed that down yet," Ganze said after a few moments, "but I have to think so. She still lives in the same mansion in Bel Air."

"Does Gillette talk to Lana?"

"No."

Boyd hesitated. "Where is he politically?"

"Registered Republican, but he voted Democrat in the last presidential election. He doesn't vote with his bank account anymore. It's so full at this point, it doesn't matter."

"How much money does he control?"

"They just closed a new fifteen-billion-dollar fund, and there's still money left over from the one before that. Plus Everest owns thirty companies. Some big-name ones." Ganze paused. "And get this. My information is that Christian's going to try to take over Apex Capital, too."

Boyd looked up. A potential pothole—and a big one. "That's interesting."

"You think it's a problem?"

"I don't know," Boyd replied calmly. "But we'll have to keep an eye on it. How about protection?"

"Protection, sir?"

"Bodyguards. Does Gillette use them?"

"All the time."

"Who does he use?"

"A firm called QS Security."

"Are they good?"

"Very. The firm's owned and run by a guy named Quentin Stiles, who's one of Gillette's inner circle. I've asked around, and he's as good as they get. Army Rangers and Secret Service before founding QS. But he's been out of commission for a while."

"Why?"

"He took a bullet to the chest last year. Finally about to get out of the hospital."

"Did he take the bullet for Gillette?"

Ganze nodded.

"Are there QS agents with Gillette all the time?" Boyd asked.

"Twenty-four/seven. Apparently, Christian and Stiles are worried about a guy named Tom Mc-Guire."

Boyd's ears perked up. "Who's Tom McGuire?"

"The muscle for Miles Whitman when Whitman tried to kill Christian last year. McGuire arranged the murder attempts." Ganze had researched everything he could find about Christian Gillette—as Boyd had instructed. "McGuire was never caught. Just like Miles Whitman wasn't."

Boyd snorted. **Miles Whitman,** he repeated, disgusted. "What an asshole. Is he still getting help from the inside?"

"Definitely."

"How much has he gotten so far?"

"About forty million dollars' worth."

"**Jesus fucking Christ.** Where is Whitman now, do you know?"

"Southern Europe, I think. I don't know exactly."

"What about Justice?" Boyd asked, still annoyed. "They must be pissed."

"It's definitely an embarrassment for them," Ganze agreed. "It's been ten months and they haven't been able to find either of those guys. The higher-ups are putting a lot of heat on people in the trenches, but it's not doing much good."

"Do you think they suspect that there's help from the inside?"

"My friend says they haven't asked yet. Too much pride."

Boyd chuckled. "Idiots." His smile faded. "Well, they'll get over their pride at some point." He thought for a moment. "Why are Gillette and Stiles so worried about this McGuire guy?"

"If the conspiracy had worked, McGuire and his brother, Vince, would have made hundreds of millions. But Gillette and Stiles figured out what was going on at the last minute and blew the thing wide open. Turned the feds onto McGuire. Like I said, McGuire was never caught, but he lost out on the money. And his brother," Ganze added.

"What happened?"

"Vince helped Tom arrange the murder attempts on Gillette, and the feds got him. He died in jail."

Boyd groaned. The last thing he needed was some psychopath out there stalking Gillette, hell-bent on revenge. "Should Gillette be worried about this guy?"

"I checked McGuire out," Ganze replied. "He's ex-FBI. A nasty son of a bitch."

"We need Gillette alive, Daniel."

"I understand, sir."

Boyd pointed at Ganze. "Monitor that situation **very** closely. We might have to move on it quickly."

"I will," Ganze promised.

Boyd glanced at Gillette's photograph once more. "When is our meeting with him?"

"Friday at eleven. I called him back this afternoon. He can do it then."

Boyd tapped the desk. "Unfortunately, something's come up since you spoke to him. I may have to go out of town on Friday. Would he come sooner?"

"He came right to the hotel."

"Mmm." Boyd took a long breath. "Think he'll cooperate with us?"

Ganze considered the question for a few moments. "You'll have to use what we've found, make him understand that we can tell him things he's been desperate to know for a long time. Then you might be able to bend him."

"But then we might have to tell him **how** we know all those things. He'll ask. He won't take us at our word. We might have to bring him inside."

Ganze shrugged. "Which is the bigger risk? Disclosing our secrets or detection from the outside?"

"Yes," Boyd said quietly. "That's the question, isn't it. Which is the bigger risk? But then, that's always the question for us."

GILLETTE DREW the pool cue through the loop of his curled forefinger, aimed at a group of three tightly packed, brightly colored balls, and fired. With the crack of the cue, the seven, twelve, and fourteen split like a molecule, atoms racing and ricocheting in all directions. Then each ball slowed to a crawl and dropped neatly into different pockets. Running the table wasn't fun anymore, so he practiced trick shots now.

He straightened up slowly and checked his watch—almost eleven. The day had started eighteen hours ago, at five this morning. It had been a long one, but as Faraday had said in the corridor, overall pretty fucking good. The new fund was closed, with an extra five billion from the Wallace Family, and they'd gotten the Vegas NFL franchise.

There'd been some challenges, too—there always were. A product liability suit had been filed by an aggressive Detroit watchdog group against Everest's Ohio-based auto parts manufacturer, and the CEO of another portfolio company headquartered in Texas had resigned suddenly for personal reasons. Truth was, the guy was banging his executive assistant on his office desk and Gillette had given him no choice but to resign. However, the attorneys for the Ohio company—the best in the country for this type of litigation—had given him airtight guarantees that the suit had zero merit, and the Texas CEO could easily be replaced by several other high-level executives at the company whom Gillette had groomed personally in case there was ever a problem. Just as he did at all their portfolio companies.

Just as he ought to be doing at Everest, he

thought ruefully, tapping the butt end of the cue stick on the floor. The conversation with Faraday this afternoon about succession had gotten him thinking. There needed to be a plan in place, especially if Tom McGuire was really lurking around out there. He owed his investors that.

Gillette snapped his fingers as he moved to rack the balls. "Damn it." He was supposed to have called Faith this evening, but it was too late now. She was at some award dinner until eleven o'clock West Coast time.

He took a deep breath and leaned against the table. He hated to admit it, but he missed Faith. She was wonderful—beautiful, sexy, caring, unpretentious despite her fame. But he didn't like missing someone, feeling so vulnerable. Didn't like caring about someone that much despite how good it made him feel inside. He'd adored—no, idolized—his father, and look where that had gotten him. Left him in an emotional abyss for years. All he could do for his father now was solve the mystery of his death. Which was why he planned to be available for Daniel Ganze whenever Ganze wanted. Ganze seemed to know something. That was enough.

Gillette glanced around the ornate billiard room, connected to his office by a short hallway. The hallway was the only access to the room, so he controlled who came and went. This was the one big perk he'd allowed himself after becoming chairman last year. He loved pool—he'd funded his trip back to the West Coast after Lana had cut him off by beating small-town patsies for fifty bucks a game. And he found there were times during stressful days that a couple of quick games against David Wright were therapeutic.

Gillette shook his head and smiled. He never had beaten his father in pool. Which he was glad about now. It seemed right.

His cell phone rang. Probably Wright, he figured. The young MD had promised to stop by and shoot a few games. During the match, Gillette was going to tell him he wouldn't be going to Los Angeles to open the office, but that he'd be promoted to managing partner. However, Wright had already left when Gillette buzzed a few hours ago, which was strange. Wright rarely missed a chance at face time.

"Hello."

"Christian?"

"Yes."

"It's Allison Wallace."

"Oh, hi. Where are you?" he asked.

"Still in New York. I'm staying at the Parker Meridien."

"I thought you and Gordon were flying back to Chicago this afternoon."

"Gordon did," she answered, "but I decided to stay the weekend to see some friends."

"How did you get this number?" Gillette asked. He hadn't given her the number, and Debbie would never give it out without permission.

"I'm Allison Wallace," she answered.

Not smugly, he noticed, just matter-of-factly. He could tell by her tone she wasn't going to say anything more about it, either. The same way he wouldn't. "Look, I—"

"Let's have lunch Monday," she suggested.

"Can't."

"Why not?"

"I'm having lunch with the commissioner of the NFL. We got the new Las Vegas franchise today, and he wants to go over a few things."

"Fantastic," she said breathlessly. "That's really exciting. You better make that investment with Everest Eight, the fund I'm going to be in."

Gillette hesitated. He was planning to make the franchise purchase out of Seven, then issue Everest-guaranteed bonds to finance stadium construction. There wouldn't be any need to use Eight for this deal. "I'm not sure how we're going to fund it yet. We still have two billion left in Seven."

"Well, I think—"

"How about breakfast," he interrupted. He could hear her tone flexing, and he didn't want to get into it now. He could understand why she'd want the NFL opportunity for the fund she was investing in—there was so much upside—but he had to be fair to all his investors. The best way to do that was to invest sequentially—use all of Seven, then go to Eight. Of course, he didn't know Allison well, and she might turn out to be emotional. She might pull the Wallace Family investment if she thought he was jerking her around so soon after committing five billion.

He took a deep breath. Conflict, always conflict in this world.

"I have a breakfast," Allison answered. "How about dinner? I could stay another night."

Gillette couldn't remember if he already had a dinner scheduled, but if he did and he couldn't remember, then it couldn't be important. "Okay."

"Great," she said, her voice turning pleasant again. "Come get me around seven at the Parker."

As he slid the phone back in his pocket, there was a knock on the hallway door. "Yes?"

"Open up!"

Gillette's gaze snapped toward the door. He knew that voice: Quentin Stiles. He hurried over and yanked on the knob. Suddenly, Stiles was standing before him.

Quentin Stiles was African American: handsome, lighter skinned, six four, and normally a rock-hard 240 pounds. He was from Harlem, a self-made man who'd never been to college but now owned a fast-growing security firm with fifty agents.

Gillette embraced him immediately, unable to remember the last time he'd been so glad to see someone.

"Hey," Stiles said, stepping back. "What are you doing?"

"I'm . . . I'm welcoming you back."

"Don't get so emotional."

"I just . . . well, I just—"

Stiles broke into a loud, good-natured laugh and wrapped his arms around Gillette. "Hey, brother, I'm just playing. It's good to be back."

"You look great," Gillette said. "A lot better than you did in the hospital bed last time I visited."

"I don't look great," Stiles answered irritably, "I look terrible. I'm down thirty pounds from my normal weight. I probably can't even bench-press three hundred at this point. Christ, none of my clothes fit. Look at me," he said, holding out his arms. The black blazer hung loosely from his frame.

"We'll fatten you up fast." Gillette moved toward two comfortable chairs in front of a plasma television screen hanging from the wall. "Sit down," he said, pointing at one of the chairs as he sat in the other, "and tell me what the hell you're doing out of the hospital. Saturday, the nurses told me it was going to be at least another two weeks before you'd be released." He watched Stiles wince as he lowered himself slowly into the chair.

"If I'd stayed in the hospital another two weeks, I'd have gone crazy," he answered. "Hell, if I'd stayed there another **ten minutes,** I'd have gone crazy. The mattress was like cement, the nurses were even harder, I hate the way hospitals smell, and the food was awful. Let me tell you something, what I need is a big fat juicy steak. How about Monday lunch?"

"I can't, I—" Gillette interrupted himself. Lunch

with the commissioner was at noon and would go no later than one-thirty. Landry's executive assistant had told Debbie that he had to catch a four o'clock flight to the West Coast and couldn't stay longer than that. "Can we do it later on? Say, one forty-five? Can you hold out till then?"

"Sure."

"How'd you know I was here?" Gillette asked, relaxing.

"I called the main number about an hour ago and Faraday picked up. He said you were going to be here for a while. He let me know where to find you," Stiles explained, looking around. "Hey, this is quite a place."

Gillette had built the pool room last spring—it had originally been O'Brien's office, but Gillette had kicked him out to get the space. Stiles had already been in the hospital several months at that point and hadn't seen it. "Thanks."

"You lost a match in here yet?" Stiles asked.

"Of course not."

"Well, what you need," Stiles declared, starting to get up, "is a good old-fashioned ass whipping on your home court."

Gillette reached over and caught Stiles, forcing him gently back into the chair. "Not now."

"Why not?"

"We need to talk."

Stiles cocked his head to the side, recognizing Gillette's serious tone. "What is it?"

"Last week I told you about a meeting I was going to have this morning with a man from Washington, remember?"

"Yeah."

During hospital visits with Stiles, Gillette had kept him up to speed with everything at Everest. Since last fall, Stiles had become as much a partner as Faraday, not just the man in charge of Gillette's personal protection.

"So how'd it go?" Stiles asked.

"It was strange; he didn't really tell me anything. I don't know much more about him or the people he represents than I did before the meeting, but I'm still going to Washington next week to meet with them."

Stiles's face contorted into a curious expression. "Sounds like he's a waste of time. Why would you bother?"

"Senator Clark arranged the meeting. I trust his judgment." Gillette hesitated. "More important, the guy I met with this morning mentioned my father's plane crash."

Gillette had told Stiles about Clayton's plane crash many times. How Gillette had been cut off from the family money immediately afterward, how he'd been born out of wedlock, and how he desperately wanted answers to so many questions surrounding all of that. "Now I get it."

"The guy also said he didn't buy the official explanation for the crash," Gillette continued. "Said pilot error seemed 'thin' to him."

"Christian, be care—"

"To others as well."

"They want something," Stiles warned.

"Everyone always does."

"I guess that's true," Stiles agreed quietly, "at least in your world."

Gillette nodded, then closed his eyes and pushed the thoughts away. "So, how are you?" he asked. "Really, shouldn't you still be in the hospital?"

"No, I'm fine."

"Well, when can you go a hundred percent? The guys you've had with me have done a great job, but I want you back full time as soon as possible." Gillette tapped the arm of the chair. "And Nigel's really raised his game. Like I told you, I'm surprised how dedicated he's gotten. This time last year, he was in at nine and gone by six, the latest. Now he's in early and here most nights until ten. I depend on him." Gillette hesitated. "But Nigel isn't you. Like I said, I need you here full time as soon as possible— but I don't want you coming back too soon, either," he added quickly. "No relapses, or worse."

"I'm fine," Stiles replied firmly. "We'll need to keep your current security detail with you because I won't be back to full speed for a few months, but they'd have had to stick around anyway. You need three to four men around you constantly."

"Amen," Gillette agreed. He'd stared down the barrel of an assassin's gun last fall, and he didn't want to do it again. "Monday at lunch we'll talk about your role at Everest. Debbie can arrange temporary space for you. It won't be great, but we'll get you into a big office quick."

"Whoa, whoa," Stiles said, holding up both hands. "Not so fast, Christian. I've got QS Security to run."

"It's done fine the last ten months without you."

"Without me?"

"Yeah."

"Are you kidding? I've been running it from the hospital. I've still been hands-on."

"I didn't know that."

"We're almost ten million in revenues at this point."

The number caught Gillette's attention, and he started going through his options. But there was only one that made sense. "Okay, I'll buy it."

"What?"

"Yeah. I'll use McGuire and Company, the security company we already own. How much do you want?"

"Jesus, Christian, is this how you negotiate? I thought you were supposed to be a hard-assed motherfucker when it came to buying and selling."

"This is different."

"Why?"

"Don't worry about it."

Stiles shook his head, fighting back a grin. "I'm not ready to sell."

Gillette did a few quick calculations. At ten million in revenues, QS Security probably netted around half a million dollars. "Any debt on the business?" he asked.

"Three hundred grand."

"Okay, I'll give you five million for it."

"Five million," Stiles repeated incredulously.

Gillette chuckled. "Now who's the bad negotiator?"

"I just didn't . . . well, I . . . I just thought—"

"Take it, Quentin," Gillette advised. "It's the best deal you're going to get, at least anytime soon. In the morning I'll call Craig West and tell him what we're doing, that we're buying you out. And I'm going to pay you a million a year here at Everest, plus bonus, plus ups."

"Christ. That's incredible, but why?" Stiles asked. "I don't know anything about finance."

"I trust you more than anyone else on the planet. From where I sit, that's worth every penny I just offered. Plus, you know a lot about running companies. You just grew one and sold it for five million dollars."

"What exactly will I do here?"

"For starters, you'll get me everything on the guy I met with this morning and the people he reports to. And you'll go with me to Washington next week."

"Why don't you have Craig West get the info and go with you?"

"Craig's a good man, but I don't trust him like I

trust you. It's not the same. And something tells me I'm going to need to be **very** careful with these people." Gillette took a deep breath. "There's something else, Quentin."

"What?"

"Faraday thought he saw Tom McGuire on Park Avenue this morning."

Stiles's eyes shot to Gillette's. "You're kidding."

"Nope."

Stiles looked down and was silent for a moment. Finally he glanced up. "Chris, I don't think a million bucks is going to cut it."

DAVID WRIGHT rose up on one elbow and ran his fingers gently through his wife's hair as she slept on the bed beside him. A half hour ago, Peggy had wanted to make love, but it hadn't happened. He was too distracted, expecting detectives from the New York Police Department to pound on their apartment door at any moment. Salivating to arrest him for the murder of the woman at the sex shop.

A half hour ago he couldn't perform; now he couldn't sleep. He kept replaying that awful scene in the bondage chamber in his mind. His foot hitting the block of wood, the awful sound of her neck snapping like a brand-new Ticonderoga pencil between two thumbs. A quick crack, then her body going limp. God, if he could only have those few seconds back.

Wright groaned and reclined slowly on the mattress until his head settled onto the pillow, listening to Peggy's heavy breathing, staring at the ceiling through the gloom. She'd tried hard to arouse him, going down on him for a full five minutes—which she didn't really like to do—but nothing. He'd blamed it on work, on Gillette being a slave driver, and she'd bought it, at least for tonight. But she wouldn't buy it for long. Typically, he couldn't go a day without sex. Soon she'd figure out something else, something more important, was wrong. Maybe the cops would have already led him off in shackles by then.

He tried to take a deep breath but couldn't. It was as if he had something heavy constantly pressing on his chest now. "Shit!" he hissed, rolling away from Peggy and grabbing the sheet. When he'd run into Gillette in the hallway at Everest this morning and talked about Hush-Hush, it was as if the older man had seen right through him. As if he'd known something was wrong. Wright still had that question ringing in his ears: "You okay?" And that look in Gillette's eyes was etched into his memory: like a spinning drill bit coming at him, ready to splay him wide open for everyone to see.

It was the damnedest thing about Gillette. It was as if he could tell exactly what you were thinking— or what you'd done. Probably one of the reasons he was chairman of Everest Capital at just thirty-seven. He was different. He had an edge others didn't. As if he were ten steps ahead of you all the time.

Well, Wright thought, forcing his eyes shut. He was going to get away for the weekend and take Monday off. He was going to avoid the apartment and Everest just in case the police decided to visit. What he'd do if he found out they'd come by either place looking for him, he wasn't sure. But there was one thing he knew: He wasn't going to jail. At least not for a few days.

Suddenly there was a furious banging, a loud fist slamming against a door over and over.

"Jesus Christ!" Wright shot up in bed.

"What's wrong?" Peggy was up instantly beside him, rubbing her eyes. "My God, what is it?"

As quickly as it had started, the banging subsided, and Wright realized that the knocking had been on the door across the hall. He swallowed hard and ran his hand over his forehead. He was sweating like a leaky faucet. "It's all right," he murmured.

"David, what's wrong?" Peggy asked fearfully, putting a hand on his shoulder.

"Nothing, baby, nothing," Wright assured her, lying back down and pulling her beside him. He wanted to tell her so badly, but he couldn't. He couldn't tell anyone. Which was the hardest part of it all.

4

THE PROJECT

"SO, YOU EXCITED?"

Gillette watched Kurt Landry shove a cell phone–size forkful of sirloin steak into his mouth as they sat at a back table of Sparks Steak House in midtown Manhattan. Landry had starred as a defensive end for the New York Jets in the eighties, then caught on with the National Football League's front office after a couple of high-profile stints—a two-year deal as a booth analyst for NBC's primary Sunday game and some heavily marketed rental car commercials. So he was instantly recognizable to the public, a perfect spokesman. Once at the league office, he'd played his cards right by doing a lot of palm pressing and behind-the-scenes lobbying at off-season meetings, and he'd been elected commissioner two years ago in a close vote by the owners. He'd beaten out the senior partner of a prominent Wall Street law firm in the election, mostly because the bloc of owners backing Landry believed he'd act as their puppet—they didn't want someone who would think independently.

Craig West had done some checking for Gillette, and apparently Landry's backers had been right, he was doing exactly as they wanted. There were strings everywhere.

But Landry's backers weren't here today.

As he watched Landry gorge, Gillette noticed how many of the man's physical features seemed oversize: his head, his mouth, his ears, his hands. He barely fit in a chair made for a normal-size man.

"How tall are you?" Gillette asked, ignoring Landry's question.

"Six seven."

"How much do you weigh?"

Landry laughed, a baritone rumble. "Two fifty, but that's forty pounds under my playing weight. I'm damn proud of myself for taking off all that weight and **keeping** it off." He scooped up a greasy spoonful of home fries and downed them with one swallow. "Come on," he said, slapping Gillette on the back with a bear paw of a hand after putting down the spoon. "You excited?"

Gillette nodded. "Sure."

"Doesn't seem like it. Hey, you've got a lot of fun coming your way with this thing. I mean, what could possibly be better than owning an NFL team?"

"I don't like getting ahead of myself."

"What does that mean?" Landry asked, scooping creamed spinach onto his plate out of a serving bowl.

"I want this to be a good investment for my partners," Gillette answered. "Four hundred and fifty million is a ton to pay for something that's never generated a dime of income. When we've done well financially, when we've made a good return on our money, then I'll get excited."

"Money-schmoney," Landry said, smirking. "Think about all the perks, especially with a Vegas franchise."

"There's a downside to that city, too."

"Hey, you're the youngest owner in the NFL," Landry pointed out, paying no attention to Gillette's caution. "Everybody wants to see you again, too, especially after that article in **People.**"

Gillette pushed his plate of half-eaten filet and steamed broccoli into the middle of the table so he could put his elbows down. "Look, I'm not the owner, Everest Capital is. And I was never even interviewed for that article. **People** did that all on their own." He was starting to feel like siccing Stiles on the guy who wrote the thing.

"I wouldn't be complaining if I were you," Landry said, wiping his mouth with a white linen napkin. "What was the story line? 'Most eligible bachelors in the country'? Jesus, most guys would die for that kind of pub. I bet that article's opened some doors, especially to some very attractive women. You've got it going on, don't you, boy?"

"You know, I'm just not into personal publicity, Kurt."

A concerned look came over Landry's face. "But you're going to be chairman of the team, right? You're going to be making the major decisions, aren't you?"

"Yes."

Landry seemed relieved. "Uh-huh, well, I would have liked it if that article had been written about me." He waved at one of the waiters, indicating that he wanted more water. "So, tell me about Everest. The **Reader's Digest** version, please, I don't know much about the investment world."

Clearly, Landry hadn't been very involved in the selection process. If he had, he wouldn't have needed the Everest primer. His minions—or the owners' minions—must have done the heavy lifting as far as analyzing the different bids. "We're an investment firm," Gillette began. "We usually buy and manage companies that manufacture things or provide services. And they've usually been around for a while before we get involved, so this situation is different for us. Which is why we have to be extra careful here. Not that we aren't always careful, but we want to be extremely cautious in this situation. Anything goes wrong with this thing and my investors will be on my ass. That's why I don't want to get ahead of myself."

"Ah, don't worry about it. You're going to make a boatload of money on this thing," Landry said confidently. "Besides, that article said you have the magic touch when it comes to investing."

"I do all right."

"There were lots of people trying to get this franchise."

"What won it for us?" Gillette asked directly. "Was it price alone, or were there other things?"

Landry put down his napkin and leaned back, folding his thick arms over his barrel chest. "I really can't comment on that, Christian. There were lots of criteria; obviously price was very important. But the owners don't want me to talk about what went on behind closed doors."

"Who were the other bidders?" Gillette asked, ignoring the soft warning.

"Mostly wealthy individuals."

"Who?"

Landry chuckled nervously.

Obviously, he wasn't used to this kind of cross-examination. In his position as commissioner, he probably didn't sit on the hot seat often. When there was a controversial issue, the owners probably handled it for him. They must have anticipated that today's lunch would be just a formality. They probably figured the winner would be so happy at getting the franchise that he wouldn't dig for information. But Gillette was always digging. Having information others didn't was a surefire way to make money. "It really would be helpful to know," he pushed. "I don't understand why it'd be a problem to tell me now that the selection process is over."

"All names I'm sure you'd recognize. I mean, there aren't that many individuals around who could afford an NFL team." Landry held up his hands. "But I, I really can't say any more. League policy." He grimaced.

Like all of a sudden the meeting wasn't going the way he thought it would, or like he wished it were one-thirty and he could leave, Gillette thought, interpreting the grimace.

"Let's talk some more logistics," Landry suggested, picking at something between his teeth.

"Okay."

"Tell me about the stadium construction. What's the timing there?"

Another indication Landry hadn't been one of the decision makers. All that information had been spelled out in the final bid package Everest had submitted to the NFL two months ago. "The architectural plans for the stadium were in the bid package. We still need to choose a primary contractor, but that shouldn't take long. There are only three or four serious players for this job. Our advisers tell us that once we've chosen the contractor, the stadium can be finished in eighteen months."

Landry rested his chin in his palm, as though he were thinking hard. "So, then, the plan is for your team to start playing not next season, but the season after that. We'll have the expansion draft a few weeks after next year's Super Bowl. That'll give you time to see what veterans you've got before the college draft." Landry grinned. "Damn, I wish I were in your shoes." His grin grew even wider. "If I were you, I'd make sure I was there for cheerleader try-outs."

Gillette broke into a halfhearted laugh. Landry had no conception of what it meant to be in charge, no idea of the pressure involved. "I'll remember that, Kurt."

"Now you're getting into the spirit," Landry said enthusiastically. "The NFL is fun, a marketing machine, the biggest damn party in all sports, and now you're at the center of it." He pointed at Gillette. "You beat out some people who've been trying to get one of these teams for a long time. There's folks out there who are pissed off right now, but the NFL made the right choice. It always does."

Gillette picked up his fork and pushed the broccoli around his plate. "Why are they so pissed off?"

"Because they lost," Landry said, as if the answer were obvious.

"Well, they didn't bid enough, so they've only got themselves to blame, right?"

Landry shrugged. "Right . . . I guess."

Suddenly, Gillette wished he could have been a fly on the wall during the selection meetings. Wished he could get his hands on all the bid packages. Something didn't smell right. "There's one more thing I want to talk to you about today," he said, glancing at his watch: one twenty-three.

"What's that?"

"Organized crime."

Landry's body went stiff in the chair, water glass halfway between the tablecloth and his mouth. "Huh?"

"The Mafia."

"What about it?" Landry kept his voice low, his eyes flickering around.

"Do you have any information about how active they are in Las Vegas?"

"No. I mean, I don't, specifically, have any information."

"Does someone else at the NFL office have that?"

Landry hesitated. "What do you mean?"

"Well, you guys must have looked at that hard before you decided it was all right to have a franchise in Las Vegas."

"Of course we did," Landry agreed emphatically. "And?"

Landry hesitated. "And I'll talk to our people who are in charge of franchise development later this week, when I get back from my trip. But what the hell are you worried about? We've never had a problem with the Mafia."

"You've never been in Las Vegas."

"No, but we're in New York, Chicago, and Florida," Landry argued. "What do you think they'd do, try to make players fix games? We monitor that very carefully. We have a team of people who review every game tape with a microscope to make certain there wasn't anything shady going on. Experts who can spot quarterbacks just barely under- or overthrowing receivers, running backs going down without really being hit, linebackers missing easy tackles, placekickers going wide on purpose. I don't understand what you're worried about."

"It has nothing to do with the actual operation of the team," Gillette explained. "I'm more concerned about the casino and them trying to influence the regulators on license renewals and things like that. And what they might gouge me for during construction of the casino and the stadium because they control the unions. You know, slowdowns and sick-outs if I don't pay them."

"Oh."

"I've done some checking," Gillette continued, "and I think they're still active out there, maybe more so than people think. I'll have better information on that in the next day or two. I'm willing to share that with you as long as you share what you have with me." He looked at Landry intently.

"Of course, of course." Landry cleared his throat as he checked his watch. "Look, maybe the best thing is for you to back off on this casino idea for a while? Get the franchise established first, then we'll talk about the casino again in a few years."

Landry suddenly seemed nervous, pulling the napkin through his fingers, bouncing one knee.

"No way," Gillette said firmly. "The only reason we offered four hundred and fifty million for the franchise was so we could build the casino. Without that, the bid doesn't make sense." Not entirely true, but Landry didn't know that. "That was clearly stated in the bid package."

"Right, right, but things change. We all know that. Everything's always up for renegotiation, right?"

"Not this," Gillette answered coldly. Landry gazed back for a few seconds, then glanced away, unable to stare Gillette down. "I hope I'm making myself clear."

"Let me get back to you."

Gillette shook his head. "No, I need an ironclad yes right now, or I go to our friends in the press and let them know you've reneged. If I do, you won't get close to four hundred fifty million when you reoffer the franchise. People will smell a problem, especially when I tell them why we backed off."

Landry blinked. "No, no, don't do that."

"What's your answer, Kurt?" Gillette demanded, glad the Wall Street lawyer hadn't won the election for commissioner. "I need to know right now."

Landry took several gulps of water, then nodded. "Okay, okay, you got your casino."

WRIGHT MOVED slowly through Saks Fifth Avenue's main entrance across from Rockefeller Center, then meandered through a maze of glass counters full of perfumes and body lotions. He gazed emptily at the perfectly made-up women behind the counters who were smiling back, ready to sell him something outrageously expensive.

He stopped and rubbed his face hard in the middle of an aisle, hoping he'd wake up in his bed beside his wife and realize that what had happened at the sex shop had all been just an awful nightmare. He took a deep breath and closed his eyes, praying, knowing he was being irrational—which he prided himself on never being—but unable to calm down. He was holding on to anything at this point, anything that might give him a shred of hope. But when he opened his eyes, he was still in Saks, still in trouble.

"You all right?" asked a pretty, dark-haired woman from behind one of the counters.

Wright glanced over at her. "Huh?" He'd been thinking about how he hadn't seen or heard anything on TV or radio about a woman being found dead between two parked cars in the West Village. Which seemed strange. The story might not be enough for CNN, but it should have made the local news.

"You look like you're having a bad day," said the saleswoman. "Girl trouble?"

Wright gazed at her, the horrible image of the woman dropping from the block of wood still vivid in his mind.

"You know," the saleswoman continued, "you

should give her something nice." She reached for a small bottle on a purple velvet cloth. "This is called Allure," she said. "It's one of our best sellers."

Wright moved to the counter slowly. "It would be for my wife," he murmured.

"Of course it would," the saleswoman said, brushing her fingers over Wright's left hand and his wedding band. "You two having a little tiff?"

"Well, we—"

"Hi, David."

Wright's gaze shot from the woman's fingers into the eyes of a man he'd never seen before. A stocky, swarthy man with dark hair and a crooked nose. "Who are you?"

The man snickered and looked at the saleswoman. "What a joker," he said in a thick New York accent, spreading his arms wide and smiling. "He always does this to me. Acts like he doesn't know me. It's his thing, ya know?"

The saleswoman shrugged.

The man patted Wright on the shoulder, then reached into his jacket, pulled out a photograph, and held it up so Wright could see.

As Wright focused on the photo, his heart rose in his throat and his upper lip curled. It was a picture of him whipping the woman as she hung from the iron rings.

"Follow me," he ordered, his tone gruff. He wheeled around and headed toward the elevators.

Wright followed him like a puppy after its

mother, head down and in the same tracks, all the way to a waiting elevator. Moving into the car obediently when the man waved him in. As the doors closed, the man turned toward Wright, resting his finger on the "stop" button. Pushing it hard when the elevator had risen a few feet, halting it between the first and second floors.

"What's going on?" Wright asked. "Please," he begged, "tell me."

The man smiled, his demeanor becoming pleasant again. "Everything's going to be fine, David, as long as you cooperate."

"How did you get that?" Wright asked, gesturing at the photo the man was still holding.

"We were there, in a side room. We saw everything. We got pictures **and** a tape of the whole thing." The man shook his head. "Poor woman."

"It was an accident," Wright muttered.

"Of course it was," the man agreed, "but the cops might not think so when they see the tape up to the point you put the noose around her neck."

Wright started to say something, but the man held up a finger and cut him off.

"Don't worry, David, your secret's safe as long as you work with us. Right now, all the cops have on their hands is a missing persons case. We picked the woman up and put her in cold storage. We took care of the owner, too, so he couldn't point the cops at you." The man chuckled snidely. "I doubt anybody will miss him, though. Pretty much a scumbag."

Wright shut his eyes tightly. "I didn't kill her," he said, gritting his teeth. "It was an accident."

"Of course it was," the man said, pulling a pocketful of pictures from his jacket and tossing them so they scattered on the floor of the elevator. "But try telling the cops that when they see these."

Wright dropped to his knees, scooping them up quickly. "This is crazy," he muttered over and over. "Crazy."

"And don't worry about the shop, we cleaned everything up." The man laughed harshly and pushed the elevator's "start" button. "The NYPD crime lab won't find nothing."

Wright picked up the last picture as the car jerked to a start. "What's going on?" he whispered, looking up at the man. "Please tell me."

The car came to a stop and the doors parted on the second floor. "We'll be in touch soon," the man said as he moved past several people waiting to get on. "By the way, David, my name's Paul. Remember that, because we're going to be talking a lot from now on."

DÉJÀ VU, Gillette thought, watching Stiles hoist a juicy piece of steak to his mouth. Stiles was sitting in the same chair Landry had used and had ordered the same meal—he'd shown up ten minutes after Landry left and hadn't stopped eating or said a word since the food was served. "Taste good?" he asked, glad to see Stiles enjoying himself.

Stiles finished chewing and swallowed, then leaned back and patted his stomach gently. "I don't think I've ever tasted anything better in my life."

"I'm just glad you **have** your life," Gillette said quietly, leaning over and touching Stiles on the shoulder. "I was worried about you." Worried was an understatement. Stiles had gone critical several times during the week after he was shot. The hospital chaplain had read him the last rites twice. "It was my fault you got hit."

Stiles pointed at Gillette. "That's crap and you know it. I signed up to protect you, you paid me a lot of money to do it, and I took the money. I did it out of my own free will, out of complete self-interest. It's my job, I'd do it again." He paused. "For a guy who's big on personal accountability, I can't believe you said that."

Stiles was right. It was his job, it was what he was supposed to do, and he had taken money. But right now, that didn't seem to matter. "I still feel bad."

"Then pay me more money."

"Yeah, good one." Gillette looked around the restaurant, checking for his security detail—over by the bus stand. Since Whitman and McGuire had tried to kill him last fall, he checked every few minutes whenever he was in public. It had been ten months, but the most dangerous person involved in the Laurel Energy conspiracy—Tom McGuire— was still out there somewhere. And if Faraday was right, McGuire might be close. "You're my friend,

Quentin, my good friend." Gillette took a measured breath. "I don't let many people in," he admitted, his voice going low. "I can't."

"I know."

"Some people think I'm lonely," Gillette murmured.

"I know," Stiles agreed. "They want the money and all the perks, but they don't know what you go through. The pressure of making so many important decisions all the time. It's got to be tough."

"It is sometimes." Stiles understood. One of the few people who did. Gillette had to at least appear to be immune to it, but there were moments when he felt the walls closing in around him, and it felt good to tell someone that.

"It could have been very different," Stiles pointed out. "The guy aimed at the first person he saw in that room. It could have been **you** in the hospital for the last ten months."

"Maybe." Gillette replayed the scene in his head for a few moments. It had been the wildest few seconds he had ever experienced. "But the most important thing is, you're okay. Judging by the way you're inhaling that steak, anyway."

"It'll be a while until I'm a hundred percent, but meals like this will definitely speed up the recovery."

"Good. Well, since you're feeling better, let's talk business."

Stiles nodded. "Sure."

"First of all, I want to close our deal."

"Our deal?"

"Yeah, for your company."

Stiles's jaw dropped. "I didn't think you were serious."

"When have you ever known me to be anything but serious about Everest business?"

"Not often."

"Try never," Gillette said sharply. "Look, McGuire and Company will pay five million dollars for a hundred percent of QS. I spoke to Craig West this morning, and he's fine with it."

"If he wasn't, he'd be fired."

"It's not like that."

"Sure it is, Chris. Craig knows where his bread's buttered."

"Whatever," Gillette muttered. But Stiles was right. It hadn't even crossed his mind that West would object to the deal.

"You're doing me a favor," Stiles said. "A five-million-dollar favor, and I don't want you getting in trouble with your investors. People get pretty crazy when it comes to money."

"You're telling **me**?" Gillette chuckled. "Look, I'm about to make my investors five billion dollars on Laurel Energy."

Stiles caught his breath. "Five **billion**?"

"Yeah, so I don't think they'll give me too much trouble over five million. That's chicken scratch to them."

"Jesus."

"And five million's a fair price for QS, anyway. It's full, but fair, and Craig and I think it'll be a nice tuck-in to round out McGuire's service offerings. McGuire has a high-end protection division, but it caters mostly to business executives. You've got connections in the sports and entertainment industry Craig doesn't. After we close, I'll expect you to work with him on those relationships, make all the introductions."

"Of course."

"Good. See, everybody wins. McGuire and Company gets a new business line at a decent price, you get five million bucks, and I get all your time. Okay?"

Stiles made a face as though he were trying to work through a calculus problem. "Okay."

Gillette could see it was all just beginning to sink in. Stiles had grown up dirt poor in Harlem, and now he was about to make five million dollars. More money than he probably could have dreamed of as a kid. But Gillette didn't want there to be any appearance of impropriety, either. They'd have to go through all the normal due diligence. "As part of the deal, you'll sign a noncompete."

"A what?"

"A noncompetition agreement. It'll stipulate that you can't start, or work for, another personal security company for at least five years."

"Well, I—"

"And you'll sign all the normal reps and warranties as part of the purchase agreement."

"The normal **whats**?"

"Representations and warranties. Promises that you alone have the power to sell the company and that you've been a good corporate citizen while you owned it. Specifically, that you're the only owner of QS stock and, if you're not, that the others can't block you, that you've paid all your corporate and personal taxes, and that you don't have any lawsuits pending against you. Things like that. If it turns out some of those things aren't accurate, and I find out about it after we do the deal, you'll owe me my money back and then some."

"So, I'm gonna need a lawyer," Stiles said glumly.

"It's all standard stuff in the deal business."

"I don't know deals, I know personal security and investigations."

"You'll be fine."

"You wouldn't take advantage of me, Chris."

Gillette grinned. "Sure I would. It's what I do. That's why you're going to get a lawyer." He could see Stiles was struggling, unsure of himself in this situation but trying to maintain his signature cool. Stiles didn't want to insult the man who was going to make him rich, but he'd sacrificed and risked a great deal to get QS where it was now, and he wasn't going to throw caution out the window for anyone. "I'd never take advantage of you,

Quentin," Gillette said seriously. "You'll get your five million, and you'll never have to pay me back anything. Unless you lie to me, and we both know you'd never do that."

"Of course not."

"I'll get the lawyers started on the documents. We should have everything finished up in thirty days, okay?"

Stiles nodded deliberately. "Thanks, Chris. This is all pretty amazing."

"Don't worry about it. You've worked hard, you deserve it. Most people fail where you've prospered." Gillette could see Stiles appreciated that someone else understood how much sacrifice it had taken to make QS successful. Just as he appreciated Stiles understanding how isolated he felt sometimes as chairman of Everest. It was one of the reasons they'd gotten so close. Each took the time to understand the other's situation.

Stiles cut another piece of steak and put it in his mouth. "How did your meeting with Landry go?"

"The guy tried to back me off on the casino."

"What?"

"Yeah. I had a feeling he'd try that," Gillette said, folding his napkin. "I figured the owners agreed to the casino initially to get the four hundred and fifty million, then thought they could jerk it away once they gave us the franchise. You know, they thought I'd be so happy to be an NFL owner, I'd do anything they wanted after the fact."

"What tipped you off that they'd try the bait and switch?"

"I figured they knew the Mafia was still active out there, and I know they don't want any chance that the same people who own one of their franchises would be tempted to get in bed with organized crime. That's one of the last things they want to see splashed across the front page of **The New York Times.**"

"Why did you think they were on to the Mob in Vegas?" Stiles asked.

"**You** were. I figured if **you** knew, **they** must."

Stiles's expression sagged. "You think their people are better than mine?"

"That's a fucking joke. You figured it out in a few hours, so I figured they could do it in a few months." Gillette pulled out his Blackberry and scrolled through his e-mails. "You find out anything more about what's going on? Anything specific about what we're likely to run into?"

Stiles nodded and leaned forward in his chair, motioning for Gillette to do the same.

"What is it?" Gillette asked, putting his elbows on the table and looking around suspiciously.

"Hey, this is Sparks Steak House," Stiles said quietly.

"Yep. Best steak place in Manhattan. So what?"

"There's probably Mob guys in here right now," Stiles said, looking around.

"Oh, come on."

"Hey, don't you remember?"

"Remember what?"

"John Gotti shot Paul Castellano dead on the steps of this place one night as Castellano was coming in to eat dinner. Castellano was god-father of the Gambino family. Ultimately, Gotti became don of the Gambinos. He used to eat here, too. Before the feds finally took Gotti down and sent him away for life." Stiles glanced around at a few tables. "But, like we all know, you take one wiseguy down and a new one takes his place, so I figure the walls here have ears."

Gillette nodded. "Yeah, but any ears in this place probably belong to the feds. If any Mob guy talked business in this place, he'd probably be killed by his own family before the feds could get to him."

"But they can hear what we're talking about if they're around, and I figure you don't want that." Stiles glanced at one table in particular, four tough-looking guys dressed in silk suits.

Gillette followed Stiles's glance. "Okay," he said quietly, "what do you have?"

"There's three families active in Vegas right now," Stiles answered. "Branches of the Chicago Treviso and Barducci families are there, but they're small-time. Penny-ante stuff, mostly, like retail 'protection.' They target off-the-strip restaurants and shops owned by foreigners who can't go to the authorities for help because most of their workers are illegal aliens and they haven't paid FICA in years. Easy pickings for extortionists who kill somebody every once in a while just to make a statement, whether he pays his arm-twist money or not. They've been targeting mainly Asians, from what I'm hearing. So, of course, the Asian Mobs see an opportunity and they're moving in to 'protect' their people. Problem is, those guys are worse than Italians. They charge more and kill for less." Stiles paused for a moment. "The family you need to watch out for in Vegas is the Carbone family. They're out of New York, and they've got all the local construction companies tied up, so you got to make certain everyone wants to work hard all the time. If you try to bring someone in from the outside who doesn't gouge you for the extra incentive, you find out your equipment breaks down real often. They're also close to the gaming commission and the other state regulators involved with the gambling industry, so you'll run into them whenever you need licenses and approvals. Don't believe the local city officials who tell you everything's clean. It isn't."

"It's all like you thought."

"Yeah, but now two other sources have confirmed it. People I trust."

"How did you find out this stuff, Quentin? Who did you talk to?"

Stiles shook his head. "Don't ask."

"Come on," Gillette pushed.

"Before I started QS, I wasn't just with the Army Rangers and the Secret Service. I worked in another area of the government, too. We had dealings with some of these people."

"What area was it?"

"I can't tell you."

"Quentin, I—"

"Don't push it, Chris. Really."

Gillette took a deep breath. "So, if I don't play ball with the Carbones, I'll have problems with the construction of both the stadium and the casino, and I might be denied the ability to operate the casino when it's ready to open."

"Exactly. But there are . . . **consulting** firms that can take care of all that for you." Stiles smirked. "If you get my drift. You pay them a flat fee for something called 'general business services,' and they make the payoffs for you. They skim a little off the top, but you don't get your hands dirty and they make sure you don't have any . . . **interruptions.**"

"I bet it isn't just a little off the top, either."

"It's not as bad as you think. Over time, markets get efficient. This one's no different. There's enough of those firms now that the skim isn't outrageous."

"The problem is," Gillette explained, "I want to bring in a construction group from the outside. There aren't any based in Vegas that can handle both jobs at the same time and get them done as fast as I want."

"I think as long as you hire one of these consulting firms, it doesn't matter that much. Might be a little more expensive, but as long as the Carbones get their pound of flesh, they don't care if you use someone outside."

Gillette brightened. "Good, then talk to a few of them for me. Are they all out in Las Vegas?"

"The ones you want to deal with."

"I'm going out there soon. Do phone interviews with the best ones and narrow it down to two, then we'll meet with them while I'm in town."

"Got it."

Gillette took another drink of water. "Some of these other New York crime families are in the paper every week. Somebody's being arrested for something, but I've never heard much about the Carbones."

"They're run by a guy named Joseph Celino who hates publicity as much as you do."

"Get some more on them from your contacts, will you? As much as you can. Specifically on Celino."

"Sure, sure." Stiles pushed his plate away, a few bites of the steak uneaten. "Man," he said loudly, "that wouldn't have happened a year ago. Wasting food like that, I mean. Hell, I would have had seconds."

"Like you said, it'll take a while." Gillette slipped the Blackberry back into his pocket. "Listen, Friday morning you and I are going to Washington. Then, in the afternoon, we're going to the Eastern Shore of Maryland to meet with the mayor of a small town down there."

"You're really going to follow up with those people in D.C.?"

There was no choice. Gillette had a gut feeling that Daniel Ganze really did know something about his father, and he wasn't going to miss even the **slightest** opportunity to find out what had happened to that plane sixteen years ago. "I'm going to meet with them at least once more," he replied. "I don't think I've got anything to lose doing that. Just the time if it turns out to be a dead end."

"I hope it's just the time."

"What do you mean?"

"I think you need to be careful."

"Always, and I'll have you there."

"Why the meeting with the mayor?" Stiles asked.

Gillette liked the fact that Stiles recognized when he didn't want to talk about something. If only most people he knew understood him so well. "She's getting in the way of a store Discount America is trying to build in her town, stirring up the natives. She's calling people in other towns, too. We can't have that."

"You going to bring her up to New York for a big, all-expenses-paid weekend? Turn on the Gillette charm at some swanky dinner? Make her an offer she can't refuse?" Stiles smiled. "If I know you, you'll have her begging you to bring that store to her town by the time the weekend's over."

"I wish." It wasn't going to be that easy—not according to Harry Stein, anyway. "I've got to get going. I've got this ground-breaking cere-mony for the new hospital wing we're building at St. Christopher's," he explained, standing. "Why don't you come with me? We can talk more about the QS deal on the way over. It would probably help for me to let you in on all the things to expect when you sell your business. There's more to it than you think."

"Sure, and thanks for lunch."

Gillette grinned as he pushed in his chair. "Lunch is on you, pal. You're about to bank five large. You can afford it."

BOYD LOOKED UP from his desk when he heard the rap on the door. "What is it, Daniel?"

"I did some checking on that Miles Whitman situation," Ganze replied, moving into the office. "Called over to Justice to see what was what."

Boyd put down the report he'd been working on. "And?"

"They're not as stupid as we thought."

"What do you mean?" Boyd asked.

"It's taken them some time, but they've started to figure out that Whitman must have had help hiding his forty million. It's hard to hide that big a money transfer these days with the way banks have to report transactions."

"That doesn't sound good."

"They've put out feelers to several different agencies, including the right one. It could take them a few days, maybe even a week, to run it high enough up the flagpole to get an answer, but they'll get a bite if they have information to trade. Then we're screwed."

"We need this."

"I know."

Boyd groaned and rubbed his eyes. "Okay, let's move."

GILLETTE STOOD behind a raised podium erected in a field beside St. Christopher's Memorial Hospital on the Upper West Side of Manhattan. It was a beautiful early fall afternoon, the sky a deep blue, the air crisp, the summer humidity gone. **Football weather,** Gillette thought as he looked out over the hundred invited guests. Several of the hospital executive officers and board members had already stepped to the microphone to thank him for his personal generosity, and it was his turn to say a few words, which included reminding everyone that it was Everest Capital making the ten-million-dollar donation, not him.

He said a few more things—he hoped the new wing could make a difference to more than a few people's lives, hoped the research lab the wing would include could produce results, and assured the hospital executives that Everest Capital would continue to support them in the future with their new projects. Gillette was close to several of the hospital executives—people he'd dealt with for years—so he knew the money would be used for the right purposes and not siphoned off into some leech's pocket. He was generous with money he controlled, but careful. Because he knew how easily money could fall into the wrong hands. It was like water, always following the path of least resistance.

As Gillette stepped down from the podium, one of the construction company's representatives moved forward with a gold shovel Gillette would use for the ceremonial ground breaking and handed it to him.

"Thanks," Gillette said.

The man smiled from beneath his yellow hard hat, not letting go of the shovel right away.

"What is it?" Gillette asked.

"We're looking forward to having you in Las Vegas, Mr. Gillette," the man said quietly. "For everybody's sake, go with the flow when you get there. Make things easy." His smile faded. "Or we can make them very hard."

5

DAVID WRIGHT drew back the pool cue, hesitated for a moment as he aimed, then struck the white ball hard. A tiny puff of blue chalk flew in the air, and the white ball raced across the table and careered into the seven, sending it toward the far corner pocket. But it skidded against the rail just in front of the pocket and bounced left, then rolled back almost a foot. "Damn it!"

"Too hard," Gillette observed, checking out the table as the seven came to rest. The ten was all he had to drop—Wright still had five balls on the table. If he knocked the ten in just right, he could set himself up perfectly for the eight and the match would be over. Three games for him—none for Wright.

"**Way** too hard," Stiles agreed. He was leaning against the wall beside the mahogany cue stand, sipping the iced tea Debbie had brought him.

"I don't need any coaching from the cheap seats," Wright snapped.

Stiles laughed. "Just trying to help, my man. I want to see your boss go down as bad as you do. He tells me he's never been beaten on this table." He winked at Gillette when Wright wasn't looking. "I get tired of hearing how good he is."

"Yeah, well, I almost beat him a couple of times, so screw you."

Wright and Stiles had just met, but Wright didn't care about first impressions, Gillette knew. He cared about winning.

"Why don't **you** play him," Wright said, gesturing at Stiles.

"I will when he's done with you," Stiles answered. "Which looks like it'll be in about thirty seconds, thanks to that last sorry-ass shot of yours. I thought Chris told me you had game."

Wright glared at Stiles. "Hey, you can—"

"Enough," Gillette interrupted, hiding a grin. He dropped the ten and eight quickly, then straightened up. "Looks like Quentin was wrong," he said. "Only took fifteen seconds."

"Yeah, well."

"Rack 'em, David," Gillette ordered. He picked up a bottled water off the table in front of the cue stand and took several swallows. "You and Quentin are going to play first," he said, wiping his mouth with the back of his hand. "One game, then the winner gets me. We're going to settle who's best right now with a little tournament, but it's my table so I get a first-round bye."

"What's he doing here, anyway?" Wright grumbled, gathering the balls into the rack.

"Quentin's in charge of my personal security."

"I thought we had a company doing that."

"Right, QS. **Quentin Stiles.** He's the one who got shot in Mississippi last fall. He's the one who saved my life down there."

Wright stopped gathering the balls and looked over at Stiles. "Oh, Jesus, I'm sorry."

Gillette had introduced Stiles to Wright only by his first name.

"I didn't put two and two together," Wright continued. "God, you're a legend around here." He hesitated. "No offense."

Stiles pulled a stick from the cue stand. "None taken. I got skin like a rhino."

Gillette sat at the table as Stiles prepared to break. "McGuire and Company is going to buy QS, and Quentin's going to join us at Everest when the deal's done. Which should be in about thirty days. I'm going to propose that he become a special partner at that time. Not a full partner like Faraday and me, but he's going to have some of the same privileges."

Wright's eyebrows rose, but he said nothing.

"One thing I'm going to do right away is give Quentin a piece of the ups on Everest Eight. You okay with that, David?" Gillette assumed Wright wouldn't be okay with that. Ups allocated to anyone meant less for everyone else, but Gillette had asked because he wanted to see Wright's reaction. "Well?"

Wright was waiting for Stiles to break. Stiles gestured for Wright to answer first.

"It's up to you, Christian," Wright replied, his voice uncharacteristically subdued. "It's your firm. If you think it's the right thing, do it. We've been damn successful with you as chairman."

But Gillette could see Wright wasn't on board a hundred percent. Which was fine—he wanted Wright to think for himself. He didn't want his most valuable people doing what they thought he wanted them to do or saying what they thought he wanted them to say. "You sure you don't have any issues with that?"

Before Wright could say anything, Stiles drew back his stick and sent the cue ball flying toward the triangle of balls at the other end of the table. It exploded with a thunderous crack and four balls dropped—three solids, one stripe.

Gillette had assumed Stiles was good—Stiles had told him how he'd hustled older guys in Harlem pool halls as a teenager, and another QS agent had said he'd been whipped by Stiles when they were on an assignment in Dallas one time—but Gillette had never actually seen Stiles in action. "Pretty good, Quentin." You could tell by the way he broke that he knew what he was doing. His stroke seemed effortless, but the cue ball had rocketed to the other end of the table. And the result had been impressive—

four balls off the break. A lot of that was because he was strong as hell, even in his weakened condition, but you still had to have the coordination to make it all come together.

"Pretty good?" Stiles ambled down one side of the table toward the spot where the cue ball had ended up. "You only wish you could break like that, Christian," he said, sizing up the way the balls lay, figuring out the best way to play things. "I'll take stripes," he announced.

"But you dropped three solids off the break," Wright pointed out.

"Yeah, but we've got to even this up somehow. If I took solids, it'd be over in two minutes, judging from what I've seen of your play." Stiles grinned. "No offense."

"None taken."

"That's the other reason I'm going to be around more," Stiles said, "to keep Chris humble when it comes to pool."

"We'll see," Gillette said.

"That would be nice," Wright mumbled.

"Chris."

The three men glanced toward the door at the sound of Debbie's voice.

"Yeah, Deb."

"Kurt Landry is on the phone. Says it'll only take a second."

"Okay. Transfer him in here."

"Right away."

When the cordless phone on the table in front of the cue stand rang, Gillette picked it up. "Hi, Kurt."

"Hello, Christian. Two quick things. First, thanks for lunch."

"Sure."

"Second, I want to let you know that I spoke to several of the owners about the casino issue, and they wanted me to assure you that you can move forward on that. Everything's fine there."

Gillette's mind raced back to the man who had handed him the shovel at the ground-breaking ceremony, wondering how that encounter fit into all of this. "Good."

"Other than that, welcome to the NFL. Don't hesitate to call me if you have any questions or issues."

"Thanks."

"What did he want?" Stiles asked as Gillette hung up.

Gillette shook his head, indicating they'd speak later about it. "So, David, no issues with Quentin joining the firm?" he asked again as Stiles bent to line up his next shot. He watched Wright struggle. It was obvious that the younger man wanted to say something, but it was also clear he understood how close Gillette and Stiles were and didn't want Gillette to think hiring Stiles was bad.

"Well . . ." Wright paused. "What exactly are you going to do for us, Quentin?"

Gillette liked the way Wright was going directly

at Stiles, shifting the conversation away from them, not using him as the intermediary. Efficiency was the key in business. And no matter what anyone else at Everest said about Wright, about his arrogance or his brash manner, he was direct as hell. People who were direct made progress, and progress—whether the results were good or bad—was the only way to get to the bottom line.

"I'm going to focus on disaster planning, risk mitigation, and recovery alternatives," Stiles answered. "I've had a lot of experience in those areas both in the private sector and when I was with the Secret Service and the Army Rangers. I've found that most entities aren't really prepared for disasters, even big corporations. Whether the threat is terrorism, internal fraud, fire, bad weather, whatever. Most companies haven't focused on protecting the entire entity against a disaster. Whether that means the physical plant, computer networks, or employees, they just haven't done enough. In some cases, they haven't even analyzed what disasters they face." He gestured toward Gillette. "Chris wants me to do a full review of all the Everest portfolio companies to make sure your investments are protected as much as possible."

Wright's gaze flickered back and forth between Gillette and Stiles. "How much of the ups are you giving him, Christian?"

"One percent." Gillette saw Wright's relief immediately. With a twenty-billion-dollar fund, one percent could be a meaningful number, but it was probably well south of what Wright had feared. "I'm going to pay Quentin a million a year in salary, too. He'll stay in charge of my personal security as well as doing all the other things he just talked about. I think a million's fair."

"Of course, of course," Wright agreed.

"Any more questions?" Gillette asked.

Wright shook his head.

"Will you back me internally on this?"

"Absolutely," Wright said, "but I'm not sure that's very important. I mean, I'll be glad to say something positive about it at the managers meeting, if that's what you want me to do. But I don't know if that'll help much."

"I'm going to have the managing partners vote on it before then," Gillette said.

"You probably don't have to do that," Wright pointed out. "This is probably something you can do on your own, as chairman. I can take a look at the partnership documents if you want. To make sure."

"Thanks, but don't bother," Gillette said. "I'm going to be extra careful here. Since Quentin's a friend, I'll feel better if the partners vote, even if the documents say I can do it on my own."

"Okay, but then what do you want me to do? I can't vote, I'm just a managing director."

"Not anymore."

Wright's eyes shot to Gillette's. "Huh?"

"David, I've got good news and bad news. Here's the bad. Nigel and I have decided to open a Los

Angeles office. I know how much you love L.A., but you won't be going." Gillette held up his hand when he saw that Wright was about to speak. "But here's the good: I've promoted you to managing partner. I need to talk to Nigel one more time about your compensation, but the promotion's done."

"Jesus," Wright whispered. "Thanks."

"You deserve it. And I will need your vote as far as Stiles goes."

"You got it."

"Of course," Gillette continued, "this means there won't be any more incidents like this morning."

"Incidents?" Wright asked hesitantly, swallowing hard.

"Not being able to reach you." Wright had finally called Gillette as he and Stiles were headed to the hospital for the ceremony. "Debbie started calling you at nine this morning, but I didn't hear from you until three-fifteen. What the hell happened?"

"Sorry."

"Where were you?"

Wright looked down. "I was shopping for my wife. Our wedding anniversary is coming up."

Gillette looked over at Stiles, who had stopped playing. "That took all day?"

"I'm buying her a diamond ring, and I was designing it with the jeweler."

"You didn't have cell phone reception at the jewelry store? Where was this place, in a fallout shelter?"

"I kept getting calls. The guy got pissed and told

me to turn it off." Wright looked up. "Sorry, it won't happen again." He took a deep breath. "Thanks again for making me a managing partner; it means a lot to me. A hell of a lot."

"You're the youngest managing partner in Everest Capital history," Gillette said, not completely satisfied with Wright's explanation. "Beat me by a year."

Wright gave Gillette a grateful nod for the comment. "Does this mean I can call you Chris from now on?"

"No. In fact, if you take more than thirty minutes to call me back again, you'll be calling me 'Mr. Gillette.' "

Wright rolled his eyes and motioned for Stiles to start playing again. "By the way, Christian, I meant to tell you, I was able to get a meeting with the Hush-Hush CEO. It's tomorrow morning. I know this is last minute, but can you come with me?"

"Sure." Faraday had already called his contact at the French clothing company. As Gillette had suspected, they'd been ecstatic about the possibility of picking up a hot U.S. women's clothing company. Gillette figured they could bang a big profit on a quick flip here, maybe three to four hundred million without a lot of work, so he wanted to make certain everything went right. "What time is the meeting?"

"Ten o'clock." Wright watched Stiles sink one striped ball after another. "It should go about two hours."

"Okay, then I want you to come with me to my Apex meeting. That's at one."

"Apex meeting?"

Until now, Gillette had discussed his plans to buy Apex only with Faraday. "Yes, I'm getting together with Russell Hughes tomorrow."

"He's the chairman, isn't he? Why are you meeting with him?"

"I'm gonna buy Apex."

Wright's mouth fell slowly open. **"Buy it?"**

"Yup."

"They aren't doing very well right now. In fact, from what I hear, they're doing awful."

"Which gives us an opportunity. Plus they've got five billion dollars of dry powder. And if we shoot some of the operating people at their dog investments and put our people in, I think we can turn those companies around fast. I've talked to the Strazzi Trust, the people who control Apex, and they're interested in my offer."

"Which is?" Wright asked.

"Par, what they have in it."

"How much is that in dollars?"

"A billion."

Wright chewed on the figure. "Doesn't seem too bad for twenty-two companies and five billion of equity commitments."

Gillette had known Wright would come around fast. The great thing about David was it was what he really thought, too. He wasn't agreeing just to ingratiate. "The trust people are worried that if they keep Hughes as chairman much longer, their investment won't be worth anything. Par sounded good."

"Why don't they fire Hughes?"

"Faraday asked the same thing. If they do, their investors will pull out," Gillette answered, "and Apex would die on the vine. The good thing for us is that a lot of Apex's investors are our investors, too. I've spoken to a number of them, and they'd support an Everest takeover of Apex. They wouldn't pull out if we were in charge."

"You mean if **you** were in charge," Wright said.

"I don't have time," Gillette replied, "I have to focus on our new fund."

"You can't keep Hughes around."

"No," Gillette confirmed. "Not for the long term, anyway."

"You going to bring in someone from the outside?" Wright asked.

"I'm bringing you in," Gillette said, smiling. "This is going to be your first assignment as a managing partner. You're going to be the next chairman of Apex Capital."

"My God," Wright whispered.

"We'll need to talk at least five or six times a day, maybe more at the beginning," Gillette continued. "Which is why I can't have another episode like this morning."

"I told you, it'll never happen again."

"The other managing partners may have a problem with this." Gillette rose from his chair. Stiles was about to finish Wright off without even letting him take a shot. "They'll think they should have been tapped. Especially Maggie. But I—"

"Screw her," Wright retorted sharply. "She couldn't handle Apex. You know I'm better than her. Better than Blair and O'Brien, too. They couldn't handle this assignment, either. I doubt even Faraday could. But you know I can."

Gillette glanced over at Stiles. "I'm worried about his self-confidence, Quentin."

Stiles smirked as he dropped the eight ball, winning the game. "I know what you mean. He just got his ass kicked at pool."

"Big fucking deal," Wright snapped, his bravado back. "I'll alert the media, I'm sure it'll be front-page news."

"Come on, Quentin, rack 'em," Gillette ordered, ignoring Wright. "Let's go."

"You sure you want to do this?" Stiles asked. "Sure you want to have your unbeaten streak on your home table go bye-bye?"

Gillette smiled, paying no attention to Stiles's attempt to get in his grill. "Just rack them," he repeated calmly, and turned back to Wright. "Where are the Hush-Hush offices?"

"In the garment district, down on Thirty-eighth Street near Penn Station."

"All right, we'll leave here at nine-thirty. You can brief me on the big issues on the way. After the meeting, we'll get a bite somewhere and talk about how we're going to handle the Russell Hughes meeting."

"Why even bother meeting with him?" Wright wanted to know. "Just go around him."

"First, the Strazzi Trust people asked me to meet with him. Like everyone else in the world, they hate confrontation, so they want me to let him know what's coming. As if he doesn't already," Gillette added. "Second, as poorly as he's run Apex, he knows more about it than anyone else simply because he's chairman. I want to get as much of a debrief out of him as we can before we lower the boom. He won't help much after that."

"Are you going to let him know he's gone tomorrow?"

"Haven't decided yet, but I will let him know that you're the new sheriff in town." Stiles had finished racking, and Gillette reached in his pocket for a quarter. "That's all, David, I—"

"There's one more thing I forgot to tell you, Christian," Wright spoke up, interrupting again. "I've got a line on another big investor, a Bermuda-based insurance company. I know you said Everest Eight was closed at the meeting, but these guys are looking to invest five hundred large. You should think about letting them in like we did with the Wallaces. They could probably do even more in Nine."

Gillette broke into a wide smile and moved to where Wright stood. "This is why I promoted him,

Quentin," he said, touching the younger man's shoulder. The same way his father had done when he'd done something well. A couple of light pats, then a squeeze. "He's the only person at this firm, besides Faraday and me, who's raised a dime for the new fund, and he's got us going in to see the Hush-Hush CEO tomorrow. Impressive, huh?"

Stiles grunted.

"What do you think about the Wallaces coming into the new fund?" Gillette asked Wright.

"The more the merrier," he answered immediately.

"I love it," Gillette said, beaming. "You worried about Allison Wallace being on the ground here at Everest?"

"Only if she starts to distract you."

"Excuse me?"

"I got a load of her the other day. She's pretty, and she's worth billions. You two would make a hell of a couple."

First Debbie, then Faraday, now Wright. This was getting old. "There's nothing to worry about," he assured Wright.

Wright shrugged. "Okay."

"Let's go," Stiles called impatiently. "I'm going to show you how to play pool, Chris."

Gillette picked up Wright's wallet off the table. Wright took it with him everywhere he went, even if he was just going to someone else's office at Everest. "You can go now."

Wright grabbed the wallet. "I want to stay. I want to see you—"

"Let him stay," Stiles said, laughing. "Every protégé needs to see his mentor go down once in a while."

Gillette smiled thinly. He knew what Stiles was trying to do, but it wasn't going to work. In fact, he was going to turn the tables on Stiles, take him where he didn't want to go. "Okay, David, you can stay. Tell you what, Quentin," he said, "let's make this interesting."

Stiles stopped chalking his cue. "What do you mean?"

Gillette grinned. Stiles knew exactly what he meant. "You're about to come into some money," he said. "Let's bet."

"How much?"

Gillette's grin widened. He had Stiles right where he wanted him. "How about a hundred grand?" A lot, but not too much.

Wright's eyes flashed to Stiles's.

"A hundred grand?" Stiles glanced at Wright, then back at Gillette.

Gillette shrugged apologetically. "Fine, fine. Let's make it two hundred."

Stiles swallowed hard. "I thought this was about pride."

"It was until you got cocky."

"Isn't pride more important than money?"

Gillette shook his head. "Pride's for pussies."

Wright laughed out loud, happy to see Stiles sweating.

Stiles leaned on the table with both hands and dropped his head. "Two hundred grand, huh?"

"Unless you want—"

"No, no. Two hundred's fine."

"Good." Gillette held up the quarter he'd pulled from his pocket. "Flip for the break?"

"Sure."

"I assume you want heads."

"Of course," Stiles confirmed. "Coins always come up heads more often than tails. That's a fact."

Gillette tossed the quarter in the air so it landed on the pool table. It bounced several times, then rolled to a stop.

Wright leaned over the table. "Tails," he announced.

Stiles glanced at the quarter and shrugged, as though he didn't really care. "Go ahead, Chris."

It was over quickly. As Stiles had done to Wright, Gillette didn't even give Stiles a chance to shoot once. He ran the table cleanly, dropping all seven solid balls, then the eight.

"Double or nothing?" Gillette asked as the eight fell into a side pocket, watching Stiles try to figure out how he'd let himself get taken for two hundred grand so easily.

"Nah."

Gillette placed his cue back in the wall rack and picked up his coat off the back of the chair. "I've got to get going, I'm taking Allison to dinner to talk about our new working relationship."

Wright whistled. "I hope Faith doesn't find out."

"Easy, David, that's how rumors get started." Gillette took a few steps toward the door, then stopped. "By the way, I want both you guys to come out on the boat this weekend. We'll board over on the West Side around noon, at the Forty-fourth Street pier. Plan to spend the night. Bring wives or sweethearts." He winked at them. "But not both. I'm inviting Nigel, too. We'll celebrate your promotion," he said, pointing at Wright.

"Thanks, Christian."

"Come on, Quentin," Gillette said, waving at Stiles. "Let's go." He followed Stiles out, then stopped at the door and leaned back in the room. "By the way, David. Call me Chris."

6

"**WHERE'S ALLISON** staying?" Stiles asked as they pushed through the crowded Park Avenue sidewalk toward a black limousine idling in front of the Everest Capital building.

"Parker Meridien," Gillette answered, checking for the two sedans—one in front and one in back of the limousine, his full security detail. They were there.

Gillette wasn't worried about Miles Whitman. He probably wasn't even in the country. He was probably in South America or Europe, living under an assumed name, living off the money he'd stolen from North America Guaranty as the feds were closing in on him last fall. He was probably much more interested in not going to prison than he was in revenge. When it really came down to it, most white-collars were.

But Tom McGuire was another story.

McGuire had spent years in the FBI as a field

agent before founding McGuire & Company. Revenge drove him, he was tough as nails, and he had no fear of prison. The feds had been watching his house on Long Island and listening to his wife's and children's telephone calls for the last ten months, but he hadn't made contact—as far as they could tell. However, Gillette had no doubt that McGuire had been in touch with them somehow. He was clever enough to keep it concealed.

And McGuire had one more big motivator—his brother, Vince. Vince had been co-CEO of McGuire & Company before the conspiracy, and he'd helped Tom with the assassination attempts. He'd been as deeply involved in the plot as Tom and Whitman. But Stiles's men had caught Vince and turned him over to the feds just as the whole conspiracy was collapsing last year, and Vince had been killed in a prison riot three months ago. Knifed in the back and left to bleed to death on a basketball court.

Gillette climbed into the limousine ahead of Stiles and eased onto the wide rear seat. "What did you think of David?" he asked as Stiles relaxed onto the bench seat along the driver's side.

"Cocky as hell." Stiles shrugged apologetically. "Hope you didn't think I was too tough on him."

"Tough? You were like a Boy Scout helping a little old lady across the street, for Christ's sake," Gillette grumbled. "You were a bigger prick to **me** with all that jawing before our game. Never seen that side before."

"I was just having fun. Besides, it didn't do me any good."

"No, it didn't."

"You know, it seemed like something was bothering Wright," Stiles observed.

"What do you mean?"

"He seemed **on edge.** Preoccupied."

"How could you tell? You've never met him."

"I've watched a lot of nervous people in my career," Stiles explained. "I'd never met most of them before, but I could still tell they were nervous. To me, Wright seemed like he was about to take a polygraph test."

Gillette gazed at Stiles for a few moments as the limousine pulled away from the curb, following the lead sedan. He was sorry to hear this, but he'd learned to trust Stiles's instincts.

"What did Kurt Landry want?" Stiles asked as they headed down Park Avenue.

Gillette had started making notes in a date book, jotting down names of people he needed to call tomorrow before the Hush-Hush meeting. "To tell me he'd spoken to the NFL owners and they were fine with the casino idea. Everything's a go there."

"Why didn't you want Wright to hear that?"

Gillette shrugged as he slipped the date book back in his pocket. "He's one of those guys who keeps asking questions until he gets answers."

"Like you," Stiles said.

That was what everyone always said. "Yeah.

Thing is, he wasn't involved in the bid process, and I didn't want to have to go through it all again. How the casino works in with the franchise and all that. He would have tried to push me on that, especially after I told him he'd been promoted." Gillette hesitated. "Hey, do you remember the guy who handed me the shovel at the ceremony this afternoon?"

"Yeah. Why?"

"When he handed it to me, he said they were looking forward to seeing me in Las Vegas. He told me not to make any waves. He said it so no one else would hear, but he definitely said it."

Stiles had been reaching for a small refrigerator across from the bench seat but stopped. "Really?"

"Think he's with the Carbones?"

"Maybe."

"How the hell would he find out so fast?"

Stiles shrugged. "People talk. That's the biggest problem with them. If they'd just shut up, everything would be fine." He shook his head. "I'll talk to my guys. I'm sure they checked everybody for weapons before they let them anywhere near you, but I guess they should have done background checks, too."

"Don't give them a hard time about it," Gillette ordered. "You're the one who always tells me if somebody really wanted to take out the president, it wouldn't be that hard."

"Sure, but—"

"Your guys do a great job. I don't want you getting on their case for that. Nothing happened. Just run a check on the guy."

"Right."

The limousine turned onto Fifty-seventh Street and headed west. Traffic had been heavy on Park, but it cleared as they made the turn.

"So, you want me to actually sit at the table with you and Allison at dinner?"

"Yup."

Stiles grinned. "I'm like your chaperone."

"More like my alibi."

"I don't get it."

"Some people are under the impression that I'm going to be distracted by Allison Wallace. You heard David. They think she's going to try to make our relationship more than just a business partnership, **and** that I'm going to let it happen. It's ridiculous, I'm not going to let it happen, even if that's what she wants. Which I doubt she does. But I want you there so I have a witness that tonight was just business."

"Okay, son."

"I know it sounds silly, but I gotta do what I gotta do." They were almost to the Parker Meridien. Gillette reached into his suit jacket. "This is for you," he said, handing a coin to Stiles.

"What the . . . ?"

"It's the quarter I flipped before our pool game, you know, to see who went first. I had it specially made while you were in the hospital. Check it out."

Stiles turned on a reading light behind his shoulder and held up the coin, then flipped it. "Son of a bitch. Tails on both sides."

Gillette laughed. "You always call heads when you flip anyone for anything. I've seen you do it so many times. And you always say I'm predictable." He gestured at Stiles. "Keep the two hundred grand, of course. Boy, it was fun to see your face when I dropped the eight."

WRIGHT TOSSED a ten-dollar bill onto the front seat of the cab, then hopped out and headed down the shadowy sidewalk toward the entrance of his apartment building.

"David."

"Jesus!" Wright's head snapped left, toward the voice, and he staggered back a few steps. Like a ghost, the man who'd shown up at Saks that morning appeared out of a darkened doorway. "What do you want, Paul?" Wright demanded angrily, trying to regain control.

"From now on, I want to know where Christian Gillette is at all times."

Suddenly Wright was exhausted. He just wanted to go to bed. "Why?" he asked, his voice hoarse.

The man pointed a thick finger at Wright, holding it inches from his face. "Listen to me good, pal. If you aren't helpful with this, the cops will get answers to all those questions they have. Missing persons questions right now, but they'll be murder questions real fast." He grabbed a crumpled piece of paper out of his coat pocket and put it in Wright's hand, then curled Wright's fingers around it. "That's my number. Don't lose it, don't be a stranger, and don't be stupid."

Wright watched Paul walk away until he faded into the darkness. This had been one of the best days of his life—and one of the worst.

GILLETTE SPOTTED Allison Wallace the moment he walked into the Parker Meridien lobby. Stunning. It was the only word. She wore a low-cut black dress, high heels at the end of her long legs, and a diamond choker—night and day from the conservative Wall Street outfit she'd worn to Everest. Two well-tailored men were trying to talk to her, but she wasn't paying much attention, giving them disinterested nods at inappropriate times in the conversation.

"Hi," she called, waving to Gillette with her champagne glass when she saw him over the men's shoulders. Spilling a little on one as she sidled between them. "What's this?" she asked, pointing at the agents standing on either side of Gillette, hands clasped behind their backs.

"Security."

She raised one eyebrow. "I'm the one worth twenty-two billion, and I don't have security. What's your excuse?"

"I'm careful."

"Think it might be a little much?"

"Nope."

"Sure you aren't compensating for a lack of something somewhere else?"

Gillette attempted a coy smile, but it didn't work. "Quite sure. There've never been any complaints about that."

"What **have** there been complaints about?"

"You can probably guess."

"Your girlfriends probably bitch about never seeing you, Mr. Workaholic."

"Very good, Captain Obvious. You win a prize."

"Which is?"

"Dinner with me."

"Whoopee. So, who pays for your security?" she asked.

"You," Gillette answered, noticing that she'd slurred her words slightly. This wasn't the night's first glass of champagne. "Now that you're an Everest limited partner." He wondered if she'd been drinking because she was nervous about dinner, if this was how she handled being worth twenty-two billion, or if she was just having fun. "Let's go."

"You have my office ready yet?" Allison asked as they walked. "I'll be there bright and early next Monday morning."

"What's 'bright and early' for you?"

"Seven o'clock."

"Sure it is. See you at nine."

"I'll beat **you** in."

"Are you going to stay here at the Parker Meridien for a few weeks until you get your apartment?" Gillette asked.

"I've already got my apartment. I move in next week."

"Oh, where is it?"

"On Fifth, right off Central Park."

Gillette jerked back as though he'd been slapped in the forehead. "Hey, I live on Fifth off the park."

"I know. I'm in the same building as you, two floors up."

He took a deep breath. "Great."

"Same elevator and all." Allison laughed. "What a coincidence, huh?"

"Yeah," he muttered, "amazing."

"You didn't answer my question," Allison said. "Is my office ready? I really am going to be there first thing next Monday morning, maybe sooner. I might not go back to Chicago at all."

They moved through the hotel's main door.

"It's ready. And it's at the other end of the hallway from mine."

"We'll just see about that," she said, climbing into the limousine ahead of Gillette. At the sight of Stiles, she jumped. "Who's this?" she demanded as Gillette eased next to her on the backseat.

Stiles leaned forward to take her hand. "Quentin Stiles."

"What are you doing here?"

"Quentin's in charge of my security," Gillette explained as the chauffeur shut the door.

"Fantastic, but what's he doing here?"

"Having dinner with us."

"Oh no, he's not." She smiled at Stiles politely. "Don't take this wrong, Mr. Stiles. I'm sure you're a very nice and interesting man, but I didn't come out tonight to have dinner with you. I'm here to have dinner with Christian. I need to talk to him about a lot of things, some of which are very confidential."

"Anything you say to me you can—"

"Don't give me that, Christian." Allison looked back at Stiles. "Could you sit in the front?" she asked courteously, reaching up and turning on the stereo. "Driver," she called over the music, "please pull over."

Stiles looked at Gillette as the chauffeur steered the limo to the curb.

"Go on," Gillette said quietly. So the real cost of the Wallace five billion wasn't going to be monetary, it was going to be something else. Something that might end up being far more expensive—his time and attention. He thought about Debbie's take on the meeting with Allison and Gordon. Maybe she'd been right after all.

"Just so we're clear, these aren't my real boobs," Allison said when Stiles was in the front seat and they were back in traffic. She put down the champagne glass in a holder in the armrest, then cupped her hands beneath her breasts. "I had the surgery two years ago."

Gillette searched for anything to look at inside the limousine besides her breasts. "Uh, why are you telling me this?"

"I noticed you staring at them."

"I wasn't staring."

"All right, you **glanced** at them a few times. But you would have stared sooner or later."

"Yeah, well, there isn't much to that dress."

"I figure it's better to be direct, about everything," she continued. "Full disclosure, you know? I just want the same thing from you."

"Well, these **are** my breasts."

"Funny."

"Thanks." This Allison Wallace was a firecracker, much different from the one he'd met at the office. Despite all the warnings, including a faint alarm going off in the back of his own head, Gillette kind of liked it.

Allison picked up her champagne again and took a long swallow, then pushed the button that elevated the partition between the front and back. "I was so flat before I got the implants. You have no idea how much better I feel about myself now."

"You're very pretty, Allison, with or without them."

"Ooh, a charmer. I like that." She held up her glass to him. "So, where are we going for dinner?" she asked after taking another sip.

"I made a reservation at a new restaurant here in midtown called Chez Madam." Gillette noticed how familiar Allison was with what buttons to push in a limousine. Which only made sense. She'd been riding in them since she was a baby. She probably didn't even have a driver's license. "It's popular, you'll like it."

"It's too quiet," she said, pushing the button that lowered the partition. "I went there on Saturday and it was a raging bore. I had to eat everything with silverware, and the bloody background music almost put me to sleep. I want to have fun tonight, I want to go off the hook. I know exactly where we're going. Driver," she called, "we're going down to TriBeCa."

Stiles looked back from the front seat. "Christian?"

Gillette shrugged, conceding. "I need to know where we're going," he said to her, "so my guys can check it out."

"It's called the Grill. It's down on Hudson Street somewhere, and it's casual. A lot more fun than Chez Madman, or whatever the heck that place is called. They do a great mahimahi, which is what **you'll** have, Christian. I know you like fish, and this thing is to die for. Franky's the head chef. He'll prepare it for you himself, as a favor to me." She ran her tongue around her lips, as if she were already savoring a bite of something. "I'm having their bacon cheeseburger, it's the best in the city." She raised the partition and Stiles disappeared again.

"You want a **cheeseburger**?" Gillette asked.

"Yeah. So?"

He smiled. "It's just surprising. You don't look like a woman who'd want a cheeseburger for dinner, much less know where the best one in the city is."

"I'm full of surprises."

"So I see. How exactly do you know where the best cheeseburger in New York is, anyway? You're from Chicago."

"When you're worth as much as I am, you're always in New York. Big as Chicago is, it isn't New York. By the way," she said, leaning down and pulling a champagne bottle from the refrigerator, "I've already had my people at the Grill for a half hour making sure everything's okay." She handed the bottle to Gillette. "Open that, please. Remember, turn the bottle, not the cork."

"I know how to open a champagne—"

"Of course you do. Look," she said, her voice turning serious, "I was kidding back at the hotel. I understand why you need protection. After our meeting at Everest, I had one of my staff back in Chicago put together a full report on what happened to you last fall. The way I see it, the guy you still have to worry about is Tom McGuire. Whitman's just trying to stay ahead of the law. Besides, based on what I read, he doesn't have the know-how or the guts to come after you. But McGuire's different. He's experienced with this stuff, and he's vindictive."

The cork popped loudly as Gillette gave the bottle a third twist. "You've been busy," he said, trying not to show her how impressed he was. "How did you know what I'd want for dinner?"

"You're in great shape, that's obvious," she said, brazenly giving him the once-over. "Guys in great shape eat healthy. And I spoke to Debbie this morning."

"You what?"

"Hey, girls gotta stick together. You wouldn't understand. Truth is, if I really want to be up to speed all the time with what's going on at Everest Capital, it's probably more important for me to have a good relationship with Debbie than you. If there's one person who might actually know more about what's going on at the firm than you, it's her." The limousine pulled up in front of the restaurant. Allison slid across the seat to the door and opened it. "Come on," she said over her shoulder.

Gillette liked that she didn't wait for the driver to get the door. He followed as she climbed out, looking away as her short dress rode high on her thighs. As he stood up, she grabbed his arm and pulled him toward the restaurant.

Then the paparazzi descended. Suddenly photographers were rushing at them from all directions and cameras were flashing everywhere. Four QS agents raced to form a wall around Gillette and Allison, then quickly ushered them into the restaurant. But not before fifty pictures had been snapped. People in the restaurant stopped and gazed as the couple came through the door, straining to see what the commotion was about.

Allison was still hanging on Gillette's arm. "Everyone's looking," she whispered. "God, this is fun."

Gillette turned around toward Stiles, who was behind them. "Go back out there and talk to one of those guys, will you? Find out how they knew we were coming."

"Right."

When Stiles was gone, the maître d' led them to a secluded table in a back corner of the place.

"You arrange this, too?" Gillette asked, sitting down.

"Of course." Allison looked up at the maître d' when she was seated. "We'll have a bottle of Veuve Clicquot," she ordered over the music.

The maître d' nodded and moved off.

"So, I'm obviously a little different than you thought," she said after they'd relaxed into their chairs. "Not that quiet thing you met at Everest."

"Well, I—"

"I do the prim and proper routine for Gordon. He goes back to my uncle and grandfather and reports on me all the time. He thinks I don't know that. Fortunately, I've got him snowed, and he tells them mostly good things. They'd probably have heart attacks if they knew the truth."

"Your uncle and grandfather aren't stupid, Allison. They know the truth. They've probably had you followed."

"No way. I'd know if they did."

"How?"

"I pay the maids and the chauffeurs at home to tell me everything."

So she wasn't beyond bribery. A rich girl who didn't hesitate to put out money when she wanted information. He'd have to be careful about that. Maybe even have to give Debbie a raise.

"And my grandfather and uncle **are** that stupid," she continued, "which is why they have Gordon. At least they've got enough brains to understand how stupid they are."

A waiter appeared quickly with the champagne. When it was poured and he was gone, Gillette raised his glass. "Here's to our partnership. At the very least, it's going to be interesting."

She tapped her glass to his and took a long swallow. "What do you mean by 'interesting'? Fun, or a pain in the ass?"

"I guess we'll find out. But I can tell you one thing: I've never been used like this before."

"Don't give me that," she snapped. "You're getting five billion dollars."

"And you're getting the education of a lifetime."

"Pretty sure of yourself, aren't you? Starting to believe the press clippings."

"I never believe press clippings. That puts

you right on the road to ruin. All I believe in is profits."

"Like I said before, you're on a roll right now. But the economy's been good the last few years. Things'll get rougher when the GDP boards the down elevator."

"We'll be fine."

Allison sighed. "Yeah, guys like you always are. You're Mr. Consistency, aren't you." She pointed at his glass.

He'd put the glass back on the table without drinking. "What do you mean?"

"You know exactly what I mean. You don't drink alcohol. I wanted to see if you'd at least put it to your lips to try to con me."

Gillette rubbed his chin for a second. He wondered if there was anything she didn't know about him. "You've done **a lot** of homework."

"I invested five billion dollars in your fund, Christian. Almost a quarter of my family's net worth." She leaned over the table, swirling the champagne around in her glass. "I love a great time, I love to go crazy every once in a while, but I'm also very careful when it comes to my family's money."

"You should be."

"I put my grandfather and uncle down, but they're watching this move carefully. Investing so much in Everest, I mean. They aren't a hundred percent convinced it's the right thing to do. I'm taking a big risk."

"Then why do it?"

"I want to leave **my** mark on my family," Allison explained, her expression hardening. "I want to take twenty-two billion and make it fifty, maybe even a hundred. I want to be the one they talk about at Christmas dinner a hundred years from now. The one that made us a true dynasty." She laughed. "I want them to raise their glasses to a big oil painting of me hanging on the wall over the table." She pointed at him. "And you're the one who's going to teach me how to do it."

Always let people talk, Gillette thought. They'll tell you so much if you just let them go.

"Of course," she continued, "I'll be wearing a dress like this in the painting, maybe even shorter. Not one of those long things. I'll probably get the painter to make my boobs look a little bigger than they really are, too. That way I'll drive the young boys crazy." She put her head back and laughed loudly at her own idea.

"I'm surprised you haven't had the painting done yet," Gillette said.

"That's a good point. I should."

He watched Allison pull out her Blackberry and send a message to herself. A reminder to have the portrait done. It took everything he had not to laugh himself. "Remind me how your family got so rich." He wanted to keep her talking, hoping he'd get a few tidbits Craig West hadn't dug up.

"You already know all that. You told Gordon."

"Come on," he pushed.

"The railroad, real estate, then my father's brother, the smart one, got us into the cell phone explosion. He's dead now, unfortunately. He wasn't a very nice man, but he was wicked smart. The only thing my generation's done is invest in the public markets. We did okay in the late nineties with the tech boom because we got a lot of opportunities to invest in IPOs, thanks to the relationships we had with the investment banks doing the offerings. But we stayed in too long. We were actually worth almost twenty-five billion at one point in 2000. Thanks to my cousin Ricky, we lost a lot of the paper gains we'd racked up when the bottom fell out of the NASDAQ."

"Ricky is one of your uncles' sons? The one that's on the family trust's board now?"

"Right."

"How many uncles do you have?"

"My father had three brothers. Uncle Tad's the one who got us into cell phones and died. Then there's the one that's on the board now, and there's another one who lives on a beach in Tahiti. Literally sleeps at night in a hammock that's tied up between two palm trees. He's useless."

"And your dad, where's he?"

"He runs a cattle ranch in Montana. It's what he always wanted to do. The ranch loses money every year, but the family trust makes it whole."

"Do you talk to him much?"

"No. We're different," Allison said, her tone softening. "And don't give me the speech about how I should talk to him all the time and count my lucky stars he's alive," she warned, her voice growing strong again. "I know about your father. I'm sorry about it, but my father and I can't make it work. We've tried and it just doesn't click."

Gillette stared back for a few moments, then cleared his throat. "How old is your cousin Ricky?"

"Thirty-one, a year older than me. My father's generation had eleven kids, but Ricky and I are the only ones really involved in the family business affairs. The rest of them are just leeches. Ricky was the golden child of my generation and on the board," she continued, "until he lost that three billion. Which is why I'm on the board now. My father and the brother that lives in Tahiti screamed bloody murder until my grandfather made the switch. Now that I'm on it, I want to show everyone what I can do. I want to make it big." She patted Gillette's arm as she stood up. "Which is where you come in."

"Where are you going?" he asked, standing with her.

"Ladies' room." She smiled at him. "I like your manners, standing up when a woman leaves the table. Somebody raised you right."

Yeah, he thought. My dad.

Gillette watched her walk through the restaurant, watched men's heads turn as though they were on swivels. She was attractive but moved as if she didn't know or care, paying no attention to the stares or the elbows being jabbed. Or maybe she paid no attention because she was so used to it. If the guys in this restaurant only knew what she was worth, they wouldn't just ogle, they'd stampede the table when she got back.

"Excuse me."

Gillette glanced to his right at the voice. A young woman was waving at him while one of the security agents kept her at bay.

"Will you sign my **People** magazine?" she called, waving it as the man stayed between her and Gillette. "Please."

Gillette nodded to the agent as Stiles sat in Allison's chair. "What did you find out?" he asked, taking a pen from the young woman. She already had the magazine opened to the article.

"Nice mug," he said, pointing at Gillette's picture on the page.

"They must have gotten it off the Internet. I didn't send them anything." He signed his name along the bottom of the page, then handed the pen and the magazine back to the woman. "There you go."

"Thank you so much."

"Sure."

"She must have thought you were the rock star they put on that list," Stiles said, nodding at the magazine. "She couldn't have thought it was you. You aren't that exciting."

Gillette grinned. "Ah, you're just jealous. So, did you find out anything?"

Stiles nodded. "Yeah, it took a few minutes and a hundred bucks, but the guys outside found out you two were coming here from Allison. One of them finally came clean."

"He said she called?" Gillette asked incredulously.

"He said the call was anonymous, but it came from the Parker Meridien, so it had to be her. Otherwise one of the operators would have had to be listening to her phone, and I doubt that happened."

"How did the guy know the call came from the Parker?"

"Caller ID."

Gillette spotted Allison coming back from the ladies' room. "Thanks."

Stiles saw her, too, and stood up. "Have fun."

"Did you miss me?" Allison asked as Gillette held out her chair.

"Sure." He noticed that she was sniffing as he sat back down. "You okay?"

"Huh?"

"You're sniffing. You okay?"

"Oh, I'm fine. It's allergies. Happens every fall."

Gillette watched her closely. Please, he thought, please tell me I didn't partner with a woman who has this problem. "Why did you call the paparazzi on us?"

She put a hand on her chest. "What?"

"Why'd you do it?"

"I didn't."

"Come on."

She squinted at him for a moment, then smiled and shrugged. "I thought it would be fun."

"And I thought you didn't want your family knowing you were such a party animal."

An irritated look came to her face. "First of all, they don't read the kind of rags those pictures will show up in. Second, even if they did find out about them, I'd say the photographers were following you because of that **People** article. I'd tell my grandfather I was appalled at the pictures and that I'd already told you to be more low-key."

"Why did you call them, Allison?"

"I told you," she said, sniffing again. "I thought it would be fun." She cased the restaurant, eyes darting from table to table. "How's that pop-star girlfriend of yours? Still peddling her CDs?"

So that was Allison's game. She wanted Faith to see pictures of them coming into the Grill arm in arm. Deb was beginning to look awfully smart. "She's doing fine."

"Where is she tonight?"

"On the West Coast doing some publicity. She's back tomorrow."

"How often do you see her? Is it an every night thing when she's in town?"

"Are you asking me if it's serious?"

"I'm just asking," Allison replied, wiping her nose with her napkin. "I'm not trying to get personal."

"Well, you are."

Allison rolled her eyes. "**Puleeease.** Don't flatter yourself. I'm not asking because I want to move in on her. Gawd, it would be awful to date you. You love your work way too much. A woman would always run second to Everest. Honestly, I just want to make sure it **stays** that way. I want my five billion to be twenty or forty billion in a few years. And for that to happen, your pecker needs to stay right where it is. In your pants."

She seemed sincere, which was good news. "Everyone will be very relieved."

"Everyone?"

"A lot of people at Everest think you're after me, and, well . . ."

"Well **what**?"

"You know."

Allison ground her teeth together for a few moments. "I'll pretend I didn't hear that."

"Okay."

"What's going on with that new NFL franchise you won?" she asked.

"Going on?"

"Like I said on the phone last night, I want Everest Eight to make that investment."

Gillette shook his head. "No, we'll do it out of Seven. It has to be that way. I've got to be fair to my investors. The ones in Seven were in first."

"So do it fifty-fifty. I want a chunk of that."

"I'll think about it."

"I mean it."

"I heard you."

Her cell phone rang, and she pulled it from her purse. "What?" she said loudly, putting her purse back on the table and pressing her hand to her ear. **"What?"** But the music was too loud and she still couldn't hear. She got up and trotted through the restaurant.

Gillette watched her until she'd moved into the restaurant foyer, then his eyes shifted to the purse she'd left on the table.

TOM MCGUIRE sat in the Explorer, parked on a darkened side street a few blocks from the Grill. Since everything had blown up last fall, he'd taken on a new identity—which wasn't hard if you knew what you were doing. He had a New Jersey driver's license, a Social Security card, and a passport—all of which made clear that he was William Cooper. He wore his hair longer now, had grown a goatee, and had put on twenty-five pounds. Even his children hadn't recognized him at first at the park on Long Island where he'd surprised them last month—the first time he'd seen them and his wife in ten months. The feds had been watching them twenty-four/seven since last November, but he'd found out from friends inside the Bureau that the tail had been called off at the end of August—almost a month ago. The feds were still listening in on calls, but not following the family anymore. It had been wonderful to see the kids.

Nigel Faraday's double take on Park Avenue the other morning was still bothering him. A stupid mistake, he thought. He shouldn't have been anywhere near there at that time of day, but he was trying to assess, trying to nail down routines. There was no need to worry, he told himself. The fat Brit probably hadn't noticed him anyway.

He shut his eyes as he sat in the SUV, clenching the steering wheel until his knuckles turned white. He and his brother had been so close to hundreds of millions, but Gillette and Stiles had destroyed everything at the last second. Now his brother was dead, and he had the rest of his life to look forward to an assumed existence and sporadic, short visits with his family.

McGuire took a deep breath. He'd been waiting ten months for tonight, and it was all coming together perfectly.

"**YOU READY TO GO?**" Gillette asked, checking his watch. It was nine-thirty, and he wanted to get home so he could go through the Hush-Hush material Wright had given him to prepare for tomorrow morning. "I'll give you a lift back to the Parker."

Allison looked at him as if he were crazy. "Are you nuts? We're going out. We'll start at the China Club, then figure out our plan from there. I don't go home at nine-thirty when I'm in New York."

Gillette checked the front of the restaurant. Through the large windows facing Hudson Street, he thought he could see the paparazzi still waiting, which seemed strange. They'd gotten their pictures, but it looked as though they were still hanging around. He motioned to Stiles.

"What's the matter?" she asked, noticing his wave.

"Nothing."

Stiles leaned down when he reached the table. The music was louder than when they had come in. "What is it, Chris?"

"Are the photographers still out front?"

"Yeah."

"But why? They got their pictures. You think they're waiting for somebody else?"

"I doubt it. This isn't a big place with celebrities. Besides, it's almost ten o'clock."

"Doesn't make any sense."

Stiles shrugged. "Nothing makes sense with these clowns."

Gillette thought for a moment. "Find out if there's a back way out of this place. I don't want any more pictures," he said, gesturing subtly at Allison. "You know?"

Stiles nodded, understanding. "There has to be another exit. It's building code, I think. When I find out, I'll have the driver bring the limo around.

I'll have him waiting for us so we'll be able to get right in."

"What if they follow the guy?"

"I don't think—"

"Let's get out there," Gillette suggested, "then call him."

"But—"

"Just do it."

Stiles nodded.

When he was gone, Allison leaned toward Gillette. "What was all that about?"

Gillette eyed her. She was still sniffing, still blaming it on allergies. "Business."

"Well, I'm your **business** partner, so talk to me."

"It wasn't that kind of business," Gillette answered, watching Stiles as he spoke to the maître d', who seemed willing to help, judging by the way he was pointing and nodding.

"Maybe not, but it brings up an important point."

"What's that?"

"As a managing partner, I need to know everything that's going on at Everest Capital."

"Then talk to Debbie. Sounds like you think she's going to be your best source of information."

"I'm being serious, **Christian.**"

"So am I."

"We need to meet every two days," she demanded, "just the two of us, to go over everything that's happening. We'll make those meetings on

Mondays, Wednesdays, and Fridays, and we'll talk one day over the weekend. Of course, if something really important happens, you'll call me right away."

The cost of Wallace money was going to be even greater than he'd expected, he thought, rubbing his eyes. "We meet once a week as a group in the main conference room. The meeting usually lasts several hours. Believe me," he said, emphasizing the words, "after a few weeks, you'll know more than you want to know about Everest Capital."

She shook her head. "That's not good enough. Nowhere near good enough."

"It's good enough for everyone else."

"Everyone else hasn't invested five billion dollars. I told you, I'm very careful with my family's money. And my family is watching this thing very closely."

"Which I understand," Gillette said calmly. "I hope you can understand that I'm busy. If I had to spend that much time talking to you, I wouldn't have enough time to run the firm."

"I want to help, too. The only way I can do that is if I know what's going on."

"You know how you could really help?"

"How?"

"Find me a deal. Find a good company for us to buy at a great price."

Allison finished the last sip of champagne in her glass and reached for the bottle in the ice bucket. But it was empty. "Let's get another bottle," she suggested.

"I told you, we're leaving."

"If you don't get another bottle, I won't tell you about the deal I've got working."

He studied her, trying to determine if there was any truth to what she'd said or if she'd tossed it out there just so he'd get another bottle. He couldn't tell; her face was impassive. "You play poker?" he asked.

She nodded. "Love to."

That figured. "Want to play sometime?"

"Absolutely. Are you in on a regular game?"

"I know a few guys who run a game every Monday night. I go once a month or so. It's a bunch of Wall Streeters. It's a serious game, so you need to know what you're doing."

"I'd love to take some money from the Hermès tie and suspender set. How about next Monday?"

"First, tell me about the deal you've got working." There probably wasn't anything to this, just smoke. After all, if the deal was so great, she'd do it using the Wallace Family Trust money so she could keep all the upside for herself.

She grinned. "I know what you're thinking. If the deal's so awesome, why share it with Everest? Well, I'm your partner, and when I partner with someone, whether it's business or personal, I commit. So, here it is. The company's name is Veramax. They're a—"

"A drug company based outside Chicago," Gillette interrupted. "Owned by a family named Mitchell." He'd been following the company for two years. "Very fast growing. They were going public last spring, but the family couldn't get the valuation they wanted because some of their new products were being held up by the FDA."

"Held up by a lot of red tape crap," Allison confirmed. "Some higher-up at the FDA doesn't like Jack Mitchell, Veramax's main shareholder. The company did over a billion dollars in revenue last year, but they could be doing three to four billion if they could just get these new products to the market. Some of them are incredible. They've got an Alzheimer's drug that's supposed to be fantastic."

"Why the bad blood between the Mitchells and the FDA?"

"I don't know exactly, but I think you could help."

"How?" he asked, becoming interested. This was another way you made money in the private equity world—bringing something to the table others couldn't.

"You and Michael Clark, the senator from California, are friends. You know him pretty well, actually."

"How do you know that?"

She groaned. "If I have to tell you how I know something every time we talk, we're never going to get anywhere, Mr. I Don't Even Have Time to Keep My Five-Billion-Dollar Partner Up to Speed."

"All right, all right," he said. "How does knowing Senator Clark help?"

"He's got pull with the FDA. One of the big guys over there is a golfing buddy of his from California."

"So, I broker a deal."

"Yes."

"What do I get in return?"

"Even if Clark can convince his buddy at the FDA to finish approving Veramax's products quickly, my understanding is that it'll still take six to nine months to get everything finished. The company has some big opportunities they need funding for, and the family wants to do some estate planning. They need money for all that, about a half a billion, and they need it **now.** You get to be that investor, then cash out in the IPO, which should be next fall if you can get the FDA in line. You'd probably make five to six times your money in the IPO. Your investors, me included, will like that."

"I won't pay a premium, especially if I'm the one who gets the FDA off its ass."

"I'm with you," Allison agreed.

"And I want control, I want at least fifty-one percent of the stock."

"I'll arrange a meeting with Jack Mitchell. Talk to him about that."

This actually sounded good, and Gillette was surprised. He hated surprises. "What's your in? Why will Mitchell listen to you?"

"First, I'm bringing you and your connection to Senator Clark. Second, our families have been friends for years. We've vacationed together on the

Upper Peninsula of Michigan ever since I was a little girl."

"When can you arrange a—"

"Chris."

Gillette looked up at Stiles. "Yes."

"Got a back door through the kitchen. Let's go."

"Okay. Send your guys out to the front, like we're about to come out."

"I think we should keep at least two of them with us."

Gillette shook his head. "We'll only be out there for a few minutes, we'll be fine. I don't want any more pictures."

"Still, I—"

"No," Gillette said sharply, standing. "And make your guys think we really are coming out that way. They'll sell it better."

Allison grabbed her purse. "Hey."

"Come on," he said, holding his arm out for her, "I'm not leaving you."

"You scared me," she said, standing up unsteadily and slipping her arm into his. "I thought you'd forgotten those beautiful manners for a second."

"You sure you want to stick to that allergy story?" he asked as they followed Stiles through the restaurant.

"Why wouldn't I?" she asked, holding on to his arm tightly as they climbed a few steps to the kitchen level. "It's the truth."

"Maybe you're getting sick."

"I feel fine."

"Then maybe it's something you're putting up your nose in the bathroom."

"**What**? Listen, I—"

"Nose drops, I don't know."

"Christian, I'm not a—"

"Look," he cut in, "if you tell me it's allergies, it's allergies. I'm not accusing you of anything. I'm just telling you, no drugs at Everest. No marijuana, no cocaine, no nothing. Got it?"

"Of course. I've never done drugs in my life, and I never will. I love to party, but I don't do that."

"Just so we're clear."

"We're clear."

"Perfectly clear?"

"**Perfectly.**"

"Then get me an appointment with Jack Mitchell."

"Maybe I will," she said testily, "and maybe I won't."

"Make it soon," he said, ignoring her. "Work with Debbie."

"Yes, sir. Is there anything else I can do for you? Maybe shine your shoes in between my snorting sessions?"

"And before we meet with him, I want to know two things," he said, ignoring her. "First, what's the source of the bad blood between Mitchell and the FDA, and second, how you know about my connection to Senator Clark."

Three steps led down from the back of the kitchen to the alley, which was littered with paper and broken glass that sparkled in the dim light cast by a single bulb affixed to the brick wall beside the door.

"This doesn't look good," Allison muttered, peering both ways.

"Come on," Stiles called, pulling his cell phone from his pocket, "I don't want to be out here long. Hustle!"

Allison tapped Gillette on the shoulder as they walked quickly to keep up with Stiles. "Just so you know, I didn't call the paparazzi."

Gillette's eyes shot to hers. "What?"

"I didn't call them."

"But you told me you did."

"You actually thought I'd go to the trouble of putting together some big plan so your girlfriend would see us together in the newspapers? You think I'm at Everest to get a husband, but I'm not. I'm here to make money for my family. That's it."

Gillette looked ahead at Stiles, who was staring at his cell phone as he walked. "Quentin, what's up?"

"The reception sucks back here. I haven't been able to get the driver or my guys."

Gillette pulled out his phone as they rounded the corner of the building at the end of the alley. "I think I've got—" He almost ran into Stiles, who'd stopped short.

"Jesus," Allison whispered.

Gillette counted five of them, about twenty feet away. Shadowy figures on the sidewalk, standing side by side, their faces obscured. His eyes darted around, looking for help, but the street was deserted. No one here but the three of them and the figures ahead—moving slowly toward them now.

"Give me a number, Quentin," he urged, stepping ahead of Allison and next to Stiles. "For one of your guys."

"We aren't going to have time for that."

Gillette looked up from the phone. The men had stopped a few feet away. They were close enough now that he could make out their faces.

"What do you want?" Stiles asked calmly.

"Your money," demanded the one in the middle. "Everything you got."

"Look, we don't want any trouble."

"We don't want no trouble, either," said the one on the far left as the others chuckled, "we just want your money."

"We don't have anything," Gillette said defiantly.

"Of course not. I can tell that by those cheap-ass threads."

As the gang laughed again, Stiles went for his gun, a Glock forty-caliber pistol in the shoulder holster inside his jacket.

"Hold it!" warned the one in the middle, raising his right arm and pointing a revolver at Stiles. "I got you covered. I'll kill you, I swear."

Stiles froze, hand over his heart.

"Down," the man ordered.

Slowly, Stiles dropped his hand back to his side. "All right, now—"

Gillette hurled his cell phone at the man in the middle, nailing him on the forehead, and rushed him as he brought both hands to his face. Gillette hunched down as he closed in, driving his shoulder into the man's gut, hurling him to the sidewalk. The man let out a loud groan as he hit the ground. As they rolled, Gillette heard the gun clatter away on the cement, and he heard Stiles yelling and Allison screaming.

Gillette was yanked up instantly. He swung blindly as he got his feet under him, clipping someone's chin, then he was tackled hard by a shoulder that felt like the front end of a Mack truck. For a moment, Gillette and his attacker were airborne, then they landed on the street in a heap, tumbling over and over. He felt hands close tightly around his throat, and he brought his arms up, breaking the hold, kneeing the guy in the stomach at the same time and tossing him away. He jumped to his feet and saw Stiles wrestling on the ground with two of the men.

"Stop it!" Allison screamed. She was clutching the gun the man had lost when Gillette tackled him. Aiming the barrel in different directions frantically— at the men attacking Stiles, at the guy on the ground beside Gillette, then at a man coming toward her. "Right now!"

The man coming at her froze a few feet away when he saw the gun.

Suddenly Gillette heard the sound of an engine roaring to life, then squealing tires.

"Christian!" Allison screamed. "Look out!"

He turned into a pair of high beams just as the man who had tackled him grabbed him around the legs, bringing him down again. He grabbed the guy by the hair and slammed his head into the pavement, then scrambled for the sidewalk as the SUV raced past, running over the man lying in the street. The man's body shook for several seconds, then went still.

The SUV screeched to a halt, and the driver's-side window began to come down. Then the driver punched the accelerator and the vehicle roared away.

"Hands behind your head!" someone yelled. "Now!"

Gillette glanced toward Stiles and saw two QS agents racing toward their boss, guns drawn. Then two sedans skidded around the corner—opposite the one the SUV was headed toward—headlights illuminating the scene brightly. The other two QS agents jumped from the sedans, guns drawn, too. It was over as quickly as it had begun.

Gillette bent over, hands on his knees as he sucked in air, watching the SUV's taillights disappear around the corner.

7

"**I GOT FIVE MINUTES,**" Gillette said to Stiles, checking his watch. "Then I have to go." He and Wright were leaving at nine-thirty to meet with the Hush-Hush CEO at the company's headquarters down in the garment district. "What did you find out?"

"Nice." Stiles pointed at the fresh scab on the left side of Gillette's head near his eye. "Not as bad as a bullet to the chest, but it'll do."

It had happened when the guy had tackled Gillette and they'd tumbled into the street.

"For a rich guy, you're pretty ballsy," Stiles continued. "Chucking your cell phone at somebody pointing a gun, then going after him like that? Most rich guys I know are pussies. Which only makes sense. Why fight your way out of something when you can buy your way out? I was impressed."

"Thanks."

"With your **guts**," Stiles said, grinning, "not your **smarts.** What in the hell were you thinking about, anyway? Two on five?"

"Those aren't bad odds when it's you and me. Besides, we had Allison. That tipped everything in our favor."

Stiles rolled his eyes.

"Look, it was my fault, Quentin. I told you not to have your men come with us. That was stupid. I had to do something. Figured all we had on our side was surprise. Besides," Gillette said with a chuckle, "the guy was aiming at **you.** Now, what did you find out?"

"Sure, sure. Those guys last night? Hired guns. According to my people inside the NYPD, they're part of a Brooklyn gang called the Fire. Pretty nasty crew. The Mob doesn't even screw with them. They admitted taking money to assault us."

"What does that mean? Were they supposed to kill us or just hurt us?"

"They weren't supposed to kill us," Stiles answered, "just beat the crap out of you and me, steal our wallets, and leave us there on the sidewalk. They were supposed to take Allison with them."

Now it made sense. "Must have been a kidnapping. Well, looks like you've got another client. She ought to pay well, too. Maybe a few hundred thousand bucks a year for everything."

"I don't think it was a kidnapping," Stiles said quietly.

"Why not?"

"The gang claimed they were supposed to drop Allison off a few blocks away, unhurt."

"What?"

"Weird, huh?"

"That doesn't make any sense. Who hired them?" Gillette asked.

"The gang never knew his name, they just took his money."

"Or your sources inside the NYPD aren't telling you the whole story," Gillette observed, flexing his right hand. His knuckles were killing him from hitting whoever's chin he'd nailed during the melee.

"No, my sources are good. The gang claimed it was an all-cash deal, everything up front. They said they'd never seen the guy before."

"Well, if it wasn't a kidnapping, there's a good chance Tom McGuire was behind it," Gillette said. "He could have tipped the paparazzi off, probably paid a Parker Meridien hotel operator to tell him where Allison was going. He would have finished us off while we were lying there on the street. Allison would have been the gang's witness that they didn't kill us, and he would have gotten her out of there so he wouldn't have had to kill her, too. He didn't care about getting her, and he wouldn't want the Wallaces on his ass."

"The gang described the guy, but it didn't sound like Tom McGuire."

"At this point, I doubt Tom McGuire looks like the Tom McGuire we knew."

"Probably not," Stiles admitted. "It's interesting," he said after a short pause. "I told you I was in a gang when I was a teenager."

"Yeah, up in Harlem. So?"

"We used to scam people by agreeing to roll a mark. Mostly guys who came to us pissed off because their girl was cheating on them, and they wanted us to beat the shit out of the other guy. We'd get the money up front, but we wouldn't actually do it. I mean, why go through the hassle? You've got the dude's cash, so what's he going to do if you don't beat the guy up? If he screws with one of your gang, he knows he's dead." Stiles paused. "But these guys from Brooklyn did it, and they're one of the toughest gangs in the city. Why would they follow through?"

"Any ideas?" Gillette asked.

"Probably supports your Tom McGuire theory."

"Why?"

"Whoever convinced them to come after us must have had something on them. You know, information he threatened them with so that if they didn't do it, they'd go to jail. That's the only way I can see it happening. McGuire might still have friends inside the FBI, people who might even be helping him stay hidden. Even with everything he did. He could have gotten information from them." Stiles hesitated. "Just a theory, but it's possible."

"Yeah," Gillette said quietly, a bad feeling snaking up his spine—as if he was being stalked. With each day that had passed without a murder attempt, he'd felt safer. Suddenly he didn't feel safe anymore, even with Stiles back. "Why would the gang have talked? Why wouldn't they just shut up and post bail?"

"Good question. Maybe they were so pissed off about losing one of their own. You know, the guy that died? They said the SUV that ran him over was driven by the guy who paid them."

"STOP WORRYING about it," Gillette said as they walked through the double glass doorway and into the Hush-Hush lobby. He'd caught Wright checking out the scab on the side of his face several times. "They want our money, they won't care about a scratch."

"What happened?" Wright asked, still staring.

"I got into it with a few idiots outside a restaurant last night." Stiles had been able to keep their names out of the newspapers. But he realized that Allison might blab about it later, so he couldn't make something up.

"What happened to your posse? The QS guys. Why weren't they around?"

They reached the receptionist desk, and Gillette motioned for Wright to speak to the young woman.

"Can I help you?" she asked, not bothering to look up from her computer. She was pretty, dressed to show it all off. Her silk top hung low over her breasts, revealing the top of a lacy dark purple bra.

"We're here to see Tony Maddox."

The young woman looked up at Wright, then Gillette, seemingly impressed with anyone who was here to see the CEO. "Your names?" she asked, giving Gillette a friendly smile, her voice more respectful.

"I'm Christian Gillette, this is David Wright."

"Thank you, Mr. Gillette. Just a moment."

"Why weren't Stiles's guys around to protect you?" Wright asked again as the woman buzzed Maddox's assistant.

Gillette glanced around the lobby. The walls were covered with pictures of women in lingerie. "I got careless; it wasn't Quentin's fault."

"What happened?"

"I told you, I got into a fight."

"How's the other guy?"

"Dead."

Wright laughed loudly. "No, seriously."

"David, let's talk about the meeting," Gillette said. "Given that you were on your phone the whole way down here and we've only got about ten seconds."

"Hey, I'm trying to get us in to see these guys at that Bermuda insurance company. They've got a big operation up here in New York, and like I said, they can probably do half a billion. I figure you want me to run that down as fast as possible, Chris."

"Do you want me to lead this meeting?"

"No, I'll do it."

"Don't screw up," Gillette warned. "I think we'll be able to flip this company in a couple of months for two to three times our investment. Faraday and I have it all arranged."

"What?"

Gillette hadn't told Wright about Faraday's connection to the French apparel company. "We'll talk about it later," he said, spotting a young woman coming toward them. Probably Maddox's assistant. "Just make sure the meeting goes well. There'll be a big bonus in this for you if the deal works out."

"Hello, gentlemen." Like the receptionist, Maddox's assistant was pretty and well dressed. "Please come this way."

They followed her down a short hallway and into an impressive office, expansive and modern-looking.

"Hey, guys," Tony Maddox called in a friendly voice, standing up and dropping the headset he was wearing onto the desk. He was short, silver haired, deeply tanned, and dressed casually. "This is Frank Hobbs, my director of corporate development."

"I know Frank," Wright said, stepping in front of Gillette and shaking Maddox's hand, then Hobbs's. "Frank and I went to business school together. How are you, pal?"

"Good." Hobbs was tall, dark, and thin and wore

plastic-rimmed glasses. Unlike Maddox, Hobbs was in a suit and tie.

"Thanks for giving me the heads-up on this, Frank."

"Sure."

"Guess it paid off to be in study group together first year, huh?"

Hobbs smiled and looked at the others. "Paid off for me," he said appreciatively. "David taught me how to value stocks. I don't know what I would have done without him."

Gillette winked at Hobbs. "Well, I hope you didn't take **everything** he said seriously. David tends to overpay. Which is why I'm here."

When the laughter had died down, Maddox stepped around Wright. "You must be Christian Gillette," he said, extending his hand.

"That's right," Gillette acknowledged, noticing Maddox's gold bracelet and pinkie ring as they shook hands. Also noticing his quick glance at the scab. But Maddox said nothing.

"I've read a lot about you lately."

"Yeah, thanks to that damn freedom of the press thing."

Maddox laughed heartily. "A real bitch, huh? Bitten me in the ass a few times, too." He pointed at two comfortable-looking couches in a corner of the office. "Let's sit down."

As they did, Maddox's assistant came back into the room and poured coffee, then picked up a

tray from a table near the couches and served crois-
sants.

As the young woman leaned over in front of
Gillette, her loose blouse hung low, exposing her
breasts. He looked away, over at Maddox, who was
smiling back.

"This is a fun business, Christian," Maddox said.
"If we can find a price that works for both of us
today, you're going to have a great time."

"Tony, what's the ownership structure of Hush-
Hush?" Wright asked.

"I own ninety-five percent," Maddox answered,
giving Wright a cursory glance, then refocusing on
Gillette. "My brother owns the other five, but he
hasn't been active in the business for a few years and
I control the board. I made the decision to sell the
company. He has to go along with whatever I say."

"Why sell now?" Wright wanted to know.

This time Maddox didn't even bother looking
over at Wright, just kept talking to Gillette. "I know
I look a lot younger, but I'm fifty-five. I'm getting
tired. This thing has been my baby for the last eight
years, and I love it, but it's worn me out. Plus, we're
growing so damn fast at this point. Faster than we
were a few years ago. The problem is—and I didn't
realize this when I started the company—but the
faster you grow, the more money you gotta put **in**
the business. I'm old, Christian, I want to be taking
money **out.**"

"Sure." Gillette could see that Wright was aggravated at the lack of attention from Maddox. "Tony," he said, pointing at Wright, "I want you to know that if we do a deal, David will be responsible for Hush-Hush. He'll be the chairman. He's just been promoted to managing partner. He's one of our top guns."

"Oh." Maddox turned slightly toward Wright and gave him a respectful nod. "I see."

"Could you give me a snapshot of the company's financials?" Wright asked.

"I'll handle that one, Tony," Hobbs spoke up. "This year we'll do around four hundred million in revenues and thirty in net income. That's up from two hundred twenty-five and ten last year."

"Sweet," Wright said, turning to Maddox. "So, what do you want for it?" he asked bluntly.

Maddox shoved his hands in his pockets and shrugged. "Jeez, I thought you'd make me an offer."

Before Wright could say anything, there was a knock on the door and Maddox's assistant stuck her head into the office. "Tony, we're ready."

"Okay." Maddox nodded. "Guys, I thought before we got into any hard-core negotiations, we'd have a little presentation. You should have a first-hand look at what we do. That okay with you, David?"

Gillette saw the gleam in Maddox's eyes and knew exactly what was coming.

"Yeah, sure."

Maddox waved at his assistant.

She pushed the door wide open, then stepped back to let a statuesque woman whisk into the room. The young brunette wore just a sheer white bra, a lacy white thong, and high heels. She walked seductively to where the men sat, hesitated in front of them for a few moments, hands on her hips, chest pushed out, then turned her back to them and stood still again for a few seconds in the same pose. As she walked out, another woman entered. A blonde this time, wearing a black teddy.

Gillette glanced over at Hobbs, who was looking down, then at Wright, whose chin was in his lap. Finally he looked at Maddox, who was grinning from ear to ear.

"YOU DID AN excellent job with the Hush-Hush meeting," Gillette said. He and Wright were headed into an elevator to go up to the Apex Capital offices for their meeting with Russell Hughes. "I liked the way you cut off the show after the third woman."

"I knew what Maddox was doing, obviously." Wright shook his head as the doors closed and the elevator began to rise. "But, Jesus, those women were incredible."

"That's the fashion business." Gillette had been worried that Wright would give away the farm, but he'd handled himself well. The way a protégé should. "Six hundred million's a fair price, especially since it's growing fast. I was proud of you for not offering too much."

Wright smiled. "Trust me, I thought about offering Maddox whatever he wanted when I saw that first woman."

Gillette laughed. "You should have seen your face. Your jaw was in your lap."

"You think he'll take six hundred?"

"I think he'll call his investment banker, who'll tell him it's worth more."

Wright nodded glumly. "Like they always do."

"But Tony's sharp," Gillette spoke up. "He'll understand that he might get more if he tried really hard. But it wouldn't be that much more, and it would take a while to get. I talked to him for a few seconds as we were leaving, and I made it clear that we could wrap things up quickly. I also told him I could get him into the White House for a personal visit with the president. He's a big Republican."

"How are you going to do that?"

"Senator Clark told me he'd help with that if we ever needed it. Only a couple of times a year max, but this is one of those times we need him."

Wright whistled. "That would be incredible."

The elevator doors parted on the forty-ninth floor.

"Better not tell your wife about Hush-Hush," Gillette joked. "She'll never let you go to work."

"Yeah," Wright said distractedly.

Gillette's cell phone rang.

"I'll let Hughes know we're here," Wright volunteered, moving to the receptionist's desk.

"Thanks." Gillette pulled the phone from his pocket and glanced at the digits: It was the Everest main number. "Hello."

"Christian, it's Nigel. Hope I'm not interrupting."

"David and I are about to head into our Apex meeting with Russell Hughes."

"Then I'll keep it quick. How did the Hush-Hush thing go?"

"Very well. David did a good job."

"Next steps?" Faraday asked.

"We offered six hundred million. It's in the CEO's court to get back to us at this point."

"Odds?"

"Fifty-fifty."

"I'm looking forward to the day you don't say that. Look"—Faraday's voice dropped—"I just wanted to give you a heads-up. One of the receptionists brought a copy of the **Daily News** into the office this morning. There's a couple of pictures of you and Allison on the celebrity page. She's hanging all over you." He hesitated. "I wanted to get to you before Faith did."

Gillette felt his jaw tighten. That was going to be tough to explain. "Thanks."

"Christian," Wright called from the receptionist's desk, "Hughes is ready for us."

"Yeah, all right." Gillette gave Wright a quick wave. "Thanks for the call, Nigel."

"Sure."

Gillette ended the call but didn't put the phone back in his pocket right away. Instead, he gazed at it for a moment, considering whether or not to call Faith. The proactive approach was always better, but—

"Christian," Wright called again impatiently.

Gillette let out a quick breath and shoved the phone in his pocket. Never enough time. "Coming."

The three men sat at a round table in Hughes's office overlooking the East River from forty-nine stories up. Hughes sat with his legs crossed at the knees, arms folded tightly across his chest, chin touching his tie. Clearly, some of his investors had alerted him to what was coming. Probably told him to try to negotiate some kind of settlement, Gillette thought. Then ride off quietly into the sunset.

"Thanks for meeting with us today," Gillette began.

"I didn't want to," Hughes answered candidly, his voice shaking with emotion. "But the Strazzi Estate people basically gave me no choice."

"They're getting impatient."

"They're getting impatient," Hughes repeated, his voice rising, "because you're going out and stirring them up. I have a plan."

"The plan's not working."

"I need time."

"Russell, I've looked at your portfolio. You got some dogs, and that's because you've let management teams stay on that you should have fired a long time ago. We have top-notch people who can step in right away and make a difference."

"You've already had in-depth discussions with the Strazzi Estate representatives," Hughes accused Gillette.

"I wouldn't call them 'in-depth.' "

"They want you to buy Apex. They want out."

"They actually said that to you?"

"They didn't have to, it was obvious." Hughes leaned forward and folded his hands on the table, head down. "Give me six months, Christian. If I haven't improved things after six months, then buy the firm. I won't put up a fight."

"There might not be anything to buy at that point."

"You'll be able to get it for almost nothing if the portfolio companies keep getting worse."

"I'm not a vulture," Gillette said. "I like buying things that have a pulse."

Hughes cleared his throat. "If you bought it, how would you run it? I mean, would you fold it into Everest?"

"Not right away. For at least the first year, I'd keep Apex independent. Like I said, I'd hire some of my own people and replace some of yours at the portfolio companies. But I wouldn't physically combine the offices or integrate the staffs of Apex and Everest."

"What about me?" Hughes asked, his voice hoarse.

"I haven't decided yet, but I know that whoever's running this for us will report to David." Gillette nodded at Wright, who up to this point had said nothing.

Hughes took a deep breath. "I know what I'm doing, David. People here respect me." He hesitated, then glanced at Wright. "I need this job."

"CHRISTIAN."

Gillette looked up from the Veramax report he was reading. The company was doing very well. If he could get the FDA off its ass, the thing would go white hot. Allison was right. "Yes, Nigel."

"Sorry to bother you, but Faith is in the lobby."

"Thanks." Faith had called earlier and asked if she could stop by. She'd just gotten in from the West Coast. "Tell her to come on back."

"Sure."

Gillette stood up and stretched. It was eight-thirty, and suddenly he realized he was hungry. He'd eaten nothing that day but a bowl of cereal for breakfast and a quick salad with Wright in between the Hush-Hush and Apex meetings. He came out from behind the desk and leaned against the front of it. When Faith called, she'd been short. He could tell by her tone something was wrong, and he was pretty sure he knew what.

The door opened and Faith Cassidy was standing in front of him. She was so vivacious, blond with large green eyes and a voluptuous figure. Not at all impressed with herself, either, even though she had every right to be since her first two albums had gone platinum. Normally, when she hadn't seen him for a while, she would have rushed right into his arms, but today she lingered by the door. Normally, her eyes sparkled when she looked at him, too, but today the fire was missing.

"What's wrong, sweetheart?" Gillette asked, moving toward her. He'd missed her. Hadn't realized until just now how much. Been too busy. "You okay?"

"I'm a little tired." Her voice was soft, subdued. "It was a long trip. You know the deal."

"You hungry?" he asked, stopping a few feet away. He wanted to give her a hug, but not if she didn't want to hug him. "Want to get something to eat?"

"I ate on the plane."

"Oh, okay." She never ate airline food. "So, the new album's doing well," Gillette said, keeping the conversation going. "I checked this afternoon with the label."

"Yeah, they're putting a ton of money into advertising on this album, even more than they did with the first two." Faith smiled stiffly. "I'm sure you had a lot to do with that."

After taking over as chairman of Everest last fall, Gillette had personally stepped in to increase the advertising budget for her second album—which had paid off in a huge way, kick-starting sales so the album jumped to the number one spot in the country for three weeks. "Actually, no, I didn't," he admitted. "Your execs figured it out all on their own this time."

She leaned slightly to get a better look at the side of his head. "Jesus, Chris, what happened?"

Gillette gave Faith his warmest smile. "I turned down one of David Wright's deals, and he didn't like it." But she didn't smile back.

"Seriously."

Normally, she would have laughed. She knew Wright, and they joked about how aggressive he was all the time. "Stiles and I got into it with some idiots outside the place we went to dinner last night. It was stupid."

"You okay?"

"It's just a scratch."

They were silent for a few moments.

"Faith, I—"

There was a sharp knock, and Allison appeared in the doorway. "Christian, I— Oh, I'm sorry," she said, "I'll come—"

"Allison," Christian interrupted, "this is Faith Cassidy. Faith, meet Allison Wallace."

Faith and Allison forced uncomfortable smiles and shook hands.

"What do you want?" Gillette asked, sensing the tension that suddenly swirled through the room.

"I heard back from Jack Mitchell," Allison answered. "You and I are going to meet him in Pittsburgh tomorrow night for dinner. He's going to be there on business." She giggled. "I've known Jack for so long. He's my dad's age. He taught me how to swim the year I was five up in Michigan. It'll be fun. He's staying at the William Penn Hotel, so I told him we'd meet him there. They have a nice restaurant. I'll make a reservation and get us rooms."

"Thanks." Gillette glanced at Faith. She was clutching her hands tightly together, the way she always did right before going onstage at one of her concerts. "Let's talk in the morning," he suggested.

"Sure. Um, do you want the door closed?"

Gillette nodded.

"Nice to meet you," Allison called sweetly to Faith as she was leaving.

"You too," said Faith. When the door was closed, she ran a finger under her eyes. "You **work** with her?" she asked, her voice full of emotion.

"Faith, it's not—"

"Can you even begin to understand how hard it was for me when the two of you were splashed across the celebrity pages of the L.A. papers? She was all over you in those pictures."

"Allison's a new managing partner here at Everest," Gillette explained. "Her family committed five billion dollars to us. We had a business dinner so we could talk about her responsibilities, that was all. You know how the damn paparazzi are."

"It didn't look like she was dressed for business to me."

"Stiles was there. Ask him about it."

She shook her head and bit her lip. "Like he'd tell me the truth," she whispered.

"What?"

"Nothing."

"Look, it isn't—"

"I want to take a break, Christian," Faith said suddenly. "Spend some time away from each other. Maybe then we'll figure out if we're really committed to each other."

"We just spent a week away from each other."

"And apparently you enjoyed yourself a lot."

"Faith, you can't be serious. I don't want that."

She moved to him and reached into her bag. Her lower eyelids were glistening. "Here," she said softly, handing him a photograph. "I found it in a knick-knack shop on Ventura when I had an afternoon to myself. I thought of you."

"Faith, let's talk about—"

But she turned and left before he could finish. He stared at the empty doorway, trying to convince himself to go after her and work it out. But he couldn't. He'd never been able to run after anyone in his life.

He looked down at what she'd given him. It was a faded picture of his father as a newly inducted senator, standing next to President Reagan.

8

"CHANGE OF PLANS," Gillette barked into the phone at Harry Stein, Discount America's CEO. "I need to meet with the mayor of that town in Maryland this afternoon, not Friday." He had to talk loudly to be heard over the whine of jet engines as he hurried up the stairs toward the larger of Everest's two planes. His directive was met with stony silence. "Did you hear me, Harry?"

"I heard you, Christian, but this is really short notice."

Gillette ducked down to enter the cabin, then eased into a wide black leather swivel chair near the front. Stiles followed him onto the plane and sat in the chair beside his. There were already three QS agents in the back of the plane, but two more appeared at the door. Stiles was taking no chances, and Gillette was glad. Especially after the other night.

"It has to be this way," Gillette said, nodding to

the agents as they headed toward the others in the back. "My meeting in Washington got moved up, and I need to do both of these things on the same day. I don't have time to make two trips down there."

Daniel Ganze had called at seven this morning and told Gillette to come to Washington immediately. Norman Boyd, Ganze's boss, had to travel unexpectedly for a week out of the country and didn't want to wait to meet until he got back. Things were too urgent, Ganze claimed. So Gillette agreed to come, though he still had no idea what they wanted.

It irritated the hell out of him to be anybody's beck-and-call boy, but there was no choice. He had to know about his father, and he had to know **now.** For the first time since Lana had cut him out of the family so long ago, he was desperate. He sensed that Ganze was real, and he'd been waiting a long time for a break like this.

"I doubt I'll reach this woman for a while," Stein complained. "Her day's probably jammed. After all, she is the mayor."

"What would the mayor of a town half the size of a New York City block possibly have to do on a Wednesday afternoon that could be so important she wouldn't juggle a few things around?"

"Beats me, but remember, she doesn't like us. She's not going to do us any favors."

"Make it happen, Harry."

"Okay, okay."

Gillette ended the call abruptly and answered one coming in from Wright's cell phone. "What's up, David?"

"I just talked to Tony Maddox at Hush-Hush. He says if we up the offer to six fifty, we got a deal. He wants a few reps and warranties that aren't standard, but I can talk him down off the ledge on those. What do you want me to do about the price tag?"

Gillette considered going back to Maddox at six twenty-five, then acknowledged that in this case, giving in to his natural urge not to leave a penny on the table would be shortsighted. There was no reason to waste time and potentially lose the deal over twenty-five million bucks. Not when they could probably flip the thing for at least a billion by March. "Hit it," he instructed, "but tell Maddox we want a signed letter of intent by three. I want him locked up this afternoon, or we pass. Tell him that's the price of a quick negotiation, got it?"

"Yup."

"After you talk to him, call me back. I'll be on the plane phone for the next hour, then on my cell again once we land at Reagan, which oughta be around nine-thirty. I'm at a meeting in D.C. starting at ten. After that, I'm going to the Eastern Shore of Maryland to meet with the mayor of a town over there."

"Is that the Discount America thing?"

"Yeah."

"What's the name of the town?" Wright asked.

"Why?"

"Oh, I've got relatives on the Eastern Shore. Just wondering if I'd recognize the name."

"It's Chatham." Gillette paused. "Mean anything to you?"

"Nope."

"It's not very big."

"Not many of them are down there."

"What town do your relatives live in?" Gillette asked.

"You know," Wright said slowly, "I can never remember. That's why I asked. Thought it might ring a bell when you said it. You coming back to New York when you leave Maryland?"

"No, after Chatham I'm going to Pittsburgh. Allison's got me hooked up with a deal that sounds pretty good. We're meeting the owner for dinner."

"What kind of company is it?"

"I'll tell you about it tomorrow if it's good." No need to go into it now in case it turned out to be nothing. "I'll probably fly back to New York after dinner, but if it goes late, I'll stay over in Pittsburgh and come back in the morning. Did you get in touch with that Bermuda insurance company?"

"Yep," Wright confirmed, "and they want to meet next week, Tuesday or Wednesday. Can you do it?"

Gillette checked his schedule on the Blackberry. "Yeah, I should be okay."

"If the meeting goes well, they want to invest five hundred million in Everest Eight. I sent them the offering memorandum and all the subscription documents by messenger fifteen minutes ago."

"Did you tell them about the Wallace Family coming in for five double-large?"

"Yeah, that was big for them."

"I bet."

"What about Apex?" Wright asked. "Where do we stand with them?"

"I spoke to the Strazzi estate people late last night. We've got a deal if we pay par."

"How much is that again?"

"A billion."

"And?"

"I told them we were in." Technically, Gillette was supposed to have a vote of the managing partners to move forward on a deal, but he knew none of them would dare fight him on it with the sale of Laurel Energy looming. They wouldn't want to be on his bad side as he was divvying up nine hundred million dollars.

"How are you going to fund it?"

Gillette thought for a second. "Five hundred out of Seven and five hundred out of Eight." He was still going to do the entire Vegas NFL franchise out of Seven, no matter what Allison said, but maybe this would help. Apex could end up being a great deal, too. "That'll leave a little over a billion left in Seven in case we need dry powder for the existing portfolio companies in Seven. You know, for add-on acquisitions or rainy day stuff."

"So from now on, all new investments will come out of Eight?"

Another major decision made. "That's right."

"What about Russell Hughes?" Wright asked. "Want me to go over there today and fire his ass?"

Gillette chuckled. He loved Wright's toughness, the way he was so damn direct. So efficient. So fearless. His father had always told him he was the same way. "Nah, let's wait. We're going to meet with him again Friday to go over a few things."

"What time? I mean, I assume you want me to go."

"Eleven. You know, we should do this every day now that we're buying Apex and Hush-Hush," Gillette suggested.

"Okay. Should I call you?"

"No, I'll call you. It'll be between seven and eight. Have your cell on if you aren't in the office or at your apartment. If you haven't heard from me by eight, then call me."

"Right."

"And great job on Hush-Hush again, David. Really. This is going to be another big win for us."

"Thanks."

Gillette hung up and glanced at Stiles.

"Everything okay?" Stiles asked.

"Yeah, fine." He pulled out his date book and went through a long list of calls he wanted to make while they were in the air. Thinking about how Wright was so much better than any of the other managing partners. "By the way, I got the lawyers started on your deal last night. Like I said, we should be done in thirty days."

Stiles shook his head. "How do you keep it all straight, pal?"

WRIGHT HUNG UP with Maddox. The Hush-Hush CEO had just agreed to sign an exclusive letter of intent after getting the news that Everest would up its offer by fifty million. All Wright had to do now was draft the letter and fax it over. Everything was beautiful, he thought, gazing at the scrawled telephone number on the crumpled piece of paper the guy calling himself "Paul" had pressed into his hand before—everything except this.

Wright dialed the number slowly, hoping Paul wouldn't pick up.

"Yeah?" the voice said gruffly.

"It's David, David Wright. You—"

"Well, hello there, Davy," Paul interrupted, "good to hear from you. You're making the right decision. So, what you got for me today? What's your boss's itinerary?"

Wright swallowed hard, wishing to God he'd never gone to that shop in the West Village. Wishing he could have controlled his urges. How many times had his wife warned him?

Christ. Peggy. If she ever found out about any of this . . .

He pushed all that from his mind. "Gillette's going to be in Washington this morning," Wright said in a low voice.

Christian, too, for God's sake. The guy had been so good to him. Why had he risked it all?

"And?"

Wright said nothing.

"Davy?"

Wright thought about hanging up and never calling again. Then he thought about the dead girl dangling by her neck and the photos they had of it. He hadn't heard a whisper on the news about a woman being found dead in the Village, and the shop was closed—he'd gone down and checked after Paul had shown up outside the apartment. Obviously, as Paul claimed, they'd taken care of the mess.

Suddenly it was clear to him. He had to play ball, because in the end it had to be about self-preservation. It was the only way. He'd fought too hard to get where he was.

"David."

"Gillette's landing at Reagan around nine-thirty for a meeting in D.C. that starts at ten. This afternoon he's going to a town on Maryland's Eastern Shore called Chatham. After that, it's out to Pittsburgh. He may or may not stay the night. Either way, it's back to New York. I think he's in the city all day tomorrow."

"What hotel in Pittsburgh is he staying at if he doesn't go back to New York tonight?"

"I don't know."

"Find out."

Wright hesitated. "All right."

"And find out what he's doing tomorrow, just in case. You hear me?"

"Yes."

"You say 'Yes, sir' to me, understand?"

Wright bit his tongue so hard that it almost bled. "Yes, sir."

Paul chuckled harshly. "Good boy, Davy, good boy. Talk to you later."

Wright hung up and put the cell phone back in his pocket slowly, wondering if Gillette would make it back to New York alive. Wondering what it meant for him if these people did anything to his boss.

THE ADDRESS Ganze had given Gillette on the phone was in Alexandria, Virginia, ten miles west of Washington. Not downtown, as Gillette had expected. And Ganze still hadn't given him the name of the company, consulting firm, or whatever it was he worked for or represented.

The place turned out to be nothing special. Just a plain suite on the fifth floor of a nondescript office building, a long walk down the corridor from the elevators. There was no receptionist, no logo, and no sign identifying what or who they were—just Ganze waiting outside the numbered door. Ganze wouldn't allow Stiles into Boyd's office for the meeting but did agree to let Stiles and another agent wait in the small reception area. There were three individual offices in the stark space, each sparsely furnished—Ganze had to lug a chair into Boyd's office from another one so they could all sit down.

"Why all the cloak-and-dagger crap?" Gillette asked as he sat, noticing that the blinds on the window behind Boyd's desk were down. "What is all this?"

"First, you need to sign something," Boyd announced, handing Gillette a single sheet of paper with a signature line at the bottom. Gillette's name was typed in bold capital letters beneath the line.

Gillette scanned the paper quickly, then handed it back to Boyd with a smile. It was a blind confidentiality agreement covering anything and everything discussed in the meeting—or at any time afterward with Boyd and Ganze. "No way I'm signing that." The penalty for violating the agreement was incarceration in a federal penitentiary for up to thirty years. "No way in hell."

"We have to know you'll keep your mouth shut," Boyd snapped. "You're going to be privy to top-secret information, information even the brass at the CIA and the FBI don't have."

"Let's assume for a moment I'd even consider signing something like that. Paragraph five says that the government has the right, in its sole discretion, to determine whether or not I've violated the agreement, and that I have no right to trial or due process." He shook his head. "You've **got** to be kidding me."

"That's the only way it works," Boyd said. "If you had the right to due process, you'd threaten to tell everybody what you knew in court, and we'd have to back down. It's for your protection, too."

"Bullshit."

"I know it seems a little over-the-top," Ganze spoke up gently, "but we've never had a problem. No one's ever gone to jail because they signed one of these."

"There's always a first time."

"Just consider it," Ganze urged.

"You've got my word," Gillette said, "and that's all you're going to get."

"That's not enough," Boyd growled.

"Too bad."

"Mr. Gillette," Ganze said, "I really think—"

"Well, this was a huge waste of time," Gillette interrupted, standing up.

"Sit down," Boyd ordered.

Gillette turned to go.

"Don't leave," Ganze pleaded.

Gillette turned back around.

"Do we have your word?" Ganze asked.

"I just told you that."

"Mr. Boyd needs to hear it once more," Ganze said, gesturing at his superior.

Gillette glanced at Boyd.

Boyd nodded.

"Okay, you've got my word."

"Prison isn't our only option," Boyd warned. "I assume you understand that."

"Come on, Norman," Ganze said. "We don't have to——"

"I understand that," Gillette said grimly, sitting down. They could always take that step whenever they wanted. But he wasn't going to give them the ability to unilaterally stick him in Leavenworth for the rest of his life. That would be worse than death.

Boyd made an irritated face and shook his head wearily.

As though he were dead tired of taking on so much responsibility, Gillette thought. At least they had that in common.

"Have you ever heard of DARPA?" Boyd asked.

Gillette thought for a second. "I'm not sure. What does it stand for?"

"The Defense Advanced Research Projects Agency."

"Oh, sure." Gillette recognized the full name. "The guys who invented GPS and the Internet, right?"

"Yeah. It's basically the Defense Department's dream tank," Ganze explained. "They contract with chemists, engineers, biochemists, physicists, and other kinds of doctors from the best universities and companies in the country, then let them loose to develop next-generation weapons and systems for the armed forces. But, as you pointed out, Christian, lots of great things they've invented have ultimately gotten into the hands of the public, too. Things that have made everyday life more efficient, safer, and, in some cases, more fun. The computer mouse, the Hummer. A lot of people don't know that the government invents this stuff, then gives it away when it's declassified."

"Sells it, too," Gillette added. "A lot of people don't know that, either."

"What's wrong with the government getting a return on its money?" Boyd demanded. "Companies do."

Ganze rolled his eyes. "Norman, don't—"

"The government isn't in business to make a profit," Gillette shot back. "At least, it isn't supposed to be."

"Don't be naïve," Boyd warned.

"Believe me," Gillette said forcefully, "I'm not. Look, I wouldn't care if those government profits reduced taxes, but from what I hear there are bureaucrats walking around D.C. making a damn good living off selling what the government invents. I doubt that's what Washington and Jefferson had in mind."

"Washington and Jefferson didn't have to worry about profits," Boyd snapped, "they were already rich."

Gillette said nothing.

Boyd fumed for a second, then put his hands flat on the desk. "Let's not get off track here. I don't want to get into some damn philosophical discussion about what the government might or might not be in business to do. Let's talk about one thing we'd all agree the government is in business to do, and that's protect our country from its enemies." He held out his arms, palms up. "All right?"

Gillette nodded.

"Good." Boyd took a moment to gather his thoughts. "Like I said, DARPA's mission is to come up with next-generation defense technologies. Star Wars stuff. Body armor that can start healing wounds even before soldiers make it to a forward hospital; telepathic command systems for fighter pilots; research on hemispheric sleep that allows one side of the brain to function while the other rests, so a soldier can effectively fight twenty-four hours a day. Darkening glass that can save at least one of a pilot's eyes during a nuclear blast. Cutting-edge projects that might seem like science fiction today but could ultimately become reality."

"Are you guys DARPA?" Gillette asked.

"Not technically," Ganze answered, "but we work closely with them. We're called GARD, the Government Advanced Research Department. We're set up to take on projects that are too secret for DARPA to handle."

"Why can't DARPA handle projects that are so secret?"

"Like most agencies," Boyd spoke up again, "over time, DARPA's developed an infrastructure and, worse, a reputation. For excellence, I'll grant you, but in this business you want to run quiet like a nuclear sub. You don't want **any** reputation. Another reason they run into problems on the supersecret stuff is the temporary nature of the agency's employees. Like I told you, we pull experts out of the private sector, which the companies and universities aren't happy about, so we have to plug them back in at some point. But that revolving door facilitates information flow, if you get my drift."

"Sure."

"So we need an agency that can handle the very top-secret stuff when there's a problem."

"Like what?" Gillette asked.

"Spies, basically. On projects that involve national security. I mean, we don't care much if our enemies find out about little things DARPA invents before they're declassified." Boyd's expression turned grave. "But there are certain projects that have to stay hidden from everyone. From terrorists right on down to some of our own senators and congressmen," he said. "I don't like hiding important things from our own lawmakers, but some of them just can't keep secrets. Sad, but true."

"I can relate to that," Gillette muttered. "I assume you have that situation now," he said, anticipating where Boyd was headed. "A spy issue, I mean."

"Right. And this project involves one of the most incredible technologies I've ever seen. We've got to keep this thing protected."

Gillette was interested now. "What is it?"

Boyd stared at Gillette evenly for several moments before answering. "Nanotechnology."

Gillette nodded. He'd heard about nanotech.

"The ability to produce structures at the molecular level," Boyd continued. "I'm talking about being able to build self-assembling micromachines with a diameter eighty thousand times smaller than the diameter of a human hair."

Gillette had talked to several venture capitalists who'd set up pools of money to fund preliminary research on nanotech. "I know there's a lot of work going on in that space, but people I talk to say that stuff is way out in the future. At least thirty to forty years before anything meaningful is developed. They say it might not even be real at all, just hype so scientists and institutes can get research dollars and maintain lifestyles. And the guys I've talked to would know."

"Forget for a second **when** and think about **what**," Boyd suggested. "Think about what it could do for us, for our military and intelligence capabilities, specifically." His eyes were flashing. "We could develop supersoldiers. Using nanotech machines, men could carry hundreds of pounds of the latest battlefield equipment but still run three times faster than the fastest men we have today. They'd be able to wear thick armor that could withstand almost anything while remaining agile. They'd be able to carry computers and heavy weapons that would make today's soldiers look like minutemen. They'd be almost invincible."

"How would nanotechnology help us develop supersoldiers?" Gillette asked.

"Scientists could develop exoskeletons, like intelligent armor that would fortify with artificial muscles what the body could do. They would synchronize with microsensors injected into the soldiers' bodies."

"But **how?**"

"The machines carry micro-microcomputers, nanocomputers, that take their cues from what the brain wants to do. They transmit those cues from the soldier's body as signals to the exoskeleton. The exoskeleton amplifies the physical abilities of the soldier. It's much faster and tremendously more effective than any kind of physical training. It's superhero shit come to life, Christian." Boyd took a breath. "Then there's the whole repair side. Scalpels and stitches will seem like butcher tools after we perfect nanotech. We'll be able to direct cells to discard the dead, then reform and renew. Fast. There'll be no such things as scars anymore, external or internal. More important, we'll be able to fight diseases at the molecular level. We'll send armies of nanoterminators into the body to kill cancer cells, AIDS cells, whatever." Boyd spread his arms wide. "Things we can't come close to doing now. The possibilities are endless."

Gillette's mind was humming. He was fascinated.

"You mentioned intelligence, too. What's the application there?"

"We'll be able to inject undetectable nanochips into the bodies of our undercover agents. Like microcameras, they'll record everything. Audio and video, so that the information can be retrieved later. Nothing will be left to memory. No mistakes will be made." He held up his hand. "Better still, in situations where we can't penetrate, we can actually use the enemy to help us without them even knowing."

"How?"

"Say we want to listen in on the Russian embassy here in Washington. We can put a nanochip into the nose drops or cold medicine of a Russian secretary who's sick, or into the aspirin of the ambassador or one of his or her staff who suffers from migraines. The machine the chip is attached to directs the chip to become lodged in a certain sector of the target's body—the eye, the ear—and suddenly we have a direct line into the embassy without the host or his associates ever knowing. No more digging tunnels beneath streets, no more clandestine missions trying to plant bugs that are detected within hours anyway and put people's lives at risk."

There were negative implications to all this, too. **How** negative was the question. "What do you want from me?" Gillette asked.

"Remember how you said that the people you talked to, those people who would know, told you that nanotechnology was decades off? That maybe it was just hype so researchers could maintain lifestyles by taking dollars from investors, including the government, who desperately want to see it happen?"

"I don't think I said all that," Gillette answered, "but I understand what you're saying."

"It isn't just hype, Christian. We're close." Boyd glanced over at Ganze. "**Very** close."

Gillette's eyes flickered between Boyd and Ganze. He wondered how many other secrets of this magnitude they kept. "How do **I** fit in?"

"I'm getting to that," Boyd answered. "So far, this project has been housed inside DARPA, not actually at DARPA's headquarters, which is over in Arlington not far from here, but at a university in the Northeast. Unfortunately, as you guessed, we think we have a spy problem. One of the senior biochemists on the project has been contacted by someone with close ties to al-Qaeda. The top people on the project don't know it, but we watch them constantly. The biochemist and the terrorist link have met three times. We haven't been able to record their conversations yet, but we don't have the luxury of time or giving our guy the benefit of the doubt."

"What are you going to do?"

"That's where you come in, Christian. We need to strip the project out of DARPA and use a cutout."

Gillette was familiar with the term. At one of their dinners, Senator Clark had described how the government sometimes used private companies to hide, or as fronts for, clandestine operations involving the CIA, the DIA, the NSA, and other intelligence agencies. How back in the sixties the International Telephone and Telegraph Company had bugged foreign embassies for the United States government, mostly in South America, while installing telephone systems for profit. How cutouts had become even more prevalent today and how typically only a few of the top officers in the company knew what was really going on. How numerous Fortune 500 companies were involved in such projects.

"You want to use an Everest company?" Gillette asked, anticipating what they were looking for.

"That's right."

"Why don't you just take the guy who's been contacted by the terrorist link off the project? Or take out the terrorist link?"

Boyd shook his head. "That would alert al-Qaeda that we know what's going on. Then they might try to get to someone else, or panic and do something crazy. We think it's a better idea to quietly lift the vital components of the nanotech project out of DARPA and slip it into one of your companies. We've already identified it."

"Which one do you want to use?"

"Beezer Johnson. Your medical products company. Specifically the division that develops and manufactures pacemakers, heart valves, and other very specialized products. That division works well for us from a number of different perspectives. First, and most important, it's based in Minneapolis. One of the leaders of the nanotech project, one of the people we trust implicitly, is from Minneapolis and has very good connections at the university's medical school and at the Mayo Clinic down in Rochester. Both will be excellent resources as the team finishes this thing. We intend to remove her and two other members of her team from the group and relocate them into space at Beezer in Minneapolis. We'll add a few people she's selected from a couple of other universities and companies in the U.S. to replace the people who will remain where the project is based now."

"Where is that?"

"Doesn't matter."

"Won't the people who stay, including the person who's been contacted by the terrorist link, won't they be suspicious when those people don't show up one day?" Gillette asked.

"No," Boyd answered quickly. "There's going to be an accident, Christian, a plane crash. No one, including their families, will know that they are really alive and well until after the project is complete. When it's done, they'll be able to go home. Hopefully within six months."

"Do these people have families? Spouses and kids, I mean."

"They're all married, and they all have children," Ganze spoke up. "Unfortunately."

Gillette groaned. "Shouldn't you at least tell the spouses what's really going on?"

"I can't risk detection," Boyd snapped.

"What if one of the spouses is so upset they commit suicide?"

"We're going to monitor that carefully," Ganze said. "Hopefully we'll recognize the signs and be able to stop anything—"

"But ultimately I can't worry about it," Boyd interrupted, his voice rising. "My job is to protect the project and this country. I can't allow what we have to get into our enemies' hands. It has to be kept secret at all costs. If someone is so weak they have to kill themselves because of the loss of a loved one, well, that's not my problem. And I won't lose a minute of sleep over it. I'm trying to make the world better for millions here, not individuals." He stuck his chin out fiercely. "Will you cooperate with us?"

"I don't know."

"You better decide fast."

Gillette eased back into his chair. "What about **my** questions?"

Boyd pointed at Ganze. "Daniel."

Ganze took out a small notepad from his jacket pocket. "Here's what I can tell you right now."

Gillette looked up. He'd been staring down, considering everything he'd heard.

"Your blood mother still lives in Los Angeles. Her name's Marilyn McRae."

"How do you know?"

Ganze held up his hand. "Don't try to contact her

yet. We need to talk to her again first. Give us twenty-four hours."

"Okay," Gillette agreed, his blood pressure ticking up with each passing moment. "What about my father?"

"What I've been able to find out, what my sources have uncovered, is that sixteen years ago your father may have stumbled onto a plot to assassinate the president. This is still sketchy, and I should know more in the next few days, but it appears that he uncovered a left-wing conspiracy to kill George Bush. Obviously, it didn't go anywhere, but your father was killed so he couldn't tell anyone."

The room blurred in front of Gillette. "What?" he whispered hoarsely.

"I know it sounds incredible, but we think that's what happened. Like I said, we should have more information in the next few days."

"So, you gonna help us?" Boyd growled.

Gillette looked across the desk.

"Well?" Boyd demanded.

Gillette glanced from Boyd to Ganze several times. He'd made a career out of taking risks. But never one like this.

THE FLIGHT TO the Eastern Shore would take no more than a few minutes. As the jet powered up and began accelerating down the runway, Gillette put his head back and tried to relax. But it was hard. So many things were running through his mind. Apparently, his father had been murdered after all. He'd felt that in his gut for so long, but now he was close to proving it. And he was finally going to meet his blood mother.

He desperately wished Faith would call him back. He couldn't tell her much about what had happened, but he wanted to share with her the part about meeting his real mother.

"What's wrong?"

Gillette swiveled toward Stiles. He stared at the other man for a few moments but said nothing.

"Come on, Chris," Stiles urged. "What happened in the meeting?"

Gillette ran both hands through his hair. "I made a deal."

"So? You make deals every day."

"Not like this." He looked out the window as the plane lifted off. It was a crystal clear day, and suddenly he had a beautiful view of Washington, D.C. "I agreed to let them use one of our companies in return for information that's only important to me." He thought about how he could justify the deal in the name of national security, but that wasn't why he'd done it. "That's a first for me, and it doesn't feel good. But I've **got** to know what happened to my dad," he said under his breath.

"Who are these guys?"

"Can't tell you."

"Why not?"

Stiles would never tell anyone anything Gillette didn't want him to, but it wasn't about that. Men like Boyd didn't make vague threats. If Boyd thought Stiles knew what he and Ganze were about, Stiles would be in danger. As long as Stiles really didn't know, he'd have a chance if things got sticky. "It's for your own good."

"Oh, come—"

"I'm not kidding."

"Did they tell you anything good?"

Gillette nodded. "Yeah. They know who my real mother is. At least they say they do," he muttered.

"When do you talk to her?"

"Tomorrow. They're going to give me her number then."

"What about your father's plane crash?" Stiles asked. "Anything about that?"

"They gave me a little information on that. They said they'd know more in the next few days."

"So they're for real?"

"I'll let you know after I talk to this woman they claim is my mother." Gillette exhaled heavily. "Quentin, I need you to do me a favor, and this has to stay very quiet."

"What?"

"I need you to check out Allison for me."

"I thought Craig West already did."

"You've got to check on something he didn't. If she's into drugs. Cocaine."

"What makes you think she might be?"

Gillette shrugged. He felt bad even bringing this up, but he had no choice. He had to protect the investors. "She was sniffing up a hurricane at dinner, especially after she came back from the restroom. She said it was allergies, but I'm not so sure."

Stiles grimaced. "You always think the worst," he said quietly.

"I have to."

"Sure," Stiles agreed, his voice intensifying, "I'll check it out. But why do you care so much? You've got her family's money. She gets caught with the white powder, you let her go, but you keep the money." He paused. "Is there something else going on here?"

Gillette knew what that meant. "No."

"Come on, Chris. Are you interested in her? You can tell me."

"It's not that, Quentin. I'm serious. What I'm thinking is, she's good. **Very** good. And she's connected as hell." Gillette paused. "She'd make a great permanent addition to Everest. Might even be capable of running the show at some point." He shook his head. "But not if she's into coke."

"**Running the show**? Where are **you** going?"

"Nowhere. Not anytime soon. At least, I hope I'm not. 'Course, as long as Tom McGuire's out there, you never know."

"I thought you were grooming David Wright. I thought he was your guy."

"Never hurts to have another option."

"Isn't it a little early to start thinking about Allison being the next chairman?" Stiles asked. "Jesus, you just met her."

"I trust my gut. You know that. My gut tells me she might be the one."

"Remember, Chris," Stiles warned, "blood's thicker than water. She's going home someday, back to Chicago." He cocked his head to one side. "You do like her, don't you? Come on. A little, right?"

Gillette fought to hide a grin but couldn't. "She's a piece of work, I'll tell you that."

"What about Faith?"

Gillette let out a long breath. "Yeah, Faith." He reached for the phone, trying to forget about how many times he'd called her last night.

Stiles leaned forward and held out a section of the newspaper he'd folded into a rectangle the size of a piece of paper. "Put the phone away, Chris. Work on this instead."

"What is it?"

"A crossword puzzle. It'll take your mind off things."

MILES WHITMAN moved onto the flowery veranda of his spacious three-bedroom villa and gazed out over the Mediterranean Sea in the fading light of another beautiful evening on the French Riviera.

Whitman had been nervous as hell on the flight from Kennedy to Milan last November. But once he'd gotten off the 747 and slipped into the airport crowd, he'd felt better. Even more relieved when he was out of the airport and in the cab headed downtown. He'd spent two weeks in Milan, two weeks in Rome, a month in Athens, and three months in Lisbon before settling in the south of France. He'd been here now for five months. Unless he did something incredibly stupid, he was safe. His cutout people, the ones who'd helped him hide the forty million dollars in return for allowing them to use North America Guaranty as their own little spy machine for the last nine years, would never roll over on him.

He took another sniff of the flowers, thinking about how Monique would be here soon. Thinking about how her heavenly twenty-four-year-old body would soon be draped all over him. Monique could do things his wife back in Connecticut would have a heart attack just thinking about. The little French kitten made for exquisite company—as long as she got to shop at the most expensive boutiques every day. C'est la vie, he thought. Everything had its price.

Whitman turned and walked back into the living room. A man he'd never seen before was waiting there, hands clasped behind his back.

Whitman took one look at him and spun around, ready to take his chances with the two-story leap from the veranda. But his path was blocked by two more large men who closed the double doors, cutting off any chance of escape. His head snapped left when another, smaller man ambled out of the bathroom, casually smoking a cigar. This man Whitman knew.

"Hello, Miles," the man said smoothly, moving directly in front of Whitman. "I'm afraid this is going to have a bad ending for you. But it can be easy, so you don't feel pain. Or it can be hard. **Very hard.** Your choice. All you have to do is answer a few questions and I promise the end will be quick and clean." He eased down into a wicker chair. "Now, let's talk."

9

"**I DON'T LIKE YOU.** At all."

Tell me how you really feel, Gillette thought. "We **just** met. You don't even know me."

"I know your **kind.**"

Becky Rouse was tall and thin, in her early forties, with shoulder-length dirty blond hair, hazel eyes, and a naturally determined expression. She was the mayor of Chatham, Maryland, a picturesque three-hundred-year-old fishing village set on the north bank of the wide Chester River a few miles upstream from where it met the Chesapeake Bay.

Becky had first been elected mayor five years ago—she was in the middle of her second four-year term. She'd moved to Chatham from Washington after a messy divorce from her lawyer husband, picking the town literally by tacking up a map of Maryland on her kitchen wall and throwing a dart. Originally from Georgia, she had no desire to go back. Her family had disowned her for marrying a Yankee.

Soon after moving to Chatham, she'd become friends with several female members of the town council who'd persuaded her to run against the incumbent, Jimmy Wilcox. Wilcox was a crotchety blue-crab captain who drank a case of Budweiser every day—winter or summer, rain or shine, healthy or sick. Thanks to the beer, he wasn't much fun to be around by the time the sun dipped low in the western sky, whether the crab pots were full that day or not.

As part of her campaign, Becky advertised that during his tenure, Jimmy had missed more than sixty percent of all town council meetings; accused him of buying a new pickup with treasury funds; and made it clear to everyone that tourist revenues were down twenty-five percent. She'd won the first election by fewer than three hundred votes, the second by a landslide.

Chatham's population was just under twenty thousand people, many of whom had never graduated from high school. Like most places, it was divided into the haves and the have-nots. The haves included families who'd owned huge tracts of land from way back; wealthy retirees who'd moved to the area from Wilmington, Baltimore, and Washington; yuppies and dinks who'd bought riverfront weekend homes; and proprietors who owned the waterfront shops. The have-nots were the fishermen, crabbers, and farmers whose families had been working the Chesapeake Bay and the land around it for years but had little to show for it.

The haves had tepidly supported Becky in the first election, not sure what to expect. But they'd become smitten with her when, soon after taking office, she attracted free state money for waterfront restoration, had the harbor dredged so large pleasure boats could tie up at the marinas and restaurants, moved the unsightly and smelly fish market to the other end of town, and advertised Chatham's new weekend festivals—her creations—in **The Washington Post** and the Baltimore **Sun.** Suddenly tourists were flocking to town. Just as suddenly, shop owners were making a killing and property values were skyrocketing.

"What **kind** do you think I am?" Gillette asked as they walked slowly along Main Street in the warm afternoon sunshine. He was wearing sunglasses, and his suit coat was slung over his shoulder.

Becky smiled sweetly at a mother and two children as they passed by, then glanced over her shoulder at the two QS agents following close behind. "You're about money. You've always had it, you always will, and the only thing that drives you is your desire to make more."

"Look, you should know that—"

"You want to put up that big discount store over on the west side of town," she continued, "and ruin what I've worked hard to build, all in the name of profits. That's what kind you are."

"How will putting up the store ruin what you've built?"

"It'll take business away from **my** waterfront."

"What it will do," Gillette said, "is give the people in this area who don't have a lot of money a nice place to shop for decent products at affordable prices. They won't have to go all the way over to Delaware to buy home supplies and toys for their kids."

Becky sniffed. "The citizens of this town are fine."

"They're not fine. I spoke to a few of them and they're ticked off that you're blocking this thing." Before meeting Becky, Gillette had walked around the docks and spoken to some of the fishermen coming in from the morning catch. "They want this store."

She pointed a bony finger at him. "Don't try to make like you're some champion of the poor. You want this store so you can stay ahead of Wal-Mart. Chatham is very strategic for you geographically, I've looked at the map. You'll draw from everywhere. Your interest here is completely selfish. Once you get this store built, you'll never set foot in Chatham again. You'll go back to your homes in Manhattan, Easthampton, the south of France. But **I** have to live **here.**"

"Why do the people who matter to you even care?" he asked. "The blue-collar folks don't shop on the waterfront. It's the rich and the tourists who come here."

"We'll become known as that town with the Discount America. I can already see the write-up in the **Post,**" she said, holding her thumb and forefinger an inch apart and moving them across in front of her face. " 'Stay away from Chatham,' it'll say, 'it's the strip mall capital of the Eastern Shore.' "

"What you'll become known as is the town that's got a healthy treasury," Gillette argued. "The property taxes alone will pay for fire, police, and EMT, not to mention the economic benefit from the jobs the DA store and the smaller stores that pop up around it will create."

As they rounded a corner, Becky stopped and put her hands on her hips. "What are you willing to offer me?"

He'd been ready for this. "What do you want?" **Never** offer first. **Always** counter.

"That jackass Harry Stein said something about an elementary school. Which is fine for starters, but rest assured, I'll want a lot more than that, Mr. Gillette."

He'd asked her several times to call him Christian, but she'd refused so he'd stopped trying. "Like what?"

"A retirement home with at least two hundred beds, three new squad cars for the police force, a rescue boat for the fire department, and a couple of school buses."

"How about a pool and a hot tub for every home in town?" Gillette shot back. "Free steaks for a year.

A hundred thousand in cash for everyone. We'll call this 'Little Kuwait.' "

She gave him a disdainful look. "Give me a couple of days. I'll come up with more."

"You know I'm not going to give you everything you just asked for, Becky. It wouldn't be worth it for me financially. No single store location is worth all that, not unless it's on the corner of Forty-second Street and Seventh Ave."

"You've got **billions,** Mr. Gillette. I checked your Web site this morning. Everest Capital just raised another huge fund. I believe it was fifteen billion dollars. And you can't buy me a few necessities for my town?" She turned and headed into O'Malley's Bar & Grill. "Please, Mr. Gillette," she called over her shoulder. "Please."

Gillette followed her into the pub, reaching for his cell phone as he went through the door. Wright was calling. "What is it, David?" he asked, tossing his coat and sunglasses on the bar.

"I got the signed letter back from Maddox," Wright answered. "We're done."

"Good." At least something was going right today.

"And Tom O'Brien wanted you to know that the city of Las Vegas called. They want you to fly out next week for a few meetings they've set up with the appropriate people."

He was sure that **"appropriate people"** meant the individuals who could help him start the casino process. "Tell him to work it out with Debbie, will you?"

"Okay."

"This is a priority, so make sure it happens. Stay on Tom and Debbie about it."

"I'll take care of it, don't worry."

"Thanks." Gillette slipped the phone back in his pocket and checked his watch. It was two-thirty; he had to get out of here soon if he was going to be in Pittsburgh by seven for dinner with Jack Mitchell.

"Here's what we'd have to deal with, Bob," Becky said loudly to the bartender, pointing at Gillette as he sat next to her. "A man who brings his security detail with him everywhere he goes, like he's really that important, and thinks cell phones are more essential than people." She took a sip from the beer she'd ordered. "Rude, too. We were in the middle of a conversation when we walked in here."

Gillette glanced at Bob, who was cleaning a mug and shaking his head.

"So where did you send Stein?" she asked, picking up the large glass of water Bob had put down beside her beer.

She was smart, Gillette realized. She wasn't going to drink more than a sip of the beer. It was a weekday afternoon, and she'd ridden her opponent about all-day drinking in her first campaign, so she couldn't do it herself. But she wanted to put money in Bob's pocket, too. "On an errand," he answered.

When they were introduced, he could tell she couldn't stand Stein, so he'd sent the CEO off to talk to more watermen.

Gillette pointed at what Becky had ordered. "Same, please, Bob. A beer and a water." He noticed an outside deck overlooking the river on the other side of the place. "Let's go outside," he suggested, picking up his sunglasses and the water glass. A couple of other people hanging around the bar seemed to be listening too carefully, and he didn't want this turning into an impromptu public forum. Becky had turned out to be cagey, and he didn't trust her motives. The move into O'Malley's had been too convenient. "Come on," he called when she didn't follow right away.

He moved through the screen door and sat at a wooden table with an umbrella, putting the water down amid the remnants of bright orange smashed steamed crab shells. The glare of the afternoon sun off the river's calm surface was brilliant, so he put his sunglasses back on, then took a deep breath, taking in the Old Bay seasoning from the crab shells, the salt water, and a trace of wood smoke from some far-off pile of burning leaves. He liked it here. Maybe he'd buy a place on the river. Someday.

A few moments later, Becky came through the door and sat on the other side of the table. "Why'd you want to come out here? It's awfully bright."

"I didn't feel like negotiating in front of half the

town council." He'd recognized two of the men from pictures Craig West had included in the prep memo he'd reviewed on the short flight from D.C.

She smiled at him for the first time. "Well, aren't you a worthy opponent."

"That's the rumor. Look, here's what I'll do," he kept going, not giving her a chance to speak up, "I'll buy you half your elementary school and the three police cruisers. For that, I get my store."

She laughed loudly. "You must be joking."

He spotted a **USA Today** lying on another table, stood up, and walked to it, leafing through the sections until he found the one containing the crossword. "I never joke about Everest business, Ms. Rouse," he said, folding the newspaper and stashing it under his arm, then moving back to where she was and standing in front of her so the sun was behind him. That way she had to squint. "If you don't agree to my offer, I'll rally the people of this town against you and you'll have the biggest shit-storm this side of the Mississippi on your hands. At my direction, they'll call for a referendum, which they're allowed to do under the town charter. My lawyers have checked, and I guarantee you I'll win. I've got the numbers as long as I get people out to vote. And believe me, I'll rent buses if I have to." He took off his sunglasses. "I'll expect your call no later than Friday at five P.M. If I don't hear from you, we'll start the referendum process." He dropped a twenty on the table in front of her. "Beers are on me."

...

TOM MCGUIRE walked along the wide, white-sand beach of Avalon, New Jersey, a quaint seaside resort town a hundred miles south of New York City. Avalon was built on a narrow strip of land that ran between the Atlantic Ocean and an extended bay in southern New Jersey. As far as anyone else knew, a man named William Cooper was renting a house on the bay side with a month-to-month lease. So far, McGuire hadn't run into any problems.

Avalon's busy season ran from Memorial Day to Labor Day. Now, in late September, the beach was almost deserted. Just a few elderly couples who'd retired to the town combing the beach for shells in the afternoon sunshine.

McGuire pulled the brim of his Baltimore Orioles baseball cap low over his sunglasses and looked down as he passed one of the older couples walking slowly the other way. He was taking no chances on being recognized. If he looked right at them, they might remember him later if they saw his picture on television. He'd already been featured once on **America's Most Wanted.**

When he passed them, he stopped and gazed out to sea, the cool water of a dying wave running over his toes just before it hissed, hesitated for a moment, then receded against his heels and washed back into the ocean. Everything had gone exactly according to plan, thanks to the hotel operator at the Parker

Meridien who had listened in on Allison Wallace's telephone calls. The photographers had shown up at the Grill right on time and Gillette had ducked out the back, headlong into the trap. But it was as if the guy had a hundred lives. Gillette and Stiles had been outnumbered and outgunned, but Gillette had turned the tables by going on the attack—something McGuire hadn't anticipated.

McGuire's expression hardened into one of resolve as another wave hissed past his feet. He was going to take care of Gillette sooner or later, one way or another.

"Afternoon."

McGuire's eyes flashed left, toward the voice. The man standing a few feet away wore a baseball cap and sunglasses, too, but he was younger, in his mid-thirties. "Hello," he answered gruffly.

"Nice day, huh?"

"Yeah. Nice."

"Looking for shells?"

"Nah, just taking a walk."

"Live here?"

"Visiting," McGuire replied.

"Where you staying?"

McGuire glanced over at the man again. He was looking out to sea intently from behind his sunglasses, watching a ship on the horizon. "Up the beach."

"Really? Could have sworn I saw you going into

a house over on the bay side yesterday. That's where I'm staying. On the bay side."

McGuire shook his head. "You got the wrong guy."

The man shrugged. "My mistake." He smiled. "Well, take care."

McGuire watched the man move off, wondering what the hell that had been about. Wondering if it was time for William Cooper to make another move.

IT WAS THE THIRD TIME since Gillette had left Chatham that he'd tried Faith on both her cell phone and her private apartment line in New York. Still no answer, and no return call. She was getting the messages—she checked her phone religiously, every fifteen minutes when he was with her—she just wasn't answering. He knew what was going on. She was trying to teach him a lesson. But he wasn't guilty. As he sat back down at the table, Allison smiled and leaned toward him.

"Everything okay?" she asked, squeezing his arm.

Allison's touch caused a shiver to race up his back and reminded him that it had been a month since he and Faith had made love. He looked over at her. She was wearing her hair up and looked pretty in an off-the-shoulders dress she'd changed into after they'd gotten to the hotel. "Everything's fine. I'm going to

Las Vegas next week to start that process we talked about." She'd taken a helicopter from Manhattan down to Chatham to meet him, and he'd brought her up to speed on the casino during the flight to Pittsburgh.

"I want to go with you on that trip," she said immediately.

"Well—"

"What do you have going on out in Las Vegas?" Jack Mitchell asked loudly. Mitchell was the CEO and controlling shareholder of Veramax. He was a big man who was nearly bald and wore large, unfashionable glasses.

Sometimes rich people did that, Gillette knew. Wore things that were out of style just to show everybody else that they didn't have to care about fashion.

"A couple of days ago, the NFL awarded us the new Las Vegas franchise," Gillette replied. He wasn't going to tell Mitchell about the casino because he didn't want other casinos in Vegas hearing about their plans yet. According to Allison, Mitchell was pretty connected, and you never knew who knew who.

Mitchell banged the table with his palm. The silverware and plates rattled, and two of the water glasses almost fell over. "Damn, that's great. If we do a deal here, maybe I could get an invite to the first game."

"If we do a deal here, you'll have a standing invite to **all** the games," Gillette assured the other man. "Tell me about Veramax's products, will you, Jack?"

Mitchell cleared his throat and took a long swallow of Scotch. "Right now, our bread and butter is basic over-the-counter medicine. But we've got some hot new proprietary drugs just rarin' to go." A natural-born salesman, Mitchell used his hands a lot in conversation. "Dynamite stuff, but these FDA guys in Washington are dragging their heels."

"What's the problem?" Gillette asked. Allison hadn't explained the FDA problem yet or how she knew of his connection to Senator Clark. He reminded himself to drill her on that after dinner. "Why are they dragging their heels?"

"Ah, it's a long story," Mitchell said, waving a hand in front of his face.

"We haven't even gotten our salads yet, Jack. We've got plenty of time."

Mitchell set his jaw. "It's a damn personal thing with one of the senior people over there. A guy named Phil Rothchild. He's from Chicago, and we had a run-in a while back. It's stupid, but that's how things go sometimes. Silly and stupid."

"What happened?"

"It's embarrassing."

Gillette drew himself up in his chair. "Jack, if we're going to be partners, there can't be any secrets between us. If you expect me to go to Senator Clark on your behalf, I need to know what the deal is."

Mitchell grimaced. "Okay. I slept with Rothchild's daughter."

Gillette's eyes raced to Allison's.

"Jack's been divorced for five years," she explained, "and Rothchild's daughter was twenty-eight. Jack didn't do anything wrong."

"Rothchild was irritated because Amy, that's his daughter," Mitchell explained, "was seeing some young Wall Street punk at the time. Some guy from a well-to-do family in the Northeast. Like I'm not good enough or something," he said with a sneer, pointing his thumbs at himself. "Like Chicago isn't good enough. And it's such crap because Rothchild is from here. It's like he's turning his back on the Midwest, like he wants to join that Ivy League set or something, and I don't like that. Besides, I have way more money than that little prick Amy was seeing, even after my divorce."

"I still don't understand what caused the war."

"Rothchild thought I wasn't serious about Amy," Mitchell explained, "and, well, Amy was engaged to the Wall Street kid."

"Oh."

"Somehow"—Mitchell shrugged and rolled his eyes as if he had no idea how it could have happened—"the kid found out about our affair and dumped her."

"How did the kid find out?" Gillette asked.

Mitchell glanced down into his lap and grinned smugly. "I might have called him."

"Jesus." Gillette flashed Allison a look. "Are you still seeing Amy?"

Mitchell broke into a chuckle. "Nah, I decided that dating twenty-eight-year-olds wasn't a good idea."

From what Gillette could tell, Mitchell was probably at least fifty-five. "Yeah, I can understand why you'd—"

"They're too old," Mitchell interrupted. "My new girlfriend's twenty-three. Hot as hell, too."

Gillette put his elbows on the table and rubbed his face. People just couldn't keep themselves out of trouble—especially men with money.

"There's one more piece to the 'war,' as you called it," Mitchell continued.

"I can't wait to hear this," Gillette muttered.

"I kept Rothchild out of the Racquet Club in New York when he applied last year," Mitchell explained. "I've belonged there for almost thirty years, and I made a few calls to the membership committee. The guy never had a chance."

The Racquet Club was one of the most exclusive athletic clubs in New York. Gillette had been a member since becoming a managing partner at Everest five years ago. "Why did you do that?"

"Because of this whole thing with his daughter. I mean, he had no right to—"

"All right, all right," Gillette interrupted, holding up his hand. "I've heard enough. Look, here's what we're going to do. **First,**" he said emphatically, staring at Mitchell, "you're going to write Rothchild a letter, apologizing for keeping him out of the Racquet Club. **Don't call him,**" Gillette warned. "That would probably start World War Three. Just write him, and e-mail me a copy of what you've written before you send it. Then, you're going to get Rothchild in there."

"Aw, Jesus."

"Jack."

"Okay," Mitchell agreed softly, "I'll do it."

"Then," Gillette continued, "I'm going to Senator Clark to get his help. I'll probably have to relocate one of Everest's companies to California, for crying out loud, but leave that to me. I promise you that within two weeks the FDA will have your products on the rocket-docket approval process, or whatever they call it there." He took a breath. "In return for my help, you're going to sell me forty-nine percent of Veramax for half a billion dollars in cash. It's a fair price given what you've gotten yourself into. Half the cash will go to you, the other half will go into the company to fund research and development of new products. I'll get new shares and they'll be nondilutive, meaning that if you issue more shares to other investors while I own mine, I'll still own forty-nine percent. The last part of my deal with you is that you'll sell me an option to buy another two percent of the company for a million dollars. I'll only be able to execute that option if you don't go public by the end of next year, at least at a valuation we both agree to in the stock purchase agreement. But if you don't go public by then, I'll execute my option and control the company. Got all that?"

Mitchell gazed at Gillette for a few moments stone-faced, then broke into a wide smile. "Get the lawyers started, my friend." He nodded at Allison. "That little girl over there told me you were sharp. She was right."

Gillette took several swallows of water. "So tell me about these hot new products. What do they deal with?"

"Alzheimer's, male impotence, a day-after pill that really works. Things like that."

"And the basic over-the-counter stuff that's your bread and butter right now. What's that?"

Mitchell glanced at Allison, then took a long guzzle of his Scotch. "Aspirin, nose drops, and cold medicines. Liquids and pills."

Though he wasn't sure why, something clicked in Gillette's brain.

"**YOU SURE?**" Gillette asked. He was talking to Stiles on his cell phone as he waited for Allison. They'd finished dinner a few minutes ago and she was saying good-bye to Mitchell by the elevators before he went upstairs to his room. "No drugs?"

"You can never be **sure**." Stiles had flown back to New York that afternoon on the helicopter that had brought Allison down to Maryland. "But I spoke to a couple of people who would know, and there's no indication she's doing that. And," he continued, "she does have a history of allergy shots."

"Guess I was wrong." Gillette was sitting on a sofa in a secluded section of the hotel lobby. He spotted Allison walking toward him. "It's amazing how you get this stuff so fast."

"I'll check a few more sources tomorrow," Stiles offered, "but I think she's clean."

"Okay."

"You coming back tonight?" Stiles wanted to know.

"No. In the morning."

"Uh-huh. Well, stay out of trouble."

Gillette glanced at two QS agents who were standing against a far wall, trying to seem inconspicuous. "I told you, it's not like that."

"It never is," Stiles said, "until it is."

Gillette groaned. "Good night, Plato."

"Night."

"Who was that?" Allison asked, sitting beside Gillette on the sofa as he closed his cell phone. "That pop-star girlfriend of yours?"

"No, Stiles."

"You two trying to dig up secrets on me?"

Gillette raised one eyebrow. "Absolutely."

"Have fun. You won't find anything." She pushed her hair back over her ears and relaxed onto the sofa. "How did you think it went tonight with Jack?"

"Fine. He needs to start taking self-control pills or he's going to get himself in trouble."

Allison waved and made a face. "He's just a harmless old flirt from a different age." She laughed. "Lord, he made a pass at me a few minutes ago. He does every time I see him."

"In this age, old flirts cause multimillion-dollar lawsuits."

"Oh, don't worry so much." She put up a hand before he could respond. "I know, I know. It's what you do. Well, don't do it tonight. Give yourself a break. By the way," she said, her voice rising, "I may have another deal for us. A friend of Jack's here in Pittsburgh owns a large truck-leasing company, and he may want to sell it. It could fit really well with that leasing company in Atlanta you already control. I'll follow up tomorrow."

Allison Wallace was young, but she was already a rainmaker. No doubt. And he wanted those talents for his own. "Would you ever consider joining Everest full time?" Gillette asked. At times, he almost got a high by being blunt. By shocking people. "Let someone else in the family take your spot on the family trust's board?"

She smiled at him coyly. "Don't beat around the bush, Christian. Why don't you just ask me to marry you?"

Gillette felt his face flush, caught off guard right back. "No, I—"

"You never know," Allison said softly, "I might be convinced to join Everest. But I'd have a few conditions."

"Such as?"

She ran her hand up the lapel of his suit jacket, then brushed the backs of her fingers across his cheek. "I'll let you know."

HE WAS IN A prison cell. On death row. Trying to make the man sitting on the chair beside him, the man wearing the white collar, understand that he hadn't killed anyone. That he was innocent. He was pleading, the desperate words cascading from his parched mouth, but the priest wouldn't listen. Then the warden and his deputies—a short parade of tall, faceless men—were outside the cell, ready to take him to the execution chamber. As they were leading him away, he turned to make one last pitiful appeal, and as he did, the priest became his father.

"Jesus!" Gillette hissed, rising to a sitting position on the bed and rubbing his eyes. His head was pounding from the intensity of the images.

After a few moments and several deep breaths, he dropped his feet to the floor and sat on the edge of the bed, still half-in, half-out of the dream. Finally, he checked the clock—3:15—then turned on the light and picked up his Blackberry off the night table. He needed a few minutes to shake the dream before he tried to go back to sleep.

The first new e-mail was from Faith, sent only an hour ago. It read:

Chris, I love you. Sorry I was such a jerk at your office the other night. I was tired from the flight, and the last thing I needed was to run straight into the woman I thought about strangling (kidding . . . sort of) the whole way back on the plane. I got your phone messages—sorry I haven't returned them. I said I was a jerk, didn't I? Please call me first thing in the morning (as soon as you wake up). I have to go to London tomorrow afternoon for a few days—should be back Sunday or Monday. More promo stuff. Ugh!! I would have called you, but I didn't want to wake you up. I know how busy you are. I love you so much.

When Gillette had finished Faith's e-mail, he put the Blackberry down slowly on the night table and rubbed his eyes again. As he did, he caught a whiff of Allison's perfume, left over from when she'd squeezed his hand tight and kissed him on the cheek before heading to her room.

PART
TWO

10

DR. SCOTT DAVIS was the chief neurosurgeon at the Medical Center of Virginia in downtown Richmond and, according to the head of anesthesiology at St. Christopher's, also a leading authority on biochemical nanotechnology research.

Gillette had handed the project of finding a nanotechnology resource to an Everest vice president named Cathy Dylan. Cathy was every bit as aggressive as David Wright, just five years younger and, importantly, much more malleable. Gillette would have handled the project himself, but he was worried that Boyd might be monitoring him—tapping phones, reading e-mails, having him followed—especially for the first few days after disclosing what they wanted. He couldn't have Wright track down an expert because Wright would ask too many questions. He needed a hunting dog, a loyal Lab who would act on orders without question. A younger person at the firm who wanted simply to please. Cathy fit the bill perfectly.

Like most Everest vice presidents, Cathy was nervous around him. But he sensed she was more street-smart than the others. Quicker on her feet with a believable truth stretcher if she needed to be.

Gillette had given Cathy a quick primer on nanotech, then the name of the anesthesiologist at St. Christopher's. The guy put her in touch with Davis right away. Which was a stroke of divine intervention as far as Gillette was concerned, because he didn't want six or seven degrees of separation on this. Casting a wider net would have given Boyd a better chance of finding out what was going on. After all, the nanotech research community couldn't be that big if most people believed commercial development of the technology was still thirty to forty years off.

Gillette had instructed Cathy not to use his or Everest's name during her search except with the anesthesiologist at St. Christopher's; to make all telephone calls related to finding an expert from a pay phone—never her SoHo apartment or Everest; not to do any nanotechnology research on her office or home computer; not to send any e-mails related to nanotech from her office or home computer; and to try to make certain the doctor she found was a practicing physician who worked long hours—someone who would be less likely to have time to be involved with DARPA. Gillette had called Cathy collect last night at seven forty-five from a pay phone in the hotel lobby, during a quick break from his dinner with Allison and Mitchell. Fourteen hours later, not only did she have a resource, she had an appointment. He was impressed.

Gillette sat in Davis's cramped and cluttered hospital office, waiting for the doctor to get out of surgery. Gillette had brought Stiles and just one other QS agent with him on the flight to Richmond and hadn't given the Everest pilot the destination until he and Stiles were on their way to LaGuardia and until the QS agent who was going with them was actually sitting beside the pilot. They'd stopped at a bodega in Harlem to call the pilot after the QS agent who was driving had made several nifty evasive maneuvers. And Gillette had warned the pilot on the call not to tell anyone but the tower where they were going.

He pulled out his Blackberry for the fourth time in the last twenty minutes and almost turned it on. But he caught himself just in time. He wasn't going to turn it or the cell phone on until he'd landed back at LaGuardia. He let out a long breath, glancing around the office as he put the Blackberry away. He hated sitting on his hands, hated wasted minutes. And he'd already been in here for half an hour.

"WHERE IS HE?" Wright demanded, frustrated that Debbie wasn't even bothering to look up from her computer.

"I don't know."

"What do you mean, you don't know? You **always** know where Chris is."

"This time I really don't. He told me he was going out this morning around nine, and that was it. He didn't say where he was going, and he didn't say when he'd be back."

"Look, I **have** to get in touch with him." Paul had called Wright an hour ago, looking for Gillette's schedule. "I have to talk to Chris about a deal point. We could lose it if I don't talk to him right away." A lie, but he had to say something.

"Then call his cell phone," Debbie snapped. "You've got his number."

"I tried, he's not picking up."

"E-mail him."

"I did that, too, of course," Wright said, "but he hasn't pinged me back. If he had, I wouldn't be here. Obviously."

Debbie finally looked up. "Well, I can't help you. If he calls me, I'll let him know you're looking for him."

Wright leaned over Debbie's desk. "You better not be lying to me," he warned. "The deal could hinge on this. I'm a managing partner now, and if you're holding back, I'll do everything I can to get you fired."

Debbie shot out of her seat. **"What is your damn problem, David?"**

Wright's cell phone went off, and he turned away,

yanking it out of his pocket. It was Paul again. He shut his eyes, fighting the urge to scream.

GILLETTE WAS reaching for a magazine on the front of the doctor's desk when the door opened.

"Hello," said the man, a curious expression on his face. "I'm Scott Davis. I . . . I was expecting a Cathy Dylan. Are you—"

"I'm Christian Gillette." He rose and shook the doctor's hand. "Cathy works for me. She made the appointment for me. Sorry about the confusion, Dr. Davis."

"Oh, well, fine. And please call me Scott. I don't go for that formal stuff."

Davis was fifty-five, of average height and build, and had intense brown eyes, thick eyebrows, dimples, and a full beard. He was still dressed in his light blue surgery smock and pants, a mask draped around his neck, a surgical cap slightly crooked on his head.

"Thanks for seeing me on such short notice."

"Jamie Robinson's a good friend of mine," Davis said, referring to the anesthesiologist at St. Christopher's who had put Cathy in touch. "We did medical school together at Johns Hopkins." He eased into his wooden desk chair with a tired groan. "Sorry to keep you waiting, but the surgery was more complex than I had anticipated."

"What was it?" Gillette noticed several dark

splotches on Davis's smock that looked like dried blood.

"A twelve-year-old boy with a brain tumor the size of an orange. It was a tricky procedure. The tumor was almost inaccessible."

Gillette winced. "That's awful."

Davis sighed, stroking his beard slowly with his thumb and forefinger, over and over, as he rocked in the creaky chair. "It is awful, but I believe we were successful. I believe the boy will recover."

Gillette liked Davis right away. He spoke in a low, soothing voice and had a calmness about him that was nearly hypnotic. "Congratulations," he said softly. "It's an incredible thing you do."

"God does it, Christian. I'm simply His conduit. But I appreciate your kind words." Davis was silent for a few moments as he continued stroking his beard. "Jamie tells me your firm has made quite a donation to his hospital. They'll be able to build a new wing for children with cancer now. That's wonderful. I believe in doing all we can for children. For everyone, of course, but particularly children."

"I'm a fortunate man, Dr. Davis." Davis had asked Gillette to call him by his first name, but somehow he couldn't. It didn't seem appropriate for a man who performed miracles every day. "I may not have the same faith in God as you, but I've been blessed in my life, and I believe in giving back."

Davis smiled serenely. "Good for you, good for you. Perhaps someday you'll find your faith."

"Perhaps."

Davis leaned forward and put his elbows on the desk. "Jamie also tells me you have an interest in nanotechnology."

"Yes."

"May I ask why?"

"I run an investment firm in New York, and I've been approached by some people about funding an opportunity in the space." He didn't like lying to Davis, but it was safer for the doctor if he didn't know the truth. Just as it was for Stiles. He'd taken a long look into Norman Boyd's eyes during their meeting yesterday and found a zealot, a man who was deeply committed to his objective and might use any means necessary to achieve it. If lying meant keeping innocent people out of jeopardy, so be it. "I need your expert advice."

"Let me be perfectly clear right from the start," Davis said candidly. "I've studied nanotechnology extensively, so I can sound dangerous. But I'm no expert. I know what atomic force microscopy is, I'm familiar with carbon nanotube transistors, and I can tell you that molecular tweezers will be very important one day. But I'm not researching day and night the way some people are, probably the way those people who are presenting you with that opportunity are." A far-off look came into his eyes. "You know, some people say I'm on the cutting edge of medicine today, but what I do will look like meatball surgery when true biochemical nanotechnology becomes reality."

"When will that be, Doctor?"

"Well . . . you hear rumors all the time."

"And?"

"Actually, there are people on the cusp of it right now."

Gillette's ears perked up.

"There's a company in San Francisco named Optimicronics," Davis went on, "basically four eye surgeons and a bioengineer. They've developed a subretinal chip that in clinical trials appears to restore sight quickly for many forms of blindness. The chip is tiny. Its diameter is about sixty times smaller than that of a **penny,** and it's about half as thick as a paintbrush bristle. Can you imagine? It's revolutionary, a major breakthrough if the trials prove out." Davis hesitated, studying Gillette's expression. "But judging from your reaction, that isn't what you're interested in."

"No, it's not."

"Then I assume your interest lies in the hard-core stuff. The ability to operate at the atomic level. In the range of ten-to-the-negative-nine meter and less."

Gillette broke into a grin, embarrassed at his ignorance. He wondered if this was how financial talk sounded sometimes to people outside the industry. "If you're talking eighty thousand times smaller than the diameter of a human hair, I think we're on the same page."

Davis nodded, chuckling. "Depending on whose

hair you're talking about and when it was last washed."

"If you say so."

"It is fascinating stuff," Davis said. "I just hope I'm around to see it."

Gillette noticed Davis's fingers moving more quickly over his beard. It was clear the topic excited him. You could tell so much about people if you really watched them. It was like the good poker players always said: Play the players, not the cards. "How far off do you think nanotech is, Doctor?"

Davis leaned back, put his hands behind his head, and gazed at the ceiling. "Twenty to thirty years to the market, but in the lab right now."

Less than what Gillette had heard from others, but still at least a generation off. "Could nanotechnology really live up to the hype?"

"Yes, absolutely. Some people pooh-pooh it, but I'm a firm believer, and I don't have an ax to grind."

Gillette wrestled with the best way to ask his question, letting out an exasperated breath before he spoke up. "Can you, I mean, I just don't know if I get—"

"Do you want the layman's version of what's going on here? Is that what you're trying to ask me, Christian?"

"Yes," he admitted with a relieved smile.

"Happy to oblige. But remember, I only know enough to **sound** dangerous."

"I'm glad to start with that at this point."

"Okay, here it is in its simplest form. The human body is made up of billions and billions of complex molecules, and the elderly, the hurt, the frail, the sick—they all have one thing in common. The atoms, and therefore the molecules, are no longer functioning correctly because of a virus or a bacteria, or maybe because the genetic material degenerated, or because some linebacker blindsided them and now their knee is snapped. Nanotechnology will enable doctors to use incredibly small machines, active inside the body, to detect the problem, or maybe to direct the repair of the body's own DNA. Initially, these machines may only work on one type of disorder, but there will be many of them sent in to attack the problem. Eventually, they'll work atom by atom, molecule by molecule, cell by cell, organ by organ, until everything's right."

"Can you give me a specific example?"

"Sure, take a heart attack. The way it works now is that scar tissue replaces dead muscle after a heart attack. But nanotech will help the heart to grow new muscle tissue and overcome the scar.

"This technology isn't like a drug that goes bouncing around your body after you swallow a pill," Davis continued, "with you and your doctor hoping by chance it runs into the right receptor molecule. This is an advanced, sleek device that is programmed to zero in on specific physiological or biological problems."

"Or screw it up," Gillette said quietly.

"Well, now you've hit on one of the great debates with nanotech. The other being the immortality issue."

"Immortality?"

"People age because, simply through the passage of time, there is a greater and greater chance of DNA becoming damaged, due to all kinds of factors. As long as DNA remains intact, it can continue to produce directives for the assembly of new proteins to regenerate damaged cells. But when the DNA itself is harmed, it can't continue to produce error-free directives. Those errors add up over time, molecules become misarranged, organs break down, and, of course, people die. Nanotechnology machines will **repair** DNA. Even when your organs break down, we'll be able to fix them. You may never die. In fact, you may not even have wrinkles when the technology is perfected. It'll be preventive, too," he added. "For example, doctors will be able to detect that blood vessels in your brain are weakening and are about to explode. In other words, you're about to have a stroke. They'll send nanomachines into the brain immediately to guide the quick growth of reinforcing fibers, and you'll never know you were about to become a vegetable."

"Incredible," Gillette said, aware that the word was woefully inadequate for what Davis was describing.

"It really is. Now, the immortality issue has two main subproblems. The first is, who gets to be immortal? The answer, at least initially, is whoever has enough money."

"Which has terrible social implications."

"Right. If you knew there was everlasting life to be had, but you didn't have the money, what would you risk to get it? Anything, of course."

Gillette nodded. "Then the second piece to the puzzle must be, what do you do when **everyone** can afford it? When the technology becomes commonplace and for twenty bucks a year nanotechnology can touch up any little physical problem you have. Forty years ago, computers cost millions, now you can have one on your desk for a few hundred bucks. Eventually, it will be like that with nanotechnology."

"The way it is with every technology," Davis agreed. "Good for you."

"What about the Big Brother aspect?" Gillette asked.

"What do you mean?"

"Could nanotechnology enable you to inject chips into the body that would allow you to remotely record what someone sees and hears, maybe even monitor what they think?"

Davis stroked his beard for several moments. "I'm convinced that anything will be possible with this technology, Christian. Anything."

"How would you do it so they wouldn't suspect?"

"You mean get the chip into their bodies?" Davis asked, making certain he was clear.

"Yes."

Davis shrugged. "All kinds of ways. You could put it in food, drinks, cold medicines, perfumes, nose sprays, air fresheners. There'd be many options. There're many ways into the body."

Gillette hesitated, almost distracted by the pulse pounding in his brain. "Could someone be close?" he asked, his voice almost inaudible.

"You always hear about secret projects, particularly inside the government," Davis replied, still rocking gently in his chair, "but I don't put much stock in those rumors."

"But could they be close?" Gillette asked again, his voice becoming stronger, his gaze focusing.

"They could."

"Then what's the barrier?"

"Primarily, the complexity of molecular structures. Do you remember those huge charts on the walls of your biology and chemistry classes?"

"Barely."

"Imagine a chart thousands of times bigger with millions of permutations. Before you can build, you must understand and then master the tools to control. It's an incredible proposition."

"But someone could be close. It is possible."

Davis stopped rocking and leaned forward. "What do you know, Christian Gillette?"

BOYD ENDED the phone call quickly when Ganze walked into his office. "What is it?"

"We lost Gillette in Harlem this morning around ten-thirty," Ganze explained. "We know at least one thing about the QS guys now, they sure as hell can drive. Our guy couldn't keep up."

Boyd cursed under his breath. "Where did he go?"

"Richmond, Virginia."

"Who did he see?"

"We don't know," Ganze replied.

"Why not?"

"We didn't find out Gillette went to Richmond until he got back to New York just a few minutes ago."

"But we have the pilots. They're supposed to let us know where he's going before he takes off so we can have people on the ground when he lands."

"The pilot couldn't call. Gillette didn't tell him where they were going until there was a QS agent sitting right next to him, and the QS agent didn't leave the pilot's side until they landed at LaGuardia. The pilot literally couldn't take a piss by himself."

"We've got to do better than that."

"I know, I'm working on it."

"What about the other thing?" Boyd asked.

"It's in motion."

"Good." Boyd thought for a second. "Did you speak to Marilyn?"

"Yes, she's ready."

They had to keep Gillette interested. Had to make him think he was so close to finding all these things he'd been trying to find for so long. "Tell Gillette it's all right to call her now." Boyd reached for the phone. "Anything more on Clayton Gillette?"

"I'm getting closer. I should have something to-morrow."

TOM McGUIRE reached into his pocket for the SUV keys. He wasn't going to stay in Avalon another day. The guy on the beach had rattled him; he'd had the look of a hunter about him, and over the last thirty years, McGuire had learned to trust his gut.

What bothered McGuire most was, if his gut was right, then who was the guy on the beach? If he was a fed, he would have arrested him. If it was some-body he'd put in prison a long time ago when he was with the Bureau who'd just gotten out, had some-how found him, and was settling a vendetta, he'd be dead. But the guy had just asked him about seashells.

McGuire pulled the SUV keys from his pocket, pushed the button to unlock the doors, then took a last look out over the bay in the late afternoon sun-light. He liked it here. It was too bad he had to go, but there was no choice.

Then he felt a burst of searing pain at the back of his neck, and everything went black.

. . .

IT WAS FIVE-THIRTY, and they were almost back to Everest after landing at LaGuardia thirty minutes earlier. Gillette was close to finishing the third crossword puzzle of the trip when his cell phone rang. He'd turned it back on when they'd landed.

"Hello."

"Christian, it's David."

"Hey."

"Christ, I've been trying to get in touch with you all day."

Wright had sent him seven e-mails. "I've been out of touch."

"No shit."

"What's the problem?" Gillette asked.

"I've got to talk to you about some of these reps and warranties Maddox wants in the Hush-Hush purchase agreement."

"Is it that urgent?"

"He really wants to—"

Gillette's phone beeped, indicating another call. "I've got to take this, David. We'll talk when I get to the office in a few minutes." He switched over. "Hello."

"Christian, it's Daniel Ganze."

"Yes," Gillette said, dropping the folded newspaper on the seat between Stiles and him.

"You can call Marilyn McRae now," Ganze said simply, relaying a number that Gillette jotted down. "She's really looking forward to talking to you. Also,

I should have more on your father tomorrow, or maybe Monday."

"Thanks."

"We'll be speaking to you next week about the move north as well. Understood?"

"Yeah."

"Good, talk to you then."

Gillette stared straight ahead for a few moments after Ganze hung up, then looked down at the Los Angeles telephone number. It was shaking in his fingers.

"You okay, Chris?" Stiles asked.

"Fine," he answered, slipping the number into his wallet.

"Not even going to give me a clue about what's up? I mean, I didn't ask why we had to do all the CIA-wheelman driving this morning on the way to the airport, and I didn't ask who it was you went to see in Richmond. I figured all that was business. But this is personal, I can tell by the look on your face. What was that call about?"

"It was one of the guys I saw in Washington yesterday," Gillette answered, his voice raspy. "He called to give me my blood mother's telephone number. Like I told you he was going to."

"Oh." Stiles looked away.

Gillette could tell Stiles was disappointed that something tangible had come of the Washington trip. Stiles didn't trust these guys. "I'll tell you how the call goes after I talk to her."

"Thanks. I'd like that."

When Gillette reached his office, he pulled Marilyn McRae's telephone number from his wallet, put it on his desk, and stared. A lifetime he'd been waiting for this, he thought as he eased into his chair. A lifetime he'd thought it would never happen, and now here it was, thanks to Boyd and Ganze. Who were these guys?

"Christian."

Allison. She was leaning into the office. Debbie must have gone to the ladies' room and left the door unguarded. She usually didn't leave until seven, and it wasn't even six yet. "Hi."

"Can I come in?"

"Um, yeah." He slid a manila folder over Marilyn's number as Allison closed the door, then came in and sat in the chair in front of his desk. "What is it?"

"I wanted to let you know that Jack called me this afternoon, and he's very excited about working with you. To quote. He believes a Veramax-Everest partnership would be 'unstoppable.' "

"Jack's a salesman."

"Sure, but all you care about is that he's retaining counsel so he can start drafting documents for your investment. And he's almost finished writing that apology letter to Rothchild for keeping him out of the Racquet Club. He's doing what you told him to do. That's good, isn't it?"

Gillette couldn't stop thinking about how easily

Mitchell had climbed on board the Everest train. How he hadn't negotiated at all. And how Veramax's bread-and-butter products—aspirin, nose drops, and cold medicine—were perfect nanotech delivery options. His mind was becoming cluttered with puzzle pieces he hoped wouldn't fit together. "Yeah, right."

"Don't get so excited."

"Do you think it's strange that he didn't negotiate with me at all?"

Allison shook her head. "Nope. I've known Jack a long time. He's a very gut-feel kind of guy. He liked you right away at dinner last night, I could tell. He must have liked your proposal, too."

"Mmm." Deals rarely went down like this.

"Jack talked to that friend of his again, too. The guy who owns the leasing company. He must have given you a great report because the guy wants to see you as soon as possible. I did some number crunching this afternoon while you were gone, and it's an even better fit with our company in Atlanta than I first thought."

Allison Wallace was a deal hound, and Gillette loved it. "Great. Talk to Debbie and set it up. It would be better if he could come here. But if not, I'll go back to Pittsburgh."

"Okay. By the way, where were you today?" she asked.

"Looking at a company."

Allison crossed her arms over her chest and leaned back into the chair. "Remember we talked about full disclosure the other night?"

"Sure."

"That explanation didn't sound like full disclosure. How about some more specifics? I **am** your partner."

Gillette picked up a pen and tapped it impatiently on the desk. "Look, I'm not going to tell you about every step I take during the day. I don't have time to keep you up to speed on every detail."

"Details, details," she repeated slowly. "You mean like when you have your security guy check with people I know to see if I'm a coke fiend?"

Gillette's eyes snapped to Allison's.

"The least you could have done was let me know what was going on," she kept going. "You didn't like it when **People** put you in that article without telling you. And that was **good** pub."

"Yeah, I—"

"So I sniffed a little over my cheeseburger," she continued, her voice rising. "I told you, I have allergies."

"I know."

"But you didn't take my word for it."

"I'm sorry."

"What?" she said, putting a hand to her ear. "I don't think I heard you."

"I'm sorry, **okay?**"

"That's it? That's all I get? An 'I'm sorry'?"

"What do you want?"

"I want to go out on the boat with you this weekend."

Gillette pursed his lips. "How did you hear about that?"

"I overheard Faraday on the phone talking about it." She hesitated. "So, do I get to go?"

"First, I want to hear about those conditions you have."

"Conditions?"

"Yeah, what you'd need from me to join Everest full time."

MCGUIRE REGAINED consciousness to a panoramic view of the stars, the loud roar of engines, the smell of salt air mixing with exhaust, and a throbbing pain at the back of his neck. He tried to move his hands, but they were secured tightly behind his back.

The engines droned on a bit longer, then he heard them power down, then shut off completely.

McGuire heard voices as the fishing boat drifted silently through the water, waves lapping at its hull, then he saw shadowy figures standing above him.

"Who are you?" he asked. But they ignored him as they bound his ankles together tightly with wire. He didn't fight them; that would have been useless.

His wrists were tied, and there were at least four of them. His best chance was to cooperate. "Talk to me, come on."

A moment later, two of the men hoisted him to his feet while another cut the rope binding his wrists.

"Now we're making some progress," he said to the one closest to him. "So, what's going on here?"

Suddenly two of the men grabbed his right arm and pinned it to a chopping block used for cutting bait. A third man snatched a meat cleaver off the fishing chair and slammed it down on McGuire's wrist.

McGuire screamed insanely, his body coursing with pain, his mind shuddering with anguish. He staggered backward as the two men who'd pinned his arm to the chopping block bent and picked up a huge anchor lying on the deck. Straining against the weight, they lugged it to the side of the boat. With a massive effort, they lifted it over the side and threw it in the ocean. It splashed loudly, disappearing into the black water, and a coil of rope began whipping after it over the side.

McGuire realized instantly that the other end of the rope was attached to his ankles, and he reached out with his left hand for the man standing next to him, but he was too late. The rope snapped tight around his ankles, sending him crashing to the deck, then yanking him over the side. He grabbed an aft cleat as he was going over, holding on with everything he had against the tremendous force pulling at his legs. One of the men moved to the cleat and with a grim look began peeling away the fingers of McGuire's left hand.

As he was about to go down, McGuire looked up into the face, expecting to see the man from the beach. But it wasn't him, it was someone else. Someone he recognized.

"You fucking—"

But that was all he got out before his hand wrenched free and he splashed into the water. He screamed as the anchor dragged him toward the depths, his voice muffled by the water. He thrashed, trying desperately to pull himself to the surface, but there was no chance; the weight was much too heavy. For a few moments, he could see the lights of the boat through the dark water, but then, as he passed fifty feet below the surface, everything faded.

GILLETTE SAT on his patio, looking out over Central Park from high above. It was a beautiful early autumn evening. Crystal clear with a chill and the wisp of wood smoke wafting over Manhattan as people with fireplaces took advantage of the first wave of cool temperatures.

He reached for the cordless phone on the table and dialed Marilyn's number. He didn't need the piece of paper anymore. He'd looked at it so many times, he could have dialed the number backward.

"Hello."

"Marilyn?"

"Yes?" Her voice was already shaking.

"It's Christian Gillette."

"Oh, my God," she whispered.

And then he heard sobs as he'd never heard sobs before.

PAUL POINTED a finger into Wright's cheek on the darkened street in front of his apartment building. "That better not ever happen again, you understand?"

"Yes, sir."

"I told you, goddamn it. I have to know where Gillette is at all times."

"Yes, sir."

"All times!"

"Yes, sir." This was way out of control, Wright thought. Maybe he ought to go down to the local precinct and turn himself in. In the long run, he'd probably be safer.

11

"**DO YOU MIND** if I smoke?" Russell Hughes asked, reaching for a pack of Marlboros in his jacket pocket.

Gillette and Wright were sitting in Hughes's office, going through the Apex portfolio company by company with him, asking the tough questions. Gillette wanted to squeeze as much information out of Hughes as possible before he sank a billion dollars into another private equity firm. There was always the chance Hughes would slip up and give away something about Apex that would make Gillette back off the deal.

The truth was, Gillette hated cigarette and cigar smoke, though he liked the smell of a pipe—his father had smoked a pipe. But Hughes was under a huge amount of stress, so he allowed the man his vice. "It's all right."

Wright's cell phone went off suddenly, ejecting a loud, shrill whistle throughout the room.

"Jesus, David," Gillette snapped, "turn that damn thing off."

Wright already had it out of his pocket and was staring at the number. "I've gotta take this," he muttered, getting up and hurrying from the room.

Gillette watched him go, irritated. Wright still had a thing or two to learn.

"Can we talk, just the two of us?" Hughes asked when Wright was gone. Hughes's eyes were rimmed with fatigue. "I'm sure David's a bright young man, but I'd rather report to you. We're closer in age, and I feel like I—"

"Russell," Gillette said gently, "save it. David's going to be running Apex. Full stop. Got it?"

Hughes nodded.

"I know this is difficult for you, but that's the way it's going to be."

"Okay," Hughes agreed quietly.

Gillette picked up the next company file off the stack—marked "XT Pharmaceuticals"—and began browsing through it. "This is one of your better investments," he said, not waiting for Wright to come back in. He had a lunch at one, it was already past eleven, and they still had twelve companies to go through. "It's a solid company, growing, with good cash flow."

"It's a **very** solid company," Hughes agreed. "So solid even the damn government's interested in it."

Gillette stopped scanning. "What do you mean?"

"There were some guys up from D.C. a while ago who wanted to use it as a cutout for a new technology they were trying to hide. Typical DOD clandestine ops kind of crap, but I called my contact at the CIA, and he said to stay away from them. I'm glad I did, too. They wanted me to sign some bullshit confidentiality agreement that could have put me in San Quentin doing hard time for the rest of my life if I'd sneezed the wrong way."

Gillette stared at Hughes for a few moments, then looked down, trying not to give away his shock. "What's 'a while ago'?"

"Few weeks."

"Did they tell you what kind of technology it was?"

"They made it seem like the biggest thing since electricity, but they didn't get into any specifics. It's probably all just hype, but like I said, I called my guy at the CIA and that was that. So I'm not sure if it was real or not."

"How do you have a CIA contact?"

Hughes fidgeted uncomfortably. "Look, I'm not supposed to tell anyone about this. It's classified."

"You want to keep your job?" Gillette asked. He didn't like to be this way, but he needed the information. Now.

Hughes nodded.

"Then tell me."

"Look, you can't say **anything** about this."

At that moment, Wright opened the door and stepped back into the office.

"David," Gillette said, "leave us alone for a few minutes."

"What?"

"I'll let you know when you can come back in."

"Chris, I—"

"David!"

Wright stalked out, shutting the door hard.

Gillette turned back around to face Hughes. "Tell me about your CIA contact, Russell."

Hughes took a measured breath. "Are you familiar with cutouts?"

"Yes."

"Well, that's why I have a CIA contact. One of our portfolio companies is a cutout."

"Which one?"

"The last one on the list." Hughes pointed at a piece of paper that had the names of every Apex portfolio company on it. "The information technology company."

"Omega IT?" Gillette asked.

"Yeah. Omega does IT consulting for financial institutions all over the world, including the Middle East. While the Omega people are installing and updating computer systems, they add a few extra options the customers don't know about. Options that let people in Washington watch money come and go."

"To track terrorist money," Gillette spoke up. "Probably al-Qaeda in particular."

"You got it."

"But why would Middle Eastern banks let a U.S. company do their IT work? That doesn't make any sense."

"They don't know it's a U.S. company. With the CIA's help, we've set up an elaborate corporate structure that winds its way through dummy relationships in Belgium and France and hides the ultimate ownership very effectively."

"I want to talk to your CIA contact," Gillette said tersely.

"If you're going to buy Apex, you'll **have** to talk to him. About Omega. In fact, he'll demand to talk to **you.** I'll set that meeting up right before we close the deal, when we're certain everything's a go."

What Gillette wanted to talk to Hughes's CIA contact about had nothing to do with Omega IT. "I don't want to wait that long. Set it up as soon as possible."

"**WHAT HAPPENED** back there, Chris?" Wright demanded. They were heading back to Everest in the limousine. "Why did you make me stay out of the room for the rest of the meeting?"

"Russell and I got into some sensitive issues about a few of the Apex employees. Severance. Stuff like that."

"Shouldn't I be in on those discussions if I'm going to run Apex?" Wright asked, his voice rising.

"Calm down, David, there's no reason to get upset."

"I'm not getting upset, I'm just trying to understand. Am I still going to run Apex?"

Gillette said nothing as he scrolled through e-mails on his Blackberry. At this point, he needed to have direct contact with Hughes, and he didn't want Wright trying to find out why.

"Chris?"

Still nothing.

"Chris?"

"Russell is going to report to me for a while, until we've had a chance to understand exactly what we have at Apex."

"What the hell happened? I thought I was the man."

"I made a decision, David. I'll let you know when you're going to take over. It'll probably be a few weeks. For now, concentrate on Hush-Hush."

"Yeah," he muttered, "I'll concentrate all right."

"CHRIS."

Gillette looked up from his computer at Debbie. "Yes?"

"I know this sounds crazy, but there's a woman in the lobby who says she's your mother."

After talking for two hours last night, Gillette and Marilyn McRae had ended their conversation with a promise to get together next week. He'd told her he'd come to Los Angeles after finishing his business in Las Vegas and they'd have dinner. So it couldn't be her. Gillette stepped out from behind his desk and started to follow Debbie to the lobby. Then it hit him. Lana.

"HEY, POP." Christian rose from the lumpy living room couch and moved toward his frail grandfather. Pop was shuffling in from the kitchen, pulling his blue oxygen tank behind him like a long-in-the-tooth hound dog on a leash. A lifetime in the coal mines of western Pennsylvania and thirty years of Camel no-filters had left him without much in the way of lungs.

"Let me help you," Christian offered, holding out his arm and guiding the old man to the couch. "How you feeling today?" They sat beside each other, Christian's palm resting atop his grandfather's gnarled fingers.

"I'm fine," the old man answered wearily, his voice like sandpaper on plywood. "I'm glad you came."

"Of course, Pop."

"I don't know how much time I have."

Mary Desmond bustled in from the kitchen carrying a tray of sandwiches and drinks. "Oh, you'll probably outlive me **and** Christian," she said, setting the tray on the coffee table in front of the couch and giving Christian a warm smile. "Pop thinks every day's his last," she blustered in a loud voice that belied her tiny frame. Mary was in her late fifties and lived next door. She often helped around the house with chores the old man couldn't handle anymore. "But it's probably good you came when you did," she admitted, her voice drifting lower as she sat in the chair next to the couch.

Christian was on his way back to the West Coast after graduating from Princeton, planning to put five thousand miles on his Ducati as he zigzagged from New Jersey to California, seeing the great expanse between the country's mountain chains. He knew the big cities on both coasts pretty well, thanks to traveling with his father, but he didn't know much about the small towns in between. So he was spending the summer on his bike until the highways and September finally forced him back to the real world. His first stop was this little house on Elmore Lane.

His father had told him it was important to do so quickly. Now he could see why.

"What are your plans?" Pop asked, taking a glass of iced tea off the tray and easing back on the couch with a low moan. "What will you do with yourself now?"

"I'm going to Stanford in the fall to get my MBA. Then I'll go to Wall Street, be an investment banker."

"Just like your daddy."

"Yeah, hopefully at Goldman Sachs."

"Why **'hopefully'**?"

"Goldman's the best investment bank in the world, so it's tough to get a job there. Everybody wants to work for them."

Pop took a labored breath. "I don't know much about Wall Street, but I know your father can get you a job anywhere you want." The old man shook his head proudly. "He's a good boy, your father. He loves you very much."

Christian felt a lump rising in his throat, the same way it had two weeks ago when his father had hugged him after graduation. Under a beautiful azure sky with the smells of freshly cut grass and blooming lilac filling his nostrils and that diploma clutched in his hand. "I know he does," he murmured.

"How's that mother of yours?" Pop spoke up, contempt surfacing in his voice.

Christian wondered if Pop knew, if that was the reason for the icy tone. Probably not. It wouldn't be like his father to share a piece of information like that with anyone—even Pop. "She's fine."

"Never did like her," the old man grumbled.

"**Now,** Pop," Mary piped up, "Lana's nice."

"She never calls or writes."

"She used to try," Mary argued, "but you wouldn't say more than two words to her."

"Didn't have anything to say."

Christian caught his grandfather's sidelong glance as the phone in the kitchen began to ring.

Mary was out of her chair quickly. "Don't forget, Christian," she said over her shoulder, "you promised to call bingo down at the lodge tonight." She laughed. "You'll drive all the old biddies crazy."

Christian smiled. He was looking forward to it. He and Pop were heading down there together. Team Gillette. Mary disappeared around the corner, and he heard her answer the phone. "Well, Pop, what are we going to do today?" he asked, settling back on the couch. "How about we wet a line in that pond down the lane? See if we can fool some bass?"

"Well, maybe in a—"

"Christian," Mary interrupted. She was standing in the kitchen doorway, a troubled expression creasing her small face. "Nikki is calling from California."

Christian moved quickly to the kitchen and took the old black receiver from Mary, who returned to the living room. "Hello."

"Chris, it's me."

Something was terribly wrong; he could tell by her tone. "What is it?"

"It's **Daddy**," she whispered. "It's Daddy."

A blast of blue flame seared Christian's chest. "What about him?" He turned toward the corner so Pop and Mary couldn't hear. But somehow he already knew.

"His plane went down a few minutes ago. On takeoff from Orange County." Nikki could barely get the words out. "He's gone."

Christian's forehead slowly came to rest against the wall. **Gone.** An awful word. He felt tears welling in his eyes, and he shut them tightly and ground his teeth together, trying to stem the tide. But the tears cascaded down his cheeks anyway, over his lip and into his mouth. They were warm and sweet, and the taste only invited more. "Oh, God," he whispered.

"I gotta go," Nikki said suddenly. "Come home, Chris. Come home."

He hung up the receiver and brought his hands to his face. The phone rang again, almost right away, and he picked it up, wondering what Nikki had forgotten to say. "Hello?"

"Christian."

It was Lana.

"I know you just talked to Nikki."

Lana's voice was so calm, Christian thought. But that was how she handled everything, good or bad. "Yes, I did."

"Then you know."

"Yes." He bit his lower lip. The last person in the world he wanted to show weakness to was Lana. "Are you okay?" he asked quietly.

"I'll be all right." Lana hesitated. "Christian, listen. You and I . . . we're not . . ." She took a breath.

"Christian, things are going to be very hard for us around here, and I'm not sure . . . I don't think you should be here."

Christian pressed the phone to his ear, uncertain he'd heard her right. Certain no one could be that cold. "**What?** I don't think I—"

"Listen," she said, now with full force, "I need to be alone with my children."

He heard it plain and clear this time: **my** children. Troy and Nikki. Not you.

"I know what your father always wanted," she kept going, "but you and I don't belong to each other." She paused. "Good-bye, Christian."

LANA WAS sitting on one of the plush couches near the receptionist's desk. The last time he'd seen her was at his father's funeral sixteen years ago. They hadn't spoken there or since.

Lana had been a striking woman in her youth, statuesque with long brunette hair. But she had a tough look about her, too, manifested by an intense, almost cruel flavor to her eyes, the way her jaw jutted out, the ramrod-stiff posture.

The first thing Gillette noticed about her was how the years had worn down that toughness. Her eyes seemed sad, the corners of her mouth were puffy, and she slumped slightly. Deep creases coursed out from the corners of her eyes into the loose skin of her cheeks, and her hands seemed old, as if they belonged to a woman in her late seventies, not her late fifties.

"Hello, Christian," she said as he moved into the lobby.

Gillette was aware that Debbie and both receptionists were watching carefully. They knew he had no relationship with his family. That had been well documented in the articles in both **The Wall Street Journal** and **People.** "Let's go to my office," he suggested.

"This is so nice, Christian," Lana said, looking around the large space as they sat on one of the couches in a corner of his office. "I love the artwork and the antiques. I can see why you make people go through that search." She'd been searched at the lobby door by a QS agent, just like everyone else who came to Everest.

"Everyone has to do that before they come in."

"I see. Well, I've been keeping up with you in the press, and friends of mine tell me what they hear about you, too. You're so successful. I knew you would be. Your father would have been so proud."

"It's been a long time, Lana," he said quietly.

"Too long." A tear trickled down her cheek, and she reached into her purse for a tissue. "I'm sorry," she said, sniffling. "For everything. I was just so . . . hurt. No excuse, I know. What I did to you was awful, so I want to thank you for seeing me." She gestured toward the door. "That's why I showed up out there without calling ahead. I figured if I tried to make an appointment, you'd ignore me. I wouldn't have blamed you, either."

"How have you been?"

"Fine."

"What about Troy and Nikki?" Troy was a half-sibling as well, a good-for-nothing older brother. "They okay?"

"Okay. We're all surviving."

"Are you still living in the Bel Air house?"

"Trying to."

"What does that mean?"

Lana dabbed her eyes with the tissue, then let out a tiny sob. "It's just hard."

"Why?"

"It's expensive, and, well . . . Oh, Christian. Nikki isn't okay." Lana sobbed again. "She has cancer. Lung cancer."

Lung cancer. The words twisted Gillette's stomach. He and Nikki had been so close right up to the day of their father's death. He'd called to borrow a few dollars to get back to the West Coast after Lana cut him off, but for some reason she'd never answered or returned his messages. He hadn't let himself think about her in a long time. But it still hurt deeply to hear this. "I'm sorry."

"What makes it even worse is that she doesn't have any health insurance. She can't pay for the treatment she needs."

"What happened?"

"That idiot she married. Peter. He kept telling her he had it, but he didn't."

Gillette hadn't been invited to Nikki's wedding. He'd heard about it from friends. "Are you going to help her?"

Lana shrugged. "What can I do? I don't have much money left."

"Dad was worth a **hundred million dollars** when he died."

"Taxes took more than half, he gave a lot to charity, and then there was your mother. Several other women, too. I only ended up with about ten million. You'd be surprised how fast that goes."

"Several other women?" Gillette asked.

"You weren't the only child he had out of wedlock, just the only one I agreed to take in."

He could tell this was still hard for her. Any shred of toughness she'd had about her when she'd come in was gone. "How many other children were there?"

The tears were flowing freely now. "One each with three other women."

Gillette's head suddenly ached. Secrets, always secrets. "Jesus."

Lana cleared her throat, trying to regain control. "Yes, your father had a problem." She shook her head quickly several times. "But I'm not here to rehash all that, I'm here to ask you to help your sister. She needs money, Christian."

"Have her call me."

"She won't, she's too proud."

"Then give me her number. I'll call her."

Lana hesitated, then reached into her pocketbook and removed a small black address book.

Gillette handed her a pen and one of his cards. "Write it on the back."

She scribbled the number, then handed the card and pen back to him. "I need money, too," she said firmly.

"Ten million is a lot, Lana. It isn't a hundred, but it's a lot. And you got the house, too. That's probably worth another ten. I don't believe you really need money. You can't."

"Well, I do."

She had always been a survivor. Whatever it took. She wasn't his real mother, but some of that had rubbed off on him. Maybe he owed her something. "I gotta give you credit, Lana. You cut me off completely the day Dad is killed, you don't speak to me for sixteen years, and you walk in here today with your hands out, looking for donations. One thing I'm sure we can agree on, you aren't proud."

"I don't have anywhere else to go," she said matter-of-factly, "and I did agree to take you in all those years ago. There is that."

"You're incredible."

"Will you help me?"

Gillette said nothing for a few moments. "I'll think about it. I'll be on the West Coast next week, we'll get together then. I'll call you."

She nodded slowly. "Okay," she whispered.

She seemed so much older, he realized. "Now I have a question for you. Who's my real mother?"

Lana looked him straight in the eyes. "I don't know."

She was always such a good liar, he remembered.

FARADAY SAT in Gillette's office, staring at the phone. It was almost five o'clock. "What's your bet?" he asked.

"She won't call," Gillette answered.

"I think she will. Chatham's too poor. She'll take what she can get."

"She's got too much pride."

"I thought you said she was smart."

"I did."

"So she'll do the right thing."

"Let's hope so."

Faraday dug a huge spoonful of rocky road ice cream out of a bowl in his lap. "How's Faith? She must be pissed about those pictures of you and Allison in the newspapers. She looked like she was going to kill someone when she stalked out of here the other night. I tried to say good-bye to her, but she blew past me without a word."

Gillette smiled, glad his girlfriend was once more a topic he was happy to discuss. "She's over it."

"Oh? So you finally spoke to her?"

"Yeah." Gillette jotted down a note to himself to

call Russell Hughes to see if he'd arranged the CIA meeting.

"Is Faith coming out on the boat tomorrow?" Faraday asked.

"No. She's in London doing some promo stuff for the next album. It's coming out soon."

"Who else is coming?"

"You, Stiles, Wright, and me," Gillette answered.

"You still inviting David even after the way he acted at the Apex meeting?"

"He's just young, Nigel."

"Uh-huh." Faraday hesitated. "You want me to bring my significant other?"

"Sure. Who is it?"

"You've never met her. Are you going to be stag since Faith is in London?" Faraday asked, his mouth full of ice cream.

Gillette didn't answer.

Faraday stopped eating. "Oh no."

Gillette glanced up. "What?"

"You're bringing Allison."

"What are you talking about?"

"I can tell."

"You can't tell anything. And, if I asked her to come, it would be just as a colleague."

The intercom buzzed. It was Debbie. "Chris, Becky Rouse is on the line."

Faraday smiled triumphantly from behind the bowl.

"Thanks." Gillette picked up. "Hello."

"Mr. Gillette, this is Becky Rouse from Chatham."

"Yes."

"I'm calling to tell you what you can do with your offer."

Gillette felt his cheeks flush. Becky was one feisty character. "And what's that?"

"I'm a lady, so I can't say what I'm thinking. You'll just have to use your imagination. Good-bye, Mr. Gillette."

Gillette hung up the phone calmly after a loud click at the other end.

"So?" Faraday asked.

"We're going to war in Maryland."

Faraday groaned. "What a waste of time."

"For everyone," Gillette agreed.

David Wright stuck his head in the door. "Sorry to interrupt. Could I talk to you, Chris?" He glanced at Faraday. "Alone."

Faraday downed another spoonful of ice cream, then rose. "See you tomorrow, Christian. I'm going home. It's been a long week."

Wright stepped aside to let Faraday pass, then closed the door.

"What is it, David?"

Wright hesitated, looking sheepish. "I came in to apologize. I'm sorry for the way I acted in the limousine, it was stupid."

Good, Gillette thought. The right thing for him to do. "I appreciate that, David." He'd be sure to tell Faraday about this. "You still coming tomorrow?"

"You sure you still want me?"

"We can't go without you. It's a celebration cruise for your promotion."

12

FROM THE WEST SIDE PIER, the Everest cruised down the Hudson, around the southern tip of Manhattan, then north up the East River. This course took it under the Brooklyn, Manhattan, Williamsburg, and Fifty-ninth Street bridges—massive suspension structures that were even more impressive from below than from street level. By noon, they'd made it to the Long Island Sound and were headed east beneath a hot Indian summer sun. At one o'clock, the temperature reached ninety-five degrees and the humidity was thick.

Stiles stood beside Gillette on the bridge, watching the captain navigate. "Tell me about this thing, Chris," he said over the hum of the two diesel engines.

"It's a hundred feet long," Gillette answered, glancing starboard toward Long Island. They were a mile offshore. "It's twenty-three feet at the beam, has two inboard engines with two thousand horses each, carries five thousand gallons of fuel, and has four staterooms. We've got a crew of three, including the captain, the cook, and a mate, and sailing on it is one of my favorite things in the world to do. It's a lot of money, Quentin, but it's worth it to me. I love it out here."

"You entertain a lot on it, too. That probably pays dividends."

"It does. Last Fourth of July, I took a hundred people into New York Harbor for the fireworks, big investors we were lining up for Everest Eight. Let them bring their wives, husbands, kids. It was a great time, and most of the people who came committed to the new fund. Maybe they would have committed anyway, but I still hear about how much fun they had."

Allison appeared on the bridge in a red bikini. "Here you go," she said, handing Gillette a big cup of soda. "Having fun, Quentin?"

"Absolutely."

"You like the boat?" she asked.

"It's incredible. Chris was just telling me about it."

"Yeah, it's cute." She winked at Gillette before turning and walking back out.

"Cute?" Stiles asked. "What's that supposed to mean?"

"The Wallace boat sails out of South Beach,"

Gillette explained. "It's **two** hundred feet long. That's a real boat to her. This is cute."

"Oh." Stiles gestured toward the door she'd gone through. "She's beautiful."

"Yeah."

"Makes that piece of sewing thread she's wearing look awfully good." Stiles cleared his throat. "Tempting, you know?"

"Uh-huh."

Stiles hesitated. "Is something happening between you two?"

Gillette looked off toward Long Island again. They were getting farther and farther away from land. "No."

"I don't mean to pry."

Gillette ran a hand through his hair. "Yes, you do." He hesitated. "Look, I'm attracted to her, Quentin, I'll admit that. Who wouldn't be, for Christ's sake? But I won't let anything happen. It's business between the two of us. That's it."

They were silent for a few moments.

"We talked about how lonely it gets at the top sometimes," Stiles finally said.

"Yeah, **and**?"

"And you've got to be careful who you get close to, especially when a lot of people are depending on you. And watching closely. Especially when there's a lot of money at stake."

"I told you, I'll **never** let that happen."

"Might be tough to resist at some point." Stiles chuckled. "It's funny how different people look in bathing suits, isn't it?" he asked, his voice growing stronger as he switched subjects. "For example"—he laughed loudly—"on the other end of the how-do-you-look-in-a-bathing-suit spectrum is Nigel Faraday, who should thank the Lord for big baggy business suits. He's white as paste, with a belly Mr. Claus would be proud of."

Gillette laughed, too. "It's the gallon a day of ice cream."

"**A gallon**? Really?"

"Just about." Gillette watched a large sailboat off the port side. There was a decent wind, and the skipper had his spinnaker up, a blue-and-gold sail that puffed out majestically off the bow. "That's beautiful, isn't it?"

"I don't like blow-boats," Stiles said. "They're too slow, and they're lots of work."

"That's how our ancestors got around."

"Yours, maybe, not mine. Mine were smart. They paddled." He motioned for Gillette to move to the back of the bridge with him. "I've got some things I want to go over with you," he said when they were out of earshot of the captain.

"What's up?"

"The first thing's kind of a shocker. This morning one of my guys found some very powerful GPS trackers on both Everest planes. They were tiny, but he found them. They were put on recently, judging by the screws used to attach them. No rust or wear."

Gillette cursed under his breath. Norman Boyd. He should have anticipated this. "It was probably the guys in Washington."

Stiles shrugged. "I don't know. You won't tell me much about them, and I'm not going to ask again. Even though, as your head of security, especially now that we found those things, I think you should come clean with me." He waited for Gillette to say something. "Anyway," he kept going when there wasn't any response, "we removed the devices."

"No," Gillette spoke up quickly. "Put them back on. Right away."

"Why?"

"Just do it."

"Okay, okay, but—" Stiles stopped short. "Oh, I get it."

"Any idea when those things were put on?"

"No, impossible to tell."

"But it was recently," Gillette pushed. "That's what you said."

"It could have been a couple of weeks ago, it could have been this morning. I'm not sure."

Gillette's mind was racing, trying to think of other ways Boyd might be watching. "What else you got?"

"We ran a background check on that guy at the hospital ground-breaking ceremony, the one who handed you the shovel. He's definitely a member of the Carbone family."

Gillette took a sip of soda. "Well, we got our answer about the Mafia in Vegas, didn't we? Did you talk to any of those consulting firms out there? The ones that can help us with our issue?"

"Almost a dozen of them, and I've narrowed it down to two. Like you wanted. After we're finished here, I'll send you an e-mail from my Blackberry with the names and numbers of the people I talked to."

"Thanks." Gillette had instructed Debbie to get Stiles a Blackberry earlier in the week. "Like I told you, we're going out there next week. We'll meet with them then. Anything else?"

"Yeah, I've been doing some more checking on the Carbones. First of all, this guy Joe Celino, the boss of the family, makes John Gotti look like a puppy dog. Celino's ruthless as hell. His nickname's 'Twenty-two,' after his weapon of choice. His list of suspected victims is long, but he's never been prosecuted. Anyway, from what I've learned, Celino gets into things for the long term. So you won't just be doing business with him during the construction phase of the stadium and the casino. He'll want a piece of the action on the team, maybe concessions, and the casino, part of the take. He's not going away."

"I was afraid of that."

"Listen," Stiles said, leaning over so he was talking right into Gillette's ear, "I'm getting close to something that involves the Carbones. I'm working with some people in Philadelphia on this. People from the old days, before I started QS. It's something we might be able to use against Celino so he can't get into your businesses. We could release it anonymously once we've got it tied up, and it would probably block him from doing anything in Vegas."

"Fantastic. What is it?"

"I don't want to talk about it now," Stiles said, glancing at the captain.

"Come on, Quentin."

"No, we'll talk about it when we're back on dry land. I should have all the information by then." Gillette started to say something but Stiles held up his hand. "One more thing, Chris."

"What?"

"I checked with a few more people about Allison Wallace. Still no indication she's ever done drugs."

"Thanks. You can call off the dogs." Gillette didn't want Allison hearing from anyone else that they were still checking on her. "By the way," he called as Stiles headed toward the stairs leading belowdecks.

"Yeah?"

"Your girlfriend's nice. I like her son, too." Stiles's girlfriend had brought her six-year-old son, Danny, on the boat. "I'm glad he came."

Stiles grinned appreciatively. "Danny's having a

blast, Chris. He's never been on a boat before. Thanks for letting him come along."

"Of course. Hey, if you see Wright, could you ask him to come see me up here?"

"Yup."

Gillette moved to where the captain stood and tapped him on the shoulder. "Billy, I need to use your cell phone."

It was lying on the shelf in front of the wheel. Billy reached up and snatched it. "Here you go."

"Thanks."

"Yours out of juice?"

"Yeah." It wasn't, but Gillette wasn't going through the whole thing for Billy. He dialed Cathy Dylan's number at her apartment in Manhattan.

"Hello."

"Cathy, it's Christian."

"Hi."

"I need a favor." The GPS devices on the planes were worrying him.

"Of course."

"I need you to call our friend in Richmond. I need you to thank him for meeting with me."

"Is that all?"

"Call me after you talk to him, and call me on this number. It's—"

"Already got it," she interrupted. "It's on my caller ID."

"Okay." Gillette wanted to make certain Scott Davis was all right, that Boyd hadn't done something crazy. He took a deep breath. He was putting people in danger, and it was wearing on him. "Thanks."

"Sure."

As Gillette hung up, Wright walked onto the bridge.

"You wanted to see me, Chris?"

"Yeah. Figured we'd do an update before people started having too much fun. What's up with Hush-Hush?"

"I'm already starting due diligence. I'm using Cathy Dylan to help me. That okay?"

Cathy Dylan was busy these days. "Fine."

"She should have a request-for-information list ready to go over to the Hush-Hush people by COB Monday. My buddy Hobbs is going to head up the team on their side. It should go pretty smoothly. Hobbs says Maddox couldn't be happier. He's already looking at real estate in the Caribbean."

"Good. Just so you know, I'm going to Las Vegas on Tuesday afternoon to see about some things related to the casino. After we meet with that insurance company you've got us set up with. I'll be out west for a few days. I'm going to the coast after I finish in Vegas. We'll talk every morning while I'm out there, just like we do now."

"Okay."

"There's one more deal I want to bring you in on. It's a company called Veramax. Are you familiar with it?"

"No."

"It's a privately held drug company based outside Chicago. Allison's introduced me to the owner out in Pittsburgh. That's why I was there. The company's growing fast and has some great new products coming out soon. Allison's family has known the family who owns Veramax for a long time. We're going to be able to get it pretty cheap because they've got some issues with the FDA I can help them with."

"Nice."

"But I want your take on it. Do some digging and tell me what you think about it when I get back from Vegas."

"I'll get right on it."

"Good. By the way, don't let Allison know I told you about this."

"Okay."

Gillette patted Wright's shoulder. "Well, that's it. Go back out and have some fun. It's nice seeing your bride again."

"Thanks." Wright turned to go, then paused. "Chris?"

"Yeah?"

"Is there something going on with you and Allison?"

My God, Gillette thought, don't these people have anything else to worry about? "Of course not."

"It's just that—"

Billy's cell phone rang before Wright could finish.

"Christian," Billy called, "it's for you."

"Excuse me, David," Gillette said, taking the phone. "Hello?"

"Christian, it's Cathy."

"Yes," he said, watching Wright head off.

"I spoke to Dr. Davis. Thanked him for meeting with you like you asked."

A wave of relief washed over Gillette. "Thanks."

JOSEPH "22" CELINO sat on the patio of his modest Staten Island home, enjoying the hazy view of lower Manhattan in the distance. It was across New York Harbor, which was dotted by pleasure craft and the two orange ferries about to pass each other. He glanced to the left at the Statue of Liberty, thinking about his Brooklyn childhood, about how the United States really was the land of opportunity—if you were willing to take risks. His father had tried to bring up nine children without taking any risks, in and out of work as a welder in the shipyards, but he'd gotten further and further behind every year, racking up huge debts, finally committing suicide when Celino was nine. As far as Celino was concerned, his father was a coward and had gotten what he deserved. No risk, no reward.

Celino had dropped out of high school to work as a bag boy in a grocery store for a buck seventy-five an hour, trying to help pay the family bills. But he'd quickly grown frustrated with the meager paycheck and agreed to make his first hit when a friend of a friend introduced him to a Mafia capo. The target was the owner of a Queens liquor store who refused to pay protection, and Celino had shot him with his twenty-two pistol as the guy was locking up one hot summer night. Celino found killing easy, sticking around a few minutes after the store owner crumpled to the ground to watch him vainly fight death, fascinated by the struggle. Celino was paid three hundred dollars later that night and never went back to the grocery store. By the time he was nineteen, Celino had murdered twenty-eight people.

Despite his small size—five six and a hundred forty pounds—he developed a reputation as one of the meanest, coldest men in New York. Never making a hit with a partner—not even another made man—so there were no witnesses. And always with his twenty-two. Now he was don of one of the most powerful Mafia families in the country—the Carbones. A name that struck fear in the heart of every other mobster and lawman in the country.

"How's Christian Gillette doing?" Celino asked, picking up a cheese-and-salami cracker from a platter in the middle of the table.

"He's going to Vegas next week." Al Scarpa was Celino's only direct report. Scarpa took care of all the details so Celino rarely had to leave the house. He was even smaller than Celino, and he carried a forty-four.

"Is he going to play?"

"I think so," Scarpa said, picking at something

under one of his fingernails. "Quentin Stiles talked to our consulting friend out there yesterday. Gillette's going to meet with him next week. And one other," Scarpa added.

"He better pick the right one."

"He will."

"Has Stiles completely recovered?" Celino asked, chewing on the cracker.

"About ninety percent."

"Even at ninety percent he's dangerous. We've known that for a long time. The Philadelphia people warned us about him."

Scarpa nodded. "I agree, but don't worry about it, boss. I got everything taken care of."

Celino's eyes narrowed. There was no reason to ask any more questions when Scarpa said he had something taken care of. Scarpa had been his under-boss for eight years, and Celino trusted the man completely. As much as a Mob boss could trust anyone. "Are we keeping up with things as agreed?"

"Yes."

"You have our top people on this, right? I can't have anything going wrong here, you understand? It's critical that we hold up our end of the bargain. Critical to many of our operations, to the advantage we have over our friends."

"I know, boss, believe me." Scarpa moved his chair to the right a few inches, to stay beneath the shade of the umbrella. "You know, I've always admired how you keep things so low-key, Joseph."

"What do you mean?"

"You're worth so much money, but your house . . . well . . . I don't want to insult you. I mean, it's a very nice house. But you could afford so much more. I know you do this so you don't bring attention to the family, but it must be frustrating sometimes when you see the Wall Street guys spreading money around on houses like its manure."

Celino waved. "Doesn't bother me at all. They work hard, just like I do. Whatever a man wants to do with his money is his business, as long as it doesn't affect me." He gazed out over the harbor again. "Now, how is Allison Wallace fitting in at Everest?"

Scarpa smiled. "Very well, boss. Very well."

GILLETTE AND PEGGY WRIGHT stood alone on the aft deck of the **Everest,** sipping drinks—Peggy her third martini, Gillette another Pepsi. They were thirty miles offshore, out of sight of land. Gillette liked seeing nothing but water. It made him feel as though he were truly unreachable, safe from the stress of business, if only temporarily.

"Thank you for promoting David." Peggy was a petite brunette with a pretty smile. "He was so happy."

"He deserved it."

"He works hard."

"Yes, he does," Gillette agreed. "And I depend on him."

Peggy looked around, making sure David wasn't anywhere in sight. "My husband thinks you walk on water, Christian. He's always saying, 'Well, Christian would look at it this way,' or, 'Christian would do it that way.' He's always thinking about Everest. Always thinking about how he can find deals or raise more money."

"That's why I promoted him. I know how dedicated he is." Gillette swirled the ice cubes in his cup. "Where are you from, Peggy?"

She'd been looking out to sea, watching a flock of seagulls diving at something dead on the surface. "Columbus, Ohio. Why?"

"We're involved in a deal on the Eastern Shore of Maryland, and David said he had relatives there. I was pretty sure his family was from Connecticut, so I thought maybe he meant the connection to Maryland was on your side."

Peggy shook her head slowly, a perplexed expression crossing her face. "I don't have any relatives in Maryland, and David's never mentioned anyone on his side who lives there." She swallowed hard when she saw the intense expression on Gillette's face. "Did I say something wrong?"

Gillette shook his head calmly. "You know what? It's my mistake. I was thinking of someone else. Sorry."

. . .

BILLY HURRIED into the yacht's large dining room and leaned down close to Gillette so the others at the table couldn't hear him. "We have a problem," he said quietly. "Come with me."

Gillette excused himself and followed Billy into the next room. "What's wrong?"

"There's a line of thunderstorms coming straight at us that's really bad. It's a freak thing. They popped up out of nowhere with all this heat and humidity."

"Jesus." Gillette moved through a sliding door onto a side deck and glanced up into the black sky. There'd been stars out an hour ago; now they were gone. "How long until we get hit?"

"About forty minutes."

"We can't make it to a harbor?"

"No way, not enough time."

"How the hell can a storm this bad form so fast?" Gillette asked.

"It doesn't happen very often, but when it does, it can be deadly. You remember what happened in Baltimore a couple of years ago? Freak storm hit the harbor, **right downtown.** Bunch of people drowned in a ferry." He checked the sky nervously. "Look, the Coast Guard's on the radio telling everybody who can't make port to batten down hatches and point their crafts due east, into the storm. They're saying we could get fifteen-foot seas, maybe higher, with sustained winds up to forty miles an hour and gusts up to a hundred. It ain't gonna last long, but it's gonna be hell while it's on us."

Gillette looked up and down the deck. He could feel the yacht beginning to pitch. "What do you want me to do?"

"Tell your guests things are gonna get real rough. Get them to put on life jackets right away."

"Where should we go? Does it matter?"

"Yeah, go to the enclosed aft quarters. I hate to say this, but I don't want you below if this thing turns over."

"Turns over?"

"I don't know how stable we'll be if we have fifteen-foot waves. I want people to be able to get clear of the boat quick if I give the order. They'll be better off in the water with a life jacket on if the thing isn't gonna last long. I know how that sounds, but I been doing this a long time, and I want to be ready."

"Do you really think it's going to be that—"

Billy held up his hands and shook his head. "I don't know, Christian, but the CG's making it sound **really** bad." He glanced over his shoulder. "I gotta get back to the bridge."

"All right, I'll get everyone ready," Gillette called, and headed back into the dining room.

People looked at him expectantly as he came back in, anticipating a problem because the boat had started to roll noticeably. "We've got a situation, folks," he said, standing behind his chair at the table.

"Mother Nature's decided to throw a fireball at us. There's a nasty line of thunderstorms heading right for us, and we need to get ready. We need to put life jackets on." He pointed at the young boy asleep on a couch, a puppy curled up in his arms. "Especially Danny."

THE *EVEREST* was being pounded by the storm. Wave crests reached twenty feet, gusts hit a hundred and ten miles an hour, and the rain and spray flew so fiercely that visibility was reduced to almost nothing. The yacht rose and fell violently as Billy fought to keep the bow pointed straight into the storm. The passengers, wrapped in bright orange life jackets, clung to anything they could as the boat plowed ahead and the engines roared belowdecks.

A massive surge of water rose off the starboard side of the bow, lifting the yacht high and then rolling it left. As the boat rolled, a wooden chair careened into the sliding glass door at the back of the room, smashing through it. At the same time, Wright, Peggy, Stiles, his girlfriend, Danny, and the puppy he was holding were tossed across the floor at the others, who were huddled against the opposite wall. As he tumbled, Danny lost his grip on the dog.

Wind and rain whipped into the room, and the terrified puppy yelped and tumbled through the smashed door onto the deck. Danny scrambled to his feet and raced after it, disappearing around the corner. His mother screamed and pointed, and Stiles was on his feet instantly, sprinting after the little boy, shielding his face against the driving rain, struggling to keep his balance.

"Quentin!" Gillette yelled, jumping to his feet just as another huge wave crashed into the boat. This time it was on the port side, and it tossed him and the others across the room. He landed heavily on the floor, then crashed into the far wall, and a searing shot of pain raced up his left arm through his shoulder. As he struggled to make it to his hands and knees, another shot of pain knifed through his left shoulder. Wincing, he glanced ahead as a wicked flash of lightning streaked the night sky. Stiles, Danny, and the dog were nowhere in sight.

"Oh God, oh God!" Stiles's girlfriend screamed. She'd seen the same thing.

Gillette crawled quickly across the wet carpet toward the smashed door, wind and driving rain in his face. He was trying to catch any sign of Stiles or Danny as the lightning continued to flash almost unceasingly. He pulled himself to his feet when he felt broken glass beneath his palms and edged toward the door, trying to keep his balance against the constant rocking, the din from outside like the sound of a freight train bearing down on him.

"What are you doing?" yelled Faraday. "You can't go out there."

Gillette burst onto the open aft deck, then dropped quickly to his hands and knees again. Staying on his feet would be impossible. He crawled around the side, the way Danny and Stiles had gone, as the yacht pitched left and knocked him toward the deck wall. He tried to protect his left arm, holding it tight to his side with his other arm as he crashed into the wall. Again he made it back onto his hands and knees. In the crackle of a lightning flash, he spotted Stiles up ahead and started to crawl forward.

The boat was rocked by another pounding swell. Gillette lunged for the bottom step of a stairway leading to an upper deck and clung to it desperately despite the pain in his arm and shoulder. When the wave had washed past, he looked up, still clinging to the stairs, his eyes stinging from the salt. Stiles was grasping the railing with one hand, Danny with the other. A burst of spray hit Gillette, and he ducked behind the stairs again. When he looked up, Stiles was heading toward him with Danny, half crawling, half sliding down the deck.

Just as Stiles reached Gillette, the boat pitched violently to starboard, then up. Gillette grabbed Danny as Stiles slid into the stairs, then past and down the deck thirty feet. As Danny wrapped both arms tightly around Gillette's neck, Gillette looked back, searching through the blinding spray for Stiles. For a moment, he saw the outline of Stiles's figure—

he'd caught a rope and was struggling to his feet, grasping for the side of the boat.

Then, just as he was raising up, Gillette saw him go down again, falling forward and losing his grasp on the side. He crumpled to the deck as another wave crashed over the side, this the biggest one yet, and Gillette had to hold on to the stairs with one arm and Danny with the other, trying mightily to keep from being swept to the back of the yacht. For almost ten seconds, the water rushed past. When it finally eased, Gillette glanced back. Stiles was gone.

For ten minutes, Gillette held on to the bottom stair with one arm and Danny with the other, clenching his teeth against the pain slicing through his left shoulder as wave after wave continued to pound the **Everest.** The young boy shrieked every time the boat rolled, grabbing Gillette around the neck as tight as he could, screaming directly into his ear when another monster crashed over the side. Every time lightning flashed, Gillette glanced back over his shoulder, hoping he'd see Stiles through the storm. But nothing.

Finally, the storm began to subside. The wind and rain eased as quickly as they'd hit. As Gillette started to crawl back toward the aft deck, Faraday and Wright appeared around the corner, hunched over as they moved onto the deck.

"Christian!" Faraday yelled. He and Wright got to Gillette quickly and helped him back inside.

"Danny!" his mother cried, hurrying to Gillette and scooping Danny out of his arms. "Thank you so much," she sobbed, kissing Danny's face over and over. "Thank you, Christian."

"I'm sorry for all this," Gillette said softly. He turned to Faraday as Allison trotted up to him and put her arms around him. "Any sign of Quentin?"

Faraday shook his head. "No."

Gillette wheeled around and headed back out onto the deck, shaking off Allison and moving around the corner. He made his way farther aft, to the spot where Stiles had gone down, yelling Stiles's name over and over and peering into the waves, hoping to spot an orange life vest. Then he headed across the deck to the other side of the boat, then ahead all the way to the bow. But there was no sign of Stiles.

He scrambled up a stairway toward the bridge and burst through the door. "Billy!"

Billy glanced over his shoulder, then back ahead, both hands still glued to the wheel. "Everyone all right back there?"

"No."

Billy's eyes shot to Gillette's.

"Stiles is gone."

"What?"

Gillette quickly explained how he and Stiles had ended up on the deck. "I followed Stiles out and we got the kid, but then he washed past me. I saw him behind me on the starboard-side deck for a second, then he went down. It was weird, he just went down.

Then a wave came over the side, and I lost sight of him."

"How 'bout the kid?"

"I got him. He's fine."

Billy's shoulders sagged. "Good. Look, Stiles is probably—"

"No," Gillette cut in, anticipating what Billy was going to say. "I've been all around the side decks. He's gone. We've got to turn around and look for him. We've got to call the Coast Guard right away."

"You check below?"

"No," Gillette admitted.

"I'll turn around, but I'm not calling the Coast Guard until we're sure he's not on board. They got their share of emergencies tonight, and I want to make sure we really got one before we call them out here."

But ten minutes later, Gillette was back on the bridge. "He's not on board."

Billy picked up the radio microphone and called the Coast Guard, relaying the information about Stiles and giving them coordinates from the GPS.

Gillette could hear the response over the loudspeaker. They had a cutter in the area, and they'd put a chopper in the air with a huge floodlight to cover the spot Billy had given them.

"You said he went down when a wave came over?" Billy asked when he hung up with the Coast Guard.

Gillette heard Billy's voice, but he was thinking

about how Quentin had gone down. One second he was standing, the next he was going down. Limp, not even putting out his hands to cushion the impact. Not as if he'd fallen at all—as if he'd been shot.

13

DERRICK WALKER sat in Gillette's office. One of the most senior QS agents, Walker was taking over Gillette's personal protection. It had been two days since the **Everest** had been caught in the storm on the sound, and Stiles was still missing.

Like Stiles, Walker was African American. His skin was darker than Stiles's, but while he wasn't as tall at six two, he weighed two hundred and fifty pounds, ten pounds more than Stiles weighed when he was healthy. Like Stiles, he had that same aura of control about him. As if things came to him, not the other way around. Gillette took a deep breath. It was almost impossible to believe that Walker was sitting in front of him—not Stiles.

"There won't be any drop in the quality of your protection," Walker began, "I assure you of that." He spoke in a low, tough monotone. "Everything will transition smoothly."

"I'm sure," Gillette said quietly.

"I'm up to speed on everything," Walker continued, "including those GPS devices that were put on your planes. And the fact that you **don't** want them removed."

"Good."

Walker hesitated. "I know Quentin was a friend of yours, a good friend."

"He was." Gillette winced as he shifted. His left arm was still hurting.

"I'm going to be candid. You and I won't have the same kind of relationship. I don't get close to my clients."

Gillette looked away, hiding a sad smile. Stiles had said the same thing when they'd first met. "I understand."

"Do you have any questions?" Walker asked.

Gillette thought for a moment. "Do you own any of QS Security?"

"Excuse me?"

He could see Walker thought it was a strange question. Walker had probably been expecting something more standard, like a rundown of his experience. But Gillette already assumed Walker's experience was excellent. Stiles would never hire anyone who didn't have that kind of background. Gillette was more interested in motivation at this point. "Did Quentin make you an owner? Did he give you any shares of QS?"

"No."

So there was nothing to keep Walker from going to another firm or, more important, being tempted by a huge bribe.

"Why do you ask?" Walker asked.

"Just curious."

"Chris." Debbie broke in on the intercom.

"Yes."

"We've got a problem in the lobby."

"What is it?"

"Just get out here," she urged.

Gillette rose from his chair. "Come on, Derrick."

They hustled to the lobby, and as they neared reception, Gillette saw two QS agents standing in the wide double-doorway entrance, blocking someone's progress. He could hear yelling from outside the doors and recognized the voice instantly. Allison Wallace.

"What's going on?" Gillette asked, pushing his way through the agents.

"These guys won't let my new assistant through," she answered angrily, pointing at the agents.

The young man standing beside her was tall and thin, with wavy, jet black hair, brown eyes, and a dark, pocked complexion. As far as Gillette could tell, he was Arab. "I'm Christian Gillette," he said, extending his hand.

"Hamid Mohamed." The young man's expression—a slight sneer—didn't change.

"He doesn't have clearance," explained one of the agents.

"What's that mean?" Allison demanded.

"Every new employee has to have a background check before he or she can work here," Walker said, stepping beside Gillette.

"You didn't have one done on me," she argued, looking at Gillette.

"We didn't need to." Gillette spied Faraday, who'd come out to see what the ruckus was about. "You know that." He gestured at Faraday. "Get everybody in the conference room for the managers meeting, Nigel."

"Right." Faraday hesitated a moment longer, then turned and headed back down the corridor.

"How long does this background check take?" Allison asked.

"Up to two weeks," Walker replied.

"Christ, look, I—"

"Allison, these guys are just following orders," Gillette interrupted. "**My orders.** I'm sure Hamid will check out fine, but until he does we go by the rules. Like we do with everyone else." He turned to Mohamed. "Please don't take offense, Hamid, it's just procedure." He pointed at Allison. "She didn't know."

Mohamed glanced deliberately at Allison, then back at Gillette. "This is ridiculous. You're doing this because I'm Iranian. This is nothing but racial profiling."

"Frankly," Gillette answered, "I had no idea you were Iranian."

"You could tell I was Arab."

Gillette moved close to Mohamed. "Listen, pal, I don't like your attitude. But as long as your background check comes up clear, if Allison wants you, you could be a Klingon for all I care." He glared at her. "Let's go, it's three o'clock, we're going to be late for the meeting." As he passed Walker, he touched his arm. "Get this guy's info and get it processed fast," he instructed. "I want his background check done by COB tomorrow."

"Yes, sir."

"Christian." Allison was running to keep up as Gillette hurried toward the conference room. **"Christian!"**

"What?"

"This is ridiculous, there's no problem with Hamid. He's been working at Citibank for the last three years. He has great references. I've talked to them."

"Then I'm sure he'll check out fine, but he still goes through what everyone else does."

"This is silly. If I say he's okay, he's okay. I'm a managing partner here, and I've invested five billion dollars."

Gillette whipped around, glaring at her. "As you constantly remind me. But you still don't get special treatment, Allison."

"All right," she said quietly, her expression softening. "I'm sorry."

"Look," he said, his tone turning less confrontational, too, "I told Walker to get Hamid's background check done by COB tomorrow. As long as everything clears, he'll be in here first thing Wednesday morning."

She nodded. "Thanks." As he turned away, she called to him.

"Yeah?"

"You okay?"

He looked at her for a few moments. "Come on," he said quietly, "we're late."

Gillette strode into the conference room, Allison trailing him. Everyone else was already seated. "Last week," he began, standing behind his chair at the head of the table and putting both hands on the back of it as the room went from noisy to silent in a heartbeat, "I told all of you that the Wallace Family had committed five billion dollars to Everest Eight, and that a member of their family, Allison Wallace, would join us as a managing partner." He gestured to his right. "For any of you who haven't met her yet, this is Allison. Please welcome her."

She got the customary applause, the rapping of knuckles on the tabletop.

"Thank you." She'd already introduced herself to all the managing partners, but to only a couple of the managing directors.

"You'll sit by Debbie today," Gillette said to Allison, "but next week you'll sit to Tom's left." He pointed at Jim Richards, a managing director, who was sitting beside O'Brien. "Everyone will move down one. And on this side," he continued, shifting his attention to the other side of the table, "David Wright will now sit next to Maggie. David's been promoted to managing partner," he announced, pulling out his chair and easing into it. Seat changes at the meeting weren't allowed until Gillette had formally announced promotions to the group. In Wright's case, the announcement and the seat changes made clear that he'd jumped over several other managing directors who'd been at Everest longer.

"I'm surprised Wright wasn't the first one in here today and didn't plop himself down in that chair beside Maggie," Faraday whispered to Gillette as people rapped their knuckles on the tabletop again—not nearly as loudly as they had for Allison. "Actually, I'm surprised he didn't send out his own e-mail announcing his promotion."

Gillette would have smiled, but his mind was elsewhere. "All right, let's go through updates. I—"

"Mr. Gillette."

Gillette turned toward the door. It was Karen, one of the receptionists. "Yes?"

"I'm sorry to interrupt, but can I see you a moment? It's important."

"Take over," Gillette muttered to Faraday, getting up. "Update them on the fact that we finalized the purchase of the Vegas franchise. Then have Wright talk about Hush-Hush and have Allison talk about Veramax." He'd told Faraday about the dinner with Jack Mitchell. "Don't mention your connection to the French company on Hush-Hush, though. I don't want people knowing about that yet. Don't say anything about Apex, either."

Faraday nodded.

"Yes, Karen," Gillette said as he reached the door, Faraday's voice piping up in the background.

"Mr. Walker needs to see you in your office right away."

Gillette headed quickly down the corridor. "What is it, Derrick?" he asked as he came through the doorway.

Walker was just putting down the phone. "That was the Coast Guard. They've called off the search."

"YOU ALL RIGHT?"

It was four-thirty, and Gillette was sitting alone in a corner booth of the Irish bar on the first floor of the Everest building. It was a bar Faraday frequented but Gillette had never been to. He was leaning forward, elbows resting on the table, hands over his eyes. At the sound of the familiar voice, he dropped his hands slowly to his mouth and opened his eyes. Faraday was sliding onto the bench seat opposite him.

It was dark and almost empty in here, just a couple of early birds at the bar and two QS agents in the next booth, drinking water. "Been better," Gillette muttered.

A waiter appeared at the table. "Hello, Nigel."

"Hi, Mickey."

"Long time since I've seen you down here this early."

"Things change."

"What'll it be?"

"Guinness."

"Not a Scotch?"

"Guinness," Faraday repeated.

"Tall or small?"

"Small."

"You got it."

Faraday glanced at the full shot glass in front of Gillette on the scratched, wooden tabletop. "Scotch?"

"Yeah."

"Been a while, hasn't it?"

Gillette nodded.

"I know this thing with Stiles is really bothering you. I know how close you two were. I'm sorry. But should you—"

"I should do what gets me through."

"Okay."

They sat in silence until the waiter returned with Faraday's beer. Faraday picked up the mug, touched it to the shot glass in front of Gillette, and took a long guzzle. "What did you need to talk to me about?" he asked, wiping his mouth with the back of his hand. "That you needed Debbie to get me out of the meeting for."

"Stiles."

Faraday took another gulp of Guinness. "Well, I . . . I mean I'm honored that you want to confide in me, Christian. I know you miss him; he was a good man."

"He was shot, Nigel."

Faraday had been looking toward the bar. His head snapped left at this. **"What?"**

In his mind, Gillette replayed the image of Stiles falling to the deck so many times. Replayed the way Stiles hadn't held out his hands to break his fall, just went down like a board. Because he was already dead when he was falling. Already shot. It had come to him after Derrick Walker had told him the search had been called off. It was almost a perfect murder, Gillette thought. The gale-force winds had drowned out the report of the gun, and visibility was so terrible that he hadn't seen blood fly from the wound or spilled on the deck afterward because the torrential rains had washed it away immediately. Whoever killed him had shot him, then tossed him overboard, assuming his body would never be found. "He was shot on board, after he saved the kid. I'm sure of it."

Faraday's face contorted into a look of disbelief. "By who?"

"I don't know."

"Why would someone shoot him?"

"Revenge." Gillette's fingers closed around the shot glass. He slowly turned it a full revolution but didn't pick it up. "I'm pretty sure Tom McGuire was behind it."

"No shit."

Gillette relayed the story of the gang attack outside the Grill and how he believed McGuire was still out for him and Stiles. "You must have really seen him that day on Park Ave."

Faraday nodded glumly. "So you think maybe he got to one of the yacht's crew."

"Yeah. Probably paid them, like Stiles and I think he paid the Brooklyn gang."

"Jesus."

"Here's the point, Nigel. If all that's true, I'm in danger, even with the QS guys around." Gillette started to pick up the shot glass but didn't. "So I've got to let you in on a few things, in case all of a sudden I'm not around."

Faraday straightened up in his seat. "Okay."

"First, we need to talk about the NFL franchise."

"What about it?"

"I think the Mafia's trying to get involved."

"How?"

"Construction initially, of both the stadium and the casino. They'll extort us to keep people on the job and the equipment running. Then they'll try to get involved with the casino and the team. The NFL doesn't think so, but Stiles did some checking and I do. I'm meeting with some consultants when I go out there this week. People who'll run interference on that, but I think it's still going to be a problem. I'll keep you informed."

"Should we just get the fuck out of it?" Faraday asked. "Tell the NFL we don't want it?"

"No. It's going to be a huge win for us, even if the Mob is involved. We just have to figure out how to handle them."

"Okay."

Gillette could see Faraday's fear. He'd never come close to dealing with the Mafia. "The second thing I want to talk to you about is Apex," he said, slowly turning the shot glass another revolution. "As you know, I've been through the Apex portfolio with Russell Hughes, and I think we have a real opportunity."

"Right."

"What you need to understand is that one of their portfolio companies is a cutout for the CIA."

"What's a fucking cutout?"

Gillette quickly explained the concept.

"Which company is it?" Faraday asked.

"Omega IT. They do computer hardware and software system installation and integration. One of Omega's foreign subsidiaries has lots of clients that are Middle Eastern banks. According to Hughes, the Omega sub installs things in the computers that the banks don't know about so people in Washington can watch money flows."

"They're trying to catch fucking terrorists."

"Exactly. Anyway, I'm supposed to meet with

Hughes's CIA contact, probably when I get back from the West Coast at the end of this week. If something happens to me, you do it. Call Hughes and tell him what you know."

"Nothing's going to happen to you, Christian."

"I hope not, but we can't be too careful at this point."

Faraday shook his head. "You deal with a lot of fucking shit, don't you."

This time Gillette almost picked up the shot glass, but again he resisted the temptation. He was testing himself, he knew. "I'd say you don't know the half of it, but now you do."

Faraday finished his beer. "Now there's something **I** want to talk to **you** about."

Gillette looked up. "What?"

"Allison."

"What about her?"

"I don't like her," Faraday said bluntly.

"You gotta be kidding me."

"Nope. I don't trust—"

"You guys want anything else?" Mickey asked, sauntering up to the table.

"I'll take another beer," Faraday said.

"What's your problem with Allison?" Gillette asked angrily when Mickey was gone.

Faraday shrugged. "Like I said, I don't trust her. It's hard to explain. Maybe it's the way she's tried to move in so fast."

"What do you mean?"

"Pushing Veramax so hard, for instance."

"It's a great deal."

"She had it teed up before she came here so you'd think she was good."

"So what?" Gillette snapped. "That's just good business. She wanted an early win. First impressions are important anywhere. She knows that, she's smart. **And,**" he continued, holding up one hand, "she's already got **another** deal going."

"Well, look who her fucking family is, for Christ's sake. It's easy for her, almost like she's cheating."

Sour grapes, Gillette thought. A normal human reaction, but he hadn't expected it from Faraday. "And we want to take advantage of that. It isn't like we're playing T-ball here and everyone gets a chance to bat. This is the big leagues."

"And I don't like the way she's tried to move on you," Faraday added. "It makes me want to puke."

"What do you mean?"

"Saturday on the boat she was all over you. And I wasn't the only one who noticed, let me tell you."

"Nothing's happened. Nothing will."

"People are talking," Faraday said. "They're worried that you and she are getting too close too fast, and that she's going to start having more and more influence on you. Maybe even helping to call the shots pretty soon. People don't like that."

"What 'people'?"

"The other managing partners."

Gillette was about to answer, but Mickey showed

up carrying Faraday's beer. When he was gone, Gillette said, "She's not going to start calling the shots."

"She's twenty-five percent of the new fund. **Five billion dollars.** That's a big advantage over everyone else here. You might get addicted to the money, and the bikini," Faraday muttered.

"I deserve more credit than that, Nigel," Gillette shot back. "I've—"

"And I don't like this thing with the Iranian guy," Faraday interrupted. "Call me prejudiced, but I don't think it makes sense to bring him in here."

"Careful."

"It's a feeling, Christian. I don't like—"

"Hi, guys."

Gillette and Faraday looked up at Allison.

She slid onto the bench seat beside Gillette. "I'm surprised, Christian," she said, "leaving the managers meeting to come to a bar. Either you've got all the newspapers in this city snowed, or there's something big going on." She put her hand on his arm. "Or you miss your friend," she said quietly. "Sorry."

"I'm going back upstairs," Faraday said, giving Allison a forced smile. "I'll take care of that stuff we talked about."

"Call me **Chris,** Nigel."

Nigel already had one foot out of the booth. He stopped. "That was one of the bravest things I've ever seen anyone do, Chris. You and Stiles going out into that storm after that little boy. I wanted you to know that. I just wish both of you had come back." He nodded at Gillette, then gave Allison another quick smile. "See you upstairs."

When Faraday was gone, Allison picked up the shot glass in front of Gillette and sniffed. "Oh, God," she said, almost gagging.

"What can I get you, ma'am?" Mickey was back again.

"Chardonnay. Your best by the glass." She put her hand on Gillette's thigh when Mickey was gone. "I'm sorry, I know it's—"

"Tell me about Hamid," Gillette interrupted, moving his leg. He didn't want any more pity. "What's his background?"

Her eyes stayed on him a moment, then she shrugged. "He worked in Citibank's mergers and acquisitions department for the last three years. Before that he went to business school at the University of Michigan. I don't remember where he was before that. Why the interrogation?"

"How did you find him?"

"Friend of a friend."

"What friend?"

"A friend from Chicago. Look, I don't have to answer—"

"How did you know I was down here?"

"Debbie told me."

So she and Debbie really were talking. "What friend in Chicago?"

She rolled her eyes. "A guy I used to date, if you

really must know. He works at Harris Fulmer. It's an investment bank."

Gillette felt a strange pang. "I know Harris." It felt like jealousy.

Mickey returned with Allison's glass of wine and set it down.

"How did this friend of yours know Hamid?" Gillette asked.

Allison was about to pick up her glass. "What's your problem? Is this really racial profiling? Was Hamid right?"

Gillette was thinking about the al-Qaeda conduit who, according to Norman Boyd, had approached one of the people on the DARPA nanotech project. And he was thinking about how uncomfortable Faraday was with Hamid. "No."

She took a sip of wine. "What's in Richmond?" she asked out of nowhere.

Gillette glanced up. "Huh?"

"Why did you go to Richmond the other day?"

"How do you know I went to Richmond?" he demanded.

"I told you," she answered calmly. "I'm Allison Wallace. Now, what were you doing there?"

"Research on a company. Like **I** told **you.**"

She sighed and took a sip of wine. "I have an idea."

"What?"

"You should sell Everest's medical products company to me."

Gillette's eyes zipped to hers.

"What's it called?" she asked.

"You mean Beezer Johnson?" It was the company with the division in Minneapolis that Boyd wanted to hide his nanotech project in.

"That's it."

Gillette turned on the bench seat so he was facing her. "Why do you think we should sell Beezer Johnson?"

"It's a great company, and it's about time you had another win."

"What are you talking about? We've had several big wins lately. Like we talked about when you, Gordon, and I met."

"Actually, it's been a few months since you've sold anything. We need some good press."

"We're about to announce our intent to sell Laurel Energy. That'll create a fantastic buzz."

"But it'll be a while until you actually sell it. Probably six months before all the documents are completed. We want to keep the positive momentum going." She took a swallow of wine. "Here's the deal. My family has an investment in a medical products company, too. I can convince the board of that firm to make a very nice offer for Beezer Johnson. Very nice. And the whole thing can be wrapped up in sixty days."

Gillette grimaced, thinking hard about what Faraday had said—that he didn't trust her. How she knew he'd been to Richmond and how there were suddenly GPS trackers on his planes. How it suddenly seemed so coincidental that she'd want to buy Beezer Johnson just as Norman Boyd wanted to use it as a cutout.

She smiled back at him. "So, what do you think?"

"It would look like an inside job," he countered. Maybe Allison wasn't protégée material after all. Maybe she was an enemy. "The market wouldn't give us credit because your family controls the buying company."

"But technically we don't control it. We made that investment through a number of different entities. No one would ever be able to figure it out. I'll prove it to you." Her smile grew broader. "**Now** what do you think?"

"I don't know."

She cocked her head to one side and leaned close to him. "Well, I'll tell you what I think," she said, her voice dropping to a whisper. "I think you and I make a great team."

IT WAS LATE, ten-thirty, and everyone else had left for the night. Gillette slipped into Cathy Dylan's cramped office and shut the door. "Hi."

She looked up from a spreadsheet she'd been working on. "Hi."

"Thanks for staying." He'd slipped her a note that afternoon.

"Sure. What do you need me to do?"

"I need you to call our doctor friend in Richmond again, and I need you to make me an appointment for Friday. Whatever time he can do it."

"Okay."

"I'll be in Las Vegas and on the West Coast most of this week, so e-mail me when you and Dr. Davis talk."

"Okay."

"But don't mention his name. I want you to call him Mr. Jones in the e-mail, and I want you to use another day, some day in the following week. The only thing that will be accurate in the e-mail will be the time. Don't tell anyone we've spoken about this. Just like before. Got it?"

"Yes," she said hesitantly.

Gillette could see it was all she could do not to ask.

Maybe someday I'll tell her, he thought. But right now, the less she knew, the safer she was. There were enough people in danger. One was already gone.

SHE SAT ON the floor of Gillette's living room, between his legs, as he sat behind her on the sofa and rubbed her shoulders. It was late—they were watching Letterman sign off—but Gillette didn't want to go to bed yet. He was tired, but he knew he'd never get to sleep. Too much on his mind.

"That feels so good, Chris." Faith moaned and ran her hands up to his, then turned and rose to her knees so she was facing him. "I've missed you so much. I'm glad we've got tonight, at least."

Faith had gotten back from London a few hours ago, and Gillette was leaving for Las Vegas tomorrow. Then he was going on to the West Coast to meet Marilyn.

She gave him a deep kiss. "Let's go to bed," she whispered, taking his chin in her fingers and shaking it gently when he didn't answer. "Hey, boy, I just propositioned you."

He smiled. All she had on was one of his dress shirts. She looked so sexy.

She hugged him. "I'm so sorry about Quentin, honey. I know you loved him."

"Yeah."

"How did it happen?" she asked. "You told me he went overboard, but how?"

"He was trying to get to his girlfriend's little boy. The kid went after his dog when the thing ran out onto the deck in the storm."

"That's awful." Faith moved onto the couch beside him and ran her fingers through his hair. "Who else went with you on the cruise?"

Gillette took a deep breath. "Faraday and his new girlfriend, David and Peggy Wright."

"That's all?"

Gillette gazed at her. He didn't want to get into it now, but he couldn't lie to her, either. "Well, I—"

"You took Allison Wallace," she said before he could finish, her posture going rigid. "Didn't you."

"Look, I—"

"Did you?"

"It wasn't like **I took** her, sweetheart. She's a partner at the firm. It was a firm outing."

Faith stood up. "It wasn't like you **took her** to dinner the other night here in New York, either, was it?" she asked. "She just came along, right? Why would you let her go with you on a cruise like that when you knew I was upset about those pictures?"

There was no winning this battle. The best thing to do was surrender immediately. "I wasn't thinking, Faith, I'm sorry."

"Did you ask your other partners? Tom, Maggie, or Blair?"

"No," he admitted.

"Did you sleep with her in Pittsburgh, Chris?"

"Of course not."

"How do I know?"

"Because I'm telling you."

Faith stared at him for a few moments, hands on her hips. Finally, she shook her head and groaned. "I love you so much, but I can't take this. We're away from each other more than we're together anyway, so I can't be thinking you're with someone else when I'm gone." With that she stalked out.

He started to get up, then fell back on the couch and put his hands over his eyes. Nothing was going right.

14

GILLETTE SAT UP groggily in the comfortable leather chair and tossed the crossword puzzle lying on his lap to the floor. They'd taken the bigger of the two Everest jets—a Gulfstream IV—to Las Vegas. "How long till we land, Derrick?" he asked, stretching. He'd slept very little since Saturday.

"We're close," Walker answered, "only about fifteen minutes out."

"Any word?" At Gillette's suggestion, the police had begun interviewing the crew about Stiles's disappearance. The cops had talked to Billy yesterday but let him go, satisfied that he knew nothing.

"Yeah, they questioned the cook this afternoon. Gave him the same bare-bulb treatment they gave Billy. They're convinced he doesn't know anything either."

"Have they found the mate yet?"

"Nope."

Walker brought the piece of gum he was chewing forward and smacked it with his front teeth for a few seconds. Something he did when he was thinking hard, Gillette had noticed.

"He's our man," Walker said. "I can feel it. But Billy doesn't know anything about him. Never even got his home address, so it's going to be tough to find him. Maybe impossible."

It was Tuesday afternoon, and Gillette hadn't heard from Daniel Ganze about his father—Ganze had said it would be early this week at the latest when he'd have more information. He spotted Wright walking toward him from the back of the plane. "Have a seat." He pointed at the big leather chair on the other side of the plane. He'd decided to bring Wright along this morning, wanting to have a second while he interviewed the consultants who were going to deal with the Carbones.

Allison hadn't been happy about not coming along, but he didn't care. He needed a break from her. Needed to clear his head and think about what Faraday had said in the bar. Needed to think about her suggestion to buy Beezer right as Boyd had made contact. How Veramax's products would make excellent nanotech delivery systems. Nothing specific here, but a lot of coincidences.

"I meant to tell you," he said to Wright, "Nigel and I talked last night, and now that you're a managing partner, we're going to give you five percent of the ups on Everest Eight, with all the normal caveats, of course."

"Jesus, thanks."

"If we only double the fund over the next few years, we keep over four billion of the profits and you get more than two hundred large of that."

"That's awesome." Wright looked out the window at the barren desert below them. "I was excited about our meeting this morning." He and Gillette had met with the Bermuda-based insurance company before heading to LaGuardia. At the end of the meeting, the firm's lead partner had committed half a billion to Everest Eight, so the fund was now $20.5 billion. "And I'm working on another lead my father gave me. Could be another five hundred large."

Wright's drive never faltered. "We've got to close this fund at some point."

"Let's try to make it an even twenty-one billion," Wright urged.

"How long will it take you to smoke these people out, to see if they're real?"

"Give me a week."

"Who are they?"

"The Ohio Teachers Pension. My dad's good friends with the woman who runs it. From college or something, I'm not sure. Anyway, they're usually very conservative, but Dad says we've got a good shot at getting money from them, especially now that the Wallaces are in for five billion."

It was the whale factor, Gillette knew. Once other investors heard that a family like the Wallaces were in big, **everyone** wanted in. "All right, go for it."

"I will. So what's going on with the investigation?" Wright asked, nodding at Walker. On the way to the airport, Gillette had told Wright what he thought had really happened to Stiles.

"We think it's the mate."

"You still think Tom McGuire is behind it? That he's the one pulling the strings?"

"Yeah," Gillette said as one of the QS agents tapped him on the shoulder. The agent was holding the plane's phone.

"For you, sir."

"Thanks. . . . Hello?"

"Christian?"

"Yes."

"This is Percy Lundergard in Chatham, Maryland."

"Hi." Lundergard was a local attorney Gillette had hired to help Everest through the referendum process, to help fight Becky Rouse. Lundergard's family had been in Chatham for two hundred years, but unlike Percy, most of them were farmers and fishermen and fell into the have-not category. Gillette had made sure of that before retaining Lundergard. "What's up?"

"I've been through all the town charter documents thoroughly, and you're right. We can call a referendum on this thing, and there's nothing Mayor Rouse can do about it." Lundergard spoke with a nasal twang. "But I have a suggestion."

"What?"

"Before you call for the vote, let's have a town meeting. Let's rile some people up. You've got the majority, Christian, but it's like any vote. You've got to get the population out there to win. Gotta get 'em interested. All the rich people will show, so you've got to get a lot of the poor folk out, too. My family can help. I've already spoken to them, but they think a town meeting at the high school would really do the trick."

"Fine. Let's do it."

"You'll need to be there."

"Oh, I'll be there. Don't you worry."

"You'll need to get up and make a speech, and you'll need to connect with them."

Gillette could hear it in Lundergard's voice: He didn't believe a big-shot Manhattanite had a chance in hell of connecting with a Chatham farmer or fisherman. Suddenly Gillette had a challenge on his hands. "I hear you, Percy. I'll see you there."

GILLETTE AND WRIGHT sat in Carmine Torino's spacious office overlooking the Vegas strip. Torino Consulting was furnished with big, gaudy pieces, and the colors were deafening—drapes bright red and the shag carpet a burnt yellow. Torino had thinning straight black hair and wore a flowered golf shirt—unbuttoned so you could see a gold medallion hanging in the dark chest hairs below his neck—and a sleeveless blue sweater. He wore a thick gold bracelet on his left wrist that jingled constantly and a Rolex on his right wrist with a face the size of a silver dollar.

"I love this view," he said, gesturing toward the wide window. The sun had just set, and the strip's neon lights were taking over. "It's the prettiest time of day. I can't imagine living anywhere else."

Gillette and Wright exchanged a subtle roll of the eyes.

"So, you guys got an NFL franchise."

Gillette nodded. He hated how slippery this whole thing felt, but it was a necessary evil. Tomorrow morning they'd meet with Federico Consulting, but Stiles had let him know that Torino was the best. If that was true, Gillette could only imagine what it would be like to sit down with Mick Federico.

"And you want to build a stadium and a casino, the stadium in eighteen months."

"Actually, I want **both** of them built in eighteen months. I want them both done at the same time. It'll be good from a marketing perspective."

"You're gonna use a local contractor, right?"

"No, I'm bringing in a group from Los Angeles that can handle both jobs."

Torino winced. "The local people won't be happy."

"That's why we're here," Wright said. "We understand the game."

Torino looked at Wright disdainfully. "It's no game, sonny, let me tell you."

"Can you take care of it?" Gillette asked.

Torino clasped his hands together, leaned back in his chair, and gazed up at the ceiling for a few moments. "I think so."

"How much?"

Torino smiled. "You're a bottom-line guy, huh? No bullshit? Well, it'll be two million a year until the shit is built, then five million a year after that."

Gillette raised both eyebrows. "Exactly what do I get for my five million a year?"

"A guarantee that you'll have no worker walkouts, because even if you bring in an outside contractor, you'll have to hire local people to be the ants. Another guarantee that your equipment won't break down more than normal. And if it does, you'll be able to get spare parts quickly, not a year later." Torino could see he wasn't impressing anybody. "What the fuck do you want, some leather-bound presentation? I thought you were a bottom-line guy."

"I am."

"Why does the fee go up when the construction is **finished**?" Wright wanted to know.

Torino chuckled. "And I thought you guys were

supposed to be these stiletto-sharp types. Sophisticated and—"

"It goes up," Gillette interrupted, "to give us assurances that the construction will actually get done on time. That we won't be held up for a ball-buster payment with a month to go before the first preseason game, and we end up having to play the whole year at UNLV. And if we miss a year, there'll be problems with the plumbing, electrical outages, bomb scares. Right, Carmine?"

Torino smiled smugly. "Exactly." His bracelet jingled as he pointed at Wright. "See, sonny, that's why he's the boss."

"Here's what I'll do," Gillette offered. "I'll pay you a million a year during construction and three million per thereafter."

Torino shook his head. "This isn't negotiable, Mr. Gillette. It is what it is. You want it, you call me by eight forty-five tomorrow morning. If I don't hear from you by then, the offer's off the table."

Something clicked, and Gillette realized Torino knew their meeting with Federico started at nine.

Torino clapped his hands together enthusiastically, as though he knew the deal were done. "I'm going to a couple of strip clubs and see some of my favorite girls. You guys wanna come?"

"No," Gillette answered quickly, standing. "But we'll be in touch. Thanks for your time."

Five minutes later, Gillette and Wright were standing in front of the building with two QS agents, waiting for the car to pull up. "So, David," Gillette asked, "how do you feel?"

"Like I want to take a shower."

WRIGHT WAS lying on the bed of his Caesar's Palace hotel room when the doorbell rang.

"Room service."

Wright sprang out of bed. He was famished. "Beautiful," he muttered. He was wearing just boxers but didn't bother putting on his pants. "You guys are fast," he said, opening the door. "I thought it would be at least another—" He stopped in midsentence. There were two men in dark suits at the door—and no food.

"We need to talk to you," said one of the men, ushering Wright back into the room before he could close the door. The other man followed and locked the door.

Wright's eyes flickered between the two of them. "What about?"

"Put some clothes on," the man ordered.

"Where are we going?" Wright asked anxiously, reaching for his pants.

"Don't worry about it."

Thirty minutes later, the two men led Wright into the living room of a suite on the top floor of the Hard Rock Hotel.

"Have a seat." One of the men pointed at a couch. "Mr. Celino will be with you in a moment."

Wright swallowed hard. He knew the name. Gillette had explained the reason for the Vegas trip— the fact that the Carbone family was probably who Carmine Torino was fronting for, that Joe Celino was don of the Carbone family, that Celino was one of the most ruthless crime bosses in Mafia history.

When Celino ambled in and sat in a chair opposite the couch, Wright rose, head tilted forward, doing his best to put on an appearance of subordination.

"Sit down."

Wright did.

"I'm Joe Celino, and I obviously know who you are." He motioned for the two men who'd brought Wright to move off. "You've met with one of my men in New York several times, the first time in Saks Fifth Avenue a couple of days ago."

"Yes." Wright's voice was instantly hoarse. "Paul."

"I trust he's been polite to you."

"Yes."

"Congratulations on the NFL franchise; that's exciting news for Everest Capital. As long as you play your cards right, you should enjoy quite a return on that investment. Both from a multiple of invested capital and an IRR perspective."

Wright nodded numbly. Celino wasn't at all what he'd expected. He wasn't macho and boorish. He was nattily dressed: wool blazer, button-down shirt, neatly pressed slacks, Gucci loafers. His English was perfect, he was well groomed, and he was painfully polite.

"You look . . . surprised. What's the matter?"

"Nothing . . . sir."

Celino patted the arm of the chair. "Yes, that was quite a coup Christian Gillette pulled off, winning the NFL franchise." He smiled. "And he wasn't even the high bidder. Imagine that."

"What? How do you know?"

"So we have a few things to talk about," Celino said, ignoring Wright's question.

"But I really—"

"And I hardly ever leave my house on Staten Island. In fact, I think it's been five months since I did. So I hope you understand, this meeting is very, very important."

"I understand."

"Good. Well, as my associate told you at Saks, we, uh . . . well, we know what you did. At the sex shop." Celino raised one finger. "And we have proof. But believe me, Mr. Wright, what a man does in his spare time is no concern of mine. Even if it's perverted. **Unless,** of course, I can take advantage of it. In this case, I can."

Wright was looking down into his lap. He felt a tear form in his left eye.

"You're going to do anything me or my men tell you to do. You're going to do it pronto, and you're going to do it **con gusto.** Are we clear?"

"Yes," Wright said, his voice so quiet that he almost didn't hear it himself.

"How clear?"

"As clear as you want."

Celino nodded his approval. "Good." He pointed at a manila folder lying on a side table next to Wright's chair. "Pick that up and open it."

Wright reached for the folder. Inside was a single eight-and-a-half-by-eleven glossy head shot of a face. The man's eyes had been cut out and his teeth removed. Wright felt a wave of bile rising from his stomach.

"He was still alive at that point, David. Both eyes and all twenty-nine teeth gone, **but he was still breathing.** That's how good my guys are. Am I getting through to you?"

Wright gagged, then nodded.

"You can put it down. Now, I need a few things from you. First, you need to keep telling us where Gillette is at all times, no exceptions. You miss one appointment of his and . . . well . . ." Celino pointed at the folder. "You don't want to end up like him, do you?"

"No."

"Second, I don't want Christian Gillette even **going** to that meeting with Mick Federico tomorrow morning. I want Carmine Torino to get the business. Gillette goes to the meeting with Federico and—"

"But—"

Celino raised his hand, and for the first time a look of rage filled his face.

"Torino will get the business," Wright said meekly.

The rage disappeared as fast as it had come, replaced by contentment. "Now we're getting somewhere, David." Celino pulled out a cigarette and lighted it. "I hope you don't mind."

"No."

"If you do, please say so."

"I love cigarettes." He hated them.

"You want one?" Celino asked, holding out the pack and smiling.

"No, thank you."

Celino put the cigarettes back in his jacket pocket. "You know, when you ask someone to take extraordinary measures for you, I believe you should tell them a little bit about what's going on." He opened his hands and gestured toward Wright. "It makes them feel like they're part of it. Like when you guys give your senior managers stock in the companies they're operating for you. It gives them a stake, right? Makes them more passionate about making things run well."

Wright nodded. That was exactly what they did for their senior managers.

"You see, I believe in the **stick**." Celino pointed at the manila folder on the table beside Wright. "But

I believe in the **carrot,** too. Call me an amateur psychiatrist, but, well, I've done okay for myself, you know?"

Wright could barely breathe. "Very okay."

"So here's the first thing I'm going to let you in on. **We** took care of Stiles. We retained the services of the mate on your partner's yacht. Of course, he's gone now, too." Celino chuckled. "It was a short engagement, and the cops won't find anything. If they do, I'll blame you."

"Why did you kill Stiles?" Wright asked, shuddering at the thought of Celino blaming him for anything.

"He was doing some poking around I didn't like. He was a very resourceful man. I'd had enough." Celino took a long puff off the cigarette. "The second thing I'm going to tell you will blow your mind."

Wright leaned forward. His stomach was feeling better.

"We're working on something big. We and the Wallace Family, that is."

Wright's mouth fell open.

Celino smiled widely. "Let me just tell you, when all this is over and Allison Wallace is running Everest Capital, there'll be a place for you. If you're a good boy." Wright started to say something, but Celino cut him off. "That's all I can tell you about that right now, but it's your big carrot. Treat Miss Wallace with great respect and do what you're told. At the end of the day, you'll be a happy man. Whatever ups Gillette has promised you will look like peanuts compared to what you could earn after he's gone."

Wright's heart was pounding. He was still in shock at what he'd heard, but he was thinking about the possibilities, too.

"There's one more thing," Celino said.

"Yes?"

"We know Gillette is starting to depend on you, but we don't think he trusts you yet. Not as much as we want him to, anyway."

"He trusts me."

Celino gave Wright a dismissive wave. "Like I said, not as much as we want him to. So we're going to set up an incident tomorrow."

"An incident?"

"Yes. You'll get details tomorrow morning after the Federico meeting is canceled. Before you and Gillette go downtown to meet with the city council representatives about the casino." Celino rose from the chair. "Do you have any questions?"

Wright thought for a moment. "There is one thing. Last week I was on the phone with Gillette, trying to find out exactly where he was going so I could report back to your . . . uh . . . associate, Paul."

"Yeah, so?"

"He was going to the Eastern Shore of Maryland, and I was trying to find out exactly what town it was. He asked me why I was so interested and I told him it was because I had family down there."

"And, of course, you don't."

"No," Wright admitted. "I wouldn't be too worried about it except he brought it up with my wife this weekend when we were out on the yacht. You see, he invited a few of us out on it to celebrate—"

"I know," Celino said coolly, "remember?"

"Right."

"You want me to solve this problem for you?"

"Yes, sir. I'm afraid it might blow everything."

Celino considered the request, then nodded. "All right, I'll do it. Now," he said loudly, pointing toward the door, "please leave."

Wright took one last glance at the manila folder on the table and headed quickly for the door.

When he was in the elevator with the doors closed, he leaned back against the walls, let out a deep breath, and shook his head. So Allison Wallace was going to be running Everest Capital.

15

IT TOOK EVERY ounce of self-control Gillette had not to smash the cell phone on the marble floor when it rang. He'd take so much pleasure watching it disintegrate into a thousand pieces. Then no one would be able to reach him on it anymore. **"What is it?"**

"We need you in that northern city we discussed when we met last week. We need you there tomorrow morning, ready to go by nine."

It was two o'clock. Gillette and Wright were sitting in the hotel lobby, waiting for the limo to take them to the Las Vegas airport. Earlier, they'd finished a grueling three-hour session with several members of the city council concerning the casino. After some horse trading, it appeared everything was a go, thanks in no small part to his having retained Carmine Torino at eight-thirty that morning, Gillette figured. He glanced over at Wright, who was in the chair beside him. David was going back to New York on a commercial flight, and he was headed to the West Coast to see Marilyn—and Lana. David had pushed so hard this morning at breakfast not to even bother with Federico.

"I can't," Gillette replied, refocusing on the call, "I've got plans."

"Cancel them," Ganze ordered. "We need to go **now.** You have to arrange for us to move into the space up there right away. Figure that out tonight or **early** tomorrow morning so we're ready to go at nine. We only need about three thousand square feet, but it's got to be remote, it's got to have its own access. We've had our people up there scoping out the facility, and there's a building near the river we think would be perfect. We can take care of security, no need for you to worry about that. All you need to do is get a heart valve research lab out of there. It's just a few people. That's the only thing in there at this point."

So Ganze had been watching the Minneapolis facility for a while. "I'm going to meet these people, right?" Gillette asked. "The three we talked about? The biochemist in charge of the project and her two top assistants?"

There was nothing but dead air.

"Ganze?"

"I have to talk to my boss about that."

"You promised me."

"I know," Ganze agreed quietly.

"I'm not doing this unless I meet them," Gillette vowed, "and unless I hear more about my father. You told me I would by now." Once again he glanced over at Wright, who was fiddling with his own cell phone. Gillette pressed the phone tightly to his ear. "You got that?"

"I'll give you more on that tomorrow after our meeting," Ganze promised. "I do have additional information."

"Tell me now."

"Not on a cell phone. Look, I know you're frustrated," Ganze said, his voice growing compassionate. "Just meet with us tomorrow. You'll be glad you did." He waited a moment. "Hello?"

"All right."

"Good. Find a hotel on the south side of the city. In Bloomington or Edina. You'll hear from me later on."

"Yeah, okay." Gillette clicked off.

"What's going on?" Wright wanted to know, stowing his cell phone away immediately.

Gillette checked the lobby for the QS agents. He didn't see them at first—just loudly dressed tourists moving in all directions. He sat up, his breath instantly short. Then he saw the agents over by a pillar. His shoulders sagged.

"Chris?"

"Damn it, David, keep your shorts on."

"Jeez, bite my head off."

Gillette relaxed into the chair. "Sorry." He sighed.

Sometimes it seemed as though his life weren't his own anymore. More and more he thought about giving it all away. "Change of plans," he explained. He'd have to call Marilyn from the plane to tell her he wasn't coming. A tough trade, he thought ruefully: meeting his real mother the first time for learning more about his father. "I'm not going to the West Coast now."

"Where are you going?"

"Something's come up."

"I thought you were seeing . . . your family."

"I was."

"Well, whatever came up must be pretty important if it's getting in the way of that."

"Drop it, David," Gillette said bluntly.

"I just thought we were going to be in contact all the time."

"We are. With cell phones and Blackberries."

"Yeah, but it would be helpful to know where you are in case—"

"Where's the damn limousine?" Gillette barked, surprising even himself.

"It'll be here soon," Wright assured him. "I talked to the QS guy in charge. Ten minutes tops. What's wrong?"

"Nothing."

"You just seem—"

"I told you, drop it."

"Okay, okay." Wright stayed quiet for a few moments. "You want to talk about our meeting with the city council people? You know, compare notes?"

Might as well do something with the downtime, Gillette figured. "Okay," he agreed, noticing a blonde who was sitting across the lobby from him. She was older—in her mid-forties—but very attractive. She smiled at him as their eyes met, and he smiled back politely.

"So, what did you think?" Wright asked.

"I thought it went pretty well," Gillette answered, trying to hide a yawn. He hadn't slept well again last night. Each night, he replayed the scene on the yacht deck in his mind, trying to figure out if he was missing something. Something that might help the police figure out what had happened to Stiles. "I think the casino's ours if we want it. The one guy in the maroon leisure suit at the other end of the table was a pain in the ass, but they'll probably send Carmine Torino to see him and that'll be that."

"It was amazing how they already knew you'd hired Torino when we got there," Wright commented.

"It's a rigged town. Always has been, always will be, no matter what anybody says." Gillette looked over at the blonde again. She was touching her chest, seemed to be breathing hard. "I want to ask you something."

"Yeah?"

"Why did you tell me you had relatives on the Eastern Shore of Maryland?"

Wright's mouth fell slowly open. "Because . . . I do."

"I talked to Peggy on the boat Saturday, and she said you've never mentioned having family there to her."

Wright shrugged. "I guess I never mentioned it to her. I mean, they're distant cousins, you know? I don't think I've seen them in ten years."

"Which side?" Gillette asked, leaning forward in his chair.

"Huh?"

"Which side of the family? Your mother's or father's?" Gillette stared at the blonde. She seemed to be trying to get up out of her seat, but she was having trouble. **"Jesus,"** he said, standing up and pointing, "I think that woman's having a heart attack."

The blonde clutched her chest as she finally made it to her feet. She staggered a few steps forward, then crumpled to the ground. Gillette, the two QS agents, and Wright rushed toward her.

As they did, a man who'd been sitting in a chair nearby stood up and drew a pistol from his jacket, aiming at Gillette.

"Chris!" Wright shouted, knocking Gillette to the ground as the first shot rang out. He sprinted at the shooter as the QS agents dropped to their knees and drew their weapons.

"Don't shoot!" Gillette yelled at the agents as Wright closed in on the assailant.

One more shot rang out, then Wright was on the

guy, knocking him down and grabbing his wrist, slamming it against the marble floor. The gun skittered away. The QS agents were on the man a heartbeat later, rolling him onto his stomach and cuffing his hands behind his back.

Gillette let his head fall back gently against the floor. Tom McGuire just wasn't going to quit.

THE PRIVATE JET lifted off from Boston's Logan Airport at six P.M. eastern. An hour and forty-five minutes later, it was flying at twenty-four thousand feet just east of Lake Michigan.

In the cabin were two men and one woman who'd been tucked away in a far, forgotten corner of Harvard Medical School for the last two years. They were the three biochemists who'd been leading the development of DARPA's nanotechnology project, which was on the edge of a major breakthrough.

A second, larger plane was fifteen minutes behind them, carrying their records, computer files, and all the equipment they'd used over the last two years—and would need to finish the project. They'd been told that there had been a breach of security in Boston and that they were being secretly transferred to another agency, GARD, that would be in charge of the project to its conclusion. They'd also been told that they wouldn't be allowed to see—even make contact with—their families for at least several weeks, maybe longer, until they'd gotten settled into their new location, which hadn't been disclosed to them. For a while, they tried to guess where they were going as they sped west, but after thirty minutes, they had settled patiently into their seats, reading magazines, newspapers, and files.

When the plane was twenty miles out over Lake Michigan, a remote-control device tripped two emergency fuel ejection valves, and fuel began pouring from the tanks. A red light went off in the cockpit thirty seconds later, indicating to the pilots that the plane was quickly losing fuel, but they were helpless to do anything. The valve wouldn't close, and they were flying on fumes. They turned the aircraft around and descended, trying desperately to get down, but at ten thousand feet the engines shut down and everything went eerily silent.

The plane stayed up for a few seconds, then rapidly lost speed, and the nose turned down. The pilots worked furiously to maintain altitude, but at five thousand feet they lost control and the plane went into a vertical dive.

When the jet hit the surface of Lake Michigan, it disintegrated—as did everything inside.

THE MAN WHO had pulled the gun in the hotel lobby sat at a small table in an interrogation room, smoking a cigarette. On the other side of the table was an armless wooden chair where he figured the cop would park his fat ass when he finally got around to making it in here. The man had been waiting an hour, and he was getting irritated. It wasn't supposed to take this long. He was supposed to have been in and out.

Finally the door opened.

"I'm Detective Jim Pearson."

"Congratulations."

Pearson tossed a folder on the table, turned the chair around so the back of it was to the table, and straddled it. "What in the hell were you doing?" he asked, crossing his forearms over the top of the chair back.

"What do you mean?"

"You try to shoot Christian Gillette in the main lobby of Caesar's Palace while he's being covered by two private security guys, not to mention all the hotel security people buzzing around. You only pop off two shots, neither one of which comes anywhere near him. You know you didn't have a chance of getting away. I'll ask you again, what were you doing?"

"Trying to kill him."

"Bullshit. If you were, then that was one stupid plan."

"Okay, I'm stupid."

"At least you could have shot that guy who tackled you. I mean, he was right in front of you."

The man took a deep breath. He was one of the best shots in the Carbone family, so it was difficult to take this. "Okay, I'm stupid **and** I'm a lousy shot."

Pearson grunted, not satisfied. "What's your name?"

"Johnny Depp."

"Fuck you."

The man shrugged. "Hey, maybe I'm stupid and a lousy shot, but give me some credit for being creative."

"Who's behind this?"

"What do you mean?"

"I don't think you've got anything against Gillette, I can't find any connection. So who does?"

The man looked down. Hopefully the detective would make something of his silence.

Pearson leaned in. "You're looking at a lot of time, pal. You're gonna be charged with attempted murder. I'd cooperate if I were you."

The man winced, then shook his head. "I can't."

"Come on, Johnny. Come clean. Maybe I can help."

"How?"

"Maybe the evidence gets lost, I don't know. I'll think of something. I want the person behind the scenes."

The man dropped his cigarette on the floor and stepped on it. "His name's Tom McGuire. He told me he used to run a company Gillette owned, and Gillette screwed him somehow. I don't know, though. I didn't get all the details. Frankly, I didn't care once he paid me."

Pearson pulled out a pen and paper. "What was that name again?"

"Tom McGuire."

"Where did McGuire approach you?"

"I don't understand."

"Did he talk to you here in Vegas first, or what?"

"No, no, it was back in Jersey. We have a mutual friend there."

"What's your friend's name?"

The man rolled his eyes. "Fucking Christ, you got to be kidding me."

"Okay, okay." Pearson backed off. "You said McGuire ran a company for Gillette?"

"Yeah."

"What's the name of the company?"

The man shrugged. "Ask Gillette."

"I will." Pearson put the pad and pen away. "How much did McGuire pay you?"

The man thought about it for a second. It had to be enough, but not too much. "A hundred grand."

THEY'D BEEN IN the air for two hours, and Gillette had finished the crossword puzzles in **The New York Times** and **USA Today** and was just about done with **The Washington Post.** When he'd gotten the last answer of the **Post**'s puzzle, he dropped the paper on the floor and looked over at Wright. Since Wright had gone after the guy in the hotel lobby, Gillette had decided to bring him along. He wouldn't be allowed into the meeting with Boyd, Ganze, and the biochemists, but he deserved to come to Minneapolis. Christ, he'd put himself in terrible danger, directly in the line of fire. He was as dedicated as Stiles had been. Suddenly he felt bad for asking Wright about his family in Maryland. For being suspicious. Wright had done nothing but continue to prove himself a worthy protégé.

"Hey, David."

"Yeah?"

"You okay?"

"What do you mean?"

"You look a little pale."

Wright smiled wanly. "I guess I'm just not much for staring down the barrel of an angry gun."

Gillette could relate to that. "Why don't you catch a nap?"

"That'd be nice, but I need to get this Hush-Hush deal done," Wright answered, pointing at the due diligence material spread out on his lap.

One of the QS agents trotted up from the back of the plane. "Phone, Mr. Gillette."

"Thanks," he said, taking the receiver. "Hello."

"Christian, it's me."

"Me" meant Allison. So they were at that stage already. She was, anyway.

"Having a good time without me?" she asked.

"Yep."

"How did it go with the Vegas city council?" Her voice turned serious. "Do we have our casino?"

"I think so. We hired one of the consultants I told you about. That was key."

"How much is it?"

"A lot." No need to get into it right now. "But it's worth it."

"Are you on your way to the West Coast?"

"No."

"Well, where are you going?"

"Something came up."

"What?"

"Something."

"What's the big secret?" she snapped. "Jesus, first Richmond, now this. I should have you tracked."

Gillette's eyes narrowed. No doubt she could if she wanted to. Maybe she already was and this conversation was just cover. "I'm going to Minneapolis." Really no reason to be so evasive. Wright was with him. She'd get it out of him.

"What happened?"

"A friend of mine called this morning. We got an opportunity. Another deal, but I have to get to Minneapolis right away." He was safe on this one. Wright had no idea why they were going to Minneapolis.

"More rush-rush."

"Always."

"Is David with you?"

"Yeah."

"Minneapolis, huh?" Allison spoke up, her voice intensifying. "That's weird. Doesn't Beezer Johnson have a division up there?"

"Uh-huh," Gillette answered hesitantly.

"Have you thought any more about my proposal?" she asked. "My family buying Beezer?"

"I haven't had a chance to really—"

"I talked to my uncle and grandfather about it," she cut in, "and they think it's a great idea. They had a couple of our analysts in Chicago take a look at it, you know, tear apart the numbers, and they think Beezer would be a nice fit with our business."

Gillette let out an exasperated breath. "How did your analysts get the numbers?"

"I had Cathy Dylan e-mail them. I didn't think you'd mind." She paused. "Do you?"

"Before you do that again, talk to me first. Those files are confidential."

"Okay." She paused again. "Let's talk price."

"It's not for sale, Allison." He didn't want to hear her price. Once he did, if it was good, he'd have a fiduciary responsibility to consider it.

But she barreled ahead anyway. "Six billion."

"Six billion?" Everest had bought Beezer Johnson a couple of years ago for just two. "At that price we'd make almost as much on Beezer as we will on Laurel Energy. But Beezer only has income of about a hundred million. That's a ridiculous multiple to pay."

"Thanks for calling my family ridiculous."

"You know what I mean." Why did they want Beezer so badly? Gillette kept asking himself. "I said the **deal** was ridiculous."

"Look, we can combine Beezer with the company we already own and generate some fantastic synergies, so our actual buy-in multiple is a lot less."

"I want to see that analysis." He could poke holes in any analysis, no matter how good it looked on a spreadsheet. He'd be able to keep her at bay for a while.

"Um, sure. I'll have our analyst e-mail it to you."

"As soon as possible."

"Yeah, sure. By the way, have you talked to Senator Clark about setting up the meeting with the FDA guy?" Allison asked, switching subjects. "Jack Mitchell e-mailed me today about that. He's still hot to trot, but he wants to see the FDA thing start moving."

"Don't worry about it."

"Okay. Well, I hope everything goes all right in Minneapolis. Whatever secret thing it is."

"Thanks."

"How's Faith?" she asked out of the blue.

"Fine."

There were a few seconds of dead air.

"I miss you, Christian," she finally said.

Gillette glanced at Wright. "Thanks," he said, then clicked off.

"Was that Allison?" Wright asked after Gillette had hung up.

"Yeah."

"You know, I really like her. She's something special."

"Not still worried that I'm going to be distracted by her?"

"Nah."

Gillette eyed Wright. "Why'd you change your mind?"

"I had a chance to talk to her for a while Saturday on the yacht. She's nice. Smart, too. And you're too much of a pro to let that happen. I know that."

Finally, he thought, someone was giving him the benefit of the doubt.

"By the way," Wright spoke up, "I remembered where my family is on the Eastern Shore of Maryland."

"Oh?"

"Yeah, it's a town called Easton. The woman is my mom's second cousin. You should go visit her when you're in Chatham next. It's like an hour away from there. Mom says the woman's a great cook. Fried chicken's her specialty."

Gillette nodded. "Maybe I will," he said, but his first instinct was to call Wright's mother to check the story out. When would he ever learn to trust anyone? "Thanks."

"Sure."

The phone in Gillette's lap rang. Hopefully, it wasn't Allison. When he saw the number, he knew it wasn't.

"Hello."

"May I speak to Christian Gillette?"

"This is Christian."

"Mr. Gillette, this is Jim Pearson. I'm a detective with the Las Vegas Police Department."

Gillette sat up in the leather chair. "Uh-huh."

"I got your number from one of the officers who responded to the shooting out at the hotel this afternoon. I need to ask you a few questions."

"All right."

"Does the name Tom McGuire mean anything to you?"

Gillette froze. "Yeah, why?"

"The guy we arrested claims McGuire paid him to kill you. Claims McGuire ran one of your companies and that you and McGuire got into it over something. Does all this make any sense to you?"

"Yes, it does."

"Good," Pearson said, sounding surprised. "Maybe we've got something to go on after all."

"McGuire ran a security company for me," Gillette explained. "He and his brother, Vince, started it. I think McGuire tried to kill me in New York City last week, too."

"You **think**?"

"It was like what happened today. Someone else

attacked me, but we think McGuire was behind it. And I . . . well, I believe he was behind the murder of my friend Quentin Stiles this past weekend, too. Anything you can get out of the guy you're holding could be very important."

"All right, good. I'm gonna question him again tomorrow morning, after he's cooled his heels in jail overnight and had a chance to think about how much trouble he's in. If I have any more questions, I want to call you, okay?"

"Sure. Let me know how the interrogation goes tomorrow morning, will you?"

"Okay."

"Who was that?" Wright asked.

"The detective who interrogated the guy you caught at the hotel."

"Really? What did he say?"

Gillette looked hard at David, mulling over his response. He needed a new confidante. Someone he could trust with anything. "Tom McGuire paid the guy to kill me."

HE'D BEEN IN this jail before, a few overnight stays for drunk and disorderly, so he knew the drill. And this wasn't it. Not even the usual route to the cells. As they turned a corner of the lonely hallway, the cop stopped, took out a key, and undid the handcuffs. Then he pushed open a door marked EMERGENCY. "Get lost."

The man didn't hesitate, just moved out into the night and quickly hailed a taxi.

"Airport and step on it," he urged, fat with pride thinking about what a great acting job he'd done for Pearson. He checked his watch. A few hours more than he'd expected, but Celino would be happy. And that was all that mattered.

WRIGHT MOVED into the bathroom at the back of the jet, then closed and locked the door behind him. He leaned over the sink and gazed into the mirror, then turned on the cold water and splashed his face. He stared at himself again, not exactly sure who was staring back.

Gillette had bought everything—just like Celino said he would: that the guy at the airport had really been trying to kill him, that Wright had saved his life, that Tom McGuire was behind everything. Wright shook his head. Celino using McGuire's name was perfect cover, a stroke of genius. McGuire was in hiding, so there was no way to confirm or deny that he was behind it.

Wright splashed more cold water on his face. Celino knew how to dangle a carrot, but it was the stick that was causing nightmares.

He turned to go but caught himself in the reflection once more. He hesitated and leaned close to the mirror, studying himself. Finally, he grimaced and headed out. He couldn't look any longer.

16

LATE SEPTEMBER and, at seven o'clock in the morning, it was just thirty-four degrees. The predicted high for the day was only forty-nine. It amazed Gillette that people actually chose to live in a place like Minneapolis. New York got cold, but not like this. He clenched his teeth, trying not to shiver. They'd come straight from Vegas, so he didn't have an overcoat. God, he hated the cold.

From the steps of a building that rose up along the banks of the Mississippi River, Gillette watched a dark blue Cadillac sedan move slowly down the single-lane road toward him. This was the original building of Beezer Johnson's Minnesota division—a quaint, three-story, redbrick structure built in the 1920s and added on to several times since. In the sixties, after several spring floods in a row, management had relocated most of the division to a newly constructed facility on high ground overlooking the area. Now there were four gleaming two-hundred-thousand-square-foot plants up there, and the only people left in the original building were the heart valve research staff. Management had kept the old building around mainly for posterity.

The Cadillac pulled to a stop in front of the steps, and a man emerged bundled up in a long overcoat. A QS agent descended the steps quickly, frisked him, then gestured for him to go up the steps.

"Hello, Mr. Gillette," said the man, holding out his hand as he reached the top step. "I'm Andrew Morgenstern."

Morgenstern was president of the Minnesota division. Gillette had never met him before, had spoken to him for the first time only last night on the plane. Typically, Gillette dealt with Beezer's CEO and CFO, whose offices were at the corporate headquarters in northern New Jersey.

"Welcome to Minnesota," Morgenstern said.

Nervously, Gillette thought.

"It's a beautiful morning, isn't it?"

"If you're a polar bear."

Morgenstern smiled, but not as though he were amused.

"Let's go inside," Gillette suggested, rubbing his hands together, his breath rising in front of him. Morgenstern's nervousness was typical for line managers when they met him, and he wanted to ease the other man's anxiety. "I appreciate your getting up early."

"You betcha." Morgenstern pulled out a set of keys and unlocked the front door. "Jeez, you ought to be wearing a coat, you know."

"I would if I had one," Gillette replied as Walker waved the QS agents in ahead of them. It didn't seem much warmer inside. "I thought you had people working in here."

"Sure, yah, we do."

"Don't you heat it for them?"

Morgenstern laughed loudly, then frowned when Gillette remained stone-faced. "Oh, you're serious."

"Yes."

"It's sixty-six degrees in here, Mr. Gillette. With sweaters on, people are fine. There's no need to cook 'em and pump up Northern State Power's revenues at the same time. We're big on cost savings around here. Turn out the lights when you're done, you know? I got signs everywhere."

"Uh-huh." Gillette glanced at the QS agents, who were moving down the tiled hallway ahead of him, checking rooms. Walker was staying right by his side. "How many people work in this building, Andrew?" he asked as they walked slowly down the corridor.

"Around twenty, I think."

"Can you move them into one of the other facilities up the hill?" Gillette asked bluntly.

"I guess. Do you mind if I ask why?"

"I'm afraid I do." He was used to politely telling people to pound salt.

Morgenstern's eyebrows floated up. "Jeez, okay."

"Look, I know how this sounds, but I need you to abandon this building until I tell you it's okay to come back. It could be a couple of weeks, it could be a year. I don't know, but that's the way it has to be."

Morgenstern shrugged. "You're the boss."

Gillette glanced at Walker, who had taken a call on his cell phone and peeled away. "I need everybody out of here by eight this morning, no later. If they leave anything behind, they'll have to call and make a special request to get it."

"**Eight o'clock?** Golly, some of the folks don't even **get** here until nine. They gotta get their kids off to school. You can understand that, can't you?"

"They won't be allowed in here after eight, Andrew. No exceptions."

"Okay, okay."

"Does this building have its own entrance to the main road?" He could see Morgenstern's curiosity was killing him, but to the man's credit, he didn't ask anything.

"Yes."

"Good."

The front door opened loudly behind them, and Gillette whipped around.

"It's all right," Walker called over his shoulder, trotting toward the door. "It's one of my guys. I just talked to him on the phone."

Gillette turned back to Morgenstern. "Andrew, you can't tell anyone what's going on here."

"I don't **know** what's going on."

"You can't tell **anyone** you've seen me or these men. You can't even tell the CEO or CFO. I'll fire you if you do."

Morgenstern's eyebrows rose. "Hey, it's your company."

"And Andrew . . ."

"Yes?"

"I need that key." Gillette pointed at the set of keys Morgenstern was holding. "And any others that go to doors in this building."

Morgenstern handed the entire set to Gillette. "Here."

"Thanks." Gillette shook Morgenstern's hand. "I appreciate your help." He spotted Walker coming back down the corridor. "Congratulations on the great job you're doing. The CEO tells me your group is way ahead of plan for the year."

"Division."

"Excuse me?"

"My **division** is way ahead of plan."

"Right." Morgenstern was a stickler, but Gillette appreciated that. "Your division. Have a profitable day, Andrew."

WHEN BOYD AND GANZE arrived, Gillette was waiting in the lobby, going through e-mails on his Blackberry, while Walker and several other

QS agents milled around—they'd finished checking the building. Gillette stowed the device in his pocket and stood up when he saw them.

"We need to go somewhere we can talk privately," Boyd said right away.

"The building's empty except for the people in this room," Gillette answered. "I don't think privacy will be a problem."

Walker started to follow them as they headed off down the corridor.

"He can't come with us, Christian," Boyd growled, "you know that."

"It's all right, Derrick," Gillette said, waving him off.

"That's not the same guy you brought to Washington last week, is it?" Boyd asked as they walked away, heels clicking on the tiles.

"No."

"Where's that guy?"

"Dead."

Boyd was headed into a vacant office when Gillette answered. He stopped in the doorway and turned around. **"What?"**

"Dead," Gillette repeated.

Boyd moved into the office. "Jesus, what happened to him?" he asked over his shoulder.

"It was a freak thing." No need to get into it.

"God, that's awful," Ganze said, shaking his head and following Gillette inside. "Sorry."

"Thanks."

"The nanotech people we've brought from DARPA are waiting outside in a van," Boyd spoke up impatiently. "I don't want to leave them there like that for long. What's the deal?"

"I met with the president of this division an hour ago," Gillette replied, "and told him he had to abandon this building until I said otherwise. And that he had to keep it quiet. That he couldn't tell anyone he'd met with me, including the top officers of the entire company."

"Good."

"What's his name?" Ganze asked, pulling out a pen and pad.

"Andrew Morgenstern," Gillette said. "He's good. Anyway, the building is yours at this point. You can do what you want with it. Now, I want to meet these people."

Boyd sat behind the desk, then motioned at Ganze. "Go get them, but I don't want anyone else seeing them, Daniel. Doors closed down the hall."

"Yes, sir."

When he was gone, Gillette sat down. "So, did you stage these people's deaths yet?"

"What?" Boyd was off in another world.

"You told me you were going to stage a plane crash," Gillette reminded him. "So other people on the nanotech project wouldn't suspect anything when the people in the van weren't around anymore."

Boyd nodded somberly. "Oh, yeah, we did that."

"Where was the crash?"

"Out in western Pennsylvania somewhere, in the mountains."

"How are you going to convince anyone that there were people on board?"

"There **were** people on board," Boyd answered.

Gillette looked at him hard. "Are you kidding me?"

"Don't get bent out of shape. We used cadavers, and the pilot bailed out before the thing went down." Boyd chuckled. "God, you actually thought I killed people?"

Gillette stifled his sudden outrage. He was disliking the man more and more all the time. "How would I know? You wanted to be able to stick me in prison for thirty years."

"Mmm."

"What about dental records and DNA? They won't match."

"It was a hell of a crash. Huge fireball. The plane was only in the air for a few minutes before it went down, so it was full of fuel. The bodies were too badly burned for anybody to make a positive identification."

"I think they can still—"

"It won't be a problem," Boyd snapped, aggravated. "Talk to Ganze if you're really that interested."

"Won't the other people on the project think it's

strange that the three of them were on the plane together?"

"Not at all. They were supposed to be on their way to a nanotech conference in Los Angeles, with a stopover in Cleveland to check out another project. They were going to catch a commercial flight from Cleveland. Small teams of them did that kind of thing all the time."

Gillette stood up as Ganze walked back in with the three biochemists. A petite Asian woman and two scholarly-looking men wearing tweed blazers.

"Dr. Evelyn Chang is our project leader," Ganze said to Gillette, introducing him to the woman, "and these are Dr. Silverstein and Dr. Rice."

Gillette shook hands with each of them.

"There," Boyd said, standing up, "you've met them. Now we've got to get them moved in."

Gillette gazed at each of them intently for a few more moments. "Welcome to the facility. I hope it works for you."

Dr. Chang shook Gillette's hand again. "Thank you very much, Mr. Gillette. We appreciate your dedication to national security, to keeping this country ahead."

"You're welcome," Gillette said quietly, thinking about how he'd gotten into this purely for selfish reasons. But now, with these three individuals standing in front of him, it seemed different. Maybe he **was** doing the right thing.

"All right," Boyd pushed, "let's go."

"What about my questions?" Gillette asked when they were out of earshot of the biochemists.

Boyd stopped. "Didn't Daniel give you Marilyn McRae's number?"

"Yes."

"Well, call her."

"I did, but I want to know about my father, too."

Boyd motioned to Ganze. "Go with him."

Gillette and Ganze moved to another office a few doors down.

"Here's the deal," Ganze said when they were inside and the door was closed. "We were right. Your father was killed by a group inside the government that was planning to assassinate President Bush. At that point, the group believed Bush would easily win another term. Of course he didn't, but they didn't have a crystal ball. He was incredibly popular when they were plotting."

"How do you know that these people killed my father?"

"So far," Ganze replied, "we have two sources. First, we have a guy who was a mechanic at the Orange County Airport at the time. He was working the day your father's plane crashed. The guy claims he knows who rigged the plane to go down. We're going out there to talk to him, in the next few days."

"I want to talk to him, too. I want to be there."

"I don't know if I can do that. I'll have to get back to you on that."

"You always have to get back to me."

Ganze looked down. "Sorry, Christian, it's all very complicated. I hope you can appreciate that."

"Who's the other source?" Gillette demanded.

"A man who was in the Secret Service back then," Ganze replied. "Same kind of situation as the mechanic. This guy has information for us about a couple of agents who were going to be involved in the assassination. We should get to him in the next few weeks."

"Why wait so long?"

"These things take time. People don't just give up this stuff that fast. We negotiate."

"The agents who were involved must have been thrown in jail. Check it out."

Ganze shook his head. "No, that's the thing. There wasn't anything to convict them of. No proof of a conspiracy, just the appearance of one. People in the service were let go, reassigned. Some were probably guilty, some weren't. It just isn't as clear cut as you and I want it to be. It may never be, especially since it's been sixteen years."

Frustration coursed through Gillette. As he'd suspected all these years, his father had been murdered, but maybe this outcome was worse. Now he **knew** there'd been foul play, but there might not be anyone to hold accountable. No one to take his anger out on.

"Look, I know you want answers fast," Ganze continued, "but you have to be patient. And for a while, maybe for good, you may have to be satisfied with the fact that your father probably saved the president's life. We think he contacted a higher-up at the White House just before the plane crash, maybe even that morning. We think he stopped the assassination. Your father's a hero."

17

"CHRIS!"

Gillette stopped short and turned around. He'd been heading toward the Everest lobby, but Faraday was jogging down the corridor toward him, puffing hard.

"Where are you going?"

"Downstairs to get something to eat," Gillette answered. It was just before two. They'd gotten back from Minnesota an hour ago. "What's up?"

"Without the QS guys?" Faraday asked loudly.

Gillette looked around furtively to see if anyone had heard him. "I was going to take the guy at the door."

Faraday's face scrunched up. "And let him leave the lobby?"

"It'll be fine for a few minutes." Gillette searched Faraday's expression for a sign of what was bothering him. "What is it?"

"Derrick Walker's got the FBI on the phone in Conference Room One. He wants you in there right away."

The FBI. Maybe they'd found out something about Stiles. "Okay."

When Gillette and Faraday entered the room, Walker was leaning against the conference room table near the speaker box, arms folded over his broad chest.

"Close the door, Nigel," Walker ordered. "George," he called loudly when Faraday had shut it, "I've got Christian Gillette in here now."

"Christian?"

"Yes."

"I'm Special Agent George Butler." Butler spoke with a heavy southern drawl. "I'm with the FBI downtown here at Twenty-six Federal Plaza in Manhattan. I've got some information you'll be very interested in."

"I hope it has to do with Quentin Stiles." Walker had told Gillette he'd been in touch with Butler about Stiles and that Butler was working with the local authorities. "That would make my day."

"Unfortunately not," Butler replied, "but it should make you sleep better."

"Go ahead."

"We believe Tom McGuire is dead."

Walker remained stone-faced, but Faraday pumped his fist.

"How do you know?" Gillette asked.

Butler hesitated. "We don't know **for sure,** but I'd say it's ninety-five percent at this point."

Gillette eased into the chair from which he ran the managers meetings. He felt as if a boulder had just tumbled off his shoulders.

"We have informants inside most of the big Mafia families," Butler explained. "**Soldatti,** usually, but sometimes more senior members. Yesterday afternoon we heard from one of those guys. He told us McGuire had been hit. Apparently, they put him in a boat, took him offshore from Jersey about forty miles, then threw him overboard. Our guy's always been very accurate about this kind of stuff."

"Why would the Mafia kill Tom McGuire?" Gillette asked.

"Revenge. We think it goes back to when McGuire was in the FBI years ago. He busted up a big drug operation in Boston."

"You guys bust the Mob on that kind of stuff all the time," Walker spoke up. "Why would they care so much about it that time?"

"Right," Gillette agreed, "and why would they kill him after so much time?"

"Good questions," Butler said. "During the Boston raid, McGuire killed the brother of a man who's now don of one of the big families. Rumor was, it wasn't during a shoot-out or in self-defense. Rumor was, McGuire took him in a bathroom and tortured him to get information. Cut off fingers, that kind of stuff. When the guy wouldn't talk,

McGuire dunked him in a tub. The last time a little too long."

"That's why they drowned McGuire," Walker said. "So he got it same way as the don's brother."

"Eye for an eye," Butler agreed. "And it gets better. Yesterday, McGuire's wife gets home from the grocery store and there's a shoebox on her front stoop. She opens it up and there's a human hand inside, a right hand. There's also a wedding ring inside the box. After the EMTs revive her, McGuire's wife identifies the wedding ring from the inscription."

"Still don't understand why they'd wait so long to kill him," Walker said.

"The guy who's the don of the family now wasn't in power when McGuire killed his brother," Butler answered. "Plus, McGuire was careful. He usually had his men around."

"That's true," Gillette agreed, remembering.

"But George, you guys couldn't find him," said Walker. "How could the Mob?"

"Derrick, didn't you tell me he hired a Brooklyn gang? A gang named the Fire?" Butler asked. "You know, the guys who attacked Christian and Stiles outside that restaurant in TriBeCa last week?"

"Yeah."

"Maybe one of the gang talked. Maybe they knew where he was."

"Maybe," Walker said skeptically.

Gillette settled into the chair. It sounded as if Tom McGuire were really dead. Maybe he could finally relax, get back to a more normal life. "Who did McGuire torture up in Boston?" he asked.

"A guy name Tony Celino. His brother is Joe Celino, aka Twenty-two, boss of the Carbone family."

Then again, Gillette thought, maybe not.

GILLETTE HUSTLED down Park Avenue to Grand Central Station. He headed through the station's north entrance, jogging past restaurants and shops to the escalators moving down to the main floor of the station. He turned right and covered the open area to the stairway leading up to the west entrance in a matter of seconds. He was up to the top of the stairway quickly, then past Michael Jordan's restaurant and out the door, his eyes flashing around, scouring the area for his contact. Suddenly there was a tap on his shoulder, and he whipped around. It was the QS agent he'd been looking for.

"Here you are, Mr. Gillette." The man handed Gillette a small package, then reached into his pocket and pulled out a set of car keys.

"Thanks." Gillette grabbed the package and the keys. "Where is it?"

The man pointed at a black Escalade parked at the curb a short distance away. It had tinted windows, as Gillette had requested.

"You didn't tell anybody about meeting me, did you?"

"No."

"Or about taking these for me?" Gillette held up the package.

"Nope."

Gillette could see the guy was anxious. "Don't worry."

"I don't want to lose my job, Mr. Gillette. I can't begin to tell you how pissed off Derrick will be if he finds out I did this."

"I'm the client. I pay you."

"Yeah, but I work for Derrick."

"Derrick won't find out. If he does, I'll make sure he knows I didn't give you any choice."

The QS agent eyed Gillette for a few seconds. "That's fine . . . if you're around to tell him."

"I'll be around," Gillette assured him. "Now, get to LaGuardia. Call me when you're there."

"**COME IN,**" Faraday called from his desk at the sound of the sharp knock.

Allison stepped into his office but didn't say anything right away.

"What do you want?" he asked. He was trying to answer a ton of e-mails, and he didn't have time for idle chitchat.

"Do you know where Christian is?" she asked, staying by the door.

Faraday shook his head. "Nope. Just that he isn't here."

"If you talk to him, will you transfer him over to me?"

"Just tell me what you want to ask him."

"That won't work," she said quickly. "Just transfer him over to me. Don't forget."

Faraday's eyes narrowed as she backed out of the office and closed the door. He didn't trust Allison Wallace one bit.

DR. DAVIS had agreed—through Cathy Dylan—to meet with him that afternoon. Gillette's cell phone rang as he passed Exit 9 on the New Jersey Turnpike, headed south toward Richmond.

"Hello."

"It's Richard."

The QS agent who'd met Gillette at Grand Central Station an hour ago. "You there?" Gillette asked.

"Yes."

"How about the other guy?"

"Yes."

"Is the door to the cabin closed?"

"Yes."

"All right, give me the pilot. Tell him I'm in the back."

There was a rustling noise and some muffled words, then the pilot came on. "Hello?"

"It's Christian."

"Yes, sir."

"We're headed to Chicago. Let's get going."

"Okay."

Gillette smiled to himself as he ended the call, satisfied. He could hear the pilot's irritation at having to wait until the last minute to get destination instructions, but it had to be this way.

Next, Gillette dialed the cell phone number of another QS agent who was sitting in the cockpit beside the pilot of the second Everest jet. Gillette instructed the second pilot to fly to Atlanta.

BOYD'S DOOR shook with a loud knock.

"What is it, Daniel?" Boyd demanded after Ganze opened the door.

"I just got a call from our mechanic friend at La-Guardia. Both Everest planes are on the move."

"Both?"

"Yes."

"Did Gillette gag the pilots again?" Boyd asked angrily. "Has he got his QS boys holding their dicks for them when they piss?"

"I guess. I haven't heard from either of them."

"Well, are we tracking the planes?"

"Of course."

"Good." Boyd put his elbows on the desk and rested his chin on the back of his hand. "Strange, isn't it? That Gillette would have both planes in the air at the same time?"

"Maybe."

"He's gotta be on one of them," Boyd observed.

"The question is, what's the other plane doing? Is it on a real mission or just decoying?" He glanced up. "Any chance they could have found the tracking devices?"

"Sure," Ganze replied. "If they know what they're doing."

"Gillette's a smart fucker. He might have left them on there just to screw with whoever he assumed put them there."

"Or to try to find out who did."

Boyd nodded. "I hope we have people on the ground wherever he lands."

I APPRECIATE your meeting with me again on such short notice, Dr. Davis."

"It's my pleasure, Christian."

"How's that boy you operated on last week?"

Davis broke into a wide smile. "Very well. Thank you for asking. Still in the ICU, but the prognosis is quite good. He's responding well."

"That's great. You really are a miracle man."

"Please don't embarrass me like that." But Davis's smile grew wider. "So, are you back for the 'intermediate' lecture on nanotechnology?" he asked. "I can give you that one, but you'll have to find someone else for the 'expert' lecture."

Gillette thought carefully about what he was going to say. He was about to bring Davis inside the circle, and judging by that look he'd seen in Boyd's

eyes at their meeting in Washington and again yesterday in Minneapolis, this could be dangerous.
"No. The 'beginner' lecture was plenty. I need something else."

"What?"

Gillette hesitated.

Davis leaned forward over his desk, stroking his
beard. He frowned. "Last time, I asked what you
knew and you stonewalled me, Christian. You gave
me a half-assed answer I knew was crap. Be straight
with me this time, son."

Gillette looked up, surprised at Davis's words,
even more so at his tone. The doctor seemed like
such a gentle man, but clearly he had an edge to
him. "I told you I was here last week because I had
an investment opportunity. That wasn't true."

"Well, I—"

"Can you keep what I'm about to tell you completely confidential? I mean, **tell no one.**"

Davis gazed at Gillette for a few moments.

"It's vital that you stay quiet . . . for a lot of people's sakes. But, Doctor, I think this is something
you'll want to hear."

Davis nodded slowly, his anger fading. "I'll keep
my mouth shut."

The other man's eyes were flashing. Gillette wondered if it was out of fear or curiosity.

"I was approached by the government," Gillette
began, "by people representing something called
GARD, the Government Advanced Research De-

partment. Don't bother going on the Internet to try to find it. I did. There's nothing."

"What did they want?" Davis asked, his voice hushed.

"Have you ever heard of DARPA, the Defense Advanced Research Projects Agency?"

"Sure. Those are the Defense Department's sci-fi geeks." Davis smiled. "And I use that term fondly. I consider myself one."

"Uh-huh. Well, they've been working on biomedical nanotech research for a few years, and they claim they're close to breaking through in a big way."

Davis's mouth dropped slowly open. "My God. Are you sure?"

"No," Gillette admitted. "I'm not sure at all. I only know what I've been told by the man who runs GARD. Or says he does," he added. He didn't really know if Boyd ran GARD or if there even was such an organization. Everything had come from Boyd or Ganze, so it was all questionable.

Davis's expression intensified. "Why did the people from GARD approach you?"

"Supposedly, they work with DARPA. They help them out when there's a problem. When something needs to go supersecret because there's a security issue with something the DARPA people are working on."

"Is that what's going on, a security problem?"

"Yes. They're worried that—"

"They're worried," Davis interrupted, "that one of the terrorist organizations is trying to get the technology."

"That's right. How did you know?"

"I didn't, but it makes sense." Davis shuddered. "If they did, biological warfare would suddenly look like something out of the Middle Ages. Once terrorists had bionanotech that worked, all they'd need is a delivery system. Then they could wipe out millions of us very quickly."

"Help me with that," Gillette said. "What do you mean? How could they wipe out millions of us?"

"Last week I told you how nanotechnology could save people. How those tiny little terminators could be programmed to kill cancer or head off a stroke by rebuilding blood vessels in the brain. Remember?"

"Of course."

"Well, those little terminators could also be programmed to kill healthy cells very easily. They can be programmed to do anything. But to make them killers of healthy cells on a massive scale, you have to have a way of getting them into lots of people's bodies without their realizing. You can't just release them into the atmosphere and hope they'll be inhaled. It doesn't work that way."

"Then what do you do?"

"If it was me, I'd buy a pharmaceutical company, then hide the nano-devils in things like nose sprays and cold medicines. Or I'd buy a food or a drink company. I'd buy something that produces things people ingest in huge quantities. Soft drinks, coffee, cookies. Anything like that."

Gillette looked past Davis and out the office window overlooking the James River, his mind flickering back to the dinner with Allison and Jack Mitchell. Veramax's primary products would make perfect nanodevil delivery systems.

"What does GARD want from you?" Davis asked.

"They want to use one of the companies we own to hide the project while they finish it up."

"**One** of the companies you own?"

Gillette gave Davis a quick overview of Everest. "Unlike GARD, you'll find Everest on the Internet," he finished.

"I'll take a look after you leave," Davis said. "Have they moved the project into the cutout yet?"

Gillette had started to explain cutouts to Davis, but the doctor was already familiar with them. "Yes, into a company we own that has a division in Minneapolis. There's a building on the division's property that was only being used by a few people. I kicked them out and let the biochemists use it. I met with them yesterday morning."

Davis tapped his forefinger on his lips. "Why are you telling me all this?" he asked. "How do I fit in?"

"I need you to find out who these people are."

"Which people?"

"The biochemists on the project," Gillette replied.

"I thought you said you met them."

"I did, and I can give you the names they gave me. What I need to do is make sure they are who they say they are."

"Being careful, are you?"

"I **have** to be, Doctor."

"You're smart. So, what's in it for Christian?" Davis asked quietly. "Why would you let these people use your company?"

Gillette had been anticipating this question. "Loyalty to the country. If these people are real and they're close to cracking the code, then I feel like I need to help if they think there's a security problem. The top executives at those financial firms who are big investors of mine would expect me to help. I'm sure some of them are already involved in the intelligence world, based on what I've learned in the last week or so, anyway." False as they were, he was glad the words were rolling off his tongue so easily.

Davis nodded. "You're in a tough position."

"Yeah," Gillette agreed, letting out a frustrated breath. "So will you help me, Doctor?"

Davis leaned back in his chair. "Now I know what's in it for you. So tell me: What's in it for me?"

WRIGHT SAT IN a taxi in downtown Richmond, outside the Medical Center of Virginia. Same taxi he'd hailed outside Grand Central Station almost eight hours ago after watching Gillette hop into the black Escalade and tear off. Wright had been forced to offer the cabbie more and more money as the day wore on and the miles added up. By the time they reached Richmond, the negotiated fare had reached a thousand dollars and his Rolex, and the guy demanded payment.

So Wright had gone to a cash machine, withdrawn the thousand dollars, and given it to the cabbie. Now the guy was happy, smacking his lips as he devoured a messy cheese steak sub in the front as they waited for Gillette to reappear.

Wright looked down at his cell phone and Blackberry, lying on the backseat beside him. He smiled. He'd simply conducted business today from the cab, not missing a beat. The Hush-Hush deal was on track—he'd spoken to the Everest associates who were crunching the numbers several times—and he'd arranged for a meeting with the Ohio Teachers Pension. Christian would be quite satisfied—and he'd never know he'd been followed.

GILLETTE FLIPPED through new e-mails as he headed north on I-95 toward Washington, D.C. He scrolled to the last one, shaking his head at the rush hour traffic crawling the other way. The background check on Allison's new assistant had come up clean, the message from Derrick Walker indicated. As Allison had said, Hamid had spent the last few years at Citibank, and his references were solid.

Gillette dropped the Blackberry on the passenger seat and picked up the package the QS agent had given him, sliding the stack of photographs out of the envelope. Picture after picture of Boyd and Ganze outside the Minneapolis Beezer Johnson facility yesterday.

He gazed to the left again, at the traffic, thinking about Stiles. The memorial was tomorrow, and Stiles's grandmother had asked him to make a speech. He'd met her several times at the hospital over the last ten months, and they'd gotten to be friends. Stiles's grandmother had raised Quentin—his mother had died when he was young—and had been responsible for him going into the army. Stiles always claimed that she had saved him from a dead-end life.

His cell phone rang. It was Walker. "Hello."

"Where are you?" Walker demanded angrily.

"I don't want to say on the cell phone."

"Look, I need to—"

"When I pull off I'll call you from a pay phone, all right?"

"Yeah, all right."

"Besides," Gillette spoke up, "McGuire's dead, remember? I'm fine."

"Which is one of the reasons I called."

"Oh?"

"Yeah, the DNA test checked out. It was definitely McGuire's hand his wife found."

"Well, he was right-handed. If somehow he's still alive, he won't be able to shoot very well."

"Very funny. Look, pull over right now so I can get a detail to you."

"I'll call you when I pull off for gas." Gillette heard Walker curse at the other end.

"Did you get my e-mail on that guy Allison Wallace wants to bring in?" Walker asked.

"Yeah, I got it."

"Sorry it took so much longer, but we wanted to be very careful. Faraday's nervous about him."

"Nigel told you that?"

"Several times."

"Jesus." That wasn't good. They didn't need the ACLU coming down on them if Hamid got wind of Faraday's suspicions. "You think the kid is okay?"

Walker was silent for a few moments.

"Derrick?"

"I don't like his attitude. More important, there's four months we can't account for."

"Four months? What do you mean?"

"The kid was at Citibank for a little over three years before Allison hired him. Before Citibank he worked at something called the Pan Arab Bank, in their New York branch here in Manhattan."

"I thought Allison said he went to the University of Michigan."

"He did, before Pan Arab. Anyway, he left Pan Arab in April, but he didn't start at Citibank until the following August."

"Did you ask him about those four months?"

"Yeah, this morning."

"And?"

"After he got through giving me attitude, he said he had traveled around the U.S. on his own during that time, sightseeing."

"On his own?"

"Yeah."

"Did you ask him where he went, what he saw?"

"He wouldn't talk about it. He hit me with the profiling thing again. And Christian?"

"What?"

"His parents still live in Iran. They work for the government."

Gillette gritted his teeth. Maybe Faraday was right to be suspicious. His other line rang. "Let me take this call. I'll be in touch later."

"Be careful."

"I will." He switched lines. "Hello."

"Christian, it's Percy Lundergard from Chatham."

"Hey, Percy."

"I set up this town meeting we talked about. So we can get your store built."

"When is it?"

"Tomorrow night at the high school auditorium."

"That doesn't leave much time to get the word out," Gillette said. "Will we get enough people there?"

"My family's been working this thing pretty good. There'll be plenty of people there."

"On a Saturday night?"

Lundergard chuckled. "Never lived in a small town, have you?"

"No."

"It'll be the social event of the month."

JOE CELINO was back in New York, back at his home in Staten Island, sitting on his veranda with Al Scarpa. They were taking in the sight of Manhattan drenched in late afternoon sunshine.

"I think you musta made a pretty good impression on David Wright," Scarpa said. "This morning he hired a taxi at Grand Central to go all the way to Richmond, Virginia, to follow Gillette. At least that's what Paul told me."

"Who did Gillette see in Richmond?"

"A doctor. A brain surgeon."

Celino looked over at Scarpa.

"Yeah, I know."

"Did we get that guy who capped Stiles for us yet?" Celino asked. "That guy who was crewing on Gillette's boat?"

Scarpa shook his head. "No."

"No?"

"Joseph, it's the strangest thing. Nobody's seen him." Scarpa shrugged. "He musta figured out he was gonna get it in the end and run."

"We only gave him half the money, right?"

"Maybe that was enough."

Celino grimaced. He didn't like the sound of this.

"Find the bastard," he snarled. "I don't care what it takes. **Find him.**"

"WHAT ARE YOU DOING?" Wright pounded on the Plexiglas separating the front seat from the backseat of the cab. They were slowing down, and the black Escalade was disappearing into the traffic ahead. "You can't lose this guy."

"There's nothing I can do," the cabbie yelled back. "The engine's crapping out. I knew I shouldn't have fucking come all the way down here."

"Shit." Wright grabbed his cell phone and dialed the number, but Gillette had already disappeared.

THE MEETING PLACE was a parking garage near the Potomac River waterfront below George-town, on the west side of Washington. Basement level, next to the elevator banks—nine P.M. sharp. Gillette had been standing in the shadows beside the Escalade for half an hour. He checked his watch in the low light: It was nine-fifteen.

A white sedan made the U-turn from the level above at the far end of the garage and approached slowly, headlights on. Gillette stepped back all the way to the wall and watched the driver swing into a spot, then climb out of the car.

The man looked around as he stood up, then closed the car door and walked toward the elevators.

From a distance, he reminded Gillette of Gordon Meade, the man who had come with Allison to Everest that first morning. He was tall and thin, slightly stooped, most likely in his fifties. Gillette spotted the bottled water the man said he'd be carrying as he stopped a few feet from the elevator banks. Gillette moved out, toward the man.

They made eye contact as soon as Gillette appeared in front of the Escalade, and they stared at each other until Gillette stopped a few feet away. "Ted Casey?" Gillette asked.

Casey nodded.

"How do you want to do this?"

"What do you mean?"

"We can stand out here in the open, or we can go in that SUV over there." Gillette pointed at the Escalade.

"Yeah," Casey agreed, eying the tinted windows, "let's do that."

When they were inside the SUV, Casey spoke first. "I looked at your Web site. You guys are big. Bigger than Apex."

"Thanks to the new fund, that's right."

"How big is that fund?"

"Twenty billion plus," Gillette answered.

Casey whistled. "Russell Hughes tells me you're going to take over Apex with some of that money."

"Yeah."

"Will you be in charge of Apex after you buy it?" Casey asked nervously.

"Initially. After a few weeks I'm going to turn it over to one of my partners, guy named David Wright. But Wright doesn't need to know about what Omega IT does in the Middle East. Ultimately he will, but not yet." Casey seemed happy to hear that.

"Good. We need to keep that circle as small as possible."

"Don't worry. What's going on at Omega is safe with me." Gillette hesitated. "Are you actually in the Directorate of Operations?"

"Yup, I'm a spook."

"How long have you been with the CIA?"

"Since I graduated from Yale thirty-five years ago. I'm a career man."

That was good. There was a better chance Casey would be able to answer his questions. "Are you responsible for a number of cutouts, or just Omega IT?"

Casey chewed on his answer. "Not just Omega."

"What else?"

"Can't tell you." Casey put the plastic water bottle in a cup holder.

He seemed to be growing more anxious by the moment, Gillette noticed.

"What did you want to ask me, Christian?" Casey asked impatiently.

"Do you know of a man named Norman Boyd?"

Casey looked over at Gillette. "Maybe. Why?"

"What do you know about him?"

Casey said nothing.

"Look," Gillette spoke up, "I'm going to keep

Omega a secret, but I need you to cooperate. I'm loyal, but it has to go both ways. If you know anything about Norman Boyd, I want to hear it."

"How do you know Boyd?" Casey asked.

"He wants me to help him the way Russell Hughes helps you, the way you want me to help you. In fact, I think Boyd approached Russell before he approached me, and you told Russell to stay away from him. Right?"

"Yes."

"Why did you tell him that?"

"Boyd's part of Defense Department intel," Casey began. "He's been around a long time over there. Got the ear of a lot of very important people at the Pentagon, people who want to see the DOD come out ahead of the CIA in the intelligence land grab that's going on right now." Casey exhaled heavily. "Maybe you've heard, there's a massive power struggle going on. Iraq, 9/11, and Osama have turned everything upside down. Everything's in chaos. No one knows who's going to end up with what. Careers will be made **and** destroyed by this."

"I've heard a little about it. But not much," Gillette admitted.

"Well, Boyd's a sacred cow over there at DOD. Always in charge of very **secret,** very **important** projects. He's aggressive about grabbing everything he can for the Pentagon. We respect that at the CIA, it's natural. But he's a renegade. He thinks he's outside the law, outside what's tolerable, maybe because he's older. But we can't accept it."

"What do you mean?" Gillette could tell that Casey was getting exasperated. "What's he done?"

Casey grimaced. "His people went too far with one of our important friends, a guy who helped us for many years."

"What do you mean, they went too far?"

"They killed him." Casey held up a hand. "Don't get me wrong, this guy was no angel. But he didn't deserve to die, and it really smacks our reputation."

Boyd's people were killers after all.

"They were interrogating him," Casey continued, "and they went too far."

"Was this guy someone you were close to?"

"No, I wasn't his handler. And you didn't hear all this from me," Casey added sternly. "I'd never admit I told you anything. I'd never admit we had this meeting. Anyway, that's why I told Hughes to stay away from Boyd. As far as I'm concerned, he's crazy."

Casey seemed believable enough, but he was CIA. Was anything he said believable? "Any question about Boyd's loyalty to the U.S.?" Gillette asked.

"None," Casey replied firmly. "Boyd bleeds red, white, and blue. But there is one thing I heard about him," he said, his voice dropping.

"What's that?"

"He's got a chip on his shoulder about how much money he could have made outside the government.

He feels like he sacrificed a lot by staying in all these years, and he wants something for it. Something big." Casey snorted. " 'Course, so do all of us." Casey picked up the water bottle from the cup holder. "There was a rumor that he was trying to move something out of one of his projects and into a private shell so he could sell it later on and make big bucks. But I haven't heard anything more about that for a while."

18

"**CHRIS.**" Debbie's voice crackled over the intercom.

Gillette was sitting behind his desk, rubbing his bloodshot eyes. He'd only gotten two hours sleep the previous night. There'd been construction on the Jersey Turnpike—causing a twelve-mile backup—after his meeting with Ted Casey in Washington. A meeting that had gone longer than he'd expected. He hadn't gotten to his apartment until three o'clock this morning—just four hours ago.

"What is it?" he answered, his voice scratchy.

"Nigel wants to see you."

"Let him in."

"Since when do I need to be announced?" Faraday blustered, bursting into the office.

"Calm down."

"Where were you yesterday?"

"Out."

"Come on, Chris, I've got to know where you are—"

"What do you want?"

Faraday stood in the middle of the room, hands on his hips, fuming. "I need to tell you something."

"Okay."

"It's about Allison."

Gillette's eyes narrowed.

"She called a few more of our investors yesterday," Faraday explained, "trying to buddy up to them. They said she made it sound like she was running Everest Capital. Or would be soon."

"I'll talk to her." Gillette wanted to believe it was just an error of enthusiasm. "She's young and aggressive, like David. That's all."

"I don't trust her."

"I know."

"She was going crazy yesterday trying to find you."

Gillette already knew that. She'd left five messages on his cell phone.

"By the way, I found out something very interesting about our NFL franchise and the bid process," Faraday said.

Gillette had been thinking about his trip west. Meeting Marilyn and seeing Lana. "What?"

"We weren't the highest bidder." Faraday hesitated. "By a long shot."

Somehow that didn't surprise him. Of course, not much did anymore. "By how much?" Gillette asked.

"Fifty million."

Gillette's mind flashed back to his lunch with Kurt Landry. He'd gotten a strange vibe about the whole deal that day. "Somebody was willing to pay five hundred million and they didn't get the deal?"

"Yup."

"How did you find out?"

"A little bird told me."

"Nigel, I have to know."

"I can't tell you, I really can't, but he's credible. He's an investment banker, a senior member of the team who put a bid together for a very wealthy family. Not **Wallace** wealthy, but wealthy."

"Did you tell him what we bid?"

"No." Faraday moved closer to Gillette's desk. "I think that's pretty strange, Chris."

"I hear you." Suddenly, there were a lot of strange things going on.

"Chris." It was Debbie on the intercom again. "Now Allison wants to see you."

Gillette met Faraday's eyes.

"I guess I better get out of here," Faraday muttered, turning to go.

"Let her in," Gillette said.

Faraday and Allison passed at the doorway, giving each other their standard quick nod.

"You never phoned last night," she said.

Gillette glanced up. "Was I supposed to?"

"I wanted an update on your day."

"I didn't get home till late. **Very** late."

Allison plopped down in the chair on the other side of his desk. "Well, I'm right upstairs now," she said, smiling widely. "That ought to make Faith happy."

Faith still hadn't called him back again. Problem was, maybe she was right this time. Maybe he shouldn't have invited Allison on the cruise while Faith was in London. Nothing had happened, but he could see how it would aggravate her. "You moved in yesterday?"

"Yeah."

"How did it go?"

"Smooth as silk. The movers took care of everything. We're as good as roommates now."

Gillette didn't want to get into this now, but he owed it to Faraday. "Have you been calling our investors?" he asked, trying to figure out if her expression was registering shock that he'd found out so fast or fear that he was going to be angry. Either way, she'd clearly been taken by surprise.

She didn't answer right away. "Yeah," she finally admitted. "So what?"

"Why'd you do it?"

"To tell them I'd joined the firm as a managing partner," she said nonchalantly, regaining her composure. "I didn't think you'd mind."

"Do me a favor and talk to Nigel before you do that again. That's his turf, and he's very sensitive about anyone stomping around on it."

"Fine," she agreed, rolling her eyes. "So, where were you last night?"

"You're not going to like my answer," he muttered. "Nobody does."

"Why not?"

"I can't tell you."

"I'm so sick of this," she snapped. "Were you with Faith?"

"No. Not that it's any of your business if I was."

"Then where were you?" Allison put both hands up. "I know, I know. Something came up. Look, I'm getting really tired of this," she said loudly. "I mean, I invest a ton of money in this place, find a great deal in Veramax, and offer to buy Beezer Johnson at a very nice price. I'm going the extra mile here, but I'm not getting anything in return."

Gillette stood up. "I appreciate—"

"Were you in Richmond again?"

He didn't answer.

She put her head back and groaned. "Is this how it is with you? Mystery after mystery?"

"Maybe."

"Was I an idiot to invest so much money in Everest?"

He wanted to come back at her with a flip remark, but discretion won out. "You're going to be very happy with your investment."

"Have you at least set up a meeting with that

FDA guy?" Allison asked. "Jack Mitchell called me **again** yesterday."

Gillette nodded, satisfied with her surprised expression. "I'm meeting with Rothchild in Washington two weeks from tomorrow. Has Mitchell written his apology letter?"

"I don't know, I—"

"Find out, and while you're at it, make sure he's doing everything he can to get Rothchild into the Racquet Club. Like he said he would. I'm going to call a friend of mine who's on the membership committee to see if he can help. If Jack hasn't done anything on that, tell him to get off his ass fast."

"I'll call him right now," she said, rising from the chair.

"Good. And Allison?"

"What?" she asked, turning back around.

"I haven't seen that analysis on Beezer Johnson yet. The one that shows how great the combination of it and your family's company would be."

"I'll get right on that, too."

Once Allison was gone, David Wright wanted time.

Wright moved into Gillette's office carrying two copies of a Hush-Hush presentation, a summary of the due diligence he'd done so far. "Over there," Gillette said, covering the phone with one hand and pointing toward the couches and the coffee table. "Give me a second."

By the time Wright had spread out the materials, Gillette was off the call. They sat together and reviewed the material for several minutes.

"Did Cathy do any sensitivity analysis on the exit multiple?" Gillette asked after scanning the financial projections.

"Doing it as we speak."

"I want to see what the return is if we can't flip Hush-Hush quickly to the French. If we have to hold it for a while."

Wright rose from the couch and headed for Gillette's desk.

"Where are you going?"

"To get your calculator so we can crunch that return," Wright answered. "Top drawer, right?"

"Yeah," Gillette said, noticing that Wright's wallet was lying on the table in the middle of the Hush-Hush due diligence material. He spotted a familiar-looking piece of paper sticking out of it. "Do me a favor after you get the calculator, will you?" he called. "Go see if Debbie has my daily planner. I think I gave it to her yesterday. I want to go over next week's schedule with you."

"Sure."

When Wright was out of the office, Gillette quickly pulled the slip of paper from the wallet. It was a toll receipt from the New Jersey Turnpike. He checked the date. Yesterday.

When Gillette was finished with Wright, he

headed for Cathy Dylan's office. "Cathy." He knocked on her door as he leaned into the office. He'd gotten her message from Debbie. "What's up?"

She motioned for him to come in and close the door. "I spoke to Dr. Davis, and he needs to talk to you as soon as possible. He says it's urgent."

Gillette stared at her intently. "Not a word of this to anyone."

"I know."

He turned to go, then stopped. "Do something else for me, will you?" For the first time, he thought he saw fear in her eyes. "Check the Internet and see if there were any small plane crashes in western Pennsylvania in the last couple of weeks."

"**DR. DAVIS.**"

"Christian? Glad you called so quickly."

Gillette was at a pay phone in the lobby of the Intercontinental Hotel. "Cathy said it was urgent."

"I tried tracking down those names you gave me from your meeting in Minneapolis. No luck. No one knows them, which is strange. You're right, the nanotech research community isn't that big. I thought someone would have recognized at least one of them. Usually, somebody went to school with somebody."

Gillette had anticipated this. Boyd didn't seem like the type to throw around crucial information haphazardly. "Well, thanks. I appreciate your help."

"Don't go so fast. That's not the only reason I called."

Gillette perked up. "Oh?"

"Maybe this is nothing, Christian, but you never know."

"Go on," Gillette urged.

"One of the people I called to check the names out with is a guy named Nathaniel Pete. Nate's in Boston. Runs with that whole Cambridge crowd. He's a biochemist graduate school professor at Harvard, and very into nanotech. He could be running one of these government nanotech programs, but he's a little flaky. Great credentials, but he wouldn't pass the gut check test. Right out of the sixties. Long hair, tie-dyed shirts. Not somebody you'd trust one of your most important projects to. But trust me, he's brilliant."

"What did he say?"

"Said the wife of a friend of his called him yesterday, very upset. She said her husband has been working on a highly confidential project for the government over the last two years, and suddenly he can't see or call her. He's going away and he's not sure how long it'll be. She said they had a two-minute conversation a few days ago, and that was it. She hasn't seen or heard from him since."

"What's his name, Doctor?"

"Matt Lee."

. . .

"**GILLETTE'S GONE!**" Wright shouted into the phone. "And I have no idea where he went."

"Calm down, Davey."

"There's only so much I can do before he gets suspicious. I can't follow him around every second."

"Easy, easy. We know that."

Wright swallowed hard. "I mean, Christ, I went all the way to Richmond yesterday in a damn cab for you guys."

"And we all appreciate that, the man you met with in Las Vegas particularly. He wanted me to tell you of his thanks. You've done a good job."

Wright started breathing a little easier. His mind had gone wild with possibilities. They'd shoot him on the street, kidnap his wife. Awful things he had no way to stop.

"Davey?"

"Yes, sir?"

"From now on, you don't need to worry about following him. All you need to be is his friend. Someone he confides in all the time."

Wright took a long breath. That I can do, he thought.

GILLETTE SPED north on I-95, toward Boston, toward Matt Lee's home. Dr. Davis was to have called Lee's wife, Mary, to prepare her for Gillette's knock on the door.

Gillette's cell phone rang. "Hello."

"Christian, it's Cathy."

"Hi."

"There was only one plane crash in western Pennsylvania in the last two weeks. The plane went down about twenty miles north of Pittsburgh last Wednesday."

"Fatalities?"

"One," she said, reading off an article on the Internet. "The other four people on board were okay, broken bones but nothing serious. It looks like the guy who died was thrown from the plane, and that's what killed him."

"Who was he?"

"A senior executive of Three River Bank. They were all TRB people on the plane."

Three River Bank was headquartered in Pittsburgh. No way that crash had anything to do with Boyd. "That's it?"

"Yup."

"Thanks, I'll talk to you later."

Gillette checked the rearview mirror as he ended the call. He'd made certain Wright was in a meeting behind closed doors before he'd left—which didn't mean somebody else wasn't back there. So he'd taken a couple of quick turns on his way out of Manhattan, and it didn't look as if anyone were following him.

He slid a disc into the CD player and tried to relax, but it was no use. He started thinking about everything that was happening. About how he was going to have to wait until Monday morning to confront Wright about the New Jersey Turnpike toll receipt. He was flying to the West Coast this afternoon, then there was Stiles's memorial service on Saturday, and he had to head to that Chatham town meeting right after the service. Besides, Wright was leaving the city with his wife for the rest of the weekend after the service. So Monday would be his first chance to talk to Wright face-to-face. He couldn't wait to hear that explanation. The stamp on the receipt registered the same time he would have been going through the same toll.

It was afternoon and the sky was a blazing blue when Gillette pulled the SUV to a stop in front of a quaint house in Concord, Massachusetts, a residential neighborhood outside Boston. He was on his cell phone, calling for the larger Everest jet, and he was using the same drill. There was a QS agent sitting beside the pilot as he relayed the destination. Gillette didn't care if somebody figured out he'd gone to Boston after the fact, when the plane landed at Logan. They'd never be able to figure out he had visited Mary Lee by that time. And he didn't care if anyone knew he was going to the West Coast—that trip was about family, not business. Nothing he needed to be careful about.

When Gillette was done talking to the pilot, he stowed the cell phone in his pocket and headed up the cement walkway toward the Lees' modest-looking, two-story home. He knocked on the door, but there was no answer right away. He checked his watch—one P.M. Exactly the time Davis had told him to be at Mary's front door. He knocked again, hoping he hadn't just wasted most of a day.

Finally, the door opened partway and a timid-looking Asian woman appeared. Most of her remained obscured behind the door.

"Mrs. Lee?"

She nodded almost imperceptibly.

"I'm Christian Gillette. Dr. Davis was supposed to call you. At the suggestion of Nathaniel Pete."

Again, the barely noticeable nod.

"Did Dr. Davis explain to you who I was?"

"Yes." Her voice was as timid as her demeanor, only slightly more than a whisper.

"Do you have Internet connection, Mrs. Lee?" Gillette asked.

"Yes."

"Then you can go online and check me out. My picture is on our Web site. I'll stay here while you do it. Our URL is—"

"I already checked the Web site," she cut in, "and I called some friends who know Wall Street. They said you were real."

"Good."

She opened the door wide. "Please come in. You can call me Mary."

"Thank you." He moved into the foyer and shut the door. "Please call me Christian," he said, gesturing around. "You have a very nice home."

"Thank you," she said, then suddenly teared up. "I'm so worried about my husband." She began to sob, putting a hand to her mouth to hide her quivering chin.

"I understand," Gillette said softly, surprising himself by putting his arms around her. For several minutes he held her, feeling the sobs racking her body.

Finally she stepped away from him. "I'm so embarrassed," she said, dabbing her eyes with a tissue.

"Please don't be," Gillette urged. "I know this is so difficult for you." He hesitated, not certain if he should say this. "I'm going to be very candid with you, Mary, I'm worried about your husband, too. But I'm going to do my best to find him."

"Thank you. It's just not like him to go off like this and not call. I've talked to him every day for the last fourteen years. Now this."

"Do you have a picture of him?"

"Yes."

She hurried to a table in the living room, picked up a frame, and returned, holding it out for Gillette as she neared him. It was a photograph of Matt and her standing together, holding hands. The man in the picture wasn't one of the two he'd met in Minneapolis.

"Does it help?"

Gillette kept staring at the photograph, unable to meet Mary's eyes. "I'm not sure."

"Men came here yesterday," Mary spoke up.

He finally looked up from the picture.

"They went through all of Matt's things while I had to sit in the kitchen with one of them. They went through his den, his closets, his clothes, everything. They took some things."

Gillette reached into his coat pocket and pulled out the pictures the QS agent had taken for him in Minneapolis. "Were either of these men here yesterday?" he asked, showing the pictures to her.

She gasped, then pointed at Ganze immediately. "Him."

Matt Lee had been part of the nanotech project. The fact that Ganze had come to the Lees' house linked them. And it was clear to Gillette that Matt wasn't coming back. The real question now: What was Norman Boyd really up to?

"What's wrong?" she asked.

Gillette grimaced. "I'm afraid there are some very bad people in charge of the project your husband was working on. I'm sorry." He could see that she understood what he was trying to say. That she'd heard him use the past tense.

"Follow me," she said suddenly.

Gillette followed Mary up the stairs to the couple's bedroom but stayed in the doorway as she moved to her dresser and opened a jewelry box. She pulled out the top drawer of the box and put it on the dresser, then removed a small package from inside. "Here," she said, moving to where he stood, holding out the package. "I don't want this."

"What is it?" Gillette asked, taking it from her shaking hands.

"A flash drive. Matt kept calling it the silver bullet."

"Flash drive?"

"A portable disk drive."

"What did he mean by 'silver bullet'?"

She shook her head and started sobbing quietly again. "I should have known something was wrong."

"Why?"

"He brought this home the night before he called to tell me he was going away. He suspected something."

"What's on it?" Gillette asked. "Did he tell you?"

"Everything the team had done up until the day he called to tell me he had to go away. He said they didn't have far to go on the project. That anyone who knew what they were doing and had this could finish it."

Gillette swallowed hard as he slipped the flash drive into his shirt pocket. "Mary," he said firmly, "you can't tell anyone I was here."

As Gillette walked down the path toward the Escalade, he thought about Boyd and remembered something from the other day in Minneapolis. When Boyd had seen Derrick Walker in the Beezer facility, he'd asked about the security guy Gillette had brought to Washington last week—meaning Stiles. It had seemed like nothing more than an innocent question at the time. Problem was, Boyd had never seen Stiles in Washington. Boyd had stayed in his office the entire time, and Stiles had never gone in—Ganze hadn't let him. Only Ganze had seen Stiles. So how the hell could Boyd know Walker was a different guy?

DR. SCOTT DAVIS sat strapped to the chair, a hood over his head. The ropes binding his wrists and ankles to the chair were extremely tight, cutting into his skin, and he moaned as the tension became excruciating.

"I want to know what you told Christian Gillette," said the man standing behind him. He was holding a knife to Davis's throat. "I want to know everything you and he talked about."

19

NIKKI LAY ON her back in the hospital bed, her eyes mere slits. Gillette watched her for a few moments from the doorway. Every breath seemed like a struggle, and she was painfully frail. He'd talked to one of the nurses and learned that Nikki's lung cancer was advancing rapidly. That she probably didn't have more than a few months. He shook his head. If they'd just caught it earlier . . . But it was too late now. He pressed his hand against the flash drive in his shirt pocket, wondering if it might hold the key to her cure.

He hadn't seen her in sixteen years. They'd been so close growing up—even though she was Lana's child—but she'd let him down when he needed her most.

"Nikki."

She turned her head slowly toward him, a wan

smile forming on her lips, her eyes glassy but joyful. "Chris," she murmured.

He took her hand. It was cold. She tried to squeeze his hand back when he took hers, but it was a feeble attempt. He leaned down and kissed her on the cheek. It was cold, too.

"How did you find out?" she asked.

"Lana showed up in New York last week out of the blue. She told me you were sick."

Nikki groaned, then coughed several times. "My husband screwed it all up. He said we had coverage, but he was lying. He's gone now. I don't know where. . . ."

"Christ, Nikki, how could you be with someone like that?"

"I didn't have you around to guide me."

"You didn't **want** me around. How many times did I call?"

"I'm not blaming you, I'm blaming myself. I've always let Lana control me."

Gillette brushed away a tear rolling down her cheek.

She tried to squeeze his hand again. "I wish I could go back and change everything, I really do. I'd give anything."

"Why didn't you call me when you got sick?" he asked.

She shrugged weakly. "How could I? I wasn't there when **you** needed **me**."

"So what? This is your life we're talking about. No second chances."

"Yeah," she said softly, "I know."

He cursed under his breath. An awful thing to say. "All right," he said in a determined voice, looking around at the other three patients. "The first thing we're going to do is get you a private room."

Two hours later, Nikki was in a private room with a beautiful view of dusk settling over downtown Los Angeles. The aroma of fresh-cut flowers filled the room, and a stack of her favorite magazines and books sat on the nightstand.

"Thanks, Christian," she said, her voice stronger. "This is nice. I feel better."

She looked better, too, he was glad to see. "Well, you should get some rest."

"How long will you be in Los Angeles?"

"I'm going back to New York in the morning." He was having dinner with Marilyn tonight, then seeing Lana after that. Stiles's memorial service started at ten Saturday morning, and he wasn't going to chance missing it.

"Will you come and see me again before you leave," she pleaded, "even if it's just for a few minutes?"

"Of course." He leaned down and kissed her on the forehead, then turned to go. But he stopped at the doorway. "I need to ask you a question," he said, moving slowly back to where she lay. "Was I the only one Dad had outside his marriage to Lana?"

Nikki took a shallow breath. "No. There were others. Daddy had a problem."

"How many others?" He had to see if he got the same answer from Nikki that he had gotten from Lana.

"Three, all from different women."

Confirmed. "God."

"Daddy started making a lot of money, and I guess he couldn't control himself. I guess he felt like it was his right. Plus, he and Mom . . . well, they had issues."

"That's no excuse."

"She was a bitch to him, Christian. She was never satisfied with anything."

"Do you know who the women were?" Gillette asked.

Nikki shook her head. "I think they were all from the Los Angeles area, but I don't know their names." She hesitated. "Mom does."

Lana had lied. So predictable. "Do you think she ever cheated on him?"

"I thought so, once."

"Why?"

"A man came to the house a couple of times in the months before Dad's plane crash, but then he stopped." Nikki smiled. "I took pictures of him sitting out on the patio with her from one of the upstairs windows one time. I was going to confront her, you know? But then Dad died . . . and that was that." She frowned. "Not that I probably ever would have been brave enough to actually do that." She looked up at him. "Do you think you'll ever get married, Christian?"

He thought about the question for a few moments, then gave her the best smile he could manage. "I don't know. But if I ever do, you better be there. You hear me?"

Her eyes filled with tears instantly, and she nodded.

GILLETTE HAD enjoyed dinner with Marilyn even more than he'd anticipated. She was pretty and dripping with diamonds. She'd gotten ten million dollars after Clayton died—as had the other three women he'd fathered children with. Gillette had been uncomfortable when he'd seen all the jewelry, but she'd assured him she'd invested most of the money wisely and didn't have any financial worries. She hadn't asked him for money, as he'd anticipated she would. Why wouldn't he expect that? Everyone else did. It was starting to seem like that was all family was about.

"It was wonderful to see you," Marilyn gushed as they finished coffee. "And to find out how successful you are."

"Thanks." Gillette had studied her all through dinner, looking for the physical similarities. He couldn't decide if he'd found any.

"We have to stay close," she urged. "Please call

me when you have time. I know you're so busy. I don't want to bother you."

"I'll call," he assured her, folding his napkin and putting it on the table. "Did you love my father?" he asked.

"So much, Christian. He was such a charismatic man." She smiled. "Like you."

Gillette smiled back. "I always remember those cigars he smoked. The Cubans. I loved the way they smelled, you know?"

Marilyn pondered his comment. Finally she sighed. "I miss that, too."

"**YOU LIED TO ME** in New York." Gillette and Lana were sitting on the patio of her Bel Air mansion.

"I don't know what you're talking about."

It was late, but in the glow of the outside lights Gillette could see that the mansion and its grounds had been neglected. There were dead trees and bushes in the large backyard, the paint on the shutters was peeling badly, and many of the stones on the patio were cracked and chipped. "You told me you didn't know the names of the women Dad had children with outside your marriage. Nikki says you do, and I believe her."

Lana stuck her chin out fiercely. "She's wrong."

"I need to know, Lana."

"Well, I can't help you."

"Then I can't help you."

Lana folded her hands tightly in her lap. "How would you help me?" she asked.

"The only way you care about. Money."

"I'm not as evil as you think I am."

"I'm not here to debate that," Gillette replied. "I have my opinion, you have yours. Let's leave it at that."

Lana bit her lower lip for a moment. "How much would you be willing to help me?"

"I'll lend you ten million dollars as long as you pledge this house to me as collateral."

"Do you have your father's curse? Does it always have to be about business?"

"That's what it is with you, Lana. Business. Always was, always will be."

"You aren't mine," she snapped.

"Wasn't **my** choice."

They were silent for a few minutes.

"Are you going to give me the names?" Gillette finally asked.

"I don't know yet." Lana picked up her wineglass and took a large gulp. "I could get in so much trouble if I do."

"Why?"

"There might still be people around who would make me pay."

Gillette's eyes narrowed. "Who?"

"Important people."

"Who?"

"People who hated your father."

"Why did they hate him?"

"He had information that could have destroyed them."

"What kind of information?"

"I don't know, they wouldn't tell me. Neither would he."

Gillette's brain began to pound. "Were they the ones who killed him?"

"The crash was an accident."

"Lana!"

"I gave them the names of the women, that's all I did."

"What did you get in return?" Gillette demanded. "I know you too well, Lana," he said when she didn't answer right away. "You don't give away anything for free."

"They said they were going to use the names of the women against your father. Publicize Clayton's infidelity in an awful way, so I'd be able to divorce him and get everything. Which sounded pretty damn good to me at that point, Christian," she said, her voice trembling. "He'd just started seeing someone else, a girl who was nineteen, for Christ's sake." She put her hands to her face. "You can't imagine what it's like to know that every time your husband walks out the door, you won't see him again until he's made love to another woman. I'd had enough. I couldn't take it anymore."

For a moment, Gillette tried to understand what

she'd endured, tried to feel sympathy for her. But it wouldn't come. He simply couldn't get past what she'd done to him. "Just give me the names."

"**DO WE HAVE** good news yet?" Boyd asked irritably.

Ganze shook his head. "No. I just came in to tell you that Gillette's been visiting his stepmother at the Bel Air house for the last thirty minutes."

Boyd's eyes rose from his desk. "Oh, my God."

GILLETTE SAT behind the desk in his father's old study, taking in the sights and smells. It had been a long time, but he was sure he could still smell the sweet aroma of the pipe.

He'd tried to work with the computer there to copy what was on the flash drive Mary Lee had given him, but the hard drive was too old and the memory insufficient to handle the transfer. He reached for the phone and dialed Nikki's direct line at the hospital.

"Hello."

Her voice was groggy, and he felt bad for calling so late. But he had to talk to her. "Nikki, it's Christian."

"Oh, hi."

"I'm sorry to wake you up."

"It's all right, what's the matter?"

"When I was there with you earlier, you told me you took pictures of a man who visited Lana at the house before Dad's plane crash. He was out on the patio with her."

"Yes. Actually I took a whole bunch of them, maybe ten."

"Do you still have them?"

She was quiet for a few moments. "I didn't take them with me when I moved out of the house. Which was like ten or eleven years ago. If they're still around, they're in a box in the bottom left-hand drawer of my desk. But Mom probably threw it out."

DAVIS LAY ON the cot, his wrists and ankles chained tightly to the frame. His captors had tortured him three separate times, hadn't given him any food or water, and had pulled one of his teeth with a pair of needle-nose pliers. But they hadn't broken him yet. Not because he had any allegiance to Christian Gillette; no, they hadn't broken him because the very fact that he'd been kidnapped and tortured proved to him that someone was close to a major breakthrough on nanotechnology—someone who shouldn't have it.

And for Gillette to stay in front of that person, he needed the biggest head start Davis could give him.

. . .

GILLETTE OPENED the drawer of Nikki's old desk and reached down for the small box. His fingers shook as he opened it. The pictures were there, as Nikki had promised, ten of them. Clear shots of Lana and the man Nikki had mentioned sitting on the patio outside the house.

Gillette exhaled heavily. Unbelievable.

There was no need for Lana to give him his mother's real name now. He just wanted to know that Marilyn McRae wasn't his real mother. Her slipup at dinner about the cigars—his father never smoked cigars—was almost enough. But the pictures gave him the answers he'd been looking for—and a lot more than that.

DAVIS HAD always had an irrational fear of water, which he assumed stemmed from a childhood incident where he'd almost drowned. He never swam and never took a bath, always showered because he hated the feeling of having any part of his body submerged in water. Now they had him kneeling in front of a tub of water, his hands tied tightly behind his back. Somehow they had figured out his Room 101—the thing he feared most in life.

As they forced his head into the water, he screamed as he'd never screamed in his life, trying desperately to get his head back up. Just as he thought he would pass out, they jerked him out of the tub.

They didn't even have to ask. He began to babble on his own, telling them every detail of the conversations he'd had with Christian Gillette.

"**NORMAN!**" Ganze yelled, bursting into Boyd's office. "They got Davis to break. A little water and he crumbled like a stale cookie."

"Excellent. Did he tell them anything important?"

"He told them that he had sent Gillette to Matt Lee's wife."

"**Jesus Christ!**" Boyd roared, shooting out of his chair. "Weren't you just there?"

"Yes. Apparently, Gillette was there on Wednesday, the day after we were."

"You searched the place, right?"

"Yes."

"But you didn't find anything?"

"No."

"Could she have told him anything important?"

"I don't know. These people aren't supposed to talk to anyone about the project, even to their spouses. But you know they do."

"Did you question her?" Boyd asked.

"No."

"Well, get back on the phone with Celino's people right now. Get them up to Boston immediately. Take any means necessary to find out what she told Gillette. Hell, have them do the same thing to Lee's wife that they just did to Davis."

"You mean—"

"Yes, damn it, I mean torture, then disposal. By now she must know something's happened to her husband anyway. We don't want her running around trying to get the newspapers interested in her story. Get her off the fucking face of the earth."

DAVID WRIGHT gazed out over the East River and Queens from the terrace of his Upper East Side apartment. It was four in the morning, but he couldn't sleep. He leaned forward in his chair and put his face in his hands. He couldn't go on like this, being a coward. It was killing him. Ratting on Gillette like some little pussy because he was so afraid Joe Celino would send the pictures to the cops or take him out. Or worst of all, do something to Peggy. That's what really kept him up, the thought of that. He shook his head. He wasn't a coward. Never had been. He'd always faced things head-on.

"David?"

Wright whipped around in the chair, toward Peggy. "Hey, Peg."

"It's four in the morning," she said, coming to him and putting a hand on his shoulder. Her face was creased with concern. "What's wrong?"

"Nothing," he lied, "I was just thinking about this deal I'm working on."

She sat on his lap and put her arms around him, sighed, then smiled at him sweetly. "I guess now's as good a time as any to tell you," she said, patting her belly.

"Tell me what?"

But before she could answer, he realized. Suddenly he had a whole new reason to get things straight.

20

LESS THAN A YEAR BEFORE, Gillette had delivered Bill Donovan's eulogy to a packed church in midtown Manhattan. This time it was Harlem, but the church was just as crowded.

"He was my best friend," Gillette said quietly. "I'll never have another friend like Quentin Stiles."

When he was finished, Gillette moved down the steps from the dais and knelt before Stiles's grandmother. Her face was soaked with tears, and he took her hand gently. "You going to be okay?"

"I'm a tough old bird," she whispered. "I'll be all right."

After he'd kissed her on the forehead, Gillette headed down the center aisle toward the back of the church, glancing at Wright as he passed. Wright's eyes were down, glued to the floor. So were Peggy's.

Outside the church, Gillette leaned back against a tree and closed his eyes, wondering if the time had come to get out. He was thirty-seven, and he'd never be able to spend all the money he'd made. Why keep working? Why deal with it anymore?

"You ready?"

Gillette opened his eyes. Derrick Walker stood in front of him.

"We got to get you down to Chatham, Christian. The meeting doesn't start until six o'clock, but I spoke to Percy Lundergard and he wants you there by four. Says he's got a lot of things he needs to cover with you before you go on."

"Yeah, okay." Over Walker's shoulder, Gillette saw Wright and Peggy walking toward their car. "Give me a second," he said, brushing past Walker. "David," he called.

Wright kept moving.

"David!"

The second time Gillette called, Wright stopped on the sidewalk and turned.

"I need to talk to you," Gillette said loudly as he neared them.

Wright gestured for Peggy to go ahead without him. "What is it?" he asked when she was gone.

The younger man seemed to be hanging his head, Gillette noticed. He seemed tired, almost beaten. "What's wrong?"

Wright shrugged. "Nothing."

"You sure?"

Wright shook his head. "I . . . I haven't been . . . I'm just . . ." He groaned. "I've just been working hard on this Hush-Hush thing. I want to get it done fast, that's all. I don't want someone else coming in and stealing it."

"That's all? You don't have anything else you want to tell me?"

"No. Why?"

"I went to Richmond."

Wright swallowed hard. "Yeah, so?"

"I drove. After I got out of the city, I went down the Jersey Turnpike."

"Makes sense. That would be the fastest way to get to Richmond if you were driving. But why are you telling me?"

Gillette hesitated, letting the pressure build. "Were you on the Jersey Turnpike this week?"

Wright shifted on his feet, then shoved his hands in his pockets. "Why would you think I was?"

"I saw a—"

"Look, I gotta go, Chris," Wright said suddenly, turning and trotting toward Peggy, who was standing by their car.

GILLETTE SWUNG the dark green Oldsmobile into a spot of the Chatham High School student parking lot and climbed out. Percy Lundergard had suggested that Gillette not come in a limousine, that he dress casually, and that his security detail be as invisible as possible. So he'd driven himself to the meeting in Lundergard's own sedan, worn a golf shirt and slacks, and been accompanied by only one QS agent, who was also casually dressed. As he made his way across the parking lot with the rest of the crowd, he thought how nice it was to blend in for once.

There was already a line forming at the front door, and as Gillette reached the back of it, he noticed a figure standing alone on the grass by the side of the building. When he took a second look, the figure seemed familiar. He stared hard for a moment. David Wright.

They locked eyes for a few moments and acknowledged each other with a subtle nod, then Wright motioned for Gillette to break away.

Gillette gave the QS agent standing beside him a tap on the shoulder. "See that guy over there?" he said, pointing at Wright.

"Yes."

"I'm going to talk to him. You're coming with me."

"Okay."

"What are you doing here, David?" Gillette asked as he neared him, aware that the people in line were watching. He and Wright clearly weren't locals. In a town as small as Chatham, everyone knew everyone. "I thought you and Peggy were going out of the city for the weekend, out to Long Island or something."

"We were," Wright mumbled, glancing at the QS agent. "Hey, can we have a little space?"

Gillette waved the agent off. "What's going on, David?"

Wright took a deep breath. "This is tough."

"Tough?"

"Look, let's not beat around the bush. You know I was on the turnpike the other day. I don't know how you know, but you know."

"Were you following me?" Gillette asked.

"Yeah."

"Why?"

"You're not going to believe this."

"Try me."

Wright put a hand to his face and rubbed his eyes. "I've been keeping tabs on you for the Carbone family."

Wright's image blurred in front of Gillette, and his throat went dry. The man he'd tabbed as his protégé, a man he'd trusted completely, was a traitor. It was almost unfathomable. "Is this about Las Vegas?" he asked, his voice hushed.

"I, I think so," Wright said hesitantly.

"Why would they care where I was so much?" Gillette asked, knowing it couldn't be just about the NFL franchise and the casino. Looking around warily, suddenly wondering if this was a setup. Wondering if Wright had really driven all the way down here to come clean.

"I don't know."

"We're paying that guy Carmine Torino his fee, which I'm sure the Carbones are getting most of."

Might as well try to dig as much information out of Wright as possible, Gillete thought. "I assume that's what they wanted. I can't understand why they'd need to know where I was all the time. There's got to be something more."

"Like I said," Wright answered shakily, "I don't know. I asked that question a lot, but I never got an answer."

"Why did you do it, David?"

"I've got a problem," Wright mumbled. "Something they're using against me. You know I didn't want to."

"What is it, what do they have on you?"

"I can't tell you."

"David, you—"

"I **really** can't tell you, Chris. You've been a great friend to me, and I couldn't look myself in the mirror anymore. I thought I could screw anyone to get ahead, to save myself, but I guess I can't after all. I suppose that's one thing I can take away from this whole mess." He kicked at a tuft of grass. "But I can't tell you what they have on me, I just can't. You'll probably hear about it on the news at some point, but I don't want to tell you now."

"It's that bad?"

"It doesn't have anything to do with Everest, though," Wright said quickly. "I want you to know that."

"Is it something I might be able to help you with?"

"No."

Gillette glanced over his shoulder at the line. It was getting long. "Look, I gotta go." He put his hand on Wright's shoulder. "Thanks for coming down here. We'll need to talk again on Monday. In depth."

"If I'm still around," Wright muttered.

"What?"

"Nothing. Look, there's more."

Gillette turned back. **"More?"**

"When we were in Vegas, I met with Joe Celino."

"What?"

" 'Met' isn't really the right word," Wright corrected himself. "I was basically hauled in front of him. He told me I was a dead man if I didn't do exactly what he wanted. He showed me a picture of this poor fucker they tortured to death to scare the shit out of me. Which it did. So I'm probably pretty much screwed at this point. I'm sure they'll find out I came to you, so when I don't show up Monday, you'll know why. But here's the point: Celino told me some things you oughta know."

"Like what?"

"First, he claimed he was working with Allison Wallace somehow."

Gillette suddenly felt as though someone had hit him in the gut with a sledgehammer. "Jesus Christ." Veramax, Dr. Davis, and Beezer Johnson raced through his mind.

"I don't know how, and I don't know on what,"

Wright continued. "But he told me she'd be running Everest at some point soon, so I ought to suck up to her. That if I cooperated with him, there'd be a place for me when she was in charge."

Probably why she was calling investors and inferring that she'd be running the show soon, Gillette thought. Setting the stage. So Faraday was right. Maybe Nigel was the guy to run Everest after all. His instincts seemed to be dead-on. "What else did Celino tell you?" Gillette asked angrily.

"He told me his people had gotten that mate on the yacht to kill Quentin Stiles."

"Are you serious?" Gillette asked incredulously. "Yes."

Gillette's mind was spinning. The Carbones had gotten Stiles. It kept echoing in his head. But somehow Norman Boyd had known in Minneapolis, without ever laying eyes on Stiles in Washington, that Derrick Walker was a different head of security. **Somehow Boyd had known that something had happened to Stiles.** The connection suddenly made sense. The Carbones were rarely ever in the news, but they were the most successful and feared crime family in the country. And Norman Boyd would need assassins, people who were good at killing. As Ted Casey had said in the Georgetown parking garage the other night. Maybe it wasn't a coincidence that the Carbones made so much money and Boyd had a reputation for being able to intimidate anyone he wanted to. Maybe there was a hideous partnership. One in which Celino's people tortured and killed for Boyd. And, in return, got cover from the government on their criminal activities, maybe even had things pushed their way every once in a while. That would also explain why the Carbones would kill Tom McGuire. Boyd couldn't have somebody out there trying to kill Gillette—not when Boyd was relying on him.

Then it hit Gillette. Boyd wouldn't need him if he had Allison in his pocket.

"Why would they want Stiles dead?" Gillette asked, barely able to hear his voice over the pounding of his heart.

"Celino said Stiles was getting too close on something. He didn't tell me what, though."

Maybe that was what Stiles had been talking about on the boat last weekend. Maybe he was getting close to linking Celino with a government agency. A connection that Celino and the Agency would certainly do almost anything to avoid having exposed. Something like that, were it revealed and proven true, would end any advantage the Carbones had over the rest of the country's Mob families. In fact, it would probably end the Carbones as a family. There would be endless congressional investigations and scrutiny that would make it almost impossible for the Carbones to continue to operate. And there'd be no telling what it would do to the United States intelligence agencies.

"Did you follow me all the way to Richmond the other day?" Gillette demanded.

Wright nodded. "In a damn cab."

"Do you know who I met with?"

"A neurosurgeon named Scott Davis."

Gillette banged his fist against the building. "Did you tell the Carbones that?"

"Yeah." Wright's voice was barely audible.

Gillette yanked his cell phone from his pocket to call Cathy Dylan. He had to get in touch with Davis immediately, to warn him. "Did you tell them about Tom McGuire, too? About McGuire coming after me?"

"Yeah."

"Christian," Percy Lundergard called, trotting across the grass toward Gillette, "you've got to get inside. It's almost time."

Gillette held up a hand, waiting for Cathy to answer, but she didn't pick up. "Damn it." He pointed at Wright as he cut the connection. "Get out of here, David. Call your wife immediately and tell her to get somewhere safe right away."

"Christian, come on," Lundergard urged, looking at Wright strangely.

"Percy, I've got an emergency. I'm not going to be able to—"

"No way," Lundergard snapped. "I've moved heaven and earth to put two thousand people in that auditorium tonight," he said, pointing at the building, "and to get the NBC affiliate to televise this thing. You're not backing out on me, Christian, not for **any** reason."

"**CELINO'S PEOPLE** got it out of Mary Lee," Ganze reported.

Boyd was standing behind his desk, squeezing the back of the chair so hard that his knuckles were white. "**What, damn it**? What did they get?"

"That she gave Gillette a flash drive with everything on it. All the work the team had generated up to the point they took off from Boston the other day. Matt gave it to her right before he got on the plane you sent into Lake Michigan. Apparently, he smuggled it out of the research lab the night before."

"Well, doesn't that make my fucking day," Boyd hissed. "Christian Gillette knows more about nanotechnology than we do at this point."

"What do you mean?" Ganze asked.

Boyd nodded at the secure telephone on his desk. "I just spoke to our lead person in Minneapolis. She says there's something missing from the research material, a vital piece of the code they can't find and can't re-create without Matt Lee. He must have figured out he wasn't getting off that plane." Boyd pounded the desk. "Get Celino's people after Gillette, **immediately.** I want that flash drive, and I want it yesterday. I don't care what they have to do to get it."

...

IT WAS GILLETTE'S turn to speak in front of the packed auditorium. Becky Rouse had made her case, telling the crowd that allowing a Discount America store into town would destroy the successful tourist trade she had developed over the past several years. Citing facts and figures that demonstrated how so many more outsiders were spending money on the waterfront. That tourists would no longer think of Chatham as quaint if it was at the center of a superstore war. That the mammoth retail outlet would suck dollars away from the waterfront, too, and attract a group of people from other towns Chatham didn't want. She was given a strong round of applause as she sat down.

Gillette took the microphone and smiled calmly at several people in the huge crowd before speaking, trying to focus. So many things were racing through his mind. "Good evening, I'm Christian Gillette," he began, wondering if someone in the audience was here to kill him. "I'm the chairman of Discount America, and I want to thank you for giving me the opportunity to speak. I realize that it's Saturday evening, so I won't keep you long. I want you to be able to get home to your families and your televisions and your parties, I really do. I just want to take a few minutes of your time and present you with a few basic facts as you decide whether or not you want our store in your town. We hope you do. We think it'll be a great partnership.

"First, the store will be built out on Route 212, at least five miles west of the waterfront. Almost a hundred percent of the tourist traffic comes from the east, they'll never see this store. Second, the store will be huge. You'll be able to buy almost anything you want, from fresh vegetables to computers. You won't have to go to Delaware to buy basic stuff anymore. Third, thanks to our ability to buy in bulk, our prices are tremendously low." Gillette motioned to the crowd. "Can someone please tell me what a four-bar pack of Ivory soap costs at Fletcher's market on the Chatham waterfront?"

A young woman raised her hand.

"Yes?"

"Five dollars and a quarter," the woman said, her voice cracking with nerves.

"Five dollars and twenty-five cents," Gillette said loudly. He shook his head. "You know what it'll cost at the new DA store? Two fifty at most."

A rumble ran through the crowd.

"Believe me," he said, acknowledging the positive response, "you want us here. It'll be a great store and a fantastic shopping experience. It'll create jobs and tax revenue. It'll be—"

"How much money will you make from the store?" Becky interrupted.

Gillete turned. Becky was out of her chair, arms folded firmly over her chest. Obviously, she'd felt the tide turning in his favor and was going to do anything she could to stop the momentum.

"Come on, Mr. Gillette, tell us all what you're going to make off this store."

"I don't have the exact figures yet, but it's—"

"At least a hundred million!" she shouted.

A murmur rolled through the auditorium.

Gillette smiled calmly and put up his arms. "It's nowhere near a hundred million." He glanced at Percy Lundergard, who had his hands over his eyes.

Becky pointed at a man in the second row. "You all know who Fred Jacobs is. The best accountant in the county. Fred looked at this for me. What do you think Mr. Gillette will make on the store, Fred?"

Jacobs stood up. He was a scholarly-looking man with wire-rimmed glasses and a crop of white hair. "I think Becky's pretty close. About a hundred million a year."

"Believe me," Gillette said loudly, "that's way off."

"Then how much is it?" an elderly woman in the middle of the crowd shouted in a high-pitched voice.

"I'm not sure right now."

The crowd groaned.

Gillette saw Lundergard running his finger across his neck.

"Mr. Gillette won't even help us with a few things we need around here," Becky spoke up. "His investors just gave him **fifteen billion dollars** and—"

"Actually, it's **twenty,**" Jacobs corrected from his

seat. "I checked the Everest Capital Web site right before I came over. Some rich family from Chicago just gave Mr. Gillette another five billion."

"Twenty billion dollars!" Becky shouted, whipping the crowd into a frenzy. "Can you imagine having that much money at your fingertips? I can't. I asked Mr. Gillette to help us build a new elementary school, and you know what he said? He said he'd build half of it. **Half** a school. Can you imagine that? Now, Mr. Gillette, which half were you thinking about? The top half or the bottom half?"

A loud chorus of cackles and boos arose from the crowd.

"What I said was—"

"I know about you, Mr. Gillette," Becky said, pointing at him and silencing the crowd as they hung on her every word. "I know there are people who question what you've done with some of the money they've given you."

"That's not true."

"I understand there's going to be an investigation," she said loudly, turning to the crowd. "This is not the kind of man we want in our town, people. Believe me. A man who'd build **half** a school and who's about to be investigated for fraud!"

GILLETTE AND BECKY ROUSE stood on a darkened, tree-lined side street a few blocks from the high school. It had been thirty minutes since the scene on the auditorium stage.

"What do you want?" she asked, grinning smugly. "What do you want to talk about?"

"Pretty proud of yourself, aren't you."

"Yup."

"You know I'm not being investigated."

She pointed back toward the high school. "Yeah, but they don't."

Gillette glanced over his shoulder. He'd parked Lundergard's car back up the street and told the QS agent to stay there. "I want a truce; I want to call off the war," he said. "I want my store, and I want you to support it." It had started to drizzle, and he spotted a couple beneath an umbrella walking down the other side of the street. "I'll give you everything you want. The elementary school, the retirement home, the squad cars. I just want this back-and-forth to be done. There's no reason for it."

"You better not go back on this," she said, her voice rising.

Gillette glanced through the darkness at the couple across the street, their silhouettes outlined by a streetlamp. "Easy," he urged, trying to calm her down, noticing that the couple had stopped and was looking toward them. "I'm not going back on it. There's no reason to think I would."

"There's **every** reason to think you would. I know your kind, Christian. You think the world revolves around you!"

"Becky, come on, that's not fair. I'm the one that ought to be upset here. With what you said to the crowd about me being investigated."

She shrugged and turned away.

"Hey, look," he said, moving to her side, "I'm just trying to—"

There was a flash and the blast of a gunshot. A bullet tore through Becky's back and out her chest, grazing Gillette's arm and hurling her against him. He tried to catch her, but she fell from his arms, dead even before she hit the street.

Another gunshot exploded, closer this time.

Gillette wheeled around and sprinted the other way. Whoever was shooting was trying to hit **him,** not Becky. Out of the corner of his eye, he saw the couple standing on the other side of the street dive for cover behind a car, then he cut right, hurdled a waist-high hedge, and darted between two homes. At the back of the house, he scaled a six-foot chain-link fence and dropped into the thick brush on the other side.

He pulled himself to his feet and waded through the raspberry bushes, thorns tugging at his clothes. Finally the bushes gave way to woods, and he raced ahead, wincing as his feet crashed through dried leaves, careful to avoid the trees in the darkness. When he reached the edge of the trees and the next street over, he hesitated, pressed behind a large oak, gazing back into the gloom of the woods, listening carefully for any sound. But there was nothing more than the consistent patter of drops as the rain began to fall more steadily.

Gillette waited ten minutes, then saw a police car cruising slowly down the wet street, lights flashing in the growing fog. A huge stroke of luck. He moved out from behind the oak tree, waving his arms as he stepped into the glare of the headlights.

The police car stopped, and the driver's-side door opened instantly.

"Down on the ground," the cop yelled. "Now!"

Gillette put his hand up over his face and squinted against the high beams. He could barely make out the officer kneeling behind the door, aiming a pistol at him over the mirror. "Officer, my name's Christian Gillette. I was just shot at. I'm not the one you're looking for."

"Get down, now! Arms and legs spread."

Gillette made a snap decision and bolted back for the woods. He heard the **pop, pop, pop** of the policeman's revolver, but he was quickly back into the cover of the trees, impossible to see in the darkness. As he hid behind another tree, he peered around the side of it.

The policeman was on the radio, calling for backup. Gillette wanted to give himself up, but the flash drive was in his pocket. The officer would have confiscated everything on him, and he wasn't going to let the flash drive go. Not for anything in the world. It could easily fall into the wrong hands.

Then he heard sirens, several of them, quickly growing louder. He turned and ran as the rain became a downpour.

21

FARADAY RELAXED into his favorite easy chair, propped his feet up on the ottoman, clicked the television on with the remote, then reached for a heaping bowl of cookie-dough ice cream sitting on the table beside the chair. He'd thought about going out tonight—he had several invitations—but he was dead tired. It had been a long week, and all he wanted to do was relax in his apartment. If the past was any indicator, he'd be asleep in an hour, wake up around midnight, and drag himself to bed.

He watched the last few minutes of **Seinfeld,** finishing the ice cream as the credits rolled and settling in for the news.

When Christian Gillette's face appeared on the screen over the anchor's shoulder, Faraday shot out of the chair, dropping the bowl to the floor. The woman relayed that the Everest Capital chairman was a fugitive. That he was wanted for the murder of

Becky Rouse, the mayor of a small town in Maryland called Chatham. That there were two witnesses to the shooting. That he had evaded an attempted arrest and was considered extremely dangerous.

GILLETTE FOUND Percy Lundergard's cell number on his phone and called. He was somewhere on the east side of Chatham, at the edge of a trailer park and a cornfield. His plan was to get off the Eastern Shore of Maryland as soon as possible—by going either north to Wilmington, Delaware, or east over the Chesapeake Bay Bridge toward Washington, D.C. He pressed his arms close to his body and stomped his feet. It was still raining, and the temperature was dropping fast.

"Hello."

"Percy?"

"Christian?"

"Yeah."

"Where are you?"

"What in the hell is going on?" he asked, ignoring the question. "Why did a Chatham cop try to arrest me an hour ago?"

"The police think you killed Becky Rouse."

"What? That's insane."

"That's exactly what I told them."

"Whoever shot her was trying to kill **me,**" Gillette said.

"The cops say they have two witnesses."

The couple walking on the other side of the street under the umbrella, Gillette assumed. They'd heard Becky shout his name.

"And," Lundergard continued, "they're saying they've got the murder weapon with your prints on it."

Planted, obviously. "What about the guy who was with me?" Gillette asked. "My bodyguard."

"No one can find him."

The guy was dead, was helping whoever shot Becky, or was the one who shot her. Gillette patted his shirt pocket, making certain the flash drive was still there. He had a pretty damn good idea of who was responsible for her death. Maybe he didn't know who'd actually pulled the trigger, but he knew who was pulling the strings.

"Why don't you come here? To my house?" Lundergard offered. "We'll figure out what to do next when you get here."

Gillette thought for a second. "Okay, see you in a little while."

FARADAY REACHED for his apartment phone, hoping it was Gillette. It wasn't. It was Allison.

"Have you heard what's going on?" she asked excitedly as soon as he picked up.

"You mean about Christian?"

"Of course that's what I mean."

"I'm watching the news right now."

"Nigel, what do you think happened?"

"Somebody's made a terrible mistake."

LUNDERGARD PUT DOWN the phone and glanced up at Jim Cochran, the Chatham chief of police, who was standing in his living room. On either side of Cochran were two men claiming to be federal agents. Lundergard hadn't seen the big gold badges for long—the agents had flipped them open and shut quickly—but Cochran seemed satisfied.

"So?" Cochran demanded gruffly.

"Gillette says he'll be here in a little while. You better get all the police cars out of here."

GILLETTE'S NEXT CALL was Derrick Walker. He'd thought long and hard about whether or not to make this call. If the agent who'd been with him in the car had turned on him, then Walker could easily have turned, too. Walker wasn't like Stiles; he didn't own QS Security—he could be bribed. But in the end, Gillette had no choice. He needed someone's help.

Walker picked up on the first ring.

"Hello," he answered fiercely. "Are you all right?"

Obviously, Walker had seen the number on the cell screen. "Where are you?" Gillette asked.

"The Chatham police station."

"Can you talk?"

"Yeah," Walker said quietly.

"I didn't shoot this woman." It was stupid to have to say it. If it had been Stiles, he wouldn't have even bothered.

"Of course you didn't."

"What happened to your guy?" Gillette asked. "The one who was with me tonight?"

"I'm pretty sure he's dead. He's not answering his phone or his pager."

"Maybe he's working with whoever shot Becky Rouse. Maybe **he** shot Becky."

"Not a chance. I've known Lionel for seven years. I'd trust my life with him. That's why I had him with you. Now what the fuck is going on?" Walker asked angrily. "Do you know?"

Gillette hesitated. "I'm pretty sure I do, but I don't want to say anything on this line." He watched as a man came out of one of the trailer homes close to where he was standing and stuffed a garbage bag in the trash can, then hurried back inside. "I need to meet up with you."

"Where?"

"At that place I told you I had that meeting yesterday."

WALKER HUNG UP with Gillette, then made another call immediately. It lasted just twenty seconds. After he slipped the cell phone back into his pocket, he stood up from the desk he'd been sitting on and turned around. Jim Cochran was directly in front of him, flanked by several deputies.

"You're under arrest, Mr. Walker. Turn around and put your hands behind your back."

"For what?" Walker demanded.

"Aiding and abetting."

"Aiding and abetting who?"

"Christian Gillette."

GILLETTE SPRINTED across the open field toward the rest stop and the idling tractor-trailer. He had no intention of going to Percy Lundergard's house or anywhere else the authorities might be waiting. He'd watched the truck driver jump down and trot toward the bathrooms through the driving rain. He shivered as he pulled himself up between the cab and the trailer. This was going to be a cold ride.

22

GILLETTE HAD BEEN waiting two hours for Derrick Walker on the ground floor of the same Georgetown parking garage where he'd met Ted Casey, the CIA cutout specialist, a few days ago. They must have gotten Walker, too, he realized. Walker had had a day and a half to get here, but he was a no-show.

Gillette had spent the last two nights outside in the elements. Saturday night, beneath a railroad bridge in southwest Washington fighting a torrential rain; last night, beneath the stars on a steam grate near the Washington Monument along with three indigents, bundled up in blankets. It had turned unusually cold for early October after the rain had passed through. He hadn't used his credit cards, cash card, or cell phone until this morning, not wanting to give anyone any clue to where he was. Now he didn't care.

It was five after ten, and he needed to get to Tysons Corner out in northern Virginia—a twenty-minute cab ride from here. He let out a frustrated breath. He really could have used Walker.

TYSONS CORNER was fifteen miles west of downtown Washington, D.C., and only a few miles from where Gillette, Boyd, and Ganze had first met. One anchor of the Dulles Corridor—the area's high-tech center stretching to Dulles Airport fifteen miles farther west—Tysons was also the location of two large, popular shopping malls—Tysons I and II—that were less than half a mile apart.

Tysons II, built on a hill overlooking the area, was a sprawling three-level structure full of upscale shops and restaurants, all attached to a Ritz-Carlton Hotel and two office buildings rising up on either side of the Ritz. Gillette had stayed at the hotel several times in the last few years for technology conferences, so he knew the mall well. Also called the Galleria, the mall would be crowded now at lunchtime, which was perfect for what he was planning.

It was twelve-twenty. Gillette had called Boyd and Ganze forty minutes ago, giving them until twelve-thirty to get here. They'd agreed to come immediately. Gillette now knew how important the flash drive was.

He grimaced. Mary was so timid, but she'd shown so much courage in giving him the drive. He had no doubt they'd gotten to her. Davis, too. Getting to Mary and Davis was the only way they could have connected the dots and known about the flash drive so fast. He just hoped they'd been merciful and ended it quickly for both of them. And he hoped that if something went wrong in the next few minutes, they'd do the same for him.

Gillette walked slowly, a Washington Nationals baseball cap pulled low over his eyes, looking around constantly as he approached PF Chang's, a popular, high-end Chinese restaurant located at the mall's northwest entrance. He wasn't worried about Boyd's people—including the Carbone family—trying to kill him. Boyd needed the flash drive almost as badly as he needed his next breath, so they weren't going to do anything stupid. Not yet, anyway. But the police or some bystander might. If he was still being accused of Becky Rouse's murder, the cops would be on the lookout for him, even over here on the western side of the bay. And if his face had been on the news, there was always the chance some do-gooder might try to take him just to get his name in the paper.

Gillette moved through the mall to the escalator and took it up to the third level, then followed the concourse to a Hallmark store in front of the south escalators. Boyd was standing in front of the store, alone, as Gillette had instructed.

"Well, well, look what the cat dragged in," Boyd said as Gillette stopped ten feet away. "You look like crap."

"But I'm alive."

"Only because I want you that way. Now give me the drive," Boyd demanded.

"Not yet."

"I told you, pal, I have a lot of friends in the right places. I can take Everest down in a heartbeat. Find something wrong with it and you in no time." He sneered. "Hell, there's already a kiddie porn aggregator on your hard drive at Everest, Christian, pulling enough nasty videos onto your machine to put you away for a few years. We installed it yesterday, remotely. But no one will ever know it was done that way. All the feds will know is that Christian Gillette is into kiddie porn. How's that gonna look in **The New York Times,** pal?"

"I have the flash drive. The rest will take care of itself. The truth will out."

"I'm glad you think so. I'm glad you're that naïve."

"You live in your world, Norman, I'll live in mine."

"And of course," Boyd continued, "you've got that little issue of murdering the Rouse woman down in Chatham."

"You know I didn't kill her."

"But the cops think you did. That's all that matters. **Now, give me the damn drive.**"

Gillette moved a few steps closer. "What? You think I'm going to just hand it over so your Carbone friends can pop out of a couple of these stores and mow me down?" He saw shock register on Boyd's face. "That would be pretty stupid, wouldn't it? Those guys don't mind making a hit in a public place. They don't mind killing anyone anywhere, right?"

Boyd shook in silent rage.

Gillette could tell he'd hit a nerve. His suspicions were dead-on. "Look, all I want is closure, Norman. That's all I've ever wanted from you."

"What do you mean?"

"I want answers. Answers you and Ganze promised to give me about my mother and father."

"I don't know anything about that. You'll have to talk to Daniel, but you didn't want him with me."

"But he's here at the mall, right?"

Boyd nodded. "Like I said, I don't know anything about those questions of yours."

"I think you do. I think you made Ganze and everyone else believe you didn't, but I think you know everything. I think you threw Marilyn McRae to Ganze and me. I'm sure she would have sworn to Ganze and me until the day she died that she really was my mother, but I know she's not. What did you give her, Norman? Money? A career? Promise her the world if she'd do a few favors for you and your government cronies? You've probably manipulated her for years." Gillette hesitated. "Like you manipulated the sale of the Vegas franchise to Everest so your

Carbone buddies could get their money through Carmine Torino, and ultimately get their claws into the casino. We were the only ones who put in a bid that included a casino, weren't we, Norman?"

Boyd smiled slightly.

"It was perfect. You're always looking for ways to pay the Carbones back for the dirty work. The tortures and the assassinations. Right? You called a few of the owners you have in your hip pocket and influenced them to give Everest the nod in the auction, even though there was another bid that was fifty million dollars higher. You rigged that thing, didn't you?"

Boyd shrugged. "You'll never prove it."

"How can you possibly influence NFL owners?"

"A favor here, a favor there. Make a woman who's about to file a palimony suit disappear, help a father when his kid gets into drug trouble. There's all kinds of ways, Christian. Everybody has their problems. As long as you know about them, you can make things go your way."

"How long have you been working with the Carbones?" Gillette asked.

"All right, that's enough. Give me the fucking drive."

Gillette stared at Boyd hard. "Is that what my father really uncovered, Norman? That you were working with the Mafia? Is that why you killed him? There wasn't any plot to kill the president. You were the plot."

Boyd's eyes flashed to Gillette's. "What?" An odd expression came over his face.

"Is that why you killed my father?" Gillette repeated, louder this time.

"Are you out of your mind? What kind of question is that?"

"I have pictures of you and Lana sitting on the patio at the house in Bel Air just weeks before my father was killed. That's when Lana gave you the names of the women my father had children with. You tried to extort my father, telling him you were going to leak the details of his affairs to the newspapers so he'd have to resign his Senate seat. But it didn't work, did it? He was going to expose you no matter what. Expose your relationship to the Carbones, all the things you'd stolen from the government, then sold. Like you're trying to steal the nanotechnology now. You've murdered innocent people in the name of national security, but it has nothing to do with national security. It's all about you. All about making you and your pals rich."

Boyd's face went blank.

Gillette moved closer, until their faces were just inches apart. "Tell me if I'm right, Norman. I have to know." He nodded slowly, submissively. "I know you can take me down. I know you can nail me for Becky Rouse's murder. I'm sure you've done a lot worse to people who've done a lot less."

"You're damn right I have."

"So tell me if I'm right. Then you get your drive."

Boyd's mouth slowly broke into a slight grin, then he chuckled. "You're a smart man, Christian. Brave, too. You could have worked for me." He took a deep breath. "Now, give me my goddamn drive."

Gillette spotted two men emerging from the Hallmark store. He slammed Boyd's chin with a right cross, then turned and raced toward the escalator, leaping four steps at a time, bowling over two men in front of him. As he reached the second floor, two more men came at him from Bebe, a woman's clothing store. One of them hit him high and the other low, and the three of them tumbled to the ground, knocking over a young woman who shrieked as she rolled away. Gillette felt them forcing his hands behind his back roughly.

Then suddenly a stream of agents poured out of several stores, wrestled the two men off Gillette, lifted them to their feet, and slammed them up against the wall facefirst.

As soon as he was free, Gillette jumped to his feet and sprinted down the concourse to the entrance to the Ritz. He raced inside it and through the main lobby to the elevators that would take him to the hotel's arrival lobby.

BOYD TOUCHED his chin and moaned. Gillette's punch had knocked him out, and he was just getting his senses back. He made it to his hands and knees groggily, then stood up slowly. As his vision cleared, he noticed a man standing in front of him.

"Hello, Mr. Boyd. I'm Ted Casey. I'm with the Central Intelligence Agency." Casey signaled to several men behind him. "Take him away."

GILLETTE MOVED through the main entrance of the Ritz-Carlton and trotted across the courtyard toward the ground floor of the office building to the right of the hotel. Once inside the revolving glass door, he turned left toward the Palm restaurant.

"Tim."

The host looked up from behind the stand. "Yes?"

"I'm Christian. I was here about an hour ago. I rented a wine box."

"Oh, of course."

"I need to get in there."

"Sure, follow me."

Tim led Christian to the wine boxes—ten across and ten high, available for personal wines people wanted to have on hand for a special meal. "Which one is yours?"

"Twelve."

Tim handed Gillette a key.

Gillette unlocked the small door and reached inside for the flash drive. It was there, exactly where he'd left it. "Thanks."

Gillette moved out of the restaurant and turned

left, past the elevators toward the parking garage. Casey was to have left him a car on the third level. He moved out the back door, then headed up the steps.

"Stop right there."

Gillette's eyes snapped up from the steps. Daniel Ganze stood in front of him on the first landing, gun drawn.

"Give me the drive, Christian."

Gillette stopped short, shocked, glancing from the gun to Ganze's eyes. Finally, he shook his head. "It's over, Ganze. Boyd's in custody by now."

"I don't give a rat's ass about Boyd."

Gillette shook his head. Ganze didn't understand. "You don't have to go down, too. It's Boyd they want."

"And it's the drive I want. We have to make sure it's protected."

"There was no spy, Ganze," Gillette assured him, "no terrorist outfit. That was all part of Boyd's cover."

Ganze smiled. "Perfect, wasn't it?"

Gillette's eyes narrowed. "Huh?"

"I can assure you that there absolutely is a terrorist connection," Ganze snapped. "And it's about to pay off." He stepped forward and grabbed the flash drive from Gillette's shirt pocket, then stepped back, raised the gun, and aimed it at Gillette.

The explosion was deafening in the stairwell. Gillette dropped to his knees, bracing for excruciating pain. But there was nothing. Nothing but the sound of Ganze falling to the ground and his gun clattering down several steps.

Gillette opened his eyes and looked up the stairway. Quentin Stiles was looking back.

23

GILLETTE AND STILES sat on a courtyard bench in front of the Ritz-Carlton. It had been three hours since Stiles had shot Daniel Ganze dead. Ted Casey's men had removed the body, and the flash drive was back in Gillette's pocket.

"Okay, thanks," Gillette said, ending the call.

"Who was that?" Stiles asked.

"Casey," Gillette replied curtly.

"Oh, yeah? What did he say?"

Gillette bit his lip. He was overjoyed that his best friend was alive, but torn up by what he'd been put through. Made to think Stiles was dead. "His people just finished interrogating one of the Carbone guys they shot at the mall."

"They find out anything good?"

Gillette stretched. In a few minutes, he was getting a room at the Ritz and sleeping for two days.

"David Wright killed a woman in a West Village sex shop a couple of weeks ago."

"Oh, Jesus."

"The Carbones knew about it. That's how Celino got Wright to do what he wanted. They had pictures and a tape of Wright doing it."

"What's going to happen to him? They gonna prosecute?"

"Casey's already turned everything over to the New York Police Department. He doesn't know anything more than that. But I'm sure David will end up behind bars."

"What about Miles Whitman?" Stiles asked.

"The Carbones killed Whitman in France at Boyd's direction. Tortured him until he told them how to find Tom McGuire. Whitman was feeding McGuire money once a month from the forty million the CIA helped him stash away before he ran last year."

"Why was the CIA helping Whitman?"

"He let them use North America Guaranty as a cutout for years. Basically helped them spy on a lot of individuals in this country, especially high net worth people."

Stiles spat. "Nice world we live in, huh?"

"Yeah."

"But why would the CIA tell Boyd where Whitman was?"

"Agencies cooperate. But the CIA brass obviously didn't know Boyd was working with the Carbones."

"What about Allison Wallace?" Stiles wanted to know. "Was she working with the Carbones like Wright told you?"

"No," Gillette answered. "That was Celino disinformation. He was just trying to manipulate Wright with that one. She's straight. Turns out her assistant, Hamid, is okay, too." He held up his hand. "Oh, wait a minute, you don't know about Hamid. You've been dead for a week."

Stiles chuckled. "Derrick Walker told me about that. How Allison was out in the lobby and my guys wouldn't let him in." He laughed louder.

"It isn't funny, Quentin."

"Come on, Chris, ease up."

"Fuck you," Gillette snapped. He'd been wanting to say that for three hours.

"Hey, I just saved your life," Stiles shot back. "You could at least be a **little** grateful."

"You put a lot of people through a lot of pain."

"I had to. It was the only way."

Gillette gritted his teeth. "Why? Why'd you do it?"

Stiles looked out over the courtyard. "My guys swept the yacht the morning of the cruise and we found a rifle in the bunkroom. We figured out pretty quick it was the mate's. We took him downstairs before you got there, did a little influencing. He came clean about how he'd agreed to kill me for the Mob, so we decided to use it. Put the guy into 'protective custody' so the Mob figured he'd run because he thought they'd knock him off. I told you, I was working something in Philly with my contacts, and I figured I might be able to find out more quickly if the guys I was investigating thought they'd killed me. What I was on to was basically what you figured out. That the Carbones were working with the government. I just didn't know which agency. Like I said, Walker kept me up to speed about was going on. He called me from Chatham right before they put him in jail. That's how I caught up with you."

Gillette shook his head and stood up. He'd heard enough, and he could barely keep his eyes open. "I'm going to bed."

"You better take a shower first," Stiles said, standing up, too. "You need one."

Gillette started to walk off without answering.

"Yo, Chris!" Stiles called.

Gillette turned around. "What is it?"

Stiles moved slowly to where Gillette stood, hesitated a moment, then embraced him. "I'm sorry, man. I'm sorry I did that to you. I was just trying to help."

Gillette took a deep breath, then hugged Stiles back. Life was too short to be angry at your best friend for long. "I know."

After a few moments, they stepped back.

Gillette swallowed hard. "Quentin, I um . . . I, well . . ." He could feel his heart pounding. He wanted to say it, but he didn't know how. "You know I—"

"Yeah, I know," Stiles interrupted, grinning.

"Thanks," Gillette said quietly, letting out a long breath. "Hey, where you going?" Stiles was heading off across the grass.

"Chatham. I gotta get Walker out of jail."

24

FAITH AND GILLETTE sat outside the Everest building on Park Avenue in the back of a limousine, saying good-bye. She was leaving on a two-week tour to promote her new album, which had just hit stores and was racing to the top of the charts. He was going back to Everest for the first time since facing off against Norman Boyd in northern Virginia.

He'd been wearing a wire that day, so everything Boyd had said was on tape. Ted Casey had more than enough to go to the Justice Department with. Casey had called to tell Gillette that Boyd was probably going to prison for the rest of his life—even with all his high-level connections. That Ganze was in the ICU of a hospital close to the mall, almost certain to follow Boyd to prison if he recovered. And that Gillette now had friends at the CIA, for life.

"I had such a wonderful time," Faith said quietly, stroking Gillette's arm as she nestled against him on the comfortable seat. They'd spent the last week together at a cozy resort in Antigua.

"Me too." He smiled down at her.

"I'll miss you. It'll be so hard not seeing you for the next couple of weeks."

"I know."

She gathered herself up on the seat so her face was close to his. "Christian?"

"Yes."

"I'm sorry for how I acted. Not calling you back those times. I was just jealous." A frustrated expression crossed her face. "I'm so embarrassed. I wanted to tell you in Antigua, but, well . . . There won't be any more episodes like that. I promise."

He shook his head. "I shouldn't have let Allison come out on the boat like that. That was—"

Faith touched her fingers to his lips. "Stop. She's your business partner. I understand that now, I really do. I'm just glad you're safe. That this thing with the people in Washington is over."

Gillette grinned wryly. "**You're** glad?"

"And it's so wonderful that Quentin's okay."

"Yeah." It was much more than wonderful, but he appreciated her saying that.

"I'm glad you have closure on your father, too."

He nodded. After sixteen years, he finally knew what had happened to his father. He thought knowing would make it easier. Make the hollow feeling go away. But it hadn't. "Thanks."

She stroked his arm a little longer. "I have to go."

"Right."

"Chris?"

"Yes?"

Faith hesitated. "I'm ready."

"For what?"

She sat up and slipped her hands around his neck. "To be yours. I want us to be committed to each other. Completely."

"**WELL, IT'S GOOD** to have you back, old man," Faraday said, beaming from the chair on the other side of Gillette's desk. Gillette had been giving him a blow-by-blow of the mall scene with Boyd and the Carbone people. "That's all I know."

Gillette glanced around the office. "It's good to **be** back." After a few days in Antigua, he'd started to miss the pace. It was great to be back in it again. "Give me a quick update, will you?" Faith hadn't allowed him to have contact with anyone from Everest while they were in the Caribbean.

"Sure. Well, I assigned Hush-Hush to Blair Johnson. I hope you're okay with that."

"Absolutely."

"Blair's doing a great job. Maddox and Hobbs love him. They haven't missed Wright at all. **And,**"

Faraday said, looking up from his notepad, "the French are bugging me every day for more info. We're going to make a killing on this one. Fast. Just like you thought."

Gillette liked the sound of that.

"Not much has happened as far as Vegas goes," Faraday continued. "You'll keep that one, I assume."

"Yup."

"As far as Apex is concerned, the Strazzi estate is still very committed to selling."

"Good. I was worried they might have second thoughts."

"And Morgan Stanley is working hard on the Laurel Energy sell-side book. They're pretty cocky about getting us a big payday."

"Have you spoken to Wright's father?"

"Yeah. He didn't bring up David at all."

Gillette nodded somberly.

"Christian." Debbie's voice blared through the intercom.

"Yes?"

"Allison wants to see you."

Faraday rolled his eyes and rose from the chair. "We still on for lunch today?"

"Yup."

"I'm not going to be preempted by Miss Wallace, am I?"

Gillette shook his head. "Never, Nigel. You're my right-hand man."

"Yeah, yeah, heard that one before."

"Well, well," Allison spoke up as she replaced Faraday in the doorway. "The conquering hero returns."

Gillette tried to hide a grin.

"Pretty proud of yourself, huh?"

"Just glad to be here."

Allison sat in the chair and sniffed. "Thought I was working with the Mob, did you?" she asked, her tone turning edgy.

"After sleeping outside for two nights, I wasn't really sure what to think," he replied, catching her quick glance at his left hand. "I was just trying to stay alive. And no, I didn't go do anything stupid in Antigua."

"What do you mean by that?"

"I didn't get married."

"What are you talking about?"

"You were looking at my ring finger," he said. "I saw you."

Allison grinned. "Oh, you did, did you?"

"Uh-huh."

"Well, why would getting married be stupid?"

Gillette shrugged. "Ah, I meant impulsive."

"Why **weren't** you impulsive?" Allison wanted to know. "Don't you love her?"

Gillette hesitated. "Why shouldn't I?"

"You **should.** A lot of guys all over the country do right now. I got a load of her on the new album cover yesterday." Allison held out her hand and shook it slowly. "Whew. She's hot."

"She does look good."

"Of course, they can do a lot of things with those digital photos now. You know, to hide the flaws."

Gillette grinned. "Well, Allison Wallace, I never would have thought you'd—"

"I want to give you a quick update," she interrupted. "Veramax is moving forward fast. Rothchild is into the Racquet Club, and **what do you know**? The company's products are on the fast track at the FDA."

"Yeah, what do you know?"

"We've got a meeting with this guy who owns the leasing company in Pittsburgh on Wednesday," she continued. "Here. Ten A.M."

"Okay."

"And I've got two other deals going. No need to go over the details with you yet. Probably another few days until we do that."

He watched her tick quickly down the list. She was such a natural-born rainmaker. "Just let me know."

Allison stood up. "That's it. Maybe we can have lunch at some point."

"Hey," Gillette called as she neared the door.

"What?"

"What about those conditions?" he asked, standing and coming out from behind the desk.

She stopped and turned around. "Conditions?"

"The things you said you'd need before you'd commit to joining Everest full time."

"Oh, right. Why are you so interested?" she asked, moving to where he stood.

"I think you're good at this," he said honestly. "People naturally listen to you." He took a deep breath. "You could be chairman of this place someday. Especially now that David's not around."

Allison's eyes went wide. "Wow."

"I'm not kidding. I've thought about it a lot. I can't promise anything, but you have a lot going for you." He held up his hand. "And think about this. You'd be doing this on your own. No family help. More respect."

"Yeah."

"So?" he pushed.

"I really only have one condition," Allison said after a few moments, her voice still subdued.

"What?"

"You don't get married for six months."

He leaned back, caught off guard. "Why?"

"I don't have to tell you **why,** I just have to tell you **what.**"

Gillette shook his head. "We're business partners. That's all it can ever—"

"Will you meet my condition or not?" she cut in.

Gillette thought about it for a second. "Okay." He had no intention of getting married soon anyway. Commitment was one thing, marriage another. "But that's it, right? I agree to that one condition and you'll sign a contract to join here."

Allison turned away and headed for the door again.

"Allison."

She stopped at the door. "As long as you put in the contract that you agree not to get married for six months. As long as that clause is in there." She winked, then disappeared through the doorway.

Gillette stood in the middle of his office, staring after her. Allison wanted the clause in there so she could show Faith. So she could demonstrate to Faith her ability to manipulate.

He shook his head as he headed back to his desk. There it was again, that tendency to always suspect there was a hidden agenda. Maybe Allison simply wanted him focused on the business. Or maybe it was her way of politely saying no, certain he'd never actually put anything about his personal life in a contract.

He eased into the chair and started reviewing a prep file Debbie had dropped on his desk earlier. He focused on it for a few seconds, but then looked at the doorway again and smiled, thinking of Allison, thinking of Faith.

There are always issues, he thought, but most men would kill for problems like mine.

WRITER'S NOTE
ON NANOTECHNOLOGY

I first heard of nanotechnology from a great friend of mine, Matt Malone, who is a top middle-market private equity professional. He reads more than anyone I know, and he'd recently seen an article in a popular national magazine on nanotech related to potential military applications—i.e., creating super-warriors who would be able to do physical things that even the strongest men and women of today couldn't dream of doing.

After Matt alerted me about it, I did some research and found the subject absolutely fascinating. I then called another friend, Teo Forcht Dagi, who is a neurosurgeon turned venture capitalist. Teo provided excellent technical assistance and introduced me to other specialists in the field; and soon I was off and running with the book.

It's incredible to think about it from a biological perspective (which is really all we can do right now), but if nanotechnology will ever be perfected to become available and allow us to live decades, maybe even centuries, longer, it will pose some terribly traumatic social questions. The weightiest of them will be: Who gets to take advantage of it? Only the wealthy? Because, like any technology, it will be extraordinarily expensive at first. Or will the government try to make it available to everyone? That, of course, would be incredibly costly. And what will happen when nanotechnology gets cheap and nearly everyone can afford it? Will funeral homes and cemeteries go out of business and beachfront property get **really** pricey?

If you're inclined to delve further and do some of your own research on the subject, here are some excellent websites to start with:

www.nanotech-now.com
www.nano.gov.com
www.nsti.com
www.nasatech.com

Enjoy!

—Stephen Frey
June 2005

ABOUT THE AUTHOR

STEPHEN FREY is a principal at a northern Virginia private equity firm. He previously worked in mergers and acquisitions at JPMorgan and as a vice president of corporate finance at an international bank in midtown Manhattan. Frey is also the bestselling author of **The Chairman, Shadow Account, Silent Partner, The Day Trader, Trust Fund, The Insider, The Legacy, The Inner Sanctum, The Vulture Fund,** and **The Takeover.**